Lecture Notes in Computer Science   2559

Edited by G. Goos, J. Hartmanis, and J. van Leeuwen

Springer
Berlin
Heidelberg
New York
Barcelona
Hong Kong
London
Milan
Paris
Tokyo

Markku Oivo   Seija Komi-Sirviö (Eds.)

Product Focused Software Process Improvement

4th International Conference, PROFES 2002
Rovaniemi, Finland, December 9-11, 2002
Proceedings

Springer

Series Editors

Gerhard Goos, Karlsruhe University, Germany
Juris Hartmanis, Cornell University, NY, USA
Jan van Leeuwen, Utrecht University, The Netherlands

Volume Editors

Markku Oivo
University of Oulu, Department of Information Processing Science
P.O. Box 3000, 90014 Oulun yliopisto, Finland
E-mail: markku.oivo@oulu.fi

Seija Komi-Sirviö
VTT Technical Research Centre of Finland, VTT Electronics
P.O. Box 1100, 90571 Oulu, Finland
E-mail: seija.komi-sirvio@vtt.fi

Cataloging-in-Publication Data applied for
A catalog record for this book is available from the Library of Congress

Bibliographic information published by Die Deutsche Bibliothek
Die Deutsche Bibliothek lists this publication in the Deutsche Nationalbibliographie;
detailed bibliographic data is available in the Internet at <http://dnb.ddb.de>.

CR Subject Classification (1998): D.2, K.6, K.4.2, J.1

ISSN 0302-9743
ISBN 3-540-00234-0 Springer-Verlag Berlin Heidelberg New York

Springer-Verlag Berlin Heidelberg New York
a member of BertelsmannSpringer Science+Business Media GmbH

http://www.springer.de

© Springer-Verlag Berlin Heidelberg 2002
Printed in Germany

Typesetting: Camera-ready by author, data conversion by DA-TeX Gerd Blumenstein
Printed on acid-free paper   SPIN: 10871796   06/3142   5 4 3 2 1 0

Preface

On behalf of the PROFES organizing committee we would like to welcome you to the 4th International Conference on Product Focused Software Process Improvement (PROFES 2002) in Rovaniemi, Finland. The conference was held on the Arctic Circle in exotic Lapland under the Northern Lights just before Christmas time, when Kaamos (the polar night is known in Finnish as "Kaamos") shows its best characteristics.

PROFES has established itself as one of the recognized international process improvement conferences. Despite the current economic downturn, PROFES has attracted a record number of submissions. A total of 70 full papers were submitted and the program committee had a difficult task in selecting the best papers to be presented at the conference.

The main theme of PROFES is professional software process improvement (SPI) motivated by product and service quality needs. SPI is facilitated by software process assessment, software measurement, process modeling, and technology transfer. It has become a practical tool for quality software engineering and management. The conference addresses both the solutions found in practice and the relevant research results from academia.

The business of developing new applications like mobile and Internet services or enhancing the functionality of a variety of products using embedded software is maturing and meeting the harsh business realities. The necessity for professional software development, quality, and cost effectiveness is becoming evident and there is a need to spread SPI beyond its traditional areas. Therefore, we have encouraged papers and discussions in new application domains in addition to more traditional SPI papers. As a result the conference has a more versatile program than before.

The purpose of the conference is to bring to light the most recent findings and results in the area and to stimulate discussion between researchers, experienced professionals, and technology providers. The large number of participants coming from industry confirms that the conference provides a variety of up-to-date topics and tackles industry problems.

This conference included top keynote speakers: Mike Phillips from SEI and Timo-Pekka Leinonen from Nokia Networks. PROFES also hosted the "Empirical Studies in Software Engineering" Workshop and several pre-conference tutorials, which all added to the value of the conference program.

We wish to thank Fraunhofer IESE, University of Oulu, Infotech, and VTT Electronics for supporting the conference. We are also grateful to the authors for high-quality papers, the program committee for their hard work in reviewing the papers, the organizing committee for making the event possible, the city of Rovaniemi and the University of Rovaniemi for local arrangements, and all the numerous supporters including Finnair who helped in organizing this conference.

Last, but not least, many thanks to Hanna Hulkko, Tarja Luukko, Sari Mäläskä, and Susanna Peltola at VTT Electronics for helping in the review process and in copyediting this volume.

October 2002

Markku Oivo
Seija Komi-Sirviö

Conference Organization

General Chair

Frank Bomarius, Fraunhofer Institut Experimentelles Software Engineering,
Kaiserslautern (Germany)

Program Co-chairs

Seija Komi-Sirviö, Fraunhofer Center for Experimental Software Engineering,
Maryland (USA)
Markku Oivo, University of Oulu, Oulu (Finland)

Organizing Chair

Matias Vierimaa, VTT Electronics, Oulu (Finland)

Tutorial and Workshop Chair

Peter Kaiser, Fraunhofer Institut Experimentelles Software Engineering,
Kaiserslautern (Germany)

Publicity Chair

Pasi Kuvaja, University of Oulu, Oulu (Finland)

USA Area Coordinator

Patricia Larsen, Fraunhofer Center for Experimental Software Engineering,
Maryland (USA)

Local Arrangements Chair

Juha Lindfors, University of Lapland, Rovaniemi (Finland)

Local Industry Coordinator

Ilkka Kamaja, University of Lapland, Rovaniemi (Finland)

Program Committee

Adriana Bicego, Etnoteam (Italy)
Andreas Birk, SD&M (Germany)
Lars Bratthall, ABB (Norway)
Richard Castanet, Université Bordeaux (France)
Reidar Conradi, NTNU (Norway)
Jacky Estublier, Centre National de la Recherche Scientifique (France)
Ilkka Haikala, Tampere University of Technology (Finland)
Tua Huomo, Cybelius Software (Finland)
Hajimu Iida, Nara Institute of Science & Technology (Japan)
Katsuro Inoue, University of Osaka (Japan)
Hannu Jaakkola, University of Lapland (Finland)
Janne Järvinen, Solid Information Technology (Finland)
Ross Jeffery, University of New South Wales (Australia)
Erik Johansson, Q-Labs (Sweden)
Natalia Juristo, Universidad Politecnica de Madrid (Spain)
Kari Känsälä, Nokia Research Center (Finland)
Jaana Kuula, Lapinliitto (Finland)
Mikael Lindval, Fraunhofer, Maryland (USA)
Kenichi Matumoto, NAIST (Japan)
Maurizio Morisio, Politecnico di Torino (Italy)
Paolo Nesi, University of Florence (Italy)
Risto Nevalainen, STTF (Finland)
Päivi Parviainen, VTT Electronics (Finland)
Teade Punter, Fraunhofer IESE (Germany)
Harri Reiman, Ericsson (Finland)
Günther Ruhe, University of Calgary (Canada)
Ioana Rus, Fraunhofer, Maryland (USA)
Kurt Schneider, Daimler-Chrysler (Germany)
Veikko Seppänen, University of Oulu (Finland)
Forrest Shull, Fraunhofer, Maryland (USA)
Dag Sjoeberg, University of Oslo (Norway)
Rini van Solingen, CMG (The Netherlands)
Reijo Sulonen, Helsinki University of Technology (Finland)
Otto Vinter, Delta (Denmark)
Giuseppe Visaggio, University of Bari (Italy)
Yingxu Wang, University of Calgary (Canada)
Isabella Wieczorek, Fraunhofer IESE (Germany)
Claes Wohlin, Blekinge Institute of Technology (Sweden)

We would also like to thank the following persons who helped in reviewing the papers: Alessandro Bianchi, Maria Teresa Baldassarre, and Danilo Caivano from the University of Bari; Desmond Greer from Queen's University of Belfast; Erik Arisholm from Simula, Ray Welland from the University of Glasgow, Torgeir

Dingsøyr from SINTEF, and Carl Fredrik Sørensen and Alf Inge Wang from NTNU; and Sari Kujala from the Helsinki University of Technology,

Table of Contents

Session 3: Software Quality

Session 4: Agile Software Development

Session 5: Process Improvement Approaches

Session 6: Methods and Techniques

Session 7: Embedded Software Process Improvement

Session 8: Process Improvement Case Studies

Session 9: Methods and Techniques

Session 10: Effective Uses of Measurements

Session 11: Wireless Services

Session 16: Process Improvement Frameworks

Session 17: Mobile Solutions

Session 18: Methods and Techniques

Keynote Address:
CMMI: Improving Processes for Better Products

CMMI Program Manager Mike Phillips

Software Engineering Institute, USA

Abstract. A year has passed since the full V1.1 CMMI Product Suite was released. How is it being employed in government and industry to better integrate the development and sustainment of software-intensive systems? Are appraisals being conducted? Are there uses of the CMMI Product Suite that we didn't anticipate? We will summarize current deployment experiences to aid organizations both considering implementation and engaged in initial use of the integrated model. Both current and planned product evolution will be highlighted, so that attendees know where the CMMI effort is going, how they can use the Product Suite, and how the community can participate in the further improvement.

Keywords: CMMI V1.1, CMMI adoption strategy, SW-CMM, EIA/IS 731, CMMI implementation strategy, transition

M. Oivo and S. Komi-Sirviö (Eds.): PROFES 2002, LNCS 2559, p. 1, 2002.
© Springer-Verlag Berlin Heidelberg 2002

Keynote Address:
SW Engineering under Tight Economic Constrains

Timo-Pekka Leinonen

Product Creation Quality, Processes and Tools, Nokia Networks, Finland

Abstract. Normally, it is challenging to find funding and to get the best R&D engineers to participate in quality and process improvement programs. The payback time is considerably long, and the benefits difficult to express reliably in monetary terms. How can you then proceed under tight business conditions: stable or declining markets with deteriorating margins?

The target of the presentation is to go through a few commonly recognized SW engineering paradigms such as the CMMI, requirements engineering, productized engineering environments, and the SW architecture process and to elaborate how we have been able to or plan to apply them in the current business environment.

M. Oivo and S. Komi-Sirviö (Eds.): PROFES 2002, LNCS 2559, p. 2, 2002.
© Springer-Verlag Berlin Heidelberg 2002

Panel

Agile Methods in a Mature Process Environment

Organized by Research Professor Richard Turner

The George Washington University, USA

Agile software development methods are gaining in popularity, especially in highly-volatile business sectors where time-to-market or time-to-implement is short and system requirements change rapidly. While some proponents of agile methods have declared process maturity as anathema, a significant number of mature organizations are interested in gaining the benefits of agile methods. How should agile methods integrate into the carefully orchestrated realm of process assets, SEPGs, and appraisals? This panel will highlight the benefits and pitfalls of agility, and discuss ways to investigate or implement agile methods without jeopardizing process improvement goals.

M. Oivo and S. Komi-Sirviö (Eds.): PROFES 2002, LNCS 2559, p. 3, 2002.
© Springer-Verlag Berlin Heidelberg 2002

A Systems Perspective on Software Process Improvement

Andreas Birk[1] and Dietmar Pfahl[2]

[1] sd&m AG, Industriestraße 5, D-70565 Stuttgart, Germany
Andreas.Birk@sdm.de
[2] Fraunhofer IESE, Sauerwiesen 6, D-67661 Kaiserslautern, Germany
Dietmar.Pfahl@iese.fhg.de

Abstract. Software process improvement often lacks strong links to project management and control activities, which are concerned with identifying the need of process change and triggering improvement initiatives. Project management, on the other hand, often fails at selecting appropriate software engineering methods and technology that help to ensure project success. This paper proposes a model that guides project managers (1) to set up a project so that it can reach its specific goals and (2) to identify corrective actions (or changes) once a project is at risk of failing its goals. The model complements established improvement methods such as CMMI, GQM, and Experience Factory and links them to those project management activities that often are the starting point of improvement initiatives.

1 Introduction

Today's software process improvement (SPI) methods offer little guidance for decision making on concrete improvement actions. For instance, when a project manager identifies a schedule overrun that threats timely product delivery, then improvement methods hardly give any specific recommendations nor guidance to get the project into schedule again. At the other hand, improvement methods are useful for emphasizing the role of software engineering methods and technology within a project, an aspect that conventional project planning widely neglects.

Instead of offering concrete problem solutions, improvement methods either guide organizations towards the identification of general improvement potential (i.e., benchmarking-based improvement) or help an organization to enhance its basic problem solving capabilities (i.e., feedback-based improvement). Examples of benchmarking-based improvement are ISO/IEC standard 9000:2000 [14] and the Software Engineering Institute's (SEI) Capability Maturity Model (CMMI) [10]. Examples of feedback-based improvement are the Experience Factory approach [2], measurement methods like Goal/Question/Metric (GQM) [3][7][18][25], the SEI's PSM [11], and the Balanced Scorecard [15], as well as knowledge management approaches to SPI (e.g., project post mortems [16][5]).

Project planning focuses on aspects like deliverables, milestones, staff and other project resources, time, budget, risk, etc. Software engineering method and

M. Oivo and S. Komi-Sirviö (Eds.): PROFES 2002, LNCS 2559, pp. 4-18, 2002.
© Springer-Verlag Berlin Heidelberg 2002

technology do usually not play a central role in project planning, although it can be crucial for project success to chose the right methods and to deploy them in the right way. For instance, an insufficient integration and testing strategy can easily make a project fail, even if all other project phases went extraordinary well.

This paper proposes a model that guides project managers (1) to set up a project so that it can reach its specific goals and (2) to identify corrective actions (or changes) once a project is at risk of failing its goals. Both aspects are equally relevant to project management and software process improvement. The model adds a focus of software engineering method and technology to project management. It also complements established software process improvement methods and grounds them stronger in core project management activities.

The model is defined as a systems model, which facilitates rapid and well-informed decision making. It also provides a framework for the detailed analysis of specific project phenomena, such as identifying root causes of schedule overruns and assessing the effects of adding new staff to the project. Throughout this paper, the model is denoted *SPI Systems Model*. This name is not fully appropriate, because we focus on the project management related aspects of SPI and do not address long-term organizational improvement activities in the first place. However, those long-term aspects of improvement are covered by most established improvement methods, and it will become clear how the proposed model integrates with them. For this reason we find it acceptable to stick with the simplifying but concise model name.

The sections of this paper briefly introduce the fundamentals of systems thinking (Section 2), present the SPI Systems Model (Section 3), and explain how the SPI Systems Model can be deployed by project management (Section 4). Section 5 discusses the presented approach with regard to project management and other SPI approaches. Section 6 summarizes the main conclusions of the paper.

2   Systems Thinking

In this paper we use systems thinking and cybernetics as a paradigm for modeling and discussing software project management and software process improvement. Systems models contain the main concepts of a phenomenon of interest (e.g., software projects) and describe how these concepts interact with each other (e.g., a project goal determines some aspects of a project plan, and an external event can impact the course of a project).

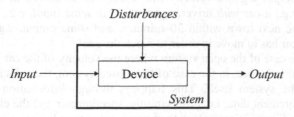

Fig. 1. Open system without feedback

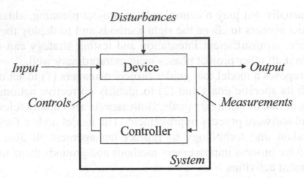

Fig. 2. Closed system with feedback and control

The usual paradigm for analyzing software projects is the process paradigm. It focuses on sequences of activities and addresses questions like "what is done when and by whom?". We want to take a different perspective: Our interest is not "what" is done, but "why" it is being done. For this purpose, systems thinking is a much better paradigm for analyzing and understanding the managerial, organizational, and socio-technical problems in software projects. It describes how *and* why systems behave the way they do.

Originating in the seminal work done by Norbert Wiener on cybernetics [28], until today there have probably been given as many definitions of systems thinking as there were scientists working in the field (e.g., Forrester [13], Checkland [8], Weinberg [27], van Bertanlaffny [4], etc.). In this paper, we follow the sufficiently broad but still concise definition given by Peter Senge who considered systems thinking the activity of contemplating the whole of a system and understanding how each part influences the rest [24]. In the case of a socio-technical system, like, for example, a car with a driver and passengers, this would include the analysis of how the actions of the individuals sitting in the car influence the behavior of the system.

An important step toward systems thinking is to recognize that the internal structure of a system and the feedback processes that govern the relationships between system elements are the explanatory factors for its overall behavior rather than external disturbances. This way of looking at the source of system behavior requires that the system be considered essentially closed and not open. An open system (cf. Figure 1) basically is considered a device, e.g., a car *without* driver and passengers, that receives some input, e.g., the pressure on the gas pedal executed by the driver, and produces some output, e.g., the velocity with which the car moves. In a closed system (cf. Figure 2), e.g., a car *with* driver, again there is some input, e.g., the request or goal to reach the next town within 30 minutes, and some output, e.g., the velocity with which the car has to move in order to reach the goal.

In contrast to the case of the open system where the velocity of the car was dependent on some external influence, in the case of the closed system, the velocity of the car is controlled by the system itself. This happens through information feedback. By collecting measurement data, i.e. observing the speedometer and the clock, the driver (the controller in Figure 2) can calculate at any point in time how fast he must drive in order to achieve the defined goal. Based on measurements and some calculations, the driver decides whether he should change the pressure on the gas pedal (the control in

Figure 2). It should be mentioned that in the case of the closed system, the controller would automatically take under consideration external disturbances (e.g. a steep hill) as long as the effect on the device is adequately reflected by the measurements – and neither misperceptions nor miscalculations occur.

3 A Systems Thinking Foundation of SPI

In the previous section we argued that systems thinking is the application of feedback control systems principles and techniques to managerial, organizational, and socio-technical problems. In this section, we will discuss further the assumptions and concepts that are important in the context of systems thinking, and – by using these concepts – we introduce the SPI Systems Model.

3.1 Control and Feedback

Control theory is based on the explicit premise that the change of a system is, or can be planned. Control is the process of ensuring that operations proceed according to some plan by reducing the difference between the plan (or goal) and reality. Control can only be exercised over the components internal to the system and cannot be affected upon the external environment. Using feedback mechanisms facilitates control over the system.

Feedback is concerned with the control of a mechanism (or device) on the basis of its past performance. It consists of procedures that determine deviations from plans and desired states and that indicate and execute corrective action regarding these deviations. This entails gathering data on the state of the output, searching for deviations from the plan, and adjusting the input based on the results of the output. It thus establishes a relatively closed system of causes and effects. It also reduces the risk of failure and the effect of residual complexity and ambiguity.

Both feedback and control presuppose planning, at least in the form of setting goals and performance levels, as plans furnish the baselines and standards of control. The pattern of goal seeking behavior exhibited by a system is then expected to stay true to the identified goal. The implicit and rather mechanistic assumption is that the plan or target does not change and that future conditions will remain identical to past conditions. In a change intensive environment these assumptions, and the resulting self-regulating mechanisms, clearly do not work and either a forward looking anticipation strategy or a double-loop feedback system must be employed.

Double-loop feedback offers a more sophisticated alternative that allows for the adjustment of the input variables to the process as well as the adjustment to plans that are used to dictate performance standards. The ability to respond to change and alter performance standards encourages adaptability and improves the chance of long-term survival. It also enables the control mechanism to benefit from most feedback data and avoid defensive routines to discredit suspect data.

Double-loop control requires long-term planning in designing the double-loop and will consume larger resources. It enables the system to become more adaptable and to do so more rapidly rather than bind itself to historical patterns. This adaptation means that the system is capable of long-term learning and continuous improvement in a search for greater efficiency. In contrast, single-loop feedback only focuses on the short-term adjustments during the duration of the control activity that will maximize the efficiency of the current product. Such improvements only apply to the current control loop and do not feed back into long-term changes to the overall process. In other words, lessons are neither learned nor retained.

The phenomenon that double-loop learning requires substantial investments which will pay-off only on a long-term time scale, while simple (isolated) single-loop feedback will only have local impact that is not sustained, is quite well reflected in the SPI literature by the duality of strategic management and project management. By offering an SPI Systems Model that has well-defined links to strategic management, we offer a perspective on organizational learning that puts the focus to the project as the heart of any sustained SPI program without de-coupling it from the strategic level.

3.2   The SPI Systems Model

Figure 3 presents the SPI Systems Model. The initiation of a software development project is triggered by business goals (BusG) from which the specific project goals (ProjG) are derived (arc 1). An example of a business goal would be: "We need to increase our market share in the database marked from 10% to 20% within the next two years". The project goals for the development of the next database release could then be: "Compared to the previous release, shorten lead time by enforcing concurrent engineering and reuse; at the same time, improve product quality by at least 20% and reduce development cost by 10%".

In order to make ProjG operational, a transformation into product goals (ProdG) and process goals (ProcG) is necessary (arcs 2). Typically, ProdG is associated with functionality and quality (i.e. functional and non-functional requirements), while ProcG is associated with time and cost (or effort). In our example, ProdG would relate to the planned increase of quality by at least 20%, while process goals would relate to the planned reduction of lead time and development cost. It should be noted that the definition of ProcG not only depends on ProjG but also on ProdG (arc 3). For example, the improvement of product quality might impose a change in the process that is going to be executed, say by increasing the inspection intensity (i.e., the number of inspections) during the design phase.

The joint set of ProdG and ProcG forms the starting point for developing ProjP (arcs 4). ProjP is the result of the planning stage and the central control for the development stage of the project. It can be seen as an instantiation of available process, product and resource models in the organization (yielding, for example, a Gantt chart, a resource allocation plan, and a high-level product architecture) that serves project management (ProjM) as an instrument to define and control development activities such as execution of processes and creation of product-related artifacts (arcs 5). The process situation (ProcS) can be determined based on observation (measurement) of project progress, i.e. activities that have been concluded, milestones that have been passed, resources that have been consumed, etc. The product situation (ProdS) can be determined based on observation (measurement) of certain characteristics (e.g., size, quality) of intermediate products and the final product. Because creation of intermediate and final products is inherently dependent on the execution of processes, and thus the current process situation, Figure 3 shows a synchronization link between ProcS and ProdS (arc 6).

The project situation is a result of combining ProcS and ProdS (arcs 7). Based on measurement data and by using adequate models, e.g., static predictive models or dynamic process simulation models, a projection can be made until project end in order to facilitate comparison with ProjG for project control. This projection is labeled with ProjS in Figure 3.

Project management (ProjM) takes the role of the controller. Its main task is to compare ProjG with ProjS (arcs 8) and to initiate a change action if needed, e.g., when project deadline or product quality are at risk. There are two types of change actions possible that would create a single-loop feedback (arcs 9 and 10). The first case (arc 9), which can only induce a corrective change of ProjP without changing ProjG is labeled "single-loop feedback (inner loop)". The second case (arc 10), which may induce a corrective change of ProjG and, due to that, a change of ProjP, is labeled "single-loop feedback (outer loop)". Since it is not realistic to assume that ProjM can simply change ProjG without asking for and receiving the agreement from higher-level management, the outer loop feedback cycle is not fully endogenous to the system.

In addition to BusG, there are two important concepts that serve as an input to the system (i.e., the software project): Information and knowledge about the Context of the project (arc 11) and Experience about planning and development (arc 12). Context information is a relevant input to many planning and development activities and thus should be reflected in ProjP. Also Experience, e.g., best practices, should be taken into account when developing ProjP. Typically, Experience is available in the form of personal and implicit mental models, or it is made explicit and stored in an experience base in the form of quantitative and qualitative models (e.g., process models, product models, and resource models) that represent the past and current state-of-practice.

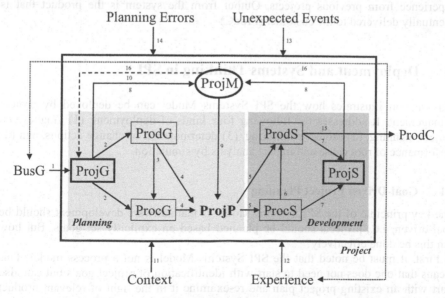

Fig. 3. SPI Systems Model with single-loop and double-loop feedback

There are two major types of disturbances that impact the system: Unexpected Events (arc 13) and Planning Errors (arc 14).

The system output (arc 15), i.e., the project outcome, is the end product that will be delivered to the customer after project end (ProdC).

By extending the system boundaries and including strategic management (dealing with BusG) and experience management (dealing with Experience) into the system under observation, i.e., the software organization is the "device" on which the "controllers" strategic and experience management work, establishment of double-loop feedback becomes possible. In the extended model, double-loop feedback is possible in two ways (arcs 16). Either observations, lessons learned and best practices resulting from the project (and reported by ProjM) are used by strategic management (StratM) to alter BusG, or they are used by experience management (ExpM) to alter the models in the experience base.

It should be noted, that the structural similarity between Figure 2 and Figure 3 is not directly visible, because in Figure 3, apart from the project plan (ProjP), which represents the control, and the project management (ProjM), which represents the controller, no real world entities are depicted that would represent the device (or mechanism) on which control is applied. In the SPI Systems Model, the device is constituted by (1) the set of real world artifacts – besides ProjP – ,i.e., process handbooks, standards and guidelines, development documents, technical documentation, test reports, user documentation, etc., and (2) all persons – besides ProjM – that assume a certain role within the project and their interaction. It can be argued, however, that project goals (ProjG), product goals (ProdG), and process goals (ProcG), are associated with the device during the planning stage, while the project situation (ProjS), process situation (ProcS), and product situation (ProdS) are associated with the device during the development stage. Inputs to the system are business goals (BusG), and – in a more indirect way – context information and experience from previous projects. Output from the system is the product that is eventually delivered to the customer (ProdC).

4   Deployment and Systems Thinking in SPI

This section illustrates how the SPI Systems Model can be deployed by project management. It addresses the following four kinds of deployment: (1) Goal-driven project planning, (2) project monitoring, (3) determination of change actions, and (4) performance of root cause and impact analysis by simulation.

4.1   Goal-Driven Project Planning

The key principle of the SPI Systems Model is that software development should be goal-driven, i.e., projects should be planned based on explicitly set goals. But how can this be done effectively?

First, it must be noted that the SPI Systems Model is not a process model. This means that one does not need to start with identification of project goals but can also start with an existing project plan and re-examine it in the light of relevant product and process goals. At the end it is important that the various goals and the project plan are consistent with each other. There are various ways through which this can be ensured.

Project goals are those that are raised by the project's customers and those set by the development company's internal authorities (e.g., product management or senior management). Each project goal should be written down together with information about who has raised it.

Table 1. Examples of product goals

Product goal	Goal category	Notes
The software system shall have a maximum downtime of 6 h / year.	Quality	This is a Reliability goal, a typical kind of Quality goal.
It shall be possible to operate the system from web browsers (via HTTP) and from mobile phones (via WAP).	Functionality	Functionality is usually defined in the system requirements; the most important such requirements should be made explicit as product goals.
The first product release shall not cost more than € 1,2 Million.	Cost	Cost and Time can also be process goals. However, here they are clearly attributed to product.
The pilot application shall be available within four months.	Time	

Table 2. Examples of process goals

Process goal	Goal category	Notes
The total project budget until product release 1 shall be € 1,04 Million.	Cost	These Cost and Time goals are attributed to process. They are associated to similar product goals.
Project duration for stage 1 (pilot application) shall be four months.	Time	
It shall be possible to introduce additional browser compatibility requirements until two months before delivery of release 2.	Flexibility	Flexibility goals usually address the project's software development process and project organization.
The entire development staff shall gain experience in development and testing of internet software.	Staff Qualification	Process goals can also relate to human resources aspects of project performance.
System tests shall document that the system will have a downtime not longer than 6 h / year.	Quality	The Quality- and Functionality-related process goals are derived from the respective product goals.
The project shall develop the system for operation with web browsers (via HTTP) as well as mobile phones (via WAP).	Functionality	

Product goals are related to functionality and quality of the product to be developed. They can also be related to cost or time. Table 1 contains several examples of product goals.

Process goals are related to project performance. They can (1) be related to cost and time, (2) address other project performance attributes (e.g., agility of the project organization, flexibility of the project processes, or work-based qualification objectives of the project staff), or (3) be derived from quality- and functionality-related product goals. Example process goals are shown in Table 2.

For defining a complete and consistent set of goals, a four-section grid can be used, which contains one section for each kind of goal: Initial project goals, product goals derived from project goals, process goals derived from project goals, and process goals derived from product goals. Each individual product and process goals should be checked for consistency with the other goals.

Once a consistent set of product and process goals is defined explicitly, a project plan can be developed that ensures that the goals can be fulfilled. For each goal, it should be possible to justify how the project plan helps attaining it. Project planning can be supported by repositories that document experience about how specific software engineering methods facilitate the achievement of certain goals (cf. [23][6]).

4.2   Project Monitoring

Project monitoring is the prerequisite for identifying the possible need for change and improvement actions. It consists of tracking product and process situation, and checking whether it is still likely that the respective goals can be attained. It is essentially based on software measurement. Therefore, indicators of goal attainment must be defined. They must allow for projecting the project situation at any given point in time to the expected situation at the end of the project. There are two basic strategies through which such project monitoring can be performed: Projection and milestone checkpoints. In practice, both strategies are usually combined with each other.

The projection strategy requires the identification of project indicators that can be identified (i.e., measured) in relatively small time intervals (e.g., on a weekly basis) to allow for sufficient projection quality. In addition, a projection function is required using which the current project indicators can be transformed into the expected project situation at project end time. Hence, in this case, monitoring is the comparison of a measurement-based estimation (e.g., derived from measurement of weekly staff effort) with the respective project goal (e.g., total effort budget of the project).

The strategy of milestone checkpoints breaks down the expected project situation at project end time into several project situations at major milestones. This requires some model from which the target values for each milestone can be derived (e.g., a model of typical effort distribution across development phases). The milestones are usually defined with time intervals of several weeks (e.g., each one or three months). Indicator measurement (e.g., measurement of accumulated staff effort) is required at least shortly before each milestone. In this case monitoring involves comparing the actual measurement data at each milestone with the previously defined target value for the respective milestone.

4.3   Determination of Change Actions

Change actions must be determined as soon as it occurs that the project is not likely to meet its goals. This can be due to two reasons: (1) The project plan is not appropriate for attaining the goals, or (2) the goals are not realistic. Both situations can happen because initial planning did not consider all relevant decision criteria, or because of the event of external changes that affect project goals or plan (e.g., customer changes strategy and wants the system to be developed on a different platform).

In the following, we will focus on the case that the project plan must be changed while the original goals can be kept. The other case (i.e., re-setting the goals) will not be considered here any further. It is widely similar to the initial project planning.

Figure 4 shows the input and output of project management activity ProjM (Determine Improvement Action), which establishes a feedback loop for project plan updates based on identified deviations of product and process situations from the respective goals. Input to the "Determine Change" activity are: Product goal and situation, process goal and situation, project plan (current status prior to change), context, and experience. Result and output of the Determine Improvement Action activity is a process change decision, which leads to a change of project plan (ProjP).

Project managers can use this decision model for delineating their own individual decision making process, or for structuring a decision-making workshop with selected team members. In both cases it is useful when product and process goals are documented explicitly, an up-to-date project plan is available, and key indicators of the product and process status are known (cf. Section 4.2). In addition, information about relevant project context as well as experience about appropriate improvement measures for specific product or process goals will be helpful.

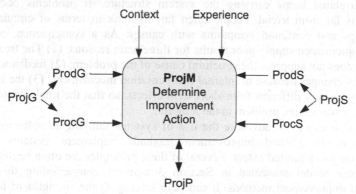

Fig. 4. Input and output of the ProjM Activity (Determine Improvement Action)

4.4   Performing Root Cause and Impact Analysis by Simulation

The SPI Systems Model provides a framework for the further refinement of model components and the relationships between them. In particular, the SPI Systems Model can be used as a blueprint for the simulation of project performance. Systematic application of simulation, in combination with measurement, can help uncover root causes of unexpected project behavior. It can also be used for evaluating planning alternatives and for performing impact analyses of proposed change actions prior to the actual implementation of the change [9][22].

The System Dynamics (SD) simulation modeling approach [12] closely follows the principles of Systems Thinking (cf. Section 2). Hence, SD is the recommended choice for building simulation models that represent and refine the SPI Systems Model [1][17][26]. SD simulation models focus on the formal (i.e., mathematical) representation of circular cause-effect structures that are held to be responsible for generating observed behavior of a system. Due to their flexibility and the possibility to combine hard data (empirical measurement) with soft data (beliefs and tacit knowledge), the SD approach allows for constructing adequate project models on different levels of detail according to the specific needs of project management. A methodology that systematically integrates measurement, quantitative modeling, process modeling, and project simulation using the SD approach has been presented in [19] under the name IMMoS (Integrated Measurement, Modeling and Simulation). Empirical evidence for the effectiveness and efficiency of the IMMoS methodology was collected in industrial case studies [20][21].

5   Discussion

The management of complex systems, like those typically underlying industrial software development processes, is very difficult. Based only on intuition and experience, it is generally not possible to comprehend the dynamic implications of so many interrelated loops carrying the system structure. If problems occur, their diagnosis is far from trivial. People often fail to think in terms of circular causal relationships and confound symptoms with causes. As a consequence, corrective policies implemented supply poor results for three main reasons: (1) The treatment of symptoms does not suppress the structural cause of the problem; (2) feedback systems resist policy changes because of internal compensation mechanisms; (3) the long term effects may be very different from short term effects, so that the implemented policy may actually worsen the problem in the long run.

For these reasons, we advocate the use of systems thinking in software process improvement. Established improvement methods implement systems thinking principles only to a limited extent. Several of these principles are often neglected. The SPI Systems Model presented in Section 3 aims at compensating this gap in established improvement methods. It can help leveraging the strengths of individual improvement methods and points out how specific improvement methods can be combined in order to receive maximum benefit for a software project or improvement program.

This section discusses the SPI Systems Model in the light of several improvement methods: CMMI-based SPI, measurement-based improvement using GQM, and the Experience Factory. Each method is compared with the SPI Systems Model, and integration possibilities of improvement method and the SPI Systems Model are outlined. The last subsection discusses appropriateness and justification of the proposed SPI Systems Model.

5.1   CMMI-Based Improvement

Improvement based on CMMI and other process assessment approaches (e.g., ISO 15504/SPICE or ISO 9001) compare (or assess) a project's or organization's software processes with a reference model of processes and evaluate the degree at which the assessed processes cover the reference model. Improvement suggestions can then be derived from the assessment results. However, the assessment methods do not include any specific recommendations on specific improvement suggestions or on the order in which possible process changes should be conducted.

From the viewpoint of the SPI Systems Model, assessment methods such as CMMI are a means for monitoring a project's process situation. They do not explicitly address any of the following concepts: Product-related aspects, project-specific process goals (i.e., other goals than those implicitly underlying the reference model of processes), specific decision making support for the identification of improvement suggestions, nor explicit support for specific project management activities. Even though it must be acknowledged that experienced process assessors usually take care of all these aspects when performing an assessment, the method itself does not address such issues.

5.2   GQM Measurement

Goal/Question/Metric (GQM) is a method for measurement and analysis in software engineering. Starting from the definition of project-specific measurement goals, appropriate measures (or metrics) are derived via a framework of question types. Usually, this is done by a measurement engineer, who acquires the needed information during interviews or group discussions with project team members. Afterwards, GQM addresses the preparation and execution of measurements and guides the analysis and interpretation of measurement results. Analysis and interpretation are usually performed in structured group discussions (so-called feedback sessions) of the project staff.

Concerning GQM's relation to the SPI Systems Model, GQM addresses the monitoring of both product and process situation with regard to individual project goals, offers a means for identifying improvement suggestions (i.e., the feedback sessions), and has been positioned as a tool for project management's monitoring and control tasks. Critics of GQM have argued that the approach is still too general, offering little specific guidance for standard measurement tasks. Likewise, it does not offer any specific decision making rules for the identification of improvement suggestions. In general, the implementation of software measurement can involve technical difficulties that make it not always easy to find a pragmatic approach to implementing measurement. For instance, it might take a relatively long time until measurement results are available and the first improvement suggestions can be made. From this viewpoint, GQM is one candidate solution (among others) for performing or supporting the measurement and control activities of the SPI Systems Model.

5.3   Experience Factory

The Experience Factory (EF) is a paradigm for experience-based (or learning-based) continuous improvement in software engineering. It builds on a cyclic process (the Quality Improvement Paradigm, QIP) of goal setting, planning, controlled action, and learning-based improvement. It also offers an organizational infrastructure that supports experience collection and deployment.

With regard to the SPI Systems Model, the EF is a conceptual framework that addresses most aspects of the SPI Systems Model. However, it does so on a relatively abstract level and does not offer operational guidance for the various tasks: The EF does not explicitly distinguish between product and process aspects, does not include specific monitoring and control mechanisms (EF implementations often use GQM for that purpose), and does not include specific improvement suggestions.

5.4   Appropriateness and Justification of the SPI Systems Model

The previous subsections have pointed out that the proposed SPI Systems Model complements established improvement methods by shifting focus on important project-related aspects of improvement. The SPI Systems Model includes key principles of systematic, feedback-based improvement: Explicit goal setting, systematic planning, informed decision making, and the need for accumulating experience (or best practice or patterns) about improvement actions that are appropriate within a specific given situation.

The importance of explicit goal setting and the separation of product goals from process goals have been emphasized by the PROFES improvement method [23]. Its relevance has been demonstrated in the PROFES application projects. The need for informed decision making, which should be supported by a sound understanding of the project situation and be based on accumulated past experience has been emphasized since the introduction of the Experience Factory. Recent contributions include the model-based simulation of software projects [19] and methods for knowledge management within SPI [6].

The SPI Systems Model formulates a project-based feedback system similar to GQM. However, it is not focusing on measurement alone and emphasizes the need for combined product and process monitoring. The SPI Systems Model also is linked to cross-project or organizational feedback (i.e., double-loop feedback) as formulated in the Experience Factory.

Concerning cross-project feedback, the SPI Systems Model addresses the core activity of identifying change actions. This is widely neglected in project management methods as well as in established SPI methods. For this reason, the SPI Systems Model guides project management's change activities and grounds established (organizational) SPI methods in software projects. It can be expected that such a link of project management and SPI helps overcome the still existing gap between both fields: Project management might gain a higher awareness of software engineering methods and technology, and SPI might easier attract project management's attention for the importance of long-term, sustained improvement activities.

6   Conclusion

This paper has introduced the SPI Systems Model that builds on explicit goal setting, separates software product from process, emphasizes monitoring of project state, and seeks for understanding the "why" of improvement needs and improvement actions.

Anchor point of all these aspects is the software project plan, which transforms project goals into appropriate planned action. For this reason, the SPI Systems Model is grounded in project management: It views SPI as a tool that enables project management to keep a project in line with its goals.

The SPI Systems Model complements established improvement methods, which are usually not rooted in project management and lack guidance for the identification of concrete improvement suggestions. The model offers a pragmatic starting point for understanding how software project phenomena interrelate with each other, and why specific improvement suggestions might be superior to others in a given project situation. In cases where additional rigor and justification of decisions are needed, the SPI Systems Model can be refined and provide the basis for simulation-based root cause and impact analysis.

References

[1]   Abdel-Hamid, T.K., Madnick, S.E.: Software Projects Dynamics – an Integrated Approach. Prentice-Hall (1991)
[2]   Basili, V.R., Caldiera, G., Rombach, D. H.: Experience Factory. In: Marciniak, J.: Encyclopedia of Software Engineering, Vol. 1, pp. 511-519, Wiley (2001)
[3]   Basili, V.R., Caldiera, G., Rombach, H.D., van Solingen, R.: Goal Question Metric (GQM) Approach. In: J. Marciniak: Encyclopedia of Software Engineering, Vol. 1, pp. 578-583, Wiley (2001)
[4]   von Bertalanffy, L.: General Systems Theory, Foundations, Development, Applications. Georges Braziller, New York (1968)
[5]   Birk, A., Dingsøyr, T., Stålhane, T.: Postmortem: Never leave a project without it. IEEE Software, 19(3), pp. 43-45, (2002)
[6]   Birk, A.: A Knowledge Management Infrastructure for Systematic Improvement in Software Engineering. PhD Theses in Experimental Software Engineering, Vol. 3, Fraunhofer IRB, Stuttgart, Germany (2001)
[7]   Briand, L.C., Differding, Ch., Rombach, H.D.: Practical Guidelines for Measurement-Based Process Improvement. Software Process Improvement and Practice 2 (4), pp. 253-280, (1996)
[8]   Checkland, P.: Systems Thinking, Systems Practice. (1981)
[9]   Christie, A.M.: Simulation: An Enabling Technology in Software Engineering. In: CROSSTALK – The Journal of Defense Software Engineering, pp. 2-7 (1999)
[10] CMMI Product Team. Capability Maturity Model Integration (CMMI), Version 1.1. Software Engineering Institute, Pittsburgh, PA (2002)
[11] Florac, W.A., Park, R.E., Carleton, A.D.: Practical Software Measurement. Software Engineering Institute, Pittsburgh, PA (1997)
[12] Forrester, J.W.: Industrial Dynamics. Productivity Press, Cambridge (1961)
[13] Forrester, J.W.: Principles of Systems. Productivity Press, Cambridge (1971)
[14] International Organization for Standardization: ISO 9001:2000: Quality Management Systems - Requirements. International Organization for Standardization (2000)

[15] Kaplan, R.S., and Norton, D.P.: The Balanced Scorecard: Translating Strategy into Action. Harvard Business School Press, Boston (1996)

[16] Kerth, N.L.: Project retrospectives: A handbook for team reviews. Dorset House, New York (2001)

[17] Lin, C.Y., Abdel-Hamid, T.K., Sherif, J.S.: Software-Engineering Process Simulation Model (SEPS). In: Journal of Systems and Software 38, pp. 263-277 (1997)

[18] van Latum, F., van Solingen, R., Oivo, M., Hoisl, B., Rombach, D.H., Ruhe, G.: Adopting GQM-based measurement in an industrial environment. IEEE Software, 15(1):78–86 (1998)

[19] Pfahl, D.: An Integrated Approach to Simulation-Based Learning in Support of Strategic and Project Management in Software Organisations. PhD Theses in Experimental Software Engineering, Vol. 8, Fraunhofer IRB, Stuttgart, Germany (2001)

[20] Pfahl, D., Lebsanft, K.: Knowledge Acquisition and Process Guidance for Building System Dynamics Simulation Models. An Experience Report from Software Industry. In: International Journal of Software Engineering and Knowledge Engineering 10, 4, pp. 487-510 (2000)

[21] Pfahl, D., Lebsanft, K.: Using Simulation to Analyse the Impact of Software Requirement Volatility on Project Performance. In: Information and Software Technology 42, 14, pp. 1001-1008 (2000)

[22] Pfahl, D., Ruhe, G.: System Dynamics as an Enabling Technology for Learning in Software Organisations. In: 13th International Conference on Software Engineering and Knowledge Engineering. SEKE'2001. Knowledge Systems Institute, Skokie, IL, pp. 355-362 (2001)

[23] The PROFES Consortium: PROFES User Manual. Fraunhofer IRB Verlag, Stuttgart, Germany (2000)

[24] Senge, P.M.: The Fifth Discipline – the Art & Practice of the Learning Organization. Doubleday, New York (1990)

[25] van Solingen, R., Berghout, E.: The Goal/Question/Metric Method: A practical guide for quality improvement of software development. McGraw-Hill, London (1999)

[26] Waeselynck, H., Pfahl, D.: System Dynamics Applied to the Modelling of Software Projects. In: Software Concepts and Tools 15, 4, pp. 162-176 (1994)

[27] Weinberg, G.M.: An Introduction to General Systems Thinking. Wiley, New York (1975)

[28] Wiener, N.: Cybernetics. Wiley, New York (1948)

Transition Management
of Software Process Improvement

Seon-ah Lee[1] and Byoungju Choi[2]

[1] Software Center, Corporate R&D Center, Samsung Electronics Co. Ltd
599-4 ShinSa-Dong, KangNam-Gu, Seoul, Korea, 135-120
salee@samsung.com

[2] Dept. of Computer Science and Engineering, Ewha Womans University
Seoul, Korea
bjchoi@ewha.ac.kr

Abstract. Process improvement studies have tended to focus on software process improvement (SPI) framework such as the generic „best practices" models (e.g., CMM and SPICE), SPI Models (e.g., PDCA and IDEAL), and Quality Improvement Paradigm (QIP). However, there are still difficulties due to the resistance within the organization and the tendency to return to the previous state. In this study, we point out it is the transition part that is overlooked in the SPI Model and explain how we apply transition management to software process improvement in the Software Center, Samsung Electronics Co. Ltd. The study also shows that considering transition management during SPI planning leads to more accurate estimation for time and goal achievement of SPI work.

1   Introduction

Past process improvement studies have concentrated on the process improvement framework. As a result, process maturity models like CMM [5] and SPICE [6] are widely used for process improvement. To use the maturity model for improving the process is a top-down approach [7]. This approach finds weak points in the organization by comparing its current process against the maturity model and sets goals on the basis of weaknesses detected. The top-down approach's strength is that it can produce a great achievement. However, as it requires a large-scale investment, it cannot work successfully unless it meets process success factors [9] such as the management commitment. On the other hand, the bottom-up approach [7] is based on the position that each project is different. NASA's SEL [8] is a representative example. The bottom-up approach specifies points to improve in the features of the targeted processes, products and organizations. A process improvement program by the bottom-up approach can lead to successful results only when one has clear insight into what needs to be improved and the ability to make proper measurements.

M. Oivo and S. Komi-Sirviö (Eds.): PROFES 2002, LNCS 2559, pp. 19-34, 2002.

Meanwhile, SPI models have been suggested which can bring changes in an organization. PDCA [4] and IDEAL [5] are general models used for an organization's process improvement. The PDCA (Plan-Do-Check-Act) model [4] explicated by Demming is one that proceeds in stages: implementing, reviewing and generalizing the improvement process. And the IDEAL (Initiating-Diagnosing-Establishing-Acting-Leveraging) model [5], which was suggested by McFeeley, is one that proceeds in stages of analyzing the current process, planning for the target and then establishing a new process.

Despite the potential of such process improvement frameworks, it is still difficult to succeed in process improvement [11,12,13,14 and 15]. Many companies have worked hard on process improvement, but few gain results, mostly due to problems like high investment cost as well as resistance and lack of participation within their organizations. This situation has prompted many studies into the causes of these failures, with researchers trying to identify factors behind a success or a failure by holding them up to the impressions of a few successful cases. However, the studies have not provided concrete strategies for deploying a new process in organizations that have yet to calculate the factors needed for success.

In general, process improvement takes a significant amount of time because it involves work to change organizational culture. The more an organization sticks to traditions laid down during its own development, the more difficult it can be to change its current culture. Meanwhile, as time to market becomes an increasingly important competitive factor, a company's success relies more and more on how quickly it can turn out high-quality products.

In this study, we suggest SPI strategies to speed up process deployment and keep conflicts within an organization to a minimum by considering how SPI affects people and how to illicit the reactions desired. For that, we introduce transition management concepts and methods aimed at helping people efficiently adjust to organizational changes. We will also use a case study conducted by the Software Center, a division of Samsung Electronics Co. Ltd, to explain how transition management can effectively reduce stress and confusion brought on by changes.

The text of this study consists of five parts. In the following section, we introduce previous study results to highlight why the primary case study under consideration was needed. Section 3 then focuses on how transition management can be introduced into SPI strategies, while Section 4 is the analysis of Samsung Electronics' SPI activities from the viewpoint of transition management. Section 5 contains the conclusion along with recommended tasks to be undertaken in future studies.

2   The Previous Studies

Previous process model and other studies have revealed SPI factors and remaining problems (2.1). We will also show the transition management (2.2) that can provide solutions to the problems discussed in the introduction.

Table 1. PDCA Model

Plan	Do	Check	Act
Identify and resolve risks	Train, adapt, consult, and remove barriers	Evaluate results, ensure success, and celebrate	Revise, develop next-level process, and convince others.

Table 2. IDEAL Model

Initiating	Diagnosing	Establishing	Acting	Leveraging
Stimulus for change	Characterize current & desired States	Set Priorities Develop approach	Create solution Pilot/Test solution	Analyze and validate Propose future actions
Set context	Develop recommendations	Plan Actions	Refine solution Implementation solution	
Build sponsorship				
Charter infrastructure				

2.1   PDCA & IDEAL Model

The PDCA model has four phases as shown in Table 1. „Plan" is the phase where vision and strategies are identified and rationalized and improvements suggested. In the „Do" phase, the timing, extent and means of improvements are made, and in the following phase, „Check", the degree of achieved improvements is measured. Finally, in the „Act" phase, activities are carried out to support standardization and stabilization of the improved process.

The IDEAL model suggests that the steps in Table 2 are required in SPI's continuous loop process. In the „Initiating" phase, the goal of SPI is defined together with the infrastructure and its roles and responsibilities. While in „Diagnosing," SPIs are laid out to reflect the vision and strategic business plans of the organization. The „Establishing" phase is where improvement activities are prioritized and measurable goals set, and in „Acting" it is necessary to create, pilot and deploy solutions for each improvement area. Finally, in the „Leveraging" phase, data from the current loop is collected as a preparation for the next IDEAL step.

Both PDCA and IDEAL models include the five key activities of the change management model:

To establish a basis on which the organization can accept changes; members of the organization need to understand clearly why such changes are necessary, what problems may occur if they do not accept the changes and what is the future of the organization.

To consider all measures that deal with opportunities or problems causing change.

To review the effects of the measures in detail, should such measures be adopted.

To choose the best measures and establish a detailed plan to implement them.

To put the plan into practice, receive feedback and revise it, if necessary.

The change management model can be properly implemented only when the organization has the factors required for successful process improvement. That is to say, the change-management model alone does not provide sufficient conditions for successful SPI implementation. Accordingly, there have been a number of failed cases in the course of the SPI process, prompting researchers to delve into the causes of the failures and uncover contributing factors.

Wiegers [12], for example, found major barriers, insufficient time, lack of knowledge, wrong motivation, arbitrary approach and lack of participation. For Myers [13], the main causes were in the resistance to change, lack of knowledge, lack of effect, failed attempts and inadequate investment, while for O'Day [14], the problem was caused by resistance, easy return to the earlier state and lack of continuity.

SPI barriers may be summarized as matters of investment, resistance and participation. In this study, we are going to introduce transition management to SPI activities as a solution for the problem of resistance.

2.2   Transition Management

The transition management concept was first asserted by William Bridges in 1980 [6]. It is the management of the psychological process people go through when changes occur [6]. It starts with the recognition that change and transition are different from each other. „Change" refers to the situation in which the external condition or environment shifts from one state to another. Meanwhile, „Transition" describes the psychological reorientation initiated by a change. Table 3 identifies the steps of transition and ways to manage them.

Table 3. Transition management model

Process	Definition	Resistance	Management
Before Progress			Define the stage of transition in which the affected individuals or a group are situated.
Ending	The 'ending', or the 'loss' of the existing world, operation method or identity	People resist the loss of identity and their world.	Establish and practice strategies to manage 'ending' and 'loss'.
Neutral Zone	The period of disorientation, confusion or dormancy coming after the ending of the existing world but without forming a new identity	People resist the experience of the neutral zone in which they are disoriented.	Establish and practice strategies to help people get over the neutral zone.
Beginning	New identity, purpose of existence, enthusiasm, and commitment	People feel uncomfortable about, fear, and resist, their new appearance and behavior.	Establish and practice strategies to help people get into the new beginning.

An organization sometime assumes that its members will adjust to changes as a matter of course if they feel that the changes are necessary, but the fact is, they suffer the psychological stage of facing stress and confusion caused by the changes rather than the stage of adjustment. As a result, the time and costs associated with a change exceed expectations. Still worse, the change can weaken, rather than strengthen, the organization, causing demoralization, confusion and decreased productivity among its members. Therefore, it is very important to understand people's state during the transition process because the strategies and measures to help them should differ according to where they are within the phases of ending, neutral zone, and new beginning. Timing is important when identifying which transition phase people are in. It is also important to reduce the possible loss of productivity and good performance among those who are undergoing a transition by minimizing guilt, resentment, anxiety, self-absorption and stress.

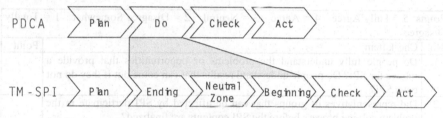

Fig 1. Idea of transition management in SPI

Table 4. Transition management in connection with process application

	Develop-ment Process	1st Development	2nd Development	3rd Development
		Small TM: Application of the 1st Process		
		Small TM: Application of the 2nd Process		
		Small TM: Application of the 3rd Process		
End-ing	Process Consolida-tion	Presentation meeting on SPI strategy and plan	Presentation meeting on SPI strategy and plan	Presentation meeting on SPI strategy and plan
Neu-tral Zone	Process Application	Application of stan-dard document tem-plates, requirements management tools, and configuration management tools	Application of re-quirements analysis techniques and analy-sis design tools.	Application of quality related policy, archi-tectural design tech-nique, and inspection technique.
Begin-ning	Process Evaluation	Analysis of defect	2nd analysis of defect, and 1st analysis of application effect	3rd analysis of defect, and 2nd analysis of application effect
	Process Establish-ment	Process map, and method of using tools for requirement man-agement and configu-ration management	Requirement analysis and design guideline, and method of analy-sis design tools	Quality related policy, architectural design guideline and inspec-tion guideline

3   TM-SPI: Transition Management of SPI

In this section, we explain how to add transition management to SPI as a means to minimize conflicts within an organization. In PDCA, transition management activities can begin after the Plan phase is complete (see Figure 1).

In putting transition management into practice, it is ideal to first break a larger transition into several smaller transitions, so that potential resistance within the organization can be kept at a controllable level. Regarding the division of a transition, we recommend the following: (1) Start from a simple procedure or product. (2) Establish an SPI plan, and reach an agreement among the affected teams. (3) Show the ROI (Return on Investment) as soon as possible. Transition management within process improvement activities is based on the above principle.

Table 5. SPI Plan Checklist

Points: 5 = Fully Agree 4 = Agree 3 = Neutral 2 = Disagree Somewhat 1 = Totally Disagree		
No.	Check Item	Point
1	Do people fully understand the problems or opportunities that provide a motive for SPI? Do people understand results that can come out if they do not enter SPI?	
2	Did representatives of groups that can be affected by SPI participate in the problem solving process before the SPI contents are finalized?	
3	Are the contents of SPI large enough?	
4	Has the extent of the organization's preparation to accept the SPI contents been analyzed?	
5	Is there a well-established communication plan that deals with, among others, the questions of what, when, and with whom information is communicated?	
6	Is there a mechanism to monitor transition? Does the mechanism contain representatives of the groups affected by SPI? Is the mechanism efficiently connected with the decision-making process?	
7	Do leaders understand the Marathon Effect[1] and are they searching for measures to fill the gap between others and themselves?	
8	Aren't unnecessary or irrelevant changes taking place during SPI?	
9	Does the SPI action plan contain well-defined weaknesses of the organization in carrying out SPI along with measures to complement such weaknesses?	
10	Has a detailed transition management plan been established and put into practice?	
Score: The score is calculated by multiplying total points by 2. If the score is lower than 60, it means that the organization is not well prepared to carry out SPI properly. It can also mean that the organization is not properly managing the transition process. (90-100 = A, 80-89 = B, 70-79 = C, 60-69 = minimum passing grade)		

---

[1] Marathon Effect expresses the idea that the speed at which individuals arrive at the „new beginning" varies widely. The reasons for the differing speeds are as follows:

1. The planners of changes start the transition process ahead of others.
2. The speed of responding to changes can vary according to personal dispositions.
3. The range and degree of influence from changes differ according to individuals and groups. Some may need a longer ending than others.

Table 4 shows the result of establishing and applying the SPI plan by dividing a project's SPI activities into several transition stages. As the process of the concerned project is iterative, each iteration is given a smaller SPI transition. If only one transition is taken up within a project, the effect may go unnoticed because several process related matters, such as project management, requirements and structure design, are closely connected. On the other hand, if many process techniques are applied simultaneously, resistance can become stronger due to delays in the development project caused by multiple learning curves. Therefore, before application, it is necessary to properly allocate and apply improvement items according to iterations calibrated to solve the current problems. At the same time, it is also necessary to analyze and report the results of the improvement activities to get systematic support required for establishing the process techniques within the organization.

Following the explanation about the measures for adding transition management to the SPI activities, we are going to describe concrete SPI checklist guidelines for the activities, from the beginning to end of the transition. Consisting of four parts, our discussion in this section contains checklists for transition management in an SPI plan (3.1) and for management during the Ending phase, where resistance to change begins to take place (3.2). We also focus on the checklist for Neutral Zone Management (3.3), which is designed to control confusion and distrust arising from the efforts to reach the targeted improvement. The Beginning Management checklist (3.4) aims to help people adapt to a new situation and will also be covered.

3.1   SPI Plan: Review of the SPI Preparation and Progress

Table 5 contains questions to be answered for affective analysis and to help determine if an organization is ready for a transition process before starting the SPI activities.

3.2   Ending Management: How to Help People Deal with Loss and Endings

Ending Management is to manage an organization in such a way that it does not return to its former state. Some people may feel difficulty about the changes taking place in their own ending process. In such a situation an SPI leader can help them manage their „ending" so that they can promptly complete the transition process. If people begin to experience loss that is the beginning of the transition process, and the leader should immediately establish a plan to manage the „ending". Table 6 shows the checklist for managing endings. It reveals the degree and extent of performance.

3.3   Neutral Zone Management: Leading People through the Neutral Zone

The neutral zone means a psychological mid-area which is neither past nor future, and neutral zone management is accordingly activities to manage confusion and distrust that can take place when nothing is clearly defined. The three core activities designed to guide people in the neutral zone via increasing their trust are communication, temporary solutions and enhancing creativity and learning. Communication is a very important element to guide people through the neutral zone. People can pass through the neutral zone rather easily when their leaders provide them clear information about the direction the organization is heading and the changes they may face on the way. Organizations in the neutral zone must exploit temporary, practical solutions. Enhancing creativity and learning is important because it makes it possible to create new knowledge, techniques and strategies which the current organization lacks. Table 7 shows a checklist that can be used for analyzing management of the neutral zone.

Table 6. Ending management checklist

Points: 5 = Fully Agree 4 = Agree 3 = Neutral 2 = Disagree Somewhat 1 = Totally Disagree		
No.	Check Item	Point
1	Do people understand what has ended, is ending, and not yet ended?	
2	Do people feel that others understand their losses?	
3	Have the elements that can be used as an excuse for returning to the past all been carefully removed?	
4	Has a clear line been drawn between present and past via a symbolic act or event that illustrates the present is definitely different from the past?	
5	Do managers accept people's complaints as a necessary and natural process?	
6	Have managers successfully made people understand problems to be solved without blaming any practice in the past?	
7	Have people been provided all the information they need? Have messages been delivered to people at least twice via a variety of media, and is the communication focused on managing the 'ending'?	
8	Do people have a fragment of the past that they want to carry to the future? The fragment may be either a practical or symbolic one?	
9	Are measures prepared to carry out changes in a gentle way by minimizing their impact on people? Have various measures to tackle loss been suggested to people?	
10	Has there been a symbolic event such as a celebration or a ritual to cut off the past?	
Score: The score is calculated by multiplying total points by 2. If the score is lower than 60, it means that the organization is not well prepared to carry out changes properly. It can also mean that the organization is not properly managing the transition process. (90-100 = A, 80-89 = B, 70-79 = C, 60-69 = minimum passing grade)		

3.4   Beginning Management: Facilitating the New Beginning

An organization normally expects people to change overnight, but the fact is, people are slow, resist, misunderstand and complain. They find it very hard to start afresh. However, if they can successfully manage the „ending" and the „neutral zone," they will actually find the „new beginning" easy to deal with. Most people gain strength after emerging from the despair and almost chaotic darkness of the „neutral zone." Table 8 shows activities that can help people cope with the „new beginning" by understanding who they are, where they are going and what they are doing.

Table 7. Neutral zone management

Points: 5 = Fully Agree 4 = Agree 3 = Neutral 2 = Disagree Somewhat 1 = Totally Disagree		
No.	Check Item	Point
1	Is there continuous communication and exchange of concerns among related people? (Connection & Concern)	
2	Are all related people provided information about the purpose of the organization, the picture of changes, future plans and their parts to be played? (Purpose, Picture, Plan & Part)	
3	Have temporary solutions been prepared for each improvement area? (Temporary Solutions)	
4	Has an environment been established in which people are encouraged to accept experimentation and risk taking? (Enhancing Creativity)	
5	Trust is an essential factor for enhancing creativity. Has trust been increased?	
6	We should press ahead with continuous improvement without over-looking even small things. Unexpected success or failure can lead to finding a clue for further development.	
7	Have people been provided opportunities to experience the view-points of other people industries, companies and businesses? (Enhancing Learning)	
8	A work environment in which people can freely exchange ideas to solve problems and are encouraged to learn and use creative techniques and processes has been created.	
9	All the members of an organization should be offered officially designated opportunities to learn. At the same time, those with outside learning should be given an opportunity to use their knowledge at the site, sharing responsibilities with others.	
10	The organization is assisting people review their duties and career in a new environment and establish a plan to acquire the necessary skills.	
Score: The score is calculated by multiplying total points by 2. If the score is lower than 60, it means that the organization is not well prepared to carry out changes properly. It can also mean that the organization is not properly managing the transition process. (90-100 = A, 80-89 = B, 70-79 = C, 60-69 = minimum passing grade)		

4   Experiences in Software Center, Samsung Electronics

In Section 4, we are going to analyze achievements made from the TM-SPI method explained in Section 3 via SPI activities carried out in the Software Center of Samsung Electronics. Software Center is a division of Samsung Electronics Co. Ltd.'s Corporate R&D Center and comprises more than 250 developers. Software Center is a leading supplier of various software components, including image processing, Internet-applications, multimedia applications, handsets and protocols. Its work ranges from small projects to very large, complex, multi-team, multi-company assignments delivering millions of lines of code. Our software process improvement culture was established in 1998 by the organization, SPI (Software Process Improvement) team.

Table 8. Beginning management

Points: 5 = Fully Agree 4 = Agree 3 = Neutral 2 = Disagree Somewhat 1 = Totally Disagree	
No.	Check Item	Point
1	Describe the details of changes you want to achieve. New attitudes and actions make such changes possible.	
2	It is important to set easily attainable goals at an early stage and to publicize and celebrate the successes.	
3	In order to establish new business roles and practices, departments and teams need to review specific charters and missions that coincide with the organization's vision and the purpose of the changes.	
4	Review and complement the compensation system to reward new techniques and acquired knowledge to encourage new attitudes and behavior.	
5	Establish a new identity for the organization, and symbolize and celebrate it through events.	
Score: The score is calculated by multiplying total points by 4. If the score is lower than 60, it means that the organization is not well prepared to carry out changes properly. It can also mean that the organization is not properly managing the transition process. (90-100 = A, 80-89 = B, 70-79 = C, 60-69 = minimum passing grade)	

4.1   SPI Activities without Transition Management: 1998~1999

In 1998, massive process improvements had just gotten underway. There was momentum for continuously propelling process improvements through the Software Center and other Samsung Electronics branches. A software process was defined based on standards from IEEE and CMM KPAs, and the organizational structure to maintain, deploy and improve processes was established.

In 1999, the Software Center began to deploy that process. An SPI team facilitated the deployment and monitored process improvement activities. Each project team designated its SCM Engineer(s) and SQA Engineer(s). Specific deployment items were (1) Project Plan and Post-Project Evaluation Report, (2) Code Inspection, (3) Coding Style Guideline, (4) SCM Plan, (5) Version Control Tool, (6) Project DB, and (7) Asset Registration for Project Asset DB. Audit teams with defined checklists twice reviewed Project Plans and SCM Plans. As a result, the Software Center, by the end of 1999, possessed the infrastructure required to proceed to CMM Level 3, such as ASP, Project DB and an SPI Team. However, the following project application problems emerged:

A delay in projects due to the unexpected need for support from other Samsung Electronics Co. divisions.

Difficulty in estimating project planning

Project management boundaries that began to blur once projects got underway

Problems caused by the retirement of developers

Insufficient documentation

Low priority for the development process due to overwork

Lack of education about and training for the process due to understaffing

Tests lingering at the user and system testing level due to the lack of employees

Lack of interest in configuration management and process

As the development process varied by project and projects underway blended with product development support projects, the need for a clear division between projects arose, hence the emergence of the specialized process.

People limited their acceptance to systems and tools, and further, the rate of Project DB or SCM tool use began to diminish. Many people expressed doubts about whether the process improvement activities would boost their productivity.

4.2   SPI Activities with Transition Management: 2000~2002

The SPI team carried out the following to solve the problems specified in section 4.1:

Table 9. SPI with transition management

	2000	2001	2002
Process Deployment	1st TM-SPI: SCM	2nd TM-SPI: Pilot Project	3rd TM-SPI: SPICE Assessment
SPI Plan	Understanding of the current SCM status Analysis of problems Establishment of execution method Presentation and discussion of SCM plan	Understanding of the develop- ment team's current level Establishment of priorities for improvement Plan for gradual process application Discussion on execution with demonstration team	Preliminary SPICE assessment and presentation Analysis of improvement items by development team Establishment of level-up plan Selection of pilot project team
Score	66	70	80
Ending Management	SCM tools Education Employment of SCM manager Solution support for each team Suspension of the source backup of team server	Essential development output documentation added Application of process for the development plan Provision of standard document form Parallel development of codes and documents	Construction and reporting of the development process web Discussions on detailed plans for each project Process tailoring for each project Weekly progress reports
Score	68	74	84
Neutral Zone Management	Regular report on each team's progress Education and consulting on SCM Application of the UCM technique Construction of the centralized SCM environment	Review of document output and feedback Education and support with CASE tools and techniques Presentation and agreement on application measures according to stages	Education of required techniques and process Inspection meeting for each document Discussion on execution method for each stage Q&A and support

Score	58	70	78
Beginning Management	Reports on successful application cases by each team Ensuring easy accessibility to source codes Celebratory event for achievement	Presentation of project improvement Planning of workbook from entire projects Writing out workbook for each project	Official evaluation of SPICE and presentation Presentation of achieved improvement and consolidation Prize awarding for participants
Score	60	64	80
Process Establishment & Construction of Organizational Infrastructure	Organization of Technical Writing Team Establishment of the project classification system	Establishment of outsourcing process Establishment of required management process Establishment of rules for the organization's operation of projects	Establishment of test process Establishment of project management process Establishment of design process Establishment of rules for organizational activities

1st TM-SPI   In the first TM-SPI, the SPI team did not consider TM when planning SPI but added it later. At that time, the SPI team encountered problems applying the improvement item, SCM, to the project. For the Neutral Zone management, the SPI Team put out and distributed a weekly report and provided each team educational programs about SCM. The SPI team finally completed construction of the organization's SCM repository, but the end result varied greatly from the initial plan.

2nd TM-SPI   As for the second TM-SPI, the SPI team carried out activities according to the SPI plan made by considering TM based on the Neutral Zone management. Here, the SPI team divided the transition into smaller parts to reduce team resistance and carried out the second TM-SPI through three mini-transitions. The first focused on standardized document templates and case tools. The second was related to analysis and design tools and SCM technique (UCM). The improvements made in the third included those in software architecture and inspection techniques. At this time, the SPI team performed an active project application by positioning experts as leaders for each process area. For example, the experts in charge of standard document templates provided templates, revised documents according to standard templates and reviewed them to find out if all the document templates were accurately filled out. Meanwhile, tool experts trained the development team in tool usage and monitored their activities to ensure compliance. The SPI team also explained the strategy behind each process application before it was initiated and produced agreement with the development team on application items.

3rd TM-SPI   When the SPI team carried out the third TM-SPI, it considered additional „ending" situations. Accordingly, the SPI team gave related members a full explanation about the problems and opportunities they might face when carrying out SPI and later organized a meeting to review possible solutions. The SPI team also prepared the repository where members could share information.

We estimated how much the transition management activities were reflected in each performance by referring to 3.1(see Table 9). The result was 63% in the first performance, 68.5% in the second and 80.5% in the third.

4.3   Analysis of Results

We analyzed TM-SPI achievement based on SPI activities carried out by Samsung Electronics' Software Center. In the first analysis, we analyzed the degree SPI success factors could be increased when the projects were carried out in TM-SPI by stages (see Table 10). In the second analysis, we analyzed the actual project period in connection with the SPI plan according to the progress of TM-SPI as well as the extent goals were achieved (see Table 11).

Table 10. Changes in SPI success factors

Points: 5 = Fully Agree 4 = Agree 3 = Neutral 2 = Disagree Somewhat 1 = Totally Disagree					
Year	1998	1999	2000	2001	2002
Success factors			TM1	TM2	TM3
1. Management commitment and support	5	2	1	2	4
2. Staff involvement	3	4	2	3	4
3. Providing enhanced understanding	3	2	2	2	4
4. Tailoring improvement initiatives	2	2	3	4	3
5. Managing the improvement project	3	3	2	4	4
6. Change agents and option leaders	4	4	4	4	4
7. Stabilizing changed processes	3	3	4	4	4
8. Encouraging communication and collaboration	4	4	3	3	4
9. Setting relevant and realistic objectives	2	2	4	4	4
10. Unfreezing the organization	3	2	1	3	4
Total Score (Totaled points X 2)	64	56	52	66	78

Table 11. Results from Each TM-SPI Performance

	TM1 (2000)	TM2 (2001)	TM3 (2002)
Improvement Items	Code management system for sources (O) Development record management system (O) Release system (O) Establishment of phase baseline (X)	Application of standard document templates (O) Application of required management tools/ techniques (O) Application of UCM (O) Application of inspection techniques (O) Application of analysis design tools/techniques (X)	Construction of standard process by linking activities in all areas (O) Designing according to design directions (O) Construction of test process (O) Construction of UCM process (O) Construction of quality control system (O) Construction of project management system (O)
Time: Actual/ Planned	11 Months/ 5 Months	10 Months/ 8 Months	6 Months/ 5 Months
Manpower	2	3	4

The results of the examination of each SPI success factor in Table 10 show the total score of success factors decreased when SPI activity was carried out without TM but began to rise from 2000 when TM was considered.

Table 11 shows the improvement items targeted for each project performance, actual and estimated time for the projects, and the number of participants. It is notable that the estimated SPI period neared the actual time taken as the project continued.

Summarizing the data from Table 9 and Table 10, Figure 2 shows the effect of TM-SPI. In 1998 when management commitment was very strong, the SPI team simultaneously introduced a new system, tools and process. But senior managers resisted the new development environment due to conflicts with traditional development culture and the lowering of efficiency. Consequently, management commitment decreased. In 2000, SPI success factors decreased because of its previous failure and lack of confidence. At that time, the SPI team started to manage transition, so they could show the ROI from SPI. The next time, the SPI team was also able to achieve its goal in a limited time by considering transition management during SPI planning.

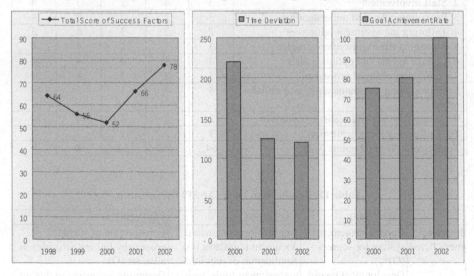

Fig 2. Analysis of the achievement via TM-SPI

5 Conclusion

Up until now, companies have often suffered difficulties in SPI projects due to unexpected delays damaging trust, a core factor for successful SPI. But the SPI team from Samsung Electronics' Software Center recently discovered that TM-SPI significantly contributes to gaining successful improvement, particularly in terms of time estimation.

The study shows that TM-SPI can substantially increase the success rate for an SPI by factoring in staff resistance. A large transition can be divided into smaller parts to hasten noticeable improvements, thus inducing active participation from development teams. By so doing, one can escalate process improvement by creating success cases from a variety of techniques in a project. We also believe one can even use TM-SPI to apply new software engineering techniques to ongoing projects. For a more efficient application of the strategy, however, one should be able to suggest the interrelationship between improvement effects and techniques before the application and explain the activities and tools that he or she will include in the application process. Also, there should be further studies on the appropriateness of the techniques, according to the development projects' distinctive features.

References

1. Humphrey, W.S., Managing the Software Process, Addison-Wesley, 1990.
2. Paulk, M. C. et al, The Capability Maturity Model: Guidelines for Improving the Software Process, Addison-Wesley, 1995.
3. ISO/IEC 15504 TR2, Software Process Assessment and Capability Determination, ISO/IEC, 1998.
4. Grady, R. B., Successful Software Process Improvement, Hewlett-Packard Company, 1997.
5. McFeeley, B., IDEAL^{SM}: A User's Guide for Software Process Improvement, CMU/SEI-96-HB-001, Feb. 1996.
6. Bridges, W., Managing Transitions, Addison-Wesley, 1991.
7. Thomas, M , McGarry F., „Top-down vs. Bottom-up Process Improvement," IEEE Software, pp.12-13, July 1994.
8. Basili, V. et al, „SEL's Software Process improvement program," IEEE Software, pp.83-87, Nov. 1995.
9. Stelzer, D., and Mellis, W., „Success Factors of Organizational Change in Software Process Improvement," Software Process Improvement and Practice, pp.227-250, 1998.
10. Rifkin, S., „Why Software Process Innovations Are Not Adopted," IEEE Software, July/Aug. 2001.
11. Bach, J., „Enough about Process: What We Need Are Heroes," IEEE Software, Mar. 1995.
12. Wiegers, K. E., „Why is Software Improvement So Hard?," Software Development , Feb. 1999.
13. Myers, W., „Why software developers refuse to improve", Computer, pp.110-112, Apr. 1998.
14. O'Day, D., „This old house [software development]", IEEE Software, pp. 72-75, Mar./Apr. 1998.
15. Pfleeger, S. L., „Realities and Rewards of Software Process Improvement", IEEE Software, pp.99-101, Nov. 1996
16. Jakobsen, A. B., „Bottom-up Process Improvement Tricks", IEEE Software, Jan./Feb. 1998.
17. Joon Sung Hong, Kang Sun Lee, ASP(A Software Process) for improving software process, APSEC, 1999.

18. Appleton, B., „Patterns for Conducting Process Improvement", Proceedings of the 4th Annual Conference on PLoP, 1997.
19. Rico, D. F., „Software Process Improvement(Impacting the Bottom Line by using Powerful „Solutions")", http://david frico.com/spipaper.pdf, Dec. 1998.
20. Hunter, R.B., Thayer, R.H. (eds.), Software Process Improvement, IEEE Computer Society Press, 2001.

Managing the Improvement of SCM Process[*]

Marcello Visconti[1] and Rodolfo Villarroel[2]

[1] Departamento de Informática, Universidad Técnica Federico Santa María
Valparaíso, Chile
visconti@inf.utfsm.cl

[2] Departamento de Computación e Informática, Universidad Católica del Maule
Talca, Chile
rvillar@spock.ucm.cl

Abstract. This article presents a framework for improving the Software Configuration Management (SCM) process, that includes a maturity model to assess software organizations and an approach to guide the transition from diagnosis to action planning. The maturity model and assessment tool are useful to identify the degree of satisfaction for practices considered key for SCM. The transition approach is also important because the application of a model to produce a diagnosis is just a first step, organizations are demanding the generation of action plans to implement the recommendations. The proposed framework has been used to assess a number of software organizations and to generate the basis to build an action plan for improvement. In summary, this article shows that the maturity model and action planning approach are instrumental to reach higher SCM control and visibility, therefore producing higher quality software.

1 Introduction

Improving product and process quality provides an important competitive edge in software industry. Quality also contributes to improve software organizations productivity, because it can heavily reduce rework costs and defects caused by poor quality. Experience in latest years has shown the tight relationship between software product quality and the processes used to build them, which motivates a shift in the approach to improve quality, because organizations are generally more concerned about product quality than about the processes being used. The key lies in having an actual picture of the way software is being developed and maintained in order to establish improvement plans. The principle is based upon improving software product quality as a result of improving the quality of the software processes in use [4].

---

[*] This research has been funded in part by the National Commission on Scientific and Technological Research of the Government of Chile, CONICYT, through research project FONDECYT #1990845.

M. Oivo and S. Komi-Sirviö (Eds.): PROFES 2002, LNCS 2559, pp. 35–48, 2002.

Software organizations have recognized the need for specific implementation guides when they adopt new software engineering methods, tools and processes. Many improvement efforts, including software process improvement, risk management, or the introduction of a new development environment, are complex and have long range effects so there is the need for specialized and systematic schemes to manage the adoption of technology during the life cycle. The Software Engineering Institute (SEI) has developed and refined the IDEAL[smt] [5] model to that end.

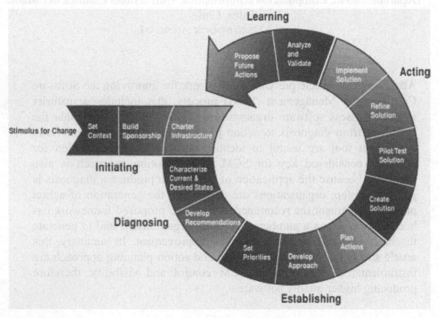

Fig. 1. The IDEAL Model

IDEAL[sm] is an organizational improvement model that is useful as a guide to initiate, plan, and implement improvement actions. Figure 1 shows the IDEAL[sm] model, composed of five phases:

I – Initiating. Laying the foundations for a successful improvement effort.

D – Diagnosing. Assessment of where an organization stands relative to a desired future state.

E – Establishing. Planning specific ways to reach the desired state.

A – Acting. Doing the work according to plan.

L – Learning. Learning from experience and improvement of skills to adopt new future technologies.

Software Configuration Management (SCM) is a software engineering discipline concerned with [2], [8]:

[†]   IDEAL[sm] is a service mark of Carnegie Mellon University.

- Identifying and documenting functional and physical characteristics of configuration items.
- Controlling changes to those characteristics, and reporting the process for those changes and their implementation status.

The problem of poor SCM quality can be considered as the inability to control the SCM process. Changes can occur at any moment, so SCM activities are useful to identify and control them, assuring their proper implementation, and informing all affected. From that standpoint, there is the need for an improvement framework that provides infrastructure and support to reach a more mature SCM process in the context proposed by the IDEAL^{sm} model. Then, the following objectives need to be satisfied:

- Development of an improvement tool (like a maturity model) and an assessment procedure for the SCM process in the context of the defined framework. The structure is based on software process concepts and the Capability Maturity Model, CMM^{sm}‡ [6], [7].
- Use of a transition approach to guide evolution from process assessment to action plan establishment in the context of the defined framework. This approach does not produce a specific action plan, it provides useful information for a particular software organization to build one.

This article is organized as follows: in the following section we present the proposed SCM process improvement framework; next, we describe a case study where we apply the proposed framework at a software organization, their results and an action list for their improvement plan; finally, we discuss the main conclusions and research projections.

2   SCM Process Improvement Framework

In this section we present the proposed framework for improving the SCM process, including maturity model, assessment instrument, assessment heuristics, assessment procedure and an approach to generate a preliminary action plan.

2.1   SCM Process Maturity Model

The maturity model presented provides the foundations for assessing the current SCM process, and guides in the identification of key practices and the required changes for their improvement. The model represents an ideal process and the assessment determines where the organization stands with respect to the model. The model and assessment tool has the main advantage of providing a deeper assessment of SCM process than other process models, such as CMM^{sm}, that only assesses the SCM process as a small part of a complete software development effort. Table 1 summarizes the model key practices and subpractices.

---

‡   CMM^{sm} is a service mark of Carnegie Mellon University.

Table 1. SCM Process Maturity Model

Level	Key Practices and Subpractices
1	**1.1 Software maintenance activities** **1.2 Backup activities**
2	**2.1 Identification and characterization of repository** • Definition and establishment of procedures associated to repository. • Establishment of services provided by repository. • Establishment of access mechanism to repository. **2.2 Establishment of code version control** • Establishment of code versions. • Characterization of code configuration items. • Documentation of code versions. **2.3 Establishment and assessment of formal change control method** • Establishment of formal change control. • Assessment of formal change control method. **2.4 Establishment of project configuration control** • Establishment of a procedure to generate software versions. • Establishment of a procedure to review and authorize changes to software versions. **2.5 Acknowledgement of importance of SCM** • Establishment of a known policy that recognizes importance of SCM. • Establishment of a procedure for adherence to established policy.
3	**3.1 Establishment of plan and procedure to implement SCM activities** • Establishment of an SCM plan. • Establishment of a procedure for implanting SCM. **3.2 Establishment of defined process to implement SCM activities** • Establishment of a written defined process for SCM implementation. • Establishment of a procedure for adherence to defined SCM process. **3.3 Establishment of SCM group** • Establishment of coordination and implementation of SCM activities. • SCM activities training. **3.4 Assessment of usefulness of SCM activities** • Individual/group perception of SCM activities usefulness. • Establishment of a procedure to get user feedback.
4	**4.1 Definition and analysis of SCM activities measurements** • Definition of SCM activities measurements for quality, productivity, complexity and risk. • Analysis of measurements for SCM activities. **4.2 Verification of implementation of SCM activities** • Change management for practices of SCM process. • Change management for technology of SCM process. **4.3 Improvement feedback for SCM process** • Record and tracking of SCM activities results. • Audits of SCM process.

Table 2. SCM Maturity model assessment instrument (partial – level 2)

2.1 Identification and characterization of repository • ....

2.2 Establishment of code version control
   2.2.1 Establishment of code versions
     • Source and executable code is subject to version control.
     • Basic software (OS, translators, etc.) is subject to version control.
     • Support software (test data, compression, etc.) is subject to version control.
   2.2.2 Characterization of code configuration items
     • Existence of naming scheme for each version.
     • Existence of a procedure to establish when a code piece enters the repository.
     • Existence of an explicit relationship for different versions of application software, basic software and support software.
   2.2.3 Documentation of each version
     • Version documentation includes configuration files.
     • Version documentation includes data files.
     • Version documentation includes computer programs.
     • Version documentation includes used libraries.
     • Version documentation includes an scheme relating previous items.

2.3 Establishment and assessment of formal change control method.
   2.3.1 Establishment of formal change control
     • Existence of change report documentation.
     • Existence of change control procedure.
     • Existence of assigned responsibilities for change control.
     • Use of tools to execute change control.
     • Existence of a procedure to prioritize change requests.
   2.3.2 Assessment of formal change control method
     • Assessment of operational impact of change.
     • Use of change control procedure.
     • Existence of reviews for change documents.
     • Record of request data and answer.
     • Record of changes performed.
     • Communication of changes performed.

2.4 Establishment of project configuration control • ....
2.5 Acknowledgement of importance of SCM • ....

2.2   Assessment Tool

The tool to be used is a checklist that contains a defined number of scenarios for each maturity level and key practice to verify if they are accomplished and their degree of satisfaction. The maturity level and degree of satisfaction for key practices are determined. The elements under consideration in the checklist are linked with the existence of an activity (*Yes/No*), with the frequency with which an activity is executed (*Never, Seldom, Most times, Always*), or whether the activity could be *Not Applicable*. With the answers to the assessment checklist we can identify the degree of satisfaction for the key practices associated to each maturity level, and according to this information elaborate an SCM process profile for the particular organization under evaluation. The SCM process profile shows the degree of satisfaction for each key practice, that is one of the following: *Very High, High, Medium, Low, and Very Low*. Each degree of satisfaction is determined with the answers to the checklist items that are associated to the particular key practice.

Table 2 shows the partial content of the assessment instrument, presenting issues to be reviewed for some subpractices in level 2 of the SCM process maturity model. Full details of assessment instrument can be found in [10].

2.3   Assessment Heuristic

The assessment heuristic has the following steps:

- Determination of score for each checklist item
- Determination of score for each subpractice
- Determination of degree of satisfaction for each key practice
- Determination of overall maturity level.

Determination of score for each checklist item. Each answer to the checklist has a possible score as shown in Table 3. The group of respondents answers according to the existence of an activity, or to how frequently that activity is carried out in the organization. They have the *Not Applicable* option too.

It is important to note that this activity is conducted at a group meeting where the participants are representatives from software organization personnel and assessment team. Each answer is reached through a consensus process among all participants, with guidance from the assessment team.

Determination of score for each subpractice. The score is computed as the average of all the answers associated to each subpractice. A score of „N" is not considered in the average computation.

Determination of degree of satisfaction for key practices. The degree of satisfaction is determined after computing the average of all associated   subpractice scores. Table 4 shows the different degrees of satisfaction.

Table 3. Assigned Score to Each Answer

Score	Frequency Answer
N	Not applicable
0	Don't know
1	Never or No
2	Seldom
3	Most times
4	Always or Yes

Table 4. Degree of Satisfaction for Key Practices

Degree of Satisfaction	Average Score for Subpractices
Very High	Score >= 3,5
High	3,0 <= Score < 3,5
Medium	2,0 <= Score < 3,0
Low	1,5 <= Score < 2,0
Very Low	Score < 1,5

Determination of maturity level. To be in a given level, every key practice for that level and the previous levels must show a degree of satisfaction of at least *High*, the only exception being level 1 (default level).

2.4   Assessment Procedure

The assessment procedure considers the following tasks:

Pre-Assessment. Preparation for the assessment. The participants are oriented about the goals for the assessment activity, and the major process improvement concepts are presented. An explanation of what is and what isn't to be expected is given, along with a description of the main potential benefits, stressing that the end goal is to assess process and not people, to avoid as much as possible any unwanted effects in the answers. Finally, the material to be used is presented.

Assessment. The appropriate group of participants is identified according to the software projects being developed at the organization. Then, the group completes the assessment checklist.

Elaboration of Report. Once the assessment tasks is completed an assessment report is produced. The contents of such a report are: assessed projects and results, maturity profiles by project, organizational process maturity profile, and recommendations to generate an action plan.

The proposed framework aims to efficiently diagnose the present status of the SCM process, which needs to be carried out without consuming too many resources on the part of the assessed organization. To that end we have proposed a simple model that reasonably represents the different scenarios for a software organization, a simple assessment tool that allows the efficient determination of the particular scenario where the organization stands according to the model, and an assessment procedure with specific and precise steps for using the model and assessment instrument towards the elaboration of a preliminary version of an action plan, in the form of process improvement recommendations operational for the specific organization.

2.5   Elaboration of a Preliminary Action Plan

According to the IDEAL^{sm} model and its prescribed phases, once the diagnosis is completed and the main improvement areas have been selected there is the need to establish the bases for the elaboration of an improvement action plan. We use an approach similar to the Goal-Question-Metric (GQM) [1] approach. GQM provides a useful way to define measurements for project progress and results, considering that a measurement program can be more appropriate when designed with the goals in mind. The questions help determining whether the goals are being met, then their answers will need to be potentially measurable. GQM involves three steps:

- GOALS: List the main goals for the measurement task.
- QUESTIONS: Derive from each goal questions that need to be answered to determine if the goals are met.
- METRICS: Decide what must be measured in order to properly answer the questions.

The approach we use, Goal-Question-Action-Activity (GQAA) [3], captures the essence of GQM but applying it for a different purpose. The main idea is that an action plan can be more successful if actions and activities are determined with the goals and key issues in mind. The proposed scheme has four steps:

- GOALS: List the main goals for the particular improvement process.
- QUESTIONS: List the main issues that determine the relevance of the defined goals.
- ACTIONS: Derive from each goal and question the actions that need to be carried out to meet the goals and address the main issues in the questions.
- ACTIVITIES: Derive from each action the specific activities that need to be executed to carry out the action; use the ETVX diagram [3], [9].

ENTRY	TASK	EXIT
Policies	Plans	Goal Satisfaction
Procedures	Actions	Assets
Resources	Metrics	Complete Products
Funds	Information	
Training		
Orientation		
Processes		
Sponsorships	**VERIFICATION**	
Responsibilities / Roles		
Databases	Reviews / Audits	
Tools / Methods	Measurements	
	Analysis	

Fig. 2. ETVX diagram

The ETVX (Entry, Task, Verification, eXit) diagram facilitates the definition of activities by considering four main activity aspects: entry criteria, tasks, verification, and exit criteria, as it is shown in Figure 2.

3   Case Study

In this section we describe a case study where we fully apply the SCM process improvement framework proposed in section 2.

3.1   Background

The study was conducted for four software companies that belong to one organization that has a highly automated software development process, building their own development environments and tools.

Each software company presents the following features:

- Company 1 provides information technology and management services, for big and medium size private companies as well as public administration
- Company 2 develops customized software for big and medium size private companies, in the client-server and internet domain
- Company 3 develops consultancy services for higher management in information technology, organizational modeling and business process redesign
- Company 4 provides solutions for public sector, mainly through the development of management information systems.

During the study we conducted four sessions:

- Pre-assessment for orientation and concept clarification
- Assessment of each company using the assessment tool
- Presentation of results, validation and prioritization of recommendations
- Preliminary application of GQAA approach to generate the bases for an action plan and the presentation of a report with final results.

The results are shown as a global profile for the SCM process in the organization, and for each of the four companies. Consequently with the results a series of recommendations is produced, which are validated and prioritized for each company, finally getting a prioritized list for the whole organization.

3.2   Process Assessment

After the orientation and concept clarification performed in the pre-assessment, the assessment was conducted with representatives (project managers and engineers) for each of the four companies. Four assessments (one for each company) were carried out, where participants belonging to one particular company provided their answers through consensus exercises, with very helpful interaction among them to clarify concepts and practices. The participants were given the opportunity to give their own recommendations as to how they thought the assessment could be improved. Some of those recommendations were incorporated in the framework presented in section 2.

Table 5. Maturity Profile for the Organization

Level	Key Practice	Key Practice Description	Key Practice Degree of Satisfaction
1	1.1	Software maintenance activities Backup activities	High
	1.2		Medium
2	2.1	Identification and characterization of repository	Very Low
	2.2	Establishment of code version control	Low
	2.3	Establishment and assessment of formal change control method	Medium
	2.4	Establishment of project configuration control	Medium
	2.5	Acknowledgement of importance of SCM	Low
3	3.1	Establishment of a plan and a procedure to implement SCM activities	Very Low
	3.2	Establishment of a defined process to implement SCM activities	Low
	3.3	Establishment of an SCM group	Low
	3.4	Assessment of usefulness of SCM activities	Low
4	4.1	Definition and analysis of SCM activities measurements	Very Low
	4.2	Verification of Implementation of SCM activities	Very Low
	4.3	Improvement feedback for SCM process	Very Low

3.3   Assessment Results

The assessment results showed that all four companies were assessed at level 1 and their maturity profiles were very similar. So, the organization was found to be at level 1. Table 5 shows the overall maturity profile for the organization. The results for all four companies showed that the organization as a whole presented the same strengths and weaknesses, so the results are shown aggregate and not for every single company. Based on these results, the following key practices were found as needing substantial improvement in order to meet the requirements for the first two levels: *Identification and characterization of repository*, *Establishment of code version control*, and

Acknowledgement of importance of SCM. Full details of the assessment results, for each company and for the organization, can be found in [10].

Table 6. Score for Improvement Recommendations

Recommendation	Score by Company				Total
1. Backup activities	6	7	1	1	15
2. Identification and characterization of repository	4	3	5	6	18
3. Establishment of code version control	7	6	7	5	25
4. Establishment and assessment of formal change control method	5	5	2	2	14
5. Establishment of project configuration control	3	2	3	3	11
6. Acknowledgement of importance of SCM	1	0	4	4	9
7. Establishment of an SCM group	2	0	6	7	15
8. Establishment of a plan and a procedure to implement SCM activities	0	4	0	0	4
9. Establishment of a defined process to implement SCM activities	0	1	0	0	1

3.4 Validation and Prioritization of Recommendations

Once the assessment results have been delivered back to the organization, they are analyzed and discussed in detail for every key practice and subpractice, for each company and for the whole organization. Representatives from each company acknowledged their limitations in some of the key practices, and they all agreed on the need to formalize those with *Medium* degree of satisfaction (*Backup activities* as an example).

Finally, seven recommendations were given back to the organization. The following list shows the recommendations according to the priority order after they were evaluated by the participants:

- Backup activities
- Identification and characterization of repository
- Establishment of code version control
- Establishment and assessment of formal change control method
- Establishment of project configuration control
- Acknowledgement of importance of SCM
- Establishment of an SCM group.

Each company was asked to assign a score between 1 and 7 to each recommendation, where a „1" means that the recommendation can be addressed last whereas a „7" means that the recommendation should be the first to be considered. Table 6 shows the score each company assigned to each recommendation, and the total score for each recommendation considering all four companies. It is interesting to note that Company 2 did not assign a score to a couple of the recommendations (6 and 7 in Table 6), they considered more important to prioritize two other recommendations (shown in Table 6 as recommendations 8 and 9) because, in their view, recommendations 6 and 7 were going to be addressed anyways when taking care of the rest of the recommendations. That's the reason why Table 6 shows 9 and not 7 recommendations.

Table 7. Questions and Answers - Goal „Establish Version Control and Backups"

Questions	Answers for the Goal Defined
Current status?	Versions are not controlled and backups are not carried out methodically
What?	Requirements, design, code and backups
Why?	Need to reduce the impact of inconsistent versions in different installations for customer and development team
Who?	A software research and development team
How?	Building a tool to automate the control of each component
When?	Short term (4 months)
Costs?	8 person-months
Benefits?	Reduced development and maintenance times, besides increased data security
Risks?	Centralization without proper security mechanisms, besides internal disposition to implant the tool

3.5   Generation of Preliminary Action Plan

With the priorities established by the organization and the dependency order for each key practice according to the maturity level they are in, the GQAA approach was used to guide the transition from these recommendations to the establishment of an action plan. In order to demonstrate the applicability of the proposed GQAA approach in this SCM process improvement context we show its use for one particular goal, defined as the highest priority by the organization. The highest-priority goal defined by them was „Establish version control and backups". Table 7 shows the questions that need to be answered in order to assess the goal relevance, importance and timeliness, and the particular answers in this case.

From the answers to these questions the company representatives agreed that the main action to carry out was „Building a tool to automate the control of each component". The particular activities needed to carry out that action followed naturally:

* Requirement integration and definition of system scope
* Building the tool
* Implanting the tool.

Figure 3 shows a partial representation of the application of the ETVX diagram to the activity „Building the tool" from the action „Building a tool to automate the control of each component", which in turn aims to satisfy the goal „Establish version control and backups". Creating a particular ETVX diagram as the one shown in Figure 3 is an iterative effort, at first the main tasks are identified, followed by the definition of entry and exit criteria; then, these criteria are useful in the specification of verification activities, but they also suggest new tasks so the cycle may start again.

This approach can be applied for every process improvement goal as an ordered scheme to produce all the necessary information to generate a complete action plan.

ENTRY	TASK	EXIT
• Requirements from each company • Personnel trained	• Design • Construction • Test • Implantation VERIFICATION Walkthroughs	Assets/products • Tool broadly used in all four companies (executable code, design documents, on-line user documentation) Goal satisfaction • Tool in use

Fig. 3. ETVX Diagram for Activity „Building the Tool"

4   Conclusions and Research Projections

This research effort and its resulting product, the SCM process improvement framework, do not solve every problem associated with the improvement of that particular process. It is only a step in the right direction, because it focuses on a very important problem providing needed guidance to move towards a solution.

The proposed maturity model addresses a host of key practices and subpractices in different scenarios or improvement levels, and an assessment tool that encompasses a series of issues that need to be considered. The scheme of key practices and subpractices allows organizations to focus more on satisfying key practices rather than reaching a given maturity level. While it may be true that the maturity level can serve as a status recognition for a software organization, the degree of satisfaction of key practices delivers more useful information for improving the process.

The checklist-based assessment procedure makes up a very efficient procedure to assess against a process model. Answering individually a questionnaire is not necessarily better, considering the many contradictions that need to be resolved later, usually at a new meeting (and extra hours of effort). The proposed scheme allows for interaction among the assessment participants, clarifying any confusion or doubt right at the moment the assessment is conducted, and looking for consensual answers.

The GQAA approach allows the systematic generation of requested actions and activities, enabling the identification of basic elements for the elaboration of a preliminary action plan. GQAA is perceived as a valid scheme to face the transition between diagnosis and action planning for any software process, because it doesn't present any feature that will limit it to a particular software process. Nonetheless, while GQAA allows the consideration of increasing detail as it is deemed necessary, the risks of generating too much detailed information that could negatively impact the action plan elaboration process must be properly managed.

The case study was carried out with the main purpose of evaluating the applicability of the proposed improvement framework to the SCM process, so a future task is the model validation, trying to correlate maturity levels with specific and measurable product and process benefits – higher visibility, increased control, higher quality, less rework -, analyzing the model predictive capability through a formal experiment. Other future research work includes: full scale application of GQAA approach, extra assessment and reassessment, development of an automated tool to facilitate the improvement effort, development of generic tools (checklists, templates, guides) for the implantation of SCM practices, development of a generic improvement action plan for small size organizations.

Acknowledgements

We are thankful to Christian Valencia for his invaluable help in reviewing and improving earlier manuscripts of this research work, and to the organization that took part in the case study described in this article.

References

1. Basily, V. and Weiss, D. A Methodology for Collecting Valid Software Engineering Data, IEEE Transactions on Software Engineering: 728-738, 1984.
2. Berlack, H. Ronald. Software Configuration Management. John Wiley and Sons, Inc. 1992.
3. Cook, C. R. and Visconti, M. What to Do After the Asessment Report. Proceedings of Pacific Northwest Software Quality Conference, Portland, Oregon, USA, October 1999.
4. Grady, R. Successful Software Process Improvement. Hewlett-Packard Professional Books, 1997.
5. McFeeley, R. IDEAL: A User's Guide for Software Process Improvement. Technical Report CMU/SEI-96-HB-001. CMU/SEI, Pittsburgh, Pennsylvania, 1996.
6. Paulk M, Curtis B, Chrissis M, Weber C. Capability Maturity Model, version 1.1, IEEE Software 10(4) : 18-27, 1993.
7. Paulk M, Curtis B, Chrissis M, Weber C. The Capability Maturity Model guidelines for improving the software process. Addison-Wesley: Reading, 1995.
8. Pfleeger, S.L. Software Engineering: Theory and Practice. Second edition. Prentice-Hall. 2001.
9. Radice, R. Getting to level 3 in the SEI's CMM. Proceedings of VISION Conference, CRIM-ASEC, Montreal, Quebec, Canada, October 1996.
10. Villarroel, R. Modelo de Madurez de Gestión de Configuración de Software. Master's Tesis, Departamento de Informática, Universidad Técnica Federico Santa María, Valparaíso, Chile, June 2000. (in Spanish)

Exploiting a Virtual Environment in a Visual PML

Kamal Zuhairi Zamli and Peter Lee

School of Computing Science, University of Newcastle upon Tyne
NE1 7RU United Kingdom
{K.Z.Zamli,P.A.Lee}@ncl.ac.uk

Abstract. This paper discusses a visual process modeling language called Virtual Reality Process Modeling Language (VRPML). Novel features have been introduced in VRPML to investigate perceived weaknesses in existing PMLs, and include support for the integration of a virtual environment, and dynamic creation and assignment of tasks and resources at the PML level. The paper describes the VRPML syntax and semantics.

1   Introduction

Software processes relate to the sequence of steps that must be carried out by humans (or „agents") to pursue the goals of software engineering. In order to have an accurate representation of what these steps actually are, software processes can be modeled using a process modeling language (PML). Some PMLs simply support the specification of the steps, while others enable the process to be executed (or enacted). When enacted, software processes can provide guidance, automation and enforcement of the software engineering practices that are embodied in the model.

While there has been much fruitful research into PMLs, their takeup by industry has not been widespread [14]. While the reasons for this lack of success may be many and varied, our research identified two areas in which PMLs may have been deficient: human dimension issues [22]; and support for addressing management and resource issues that might arise dynamically when a PML is being enacted.

Paradoxically, human dimension issues have always been a major concern in research into software processes [1]. However, current trends in the way software engineers work (e.g. cross organizational boundary, geographically and temporally distributed locations) suggest that much more could be done to address the human dimension issues in terms of providing support for engineers (e.g. enactment within a virtual environment, process awareness support and process visualization), and in reflecting that support in the features provided in a PML. Issues from related research areas such as Collaborative Virtual Environment (CVE), a subset of Computer Supported Cooperative Work (CSCW) and Visual Language community, seem particularly appropriate [9,22].

Software processes are highly dynamic and rarely can they be completely specified ahead of time. An example of such dynamic behavior can be seen in the case when a

M. Oivo and S. Komi-Sirviö (Eds.): PROFES 2002, LNCS 2559, pp. 49-62, 2002.

software engineer leaves their job in the middle of a software development project and a new assignment of tasks needs to be made.

Our research is developing a new PML, called Virtual Reality Process Modeling Language (VRPML), as a research vehicle for investigating these issues. The novel contribution of VRPML includes exploiting a virtual environment in its enactment and allowing dynamic creation and assignment of tasks and resources.

2   Related Work

A significant number of PMLs have been proposed in the last 12 years. Surveys of the majority of the languages are provided elsewhere [5, 13, 21]; here we concentrate briefly on the novel features in VRPML.

Integrating a virtual environment into software processes in itself is not new. Most commonly, virtual environments have been used as part of the support environment for a PML - Process Centered Software Engineering Environments (PSEE) [4, 7, 8]. Dopke [7] developed a prototype proscriptive PSEE called PROMO, which demonstrated a mapping of software processes into a virtual environment. A similar prototype PSEE was also produced by Becattini [4]. In other work, Dossick and Kaiser [8] developed a (persistent) software engineering support environment in a virtual environment.

VRPML differs from the above in that it provides language support for identifying virtual environments as resources that can be used in the process modeling, and then uses those resources at enactment time. A simple example would be a step in a process that requires geographically separated engineers to meet. VRPML permits a virtual meeting room to be specified as a resource, with the obvious realization at enactment time. Further examples are given below.

3   Overview of VRPML

The ISPW-6 problem [15] is often used as a common example of a software process for illustrating the features of a PML. Fig. 1 presents a partial solution to this problem using VRPML, and is discussed briefly here with more detailed descriptions of the various VRML features given in Section 4.

As can be seen, VRPML has a visual syntax, with the enactment model being based on the flow of control flow signals between nodes. Software processes are written in VRPML as graphs, by interconnecting nodes from top to bottom using arcs carrying control flow signals. In VRPML, software processes are modeled generically, in the sense that while the model identifies the steps, the particular resources required for an instantiation (in terms of agents, artifacts and tools) can be dynamically assigned and customized for specific projects.

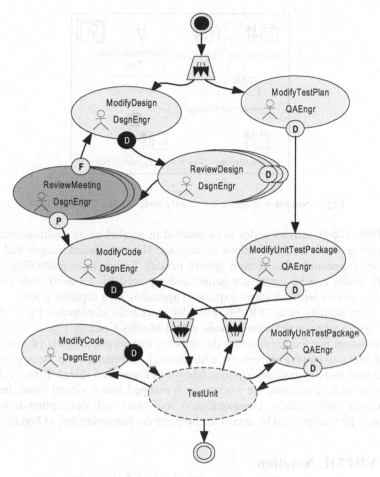

Fig. 1. Partial solution of the ISPW-6 problem

As in JIL [17] and Little JIL [19], software processes in VRPML are described using process steps, which represent the most atomic portion of a software process (i.e. the actual task that agents are expected to perform). These process steps are represented as nodes on a graph, called *activity nodes* (shown as small ovals with a stick figure). VRPML support a number of different kinds of activity nodes – some examples are in Fig.1, but are discussed further in Section 4.

The firing of activity nodes is controlled by the arrival of a control flow signal. Control flow signals may be generated at the completion of a node, often from special completion events called *transitions* (shown as small white circles with a capital letter, attached to an activity node) or *decomposable transitions* (small black circles with a capital letter). An initial control flow signal is always be generated from a *start node* (a white circle enclosing a small black circle). A *stop node* (a white circle enclosing another white circle) does not generate any control flow signals.

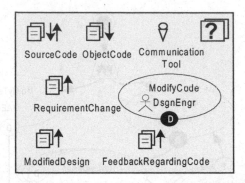

Fig. 2. Sample workspace for activity node Modify Code in Fig. 1

VRPML allows activity nodes to be enacted in parallel using multi-instance nodes (overlapping ovals) or combinations of language elements called *merger* and *replicator nodes* (trapezoidal boxes with arrows inside). To improve readability, a set of VRPML nodes can be grouped together and replaced by a *macro node* (shown as dotted line ovals), with the macro expansion appearing on a separate graph.

For every activity node, VRPML provides a separate *workspace*. Fig. 2 depicts a sample workspace for the activity node called Modify Code in Fig. 1. A workspace hosts resources needed for enacting the activity: transitions, artifacts (shown as overlapping two overlapping documents with arrows), communication tools (shown as a microphone) and any task descriptions (shown as a question mark). Effectively, when an activity node is enacted, the workspace is mapped into a virtual room, transitions into buttons, and artifacts, communication tools and task description into objects which may be manipulated by agents to complete the particular task at hand.

4   VRPML Notation

As VRPML uses a control flow model, it is necessary to be able to describe the generation and propagation of control flow signals. Besides the use of transitions (described below), VRPML provides and handles control flow signals through start nodes, stop nodes and re-enabled nodes. The notation for these nodes is given in Fig. 3.

A start node generates an initial control flow signal when the VRPML graph is first enacted. A stop node serves as an exit point for control flow signals. A re-enabled node behaves like a stop node allowing the control flow signal to exit and permitting the same control flow signal to re-enable its own parent's activity node - their use will be clarified when decomposable transitions are explained below.

Fig. 3. Start, Stop and Re-enabled nodes

Fig. 4. Arc

In VRPML, arcs are conduits for control flow signals. Arcs depict dependencies amongst activity node and their proper sequencing. Arcs are unidirectional and only one control flow signal may flow on a particular arc at any particular time. The obvious notation for arcs is given in Fig. 4.

Process steps are used as the main abstraction for software processes in VRPML, as in JIL and Little JIL. They are represented as activity nodes and workspaces, and for every activity node, a workspace must exist.

In general, an activity node is a parameterised node, accepting a role assignment as a parameter which may be used to allocate a specific engineer to the task. For a particular activity node, a workspace hosts transitions, and artifacts and communication tools for completing the activity. In addition, for every workspace, a task description can be optionally specified to informally describe the activity in natural language and be made available during enactment to guide the agent. In VRPML, the concept of workspaces can be seen as a step toward supporting process visualization.

There are three kinds of activity nodes supported by VRPML. They are a *general-purpose activity node*, a *multi-instance activity node* and a *meeting activity node*. The visual representation of activity nodes and their workspaces is given in Fig. 5.

A general-purpose activity node represents the most atomic part of software processes which an agent is expected to perform. A multi-instance activity node, a concept borrowed from APEL [6], is a collection of identical process steps performed by more than one agent. A meeting activity node allows multiple agents to meet virtually to make some collective decision. Both multi-instance activity and meeting activity nodes have an associated depth, indicating the actual number of agents involved (and also the number of identical activities in the case of multi-instance activity). Depths of multi-instance activity and meeting activity nodes can be specified during instantiation or dynamically.

As exemplified in Fig. 5, workspaces for different kinds of activity nodes are unique. The reason for having a unique workspace is to support a sense of process awareness during process enactment. For instance, agents are able to distinguish whether the process steps that they are undertaking also concurrently involve other agents - the case for multi-instance activities. Such awareness should encourage inter-agent communications, which is seen as one of the important aspect of supporting collaborative work [20].

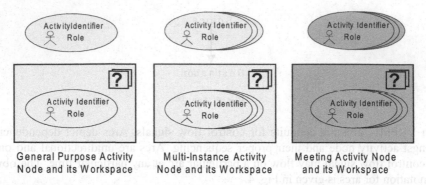

General Purpose Activity   Multi-Instance Activity   Meeting Activity Node
Node and its Workspace   Node and its Workspace   and its Workspace

Fig. 5. Activity nodes and their workspaces

When a process step specified by an activity node is undertaken in its workspace, there is obviously a need to be able to indicate its completion (success or failure) or cancellation. The way VRPML support such events is through *transitions* (similar to options in VPL [18]). Effectively, transitions give an agent some flexibility and choice of control over what happen next. This is an important characteristic, which can also be seen in other PMLs, particularly Little JIL[19]. In term of semantics, a transition is similar to a button (in the agent's virtual room), which responds to a click-event. On pressing a transition, a single control flow signal is generated.

In the case where certain post-conditions would have to be satisfied or some automated steps would need to be performed before allowing the completion or cancellation of a process step, VRPML allows transitions to be decomposable. *Decomposable transitions* enable automation scripts or sub-graphs to be specified (and executed if selected). An example of a transition labelled D (representing a 'done' transition) and a decomposable transition labelled A (representing an 'abort' transition) is given in Fig. 6.

The re-enabled node introduced earlier behaves like a stop node allowing a control flow signal to exit through in a decomposable transition and permitting the same control flow signal to re-enable its parent's activity node. To illustrate the behavior of a re-enabled node, Fig. 7 depicts a sub-graph representing the decomposable transition labelled D (for Done) for the activity node Modify Code in Fig. 1. If the transition representing Redo (labelled R) in the activity node Check Compilation in Fig. 7 is pressed by the agent, a control flow signal will be generated and will re-enable its parent activity node Modify Code.

Fig. 6. Example of a transition and a decomposable transition

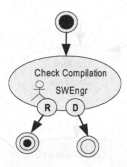

Fig. 7. Example usage of a Re-enabled node

The access given to the assigned agent for transitions is handled differently for different kinds of activity nodes. In a general-purpose activity node, an assigned agent has sole access to the transitions in that node. In a multi-instance activity node, each assigned agent also has sole access to their instance of the transitions but only one control flow signal will be generated eventually from the node. For this signal to be generated, all of the multi-instance transitions must be completed. Control flows generated for each of these transitions can be thought of as passing through a merger node (described below).

In a *meeting activity node*, access to transitions is only given to a designated agent who is expected to moderate the meeting. By convention, the agent assigned to the top general-purpose activity node in a meeting activity node is assumed to be the moderator. Meeting activity nodes can also be used to support process steps involving multiple agents, but access to transitions will be centrally controlled by the moderator.

To support modularization of its graphs, VRPML provides a macro facility. A *macro node* can group one or more nodes together and replace them with a single node, to reduce the graph complexity. Semantically, a macro node behaves like a textual macro in the C programming language. When a control flow signal encounters a macro node, the enacted VRPML graph is rewritten to include the graph contained in that macro. In this way, a macro may be used in different parts of VRPML graphs. The visual representation of a macro node is given in Fig. 8.

To illustrate the usage of a macro node, Fig. 9 shows the expansion of the macro node called Test Unit in Fig. 1.

Fig. 8. Macro node

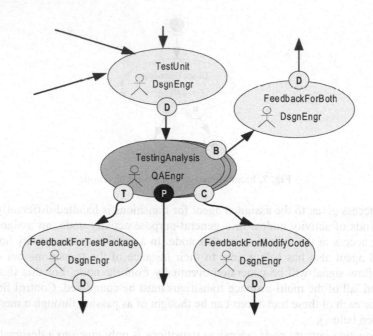

Fig. 9. Macro expansion for Test Unit (see Fig. 1)

Since software processes in reality are never performed in a sequential manner, a PML needs to support process steps running in parallel. As well as the use of multi-instance nodes, in VRPML this parallelism support is enabled using *replicator* and *merger nodes*. Replicator nodes accept a control flow signal and replicate it as many times as specified by arcs leaving it. Merger nodes accept many control flow signals and convert them into a single signal. In doing so, a merger node blocks execution until it receives the control flow signals on all of its input arcs. The visual representation of replicator and merger nodes is given in Fig. 10.

Artifact icons provide access to the actual artifacts and tools needed to complete the particular process step, and can only be defined inside a workspace. An artifact has two formal parameters. These parameters are associated with the actual location of the artifact (e.g. a particular source file) and the corresponding tool and its actual location (e.g. the compiler to use). Typically, these parameters are set either during instantiation or dynamically during enactment. Artifacts have 5 modes of access: read only, read and write, write only, local and exclusive. The default mode of access for artifacts is read and write. With the exception of exclusive, other modes of access are similar to Little JIL. Exclusive access mode is needed in the case of multi-instance activity nodes and meeting activity nodes where artifacts are by default shared amongst assigned agents. By using the exclusive access mode, certain shared artifacts can be made exclusively accessible to a particular agent. The visual representation of artifacts and their modes of access is given in Fig. 11.

Fig. 10. Replicator and Merger nodes

Read   Read/Write   Write   Local   Exclusive

Fig. 11. Artifacts and their access rights

Communication tools support interactions amongst agents, which is an important element when geographically and temporally distributed software engineering teams are involved in the processes. Synchronous (e.g. teleconferencing programs or chat-like programs) and asynchronous (e.g. email or messaging programs) tools are provided as icons and have one formal parameter. This parameter, which may be set during instantiation or dynamically, relates to the actual tool and its location. Just as with artifacts, communication tools must be defined inside a workspace. One way of providing user awareness support is to use videoconferencing-like systems as the main synchronous communication tool. The visual notation for synchronous and asynchronous communication tools is given in Fig. 12.

Finally, like other PMLs, VRPML also provides support for specifying comments. In general, comments allow extra documentation, and provide some justification pertaining to the chosen approach in the source code. In VRPML, comments can be placed anywhere. The visual representation of a comment is given in Fig. 13.

5   Enactment Model

As mentioned in the previous section, resources in VRPML include agents (e.g. for roles assignment), artifacts and tools (including synchronous and asynchronous communication tools), and are specified as part of a workspace. Since software processes are highly dynamic, resources can rarely be specified completely during instantiation, and require dynamic support during enactment. VRPML exploits a resource exception handling mechanism to provide this support.

Fig. 12. Synchronous and asynchronous communication tools

Fig. 13. Comments

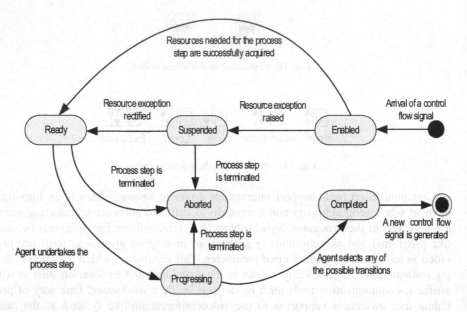

Fig. 14. VRPML enactment model

As in Little JIL [19], there are two types of resource exceptions supported by VRPML:

- Resource unknown; and
- Resource unavailable.

Resource unknown exceptions are thrown if no matching resources can be identified (e.g. in the case of failure to assign activity node to agents, or a failure to locate the artifacts/tools needed in a workspace). Resource unavailable exceptions are thrown if no matching resources can be acquired (e.g. in the case of shared artifacts with exclusive mode of access).

Whenever a resource exception is thrown, VRPML blocks further enactment of the graph. As software processes are typically long-lived, blocking removes the need to roll-back and recover from the effect of previously completed process steps, thus, allowing online rectification of an exception. In this way, enactment of a generic software process model can be allowed even if resources have not yet been assigned.

Fig. 14 depicts the enactment model for an activity node in VRPML expressed in terms of a state transition diagram. The behavior of the runtime system supporting such an enactment model can be thought of as consisting of a single producer (VRPML interpreter) and multiple consumers (VRPML agents) communicating using a shared tuple space as in Linda [10].

Upon the arrival of a control flow signal, an activity node will be in an **enabled** state. This is where the VRPML interpreter attempts to acquire resources that the activity node needs. If resources are successfully acquired, the VRPML interpreter then „produces" the process step corresponding to that activity node in the tuple space. The agent's runtime support system then „consumes" the process step putting it into a **ready** state. Ideally, in this state, the process step is made available in the to-do-list of the assigned agent. If for any reason, the VRPML interpreter fails to acquire resources it needs, a resource exception (i.e. resource unknown or resource unavailable) will be thrown putting the enactment of that particular process step in the VRPML graph into a **suspended** state. In this state, the interpreter automatically produces a process step in the tuple space for the administrator agent (in this case, it may be the project manager) to permit them to rectify the resource exception or terminate the process step (putting it in an **aborted** state). If a process step is terminated, the administrator agent may optionally terminate the overall enactment of the particular VRPML graph in question or manually re-enact connecting and enclosing nodes (e.g. in a decomposable transition) by providing the necessary control flow signals that they need to fire. If the resource exception is rectified, enactment of the particular VRPML graph can continue allowing VRPML interpreter again to „produce" the process step in the tuple space. This process step can then be put into a **ready** state once the agent's runtime support system has consumed it. If an agent selects that particular process step (in the **progressing** state), a workspace for that process step will appear as a virtual room with artifacts, transitions and communication tools as objects which agent can manipulate to complete the task. The process step is in the **completed** state when the agent selects any one of the possible transitions.

6   Discussion

It is hoped that the explanation of VRPML in sections 4 and 5 now permit the reader to understand more fully the (partial) solution to the ISPW-6 problem introduced earlier. In a small research (PhD) project such as this, it is impossible to build a complete system supporting VRPML with a virtual environment, and to conduct meaningful software engineering experiments to evaluate the new features that VRPML supports. A prototype VRPML interpreter has been implemented which supports the enactment of VRPML graphs (although the graphs have to be converted by hand to an intermediate form) and which links to a simple Virtual Reality Modeling Language (VRML) generator. This prototype has been used to verify that the enactment of graphs behaves as expected, and hence that the semantics of the VRPML features are sound. Some informal discussion points can be reported.

In our research, we have designed VRPML to address some of the issues relating to the human dimension and dynamic issues inherent in software processes at the PML level. While there are already a number of PMLs which also employing visual notations (e.g. Slang [3], APEL [6], EVPL [11], PROMENADE [16] and Little JIL [19]), our approach breaks away from the approach taken by these languages in that software processes are described not only in term of tasks but also in terms of their workspaces which accommodate resources, artifacts and communication tools needed to complete the tasks in a virtual environment. We believe that VRPML permits an easy to understand representation of a software process to be generated, and naturally supports many of the aspects of modeling a software process that are required.

The concept of a workspace in VRPML is perhaps comparable to the desktop paradigm in APEL. In APEL each task and their sub-tasks „graphs" are made available to an assigned agent during enactment showing the data and control flow dependencies relating to that particular task, together with some defined operations and tools for manipulating artifacts. While a desktop paradigm may be useful for providing process awareness, a counter argument suggests that it may be too low level and perhaps not sufficiently user friendly. Agents may well be forced to learn APEL to make sense out of such representation. In contrast, a workspace consisting of a virtual room populated by artifacts and tools as objects in a virtual environment, as in VRPML, seems to provide more intuition and realism, abstracting its graph complexities to specialist programmers.

In terms of its general features, many VRPML language elements have been inspired by Little JIL, VPL and APEL. For example, like Little JIL, software processes in VRPML are described using process step abstractions. Syntactically, an activity node is similar to stages in VPL and transitions are similar to options. The concept of multi-instance activity node is borrowed from APEL.

In terms of achieving its dynamic behavior to support dynamic creation (i.e. in the case of multi-instance and meeting activity nodes) and assignment of tasks and resources, VRPML exploits its resource exception handling mechanism. Exceptions can be interactively rectified allowing enactment to be resumed. This feature removes the need to restart an activity which also requires possibly complex recovery from the effect of previously completed process steps.

In Dynamite [12], support for dynamic creation of tasks can also be achieved by exploiting its support for on-the-fly evolution using graph rewriting system. Indeed, the support for dynamic creation of tasks in Dynamite is very powerful but it is perhaps not an „ideal" solution. For instance, in the straightforward case, where multiple agents need to collaborate on similar activities (e.g. multi-instance or meeting activities) and the actual number of agents involved depends on the dynamic needs of a particular project, utilizing on-the-fly process evolution to support the dynamic creation of tasks may be difficult (or expensive) to achieve because of the need to ensure that there are no side effects or no ad-hoc changes that will be introduced in the process. In VRPML, such a case can be easily handled by exploiting resource exception handling mechanism, allowing the activities depths (e.g. for multi-instance and meeting activity nodes) to be dynamically specified.

7   Conclusion

Although a number of PMLs have been proposed in the last 12 years, their adoption has not been widespread. One reason might be that the human dimension issues and dynamic aspects of software processes have not been sufficiently supported in the design of existing PMLs. VRPML, which integrates a virtual environment in its visual language elements and enactment model, is being developed to address some of these issues.

Our long-term goal is to provide a PSEE to facilitate the construction and enactment of a software process using VRPML, and to allow support for process evolution.

Experiments are also planned to address a more general form of collaborative work such as the Workflow Management Systems (WFMS).

References

1. Arbaoui, S., Lonchamp, J., Montangero, C.: The Human Dimension of the Software Process. In: Derniame, J.C., Kaba, B.A., Wastell, D. (eds.): Software Process: Principles, Methodology and Technology. Lecture Notes in Computer Science, Vol. 1500. Springer-Verlag, Berlin Heidelberg New York (1999) 165-196
2. Baldi, M., Gai, S., Jaccheri, M.L., Lago, P.: Object Oriented Software Process Model Design in E3. In: Finkelstein, A., Kramer, J., Nuseibeh, B. (eds.): Software Process Modelling and Technology. Research Studies Press, Taunton, England (1994) 279-290
3. Bandinelli, S., Fuggetta, A., Ghezzi, C., Lavazza, L.: SPADE: An Environment for Software Process Analysis, Design, and Enactment". In: Finkelstein, A., Kramer, J., Nuseibeh, B. (eds.): Software Process Modelling and Technology. Research Studies Press, Taunton, England (1994) 223-247
4. Becattini, F., Nitto, E.D., Fuggetta, A., Valetto, G.: Exploiting MOOs to Provide Multiple Views for Software Process Support. In: Proc. of Intl. Process Technology Workshop, Villard de Lans – Grenoble, France (1999)
5. Conradi, R., Jaccheri, M.J.: Process Modelling Languages. In: Derniame, J.C., Kaba, D.A., Wastell, D. (eds.): Software Process: Principles, Methodology and Technology. Lecture Notes in Computer Science, Vol. 1500. Springer-Verlag, Berlin Heidelberg New York (1999) 27-51
6. Dami, S., Estublier, J., Amiour, M.: APEL: a Graphical Yet Executable Formalism for Process Modeling. Automated Software Engineering 5, 1 (January 1998) 61-96
7. Doppke, J.C., Heimbigner, D., Wolf, A.L.: Software Process Modeling and Execution within Virtual Environments. ACM Transactions on Software Engineering and Methodology 7, 1 (January 1998) 1-40
8. Dossick, S.E., Kaiser, G.: CHIME: A Metadata-Based Distributed Software Development Environments. In: Nierstrasz, O., Lemoine, M. (eds.): Proc. of the Joint 7th European Software Engineering Conf. and Foundation of Software Engineering (ESEC/FSE99). Lecture Notes in Computer Science, Vol. 1687. Springer-Verlag, Berlin Heidelberg New York (1999) 464-475
9. Fuggetta, A.: Software Process: A Roadmap. In: Finkelstein, A. (ed.): The Future of Software Engineering (FOSE 2000) in conjunction with the Proc. of the 22nd Intl. Conf. on Software Engineering (ICSE 2000). Limerick, Ireland, June 2000. ACM Press (2000).
10. Gelernter, D.: Generative Communication in Linda. ACM Transactions on Programming Languages and Systems 7, 1 (January 1985) 80-112
11. Grundy, J.C., Hosking, J.G.: Serendipity: Integrated Environment Support for Process Modeling, Enactment and Work Coordination. Automated Software Engineering 5, 1 (January, 1998) 27-60

12. Heiman, P., Joeris, G., Krapp, C.A., Westfechtel, B.: DYNAMITE: Dynamic Task Nets for Software Process Management. In: Proc. of the 18th Intl. Conf. on Software Engineering, Berlin, Germany. IEEE Computer Press. (March 1996) 331-341

13. Huff, K.E.: Software Process Modeling. In: Fuggetta, A., Wolf, A. (eds.): Trends in Software Process. John Wiley & Sons (1996) 1-24.

14. Jaccheri, M.J., Conradi, R., Drynes, B.H.: Software Process Technology and Software Organisations. In: Conradi, R. (ed.): Proc. of 7th European Workshop on Software Process Technology (EWSPT 2000), Kaprun, Austria. Springer-Verlag, Berlin Heidelberg New York (February 2000) 96-108

15. Kellner, M.I., Feiler, P.H., Finkelstein, A., Katayama, T., Osterweil, L.J., Penedo, M.H., Rombach, H.D.: Software Process Modeling Example Problem. In: Katayama, T. (ed.): Proc. of the 6th Intl. Software Process Workshop, Hakodate, Hokkaido, Japan. IEEE Computer Society Press (October 1990)

16. Ribo, J.M., Franch, X.: PROMENADE: A PML Intended to Enhance Standarization, Expressiveness and Modularity in Software Process Modelling. Research Report LSI-00-34-R, Llenguatges I Sistemes Informatics, Politechnical of Catalonia (2000)

17. Sutton Jr, S., Osterweil, L.J.: The Design of a Next-Generation Process Language. In: Proc. of the Joint 6th European Software Engineering Conf. and the 5th ACM SIGSOFT Symposium on the Foundation of Software Engineering. Lecture Notes in Computer Science, Vol. 1301. Springer-Verlag, Berlin Heidelberg New York (1997) 142-158

18. Swenson, K.D. :A Visual Language to Describe Collaborative Work. In: Proc. of the 1993 IEEE Symposium on Visual Languages. IEEE Computer Society Press (1993) 298-303

19. Wise, A.: Little JIL 1.0 Language Report. Technical Report 98-24, Department of Computer Science, University of Massachusetts at Amherst (April 1998)

20. Yang, Y.: Coordination for Process Support is Not Enough. In: Proc. of the 4th European Workshop on Software Process Technology. Lecture Notes in Computer Science, Vol. 913. Springer-Verlag, Berlin Heidelberg New York (1995) 205-208

21. Zamli, K.Z.: Process Modeling Languages: A Literature Review. Malaysian Journal of Computer Science 14, 2 (December 2001)

22. Zamli, K.Z., Lee, P.A.: Taxonomy of Process Modeling Languages. In: Proc. of the ACS/IEEE International Conference on Computer Systems and Applications. IEEE Computer Society Press (June 2001) 435-437

Integrating Dynamic Models for CMM-Based Software Process Improvement

Mercedes Ruiz[1], Isabel Ramos[2], and Miguel Toro[2]

[1] Department of Computer Languages and Systems
Escuela Superior de Ingeniería. University of Cádiz
C/ Chile, n°1. 11003 – Cádiz, Spain
mercedes.ruiz@uca.es
[2] Department of Computer Languages and Systems
Escuela Técnica Superior de Ingeniería Informática. University of Seville
Avda. Reina Mercedes, s/n. 41012 – Seville. Spain
{isabel.ramos,mtoro}@lsi.us.es

Abstract. During the last decade software process simulation has been used to address a wide diversity of management problems. Some of these problems are related to strategic management, technology adoption, understanding, training and learning, and risk management, among others. In this work a dynamic integrated framework for software process improvement is presented. This framework combines traditional estimation static models with an intensive utilization of dynamic simulation models of the software process. The aim of this framework is to support a qualitative and quantitative assessment for software process improvement and decision making to achieve a higher software development process capability according to the Capability Maturity Model. The paper describes the concepts underlying this framework, its implementation, the dynamic approach followed to systematically develop the dynamic modules, and an example of its potential use and benefits.

1   Introduction

World-wide the demand for high complex software has significantly increased in such a way that software has replaced hardware as having the principal responsibility for much of the functionality provided by current systems. The rapid pace in which this software is required, the problems related to cost and schedule overruns, and the customer perception of low product quality have changed the focus of attention towards the maturity of software development practices. Over the last few decades, the software industry has received a significant help by means of CASE tools, new programming languages and approaches, and more advanced and complex machines. However, it is widely accepted that the potential benefit of a better technology cannot be translated into a more successful project if the processes used to execute it are not

M. Oivo and S. Komi-Sirviö (Eds.): PROFES 2002, LNCS 2559, pp. 63–77, 2002.

well defined, established, and executed. Proper processes are essential for an organization to consistently deliver high quality products with a high productivity.

Currently, many frameworks are available for software processes, being CMM [1] and ISO 9001[2] the most influential and widely used. Although ISO 9001 is a standard, and has been interpreted for a software organization in ISO 9000-3 [3], it has been written from the customer and external auditor's perspective. On the other hand, CMM is not a binary certification process, but a framework that categorizes software process in five levels of maturity and provides roadmaps to evaluate the software process of an organization as well as planning software process improvements.

Dynamic modeling and simulation as process improvement tools have been intensively used in the manufacturing area. Currently, software process modeling and simulation are gaining an increasing interest among researchers and practitioners as an approach to analyze complex business and solve policy questions. However, simulation is only effective if both the model and the data used to drive it, accurately reflect the real world. As a consequence, it is possible to say that the construction of a dynamic model for software process itself points to what metric data must be required and, hence, collected, providing clear guidelines on what to collect.

After having applied the system dynamics approach to model and assess software process improvement in a local organization [4], lessons learnt from this experience moved us towards the development of, initially, a framework and, then, a working environment which combines the traditional and static techniques used in project management with the process dynamic modeling and simulation.

The aim of this paper is to present this combination to build a framework to support a qualitative and quantitative assessment for software process improvement and decision making. The purpose of this dynamic framework is to help organizations to achieve a higher software development process capability according to the Capability Maturity Model [1]. The dynamic models built inside this framework provide the capability of gaining insight over the whole life cycle at different levels of abstraction. The level of abstraction used in a certain organization will depend on its maturity level. For instance, in a level 1 organization the simulator can establish a baseline according to traditional estimation models from an initial estimate of the size of the project. With this baseline, the software manager can analyze the results obtained with the simulation of different process improvements and study the outcomes of over or underestimate of cost or schedule. During the simulation metric data are saved. These data conform to the SEI core measures [5] recommendation and are mainly related to cost, schedule and quality.

The structure of the paper is as follows. Section 2 describes in detail the dynamic framework proposed. It includes the motivation we found to design and develop it, the conceptual approach followed, the potential uses of the framework, its architecture, a brief description of the different techniques which have been integrated in the framework, and how it has been implemented to develop a fully functional working tool. In Section 3 an example of how the framework may be used to design and evaluate the effect of a certain process improvement is presented. The example shows the use of the integrated techniques together with the dynamic modules inside the framework. Finally, Section 4 summarizes the paper and draws the conclusions and lessons learnt.

2 Description of the Framework

2.1 Motivation

The Dynamic Integrated Framework for Software Process Improvement (DIFSPI) has been designed with the aim of creating both a conceptual framework and a working environment to help in the achievement of higher maturity levels according to CMM. Traditionally, system dynamics and simulation have been considered as helpful tools to design and evaluate software process improvements. In fact, some real applications can be found in the literature regarding the application of this approach inside software development organizations [6]. All these applications share a common characteristic: they conclude that for a successful system dynamics application, it is a requirement for the organization to have their processes well defined and structured, as well as defined metric programs to provide the models with accurate data. It is absolutely true that dynamic models are only useful if the data used to drive their numerical parameters are available in the organization, and that the availability of these data is only possible if a metric process is applied to the software process executed at the organization. As a consequence, many of the applications of system dynamics in the field of process improvement have required from organizations a certain level of maturity in their processes, typically level 3 or above according to CMM.

In order to design a software process dynamic model is necessary to know the features of the process which is going to be modeled. It becomes apparent that the higher the maturity level, the better the process is defined and established, the easier to obtain information to develop the dynamic model, and, therefore, the better results are obtained when using the model as a tool for evaluating software process improvements. Bearing this statement in mind, our interest is to help organizations with less mature processes to design and execute the process improvements which could help them to achieve upper levels of maturity.

Thus, we propose an approach which is mainly focussed on the development of dynamic models, using them to trigger a process inside the organization aimed to increase the level of knowledge it has about its software process, and to design a software metrics collection program which can be applied to obtain the required data to drive the parameters of the dynamic model. This metric collection is not only useful for the dynamic models; it also serves as an invaluable opportunity to obtain a real knowledge of the state of the software processes inside an organization. This knowledge is essential before tackling any process improvement. The utilization of dynamic models is the main technique in the framework, but it is not the only. Static or traditional algorithmic models are integrated with the dynamic models in order to supply important information during the early stages of the life cycle simulated. Other recommendations and techniques are also used inside the framework to provide useful tools of analysis and evaluation of the results obtained through simulation.

2.2   Conceptual Approach of the Framework

Static models use empirically obtained formulas to compute some project estimates as a function of some project initial estimation, typically the size. The empirical data that support these models come from a limited sample of projects, and this requires a careful utilization of these models, as only if the features of the project under estimation are similar to those of the projects used to calibrate the static models, the results obtained will be reliable. Although static methods for software project management have revealed during the last decades their weaknesses, there is common agreement that they are still useful. At least, in lower maturity organizations they are useful to establish an initial baseline for the project with which evaluate the results of the project and the process improvement tentative. Static and dynamic models have similar objectives, yet the perspective under which they work is completely different. Static models are normally based on a top-down decomposition of the software project, while the dynamic models can be characterized by the aggregation process they are focussed on, according to which some features of a project are joined together under a simulation model. In accordance with what has been said, it can be deduced that dynamic models are suitable to deal with problems placed at the strategic level, while traditional methods are useful at the operational level of software projects. By combining both approaches in a common framework, a useful methodology and even a working tool can be developed to provide insight into the software process and to help in the achievement of upper maturity levels. Nevertheless, the achievement of higher maturity levels can only be possible if the data that enable the evaluation of the results of the process improvement practices are available. Therefore, the design of a proper metrics collection program for the organization is mandatory. The metrics collected are useful in many different aspects:

1. The metrics collected must be used to calibrate and initialize the dynamic models. Lower maturity organizations are characterized by the absence of metric programs and historical databases. In this case, it is completely necessary to begin identifying the general processes and the information that has to be collected about them. The questions of what to collect, at what frequency and with what accuracy have to be answered at this moment. The design process of dynamic models helps to come to a solution to these questions. When developing a dynamic model it is required to know: a) what is intended to be modeled, b) the scope of the model, and c) what behaviors need to be analyzed. Once the model is developed, it needs to be initialized with a set of initial conditions in order to execute the runs and obtain the simulated behaviors. These initial conditions customize the model to the project and to the organization to be simulated, and are effectively implemented by a set of initial parameters. These parameters that rule the evolution of the model runs answer precisely the former question of what data collect: those data required to initialize and validate the model will be the main components of the metrics collection program.

2. Once the components of the metrics collection program have been defined it can be implemented inside the organization. This process will lead to the achievement of a historical database. The data gathered can then be used to simulate and empirically validate the dynamic model. When the dynamic model has been validated, the results of its runs can be used to generate a simulated

database; with this database it is possible to perform process improvement analyses.

An increase in the complexity of the actions intended to be analyzed will directly lead to an increase in the complexity of the dynamic model required and, therefore, to a new metrics collection program for the new simulation modules. Thinking from a perspective of causal loops, what has been described is no more than the translation of a positive reinforce causal loop which is shown in Figure 1.

The benefits of using dynamic models have been widely discussed in the literature [7]. It can be concluded that the use of these models leads to better prediction activities, more accurate cost predictions, and more effective process improvement initiatives. Three factors which are known to drive organizations towards upper maturity levels according to CMM.

2.3   Potential Use of the Framework

Dynamic models help to understand the integrated nature of project management as they describe it through different processes, structures and main interrelationships. In the framework proposed here, project management is considered as a set of dynamic interrelated processes. Projects are composed of processes. Each process is composed of a series of activities designed for the achievement of an objective [1]. From a general point of view, it could be said that projects are composed of processes which fall in one of the following categories:

Management process. This category collects all those processes related to the description, organization and control of the project.

Engineering process. All those processes related to the specification and development activities of the software product are collected in this category.

Both categories interact during the lifecycle of the project. From an initial plan performed by the project management processes, engineering processes begin to be executed. Using the information gathered about the progress of this second group of processes, project management processes determine the modifications that need to be made to the plan in order to achieve the project objectives. The DIFSPI proposed follows this same classification and it is structured attending to project management and engineering processes. In both levels, the utilization of dynamic models to simulate the real processes and to define and develop a historical database will be the main feature.

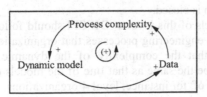

Fig. 1. Causal diagram

2.3.1   Engineering Processes in the Framework

On this level the dynamic models simulate the life cycle of the software product. Figure 2 shows a schematic representation of how DIFSPI may be used inside an organization. In low maturity organizations, the amount of information required to begin running simulations is relatively small and mainly focussed on the initial estimations, that is the estimated size of the project, and the initial size of the working team. Depending on the paradigm followed to develop the software product and the maturity level of the organization, the suitable dynamic model is simulated. The main paradigms that can be simulated inside the framework are the traditional waterfall and COTS paradigms. Depending on the paradigm chosen, different dynamic modules will be joined in order to create a final and fully operational dynamic model. Once the simulation has been run, it provides data that are saved in a simulated database. These initial data contain the results of the simulation together with a set of initial estimations resulting from the computation of the static models. These initial estimations establish the base line for the project, and the simulated data obtained represent the dynamic evolution of the project variables along the whole life cycle. As well as the initial baseline and the simulated data, the so-called simulated database contains a third component. This third component contains the results of applying some other techniques during the simulation of the project, which are oriented towards the gaining of insight into the process under simulation. These techniques, which have been integrated with the dynamic modules, are described in Section 2.5.

As it was mentioned before, the process of modeling the software process requires a good knowledge of the software process itself, and triggers a metrics collection program which can then be used to initialize the parameters of the model and increment the level of visibility the model has about the process. All that has been simulated so far, must be taken into practice. After having determined the initial estimates and run the simulations to establish the initial base line, it is possible to run different scenarios in order to find out the outcomes of different initial values for the project estimates. This reflects, of course, the level of uncertainty low maturity organizations have at the initial stages of a project. When the real project begins, the metrics collection program may be applied to gather real information about the progress. These real data are also saved in the database, enabling the development of a historical database. As these data become available, it is possible to perform analysis and calibrate the functions and parameters of the dynamic modules so that their accuracy may be improved. Improving the accuracy of the dynamic modules may require an improvement in the knowledge we have about the software process and, this way, the loop is closed.

The dynamic models of this level at DIFSPI should follow the levels of visibility and knowledge of the engineering processes that organizations have at each maturity level. It is obvious that the complexity of the dynamic model used in level 1 organizations cannot be the same as that one of the models capable of simulating the engineering processes of, for instance, level 4 organizations.

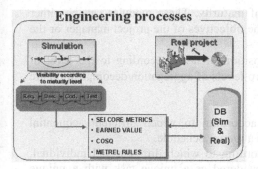

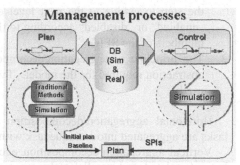

Fig. 2. Engineering processes in DIFSPI   **Fig. 3.** Management processes in DIFSPI

2.3.2 Project Management Processes in the Framework

Inside the framework, management processes are divided into two main categories:

Plan. It groups the processes devoted to the design of the initial plan and the required modifications when the progress reports indicate the appearance of problems. The models of this group integrate traditional estimation and planning techniques together with dynamic ones.

Control. In this group all the models designed for the monitoring and tracking activities are gathered. These models will also have the responsibility of determining the corrective actions to the project plan. Therefore, the simulation of process improvements will be of an enormous importance.

Figure 3 shows the utilization of DIFSPI at this level. As it was mentioned before, the initial baseline for the project is established using the static models built inside the framework. The dynamic modules that model the planning activities performed in the organization have not only the differential equations to model these activities, but the equations of the traditional static estimation models. In order to gain a useful information from these static models, the same knowledge about the software process which is required to use these models is necessary at this moment.

The control modules model and simulate all the activities which determine the progress of the project, and make the corrective decisions which are required to meet the project objectives. These modules have a great importance in the design of the process improvements.

2.4   Dynamic Modules Architecture

The approach followed in the construction of the dynamic models is based on two fundamental principles:

1.   The principle of extensibility of dynamic models. According to this principle, different dynamic modules are joined to an initial and basic dynamic model. This initial model models the fundamental behavior of a software project. Each one of the dynamic modules models each one of the key process areas which conform

the step to evolve to the next level of maturity. These modules can be either „enabled" or „disabled" according to the objectives of the project manager or the members of the SEIG.

2. The principle of aggregation/decomposition of tasks according to the level of abstraction required for the model. Two levels of aggregation/decomposition are used:

Horizontal aggregation/decomposition according to which different sequential tasks are aggregated into a unique task with a unique schedule.

Vertical aggregation/decomposition according to which different and individual, but interrelated and parallel tasks are considered as a unique task with a unique scheduled too.

The definition of the right level of aggregation and/or decomposition for the tasks mainly affects the modeling of the engineering activities and principally depends on the maturity level of the process intended to be simulated.

To define the initial dynamic model the common feedback loops among the software projects were taken into account. The objective of this approach was to achieve a generic model and avoided modeling specific behaviors of concrete organizations which might limit the flexibility of DIFSPI. To initialize the functions and parameters of the initial model, data originating of historical databases collected in the available literature were used [8]. Figure 4 shows the main structure of the initial model. Four dynamic modules are joined together to develop an operational model that provides the set of final differential equations to generically simulate the software process in low maturity organizations.

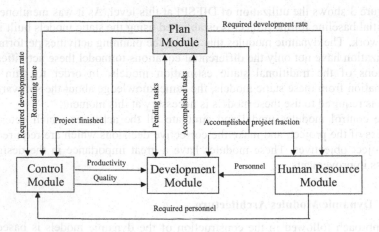

Fig. 4. Submodules architecture of the initial model

By replicating some of the equations of the initial model it is possible to model the progress to higher maturity levels. The initial model can be used to simulate software projects developed in organizations progressing to level 2. Generally speaking, the software product development process can be considered as follows. The number of tasks to be developed is determined from an initial estimate of the size of the project. These pending tasks become accomplished tasks according to the development rate. During this process, errors can be committed. Thus, in accordance to the desired quality objective for the project, the quality rate and the revision rate are determined. These two rates govern the number of tasks that are revised. To model the progress to level 3, the model will make use of a horizontal decomposition, creating as many substructures as phases or activities are present in the task breakdown structure of the project (analysis, design, code and test, in the waterfall paradigm). According to this approach, each time a complete model or some part of it is replicated, it will be necessary to define the new fixing mechanisms (dynamic modules) for the new structures. These mechanisms effectively implement the principle of aggregation/decomposition previously mentioned. The replication of structures also provides the possibility of replicating the modules related to the project management processes. This replication is especially useful for high maturity level organizations, which will be able to establish process improvement practices for each certain activity of the life cycle.

2.5   Integrated Techniques

As it was mentioned before, our aim is to develop a working environment where the simulation of different scenarios can be used to generate the simulated database where managers can experiment different process improvements and activities focussed on the implementation of metrics programs and value analysis. The following techniques and methods are currently successfully implemented in DIFSPI:

Traditional Estimation Techniques. Traditional algorithmic estimation models have been implemented inside this framework with the aim of providing an initial baseline for software projects carried out in low maturity level organizations [9] and [10].

SEI Core Measures. Recent studies and experiences highlight the benefits of the application of these four core measures to the software life cycle. The main aspects of the product and process (quality, time, size and cost) are monitored and tracked to facilitate project success and higher maturity achievement. Inside this framework theses four measures constitute the basics for both, the dynamic models and the graphical representation of the process performance [5].

Metrel Rules. Given the dynamical nature of the DIFSPI proposed, we consider it could be useful to integrate a taxonomy of software metrics which is derived from the needs of users, developers, and management. Among all the advantages that can be obtained with the use of this system of metrics, we would like to point out the dynamic performance of these metrics, that is, how their accuracy, precision, and utility changes over the duration of a project, the life of a product or the strategic plan of an organization. In DIFPSPI Metrel rules have been used as an efficient method for depicting on one graph the information needed for management, staff, and customers to view or predict process performance results. We consider that Metrel rules are particularly important in the field of software process modeling as their application provides a formal procedure for the expansion and transformation of models. By employing simple mechanisms as derivative or integration (over time, phases or even projects), a mathematical model for one level can be transformed into another for another level, providing a simple but powerful extension for the analysis processes [11].

CoSQ. The basis for the Cost of Software Quality (CoSQ) is the accounting of two kinds of costs: those which are due to a lack of quality and those which are due to the achievement of quality. These costs have an inverse relationship that is normally shown as a set of two-dimensional curves that plot costs against a measure of quality. We think that CoSQ can help not only to justify quality initiatives, but also to a number of other benefits. Among them, we would like to point out that CoSQ provides the basics for measuring and comparing the cost effectiveness of the quality improvements undertaken by an organization [12].

Earned Value Analysis. Earned value analysis has been chosen as the method for performance measurement as it integrates scope, cost, and schedule measures to help managers assess process performance. The three main values and the derived efficiency indexes are used in combination to provide measures of whether or not work is being accomplished as planned. Furthermore, the earned value analysis is used to evaluate the performance of different software process improvements inside DIFSPI [13].

Statistical Process Control. Current software process models (CMM, SPICE, etc.) strongly recommend the applications of statistical control. In the framework, Statistical Process Control (SPC) is used to obtain run charts and control charts with the aim of helping software managers to find an answer for questions such as "How do I know if my software development process is in control?" SPC is also used to test the capability of the process. In order to do that, SPC and earned value techniques have been merged in the way [14] suggests.

2.6   Implementation of the Framework

The conceptual ideas presented above were firstly implemented using VemSim® [15] which was used for developing and analyzing the different dynamic models. However, there are some limitations to using this tool. This simulation environment provides a crude way of modularization, there is no easy way to both overlay objects for abstraction and to generate a generic sub-model so that it can be instantiated multiple times without duplicating the effort, and since there is no scoping mechanism, all the elements are global to each other. Like traditional programming languages, a mechanism to allow data encapsulation and modularity is essential to handle the complexity in large and complex models. Due to this reason, the complete framework is currently being re-engineered using Java™ technology. The purpose of this process is to develop a library of classes, each of which represents a simple dynamic module. When using this tool, a suitable dynamic model is made of the required objects. This way, the abstraction aspect and standardization of the interface of these defined modules may be taken to the point where project managers could transparently „plug-in" the modules regarding the software process improvement they would like to analyze. This approach implies a special effort at the interfacing mechanism of these different modules when they are plugged together. Nevertheless, the results obtained after the first functional prototype have been successful and encouraging.

3   Example of Utilization of the Framework

In this section we present the results obtained when using the framework to design and evaluate a specific software process improvement, as well, as quantifying the return on investment of tackling this SPI and its benefits. This example pretends to show the utilization of the different integrated techniques in the SPI field. The approach to the SPI considered is the realization of software inspection activities which is a key factor for level 3 organizations.

Inspections are aimed to objectively identify the maximum number of software defects. Different studies have mentioned the problems and the benefits of these kinds of challenging activities [16]. Figure 5 uses system dynamics notation to illustrate the dynamics of the inspection process module.

The inspections module implements the general steps of the inspection process, the allocation of manpower to the inspection activities, the amount of errors found during inspection, and the defect prevention resulting from the inspection process. The most important factor to be considered here is how the module is obtained, that is, the

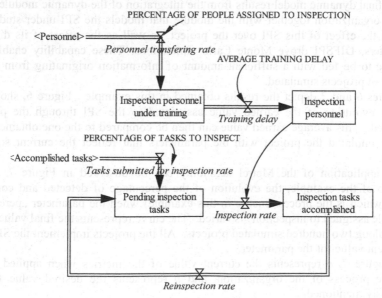

Fig. 5. Inspection module dynamics

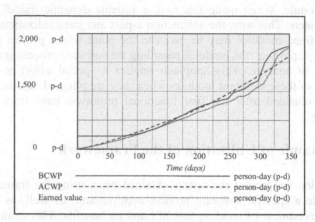

Fig. 6. Average earned value evolution

revision process module itself is the instantiation of other dynamic modules. In fact, the modeling of the workforce allocation, and personnel training which is oriented towards providing them the required abilities to perform the inspection activities, is no more than an instantiation of the generic human resource workforce of the initial model. The modeling of the development of the inspection activities is an instantiation of the generic development model, described in Section 2.4. Other parameters are necessary to model and determine the costs of performing this activity. These parameters have not been graphically represented to simplify the figure but have been coded in the equations of the model.

The final dynamic model results from the integration of the dynamic modules for a level 3 organization together with the module that models the SPI under study. To analyze the effect of this SPI over the project, as well as the effect of its different parameters, DIFSPI drove Monte Carlo simulations. These capability enables the database to be fed with a sufficient amount of information originating from a high number of projects simulated.

Figures 6 and 7 depict the results obtained in this example. Figure 6, shows the average evolution of the earned value associated to the SPI through the projects simulated. This average earned value can then be compared to the one obtained after having simulated the project with the parameters that reflect the current software process.

The application of the Metrel taxonomy can be observed in Figure 7. In the scenario of the example, the evolution of the percentage of detected and corrected errors (which is the process metric in this example) when the parameter „percentage of people assigned to inspection" is varied. The curve represents the final value of the metric along two hundred simulated projects. All the projects implement the SPI with a different value for the parameter.

In Figure 7, c represents the current value of the metrics when applied to the software process of the organization, and b represents the desired value for the previously mentioned.

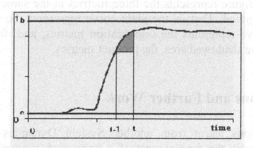

Fig. 7. Number of defects detected and correct due to the SPI

Once the model is simulated and their results graphically represented, it becomes apparent that the potential effect of the SPI in the whole software process follows a model which is determined by the Equation 1.

$$f(t) = b - (b - c)(1 - g)^t . \tag{1}$$

According to this model $f(0) = c$ and $f(1) = c + (b-c)*g$, where g is the gain of the SPI. Let's assume that currently 60% of software errors are detected and corrected and that the objective of the organization is to get 80%. According to this objective, $b - 0.8$, and $c - 0.6$. Let's assume that the final value of the metric is $f(1) = 0.7$. With these values, the quantified improvement of the process is: $g = (0.7 - 0.6) / (0.8 - 0.6) = 0.5$.

This value is computed during the simulation of each project of the set that integrates the Monte Carlo simulation. It serves as an indicator of the capacity of the organization regarding this process improvement. Besides, and according to the Metrel taxonomy, a process metric as the one that has been used here, can be easily transformed by means of integration and derivative processes, in a metrics of the organization or the product. Equation 2 describes the model of the metric for the organization.

$$f'(t) = -(b - c)(1 - g)^t \operatorname{Ln}(1-g) . \tag{2}$$

In this example, given the values for b, c, and g, the obtained model is: $f'(t) = 0.14 (0.5)^t$

$$\int f(t)dt = bt - (b - c)(1 - g)^t / Ln(1 - g) . \tag{3}$$

As far as the metric of the product is concerned, the integral of f(t) along a time interval provides a metric for the number of software errors detected and corrected during that time interval. This value is represented by the shadowed area in Figure 7.

In fact, this same Figure represents the three metrics at the same time, according to the taxonomy integrated. That is, the main curve represents the process metric, the tangent of this curve represents the organization metrics, and, finally and as it has been said before, the shadowed area, the product metrics.

4   Conclusions and Further Work

Motivated by lessons learnt from another System Dynamics application in an industrial environment, the development of a framework to combine the traditional static estimation tools with the dynamic approach has been initiated. The main objective of this dynamic framework is to assess project managers and members of the SEIG to define, evaluate and implement process improvements to achieve higher levels of maturity. The whole process of development of the framework also helps to design a specific metrics collection program which, once implemented, contributes to build and feed a historical database inside an organization.

With the application of DIFSPI some important benefits are expected to be obtained. First, during the process of model building, the project manager may gain much new insight into those aspects of the development process that mostly influence the success of the project (time, cost and quality). Second, having the possibility of gaming with the DIFSPI, it allows project managers to better understand the underlying dynamics of the software process. As a consequence, several process improvement suggestions may easily be designed and, most importantly, analyzed using simulation of scenarios. Third, templates and guidelines for a metrics collection program may almost automatically derived from the requirements of the dynamic modules. Fourth, the approach of abstraction and encapsulation followed to develop the dynamic modules makes it possible to easily instantiate a dynamic model using different dynamic modules which can be plugged in the final model. Finally, the combination of the dynamic approach with other techniques allow project managers to perform complete analysis and quantification of the effects and the benefits of different software process improvements. All these features combined in the framework intend to help organizations to design and execute more mature process and, therefore, to increase their maturity level.

Our future work will mainly concentrate on research towards a full development of the dynamic modules that implement the key process areas of the higher maturity levels. Once this development has been accomplished it is intended to validate the complete DIFSPI in real industrial environments.

Acknowledgements

The authors wish to thank the Comisión Interministerial de Ciencia y Tecnología, Spain, (under grant TIC2001-1143-C03-02) for supporting this research effort.

References

1. Paulk M., Garcia S.M., Chrissis M.B., Bush. M.: Key practices of the capability maturity model. Version 1.1 Technical Report CMU/SEI-93-TR-25. Software Engineering Institute, Carnegie Mellon University, Pittsburg, PA (1993)
2. International Standards Organization.: ISO 9001, Quality Systems – Model for Quality Assurance in Design/Development, Production, Installation, and Services (1987)
3. International Standards Organization.: ISO 9000-3, Guideliness for the Application of ISO9001 to the Development, Supply, and Maintenance of Software (1991)
4. Ruiz M., Ramos I., Toro M.: A simplified model of software project dynamics. Journal of Systems and Software, Vol. 59, No 3 (2001) 299-309
5. Carleton A., Park R.E., Goethert W.B., Florac W.A., Bailey E.K., Pfleeger S.L.: Software measurement for DoD systems: recommendations for initial core measures. Technical Report CMU/SEI-92-TR-19. Software Engineering Institute, Carnegie Mellon University, Pittsburg, PA (1992)
6. Prosim 200 workshop Proceedings. July, 12-14 2000. London UK
7. Christie AM. Simulation – An enabling technology in software engineering. http://www.sei.cmu.edu/publications/articles/christie-apr1999/christie-apr1999.html
8. Putnam L.H.: Measures for excellence: reliable software, on time, within budget. Prentice-Hall, New York (1992)
9. Boehm B.: Software Engineering Economics. Prentice-Hall Inc. (1981)
10. Boehm B., Horowitz E., Madachy R., Reifer D., Clark, B.K., Steece B., Brown A.W., Chulani S., Abts, C.: Software Cost Estimation with COCOMO II. Prentice-Hall Inc. (2000)
11. Woodings T.L.: A Taxonomy of Software Metrics. Software Process Improvement Network (SPIN) (1995)
12. Knox S.T.: Modeling the Cost of Software Quality. Digital Technical Journal, Vol. 5, No 4 (fall 1993), 9-16
13. Fleming Q.W., Koppelman JM.: Earned Value Project Management, 2nd Edition, Newton Square, Project Management Institute (1999)
14. Lipke W., Jennin, M.: Software Project Planning, Statistics, and Earned Value. Crosstalk (December 2000)
15. Vensim. Ventana Simulation Environment. Reference Manual, version 4, Belmont, MA (2000)
16. Siy H.P.: Identifying the mechanisms driving code inspection costs and benefits. Unpublished doctoral dissertation, University of Maryland, College Park (1996)

Simulation-Based Risk Reduction
for Planning Inspections

Holger Neu[1], Thomas Hanne[2], Jürgen Münch[1], Stefan Nickel[2], and
Andreas Wirsen[2]

[1] Fraunhofer Institute for Experimental Software Engineering
Sauerwiesen 6, 67661 Kaiserslautern, Germany
{neu,muench}@iese.fhg.de
[2] Fraunhofer Institute for Industrial Mathematics
Gottlieb-Daimler-Str. 49, 67663 Kaiserslautern, Germany
{hanne,nickel,wirsen}@itwm.fhg.de

Abstract. Organizations that develop software have recognized that
software process models are particularly useful for maintaining a high
standard of quality. In the last decade, simulations of software
processes were used in several settings and environments. This paper
gives a short overview of the benefits of software process simulation
and describes the development of a discrete-event model, a technique
rarely used before in that field. The model introduced in this paper
captures the behavior of a detailed code inspection process. It aims at
reducing the risks inherent in implementing inspection processes and
techniques in the overall development process. The determination of the
underlying cause-effect relations using data mining techniques and
empirical data is explained. Finally, the paper gives an outlook on our
future work.

Keywords: Risk reduction, simulation, software inspection, software
process modeling, software process improvement, and discrete-event
simulation

1   Introduction

The software industry is facing increasing demands to reduce time and costs for
software products while increasing quality. Besides hiring better or more personnel
and using more sophisticated tools and techniques, the improvement of the process
itself is a crucial part of improving software development. Assessments and programs
like CMM or SPICE address the maturity of the software development process. To
achieve higher CMM or SPICE levels, the description and later the improvement of
the process is important.

Usually, the key drivers for improving the software development process are time,
cost, and product quality. Process improvement implies process change. Changing a

M. Oivo and S. Komi-Sirviö (Eds.): PROFES 2002, LNCS 2559, pp. 78–93, 2002.

software development process often leads to unpredictable results and therefore implies high risks. Occasionally, the change results in a worsening that is expensive to correct. Experienced personnel and a sufficiently valid software process model can reduce, but not eliminate, the risks. However, in practice, this only becomes evident after the implementation of the change.

Models help to understand the software development process and are a prerequisite for producing software with predictable quality and effort, but the models used and required often show only a static view of the process. The development of software is mainly a human-based activity and the related dynamic effects are often not considered when the process is changed.

Here, simulation can help to understand the current process and predict the effects of a process change before the change is implemented and the money is spent. Simulation can help to judge whether the change is an improvement of the process or, if several alternatives are available, to identify the alternative with the greatest benefit (e.g., selecting the appropriate inspection technique).

This paper is organized as follows: Section 2 gives an overview of simulation in the software engineering domain. In Section 3, we explain why we use a discrete-event model as modeling approach. Section 4 describes related work in this area. Section 5 explains our model and its goals. The input and the results of the simulation are discussed in Section 6. Finally, we give a summary and an outlook.

2   Background

In general, simulation can be used for planning a system a priori (e.g., before implementing it), for controlling a system (e.g., for operative or online usage), or for analyzing it (a posterior application). In the case of software development processes, a simulation model can support decision-making and risk reduction through a better understanding of the process. The reasons why a simulation model is created have been clustered in six categories of purpose [9]: strategic management, planning, control and operational management, process improvement and technology adoption, understanding, training and learning.

The simulation model we have developed can be used for planning, process improvement, technology adoption and understanding. Planning has two perspectives; one perspective is thorough planning to make forecasts about such things as effort/cost, schedule and product quality, staffing levels needed, or resource allocation. The other planning perspective is to help select, customize and tailor processes for a specific context, e.g., for deciding which process alternative should be used, or which parts of the process can be skipped without quality loss. For the planning perspective, cost/effort, time and quality are often the dimensions of interest. However, for this purpose the model has to be more detailed than for other purposes, and it needs more precise input data.

Process improvement and technology adoption also have a planning perspective. Here, simulation can be useful if the process is to be changed according to suggestions, never tested in the considered environment, or technologies not used before. The decision is more difficult if several improvement alternatives are possible. Forecasting the impact with the simulation contributes to the improvement decision.

If new technologies are to be introduced, at least some of the data has to be estimated or obtained from literature. The simulation results have to be compared with the actual process baseline (if available) or with alternative changes in order to decide on which change to implement.

In addition to making it easier to understand the software process, simulation helps to illustrate the process flow, the effects of feedback loops, and delays inherent in the process. Many project managers and experienced software professionals face problems when they try to explain these effects by themselves, which is due to their complicated dynamic behavior over time.

Before building a simulation model, the scope of the model has to be defined in accordance with the result variables, the process abstraction, and the input parameters. In general, the model scope (which usually fits one of the following definitions: portion of the life cycle, development project, multiple, concurrent projects, long-term product evolution or long-term organization) has two dimensions, time and organizational breadth. Time is the duration of the real process to be simulated and the breadth is the number of people or project teams involved [9].

The result variables and the input parameters depend on the information and data available or needed. Typical result variables are: effort/cost, cycle time, defects, staffing, cost/benefit. Input parameters are the amount of work, defect detection efficiency, code rework effort, etc.

For the process abstraction, the model builder has to identify the key elements of the process, the relations between these elements and the behavior of these elements in the context of the simulation model. Obviously, the relevant elements are those necessary for fulfilling the purpose of the model. Important elements to identify are the key activities and tasks, objects (code units, designs, reports), resources (staff, hardware), dependencies of activities and flow of objects, loops and decisions (iteration, feedback), and other important interrelations.

To run a simulation model, the input parameters need to be initialized and the model has to be calibrated and validated to the target organization. Validation can be done through reviews and inspections of the model. However, in order to make a model fit an organization, the input data has to come from the organization. The quality of the simulation results depends on the accuracy of the input data. In an industrial setting the data is often not available because the metric data needed was not captured or different measures were collected. Useful strategies for handling these situations can be found in [8]. Problems with the availability of data and also with the acceptance of simulation techniques when those are introduced are well known from other areas of application, but experience has shown that such difficulties can be overcome [19].

3   Approach

This paper focuses on the analytical processes in software development, especially the inspection processes. These processes are important for producing high quality products, and they are suited for building a simulation model, since a large amount of empirical data and knowledge exists for these processes. The simulation model can be used to play so-called „What If" games, for experimenting where real-life experiments are too expensive and time consuming, or even too dangerous or just impossible.

In the following, we explain why we use the discrete-event instead of the system dynamics approach for simulating the inspection-focused model.

Various simulation approaches have been used so far in the software engineering domain. These include system dynamics (or continuous simulation), discrete-event simulation, state-based process models, rule-based languages, and petri nets, among other approaches. System Dynamics (SD) is the simulation technique that was used in most cases for modeling software development processes. The first time SD was extensively used in that context was in the model of Abdel-Hamid and Madnick [1]. After that, many SD models were built in the SE domain for different purposes. Regarding software inspections, a well-elaborated system dynamics model can be found in [16] and [15].

A few models [17], [5], [18], [22] use two simulation techniques, usually a continuous and a discrete approach, and are, therefore, called hybrid models. A pure discrete-event simulation was used in [4].

[17] give a good overview of the advantages and disadvantages of system dynamics and discrete-event simulation, especially if they are combined in a hybrid model.

System dynamics (SD) models usually focus on macro modeling levels and represent aggregated variables. The construction of an SD model of a software development process might be rather obvious by using nodes for representing aggregated variables such as total lines of code, total number of defects, or total effort. Arrows represent relationships between these variables. With SD models, it is easy to model feedback cycles caused by human effects such as fatigue, experience levels, schedule pressure or other dynamic influences. SD models are valuable for finding situations where models become unstable (because of feedback loops), and in predicting unanticipated side effects, if, for instance, the value of a variable is changed. However, explicit representations of objects such as team members or tasks to be done are not or not easily possible.

The nature of system dynamics models implies no specific process steps. If some design was done, coding starts immediately. To describe process steps such as „finish design before coding", additional mechanisms have to be modeled. In discrete-event simulation, a more detailed level with an explicit representation of objects is supported in a user-friendly way [3]. Thus, discrete-event models usually require higher complexity in modeling than SD models.

On the visual level, discrete-event models are more concrete than SD models because they represent static objects in reality by static blocks in the model, and transitory objects by moving units (MUs) similar to logistics simulation. In that area, MUs are, for instance, goods being transported by conveyors to a working station for processing them. SD models do not visualize such realistic operations but show logical relationships between the aggregated variables, in a way similar to that of cause-effect diagrams. While activities that occur in parallel are easier to model in SD models the idea of the simultaneous representation of one MU in two activities is difficult. For discrete-event models, the sequence of activities in a software process is easy to model, therefore this technique is extensively used for simulating manufacturing lines. The MUs flowing through the model represent items (design documents, code units) or persons. This representation is more flexible than representing MUs by static objects, especially with respect to a variable number of these objects. Discrete models allow individual attributes for each MU that can capture variations, for instance, in code size, difficulty, or personal productivity and experience. With these individual item attributes, we can determine, for example, an individual coding time for a code unit and a specific person. In addition, the values of the item's attributes can be sampled from distributions for capturing uncertainties in measuring the attributes.

The support of stochastic modeling is a seminal feature of tools for discrete-event simulation, e.g., by providing random number generators for various distribution functions. In SD tools, on the other hand, the representation of stochastic influences is usually less well supported.

In summary, SD is usually applied for rather general predictions, while discrete-event simulation is recognized as a reliable instrument for planning (e.g., in production and logistics). Since we focus on real-life applications of the model to specific industrial software development processes, we use the discrete-event simulation concept for our model. This provides us the possibility of characterizing the project items and persons by attributes. By doing so, the model can be used for a posteriori analysis with the data measured during the process. It is also possible to use historical data about items and persons to use the model to make predictions and planning for future projects.

The software package Extend has been chosen as a simulation tool for modeling software processes because it supports discrete-event modeling as well as time-continuous modeling in a systems dynamics fashion [10]. Although we focus on building a time-discrete type of model analogous to logistics simulation, we also have the possibility to model specific parts of a software development process in a time-continuous way.

4   Related Work

Empirical studies about software inspections are an established discipline. A multitude of controlled experiments and case studies has been reported in literature (e.g., [11]). Moreover, modeling and simulation are increasingly applied to software processes and widen their understanding. Raffo et al. [23] describe the multifaceted relationships between empirical studies and the building, deployment and usage of process and simulation models. Several models for simulating inspections are described. They mainly differ with regard to the intended purpose (e.g., prediction, control), the dependent variables of interest (e.g., cycle time, reliability), the development phases considered (e.g., design, all phases), the simulation technique, and the degree of combining simulation with other techniques that support process understanding (e.g., descriptive process modeling, GQM). In the following, some essential contributions are sketched.

Rus *et al.* [22] present a process simulator for decision support that focuses on the impact of engineering practices on software reliability. The simulator consists of a system dynamics model and a discrete-event model. The continuous model is intended to support project planning and predict the impact of management and reliability engineering decisions. The discrete-event model is more suited for supporting project controlling. One main purpose of the discrete-event model is to predict, track, and control software defects and failure through out a specified period.

Madachy [16] sketches a system dynamics simulation model of an inspection-based lifecycle process that demonstrates the effects of performing inspections or not performing them, the effectiveness of varied inspection policies, and the effects of other managerial decisions such as resource allocation. The model does not take into account schedule pressure effects and personnel mix.

Tvedt and Collofello [27] describe a system dynamics model aiming at decision support with regard to several process improvement alternatives. The dependant variable of interest is cycle time. The model is intended for understanding cause-effect-relationships such as the influence of the implementation of inspections on cycle time reduction. The modeling approach distinguishes between a base model and several modular process improvement models (i.e., one for each improvement alternative).

Pfahl and Lebsanft [21] combine process simulation techniques with static modeling methods, namely software process modeling and measurement-based quantitative modeling. They propose the IMMoS approach that integrates system dynamics modeling with descriptive process modeling and goal oriented measurement. The descriptive process model is used as a starting point for identifying causal relationships. Goal-oriented measurement is used for deriving measures from goals that are determined by the needs of a system dynamics model. Benefits of this combination are synergy effects from using already existing and proven methods and overcoming weaknesses of system dynamics model building.

In contrast to these contributions, the simulation model described in this paper focuses more strongly on the organizational and personal influence factors on inspections. It is mainly developed for risk reduction purposes. This model is much more detailed than other models described in the literature, and it is based on expert knowledge and partly on empirical data.

5   A Simulation Model for Analyzing the Effects of Inspections

A model is a more or less simplified representation of a real object, system, or any other subset of reality, but still similar with respect to certain aspects. It supports a better understanding and the analysis of the actual subject. Therefore, the model has to represent the essential information of the real process regarding static and dynamic relations. (See above) A guideline for developing discrete-event simulation models can be found in [20].

In the following, we will show the development steps of the simulation model. At first we started with a static representation of the inspection model, which can usually be found in descriptive process models. These define the sequence of steps or activities, the products produced and changed, and the roles involved. For instance, an elicitation-based method [2] and the tool SPEARMINT [26] can be used. The inspection process used for modeling is described in [6].

To capture the dynamic behavior not described in a process model, we used, in a second step, cause effect (see Fig. 1) or casual loop diagrams [25]. The variables of

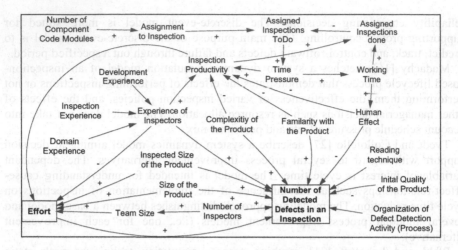

Fig. 1. Cause-effect diagram for effort and number of detected defects

the cause effect diagrams depend on the goal of the simulation, e.g. ,the human effects like skills or productivities are important if effort, time and defects are of interest. The cause effect diagrams structure the assumptions of the dynamics inherent in the process.

In the next step, the static model was used to build the structure of the discrete event model while the cause effect diagram was used to define the elements of the equations for computing the variables of interest, e.g., coding time, defects, etc.

All variables appearing in the process model and cause effect diagrams of all sub-processes were classified with respect to their usage in an activity block or a moving unit. If a variable does not clearly belong to one of these groups it is classified as general process variable.

The following groups were identified: Process variables, person variables, item variables, inspection specific variables, design, rework and coding specific variables. A person object, for example, consists of all attributes one would associate with humans, i.e., fatigue, skills in programming and inspection, personal productivity in coding and inspection, and a personal defect generation factor. General process variables include, e.g., information about factors for maximal productivity or quality measures used for computing the time an individual needs for performing an activity. The initial values of these attributes are usually inputs for the simulation model that have to be calibrated for a specific application of the model. A manager, for example, can use this freedom of choice of the parameters for studying the impact of introducing a software inspection into a concrete software development process in his or her company.

Now the functional dependencies between the different moving units in each sub-process have to be determined. It is obvious that these dependencies will differ with respect to the tasks of the MUs in the different sub-processes. For example, the interaction of persons and items (documents) depends on the process and on their role in it, i.e., in the coding sub-process a person is acting as a programmer, whereas in the inspection process, the same person can be an inspector or a moderator of the inspection of another item.

To specify the simulation model, the relationships qualitatively described in the cause-effect diagrams of all sub-processes and process models have to be quantified. Possible methods for quantifing the relationships are expert interviews, pragmatic models, stochastic analysis, and data mining techniques. Here one has to distinguish between the quantification of known relationships, i.e., exact linguistic descriptions that are available and have to be transformed to mathematical functions, and the generation of new rules by applying data mining techniques to describe relations that are not obvious or were not considered up to now in simulations of the software development process. The choice of the data mining techniques for quantification depends on the data or information available from experiments. The data will also be used for the validation of functional relations known from literature.

Up to now we have been using neural networks and classification trees for the quantification of the qualitatively known relations. The neural networks used are feed forward neural networks with one hidden layer and a single output [28], [29]. The neural network function is given by

$$f(x,\Theta) = v_0 + \sum_{k=1}^{n} v_k g(xw_h) \tag{1}$$

where $\Theta = (w_1', \ldots w_h', v_0, \ldots v_h)$ is the vector of network weights, while $w_h' = (w_{0h}, \ldots, w_{dh})$, $h=1,\ldots,n$, g is the activation function from each hidden unit and $x = (1, x^1, \ldots x^d)$ is the vector of inputs. The network weights in our simulation model were estimated from industrial data.

Additionally, relevance measures [24] were used to determine the impact of each explaining (input) variable with respect to the explained (output) variable. The relevance measure here, denoted as $R(f,x)$, was computed as the partial derivatives of the trained network function $f(x,\Theta)$ with respect to explaining input variables x^k, i.e.,

$$R(f, x^k) = \frac{\partial f(x,\Theta)}{\partial x^k}. \tag{2}$$

Applying these measures, one can easily verify whether the estimated functional dependencies describe the input/output relation in a sufficient manner, or whether an explaining variable is missing. In the latter case, a new rule has to be generated for applying data mining techniques. Thus, a relevance measure can also be used to validate the qualitative description of the dependencies given in the cause-effect diagrams.

The second technique applied for the quantification of the relationships we used are classification trees determined by the software tool XpertRule Miner [30]. Based on the information gain technique, a classification tree for an explained variable is calculated on the data set. The tree can be read from root to a leaf as a rule for the input/output relation. A leaf of the tree contains information about the percentage, variance, mean and standard deviation for the explained variable when applying the corresponding rule. Thus, the root of the tree denotes the variable with the greatest impact with respect to the explained variable. The splitting criterion used is based on the normalized standard deviation [30].

In the following, we will describe the simulation model, which is being developed for decision support on organizing inspection processes. We focus on the variables size and percentage of modules to be inspected, number of inspectors and inspection effort.

The sub-processes of the process diagram pre-structure the sequence of tasks (design, coding, inspection, test, etc.) to be performed during a software development process. Similar to lines in material flow systems the activity blocks and other modeling blocks are connected for guiding items and persons through the system.

The general idea of directing MUs through the system is as follows: Before specific tasks can be performed, items and persons have to be assigned. In Extend, a block creating a compound MU, which represents an item together with an assigned person, supports this. Up to now, one main assumption of the model is that the assignment of tasks to persons is done in an arbitrary way or, more precisely, persons are selected from a staff pool in a "first come, first serve" fashion.

After accomplishing a task, linked items and persons are un-batched. Persons are then directed back to the pool where they are waiting for new tasks to be assigned to them. Items are directed to the subsequent sub-process, e.g., from design to coding or from inspection to rework. In some cases, there are alternatives for routing an item. For instance, rules may be applied for deciding on whether an item is subject to inspection or not. Moreover, switches can be used for activating or deactivating some parts of the model, e.g., the inspections, the design, or the testing and rework activity. In general, the connections of processes and sub-processes and the routing logic for the MUs represent organizational rules of a considered real-life company. Because of the complex nature of the processes to be modeled, it is hardly possible to represent many details of a real-life software development process. For instance, meetings prior to an inspection are not represented in the model. Let us note that the sub-processes outside our model focus are modeled in a rougher way. Similarly, aspects outside the considered project are neglected, for instance the involvement of persons in other tasks. It would, in principle, be possible to have a pre-specified timetable for each person defining the availability of the person for the current project.

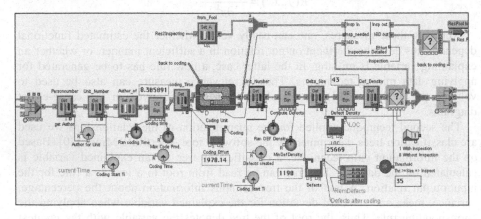

Fig. 2. Excerpt from the Extend visual Interface of the model. Coding with the inspection of selected code items

Most of the blocks used for representing a sub-process (see Fig. 2) are for accessing attributes or variables and for calculating and assigning new values. For instance, in the coding process, the number of defects produced is calculated; in the inspection and test processes, the number of defects found is calculated, and in the rework processes, the number of defects is updated (considering new defects produced during rework). The most important block of a sub-process is, however, a working unit representing the activity of that sub-process in a narrower sense. When a compound MU reaches this block, it stays there for a specific time. This working time has to be calculated beforehand.

The most important issue in each sub-process is to represent the quantitative relationships of the model in a valid way, especially those output values that are most interesting for the user, i.e., changes in the number of defects and time consumed by the various activities. In general, these values are determined by attributes of the items, by attributes of the persons, and by general or project-specific factors. For some of the relevant data it is hardly possible to determine the necessary information in real-life projects. For instance, details on the specific experiences, skills, and productivities of persons are usually not available. Therefore, we have elaborated approaches for taking such human attributes into account, which are not directly observable, and for considering them in the quantitative logic of the model. For instance, a logistic learning model has been adapted and implemented in the simulation model. This is based on various skills that increase with experience and that affect the (ex post) productivity of a person. In a similar way, a model for considering time pressure and its influence on the productivity has been worked out.

Even after careful refinement of the quantitative relations, there are essential effects in a software development process that cannot be fully determined a priori, for instance, human effects such as fatigue, boredom, and other physical and mental factors. These human effects are be considered by having stochastic elements in the process, which influence, for instance, the working times and numbers of defects produced.

As input data, the simulation model requires a specification of a software development project. Roughly said, such a project consists of item-specific data, person-specific data, and project-specific or general data. For each item to be produced (e.g. the source code of a module), the item-specific data includes the number of lines of code (or new/changed lines of code in case the item existed before) and a complexity measure assumed to be around 1. The person-specific data consists of estimates for skills or productivities of all members of the development team.

General or project-specific data are, for instance, average and maximum productivity values or person costs per hour. Alternatively, it is possible to generate a stack of tasks (items) and a pool of persons randomly for applying the model unrelated to a given project, e.g., for educational purposes. Input and output data are stored in a text file linked via SDI Interface with the Extend simulation software. An internal DB stores values for used distributions that can be changed if the model is to be fitted for a specific context.

When the input data are defined, the simulation can simply be started and runs automatically. If the animation is switched on, one can observe people and items moving through the various sub-processes represented in the model similar to a logistics simulation. The overall information value of the animation is, however, rather small. Worthwhile tools for keeping the user informed about the dynamics of the model are plotter blocks, which show the charts of specified variables. Additionally, various variable values are displayed within the window of the simulation model. During the model run, values of various variables are written to the file for further processing. These output variables are, for instance, the number of defects of each item produced during coding, found during inspections, produced during rework and so on, data on the required working times, and effort spent for each task.

If the user is mainly interested in the results of a simulation run, he or she may just consider the output data. In that case, it is possible to switch off the time-consuming animation for getting the results more quickly. It is then possible to use such a model in an online fashion, e.g., for quickly analyzing the effects of varying model parameters. It is planned to equip the model with a simulation cockpit for providing a user-friendly, custom-made interface to the simulation model.

6   Results of the Simulation Model

In this Section, we use the simulation model for two experiment series on variants of the software development process. In both series, the objectives 'duration' and 'overall effort' are considered. For facilitating comparisons, the third objective, product quality, is assumed to be constant. This is achieved by requiring the test phase to continue until a minimum level for the defect density is reached. This means that products with more defects entering the test phase require more test and rework effort.

For the sub-processes testing and rework, it is calculated how much time the test activity requires to get a desired defects density. Thus, the rework effort depends on the number of defects to be found in test, and after testing, the resulting number of remaining defects is always the same.

In 6.1, we analyze whether inspections of all or selected items are useful compared to a software development process without inspections. In 6.2, we analyze the question of what an optimal size of an inspection team might be.

Of course, there are further parameters of the simulation model that influence the effectiveness of inspections and that could be analyzed by the simulation model, e.g., the inspection technique. Corresponding studies based on the simulation model will be performed in the future.

6.1   The Selection of Items for Inspection

One of the key questions in introducing and planning inspections concerns the selection of items to be inspected. In order to compare different policies, we look at a project for producing software (creating new features for an existing product) with 100 items of different size, with 20 developers, and compare the overall effort and time spent for a specific defect density. We consider three variants of a software development process: a) without any inspections, b) with inspecting all items, and c) with inspecting all items with a defect density larger than 35 defects per KLOC. This defect density threshold turned out to be reasonable according to the given defect distribution. Usually the number of defects in a piece of code is not known. This assumption can give a baseline for the effects of an optimal selection of code units for the inspection. Alternatively, other rules could be used, for instance, rules based on the size of the document.

Table 1 shows the simulation results for 100 items with a purposed defect density of 1.5 defects per 1000 lines of code. The model shows that the introduction of inspections increases the effort spent for the coding phase but if the inspections are executed, the effort spent for testing and rework is reduced.

The overall effort is less for the simulation runs with inspections. Also, the duration of the project is shorter if inspections are executed.

These results are in accordance with the literature [FrW90], which suggests that the effort spent for inspections is less than the effort saved for testing. The results of the simulation runs for items selected for inspections show that with such a policy the overall effort can be further decreased, but only with some increase the project duration.

As an alternative to the used testing policy, it would be possible to specify a time frame for how long a code item is tested (instead of specifying a desired defect density) so that the effort spent on testing could be kept constant. In that case, software development processes with inspections would result in better product quality at the end of the software development process.

Table 1. Average results of 20 simulation runs

Alternatives	Size	Defects coded	Defects found during inspection	Defects after insp.	Defects	Overall Effort	Duration
No inspections	25669	1135	552	485	33	9885.64	732.7981
All inspected	25669	1149	650	564	33	9538.59	614.6752
Select item for inspection	25669	1137	578	503	33	9534.09	619.104

6.2   The Influence of the Team Size

The number of found defects and the effort in the overall process (especially coding and test) depend on the number of inspectors involved in the inspection of one code item. For analyzing these effects we perform simulation runs of the model with the size of the inspection team varying from 1 to 10.

In Fig. 3 the graph shows the overall effort needed for the process. It significantly increases for more than four inspectors. Similar increases are shown for the duration for the overall process. If we consider the effort and the duration, the optimal number of inspectors is between two and four.

The other two lines in the graph show the number of defects found and missed during the inspection. Here we can see that increasing the number of inspectors does increase the number of defects found, but only degressively. With more than seven inspectors the number of found defects does not increase significantly. Therefore, an inspection team size of more than seven inspectors is not useful for increasing the product quality.

As stated in [LLS+99], increasing the number of reviewers has a ceiling effect because the probability that defects are found by two or more inspectors increases with the number of inspectors. Therefore, adding inspectors does not increase the number of defects detected significantly and mainly increases the effort and time spent.

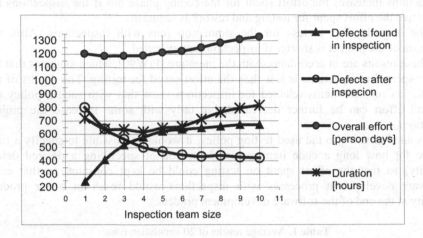

Fig. 3. Defects, duration and effort with respect to different numbers of inspectors (average values for 20 simulation runs)

7   Summary and Outlook

In this article, we have described the development and usage of a simulation model for software development processes. This model can be applied for various purposes such as improving the understanding of these processes, and for planning in an industrial setting. Unlike most existing work in that area, our model is based on discrete-event simulation and supports a more detailed representation of analytical processes with a focus on inspections. Techniques used for developing the model were static process models, cause-effect diagrams, general models documented in the literature, and tools for data analysis. As we have seen, the questions of calibrating and validating are among the main issues for modeling.

For this purpose, we have used various kinds of data such as data from industrial companies, but also general results taken from the relevant literature. In practical settings, data required for model calibration is usually not complete, in particular with respect to human effects, i.e., experience and fatigue. Because of this reason, the modeling of stochastic effects is a significant feature of the model, especially for adequately considering the risks when changing the software development processes in a company. In any case, the employment of rules generated by advanced data mining tools and techniques like fuzzy logic and rough sets for rule generation will be an important issue for further development of the model.

Some exemplary applications of the model led to results similar to those expected from the literature, i.e., emphasizing the usefulness of inspections in software development. We cannot directly compare the overall effort and duration with the defects found during inspection, because the test policy (see above) is not elaborated enough.

For future development of the model, we plan to apply some optimization tools especially for calculating a load balancing assignment and for scheduling staff in an online fashion [7], [14], which should lead to more efficient results than the current arbitrary mechanism used in the simulation model.

It is planned to apply the model in an industrial application for a case study. For this purpose, further refinements of the model will include the provision of modular models and the modeling of other sub-processes that are currently not or just roughly included in the model.

Acknowledgements

The main work for this paper was done in connection with the SEV project and the ProSim project. The projects where supported by the German Bundesministerium für Bildung und Forschung (SEV) and the Stiftung Rheinland-Pfalz für Innovation (ProSim, project no.: 559)

We would like to thank Sonnhild Namingha from the Fraunhofer Institute for Experimental Software Engineering (IESE) for reviewing the first version of the article.

References

1. T. Abdel-Hamid, S. E. Madnick: Software Project Dynamics. An Integrated Approach. Prentice Hall, Englewood Cliffs 1991.
2. U. Becker-Kornstaedt: Towards systematic knowledge elicitation for descriptive software process modeling. F. Bomarius, S. Komi-Sirviö (Eds.): Proceedings of the Third International Conference on Product–Focused Software Processes Improvement (PROFES), Kaiserslautern, September 2001. Lecture Notes in Computer Science 2188, Springer, Berlin 2001, 312–325.
3. J. Banks, J. S. Carson, II: Discrete-Event System Simulation. Prentice-Hall, Englewood Cliffs 1984.
4. M. Christie, M. J. Staley: Organizational and social simulation of a software requirements development process. Software Process Improvement and Practice, 2000, 103-110.
5. P. Donzelli, G. Iazeolla: Hybrid simulation modelling of the software process. Journal of Systems and Software 59, 3, 2001, 227-235.
6. Ebenau, Robert G.; Strauss, Susan H.: Software Inspection Process. New York: McGraw-Hill, Inc., 1994.
7. A. Fiat, G. J. Woeginger (Eds.): Online Algorithms: The State of the Art, Springer, Berlin 1998.

8. M. Kellner, D. Raffo: Measurement issues in quantitative simulations of process models. Proceedings of the Workshop on Process Modelling and Empirical Studies of Software Evolution (in conjunction with the 19th International Conference on Software Engineering), Boston, Massachusetts, May 18, 1997. 33-37.
9. M. I. Kellner, R. J. Madachy, D. M. Raffo: Software process simulation modeling: Why? What? How? Journal of Systems and Software 46, 2-3, 1999, 91-105.
10. D. Krahl: The Extend simulation environment. J.A. Joines, R. R. Barton, K. Kang, P. A. Fishwick (Eds.): Proceedings of the 2000 Winter Simulation Conference. IEEE Press, 2000, 280-289.
11. O. Laitenberger, J.-M. DeBaud: An encompassing life-cycle centric survey of software inspection. Journal of Systems and Software 50, 1, 2000, 5-31.
12. O. Laitenberger, K. El Emam, T. Harbich: An Internally Replicated Quasi-Experimental Comparison of Checklist and Perspective-Based Reading of Code Documents. IEEE Transactions on Software Engineering 27, 5, 2001, 387-421.
13. M. M. Lehman, J. F. Ramil: The impact of feedback in the global software process. Journal of Systems and Software 46, 2-3, 1999, 123-134.
14. A. Lavrov, S. Nickel: Simulation und Optimierung zur Planung und Steuerung von Kommissioniersystemen. VDI-Wissensforum Optimierte Kommissionier-systeme, March 2002, K. 10, 1- 16.
15. R. J. Madachy: A Software Process Dynamics Model for Process Cost, Schedule and Risk Assessment, PhD Dissertation, Department of Industrial and Systems Engineering, USC, December, 1994.
16. R. J. Madachy: System dynamics modeling of an inspection-based process. Proceedings of the Eighteenth International Conference on Software Engineering, IEEE Computer Society Press, Berlin, Germany, March 1996, 376-386.
17. R. H. Martin, D. Raffo: A model of the software development process using both continuous and discrete models. Software Process Improvement and Practice, 2000, 147-157.
18. R. Martin, D. Raffo: Application of a hybrid process simulation model to a software development project. Journal of Systems and Software 59, 3, 2001, 237-246.
19. F. McGuire: Simulation in healthcare. J. Banks (Ed.): Handbook of Simulation. Wiley, New York 1998, 605-627.
20. K. J. Musselman: Guidelines for success. J. Banks (Ed.): Handbook of Simulation. Wiley, New York 1998, 721-743.
21. D. Pfahl, K. Lebsanft: Integration of system dynamics modelling with descriptive process modelling and goal-oriented measurement. The Journal of Systems and Software 46, 1999, 135-150.
22. I. Rus, J. Collofello, P. Lakey: Software process simulation for reliability management. Journal of Systems and Software 46, 2-3, 1999, 173-182.
23. D. Raffo, T. Kaltio, D. Partridge, K. Phalp, J. F. Ramil: Empirical studies applied to software process models. International Journal on Empirical Software Engineering 4, 4, 1999, 351-367.
24. A. Sarishvili: Neural Network Based Lag Selection for Multivariate Time Series. Phd. Thesis, University of Kaiserslautern, 2002.

25. J. D. Sterman: Busines Dynamics – Systems Thinking and Modeling for a Complex World, Irwin McGraw-Hill, 2000.
26. The SPEARMINT web site: www.iese.fraunhofer.de/Spearmint_EPG.
27. J. D. Tvedt, J. S. Collofello: Evaluating the effectiveness of process improvements on software development cycle time via system dynamics modeling. Proceedings of the Computer Software and Applications Conference (CompSAC'95), 1995, 318-325.
28. H. White: Learning in artificial neural networks: A statistical perspective. Neural Computation 1, 1989, 425-464.
29. H. White: Connectionist nonparametric regression: multi layer feed forward networks can learn arbitrary mappings. Neural Networks 3, 1990, 535-549.
30. XpertRule Miner, Attar Software GmbH: www.attar.com.

Introducing Object Validation and Navigation in Software Process to Improve Software Quality

Gopalakrishna Raghavan

Nokia Research Center
5 Wayside Road, Burlington MA 01803, USA
gopal.raghavan@nokia.com

Abstract. Software quality can be judged by various factors [1,2,3,4]. *Correctness* is one of the important factors that signify the capability of software to satisfy its specifications and meet customer needs. One of the means for improving correctness is by performing verification and validation. Validation can be performed at various levels, but is most effective when it is coherent with the implementation. This paper presents a process called *Ucita*, which supports validation using certain domain specific rules and also enhances system comprehension with navigational aids. The process does not impede regular development cycle but adds value to it by precisely validating existing implementation and providing means for generating validated source. In order to facilitate this process an experimental toolset was developed at Nokia Research Center and successfully applied on a mobile software component. The proposed process, tools and benefits of Ucita are highlighted in this paper.

1   Introduction

There are several ways in which errors could creep into software. Some can be avoided by following systematic process and development techniques. There are others that cannot be easily avoided but can be detected by using formal verification and validation techniques. Formal verification is an activity that ensures that the specification satisfies system properties and formal validation is an activity that ensures that the specification captures users needs [5,6]. In the simplest form, verification can be conducted by design walkthrough and code inspections. In a more elaborate form it involves rigorous testing and simulation. At the highest level, formal verification involves application of mathematical deduction for proving system properties. There is also another class of errors that are hard to avoid and detect. Systematic approaches go a long way in eliminating defects in the system. This paper presents a mechanism to avoid defect injection in the system by introducing some lightweight validations without hindering existing development process. Validations are based on some invariant rules. The system is analyzed and checked against these rules for conformance.

M. Oivo and S. Komi-Sirviö (Eds.): PROFES 2002, LNCS 2559, pp. 94-102, 2002.

Embedded devices have limited resources but have rapidly growing applications. They have strict constraints for memory and CPU utilization. It is therefore essential to develop software that is efficient in memory usage and completes tasks as per schedule. In order to achieve better performance, most embedded applications are developed using C language or low-level assembly. But recently C++ and Java based compilers are available for several micro architectures [7,8]. However, since most legacy systems are developed with C, the migration process to C++ is still gradual and controlled. In the mean time object-oriented enthusiasts have not sat back and relaxed waiting for their teams to adopt C++ as their primary development language. There has been a lot of work in incorporating object-oriented concepts like inheritance, aggregation and data hiding, using non-object-oriented languages like C [9]. Reuse has been a powerful concept that has attracted a lot of developers in this direction. These concepts are implemented in C language primarily by means of naming conventions and macro definitions. The advantage ofcourse is the availability of some powerful object-oriented concepts that fit well within the framework of legacy components. However, the downside is the need to handle the implementation intricacies manually. Many don't foresee this as a drawback because they have access to another amazing tool called *cut-and-paste*. Cut-and-Paste feature has facilitated faster reproduction of large code segments. It has also been a source point for a lot of negligent errors.

The major outcome of this project was an improved process with appropriate tool support to facilitate validation and navigation. The process framework and tool support facilitate early detection of defects. The framework is quite generic and could fit well within most development processes. Section 2 presents the software process framework. The automated tool support used is described in Section 3. Various associated benefits are discussed in Section 4. Section 5 provides concluding remarks.

2   Software Process Framework

Every software development organization has its own convention for developing software. Although most organizations use standard development processes like the waterfall model, spiral model [1] or rational unified process [10], it is difficult to strictly follow and adhere to these procedures. Agile software development methods encourage any process that can take them closer to meeting customer needs [11,12,13]. Most development organizations consider working software as a measure of progress. Developers spend most of their time in achieving this measure by concentrating on implementation. Very small portion of their time is spent in requirements analysis or design. Design level validation would not add much value in an environment that is primarily implementation oriented. Also, the ones that are concerned about design need to make sure their models are realistic and up-to-date. If the conceptual models and implementation were fragmented, developers would shun from design activities since it does not contribute to the overall progress. It is therefore important to keep these artifacts coherent. In order to achieve this coherence, some organizations spend most of their time in design activities and use auto-code generation for implementation. This again is not very straightforward if you have to deal with a lot of legacy components. The conventional development process is generalized in the subsection 2.1. Sub-section 2.2 presents an improved process that incorporates the validation framework.

2.1   Conventional Software Creation Process

In general, developers understand that it is a good practice to do requirements analysis first, followed by design and then to get into implementation. But in reality they delve into coding and try to get the system working. Lot of effort is put into system development since it is definitely rewarding and gets attention. By some ad hoc means the system is divided into various functions and the effort is distributed among developers. Initially there is a lot of slack time for developers to explore various possibilities, but very soon they get into a burst mode. Individual developers run their unit test and submit their module for integration. Various smaller pieces are integrated and an overall integration test is performed. If the system passes some satisfactory level of testing then the product is released and the next phase of development begins. Requirements and design documents get some attention at release time. In some cases the design might even be based on implementation. Although an oversimplified picture is presented here, in reality it is developer attitude to work out a rough design mentally and start coding. Many software engineering researches suggest that such process could only bring short-term gains and result in higher long-term costs.

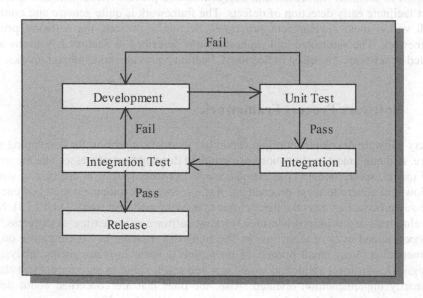

Fig. 1. Conventional software creation process

2.2   Proposed Software Creation Process – „Ucita"

The goal of Ucita is to achieve better precision and quality. It is definitely worthwhile to follow all the good software engineering principles. Management has a vital role in enforcing, encouraging and rewarding developers who adopt good development practices. Managers themselves are pressurized to deliver tangible results regularly. When it comes to software product release, source code appears to be the striking tangible outcome. It is therefore important to have a systematic process to ensure that this significant tangible product meets or exceeds expectations. The proposed process supports implementation level validation that can be performed in parallel to the regular development process and thereby avoiding any hindrance. Validation is performed by first defining a set of rules that the system must comply with. The validation rule precisely specifies the requirement. The implementation is parsed and its meta-data is elicited. Validation rules are applied against the parsed information to ensure that the implementation meets these criteria. The meta-data as such is organized in a systematic fashion to facilitate easy navigation of various objects, attributes and functions in the system. Since most legacy systems are not structured into efficient and maintainable parts, it is not easy to navigate to various component parts and understand them. The proposed process incorporates navigation and promotes structural organization. It also strongly recommends auto code generation whenever applicable. With meta-data and structural organization in place, most of the static information can be easily generated. The generation approach not only speeds up the development process but also ensures that the implementation meets the coding style and standards, since they are pro validated. It is possible to fully automate the process thereby eliminating possible error intrusion due to human negligence.

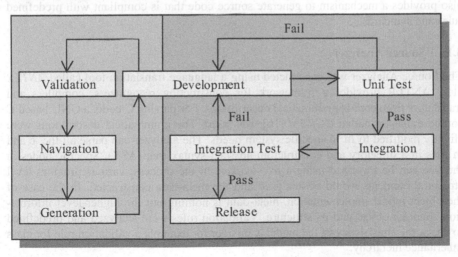

Fig. 2. Proposed improvements to software creation process

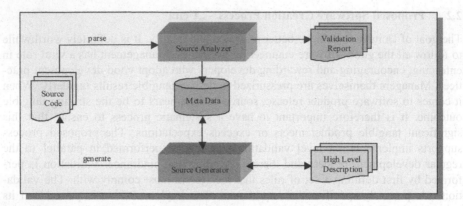

Fig. 3. Tool support for Ucita

3   Automated Tool Support for Ucita

The tool support for Ucita primarily consists of two major parts: Source Analyzer (SA) and Source Generator (SG). The source analyzer parses the source code and transforms it into an internal representation. Traversing a subset of the internal representation would produce the meta-data. Validations would be conducted at this level and appropriate reports generated. The meta-data would be shared with the Source Generator, which uses this information to visually organize various objects in the system. It provides high-level interface to navigate and populate new information. It also provides a mechanism to generate source code that is compliant with predefined rules and standards.

3.1   Source Analyzer

The Source Analyzer was constructed using a language translation tool called *ANTLR* [15]. ANTLR provides a framework for constructing recognizers, compilers and translators from certain grammatical descriptions. For parsing C code, a GNU based C source translator called *CGRAM* [16], was used. The grammatical descriptions were slightly modified to fit to specific system needs. The analyzer can parse all the .c and .h files in a directory and construct an abstract syntax tree (AST). Specific nodes in the tree can be traversed using a *tree-walker*. In the process, various program level structural elements would be analyzed and the meta-data constructed. In the case of the object model implementation, meta-data is nothing but the higher-level information about an object and its structure. Validation rules were analyzed and predefined to check the consistency of the model. Consider for example a validation rule for class inheritance hierarchy.

Rule: Consistent class inheritance hierarchy: It should be possible to successfully traverse from the leaf node to the root node. The leaf node should be the sub-class and the root node should be the top-level super-class. If it is not possible to successfully traverse the tree in this fashion, it means that the class inheritance hierarchy is broken.

It is pretty simple to write a validation routine for this rule. The routine would actually do the traversing by calling the super member. The traversing steps would be recorded until it reaches the root node. The validation would pass if the root node were successfully reached; else the validation fails. This specific rule is an invariant and has to be strictly followed regardless of the level at which the object is inherited. For a C++ programmer, this rule seems pretty trivial and unnecessary to be on the validation list. True, but its not the same case if this has to be implemented in C since the inheritance hierarchy has to be defined in a structure and has to be updated every time it changes. C++ handles all this behind the scene. But if programmer were to handle this manually, there are all possibilities for errors to creep in. The illustrated rule is very specific for an object model system. However, a similar rule can be created for practically any situation and validated in a similar manner. The validation rules basically match certain requirements with the actual implementation. Unlike certain model level validations, this technique is at the implementation. The validations are not only coherent with the requirements but are also specified in the same paradigm as the implementation.

3.2   Source Generator

The meta-data captured by the Source Analyzer is shared with the Source Generator. In addition to code generation, it supports a valuable navigation mechanism. This component primarily classifies and organizes various objects in the system. For example in the object model implementation, the meta data specifies various packages, subsystems, components, classes, attributes, methods and interfaces. In order to support the navigation, this component establishes systematic organization. The visual representation would facilitate viewing and navigating to specific objects in the system. It also presents various relationships, like inheritance and aggregation. This information is a higher-level replication of the implementation. If C++ were used for development, tools like MS VC++ would already establish some of this class organization. However, object implementation in C is primarily in terms of macros and there are no source browsers available to organize this information efficiently. Without this tool support, developers have to spend hours of effort in searching, examining source code and navigating to various objects to understand the system. Again this navigational scheme is not specific to the object model considered here. If the meta-data has sufficient information to support structural organization, any system can be specified using a similar technique. In addition to navigation, the tool also facilitates addition of new objects in the system. For the considered object model one could actually go to a specific class, view it as tree structure, create a new sub-class visually and add its attributes or methods. The visual navigational tool establishes all these links behind the scene and uses this information during code generation. Source code generation is another important feature of this tool, which facilitates generation of certain model definitions. Some of the object definitions in the system follow a standard pattern and are reproducible. These definitions can be generalized and used along with the meta-data information to generate new object definitions. This not only saves time but also reduces the chances of error while implementing repeated definitions.

4   Benefits of Using Ucita

Formal validations are involved, mathematical and proof based. It is not only hard to specify and validate the models but it is also non-trivial to connect the verified models to the implementation. Developers shun from formalism due to its complexity and intricacy. Medium weight formalization using UML or SDL based validation [17,18] along with auto-code generation is also not very popular among developers since they have to shift paradigms and most importantly their trust in generated code is low. Ucita being a domain specific lightweight validation scheme has several advantages:

Capability to validate current implementation: The Source Analyzer parses current implementation to perform validation. Since the validation process is automated it can be attached to nightly builds and the reports generated could be reviewed periodically. This process can catch defects earlier in the life cycle and cost less to fix defects.

Ensures correct usage of a model: The validation rules capture the constraints of a domain specific model. The implementation needs to strictly adhere to this model. The first level validation ensures this and subsequent model elements created through the Source Generator interface would also make certain that the generated code is compliant with the predefined rule sets.

Capability to produce reliable software faster: Automation always speeds things up. Since Ucita is fully automatable, the validation, navigation and source generation can be done faster. Validating the implementation goes a long way in producing quality software much quicker. It alleviates a lot of effort that goes into test-debug cycle.

Capability to navigate to different class information: It is usually a wearying activity in legacy system to identify various classes, their associated attributes and interrelations between different classes. Lack of documentation and object navigational capability in non-object-oriented languages not only consumes lot of time but also adds to confusion.

Separates concerns: The validation process should not hinder regular development in any respect. Any proposed solution should be complementary to existing ones and provide significant improvement to the overall process. Ucita deals with the concerns of development and validation separately and yet in a consistent fashion.

Coherent solution: The validation models and implementation should be in the same plane or at least have a sound mapping. It should be possible to easily specify and apply validation rules. If models are formally specified in SDL and implementation is in C language, then validation models cannot be effectively utilized without suitable roundtrip mapping. The proposed tool support defines rules at implementation level and is capable of validating existing implementation.

5   Conclusion

Software quality improvements can be realized by following an efficient validation process. Software validation assists in eliminating errors and ensures that the implementation meets the requirements. A process called Ucita is proposed in this paper, which promotes validation, navigation and source generation as a parallel activity to development. It avoids any hindrance with conventional development process and at the same time contributes to it by verifying the implementation. The verification strategy employed is at implementation level, which makes the validation rules consistent with the source. This validation framework aims at keeping the discontinuities low and achieving realistic results. The validation is lightweight and does not involve any complex proof techniques.

The Ucita framework was applied on a mobile software component at Nokia Research Center using a tool support that consists of a Source Analyzer and Source Generator. The analyzer parses the source code and validates it using predefined domain specific rules. It also constructs a meta-data that is a higher-level representation of the implementation model. The meta-data is shared with the generator, which organizes the information in an easily navigable form and also facilitates source code generation. There are several benefits in using this framework and associated tool support, like improved correctness and capability to produce reliable software faster. However the only caveat lies in the rule specification format. In the future, we plan to enhance this by adding a more generic framework.

Acknowledgement

I gratefully acknowledge the support from members of Software Architecture Group at Nokia Research Center. I would also like to extend my sincere thanks to several product creation experts who provided excellent domain support.

Reference

1. R. S. Pressman, Software Engineering A Practitioner's approach, 5th ed., McGraw-Hill Series in Computer Science (2001)
2. J. McCall and P. Richards, G. Walters, Factors in Software Quality, three volumes, NTIS AD-A049-014, 015, 055 (1977)
3. J.P. Cavano and J.A. McCall, A Framework for Measurement of Software Quality, Proceedings of ACM Software Quality Assurance Workshop (1978)
4. ISO/IEC 9126, Information Technology – Software Product Quality, Part 1-4, ISO/IEC JTC1/SC7/WG6 (1998)
5. C. Heitmeyer, D. Mandrioli, Formal Methods for Real-Time Computing: An Overview, John-Wiley & Sons (1995)
6. G. Raghavan, Industrial Strength Formalization of Object-Oriented Real-time System, PhD Dissertation, Florida Atlantic University, Boca Raton, Florida (2000)
7. ARM Developer Suite, http://www.arm.com
8. Code Composer Studio, http://www.ti.com
9. B. Cox, Object C, http://www.virtualschool.edu/lang/objectivec/index.html
10. P. Kruchten, Rational Unified Process-An Introduction, Addison-Wesley (2000)

11. K. Beck, Extreme Programming Explained – Embrace Change, 1st ed., Addison-Wesley (1999)
12. Cockburn, Agile Software Development, 1st ed., Addison-Wesley (2001)
13. Agile Alliance, http://www.agilealliance.org/home
14. T. Gilb, Principles of Software Engineering Management, Addison-Wesley (1988)
15. ANTLR, Complete Language Translation Solutions, http://www.antlr.org
16. CGRAM, ANSI C and GCC Source Translator, http://www.antlr.org/grammars/cgram
17. Rhapsody I-Logix, http://www.ilogix.com
18. Telelogic AB., Telelogic Tau 4.2: SDT Manual (2000)

A Framework for Software Quality Evaluation

Bernard Wong[1] and Ross Jeffery[2]

[1] Faculty of Information Technology, University of Technology, Sydney
PO Box 123, Broadway, NSW 2007, Australia
bernard@it.uts.edu.au
[2] School of Computer Science & Engineering, University of New South Wales
Sydney, NSW 2052, Australia
rossj@cse.unsw.edu.au

Abstract. The primary objective of this paper was to propose and empirically test a theoretical model for Software Quality Evaluation based on Gutman's Means-End Chain Model. Recent studies of Gutman's Model have found it significant for software quality evaluation. As such the proposed framework introduces the first theoretical model for software quality evaluation, which considers the motivation behind the quality evaluation, and the utilization of cognitive structures to describe these relationships. The framework not only gives the rationale for the choice of characteristics used in software quality evaluation, but also introduces the possibility that the characteristics can be used to measure the capability for attaining desired consequences and sought after values. To test this proposed framework, a study of 22 commercial Australian companies was conducted and analyzed with Path Analysis. Results of the analysis provided a number of important insights and suggest several conclusions. The study showed (1) that there is support for applying Gutman's Means-end chain model as the theoretical foundation for a framework on software quality evaluation; (2) that characteristics can be used as a measure to predict the capability of the software on desired consequences and values; (3) that non-ISO9126 characteristics are also important for software evaluation; (4) that the characteristic, consequence, value relationship can be valuable to benefit the Goal Question Metric model

1 Introduction

One finds almost as many definitions of quality as writers on the subject. Perhaps, fortunately, the latter have been remarkably few in number considering the obvious importance of the concept and the frequent appearance of the term quality in everyday language. Though the topic of software quality has been around for decades, software product quality research is still relatively immature, and today it is still difficult for a user to compare software quality across products. Researchers are still not clear as to

M. Oivo and S. Komi-Sirviö (Eds.): PROFES 2002, LNCS 2559, pp. 103–118, 2002.
© Springer-Verlag Berlin Heidelberg 2002

what is a good measure of software quality because of the variety of interpretations of the meaning of quality, of the meanings of terms to describe its aspects, of criteria for including or excluding aspects in a model of software, and of the degree to which software development procedures should be included in the definition. A particularly important distinction is between what represents quality for the user and what represents quality for the developer of a software product.

The paper introduces a framework for software evaluation, which gives the rationale for the choice of characteristics used in the evaluation, whilst also supplying the underpinning explanation for the multiple views of quality. The framework has its theoretical foundations on value-chain models, found in the disciplines of cognitive psychology and consumer research, and introduces the use of cognitive structures as a means of describing the many definitions of quality, whilst also showing the rationale behind these differences.

This paper is the third in a series of papers covering studies on Gutman's Means-End Chain Model. In the first paper, focus was placed on exploring, through a qualitative study, the use of cognitive structures as a means of describing Gutman's means-end chain relationship [1], and in the second paper, the results of a larger quantitative study on the appropriateness of Gutman's model in software quality evaluation was reported [2]. This paper differs from these past papers, in that it introduces a framework for software quality evaluation, whilst also describing the quantitative results, which validate the cognitive structures introduced in the earlier qualitative study [1].

The paper reports on a quantitative study of stakeholders' understanding of software quality. The study involved 403 subjects from 22 Australian organisations. It should be noted that whilst there are many more stakeholders than just users and developers, this study followed the previous qualitative study by focusing on only the users and developers. The study involved both users and developers of in-house developed software, and sought to study the stakeholders' understanding of software quality. Utilizing Path Analysis, the cognitive structures derived in the qualitative study are validated and the framework introduced in this paper tested.

2   Software Quality Evaluation Framework

Whilst there have been many studies on the topic of software quality, there have been none on a framework for software quality which considers the motivation behind the evaluation process. The recent studies of Wong & Jeffery ([1], [2]) provide the premise to the framework introduced here in this paper. It is proposed that a framework be based on the notion that software evaluators are influenced by their job roles. This is supported by earlier studies ([3], [4]) where stakeholders with different job roles were found to focus on different sets of software characteristics when evaluating software quality. What motivates these differences is found within the broader context of value, where studies have shown that values are a powerful force in influencing the behavior of individuals ([5], [6]).

The theoretical basis for developing such a framework was based on the theory found in cognitive psychology, and adopted Gutman's Means-End Chain Model ([7], [8], [9], [10], [11]), which posits that linkages between product characteristics, consequences produced through usage, and personal values of users underlie the decision-making process, or in this case, the software quality evaluation process. It is proposed in this research, that a framework be introduced for software quality evaluation, which focuses on the relationships between the characteristics, the consequences and the values, as introduced by Gutman's Model. It is the aim of the framework to not only show the relationships between the characteristics and software quality, but also show that there are relationships between the characteristics and the desired consequences, and between the characteristics and the sought after values.

As highlighted in the literature, the benefit of utilizing Gutman's model in the framework is that it shows how the desired values influence the behaviors of individuals in all aspects of their lives ([5], [6], [7]).   Gutman's Model suggests that the desired consequences and the values sought are the motivators behind the choice of characteristic for software evaluation. In addition to this, the framework also highlights the significants of this relationship through the relationships between characteristics and consequences and also between the characteristics and value. It is through these relationships that allow the possibility of using the characteristics to evaluate each consequence and value.

The framework distinguished individual responses in terms of three broad classes of elements: characteristics, consequences and value. This framework provided a good foundation for developing relevant hypothesis for this study. The results elicited the various combinations of characteristics, consequences and values for each person.

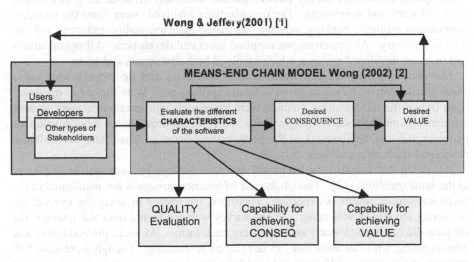

Fig. 1. Software Quality Evaluation Framework

The framework shown in figure 1. is based on Gutman's Means-End Chain Model. As can be seen in this diagram, the framework consists of a number of boxes describing the three elements of Gutman's Model, the stakeholders who evaluate the software quality, the outcome for the Quality evaluation, and the arrows linking these elements, whilst also describing the direction of the influence. The Means-End Chain Model has been placed in the main box, as it is proposed, in this framework, to be the central influence for the choice of characteristics used in software evaluation, and the influence for the differences found between stakeholders. Parts of this framework have already been investigated and have been reported in recent papers ([1], [2]). An exploratory study by Wong & Jeffery [1], utilized a qualitative approach to explore the influence of value on the choice of characteristics, and to determine whether cognitive structures could be used as a tool to represent the links between the characteristics, consequences and values. This study also supported earlier pilot studies on stakeholder differences ([3], [4]), identifying different cognitive structures for users and developers. A more recent paper by Wong [2] reported on a large quantitative study, which tested the appropriateness of utilizing Gutman's Model in software evaluation. What this paper will focus on will be to validate the cognitive structures introduced in the qualitative study [1], and to introduce a framework for software quality, which introduces the possible measurements by characteristics on each desired consequence and value.

3   Data Collection and Analysis

In order to investigate the framework, and validate the cognitive structures of the recent qualitative study, a survey was conducted. The study involved 22 organizations with 530 users and developers. The organizations involved, were from the telecommunications industry, banking industry, insurance industry, airline industry, and the dot.com industry. All organizations supplied users and developers. All organizations had in-house developed systems, which involved both developers and users.

The questionnaire was distributed to over 600 users and developers who had a close relationship with their in-house software applications. With the aid of organizations from different industries, contacts were made with appropriate managers, to seek assistance from their staff. Respondents were sought from those who develop or maintain in-house applications in the participating firms or those who use in-house developed applications in their daily job.

It is noted that face to face, telephone, and mail surveys produce similar responses to the same questions [12]. Though the use of internet surveys is not mentioned in the literature, similar results is expected. Therefore, the choice of using the internet for delivering the survey was made. As the survey was conducted over the internet, the subjects did not have to worry about mailing back forms. As such, the end result was most pleasing, with 210 users and 193 developers responding. Though there were 530 attempts at the survey, 127 were not usable, either because no attempt was made at any of the questions, or only a small percentage of questions were attempted. In total, 403 usable results were collected from 22 organizations.

The questionnaire was based upon the findings of previous research ([3], [4]), a previous qualitative study [1], survey questions from value studies ([9], [10]), and designed upon established principles [8].

Questions of similar design were put together, and distinctive typefaces were used for questions, answers and directions [13]. Question referring to Value were placed at the start of the survey, requesting subjects to identify the level of importance for each value. The subjects were then asked to rate the effect of the software on these values. The personal questions about respondents were placed at the end of the survey.

The questions are highly structured in order to make completion and comparative analysis easier. Because open questions are more likely to cause problems of categorization and so lead to false conclusions, or to over-represent the more convinced and more articulate [14], the great majority of responses involve selecting an appropriate box.

The questionnaire consisted of 80 questions. There were 9 questions on the List of Values, 9 questions on the quality of the software being evaluated, 6 questions covering the background of the respondent and 56 questions for the respondent to rate their satisfaction with 56 different measures of the software product. The questions are in no particular order. It is common practice for questionnaires to use several questions to ask what is essentially the same question, and then to average the results per case to form an index, as such a number of questions may refer to the same characteristic. There are two main reasons for this. Firstly, in order to avoid the problem of omitted variable bias ([15]), or variable selection bias [16], a question is included for *every* measurement required from the qualitative study. This means that 56 questions need to be asked, and it is likely that the fatigue induced by asking each question more than once would outweigh the advantage of creating an index. It is also likely that the completion and response rate of a longer form would be lower. Secondly, this technique of indexing is normally used because having only one measure is often unreliable, but the presumption that several sources are more reliable is a statistical argument based upon sampling theory [17]. The method assumes that each measure used in an index has the same variability, and that this is due solely to random error. If either of these assumptions is false, and it is unlikely that either would hold in much published work, using only one question can, in fact, be more accurate [17]. Any decision here is in the nature of a compromise, but although it is recognized that there will be a substantial error component in the responses, there seems little point in repeating the substance of the questions.

Unfortunately, the limitation on the length of this paper prohibits further details of the research instrument and method. For further details please refer to the doctoral thesis of Wong [18].

It is the purpose of this paper to determine whether cognitive structures can be derived, similar to those described in the qualitative study. Using the data from the quantitative study, an investigation of the cognitive structures was conducted, analyzing the direct and indirect effects of the characteristics, the desired consequences and the values. In order to achieve this, structural equation modeling is used.

Structural equation modeling, often loosely termed causal modeling, is an approach used to test multivariate models with empirical data. In this section, results of path analysis, a structural equation modeling technique, are presented. The main advantage of path analysis over simple correlation analysis, or regression analysis alone, is that it enables the decomposition of the correlations between the model variables into direct and indirect effects.

Structural Equation Modeling grows out of and serves purposes similar to multiple regression, but in a more powerful way which takes into account the modeling of interactions, nonlinearities, correlated independents, measurement error, correlated error terms, multiple indicators, and one or more latent dependents also each with multiple indicators. Advantages of Structural Equation Modeling compared to multiple regression include more flexible assumptions (particularly allowing interpretation even in the face of multi-collinearity), use of confirmatory factor analysis to reduce measurement error by having multiple indicators per latent variable, the Structural Equation Model's graphical modeling interface, the desirability of testing models overall rather than coefficients individually, the ability to model error terms, the ability to test coefficients across multiple between-subject groups and ability to handle difficult data (time series with auto-correlated error, non-normal data, incomplete data).

Path analysis was developed by Sewall Wright [19], as a method for studying the direct and indirect effects of variables hypothesized as causes, of variables treated as effects. It is a subset of Structural Equation Modeling (SEM), the multivariate procedure. Ullman [20] describes Structural Equation Modeling as a technique which allows examination of a set of relationships between one or more independent variables, and one or more dependent variables.

Structural equation modeling deals with BOTH measured and latent variables, whereas path analysis deals with only measured variables. A measured variable is a variable that can be observed directly and is measurable. Measured variables are also known as observed variables, indicators or manifest variables. A latent variable is a variable that cannot be observed directly and must be inferred from measured variables. Latent variables are implied by the covariance among two or more measured variables. They are also known as factors, constructs or unobserved variables.

With path analysis, the ability to quantitatively distinguish direct from indirect effects enhances the interpretation of relations as well as interpretation of the pattern of the effects of variables on each other. The path coefficients or regression beta coefficients of the path diagram represent direct effects. An indirect effect is simply the effect of one variable on another via mediating variable. The sum of the indirect and direct effects of one variable on another is termed the total effect. Path analysis addresses the structural model alone, whilst factor analysis aims at assessing the measurement model alone, and structural equation modeling is a way of addressing both techniques simultaneously. As such, path analysis is the most appropriate for what is required in this study. It has the benefit of assessing ALL the observed variables significant to the cognitive structure, identifying the direct and indirect effects of each variable on each other.

In path analysis, fit statistics are used to evaluate the research model. A model is said to „fit" the data if the difference between the actual and reproduced covariance matrices is within a predefined range. Since there is little consensus as to what the best overall measure of model fit, a menu of fit statistics is reported ([21], [22], [23], [24]). However, if a model is „successful at explaining the relationships behind the data, there should be some degree of consistency across the various fit indices. One of the difficulties in SEM analysis is the over-reliance towards overall model fit or goodness of fit [25]. „Where is the goodness of fit measure?" has become the 1990s focus for any SEM-based study. It should be clear that the existing goodness of fit measures relate to the ability of the model to account for the sample covariance and therefore assume that all measures are reflective. SEM procedures that have different objective functions and/or allow for formative measures would, by definition, not be able to provide such fit measures. In turn, reviewers and researchers often reject articles using such alternate procedures because simply, the model fit indices are not available. As such, Cognitive Structures with poor goodness of fit were rejected. It should be highlighted, that for any given SEM model, there might be a number of alternative models that are equivalent in terms of overall model fit. Such models produce substantially different explanations of the data. MacCallum et al [26] showed that such equivalent models exist in published studies, often in large numbers. Whereas Breckler's 1990 survey indicated that all but one of 72 published studies, acknowledged the possibility of alternative models [27].

The cognitive structures derived from the qualitative study were both tested with Path Analysis. Path Analysis has been used to confirm structural models, and to compare or anlayse alternative, competing models [28]. However, Joreskog and Sorbom states that the most common practice is to assist in improving a tentative initial model. They highlight that it is very rare to find researchers being content with just rejecting a given model without suggesting an alternative model. Breckler supports this through the results of a review of 72 articles, in which SEM was applied and found that only one acknowledged the existence of a specific model [27]. Bentler [29] asserted that in practice, most initially specified models do not fit the data and it becomes essential to make adjustments by adding new parameters, or by dropping insignificant ones. As such, alternative models were applied to improve the goodness of fit.

4   Results

The fit of the hypothesized models were assessed by using the maximum likelihood estimation technique in LISREL 8.5 [28]. In accordance with the recommendations of Hoyle and Panter [24], the following fit indexes were used to assess the fit of the hypothesized model: the goodness-of-fit index (GFI, [28]), the nonnormed fit index (NNFI, [30]), the incremental fit index (IFI, [21]), and the comparative fit index (CFI, [31]). The use of multiple fit indexes is generally advisable in order to provide convergent evidence of model fit. The values of GFI, NNFI, IFI, and CFI range from 0 to 1.0. It has been argued that only values above 0.90 indicate acceptable model fit ([24], [30]), however, this value has often been disputed and disregarded ([21], [22], [23], [24]), and values below 0.90 been accepted as an appropriate fit. Cohen [32], for example, suggested a minimum of 0.80. Bollen [21] observes that cutoffs are arbitrary and states that a more salient criterion may be to compare the fit of one model to the fit of another, prior model of the same phenomenon. For example, a CFI of 0.85 may represent progress in a field where the best prior model had a fit of 0.70. As the literature points out, there is no such animal as "good fit" ([24], [30]). The aim is to find a meaningful pattern of loadings (and paths) to best reproduce the original covariances. The emphasis, thus, is on meaningfulness. A model with a fit index of 0.8 may be the very best that can be achieved - given the status of the theory, given the adequacy of the measures, and given the representativeness of the sample. On the other hand, you can get a fit index of 0.95 simply by over-factoring the data. The aim of fit indices is to assist in the development of meaningful theory. The cognitive structures derived from the qualitative study, figures 2 and 3, both obtained appropriately good fit.

Table 1. FIT Statistics for User & Developer Cognitive Structures

FIT INDEX	USER COGNITIVE STRUCTURE FIT	DEVELOPER COGNITIVE STRUCTURE FIT
GFI	0.89	0.84
NNFI	0.90	0.83
IFI	0.89	0.82
CFI	0.89	0.84

Both models depict a number of hypothesized relationships involving the software characteristics, the software quality, the consequences and values. The causal order is read from bottom to top. Each line in the model is called a path and each has a path coefficient obtained from LISREL 8.5 ([28]). Figures 2 and 3, show the structures derived from the qualitative study [1]. However, it must be noted that there is one difference between these structures and the ones from the qualitative study. In order to conduct a thorough analysis on the effects of the characteristics, the structures described here, include all the characteristics, rather than just the characteristics found to be significant in the qualitative study.

The values listed in table 1, revealed that there is an acceptable fit between the hypothesized models and the observed data. The degree of fit, compared with the suggested minimum fit of Cohen [32], 0.80, confirms that the configurations of the research models are both appropriate.

As described before, the goodness of fit has often been disputed in regards to the cutoff value ([21], [22], [23], [24]). Though 0.90 has often being cited as the accepted measure for a good fit ([24], [30]), suggestions have been found in literature that a minimum value of 0.80 is also an acceptable cutoff [32].

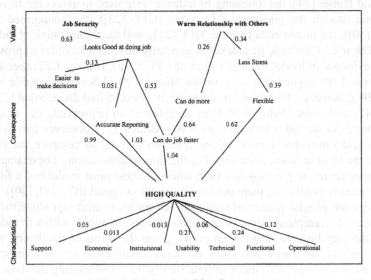

Fig. 2. Users' Cognitive Structure

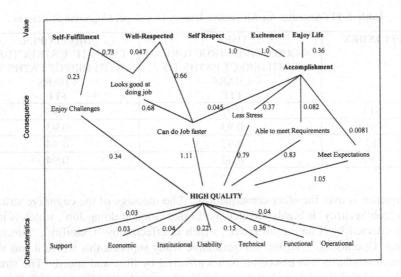

Fig. 3. Developers' Cognitive Structure

The structural models were assessed for the explanatory power of the independent variables, and an examination of the size and significance of the path coefficients. These path coefficients are standardized regression coefficients (beta weights), showing the direct effect of an independent variable on a dependent variable in the path model. Thus, when the models have two or more causal variables, path coefficients are partial regression coefficients, which measure the extent of effect of one variable on another. Therefore, these path coefficients can be interpreted in similar ways to the regression coefficients of regression analysis, that is, the higher the value the stronger the effect given by the variable.

The users' structural model (figure 2) as tested here with Path Analysis, adopted the structure from the qualitative study. Whilst the qualitative study was rich with data explaining the cause and effect for each consequence and value, the quantitative study was able to show the effects of each path between each variable.

The results showed that the values 'Job Security' and 'Warm Relationship with Others', were perceived by Users to be affected by the use of the software. These values were identified in the qualitative study as the values significant in the user's cognitive structure. The path coefficients showed that 'Job Security' is far more important than 'Warm Relationships with Others'. This was evident during the qualitative study as well, where job security and issues like 'Status', 'Job is Safe', 'In Control', and 'Feel Confident' were dominant issues during the interview of users. However, the strength of Path Analysis is that it shows the amount of effect between the paths not just the paths.

The cognitive structure showed strong path coefficients for 'Easier to Make Decisions', 'Accurate Reporting', and 'Can do Job Faster', supporting the qualitative results which showed that these variables are extremely important to the user. The extremely high path coefficient of 'Can do Job Faster' clearly shows how important this

Table 2. FIT Statistics for Alternative User & Developer Cognitive Structures

FIT INDEX	USER COGNITIVE STRUCTURE WITH DIRECT PATHS TO CHARS FIT	DEVELOPER COGNITIVE STRUCTURE WITH DIRECT PATHS TO CHARS FIT
GFI	0.92	0.94
NNFI	0.93	0.93
IFI	0.92	0.94
CFI	0.92	0.94

consequence is over the other consequences. The message of the cognitive structures is that 'Job Security' is highly effected by 'Looks Good at doing Job', which is in turn highly effected by 'Can do job faster', which is effected by 'Usability', 'Functionality', and 'Operational'. Again, the qualitative study supports this where it was shown that much emphasis was placed on issues affected by time and speed. The structure also showed that 'Looks good at doing Job' had a significant effect on 'Job Security', and that 'Easier to Make Decisions' had only small effects on 'Looks Good at doing Job', as compared to 'Can do Job Faster'. The results showed that 'Can do Job Faster' had a strong effect on 'Can Do More', and that 'Flexible' resulted in 'Less Stress', again similar to the qualitative study. It is also highlighted that the following consequences, 'Easier to Make Decisions', 'Accurate Reporting', 'Can do Job Faster', and 'Flexible', are highly affected by software quality.

However, the characteristics affecting software quality are found to contain slight differences to the user cognitive structure of the qualitative study. Like the qualitative study, Technical characteristics gave minimal effect, whilst, Usability, Functional, and Operational characteristics showed significant effects on software quality. However, the Path Analysis showed that the effects of Support, Economic and Institutional characteristics on quality evaluation differed from the results of the qualitative study. The results of the Path Analysis showed that these variables had minimal effect on software quality evaluation, whilst the qualitative study showed that these characteristics gave significant effects on quality. Earlier studies ([3], [4]) support these results, where it was found that these characteristics were borderline in regards to their contribution to quality evaluation. These earlier studies found small amounts of support from users who were middle managers or more senior in their job, but no support for these characteristics from users who were lower in the company structure. Perhaps further studies on other user groups will clarify the role of these three characteristics on quality evaluation.

As with the users, figure 3 shows a similar structure to that derived from the qualitative study except that all characteristics are included for the Path Analysis so as to test the effects of the characteristics on quality.

The results showed that the value, 'Self-fulfillment' was highly affected by 'Looking good at doing job', whilst the consequence 'Enjoying Challenges' gave only minimal effect. The value 'Well-respected' was highly effected by 'Being able to do job faster', but only effected in a very small way by 'Looking Good at doing job'.

The value Accomplishment is most effected by 'Less Stress', with very slight effects from 'Can do job faster', 'Able to Meet Requirements' and 'Meet Expectations'. Quality Software effects all the consequences with 'Can do job faster' and 'Meet Expectations' being the most effected, whilst 'Enjoy Challenges' being only relatively effected. The qualitative study supported these same results with strong focus placed on 'Meet Expectations' and 'Can do job faster'.

As to the Characteristics, similar effects were discovered as described in the qualitative study [1]. Usability, Functional and Technical dominated the effects on quality software. Though Support and Operational were part of the qualitative study's Cognitive structure, it must be highlighted that very minimal effects on software quality were found in this study. Unfortunately, no obvious reasons could be identified for these differences.

Whilst the path analysis can only show the strength of an effect, it fails to show the personal, subjective reasons behind these effects. As the literature has highlighted ([24], [30]), the fact there exists significant path coefficients or correlations does not guarantee causal effect. For this reason, the results from the qualitative study are valuable to help understand the quantitative results.

Alternative structure was also tested for both users and developers, introducing new paths between the characteristics, and each of the consequences and values. As can be seen here in table 2, the Goodness of Fit was improved, highlighting the significance of these new paths to the structure. The framework described in figure 1, proposed that characteristics could be used to not only evaluate software quality, but also to measure the capability of attaining a desired consequence or sought after value. This introduces further benefit for applying Gutman's Model to software evaluation.

Table 3. The Effect of Characteristics on Consequences & Values as per Users

CONSEQUENCES & VALUES	ECONOMIC	FUNCTIONAL	INSTITUTIONAL	OPERATIONAL	SUPPORT	TECHNICAL	USABILITY
JOB SECURITY	0.033	0.99	0.0015	0.046	0.024	0.038	0.086
WARM RELATIONSHIP WITH OTHERS	0.28	0.24	0.037	0.046	0.011	0.11	0.65
LOOKS GOOD AT DOING JOB	0.11	0.49	0.044	0.21	0.084	0.12	0.26
EASIER TO MAKE DECISIONS	0.0074	0.82	0.061	0.059	0.093	0.013	0.086
ACCURATE REPORTING	0.0014	0.92	0.041	0.30	0.10	0.019	0.29
CAN DO JOB FASTER	0.10	0.86	0.0041	0.19	0.075	0.096	0.42
LESS STRESS	0.049	0.16	0.013	0.08	0.063	0.11	0.66
CAN DO MORE	0.035	0.08	0.12	0.033	0.16	0.26	0.56
FLEXIBLE	0.094	0.61	0.0026	0.39	0.0046	0.051	0.48

The characteristics are seen here to improve the goodness of fit from 0.89 to 0.92 for the users and from 0.84 to 0.94 for the developers, implying that the relationships between the characteristics and the consequences, and the relationships between the characteristics and the values are important for the cognitive structure. The following two tables list the effects of each characteristic on every consequence and value for users (table 3) and developers (table 4). The effects are measured between 0 and 1, where a measure close to 1 signifies a greater effect, and a measure that is closer to 0 signifies a smaller effect.

The results show that there is a clear dominant effect from functionality and usability for both users and developers. Whilst operational and economic were occasionally seen as having significant effect for users, technical was occasionally seen as having significant effect for developers. These results are supported by previous studies ([1], [2], [3], [4]). It should be also pointed out that these tables do not list the effects from the paths of the cognitive structures in figures 2 and 3. The alternative path analysis with the improved Goodness of Fit also includes the effect along these paths. Though most of them have very small effects compared with the characteristics listed in the tables, a number of the consequences „Looks good at doing job" and „Can do job faster" do have relatively significant effects, highlighting their importance to the stakeholders. Whilst the potential exists to use these effects with the characteristics, as a means to calculate the capability of achieving desired consequences and values, it should be noted that the paths discussed here only highlight the effects and are not equations for measuring the consequences and values. Further studies are required to achieve this.

Table 4. The Effect of Characteristics on Consequences & Values as per Developers

CONSEQUENCES & VALUES	CHARACTERISTICS						
	ECONOMIC	FUNCTIONAL	INSTITUTIONAL	OPERATIONAL	SUPPORT	TECHNICAL	USABILITY
SELF FULFILLMENT	0.029	0.012	0.0013	0.13	0.017	0.062	0.8
WELL-RESPECTED	0.04	0.75	0.072	0.12	0.0096	0.15	0.21
SELF-RESPECTED	0.044	0.18	0.0098	0.27	0.0094	0.98	0.021
EXCITEMENT	0.044	0.18	0.0098	0.27	0.0094	0.98	0.021
ENJOY LIFE	0.036	0.98	0.054	0.059	0.084	0.028	0.20
ACCOMPLISHMENT	0.044	0.18	0.0098	0.27	0.0094	0.98	0.021
LOOKS GOOD AT DOING JOB	0.073	0.12	0.091	0.17	0.0095	0.30	0.45
ENJOY CHALLENGES	0.10	0.52	0.0046	0.090	0.024	0.074	0.021
LESS STRESS	0.0036	0.035	0.078	0.14	0.023	0.418	0.56
CAN DO JOB FASTER	0.07	0.85	0.12	0.076	0.085	0.13	0.49
ABLE TO MEET REQUIREMENTS	0.038	0.13	0.048	0.069	0.11	0.26	0.68
MEET EXPECTATIONS	0.027	0.14	0.0086	0.21	0.019	0.16	0.69

5   Discussion

The results of this paper support the use of Gutman's Model in the proposed framework, as have the previous studies ([1], [2]). Like the qualitative study [1], the cognitive structures provided the means to describe the paths between the characteristics, the consequences and the values. Whilst this is significant to the framework, it is more important to highlight how this study has benefited from the strength of Path Analysis, in that it not only showed the structure and provided a measure of its goodness of fit, but was also able to show the effects between the paths, therefore describing how some paths are more important than others.

The benefit of the framework is not only in being able to identify a link between the characteristics and software quality, but more importantly, identify the characteristics which have significant effect on the individual consequences, and values. This is extremely important in the evaluation of software, as it introduces measurements more focused on the user or developer needs. Though this study has introduced the paths between characteristics and consequences and between characteristics and values, more study is required to validate the relationships and to develop appropriate equations.

Software Quality has been described as a combination of characteristics, with ISO9126 being adopted as the current international standard. However, though support for ISO9126 appeared in some of the results, evidence suggests that non-ISO9126 characteristics are also important when evaluating software quality. This is supported by the recent qualitative study [1], the results of earlier studies of Wong & Jeffery ([3], [4]). The results found that ISO9126 characteristics, usability and functionality strongly effect software quality for both developers and users, whilst technical characteristics, like portability and maintainability were only significant for the developers. However, the results surprisingly found operational characteristics, like efficiency and reliability, to minimally affect software quality. This result was not expected since many of the measurements for software quality, like defects and failures, focus on reliability. As to the non-ISO9126 characteristics, support was found to be important for both users and developers, whilst the characteristics economic and institutional were only relevant for users. It is evident from this study that further work is required to identify whether the non-ISO9126 characteristics should be part of the ISO9126 set of characteristics.

The result of this study also introduces a valuable addition to the Goal Question Metric Method (GQM) ([33]). The most notable feature of GQM, is the central role of a goal, focusing on the fact that there must be a reason for measuring, and that without goals, patterns are unlikely to be visible, since the data collected will be unfocused. Basili rejects the notion of fixed sets of metrics, which many of the earlier models of quality are based on, but instead offers a method to assist tailoring sets of metrics to specific goals. However, it has been generally accepted that the progression from the goals to the questions is the most difficult aspect of GQM. The method provides little guidance, relying instead upon the judgment, experience and insight of those involved with measurement to identify useful questions. There exists a multiplicity of questions that could be asked about virtually any goal. The research described in this paper, solves this problem for software quality evaluation through the use of cognitive structures. Values sought by the stakeholders are appropriate goals, with the cognitive structures supplying related questions, which are associated with these goals. This results in creating the purpose for measurement, setting in place the progression from the goals, to the questions and finally to the metrics, which are associated with the software characteristics.

6   Conclusion

The results elicited the various combinations of characteristics, consequences and values for each person, indicating the presence of these types of cognitive elements when dealing with software quality evaluation.

The framework gives rationale for the selection of characteristics. It introduces the means to describe this rationale. It also showed that the rationale for different views of quality exist and allows the motivation to be described. The framework supports the means-end chain model of Gutman, and shows that the means-end chain model can be used in software evaluation. Through the use of these cognitive structures a better understanding of the characteristics selected during quality evaluation, and how they are related to what the evaluator values is achieved. The evidence from the study supports the view that evaluators of software choose certain characteristics because of this relationship.

Several implications for researchers can be derived from the study reported here. First, the research shows the validity of the cognitive structures, which supports the application of Gutman's Means-End Chain Analysis applied to software quality evaluation. Second, the results of both this study and the previous Wong & Jeffery qualitative study, introduce a valuable addition to the Goal Question Metric Model. The research shows that Values sought by the stakeholder are appropriate goals for software evaluation, highlighting not only that users and developers have different goals, but also what these goals are. Third, the cognitive structures describe the related questions, which are associated with both the goals and the characteristics where the metrics would come from, showing clearly the linkages between them. Fourth, the use of these cognitive structures can better the understanding of the characteristics selected during quality evaluation, and how they are related to what the evaluator values. Fifth, the results are valuable for developers; to better their understanding of the users they are developing software for. Sixth, the framework introduces a whole new area of measurement, which focuses on assessing capability of the software in its effect on desired consequences and values based on measurements of the software characteristics. And lastly, the study provides the empirical research that gives explanation to the choice of characteristics for software evaluation, showing that both ISO9126 and non-ISO9126 characteristics are required for software evaluation, whilst describing clearly the differences between the users and developers.

References

1. Wong, B. & Jeffery, R.: Cognitive Structures of Software Evaluation: A Means-End Chain Analysis of Quality, Proceedings of the Third International Conference, PROFES 2001, 2001, pp 6-26.
2. Wong, B: The Appropriateness of Gutman's Means End Chain Model in Software Evaluation, Proceedings of the 2002 International Symposium on Empirical Software Engineering, ISESE 2002, pp 56-65.
3. Wong, B. & Jeffery, R.: Quality Metrics: ISO9126 and Stakeholder Perceptions, Proceedings of the Second Australian Conference on Software Metrics, 1995, pp 54-65.
4. Wong, B. & Jeffery, R.: A Pilot Study of Stakeholder Perceptions of Quality, Technical Report, CSIRO, 1996.
5. Rokeach: Beliefs, Attitudes and Values, San Francisco: Jossey Bass, 1968.
6. Yankelovich: New Rules, New York: Random House.
7. Gutman,J.: A Means-End Chain Model Based on Consumer Categorization Processes, Journal of Marketing, 46 (Spring): 60-72.
8. Gutman.J. : Means-End Chains as Goal Hierarchies, Psychology & Marketing, 14 (6):1997 545-560.
9. Bagozzi, R.: Goal-directed behaviours in marketing: cognitive and emotional, Psychology & Marketing, 14, Sept 1997, pp 539-543.
10. Valette-Florence, P.: A Causal Analysis of Means-End Hierarchies in a Cross-cultural Context: Metholodogical Refinements, Journal of Business Research, v 42 No 2 June 1998, pp161-166.
11. Bagozzi, R. and Dabholkar, P.: Discursive psychology: an alternative conceptual foundation to means-end chain theory, Psychology & Marketing, 17, July 2000, pp 535-586.
12. Kahle L, Beatty S and Homer P.: Alternative Measurement Approaches to Consumer Values: The List of Values (LOV) and Values and Life Style (VALS), Journal of Consumer Research, 13 December, 1986, 405-409.
13. Oppenheim A: Questionnaire Design, Interviewing and Attitude Measurement, London: Pinter, 1992.
14. Payne S: The Art of Asking Questions, New Jersey: Princeton University, 1951.
15. Maddala G: Introduction to Econometrics, New York: Macmillan, 1992.
16. Kim J and Mueller C: Introduction to Factor Analysis. What it is and how to do it, London: Sage, 1978.
17. Anderson T and Zelditch M: Basic Course in Statistics, New York: Holt, Rinehart and Winston, 1968.
18. Wong, B: An Investigation of the Cognitive Structures used in Software Quality Evaluation, Unpublished PhD Thesis, University of New South Wales, 2002.
19. Wright S: The Method of Path Coefficients, Annals of Mathematical Statistics, 5, 1934, pp. 161-215.
20. Ullman J B: Structural Equation Modeling (in Using Multivariate Statistics, Third Edition, BG Tabachnick and LS Fidell Eds), HarperCollins College Publishers, New York, NY, 1996, pp. 709-819.

21. Bollen K A: Structural Equations with Latent Variables, John Wiley & Sons, New York, 1989.
22. Marsh H W, Balla J R and McDonald R P: Goodness of Fit Indices in Confirmatory Factor Analysis: The Effect of Samle Size, Psychological Bulletin, 103(3), 1988, pp. 391-410.
23. Tanaka J S: Multifaceted Conceptions of Fit in Structural Equation Model, in K.A. Bollen & J.Scott Long (Editors), Testing Structural Equation Models, Newbury Park, CA: Sage, 1993, pp. 10-39.
24. Hoyle R and Panter A: Writing About Structural Equation Models, in Structural Equation Modeling, Concepts, Issues and Applications, R.H. Hoyle (ed), Sage Publications, Thousand Oaks, CA 1995, pp. 158-176.
25. Chin W W: Issues and Opinion on Structural Equation Modeling, Management Information Systems Quarterly, 22(1), Mar 1998.
26. MacCallum R C, Wegener D T, Uchino B N, Fagbrigar L R: The Problem of Equivalent Models in Applications of Covaraiance Structure Analysis, *Psychological Bulletin,* **114(1)**, 1993, pp.185-199.
27. Breckler S J: Application of Covariance Structure Modeling in Psychology: Cause for Concern?, *Psychological Bulletin*, **107(2)**, 1990, pp. 260-372.
28. Jöreskog K G & Sörbom D: *Lisrel 8: User's Reference Guide*, Chicago: Scientific Software, 1993.
29. Bentler P M: Drug use and personality in Adolescence and Young Adulthood: Structural Model with Nonnormal Variables, *Child Development*, **58**, 1987, pp. 65-79.
30. Bentler P M & Bonnett D G: Significance Tests and Goodness of Fit in the Analysis of Covariance Structures, *Psychological Bulletin*, **88**, 1980, pp. 588-606.
31. Bentler P M: Comparative Fit Indexes in Structural Model, *Psychological Bulletin*, **107**, 1990, pp. 238-246.
32. Cohen J: *Statistical Power Analysis for the Behavioural Sciences*, 2nd Edition, Hillsdale,NJ: L. Erlbaum Associates, 1988.
33. Rombach D and Basili V: Practical Benefits of Goal-Oriented Measurement, Proceedings Annual Workshop of the Centre for Software Reliability: Reliability and Measurement, Garmisch-Partenkirchen, Germany: Elsevier, 1990.

Component Certification – What is the Value?

Lars Bratthall[1], Johan Hasselberg[2], Brad Hoffman[3], Zbigniew Korendo[4],
Bruno Schilli[5], and Lars Gundersen[1]

[1] ABB, Corporate Research Center, N-1375 Billingstad, Norway
[2] ABB Automation Technology Products, S-721 67 Västerås, Sweden
[3] ABB Automation Technology Products, CH-8050 Zürich, Switzerland
[4] ABB, Corporate Research Center, 31-038 Kraków, Poland
[5] ABB, Corporate Research Center, D-68526 Ladenburg, Germany

Abstract. Component-based software is becoming increasingly popular
as a means to create value through improved integration across multiple
parts of a plant or business. However, sometimes components that are
supposed to be integrated cannot be integrated in the same way that the
user envisions at time of acquiring the component. Certification of
components is one way of ensuring that components adhere to certain
standards for integration. This study presents findings from two case
studies assessing the value of one particular certification program from
ABB, called Industrial IT Enabled. A method for facilitating complex
decision-making, Incomplete Pairwise Comparison (IPC), has been
used to identify the relative value of Industrial IT Enabled for
customers, as well as for ABB itself. Results indicate that the
certification provides practically significant added value to customers,
as well as to ABB. It is believed that these results, to some extent, can
be valid in other similar certification programs.

1   Introduction

Very large enterprises face the challenge of offering value through drawing on the
power of the large company, while maintaining the agility and speed of the small
firm. One way to balance these requirements is to deploy a common extendable
system architecture throughout the enterprise, where products from different parts of
the organization are easy to plug in and the architecture facilitates integration.

ABB, an enterprise with more than 130 000 employees worldwide, has launched
the Industrial IT initiative to achieve this goal. Industrial IT is a commitment to
providing real-time automation and information across the business enterprise.
Industrial IT includes a set of compatible products, a common architecture for
integration, and a corporate mind set geared to value-added solutions. Industrial IT
spans multiple business layers, including process automation, asset optimization and
collaborative business processes. It includes functionality ranging from field devices
(products with lots of embedded software and network communication capabilities) to
business systems, focused on supporting decisions and improving customer

M. Oivo and S. Komi-Sirviö (Eds.): PROFES 2002, LNCS 2559, pp. 119-133, 2002.

productivity and asset utilization, from the first phases of design, through installation, commissioning, operation, maintenance and asset optimization as shown in Fig. 1.

Evolving a very large organization – and its subcontractors – to conform to a single architecture can be a daunting task [1], considering there may be thousands of products that are being integrated, or ported to the new architecture. But what does „integration" really mean? For example, one may claim that Microsoft® Notepad is integrated with Microsoft® Word, as Notepad can open a Word file. On the other hand, integration is not perceived as complete, as Notepad mainly displays unreadable signs when a Word file is opened.

Thus, a way of measuring „how complete" the integration is, is needed, and the business value of different such measurements has to be known when choosing what „completeness" of integration is needed. This paper presents how „completeness of integration" is determined and certified for Industrial IT products from ABB and its partners, allowing them to deploy the Industrial IT Enabled symbol. In particular, value to ABB, as well as value to its customers, is assessed through two case studies of current industrial projects.

The paper is outlined as follows. In Sect. 2, the Industrial IT architecture, as well as how ABB measures and certifies how well a particular product is integrated with the architecture is discussed. In Sect. 3, we outline the method used to determine the value of certification to ABB and its customers. Individual results are reported in Sect. 4, and these are used to build a comprehensive valuation of the certification program summarized in Sect. 5.

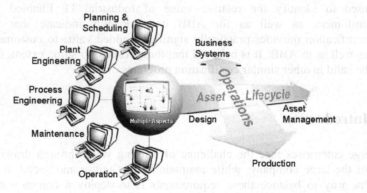

Fig. 1. The scope of the Industrial IT commitment

2   Background

2.1   The Industrial IT Architecture

In order to understand the certification process for Industrial IT products, the Industrial IT architecture must be understood to some extent. Below, a very brief summary is given.

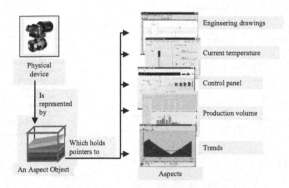

Fig. 2. Simple example instantiation

The Aspect Object Model. In the Industrial IT architecture, each real-world device is represented by a software model called an Aspect Object. The software object holds pointers to various software entities representing aspects – or characteristics – of the real-world object. For example, the Aspect Object for a typical plant device might have a documentation aspect, an error log aspect and a replacement availability aspect. An example of one device (typically a combined mechanical/embedded software device) represented by an Aspect Object with multiple aspects is shown in Fig. 2.

Each aspect incorporates various data belonging to the complete system rather than the individual application (called Aspect System) that operates on the data. For example, a spare parts aspect might have a URL to a site for online orders as its only data, and a web browser could be the Aspect System that operates on the data.

Each physical object has distinct relationships to other physical objects. For example, a given set of objects might have location relationships (same room/different rooms), or they might participate in same/different production processes. In the Industrial IT software representation, each object may participate in different structures such as the location structure, functional structure, maintenance structure, etc. The idea of placing the same object in multiple structures is based on [8], [9]. This approach makes it easy to add new structures. For example, one may want an electrical structure to keep track of which power-consuming devices are attached to the same power generators, a control-system structure to show which outputs and signals influence control of the given components, etc. Although a given object may reside in multiple structures, aspect data need only be provided once as the Industrial IT architecture permits easy instantiation. Fig. 3 shows an instantiation of one valve in multiple structures.

During operation, a plant operator (or, a vessel captain, or a mill maintenance staff-member) is presented with an easy-to-understand, object-oriented view of the real-world objects. An example is shown in Fig. 4. This view is completely customizable, since usability needs may differ very much between different user groups. For example, a plant control operator may need to access much more information than the engine room operators on a marine vessel. A cost accountant will have different informational needs for a plant process than will a maintenance engineer. Etc.

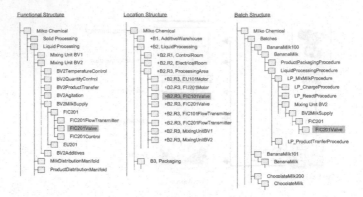

Fig. 3. One valve in three structures

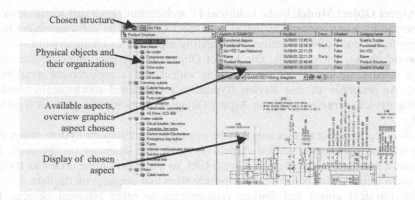

Fig. 4. Example of a workplace. Here a compressor is modeled, and the Wiring Diagram for a part is displayed

2.2 Testing and Certification of Industrial IT Enabled Products

The purpose of certifying products to the Industrial IT Enabled standard is to make sure customers that standardize on Industrial IT can benefit from its value with a minimum of integration challenges, despite the fact that different products may come from different vendors. This is much like the Microsoft Certified Partner Program, or Novell® certification program, or Bluetooth qualification, which are other vendor/product specific product certification programs intended to increase customer value of products that operate in partly heterogeneous, distributed integrated environments.

The Industrial IT certification process was shaped by three main requirements:

1. The certification process should facilitate a step-wise transition from older systems to newer systems. For example, an older legacy system may be hard to change substantially. Modular addition of new compatible products, however, can help to evolve the full system toward the new standard.

2. As certification is intended to increase customers' value of their Industrial IT investments, a customer perspective should be taken. Typically, customers will include several types of users as well as sponsors. Thus, certification is not only about conformance to the Industrial IT architecture, but also it should ensure that supporting documents and processes are in place. In particular, a certified product should be easy to purchase, integrate, engineer, install, commission, operate, maintain, and de-install. These process areas cover a product's life cycle as seen from a customer's point of view, so that total cost of ownership (TCO) can be optimized.

3. Viable procedures for testing and certification must be in place, so that certification does not become a time-to-market bottleneck for new products.

Table 1. The four levels of Industrial IT Enabling

Level	Description
0. Information	• Unique identification of the product • Developed, produced, etc. with adequate quality control • Environmental impact and immunity must be stated for hardware products • Global product support must be available • Aspect Object Types are provided with at least the Basic set of Aspects • Additional requirements apply to ABB products.
1. Connectivity (as Information plus...)	• Hardware can be physically connected via defined interfaces • Software is installed and handled in a consistent way. (Usually, this implies the Microsoft Installer (MSI).) • Basic interoperability of the product in the environment it is inserted in • Basic product data can be exchanged via defined protocols. Example: Device Identity, Device type and process values can be read via a defined protocol such as OPC (OLE for Process Control, an industry standard)
2. Integration (as Connectivity plus...)	• Aspect Object Types are provided with the Basic set of Aspects (configuration tools, specs, drawings, documents etc) • Extended aspect data (status, maintenance needs etc) can be exchanged via defined protocols such as OPC • Relevant functionality is available as Aspect Systems
3. Optimization (as Integration plus...)	• Aspect Object Types are provided with at least the Extended set of Aspects • Relevant functionality is available as Aspect Systems on integration level 3 • The product is handled in a consistent manner throughout the life cycle and value chain.

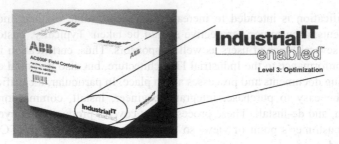

Fig. 5. The Industrial IT Enabled symbol

Given these main requirements, the Industrial IT certification process was defined as a ladder certification process, where key areas on a lower level must be achieved before a product can be certified on a higher level, much like the Capability Maturity Model® for Software (SW-CMM®) [13].

Certification does not evaluate the functionality, capacity or performance of the product in a given task. It only deals with integration properties, i.e. how well the product behaves in an Industrial IT environment. Thus, certification does not repeat product testing, but it verifies to a large extent conformance to standards (international and ABB internal). Certification is made in a well-defined system environment. This means that a product is certified for integration in this specific environment.

Only properties that are applicable for a certain product are tested. For example, statements about environmental immunity are obviously only valid for products that include hardware. The actual Industrial IT Enabled specifications evolve over time. It is expected that there will be regular (e.g. annual) versions of the Industrial IT Enabled itself. An official steering body for the Industrial IT Enabled governs this. The body has the ruling power in case of disagreements regarding test results, properties to be tested, validity of signed checklists etc.

The certification is valid until the next major release of the tested product. With a major release a renewed certification has to be made in order to keep the certified status. Certified products, and only those, are allowed to display the Industrial IT Enabled symbol, as shown in Fig. 5

The process for certification of Information level products is streamlined: The developer of a product, or solution, creates a number of files, such as user manual, technical manuals etc according to a checklist provided. When those are ready, a software tool adds these as aspects of the aspect object representing the product. Thus, they become part of the product itself, and can be consistently handled in any Industrial IT based system. The tool does not allow incomplete sets of documents. Finally, the tool enlists the product as an Information Enabled product in ABB's central database. This ensures that other developers gets immediate access to information about the product.

For the higher levels of Industrial IT Enabled, there is more documentation needed. There are checklists for a number of categories of products that guide the development organization to create the information needed. This information, together with the completed and signed checklist, is sent to any of ABBs accredited certification centers. These evaluate the delivered information and eventually certify the product. The reason for why self-assessment is not allowed is that it can be fairly complex to determine how, for example, partial NLS (partial localized language support due to use of COTS software) should be judged. The accredited centers continually monitors such issues, and creates and maintains common practices for this purpose.

Table 2. Customer key processes investigated[1]

PURCHASE	An Industrial IT Enabled product is easier to purchase for a customer than a non certified product, because it is easier to identify the right product, assess it, and handle the administration side of purchasing of the product.
INTEGRAT	An Industrial IT Enabled product is easier to integrate with other current and future systems, than a non-certified product.
ENGINEER	An Industrial IT Enabled product is easier to use in engineering than a non-certified product.
INSTALL	An Industrial IT Enabled product is easier to install than a non-certified product.
COMMISION	An Industrial IT Enabled product is easier during commissioning than a non-certified product.
OPERATE	An Industrial IT Enabled product is easier to operate, compared to a non-certified product, because certified products share a common „look and feel".
MAINTAIN	An Industrial IT Enabled product is easier to maintain after commissioning than a non-certified product. Maintenance may involve, e.g., product replacement, and integration with other systems anywhere in the world.
DEINSTAL	An Industrial IT Enabled product is easier to deinstall than a non-certified product.

3 Method for Investigation

In this section, the method used to conduct this study is outlined. In Sect. 3.1, the two questions that this study attempts to answer are defined. The way data is collected is outlined in Sect. 3.2. The two organizations studied are described in Sect. 3.3, to illustrate the type of organizations where findings are highly likely to be valid. Analysis of data is described in Sect. 3.4, and threats to the validity of this study are described in Sect. 3.5.

3.1 Research Definition

Based on the research focus stated in Sect. 1, the following research questions have been derived:

---

[1] Some of the vocabulary here has particular meaning within ABB. However, this is very similar among the participants in this study, though it may differ from other organizations.

RQ1: Industrial IT Enabled products should add value to customers. In which key processes do Industrial IT Enabled products add the most value for a customer? Customer key processes investigated are found in Table 2. These cover a product's life-cycle as seen from a customer's point of view.

RQ2: Where is the value for ABB in investing in Industrial IT enabling its products? Value sources investigated are found in Table 3. These sources are considered some of the main sources for ABB.

3.2   Operation

This study has been conducted as follows. First, a number of value sources and customer key processes were identified by discussing with ABB employees in research, marketing, strategic management, as well as with customers. These value sources are stated in Sect. 3.1.

The definition of these sources were reviewed by having two independent ABB employees review the definitions for clarity and preciseness in their contexts, prior to the definitions being exposed to others. These two employees do not contribute to the real data collection. The research questions and the variables were then used in a questionnaire template that has been used several times before, for example in [2], [10].

The questionnaire was distributed to ABB employees working in two current industrial customer projects (described below), where Industrial IT plays an important role. The projects were selected because of availability; thus, a kind of convenience sampling has been used. However, the two cases are considered representative for current work. There were five respondents in project A, and seven in project B. Written instructions regarding how to fill in the questionnaire were included.

Table 3. Value sources for ABB investigated

LR_SALES	An Industrial IT Enabled product is verified to work together with products from other domains. Thus it is a lower risk choice than a non-certified product for customers who have Industrial IT installations. This may result in higher sales for ABB.
EXPOSURE	An Industrial IT Enabled product is exposed to a wide market through Industrial IT product family marketing. Thus the market exposure is larger than for a non-certified product. This may result in higher sales for ABB compared to competitors.
REUSE	An Industrial IT Enabled product can to some extent be reused across business areas. Thus there is less need for rework. Thus development needs are reduced, resulting in lower costs.
BIGSCOPE	As there are many (currently almost 4000) Industrial IT enabled products, the scope of ABB deliverables can be enlarged. Thus more – and larger – integration contracts can be captured.
PREMPRIC	The Industrial IT Enabled symbol tells a user that a product has extra value added throughout the entire product lifecycle. Thus customers may be willing to pay a higher price for the product than otherwise.

After filling in the questionnaires, the respondents were given the possibility to comment further in an open-ended interview [5], i.e. an interview with no predetermined set of questions.

3.3   Description of Cases

Project A: Co engineering of Compressors ABB – Atlas Copco. Atlas Copco is a global industry group with more than 25000 employees. One of their business domains is heavy duty compressors. These are complex products requiring many different competencies. ABB provides some of these as a subcontractor, and competencies come from different parts of ABB. Atlas Copco expects from ABB:

- effective business relationships in terms of a single electronic interface to all ABB businesses, delivery of full systems, and high quality of delivery.
- collaboration in terms of multi-functional project teams in engineering, common specification for product development, and frequent data exchange.
- an optimized product in terms of highly customized products, fast and cheap delivery of components. The products should be designed for optimized service costs.

The cooperation requires intensive information exchange at several stages of the product life cycle of a compressor. When ABB is delivering a complete electrical system, close co-operation between engineering of the mechanical components within Atlas Copco is required to design the interaction between the components of the compressor. During engineering of the compressor, all information that later is required during ordering, production and operation is created. This information includes, for example, in case of delivering ordering information

- An Atlas Copco order number for the motor starter and a part list with dual part numbers.
- The agreed price and delivery time.

All information described above is part of the „Ordering Aspect", of Industrial IT Enabled product information.

Project B: Industrial IT Enabled Substation. Though plant documentation may not be a product in itself, it plays an essential role in a customer's overall reception of products acquired for the plant. Customers require comprehensive and up-to-date documentation that is accessible in a natural and efficient manner. Providing paper documents in electronic format offers only a partial answer to these requirements. Therefore, a comprehensive product information environment, with a variety of tools to access the documents is of great value.

In an upcoming delivery of a high-voltage modular substation (PS1) for Electrica S.A., an electrical utility in Romania, such an environment is developed using Industrial IT Aspect Objects. The customer benefits from a complete Industrial IT based model of the ordered PS1 substation with the whole documentation embedded into a collection of Aspect Objects. No longer a plain set of document folders on a CD, but a flexible information system where maintenance manuals are retrievable within seconds by a click on the corresponding apparatus in the single line diagram.

The solution features immediate access to complete substation documentation on various levels and structured in various ways (different user profiles – operator, maintenance). It is expected that this will result in essential improvement of several of Electrica's internal processes. Also, synergy with future substation operation solutions through the existence of standardized object model representation (common object/data engineering) is foreseen.

3.4   Analysis

As the ranking of multiple items is a cognitively complex task, the AHP/IPC [14], [6], [7] data analysis techniques have been used to calculate the relative impact of the factors identified in Sect. 3.1 by pair-wise comparing them. The Analytic Hierarchy Process (AHP) was constructed to facilitate complex decision making, and the IPC is a method that is used to decrease the number of questions asked to determine the relationship between factors. This decreases the risk for maturation effects. Aggregating data from multiple participants that use the AHP/IPC individually is explained in [4] and the circumstances during which the IPC produces correct answers are explained in [3]. In the software engineering domain, the AHP/IPC has previously been used in, e.g., [2], [10], [11], [12]. The method has been suggested as part of a method for identifying key project success factors by [15].

3.5   Threats to Validity

The questionnaire layout has been used before in several studies, so its structure should not be a problem. As all participants have received the same training in how to fill in the questionnaire, there should be good reliability of measures. Selection effects should have been avoided by sampling participants from a wide variety of technical backgrounds. Since the participants were asked not to discuss the questionnaire until all participants had finished the task, there should not be any imitation of answers between the participants. There is some mono-method bias: Only the AHP/IPC is used to prioritize the findings in this study. On the other hand, these techniques were developed with complex decision making in mind. Therefore, this should not be a threat to this study. Since the respondents are anonymous, there should be no social pressure to answer in a particular way. As this is a dual case study, validity should be increased compared to a single case study. We believe that the biggest threat to validity is that it is hard to estimate the value of such complex items as in this study. We have countered this threat by a) Only allowing senior engineers (many with PhD degrees) to participate in the study, in two non-related projects that has unusually good knowledge of Industrial IT Enabled products; and b) Using the AHP/IPC to simplify questions.

4   Results

In this section, raw data and individual findings are presented. These findings are used to contribute to a comprehensive body of knowledge in Sect. 5.

4.1 Value for Customers of Industrial IT Enabled Products

First, it was assessed if the participants perceived that there is a value *at all* for a customer in different processes for an Industrial IT Enabled product, compared to if they instead used a non-certified product. Results are shown in Figures 6 and 7. In the boxplots, individual datapoints are denoted by a ring, outliers by a cross, and the box shows where 75% of the results are located. A median bar is added as well.

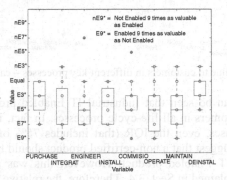

Fig. 6. Value of Industrial IT Enabled products for ABBs customers – all participants

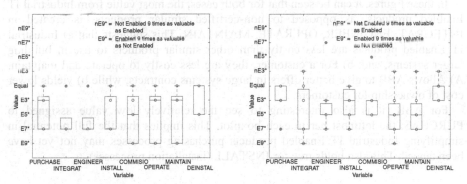

Fig. 7. Value of Industrial IT Enabled products for ABBs customers – cases A (left) and B

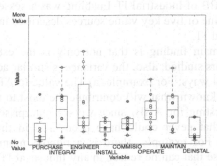

Fig. 8. Relative value to customers in different key processes – all participants

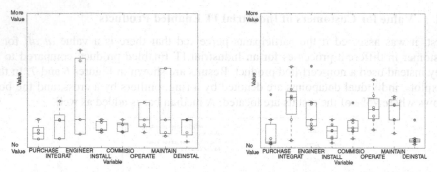

Fig. 9. Relative value to customers in different key processes – cases A (left) and B

In the figures it can be seen that Industrial IT Enabled products are considered more valuable to customers in all life-cycle processes. In fact, in no process area, in neither of the two cases, even the IQR (that includes 75% of individual answers) includes values that suggest that a non-certified product should be more valuable than a similar Industrial IT Enabled product. However, this was assessed without the support of the IPC explained in Sect. 3.4. Therefore, the relative value to customers in different key process areas was assessed. These results are shown in Figures 8 and 9. ·

In these figures, it can be seen that for both cases, the most value from Industrial IT Enabled products, as opposed to non-certified similar products, is created in INTEGRAT, ENGINEER, OPERATE, MAINTAIN. This suggests that a) Industrial IT Enabled products are less costly than other similar products to use in building larger systems, and; b) For a customer, they are less costly to operate and maintain. A) Allows ABB to give better offers in large systems contracts, while b) yields lower cost of ownership for customers.

For ABB, it is also interesting to see the relatively low value assigned to PURCHAS, the leftmost bar in each boxplot. This implies that the full potential in simplifying Industrial IT Enabled products purchasing processes may not yet have been tapped. This also holds true for INSTALL (installation processes).

4.2   Value for ABB of Industrial IT Enabled Products

The relative value to ABB of Industrial IT Enabling was assessed by using the IPC to compute the relative value of five key value sources described in Sect. 3.1. Results are shown in Figures 10 and 11.

In these figures, a main finding is that not only is the estimated median value similar for all five factors studied, also, the variance is similar across factors. This can be interpreted in several ways; For example, a) The value to ABB from the factors is similar; and b) It is not known what will contribute the most to value. If a) holds true, this is extremely interesting for ABB, since we see enterprise-wide reuse (REUSE variable) of software that never could have been used in that way, before being Industrial IT Enabled. For example, there is a remote monitoring aspect system developed for marine use that can be reused in any Industrial IT Enabled system. The saving from this is considered very large, and given the results of this investigation ABB should also expect similar gains from the other value sources investigated.

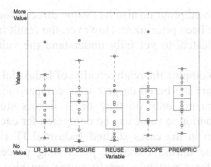

Fig. 10. Relative sources of value to ABB – all participants

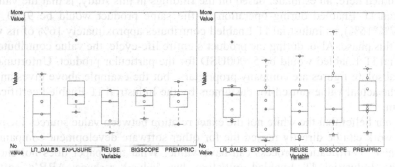

Fig. 11. Relative sources of value to ABB – cases A (left) and B

4.3   Results From Open-Ended Interviews

Several participants commented that it was hard to assess the actual value of the Industrial IT Enabled certification program, because there was always a possibility that a customer did not utilize the value of an Enabled component to its full extent.

5   Summary and Discussion

Industrial IT Enabled is a product certification program that all ABB products are required to pass. It is intended to provide customer value, and thus it focuses on how well a product is integrated with a number of customer process areas – including, but not limited to software interfaces.

Through two case studies based on questionnaires and interviews, this study suggests that the Industrial IT Enabled program provides measurable value to customers in their integration, engineering, operation and maintenance processes. The two first process areas allows ABB to make competitive offers to large integration projects, while the latter gives a low cost of ownership for customers standardizing on Industrial IT Enabled products.

The Industrial IT Enabled program also has value directly for ABB. Five important contributing factors have been prioritized. However, the result indicates that it may be too early, or too complicated, to yet fully understand the value of the certification program to ABB.

The methods used to compute the relative value of Industrial IT Enabled in various customer process areas are the based on pair-wise comparisons. A particular trait of the methods used is that not only do they order factors studied, but the median *relative* degree of contribution to value can be computed for each factor. For example, it is seen that in median in the cases studied Industrial IT Enabled contributes, in median, 7% of its value during customer purchasing processes. If this value is estimated at 4000USD for a particular product, one can also estimate the value of Industrial IT Enabled in other customer processes. For example, in cases similar to the ones studied here, an estimate, based on the findings in this study, is that the value of Industrial IT Enabled during operation of the same product would be 9100 USD (4000/7%*16%), as Industrial IT Enabled contributes approximately 16% of its value during this phase. Also, during the product's entire life-cycle, the value contributed by Industrial IT Enabled would be 57000USD for the particular product. Unfortunately, actual absolute figures are company proprietary, but the example above gives an idea about the actual value caused for customers by the Industrial IT Enabled certification program.

It is our belief that the while not the exact relation between value sources identified in this work can be directly reused the for other software development companies, a component certification process can have value. What this paper does not show is how the Industrial IT Enabled initiative has helped reshape ABB's software development processes, globally: All approx 25000 software developers now develop documentation with a common format. It is uniformly checked, resulting in that customers can reduce learning needs, if they use Industrial IT enabled products. Such achievements should be possible for other certification approaches as well.

References

1. Bratthall, L., van der Geest, R., Hofmann, H., Jellum, E., Korendo, Z., Martinez, R., Orkiz, M., Zeidler, C., Andersson, J. A. „Integrating Hundreds of Products through One Architecture – The Industrial IT Architecture". In Proc. Int'l Conf. Software Engineering, 2002
2. Bratthall, L., Runeson, P., Adelswärd, K., Eriksson, W. „A Survey of Lead-time Challenges in the Development and Evolution of Distributed Real-time Systems". Information and Software Technology, Vol. 43, No. 13, pp. 947-58. 2000
3. Carmone, F. J., Kara, A., Zanakis, S. H. „A Monte Carlo Investigation of Incomplete Pairwise Comparison Matrices in AHP". European Journal of Operational Research. Vol. 102, No. 3, pp 538-53. Nov. 1997
4. Forman, E., Peniwati, K. „Aggregating Individual Judgements and Priorities with the Analytic Hierachy Process". European Journal of Operational Research. Vol.108, No. 1, pp. 165-169. July, 1998
5. Frankfort-Nachmias, C., Nachmias, D. Research Methods in the Social Sciences, Fourth Edition. St. Martin's Press, United Kingdom. 1992

6. Harker, P. T. "Incomplete Pairwise Comparison in the Analytic Hierarchy Process", Mathematical Modelling, Vol. 9, No. 11, pp. 837-848. 1987
7. Harker, P. T. "Alternative Modes of Questioning in the Analytic Hierarchy Process", Mathematical Modelling, Vol. 9, No. 35, pp. 353-360. 1987
8. IEC Standard 61346: Structuring principles and reference designations. 1996
9. IEC Standard 61355: Classification and Designation of documents for plants, systems and equipment. 1997
10. Johansson, E., Bratthall, L., Wesslén, A., Höst, M. „A Survey on the Importance of Quality Requirements for Different Stakeholders in Software Architecture Development". In Proc. 34rd Hawaii International Conference on System Sciences (HICSS-34). January, 2001
11. Karlsson, J., Ryan, K. „A Cost-Value Approach for Prioritizing Requirements". IEEE Software, Vol. 14, No. 5. 1997
12. Miranda, E. „An evaluation of the paired comparison method for software sizing". Proc. Int'l Conf. Software Engineering, pp. 597-604. Limerick, Ireland. 2000
13. Paulk, M. C., Weber, C. V., Curtis, B. The Capability Maturity Model: Guidelines for Improving the Software Process. Addison-Wesley. 1995
14. Saaty, T. Multicriteria Decision Making: The Analytic Hierarchy Process. RWS Publications. 1996
15. Wohlin, C., von Mayrhauser, A. „Assessing Project Success using Subjective Evaluation Factors". Accepted for publication in Software Quality Journal. 2000

Agile Development: Good Process or Bad Attitude?

Richard Turner

The George Washington University, Washington, DC 20052
turner@seas.gwu.edu

Abstract. Agile development methods are gaining adherents in a wide variety of industries. Agile proponents and those who support traditional process improvement have been equally vocal in their disdain for each other. However, it is unclear whether or not agile methods constitute an improvable „process." This paper discusses the relationship between agile methods and process improvement goals and values and evaluates the components of the Capability Maturity Model Integration[SM] (CMMI[SM]) Systems Engineering/Software Engineering/Integrated Product and Process Model[1] for their support of agile methods.

1   Introduction

The Capability Maturity Model® for Software (CMM®) [1] and process improvement have received a great deal of derision from the proponents of agile methods. Likewise, process improvement professionals have labeled agile methods as no better than hacking. [2] Although attempts to reconcile the positions appear in the literature, [1, 3-5] the two approaches have been informally characterized as having the same relationship as oil and water. This paper discusses how a thoughtful comparison and a closer look at the fundamental tenets of both schools of thought yield a better understanding of their relationship.

2   Fundamentals of Process Improvement

Process improvement grew out of the quality movement and the work of Crosby, [6] Deming, [7] and Juran, [8] and is aimed at increasing the capability of work processes. By increasing the capability of its processes, an organization becomes more mature and so operates at a higher level of effectiveness.

One means of achieving this focus on process is by using a capability model to guide and measure the improvement. Assessments against the model provide findings that initiate corrective actions that result in better processes. Models often are

---

[1] The following Carnegie Mellon University service marks and registered marks are used in this paper: Capability Maturity Model®, CMM®, CMM Integration[SM], and CMMI[SM].

M. Oivo and S. Komi-Sirviö (Eds.): PROFES 2002, LNCS 2559, pp. 134–144, 2002.

organized so that there is a proven, well-defined order by which processes are improved based on the experience of successful projects and organizations. The first model of this type was the Software Engineering Institute's Capability Maturity Model for Software. The latest in capability model thinking is represented in the Capability Maturity Model Integration (CMMI) effort and the product suite it has developed [9, 10].

CMMI is essentially a set of requirements for engineering processes, particularly those involved in product development. It consists of two kinds of information – process areas (PAs) that describe the goals and activities that make up process requirements in a specific focus area, and generic practices (GPs) that are applied across the process areas to guide improvement in process capability.

The process areas include requirements for

- basic project management and control
  - basic engineering life-cycle processes
  - fundamental support processes
  - process monitoring and improvement processes (similar to SW-CMM)
  - integrated development using teams

The second type of information CMMI provides is a set of generic practices that support the improvement of the processes established under the Process Areas. The generic practices are associated with a six-level capability scale that describes relative capabilities as follows:

1. Not performed (Not even doing the basics)
2. Performed (just doing it)
3. Managed (fundamental infrastructure to accomplish the process generally at the project level)
4. Defined (institutionalizes a standard version of the process for tailoring by projects)
5. Quantitatively managed process (uses quantitative measures to monitor and control selected sub-processes)
6. Optimizing (constant adaptation of processes based on quantitative measures)

CMMI users apply these two kinds of information to establish, refine and manage the processes used to meet organizational goals. The specific goals of the process areas and generic practices are considered the primary means of evaluating organizational capability, while the specific practices are used to provide requirements for meeting the goals.

3   Fundamentals of Agile Methods

Agile methods are an outgrowth of rapid prototyping experiences and a response to the experience of dehumanizing „Taylorian" application of traditional, process-based software development. They are targeted at solving the problem of long development cycles yielding poorly written code that does not meet user expectations. In general, agile methods are very lightweight processes that employ short iterative cycles, use testing to establish and verify requirements, actively involve users, and rely on tacit knowledge within a team as opposed to documentation. Examples of agile methods include Extreme Programming (XP), [11] Scrum, [12] and Crystal. [13] The Agile Manifesto, [14] a document developed and signed by a wide group of agile proponents, defines the agile values as follows:

> *We have come to value*
> - *Individuals and interactions over process and tools*
> - *Working software over comprehensive documentation*
> - *Customer collaboration over contract negotiation*
> - *Responding to change over following a plan*
>
> *That is, while there is value in the items on the right, we value the items on the left more.*

As we shall see, it is important to note that these are relative statements, not absolutes. Alistair Cockburn has described agile values as „would-be" – that is, they represent an attitude more than a state of accomplishment. [15]

The practices which are espoused to support these values vary with the method, but can be generally classified as belonging to three general areas:

1. Communication (e.g. metaphor, collaboration, pair-programming, daily stand-up meetings, customer involvement)
2. Management (e.g. planning game, collective ownership, 40-hour work week, short iterations with working releases, trust, coaches, metrics, tracking)
3. Technical (e.g. simple design, test-first, refactoring, continuous integration, coding standards, reflection)
   Many of these practices have long histories and should be familiar to both process improvement advocates and software engineers. The key is that they are applied rigorously and most importantly, intelligently to the development cycle. Kent Beck describes this as a „mentality of sufficiency" – doing only what is necessary. [11] Jim Highsmith calls it „barely sufficient." [16]Highsmith also coined the term „chaordic" for work which unifies chaos and order in a way that defies management by normal, traditional, linear planning and processes.

4   Summary of CMMI Support for Agile from the USC Workshop

A workshop on agile methods was held as part of the annual review of the research conducted by the Center for Software Engineering, located at the University of Southern California. [5] Over 40 participants attended, including researchers, research sponsors, and affiliates as well as invited experts on agile methods. One of four breakout groups was asked to look at agile methods in the context of CMMI and process improvement. The USC group classified each CMMI component as in conflict with (C), of no consequence to (N), or supportive of agile methods in general (S). Table 1 shows the findings from the USC workshop. Summarizing the results, we find:

- 7 components are seen as clearly in conflict
- 10 components are seen as possibly in conflict
- 11 components are seen as clearly supportive
- 11 components are seen as no worse than neutral
- 1 component had no consensus finding

Only 17 of the 40 components were considered in conflict or possible conflict. Twenty two components were seen to be supportive of or neutral to agile methods.

I believe some of the „findings" of the USC workshop are debatable, and represent misperceptions on the part of the group. The next section presents my more detailed analysis based on reading and discussions with agile practitioners, including Kent Beck, Martin Fowler, and Alistair Cockburn.

5   Discussion of the CMMI Components with Respect to Agile Methods

The CMMI scope extends farther into the engineering, development, and teaming practices than the original Software CMM, and so maps better into the agile methods. Since agile methods are very much „how to do" rather than the CMM's "what to do," the best method-to-method mapping would probably be to the Personal Software Process [17] and Team Software Process. [18] However, the controversy seems to revolve around CMMs, so I believe it is more useful to compare agile methods to the more widely-applied organizational model.

One significant aspect (that some consider a flaw) of CMMI is that in it's description of „what" it often assumes an aerospace engineering „how." CMM was similarly prejudiced toward projects where requirements were furnished fully formed to a software development team. This makes some of the goals difficult to translate into the agile world.

5.1   CMMI Process Management Process Areas

The process management PAs are by far the most problematic when considering agile methods. Agile philosophy is aimed primarily at the team creating the software – not at the organization that supports it. While there are definite infrastructure requirements for successful agile projects, there is little in agile method descriptions that directly apply at the organizational level. This does not mean, however, that such an organizational approach would be inappropriate, only that it is not specifically addressed.

Table 1. Agile methods vs. CMMI conflict findings

Process Area	Survey Finding	CMMI Generic Practices	Survey Finding
Organizational Process Focus	C	2.1 Establish an Organizational Policy	N-S
Organizational Process Definition	C-N	2.2 Plan the Process	N-S
Organizational Training	N-S	2.3 Provide Resources	N-S
Organizational Process Performance	C	2.4 Assign Responsibility	S
Organizational Innovation and Deployment	C-S	2.5 Train People	N
Project Planning	S	2.6 Manage Configurations	C-S
Project Monitoring and Control	S	2.7 Identify and Involve Relevant Stakeholders	S
Supplier Agreement Management	N	2.8 Monitor and Control the Process	N
Integrated Project Management	S	2.9 Objectively Evaluate Adherence	C
Risk Management	N	2.10 Review Status with Higher Level Management	N-S
Integrated Teaming	S	3.1 Establish a Defined Process	C
Quantitative Project Management	C	3.2 Collect Improvement Information	C
Requirements Management	N	4.1 Establish Quantitative Objectives for the Process	N
Requirements Development	S	4.2 Stabilize Subprocess Performance	C-N
Technical Solution	S	5.1 Ensure Continuous Process Improvement	C-N
Product Integration	S	5.2 Correct Root Causes of Problems	N
Verification	S		
Validation	S		
Configuration Management	None		
Process and Product Quality Assurance	C-N		
Measurement and Analysis	C-N		
Decision Analysis and Resolution	C		
Organizational Environment for Integration	S		
Causal Analysis and Resolution	N		

Organizational Process Focus
The goals of this PA are „Strengths, weaknesses, and improvement opportunities for the organization's processes are identified periodically and as needed; Improvements are planned and implemented, organizational process assets are deployed, and process-related experiences are incorporated into the organizational process assets." The goals seem to imply an infrastructure. Agile processes evolve, but they generally do so via their own experience, generally within a team or a project. There is nothing to prevent the organization from actively supporting improvement.   The conflict comes in the way traditional PI initiatives have been implemented – gap assessments, detailed plans, SEPGs, and so forth do not fit well into the fluid agile environment. In order to meet the goals, agile organizations will probably need to document the ways they improve. Agile practices that relate to this PA include reflection and collaboration.

Organizational Process Definition
Can an agile method or ecosystem be considered a process asset repository, albeit perhaps an informal one? Agile organizations do generally have an organizational process (the agile method or ecosystem) within which improvements take place. The tacit knowledge and experience in the team members work toward discovering and sharing successful techniques, tools, and patterns. From a development viewpoint, the shared code and objects that result from pair-programming and refactoring act as a development asset as well as a process asset. My feeling is that the agile process, while perhaps not formally defined, is effectively and continuously tailored for each project.

Organizational Training
Agile methods rely on practitioners trained in the method. The agile manifesto values individuals over processes and tools, and so strongly supports training and mentoring. There is no requirement in the PA for complex infrastructure – simply that the capability exists and is maintained. Pair-programming, reflection, coaching and collaboration are all methods of training.

Organizational Process Performance
The idea of measuring a process and maintaining baselines and models seems certainly in conflict with the agile manifesto. However, some of the agile methods, Scrum [12] and XP [11] for example, have metrics which could be characterized as process metrics. Since the agile development process and its outcome are tied to achieving well-specified goals in a short period of time, it may be that the measurement of cycle success is a suitable surrogate process measure, given that plans and results are constantly updated through the development activity.

Organizational Innovation and Deployment
In some ways, this PA captures the essence of agile development. The goals are „Process and technology improvements that contribute to meeting quality and process-performance objectives are selected. Measurable improvements to the organization's processes and technologies are continually and systematically deployed." There may be some difficulty in demonstrating systematic deployment or effective measurement, but as in OPP, successful iterations are strong contenders for relevant data.

5.2   CMMI Project Management Process Areas

Project Planning
Most agile methods require a high level of start-up planning, task prioritization, cycle scheduling and risk assessment. While the planning is accomplished and used in different ways, it is vital to the success of agile methods.

Project Monitoring and Control
There is opportunity to argue the level and rigor of the monitoring and control activities in an agile method, but the level of visibility given to planning dates and tasks is high within the development team. The reflection and post-mortem that occurs at the end of a cycle in most of the agile methods provide timely discovery of issues and the means for their resolution.

Supplier Agreement Management
This PA is rarely applicable in agile projects due to the nature of the teams and the development focus of the work. A considerable amount of COTS or legacy code over which the team has little control could require that agreements be established.

Integrated Project Management
Agile methods are generally team-based and integrate the developers, validators and customers. The goals here are essentially the same as those espoused by the agile methods. It is unfortunate that the goals also echo so much of the Organizational Process Definition PA.

Risk Management
Most agile methods are designed to mitigate certain types of risks, particularly those from changing requirements and schedules. It is less obvious whether agile addresses long-term risk. A strong case can be made that the minimalist nature of agile reduces short-term risk, but the lack of specific documentation or architecture that is part of some agile methods may increase risk later in the life cycle. There have been few studies and little experience in this area. It is not difficult to see that agile methods probably don't strictly follow the CMMI process of identifying, analyzing and tracking risks. This is one of the places that the „what" in some ways assumes the „how."

Integrated Teaming
Integrated teaming is a key facet of all of the agile methodologies. Collaboration, valuing teamwork, trust, and pair-programming are exemplary practices.

Quantitative Project Management
The goals of this PA are „The project is quantitatively managed using quality and process-performance objectives. The performance of selected subprocesses within the project's defined process is statistically managed." While agile methods don't specifically address these activities, there is nothing in the agile manifesto that precludes their performance. However, there is considerable feeling in the agile camp that statistical management is for machines, not people. This attitude virtually precludes its use in mainstream agile projects. This is one of the few major trouble spots for agile projects in meeting CMMI requirements.

5.3 CMMI Engineering Process Areas

Requirements Management and Requirements Development

Agile focuses heavily on customer involvement and requires iterative development both of which directly relate to requirements development and management. The test-first practice can be seen as a way of demonstrating that the requirements are understood at the unit and product level, and for tracking changes to the requirements. In fact, agile methods were developed to embrace and take advantage of changing requirements. Unfortunately, the language in the CMMI goals implies (though doesn't require) a single „definition of required functionality," which could lead some appraisers to overlook the iterative nature of agile processes.

Technical Solution

Agile methods are designed to „Design, develop, and implement solutions to requirements." Agile projects continuously meet this PA's goals „Product or product-component solutions are selected from alternative solutions; Product or product-component designs are developed; Product components, and associated support documentation, are implemented from their designs." The only possible difficulty is the support documentation – something that some agile methodologies consider superfluous.

Product Integration

If considered as strictly software integration (or the integration of software into the target environment), agile projects should have no problem meeting the goals of this PA. The test-first and build frequently practices result in continuous validation and integration throughout the agile project.

Verification

Peer reviews are closely aligned with pair programming. Early agile methods did not specifically address non-functional requirements, but performance and quality stories are being used more and more.

Validation

The close relationship with the customer and the desire to produce software that, as Martin Fowler puts it, „delights" the customer, strongly correlates with this PA.

5.4 CMMI Support Process Areas

Configuration Management

Software CM is strongly supported in agile processes through tools and frequent builds. The absence of other documentation negates the need for much of the traditional CM of designs and specifications. Requirements stories are generally only needed for the cycle in which they are implemented, so long term CM may not be appropriate. Likewise, tests are the technical requirements artifact and are under close CM. There may be a need to look carefully at how strict a CM process needs to be to meet the PA goal

Process and Product Quality Assurance
Product quality assurance is an intrinsic part of agile methodologies. Process quality assurance is a bit more difficult. Since the process is designed to evolve as the project needs change, there is very little use for „process police." Rather, the management (in the roles of coach or Scrum master) makes sure that the overall process is maintained and that organizational distractions are kept to minimum.

Measurement and Analysis
Many people have expressed the view that the concept of measurement and analysis is not a part of the agile approach. However, the PA goals are „Measurement objectives and activities are aligned with identified information needs and objectives. Measurement results that address identified information needs and objectives are provided." This is one of the best of the PAs in CMMI, in that it clearly establishes that the activities be strongly liked to business or project need. I assert that the philosophy of agile methods speaks strongly to this PA, and that the few measurements needed for meeting the schedule and delivering an acceptable product to the user are sufficient to meet this PA.

Decision Analysis and Resolution
This PA's focus on establishing specific processes for team functions is in conflict with the spirit of agility. To be agile means to be able to adapt quickly to the situation rather than be bound to pre-conceived criteria and a strict alternative evaluation or decision analysis process. Even though the level of communication and collaboration in most successful agile teams provides for efficient consensus-building, this is another PA that will cause major problems.

Organizational Environment for Integration
Most of the agile methods are supported by a person-friendly, „whatever the developer needs" environment which mirrors the CMMI goals.

5.5   CMMI Generic Practices

The generic practices provide the means of improving (e.g. making more predictable) the processes established to accomplish the process area goals. Since most have obvious interpretations for agile methods, only a few of the more interesting GPs are addressed.

GP 2.1 Establish an Organizational Policy
While not an important part of agile methods, policy is not necessarily in conflict with their intent. The move to agile often requires support by management that may be enhanced through policy.

GP 2.3 Provide Resources
Providing the resources necessary to complete the work is certainly not in conflict with agile values. The team lead's responsibility includes making sure everything necessary to succeed is available and that the organizational interference with the project is kept to a minimum.

GP 2.4 Assign Responsibility
Assignment of responsibilities is a part of the daily stand-up meetings. This allows the best person or persons to be working on the most appropriate work every day. There is little need of complicated scheduling or tasking statements..

GP 2.9 Objectively Evaluate Adherence
The idea of a process mafia that checked on how the developers developed may be as significant barrier to agile methods. However, in XP and other more strictly defined methods, there is a sense that the team lead/coach/facilitator performs this function on a person-by-person basis.

GP 2.10 Review Status with Higher Level Management
The implementation of frequent deliveries makes the communication with upper management much more accurate.

GP 3.2 Collect Improvement Information
Most agile methods assume that improvement ideas are not collected and analyzed but are implemented and validated. This meets the same goals far more efficiently.

GP 4.1 Establish Quantitative Objectives for the Process
Quantitative objectives for the process seems not in the spirit of agile concepts. Rather, the product being delivered on time with the correct functionality precludes the need for this type of information.

GP 4.2 Stabilize Subprocess Performance
This practice is closely related to statistical process control and so borders on anathema within the agile community.

GP 5.1 Ensure Continuous Process Improvement
Continuous improvement is one of the goals of agile methods.

GP 5.2 Correct Root Causes of Problems
Root cause analysis, while a worthwhile endeavor, is neither recommended nor proscribed by agile methods.

6   Analysis and Conclusions

In researching agile methods I have been struck by the caliber of people developing the methods and by the up swell of support for practices that are sometimes difficult and often unnatural for many developers. Agile methods address some of the fundamental software issues (e.g. requirements volatility, quality and complexity), and software engineering will greatly benefit from the studies and experiences of agile projects. The pendulum continues to swing between order and chaos in software development. Perhaps „chaordic" approaches can reconcile the two extremes.

The agile world gains much of its fervor from the experiences of talented and creative people who have been shoehorned into statistically-controlled process boxes and made to feel as if they were replaceable parts on an assembly line. Agile methods are a way to provide value to the developers as well as to the customer.

As is suggested by the discussions in section 5, I believe that agile processes can fit quite nicely into the realm of process improvement. To do this, however, requires CMMI to be interpreted in a more essential and less literal manner. If CMMI is applied in the same manner as the CMM has traditionally been applied, the agile world may simply forgo any benefit from process improvement because it threatens their perceived liberation. This would be a loss to both communities. I challenge the process improvement community to carefully investigate agile methodologies and begin to incorporate their practices and approaches into our mental models.

References

1.   Paulk, M., *Extreme Programming from a CMM Perspective.* IEEE Software, 2001.
2.   Rakitin, S., *Manifesto Elicits Cynicism.* Computer, 2001(December): p. 4.
3.   Boehm, B.W., Get Ready for Agile Methods, with Care. IEEE Computer, 2002.
4.   Glass, R.L., *Agile versus Traditional: Make Love not War.* Cutter IT Journal, 2001. **Vol. 14, No. 12**(December): p. 12-18.
5.   Turner, R. and A. Jain. Agile Meets CMMI: Culture Clash or Common Cause? in Extreme Programming and Agile Mathods - XP/Agile Universe 2002. 2002. Chicago, IL: Springer-Verlag.
6.   Crosby, P.B., *Quality is Free: The Art of Making Quality Certain.* 1979, New York, NY: MacGraw-Hill.
7.   Deming, W.E., *Out of Crisis.* 1986, Cambridge, MA: MIT Center for Advanced Engineering.
8.   Juran, J.M., *Juran on Planning for Quality.* 1988, New York, NY: MacMillan.
9.   Ahern, D.M., A. Clouse, and R. Turner, *CMMI distilled : a practical introduction to integrated process improvement.* The SEI series in software engineering. 2001, Boston: Addison-Wesley. xv, 306.
10. CMMI Development Team, CMMI-SE/SW/IPPD, V1.1 : Capability Maturity Model Integrated for Systems Engineering, Software Engineering and Integrated Product and Process Development, Version 1.1 : continuous representation.. 2001, Software Engineering Institute, Carnegie Mellon University: Pittsburgh, PA. p. 688.
11. Beck, K., *Extreme Programming Explained.* 1999, Boston: Addison-Wesley.
12. Schwaber, K. and M. Beedle, *Agile Software Development with Scrum.* 2002, Upper Saddle River, N. J.: Prentice Hall.
13. Cockburn, A., *Agile Software Development.* 2002, Boston: Addison-Wesley.
14. Agile Alliance, Manifesto for Agile Software Development. 2001.
15. Cockburn, A., *Agile Software Development Joins the "Would-be Crowd,".* Cutter IT Journal, 2002. **15**(1): p. 6-12.
16. Highsmith, J., *Agile Software Development Ecosystems.* 2002, Boston: Addison-Wesley.
17. Humphrey, W.S., *Introduction to the Personal Software Process^{SM}.* 1997, Boston: Addison-Wesley.
18. Humphrey, W.S., *Introduction to the Team Software Process^{SM}.* 2000, Boston: Addison-Wesley.

Organisational Culture in Agile Software Development

Peter Wendorff

ASSET GmbH, Am Flasdieck 5
46147 Oberhausen, Germany
P.Wendorff@t-online.de

Abstract. Recently a number of so-called "agile" software development methods have been proposed. Interestingly, these approaches have been met with "both enthusiastic support and equally vigorous criticism" among experts in the field. At present the software engineering community is split, and seemingly irreconcilable "schools of thought" have emerged. In this paper we identify an important characteristic of any software engineering method: its set of tacit basic assumptions. We retrieve some important basic assumption that underly agile software development and discuss an example to illustrate in detail how conflicting basic assumptions can lead to fundamental disagreement about software development methods.

1 Introduction

A software development method (SDM) provides a prescriptive, systematic, and explicit description of resources, activities, and artefacts in order to produce software. In the late 1990s a number of so-called "agile" SDMs have been proposed, for example "Extreme Programming" (XP) [2], the "Crystal" family [5], or "Adaptive Software Development" (ASD) [7]. They claim to be superior to other methods in some situations that are characterised by vague requirements and rapid change. They share a core of values and principles published as the "Manifesto for Agile Software Development" on the World Wide Web [1]. XP is by far the most widely used agile SDM at the moment, and even the first ever dynabook of the Institute of Electrical and Electronics Engineers (IEEE) has been devoted to it [9].

Agile SDMs have quickly gained a remarkable degree of acceptance in parts of the software engineering community. Interestingly, they have provoked a vivid and often controversial exchange of opinions, for example, published in the dynabook mentioned above. The observation by Jawed Siddiqi of "both enthusiastic support and equally vigorous criticism" of XP in the dynabook [9] extends to agile SDMs in general [8].

Highsmith introduces the term "rigorous" software development method [8] for most methods that do not explicitly focus on agility, and we will adopt his terminology in this paper.

M. Oivo and S. Komi-Sirviö (Eds.): PROFES 2002, LNCS 2559, pp. 145-157, 2002.

There is yet no convincing empirical evidence that agile SDMs outperform other approaches, but there is equally little empirical evidence to suggest the opposite. This situation of uncertainty calls for an unprejudiced discussion of agile methods, but the debate has become weirdly polarised and opinionated in many instances (cf. [9]).

Jim Highsmith makes an important point when he remarks: "Many of the debates about Agile versus rigorous practices have no basis in fact - they are purely emotional and based on one's culture, one's values and beliefs. Now, emotion-based reactions are at least as valid as fact-based ones, but they do tend to create high-volume rhetoric" [8, p. 167].

We agree with Highsmith's view that much of the debate aboute agile software development is due to cultural differences. We believe that in order to understand and appreciate any software development method it is necessary to understand its underlying culture. The cultural perspective illuminates the influence of conflicting, unconscious basic assumptions as a primary source of disagreement over different software development methods. Basic assumptions derive much of their power from the fact that they operate outside awareness. They are the sublime result of complex and prolonged learning processes and therefore difficult to detect and decipher.

Agile software development is based on some basic assumptions that seem to contradict the basic assumptions on which many other approaches are based. We believe that a clear elaboration of these basic assumptions is a necessary prerequiste for an unprejudiced discussion of agile software development within the whole software engineering community. The aim of this paper is to contribute to this process of elaboration by suggesting some basic assumptions of agile software development.

In section 2 we will present a brief description of organisational culture and the model developed by Schein, that will be used as conceptual framework in subsequent sections. In section 3 we will elaborate some basic assumptions that underly agile software development.

2   Organisational Culture

The concept of organisational culture has attracted much attention from scholars as well as managers recently. Much of this interest has been due to the apparent failure of traditional organisational analysis to explain phenomena in organisations based on objective and formal structural characteristics.

The culture perspective uses established ideas from fields like anthropology, psychology, and sociology. One of its central assumptions is, that organisations cannot be understood comprehensively in terms of their formal characteristics alone, but that there exist influential informal elements in organisations. Informal elements within organisations may include myths, heroes, traditions, mental models, animosi-ties, patterns of behaviour, social perceptions, bias, groupthink, group dynamics, politics, coalitions, friendship, revenge, etc. The culture perspective emphasises the importance of these informal aspects of organisations for the analysis of organisa-tional life. Much of the informality in organisations results from the fact that their members are human beings, and that human behaviour defies a definition in purely formal and rational terms. Therefore, the analysis of processes in organisations should take these informal aspects into account.

2.1 Elements of Organisational Culture

A look at contemporary textbooks on management shows, that there is no single, universally accepted definition of organisational culture. Nevertheless, most defini-tions refer to some points in the following definition:

Organisational culture refers to

- a common set of beliefs, attitudes, perceptions, assumptions, and values,
- that is shared by the majority of an organisation's members,
- where it is clearly observable who shares in the culture and who does not,
- while it reflects accumulated common learning by organisational members,
- who develop it as a response to perceived internal or external requirements,
- regarding it as a valid source of appropriate explanations for relevant situations,
- for which it suggests or prescribes a range of acceptable behaviour,
- that is taught to new members to facilitate their understanding and integration,
- and is therefore stable and persistent over long periods of time.

As organisational culture is a theoretical artefact, that can only be measured indirectly, it is important to identify elements of an organisation that indicate its culture. A popular layered conceptualisation of organisational culture has been introduced by Schein [10], who differentiates three levels of manifestation. At the first level there are "artefacts", that are most easily discernible by an observer. At the second level there are "espoused values", that are more difficult to observe. The third level are "basic assumptions", that are most difficult to detect and express. We will now briefly explain these three levels.

Artefacts are the most visible manifestations of organisational culture. Usually they are created by humans in order to solve a problem. Artefacts comprise rules, jargon, stories, symbols, office layouts, and ceremonies. These elements of a culture are visible to an outside observer directly by watching the behaviour of the organisational members.

Espoused Values are consciously held reasons for behaviour. They are strongly related to ethical codes, and they express what ought to be done. Values are not directly discernible for an outside observer, instead they can only be investigated indirectly through interpersonal communication.

Basic assumptions are the least obvious manifestation of culture. They comprise reasons for behaviour that are not consciously held by organisational members, because they are taken for granted. Basic assumptions are not confrontable or debatable, and examples include the basis on which individuals are respected, whether cooperation or competition is desirable as mode of behaviour, and how decisions are made. These unconsciously held assumptions guide human behaviour, and they are not directly observable for an outside person.

The relationship between the three levels of organisational culture described above can be demonstrated by the following example. We assume two basic assumptions, namely (a) humans are generally lazy and try to avoid effort, or (b) humans are generally motivated and enjoy to do good work. Depending on our basic assumption we could then proceed to the level of values and find that (a) strict control of procedures is desirable, because it leads to productivity, or (b) a motivating workplace that provides opportunity is desirable, because it leads to productivity. Depending on these values, we might then choose an appropriate artefact to serve our value, for example, by (a) using a production line, or (b) forming a semi-autonomous work team.

2.2   Functions of Organisational Culture

The importance of culture for the smooth functioning of organisations has been emphasised by many writers. Organisations provide venues where people with differing backgrounds meet, and clearly this creates a potential for disagreement. In order to act effectively, an organisation has to achieve some degree of consensus and cooperation, for example, through formal regulations. This formal approach often results in organisational designs that rely on extrinsic motivation of organisational members. There is strong evidence that common and intrinsic motivation of members does often increase the effectiveness of organisations. An organisational culture represents a shared basic mindset, and therefore it can motivate action, facilitate agreement, and encourage cooperation. In this way it can lead to intrinsic motivation, thereby reducing the need for extrinsic motivation [4, pp. 89].

3   Organisational Culture in Agile Software Development

In February 2001 many of the leading inventors and proponents of agile SDMs met to identify common core elements of agile SDMs. This has led to the formulation and publication of the "Manifesto for Agile Software Development" on the World Wide Web [1]. An annotated version of the Manifesto can be found in [5]. This manifesto is still the most up-to-date and most comprehensive attempt to compile and publish the defining commonalities of different agile SDMs. The manifesto defines 4 values and 12 principles.

On the backcloth of Schein's layered conceptualisation of organisational culture the 12 principles from the manifesto clearly qualify as artefacts in Schein's hierarchy, while the 4 values from the manifesto are in fact espoused values according to Schein. But there is one layer in Schein's model of organisational culture that is not matched by any material provided in the Manifesto: the underlying basic assumptions of agile software development.

In the following subsections we will attempt to recover some basic assumptions underlying agile software engineering. We have mainly relied on the books by Highsmith [7], Cockburn [5], and Beck [2], as well as material from the manifesto.

The following six subsections all correspond to the same structural pattern. First, the headings of the subsections correspond to the six categories defined by Schein to categorise basic assumptions [10, pp. 94]. After a short introduction of the general category we narrow the context to a subject with particular relevance to our discussion. After that we present some references that illustrate some aspects of different agile SDMs regarding the given context. Then we present a brief summary of our deliberations, and finally we formulate a basic assumption.

Generally, our work does owe much credit to the book [8] by Jim Highsmith, in which he presents a very readable overview of many current agile SDMs as well as material on the biographies of their founders.

3.1   Assumptions about the Nature of Reality and Truth

Assumptions about reality are a cornerstone of any culture. The members of the culture share an understanding of what is real, how things are perceived, what is important and what is not, how to gather and use information, when and how to act, etc.

Context. An important distinction can be made due to different levels of reality. For example, external physical reality can be determined empirically by objective tests, while subjective perceptions shared by a group of people, that cannot be tested empirically, are referred to as social reality. Not all questions concerning reality and truth can be answered at the level of external physical reality, and indeed it is one of the important functions of culture to provide orientation in these cases where objective tests are impossible or too difficult to construct [10, pp. 97].

References. Fenton and Pfleeger use a quotation from a popular book by DeMarco, "You cannot control what you cannot measure" [6, p. 11] to express their belief that classical engineering techniques like scientific measurement should be adopted in software engineering. They explain: "Even when a project is not in trouble, measurement is not only useful but necessary. After all, how can you tell if your project is healthy if you have no measures of its health? So measurement is needed at least for assessing the status of your projects, products, processes, and resources" [6, p. 11]. In their book, "Software Metrics - A Rigorous and Practical Approach," they describe the quest in rigorous software development for objective definitions of software quality attributes like size, structure, complexity, understandability, etc. Unfortunately, there is good reason to believe that these objective definitions are not feasible, because concepts like complexity are in fact highly subjective, and for example, often one person's simplicity is another person's complexity [6]. Many software developers are quite opinionated regarding software quality attributes, and this is a constant source of disagreement in software projects.

Highsmith notes that in agile software development decision making is generally based on power sharing. If decision-making authority is delegated, then it is granted from below, not from above [7, pp. 214]. Different opinions must be reconciled through compromise, and Highsmith regards the willingness to compromise as necessary behaviour of developers. He notes that, for example, in the field of software quality attributes trade-offs are often unavoidable, and that these necessitate the involvement of relevant stakeholders. Given the fuzzy nature of software quality attributes he concedes that "compromising on values and beliefs is much stickier" [7, p. 217]. Highsmith proposes three types of compromise, namely synergy, mutual concession, and appeasement. Obviously, all of these three types of compromise are primarily based on intensive social interaction among equals, not on coercive authority or authoritative science.

Cockburn observes, "on an effective team, the people pull approximately in the same direction. They actually all pull in slightly different directions, according to their personal goals, personal knowledge, stubbornness, and so on. They work together at times and against each other at times" [5, p. 99]. In order to increase alignment within the team he recommends "microtouch" intervention by the team leader, where a small increase in alignment of all team members can effect large changes in team performance. On the role of conflict within an organisation Cockburn notes that conflict is even desirable in some instances, for example in order to alert the team to design problems. Accordingly, he contemplates "the intentional use of small doses of conflict to get people to meet and learn to talk with each other" [5, p. 101].

Beck gives an important role to the concept of simplicity in XP, as it is one of the four values [2, pp. 30], one of the basic principles [2, p. 38], and one of the core practices [2, p. 54]. Beck does not provide any sophisticated, objective definition of the concept of simplicity, and the explanations he gives (cf. [2, p. 57 and p. 109]) are vague and questionable. So, how can simplicity be a meaningful concept in XP if there is no objective definition? Beck provides the answer referring to the levelling effect of communication: "The more you communicate, the clearer you can see exactly what needs to be done and the more confidence you have about what really doesn't need to be done" [2, p. 31]. The core practice of pair programming, where two developers sit in front of a single computer and work together, increases the mental alignment of the two programmers and thereby increases the mutual understanding of the two persons [2, pp. 66 and pp. 100].

The following practices taken from the Manifesto [1] relate to the assumptions about the nature of reality and truth in agile software development.

- Working software is the primary measure of progress.
- Continuous attention to technical excellence and good design enhances agility.
- Simplicity – the art of maximizing the amount of work not done – is essential.
- The best architectures, requirements, and designs emerge from self-organizing teams.

These principles are based on terms like "working software", "technical excellence", "good design", "simplicity", and "best architectures, requirements, and designs". It is obvious, that there doesn't exist any consensus in the software engineering community about the definition of these terms. Nevertheless, because many crucial artefacts in the Manifesto rely on these notions, it is necessary that some consensus about these concepts exists, at least at the level of social reality.

Discussion. Rigorous software development has a low tolerance toward ambiguity, and the obvious solution is to adopt traditional engineering practices, e.g. scientific software measurement, to reduce ambiguity. Thus, consensus is established on the basis of scientific authority at the level of external physical reality. Nevertheless, this approach suffers from a number of inevitable drawbacks, and admittedly, many software measures that have been proposed are of questionable practical value [6]. The culture of agile software development is more tolerant toward ambiguity, and, for example, a concept like simplicity is obviously regarded as useful. In the absence of a convincing objective, scientific definition for such a concept agile methods rely on the emergence of consensus at the level of social reality. This desired consensus emerges over time as the result of intensive social interaction, and that is one of the reasons why agile methods try to sustain a high level of social interaction.

Basic Assumption. "Social interaction leads to consensus."

3.2   Assumptions about the Nature of Time

A "natural" notion of time is taken for granted in most cultures, yet there exist different assumptions about the nature of time in different cultures. One aspect of this is the perception of "being on time", obviously an important issue in software engineering that is traditionally focused on deadlines.

Context. A shared notion of time is important to synchronise activities in an organisation in an orderly way. If different assumptions about time exist within an organisation, tremendous problems can emerge. For example, in a biotechnology company serious communication problems developed because managers used a notion of time that might be called "planning time", while scientists used a different notion of time that might be called "development time" [10, p. 109].

References. Boehm, in his landmark book "Software Engineering Economics" [3], used classical engineering practices and ecomomic models as basis for a rigorous approach to software effort estimation. His work has influenced generations of managers and developers since then. It is fundamentally based on the notion of "monochronic time" [10, p. 107], where time is measured by hours, where a man-hour is a standardised measure of production capacity, and hitting a deadline is the ultimate measure of success. Effort is meticulously calculated in hours, and completion dates are set as precise calendar dates. Time is seen as a linear resource that is compartmentalised into appropriate assignments that are then completed according to plan. The COCOMO model developed by Boehm has later been refined, and it is one of the most popular frameworks for effort estimation and project planning in software development. COCOMO, as well as many other frameworks of its kind, heavily relies on data of past projects that are regarded as a valid predictor for future projects.

Highsmith contrasts workflow-oriented models that focus on tasks, as the basis of rigorous software engineering, to workstate-oriented models that focus on resulting artefacts, as the basis of agile software development [7, pp. 235]. He continues: "The workstate approach says, 'Don't bother me with the detailed activities, just let me know when the work product (component) has reached a certain completion state' [7, p. 238]. He claims that a workstate-oriented approach works better in many areas of software development where "activities are concurrent, with partial completion and later refinement being the norm" [7, p. 239]. Concurrent development is an inherent management challenge in adaptive software development, that requires intensive interaction to synchronise activities, according to Highsmith.

Cockburn declares: "Software development is therefore a cooperative game of *invention and communication*. There is nothing in the game but people's ideas and the communication of those ideas to their colleagues and to the computer" [5, p. 28]. In a game the moves of players are not predetermined by a schedule, instead they are coordinated by interaction. Therefore, "the purpose of each activity is to move the game forward. Work products of every sort are sufficiently good as soon as they permit the next move" [5, p. 33]. Cockburn applies this viewpoint to the inevitable bottleneck activities of a software project and concludes that these are the areas where synchronisation of activities based on interaction promises huge performance gains: "The shifting bottlenecks in the system determine the use of overlapped work and 'sticky' information holders" [5, p. 201]. He regards this technique as valuable for any software engineering methodology and makes it a cornerstone of his own Crystal family of methodologies.

Beck denotes the planning technique used in XP "planning game" [2, p. 86]. The planning game is a highly interactive, incremental, and iterative technique used to match software requirements to development capacity. At any time plans can be revised in subsequent iterations as soon as deviations arise.

Discussion. One important function of time is the synchronisation of activities. The notion of time used in rigorous software engineering can appropriately be described as "monochronic time", for example implicitly assumed by Boehm. An alternative to monochronic time is "polychronic time" [10, p. 107]. If time is perceived as polychronic, then it is not seen as a linear resource that is divided into time units that can be matched to particular activities, instead several activities may run concurrently in order to accomplish a task at hand. The above references indicate that in agile software development monochronic time is seen as a less useful concept, instead the concept of time used is rather close to polychronic time, where synchronisation does preferably occur through interaction rather than a clock.

Basic Assumption. "Social interaction synchronises activities."

3.3   Assumptions about the Nature of Space

The use of space is highly visible in organisations and often it does have a powerful symbolic meaning. One obvious reason is that space is a scarce resource in most organisations, and therefore its allocation can symbolise the status of a person.

Context. An open-plan office may stimulate communication, but it limits the degree of privacy, and the opportunity for individual expression. A private office, on the other hand, provides a high degree of privacy and enables more individual expression, but it may become a barrier for spontaneous communication [10, pp. 115].

References. Highsmith stresses the role of a shared work space for a team: "A factor contributing to adaptive project success is shared work space - a war room or team meeting place. [...] Adaptive teams need a team-owned place in cyberspace where the team can share context and content, where team members can interact one-on-one or in groups, where information can be both public and private, where there is an element of both work and play - a comfortable site to visit and to use." [7, p. 277]

Cockburn remarks that larger teams are often split into groups, and the groups are then assigned to different, scattered offices. This is a frequent source of problems because "each group forms its own community and usually complains about the other group. The chitchat in the osmotic communication is filled with these complaints, interfering with the ability of people in each group to work with each other in an amicable way" [5, p. 82]

Beck recommends an open workspace that combines a common workspace with small private spaces for XP. The reason for this arrangement is that, "XP is a communal software development discipline" [2, p. 79].

Discussion. The above references indicate that in agile software development the work space is not merely a place where people perform their professional duties. Instead it is rather seen as a venue where many different social functions, professional as well as private, take place. This is also reflected in the idea expressed by Cockburn and Beck that the workspace should provide room where people can socialise or prepare food. This deliberate integration of social needs into the professional environment is not accidental, instead it is intended to encourage communal life that leads to a cohesive team and effective communication.

Basic Assumption. "The workspace is a social venue."

3.4   Assumptions about the Nature of Humans

Every culture conveys assumptions about the nature of humans, for example about mission, motivation, ability, etc. The view that is hold about human nature inevitably has a strong influence on the fabric of society and organisations.

Context. The efforts of an organisation to effect certain behaviour will naturally be based on its prevailing set of assumptions about human nature, for example, its control and reward systems will be designed accordingly [10, p. 123].

References. Highsmith builds his theory of adaptive software development around the themes of self-organisation, emergence, and collaboration. In his discussion of effective collaboration he refers to attitudes like trust, respect, participation, and commitment [7, pp. 129]. He regards these attitudes as inherent in all humans to different degree and that the management challenge for an organisation is to activate this potential. He points out that the willingness of individuals to volunteer high performance in the workplace depends on the satisfaction of their own physical needs, emotional needs, and self-interest. Success requires both, ability and motivation [7, p. 133].

Cockburn describes common "failure modes" [5, pp. 48] and "success modes" [5, pp. 67], but he warns that these generalising statements do only apply to some degree to any individual [5, pp. 46]. It is the primary management task of an organisation to create an environment where the success modes of individuals can take effect, and where the need to control their failure modes can be reduced [5, p. 73].

Beck devises in his book on XP to "Work with people's instincts, not against them" [2, p. 41]. Indeed, it is one of Becks claims that XP is a methodology that reconciles the instincts of programmers and the interests of the organisation [2, p. xviii].

Discussion. The above references indicate that in agile software development the individual is seen as a valuable human resource with high potential for productive work. The exploitation of this potential should not be taken for granted by an organisation, however, because it is ultimately at the discretion of the individual to put these capabilities to a productive use for the organisation. Therefore, an organisation must take human needs into consideration that go far beyond payment.

Basic Assumption. "Happy people do good work."

3.5   Assumptions about the Nature of Human Activity

Humans do not exist in isolation, instead they interact with their environment. A culture entails assumptions about the appropriate way of interaction with the environment for individuals and groups.

Context. At the organisational level a key question is whether members are encouraged to behave proactively, or whether they are assigned a rather passive role [10, pp. 127].

References. Highsmith states, "Speed is often the least risky course of action" [7, p. 203].

Cockburn, too, expresses a strong preference for action, and regards the willingness to take initiative as one of the success modes of humans. Referring to the other success modes of humans he continues, "With these, we see people taking initiative to get the job done every day, an ongoing activity that keeps the project operating at peak form" [5, p. 70].

Beck uses the metaphor of learning to drive a car to explain the management philosophy used by XP. The idea is to start early, act small, and prepare for corrections: "We need to control the development of software by making many small adjustments, not by making a few large adjustments, kind of like driving a car. This means that we will need the feedback to know when we are a little off, we will need many opportunities to make corrections, and we will have to be able to make those corrections at a reasonable cost" [2, p. 27].

Discussion. The above references indicate that agile software development is strongly biased in favour of action. In a situation where only incomplete information is available action is preferred to waiting for more complete information. The general attitude is that action is preferred to inaction. This may increase the possibility of undesired effects, but it is assumed that these effects can be rolled back without difficulties. Early action usually results in higher risk, and therefore the importance of rapid feedback increases, to stop inappropriate action quickly.

Basic Assumption. "Action makes a project work."

3.6   Assumptions about the Nature of Human Relationships

A culture contains many assumptions about acceptable forms of human relationships. Important issues that must be addressed are the distribution of power and authority, and the nature of peer relationships.

Context. An important characteristic of culture is the dimension of "power distance" [10, pp. 132]. A fundamental question in this respect is the degree of power distance that is regarded as acceptable. If, for example, a low power distance is taken for granted in a culture then a manager may choose to substitute group-decisions for his own authority.

References. Highsmith notes that agile software development needs strong leadership: "While the following fact may seem paradoxical, adaptive environments require much stronger leaders than do deterministic ones" [7, p. 209]. Concerning the expectations of followers he adds: "Teams want a clear sense of direction and decisiveness from their leaders; they do not want arbitrariness or authoritarianism" [7, p. 210]. According to Highsmith the leader is empowered by the team to make decisions, and likewise the leader empowers the team members [7, p. 215].

Cockburn does give numerous examples of successful leadership in [5], but he does not provide a comprehensive discussion of leadership issues.

Beck vaguely describes the decision-making process in XP as "more like decentralized decision making than centralized control" [2, p. 72]. He has included a special role, called "coach", in XP: "What most folks think of as management is divided into two roles in XP: the coach and the tracker (these may or may not be filled by the same person). [...] The measure of a coach is how few technical decisions he or she makes: The job is to get everybody else making good decisions" [2, p. 73]

The following two practices taken from the Manifesto [1] relate to the assumptions about the nature of human relationships in agile software development.

- Build projects around motivated individuals. Give them the environment and support they need, and trust them to get the job done.
- The best architectures, requirements, and designs emerge from self-organizing teams.

These principles clearly favour a high degree of autonomy of a team, and this may imply that the team decides on the issue of leadership itself.

Discussion. The above references indicate that agile software development is leadership-centric. A manager has formal authority granted by an organisation to act in certain situations, for example, to demand certain behaviour from others. A leader has the ability to influence the behaviour of others without using formal authority. The roles of leader and manager are independent, for example a manager may also act as leader in a certain situation. Generally, agile software development does not necessarily rely on strong formal authority, much in contrast to a traditional, hierarchical team structure with a single, appointed team manager who carries all responsibility. Nevertheless, in almost all published material about management in agile projects the figure of a strong and competent leader lurks underneath the egaliterian surface. This leader is usually described as very competent and successful. The relation between the leader and his followers is described as very harmonious and respectful. The impression is that in agile software development leaders are substituted for managers in a sucessful way, although it remains unclear why and how these leaders develop.

Basic Assumption. "Leaders influence followers."

4   Conclusion

Organisations provide venues where people meet, learn, and interact. Over time these social processes often result in organisational cultures that define "how things are done here". Schein has proposed a layered conceptualisation of organisational culture where basic assumptions are the least visible yet most influential element of the culture. Only if these tacit basic assumptions are uncovered it is possible to decipher and understand the observable behaviour of an organisation.

In this paper we have applied the perspective of organisational culture to agile software development. Using Schein's model we have retrieved the following six basic assumptions:

-   Social interaction leads to consensus.
-   Social interaction synchronises activities.
-   The workspace is a social venue.
-   Happy people do good work.
-   Action makes a project work.
-   Leaders influence followers.

We suppose that these basic assumptions are unconsciously held by many proponents of agile SDMs. Basic assumptions refer to the most fundamental way we expect the world to be, and therefore they inform our thinking. We can think about them, we can discuss them, but we are extremely unlikely to change our own basic assumptions. They give us orientation in a complex world, and therefore, powerful, unconscious defence mechanisms fight anything that might violate or invalidate them. We treat a challenge of our basic assumptions as a threat to our identity. Because our defense mechanisms work unconsciously, we are often not even aware when they operate. This can make us vulnerable to stagnation, because we may reject new ideas not on the basis of a careful evaluation, but out of uncontrolled fear.

A look at the concept of simplicity in XP can be used to illustrate the importance of basic assumptions for our understanding. Assume, for example, a hypothetical software engineer who becomes interested in XP, buys a book on the subject, and starts reading. He will soon read about the core practices in XP, and simple design is one of these core practices. He looks for an objective, operational definition of the concept in the book, but he does not find any. He recognises that the core practice qualifies as a rule, which according to Schein is an artefact, but he cannot make much sense out of it, because a proper definition is missing. But why is this artefact there in the book, even in the form of a core practice, if it is indeed useless? Our hypothetical software engineer proceeds to the level of espoused values then, just to find that simplicity is indeed listed there. He feels that he cannot accept the use of such a fuzzy concept without definition. So he might get the impression that XP is disorganised and unscientific, because it relies on a concept that is not properly defined in an objective way. Without further consideration he might decide that he had enough of it and dismiss XP completely.

What is this engineer's basic assumption that unconsciously informed his thinking? In the best tradition of rigorous software engineering he is searching for an objective, scientific definition of the concept of simplicity. That is perfectly reasonable behaviour, he thinks.

What is the corresponding basic assumption that informs XP as well as agile software development in general? It says, "Social interaction leads to consensus." In this statement "social interaction" is assumed to be trustful, collaborative, and competent interaction, of course. The term "leads to" refers to a process that takes some time before palpable results are obtained. The term "consensus" refers to social reality, basically it is assumed that the relevant team members align their notions of the concept of simplicity sufficiently, but it does not require that people outside the team agree. The result is a useful, barely sufficient means of communication in the context of the team.

It does become clear now, that the rejection of XP by our hypothetical engineer was caused by basic assumptions that he has held, that conflict with those that underly XP. For example, he is arguing at the level of external physical reality, whereas XP does only address the level of social reality in this case. This case shows that these subtle differences in basic assumptions can only be detected when the basic assumptions are retrieved, elaborated, and subjected to analysis.

Agile software development is based on many basic assumptions that conflict with the school of rigorous software development. We think that this is the cause for the sometimes strong rejection of agile practices in the software engineering community. An open, unprejudiced discussion and appreciation of agile software development is, therefore, dependent on a thorough analysis of basic assumptions in both communities. In this paper we have presented some of the important basic assumptions in agile software development, but there exist many more.

References

1. The Agile Alliance: Manifesto for Agile Software Development. http://agilemanifesto.org/ (last visited on 16/06/2002), 2001.
2. Beck, K.: Extreme Programming Explained: Embrace Change. Longman Higher Education, 2000.
3. Boehm, B. W.: Software Engineering Economics. Prentice-Hall, 1981.
4. Brown, A.: Organisational Culture. Prentice-Hall, 1998.
5. Cockburn, A.: Agile Software Development. Pearson Education, 2001.
6. Fenton, N. and Pfleeger, S. L.: Software Metrics. International Thomson Computer Press, 1996.
7. Highsmith, J. A.: Adaptive Software Development. Dorset House Publishing, 2000.
8. Highsmith, J. A.: Agile Software Development Ecosystems. Pearson Education, 2002.
9. Institute of Electrical and Electronics Engineers: Dynabook on Extreme Programming. http://computer.org/seweb/dynabook/Index.htm (last visited on 16/06/2002), 2000.
10. Schein, E. H.: Organizational Culture and Leadership. Jossey-Bass Publishers, 1992.

Making a Method Work for a Project Situation in the Context of CMM

Mehmet N. Aydin[1] and Frank Harmsen[2]

[1] University of Twente
Department of Business Information Systems
P.O. Box 217
7500 AE Enschede, The Netherlands
m.n.aydin@sms.utwente.nl
[2] Cap Gemini Ernst & Young
IT Process Consulting Group
P.O. Box 2575
3500 GN Utrecht, The Netherlands
frank.harmsen@cgey.nl

Abstract. Adaptation of Information Systems Development (ISD) methods has been a very important issue as it promises 'making a method work for a project situation' rather then bringing on 'hard-constraints' for practitioners. This is especially true for those organizations that target a business centered system development in new application domains. The goal of this paper is to show the best practices pertaining to tailoring a method on project-by-project basis in an organization. The best practices regarding tailoring a method correspond to some of the activities defined in Software Product Engineering, one of the key process areas in CMM Level 3. The paper also addresses a model available in method engineering domain as an underlying rationale behind the best practices used in the organization. By doing so, we intend to show how the best practices are backed by a theory and what possible enhancements in the area of ISD are foresighted in the coming future in the organization.

1 Introduction

For years, executives in the IS world have understood a compelling business value for having a superior solution delivery capability, which leads to better, cheaper, faster IS development projects. Astonishingly, various analysts' reports and researches are indicating a high percentage of failures [20]. The bottom line impacts of such failures are large and measurable in terms of cost of over time, over budget, inefficient use of available resources like human resources, methods, tools. Furthermore, even when projects are completed within time and budget proposed solutions do not really fit the company's specific needs and do not fulfill expectations of involved actors in the project. This issue may be called fitness-for-business purpose.

M. Oivo and S. Komi-Sirviö (Eds.): PROFES 2002, LNCS 2559, pp. 158-171, 2002.

Methodological supports are aimed at achieving a desired outcome via executing a proposed solution successfully, in a fast and reliable way [12]. However, in practice, traditional one-size-fits-all approaches may not fit specific organizational situations. Indeed, they seem to be far away from supporting practitioners in a more complex, dynamic environment, and such approaches must change from this as-is paradigm [10]. New application domains that support business transactions across organization boundaries and/or units call for more attentions on the issue of fitness-for-business purpose because of diverse or, sometimes, conflict interests of involved stakeholders in the projects and unclarity and/or instability of business requirements.

The truth is that despite our best endeavors ISD projects are not risk free and we need to investigate continuously a better way of gaining a solution delivery capability and reducing risk of failures.

Organizational maturity frameworks such as Capability Maturity Model (CMM) [18] have been used to improve organizations' software process and in turn achieving better software products.

The paper, in the first session, highlights the background of the need of making an ISD method work for a project situation in the line with CMM and ME. In section 2, we further elaborate a context of tailoring a method (DSDM) using ME principles. That section also includes details of research methodology, current IT development situation in an organization and applied research method. Section 3 describes an organization's approach to tailoring a method and its related activities, which are perceived as best practices in the organization. Particularly, coaching activities will be illuminated in the same section. The last section concludes the paper with further implications of best practices and our future research activities in the organization.

2   Tailoring a Method (DSDM) within the Context of CMM and Method Engineering

2.1   Tailoring a Method and CMM

At CMM Level 3 the software process for management and engineering activities is documented, standardized, and integrated into an organization-wide software process [18]. Among seven key process areas software product engineering (SPE) indicates the need of tailoring a method. SPE distinguishes itself from management activities in the projects. SPE involves performing the engineering tasks to build and maintain the software using the project's defined software and *appropriate methods and tool.* However, CMM does neither tell how to decide *appropriateness of methods, tools* nor *how to make it appropriate for a project situation.* The former task refers to suitability of a method to a project situation and the later task indicates an approach to adapt a method if not completely suitable. In the following section we elaborate both tasks by referring best practices gained in an organization.

2.2   Tailoring a Method and Method Engineering

The notion of SPE is reflecting the principles of method(ology) engineering (ME) introduced by Kumar and Welke [16]. The concept of methodology engineering was proposed a solution to engineering IS development method by taking into account uniqueness of a project situation [16]. Later, method engineering is defined as an engineering discipline to design, construct and adapt methods, techniques and tools for development of information systems. Method Engineering includes routemap configuration [21][22], aiming at tuning and extending method fragments to obtain a situated method. A routemap can be configured by considering *the situation* in which the resulting *situated method* will be applied and *the success* one wants to achieve with the situated method [15]. This so-called S^3 model (Situation, Scenario, Success) [8] provides heuristics that guide method engineers in constructing and tailoring a method.

An important aspect of Method Engineering is capturing and distributing knowledge and experience of practitioners, in particular project managers, to improve routemaps, situated methods and the process to construct situated methods [12][19]. Experience factory as a project-independent unit within an organization has been proposed a way to capture and process project experiences of all kind and to actively support the project by providing suitable experiences from the past projects [3]. In that respect a case-based approach is used as a technique to employ accumulated project experiences for tailoring the software process [1]. Eliciting project characteristics, combined with identifying the required project success are identified as essential activities in such a tailoring process [9]. All these approaches to Method Engineering stress the importance of a sound decision-making process leading to a situated method. This decision-making process should be facilitated by knowledge support, to improve both the efficiency of the process itself and the effectiveness of the resulting situated method

Suitability and adaptation of a method to a given situation has been elaborated by [8] [21].[24] Suitability of an approach or a method indicates its fitness to a project situation. Choosing an inappropriate approach is one of the major risks of failure for ISD projects [13]. A situation as we adopt the definition of [5] resembles a 'snapshot' of a perceived object system, which is a state at a particular time, a combination of circumstances, conditions, and facts having an effect on an organization. Notice that such fitness can be analyzed at an organizational and a project level. In this paper we mainly focus on a project level. Even though an approach or a method is suitable to a situation at hand it still needs to be tailored or customized according to project specifications during the project.

2.3   About a Method (DSDM) to Be Tailored

DSDM (Dynamic Systems Development Method, 1997) [6] is a method for RAD, Rapid Application Development [17][18]. In the UK and in the Benelux, DSDM, which is supported by a consortium of over 600 organizations, has become a de-facto market standard. The method highly emphasizes the notions of suitability and adaptability – DSDM is to a certain extent suitable for a project or organization and is adaptable if not completely suitable. For the purpose of this research, we have considered three components of DSDM: its underlying philosophy, its framework and its techniques. In practice, each of these components can be applied separately, and subsets of the components can be applied on their own as well. DSDM framework suggests a complete project approach including key phases, products and roles, which should be customized according to a project situation. In this manner, DSDM is highly adaptable – it is possible to use full-fledged DSDM, but individual techniques or just terminology are still meaningful to be used.

Philosophy of DSDM. The underlying philosophy or way of thinking of DSDM is captured in nine principles [23], stressing typical RAD features like iterative development, integrated testing, user involvement in the development team and fitness for business purpose. DSDM has a lifecycle model of which the core consists of five phases. Important techniques of DSDM are timeboxing, facilitated workshops, prioritisation and prototyping. Timeboxing refers to setting a deadline by which a predefined objective must be met, instead of describing when a task must be completed. MoSCoW, which is abbreviation for Must, Should, Could have and Want to have but won't have this round, is a way to prioritise requirements of the system. Modeling techniques are not included in DSDM, as they often are part of modeling tool sets, which are not part of the method. However, suggestions for modeling techniques to be used are described.

2.4   Research Methodology

An Investigation in an Organization. The organization, we have investigated, is one of the leading financial institutions in Europe and operates in a dynamic business environment. IT Development is one of the departments employing 2000 people who are involved in IT projects. The department has considerable method use experiences and continuously invests in software process improvements.

This department is organized in terms of clusters for each business characteristics can be defined. For instance, one of them is *process cluster*, which aims to supporting and improve business processes. Another one is *e-channel cluster*, which reflects flexibility and an innovative face of the organization to its customers. Clusters are further divided into application domains, which distinguish themselves in terms of business and application characteristics. Business characteristics are related to business value added aspects of the application and application characteristics primarily include technical aspects. To give an example of how business characteristics used in a domain consider *core business process* application domain in *the process* cluster. This domain has an essential role of executing all business transactions properly. Business transactions are running across organizational units and they usually need to be re-engineered to respond to changes in organizational structures. The other domain, *customer contact domain,* often requires innovative development environment and tools.

Recently, DSDM has been chosen a method of choice for all clusters in the department and a big programme including several projects are launched. One of them aims at coaching project managers in tailoring DSDM with the help of experts and several instruments developed in the organizations. Experts have extensive project experiences and are subject matter experts in DSDM (certified DSDM trainers and/or trained in DSDM area). They are coaching project managers to make better decisions about the suitability of DSDM and a degree of adaptation of DSDM to their project. Basically, there are two important roles essential in tailoring DSDM: the project coaching role and the project leading role. DSDM coaches assist project managers in tailoring and applying DSDM whereas project managers are fully responsible for the project execution and they are final decision makers for the selection of parts (fragments) of DSDM.

DSDM implementation projects start with a 'go' instruction from the Portfolio Manager who is accountable for all DSDM implementation projects. Then, a project coach is assigned to the project for which s/he arranges several meetings with two project managers; one from business side and the other represents technology side. These meetings result in an advice, which includes adaptation of DSDM, possible risk factors and several ways to mitigate them, etc.

The Research Method. Our research method is a combination of several rounds in-depth semi-structured interviews with those stakeholders who are responsible for execution of the projects and documentary analysis of project deliverables.

In the first round interviews, we chose five DSDM coaches, who have different degree of project experiences in general and coaching experiences specific to DSDM. The goal of this first round interview was to identify commonalities and differences in tailoring DSDM. Semi-structured interviews include several questions. Among them two key questions were essential:

- How do you go about tailoring a method for a project?
- What do you look for and take into account while tailoring DSDM for a project?

In the second round, we interviewed all coaches. At this stage, we zoomed in identified common activities, factors and heuristics used in tailoring a method. To get more rich understanding of coaching activities we decided to conduct interviews with project managers and executives as well.

Third round interviews included project managers from technology side, project managers from the business side and portfolio managers. Selection of columns, domains, projects, project managers were done carefully so that good representatives were interviewed.

- Column selection was done in terms of a degree of DSDM project experiences in the columns
- Domain selection was based on application characteristics and profile of project managers involved in the projects.
- During the selection of projects we included at least four types of application characteristics: typical software package implementation, component based system development (CBD), migration and application integration type project, and projects including combination of CBD and package implementation and system integration.
- We selected project managers after consultation with those DSDM coaches and other project executives involved in the same projects with project managers.

To enhance our interview sessions we gained more insight on the projects by doing in-dept documentary analysis. Following project deliverables were examined: project proposal, business area definition, system architecture definition, prioritized requirements list, development plan.

3   Best Practices Pertaining to Tailoring a Method in an Organization

In this section we will show how tailoring mechanism is applied in the organization. Figure 1 summarizes key activities are performed by coaches.

3.1   Suitability of DSDM and Coaching Activity

DSDM clearly states in which situations DSDM is applicable, and in which situations the method should be tailored. For this, an instrument called 'suitability filter' is available in the manual [6]. The filter considers the critical success factors for DSDM and characteristics of projects that are especially effective for DSDM. Each potential project should be judged individually using the filter. If the project provides a good match against the filter, then DSDM can be considered the appropriate development approach. Inability to satisfy all of the criteria results in modification of the method.

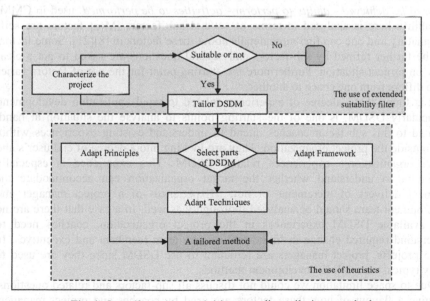

Fig. 1. Overall coaching activities regarding tailoring a method

3.2   Characterizing the Situation at Hand
by Using the Extended Suitability Filter

Coaching experiences have been evolving to a set of best practices. One of them is the extended suitability filter, which is our main focus in this paper. The organization has very extensive experiences about the questions in the extended suitability filter. During early stages of DSDM implementation in the organization coaches had used original DSDM suitability filter questions that can be found in DSDM Manual. Later on they have experienced with them, some questions were extended, clarified and furthermore for each question working instructions, measurements, useful hints & tips were added. The filter became a sort of a 'working' document and now is acting like an instrument, which provides a baseline for advices to be written for every project. From our interviews with both DSDM coaches and project managers they agree on the significance of using this instrument. Our investigation shows both coaches and project managers agree on high relevance of the factors for the characterization of the project situation. The instrument provides a common ground for characterizing a project situation and facilitates a discussion for which aspects of DSDM can be fully or partly utilized and leads to a tailored method.

Figure 2 provides an overview of the factors used to characterize the situation at hand. Critical success factors defined by DSDM can be associated with these factors. Basically factors are clustered under two notions: *capability and solution*. *Capability* indicates a degree of ability a project organization possesses and an extent to which a desired solution can be delivered. Thus, this picture is consistent with the notion of *'goal to be achieved - ability to perform - activities to be performed'* used in CMM. Capability here is analysed in terms of several sub-factors. Most factors are self-explanatory and one can find more details about these factors in [8][21]. Some factors can be further refined by sub-factors and several questions are asked to get a clear view on project situation. Furthermore the starting point for the use of factors varies from differs from one coach to another.

It is found that a degree of experience related to rapid application development, particularly DSDM, is one of the starting points to analyse the situation at hand. Related to this sub-factor coaches intend to understand existing experiences within and outside the project organization. They are looking into a degree of end user's and target organization's experiences related DSDM. This experience is especially important to understand whether the target organization can accommodate the frequent delivery of increments or not.   Experiences of a project manager and development team should be analysed thoroughly as well. In a case that there are no any available DSDM experiences in the project organization, coaches need to understand required change in 'mind-set' of core team members and executives. In some projects, project managers are reluctant to use DSDM since they are used to apply typical waterfall IS development methods.

Due to space limitation we could not discuss all sub-factors and related questions. To give a flavour of how these factors are used by coaches and project managers consider *commitment, empowerment* and *a degree of end user involvement* in a project. These three factors are also pointed out in DSDM principles.

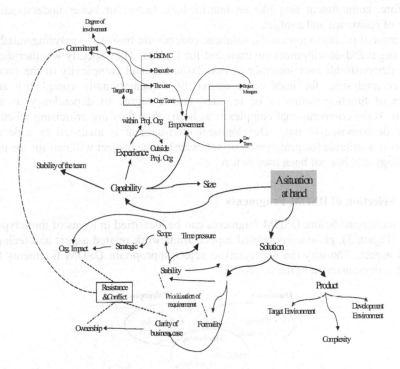

Fig. 2. The extended suitability filter factors (situation factors) used for characterising project situation

Commitment needs to be taken into account from executives', the end user's and the target organization's perspectives. Commitment of end user can be linked to *a degree of involvement of end-user*. Four end user involvement variants are often considered: no end-user-participation, consultation (advisor), representation and consensus (ambassador), and end-user computing. Related to the linkage between commitment and end-user involvement coaches want to know whether there is a senior user commitment to provide end user involvement or not. *Empowerment*, as another sub-factor, is used to point out whether project managers and the development team will be empowered to make decisions on behalf of their communities.

The second notion is related to the desired solution. There are two views on the solution: *business view* indicating business value added aspect of the solution and *the product view*, which refers to its functionality including technical aspects to be required.

In terms of business view on the solution, project managers are supposed to clearly demonstrate a business case behind the project. Clarity of business case, stability and formality of business processes to be analysed are other sub-factors related to the business view of the solution. An important factor is a level of resistance and conflict. This factor cannot be isolated from a degree of impact of the solution at strategic and operational level. To get more rich understanding of the degree of resistance and conflict coaches are looking into a level of commitment that can be secured.

Therefore, commitment acts like an intermediate factor for better understanding a degree of resistance and conflict.

In terms of product view on the solution, coaches are basically analysing suitability of the target and development environment for DSDM. They specify whether there is highly demonstrable user interface or not. To understand complexity of the product, they are analysing, for instance, a degree of computationally complexity and a number of function points to be required and a degree of dependency to under systems. If the computational complexity is high,, then they are criticising whether it can be decomposed or not. Development environment is analysed to understand whether it is suitable for prototyping or not, whether the project will call for the use of technology that has not been used before.

3.3   Selection of DSDM Fragments

As we mentioned before DSDM fragments can be identified in terms of three types of aspect (Figure 3): philosophy related aspect, framework related aspect and technique related aspect. The way (an approach) to select appropriate DSDM fragments for a project is demonstrated in the following:

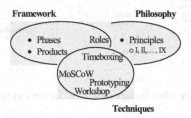

Fig. 3. Three types of DSDM aspects

Based on the analysis of the situation at hand coaches and project managers decide which aspects can fully realized. For instance, if we are talking about DSDM principles, which is related to philosophy aspect then the key question to be answered is: *To what extent the situation at hand is suitable to realize the principles.* In that case, they assume that the more critical success factors (CSF) the project organization owns, the more principles they can realize. CSF are already found in DSDM manual and are linked to principles. Furthermore, the factors presented in figure 2 cover CSF.

To understand how the relationships between DSDM aspect, CSF and suitability filter factors work consider the following example: Incremental delivery is one of the critical success factors to realize two DSDM principles: principle of 'a product based approach' and 'fitness for business purpose'. Now, the question remains to what extent the situation at hand is suitable to realize two principles by means of achieving 'incremental delivery' as one of the CSF. To answer this question we need to analyse our capability for incremental delivery and whether the solution can be delivered incrementally or not. The factors in figure 2 will help us answer the question from different perspectives. Some factors are more relevant than others and need more attention to get deeper understanding of the situation. For instance, if the requirements cannot be prioritised than the incremental delivery will be hardly possible. Indeed, DSDM provides a technique to prioritise requirements, which is called MoSCoW. So, we need to look at whether MoSCoW can be used in the project or not. MoSCoW is representing one of the fragments of technical aspect of DSDM. It means that now we should answer the key question again, which is 'to what extent the situation at hand is suitable to use MoSCoW'.

In many project cases, coaches face difficulty of prioritising requirements. End user and project managers usually think that all requirements are 'must haves' ('M' of MoSCoW). The idea behind the technique is to determine which requirements have high business values and critical so that the project will focus on these requirements and guarantees at least delivery of 'must haves and should have' and maybe 'could haves' in incrementally rather than one-shot manner. It means that MoSCoW (the prioritisation technique) should be used to reveal business values behind the requirements. According to DSDM coaches, in some projects it has been very difficult to convince project members a need of focusing business value rather than functionalities of the system while prioritising the requirements. And, they believe that even all requirements are 'must haves' they can still be prioritised.

3.4   The Use of Heuristics and Writing an Advice

Having said the importance of situation factors, we now give on example of the use heuristics documented in advices (Table 1). In this example, the heuristics are used for determining an appropriate development process variant for a project. Furthermore, the advice will be given for the suitability of two DSDM techniques.

In terms of development process, we found that project managers have often used the following development process variants (options) [6]:

- One increment - one iteration (typical waterfall type (linear) development process),
- One increment –many iterations (1-pass DSDM),
- Many increments – many iterations (typical DSDM development process variant)
- Many increments – many iterations (some increments are done in linear way) (Hybrid DSDM)

The increment, here, refers to a part of the total system that is delivered and used by the business before the total system is operational or a part of the total system that develops and delivers an implementable part of the total system, e.g. a set of Functional Model Iteration, Design and Build Iteration and Implementation phases. An iteration follows one cycle of identify what is to be produced and its acceptance criteria and plan how to do it, check that it is satisfactory by reviewing or testing the product against the acceptance criteria (DSDM Manual).

Now, given the project situation in the left part of Table 1 the heuristic will help project managers decide which development process variant is more appropriate for the project. For the sake of simplicity we kept the project situation short and heuristic is not complete and it is just an extraction from an existing heuristic.

Table 1. An example of the use of heuristics in an advice

About the project situation and one decision point (just an extraction from a real project history)	*About the appropriate DSDM development process option and a part of an advice*
(...) If we know that requirements are almost clear, stable and they are hardly possible to be prioritised and there is no clear user interface and there is high computational complexity, the timeline is not clear and the resource availability (in terms of developers, end user) is not known yet the total resources can be fixed, then we would like to know which development process variant is more appropriate and what kind of consequences we may anticipate in the later DSDM phases if we choose one of the DSDM process variants?	It *seems* that hybrid development process variant is more appropriate compare to other options. The reason is the following: Even though all requirements are 'must haves' we can still partly prioritise them and for those requirements that are firmly stable we may plan one increment for which DSDM phases will covered in a more linear way (i.e. no iteration for this increment), for the rest of requirements we may plan other increment(s) for which many iterations will be done (...) *(more explanation follows)*
	About some issues related to two techniques of DSDM and related risks
	As the case indicates, MoSCoW (one DSDM technique) appears to be not very suitable for this situation due to difficulty of prioritising requirements. The same holds for timeboxing for which there must be fixed date for the project or for an increment or for an iteration. For both anticipated issues there may be some ways to use these two techniques in different ways. Indeed, DSDM coaches have been already experienced about such ways and they successfully use the philosophies behind MoSCoW and Timeboxing in real projects situations (...)*(More information follows)*

In terms of suitability of two DSDM techniques, the heuristic is again used to make project managers aware of pros and cons of MoSCoW and timeboxing. Especially, hints related to use of these techniques in different ways are found to be very useful for project managers.

4   Conclusions and Further Research

Tailoring includes several compromises and trade offs between a tailored method and changes in a project situation. Our investigation in the organization shows that project managers have different levels of awareness about the tailoring process. Some project managers are already ready to go through tailoring steps smoothly. Others need to be convinced about a need of tailoring a method. We also found that some managers perceive tailoring mechanism as very formal decision-making process. Even though achieving CMM Level 3 in an organization provides a baseline to have formal system development processes we found that most decisions related to tailoring a method are made implicitly or ad hoc. In that case, coaching activities aim at increasing a degree of awareness for tailoring a method. Coaches walk through each step of tailoring mechanism with project managers. It means coaches are facilitating project managers to get use explicit decision-making process. Once project managers get the essence of tailoring mechanism then they can, to some degree, coach themselves. Indeed, the organization has already achieved a degree of awareness and readiness for self-coaching. Such self-coaching mechanism can be supported by an instrument, which acts like an interface between project managers and coaches. The development of an instrument is our major goal for the future.

Acknowledgements

The authors would like to thank Jean Kleijnen, Inspiration Program Manager and DSDM Coaches involved in DSDM Implementation at ABN AMRO Bank in the Netherlands. They supported and spent a lot of time in facilitating this research. We would also like to thank Robert Stegwee and Kees van Slooten from University of Twente, who helped guide us in our efforts.

References

1. Althoff, K. –D., Birk, A., Greese von Wangenheim, C., Tautz C.: Case-Based Reasoning for Experimental Software Engineering. In: M. Lenz, B. Bartch-Sporl, H.-D. Burkhard, S, Wess (eds.), Case-Based Reasoning Technology, Springer Verlag, (1998) 235-254
2. Barki, H., Rivard, S., Talbot, J.: Toward an Assessment of Software Development Risk. Journal of MIS, 10(2), Fall, (1993) 203-225
3. Basili, V. R., Caldiera, G. Rombach, H. D.: Experience Factory. In J.J. Marciniak (ed.): Encyclopedia of Software Engineering, Volume 1, John Wiley & Sons (1994).
4. Boehm, B: Making RAD Work for Your Project, IEEE Computer, March, pp. 113-117(1999)
5. Brinkkemper, S.: Method Engineering: Engineering of Information Systems Development Methods and Tools. Information and Software Technology, 38, (1996) 275-280
6. DSDM Dynamic Systems Development Method Manual: Version 3, http://www.dsdm.org (1997)
7. Harmsen, F., Brinkkemper, S., Oei, H.: Situational Method Engineering for Information Systems Project. In: Olle, T. W., Stuarts, A.A. V. (eds.): Methods and Associated Tools for the Information Systems Life Cycle, Proceedings of the IFIP WG 8.1, Int. Conference CRIS'94, Amsterdam, North-Holland, (1994) 169-194
8. Harmsen, F., Lubbers, I., Wijers, G.: Success-Driven Selection of Fragments for Situational Methods: The S3 Model. In: Pohl, K., and P. Peters (eds.): Proceedings of the Second International Workshop on Requirements Engineering: Foundations of Software Quality, Aachener Beitrage zur Informatik, Band 13, (1995) 104-115

9. Henninger, S. and Baumgarten, K. A.: Case-Based Approach to Tailoring Software Processes. In: Aha, D.W., Watson, I., Yang, Q. (eds.): Proceedings of the 4th International Conference on Case-Based Reasoning, ICCBR-2001. Vancouver, Canada, 30 July - 2 August 2001. Springer, Lecture Notes in Artificial Intelligence
10. Hidding, G. J.: Reinventing Methodology. Communications of the ACM, Vol. 40, No.11, November (1997)
11. Hoef, R. van de, Harmsen, F., Wijers, G.: Situation, Scenario, and Success. Memoranda Informatica 95-12, University of Twente, Enschede (1995)
12. Jarke, M., Pohl, K., Rolland, C., Schmitt, J. R.: Experience-Based Method Evaluation and Improvement: A process modeling approach. Proceedings of the Int. IFIP WG 8.1 Conf. In CRIS Series: Method and Associated Tools for the Information Systems Life Cycle, North Holland (1994)
13. Jiang, J. J., Klein, G., Discenza, R: Information Systems Success as Impacted by Risks and Development Strategies. IEEE Transactions on Engineering Management, Vol.48, No.1, February (2001)
14. Kettinger, W. J., Teng, J. T. C., Quha, S.: Business Process Change: A Study of Methodologies, Techniques, and Tools, MIS Quarterly, March (1997)
15. Klooster, M., Brinkkemper, S., Harmsen, F. and Wijers, G.: Intranet Facilitated Knowledge Management: A Theory and Tool for Defining Situational Methods In: Olivé, A., Pastor, J.A.: Advanced Information Systems Engineering. Proceedings of the 9th International Conference CAiSE'97, Barcelona, Spain, Lecture Notes in Computer Science 1250, pp. 303-317, Springer Verlag (1997).
16. Kumar, K., Welke, R. J.: Methodology Engineering: A Proposal for Situation-Specific Methodology Construction. In: Cotterman, W.W., Senn, J. A. (ed.): Challenges and Strategies for Research in Systems Development, Wiley& Sons Ltd (1992).
17. Martin, J.: Rapid Application Development. Macmillan Publishing, New York (1991)
18. Paulk, M. C., Weber, C. V., Curtis, B, Chrissis, M. B. (eds): The Capability Maturity Model: Guidelines for Improving the Software Process. SEI Series in Software Engineering, Carnegie Mellon University, Addison-Wesley (1994)
19. Rolland, C., Prakash, N. A proposal for context-specific method engineering, In: Brinkkemper, S., Lyytinen, K. and Welke, R. W. (eds.): Method Engineering: Principles of Method Construction and Tool Support. Proceedings of the IFIP WG 8.1, Atlanta, Chapman & Hall, ISBN 0-412-79750-X (1996)
20. Schmidt, R., Lyytinen, K., Keil, M., Cule, P.: Identifying Software Project Risks: An International Delphi Study. Journal of MIS, Spring, Vol.17, No.4, (2001) 5-36
21. Slooten, C., Brinkkemper, S., A Method Engineering Approach to Information Systems Development. In: Prakash, N. C., Rolland, C., Pernici,B. (eds.): Information System Development Process. Proceedings of the IFIP WG 8.1, Como, pp.167-186, Elsevier Science Publishers B.V., North Holland, ISBN 0-444-81594-5 (1993)

22. Slooten, C. , Hodes, B.: Characterizing IS Development Projects. In: Brinkkemper, S., Lyytinen, K. and Welke, R. W. (eds.): Method Engineering: Principles of Method Construction and Tool Support. Proceedings of the IFIP WG 8.1, Atlanta, Chapman & Hall, ISBN 0-412-79750-X (1996)
23. Stapleton, J.: Dynamic Systems Development Method – The Method in Practice. Addison-Wesley, 1997.
24. Tolvanen, J.-P.: Incremental Method Engineering with Modeling Tools: Theoretical Principles and Empirical Evidence, Dissertation, University of Jyväskylä, Finland, ISBN 951-39-0303-6 (1998)

A Practical Application of the IDEAL Model

Valentine Casey and Ita Richardson

Department of Computer Science and Information Systems
University of Limerick
Limerick, Ireland
{Val.Casey,Ita.Richardson}@ul.ie

Abstract. The focus of this paper is to outline the experience of a European based software organization utilizing the IDEAL model, while implementing a tailored Capability Maturity Model (CMM) software process improvement program. The goal was to achieve process improvement rather than a specific CMM maturity level. In doing this, the IDEAL model was extensively researched and employed. The benefits and limitations of the IDEAL model are presented as experienced. Further details on this research are available in [1]. Research was carried out on a number of software process improvement paradigms prior to the selection of the CMM. A key element of this approach was to see the requirements of the organization as paramount and immediate. It was deemed important to achieve process improvement in specific Key Process Areas regardless of their position in the CMM. This provided the flexibility for future investment in SPI to capitalize on the current work.

1   Introduction

Software process improvement (SPI) is a complex and expensive exercise, which should not be entered into lightly and without due preparation. Therefore the correct implementation of any improvement initiative is an important undertaking. To implement an improvement plan, companies must consider how they should go about it. This is particularly important for the small to medium sized enterprises (SME), where the company needs to have fast return on investment [2]. No company, regardless of whether they are large or small, is willing to undertake any project without being assured that the resources expended will in fact give maximum value for money. The research project presented here demonstrates an implementation of the IDEAL model in an SME, ensuring that the organization's business requirements are top priority.

2   Research Project

The action research five-phase cyclical process based approach as defined by Susman and Evered [3] and Baserville [4] was used during this research project.   This

M. Oivo and S. Komi-Sirviö (Eds.): PROFES 2002, LNCS 2559, pp. 172-184, 2002.
© Springer-Verlag Berlin Heidelberg 2002

approach allowed one of the authors perform the role of assessor in the process improvement program detailed in this paper. It also provided both authors with the objectivity and structure to effectively perform their work.

The project was carried out within a subsidiary of a software company employing 120 people. It was focused on two teams with a total staff of 20, running an independent process. It had its own Project Manager who reported directly to senior management and was financed as an independent profit centre. This subsidiary, given its independent mode of operation meets the criteria necessary to be defined as a SME.

The questions being researched in this project include:

- Can standard models work within SME companies?
- Do process improvement models   make a meaningful contribution, or do they add unnecessary levels of bureaucracy?
- Does the IDEAL model work?
- How does the research undertaken in this project compare with the findings on the IDEAL model presented by Bill Curtis at the ICSE 2000[5]?

3   Background of the Organization

The organization, Software Future Technologies (pseudonym) is based in the Republic of Ireland and while having an Irish management team, is part of a multinational whose parent is in the United States. The parent organization established a mainframe software application development and maintenance company in Ireland in the nineteen nineties. While mainframe application development and maintenance continued to be a significant part of the organization's business, by 1999 the technological focus of the Irish operation had evolved to include the development and maintenance of applications on a number of diverse platforms, including client server, web-based and CASE tool technologies.   Software Future Technologies developed and expanded its market share in Europe and the US, and while this research was being carried out, employed 120 staff.

3.1   History of the Process Improvement within the Organization

In 1998 the parent organization took the strategic decision to develop a CMM-compliant process for all its software development and maintenance activities. Plans were drawn up for a US based assessment to take place. A CMM assessment of the Irish operation was also scheduled to take place. SEI-approved CMM assessor training was provided to key members of staff, including one of the authors. However, due to a sudden change in corporate strategy, the CMM initiative was dropped for both the US and the Irish division.

3.2   Software Future Technologies Process

On establishing Software Future Technologies a defined process had been documented for mainframe software application development and maintenance. The documented process was stored on the company's intranet.   This proved very successful. Despite the introduction of projects for other platforms no new defined processes were developed. Basic Requirements Management (Key Process Area (KPA) at Level 2 of the CMM) was in place as was limited Project Planning (KPA at Level 2) and Project Tracking and Oversight (KPA at Level 2). A number of methods of Configuration Management (KPA at Level 2) were employed, but this did not extend to documentation or specifications and was not used on all projects. An extensive Training Program (KPA at Level 3) was in place and Peer Reviews (KPA at Level 3) were carried out from the establishment of Software Future Technologies in Ireland. While some basic Software Quality Assurance Key Process Area practices were in place, defect reoccurrence had been identified as a major problem area. Any process improvement initiative in Software Future Technologies would have to address this problem.

Having reviewed customer and prospective customer quality expectations, it was determined by the Marketing department that there was no demand for the organization to achieve any specific external certified quality standard, or the achievement of a specific maturity level. This allowed the assessor to review and evaluate a number of standards for application in the process improvement initiative.

4   Selection of the CMM

A number of process improvement models were reviewed prior to the selection of the CMM as the basis for this initiative, including ISO 9001 and ISO/IEC 15504 (SPICE). The goal of this review was to determine the most suitable and flexible model for the organization to implement. Each model was extensively compared and their strengths and weaknesses explored.

The CMM and ISO 9001 are the most popular frameworks for process improvement within the software industry [6]. Indeed it has been recognised there is a strong correlation between ISO 9001 and the CMM [7]. That stated, clear differences have been recognised in each approach [6], [8], [9]. Given the organization's European location, ISO 9001 was a strong contender.

Based on the organizations goals an extensive comparison was made between the CMM and ISO. This included the examination of Paulk [7] and O'Tinney [8]. The final decision to choose the CMM was reached because ISO 9001 had specific limitations from the organization's perspective. In particular the ISO standard provided only a minimum quality baseline for software organizations [7]. ISO 9001 placed an emphasis on meeting minimum requirements rather then promoting continued process improvement.

ISO/IEC 15504 (SPICE) was also considered. This standard was in beta test at the time the initiative was undertaken. It did offer advantages; these included the separation of process and capability into two dimensions and the consistency of results between ISO/IEC 15504 and CMM [10]. The problem identified with this option was that there was only an academic knowledge of the model within the organization and the cost of further training and outside support would be high.

On the other hand the CMM offered a comprehensive approach to process improvement. There was also the advantage of the opportunity to leverage any formal CMM assessment that might take place in the medium to long term utilising

ISO/IEC 15504 to generate an internationally standardised rating. The compatibility between ISO/IEC 15504 and the CMM was seen as a further advantage offered for utilising the CMM. While ISO/IEC 15504 was the up and coming standard, the CMM was the proven market leader. A commitment to continued process improvement was a key element in the initiative undertaken. It was also determined that given the location of a number of the organization's customers in the US, a US centric improvement paradigm with acceptance in Europe would be the perfect model to apply.

The process improvement initiative had to be performed under a number of constraints and within a defined scope to achieve clear goals and objectives. The scope, objectives and constraints had only been verbally discussed. It was understood there was need for clear guidance on the implementation of the process improvement initiative. That guidance appeared to be provided by the IDEAL model [11]. The initial selection of the IDEAL model as the life cycle approach to the process improvement initiative went hand in hand with the selection of the CMM [12].

5   The IDEAL Model

The IDEAL model [13] is defined as „ *A life Cycle approach for process improvement*". It was developed by the Software Engineering Institute (SEI) and based on the CMM [14]. The model clearly has its roots in the Shewart/Deming cycle Plan Do Check Act approach [9]. It offers specific and practical implementation guidelines for the adoption of new software processes and methods. It addresses the essential phases, activities, and resources required for effective process improvement to take place. Given the potential offered by the IDEAL model for general application the SEI have revised it and Version 1.1 has been used in this project.

The model consists of five phases (See Fig. 1):

Initiating	Laying the groundwork
Diagnosing	Determining where you are and your future goals
Establishing	Planning how you are going to achieve your goals
Acting	Doing the work required to reach the defined goals
Learning	Learning from what has been done for the next iteration
/Leveraging[1]	of the process improvement cycle

The five phases consist of a total of fourteen activities, which address the specific requirements of one complete cycle of the model. The length of time taken to complete a cycle depends on the resources and the agreed time frame defined for each iteration by the organization.

Each phase is made up of a number of activities. In the Initiating phase the business reasons for undertaking the initiative are recognized and defined. The whole effort is put in context within the organization's business goals and objectives. The benefits, which will result from the effort are defined and articulated. Senior

---

[1] The letter 'L' of IDEAL is referred to as Leveraging in [9], [11], [13] and Learning in [14]

management sponsorship is established. To manage the initiative a Management Steering Group and Software Engineering Process Group are formed.

During the Diagnosing phase the current state of the organization is determined and a baseline established. The recommendations that arise from this activity provide the basis for a draft improvement action plan.

The purpose of the Establishing phase is to develop a detailed action plan. Priorities are determined which take external and internal factors into account. Once these priorities have been set a strategy is developed and a detailed action plan is prepared. This plan includes milestone metrics, decision points, responsibilities, resources and all other elements, which are essential for the success of the initiative.

During the Acting phase all the key elements are brought together and a best guess solution is identified. The solution is then piloted and modified through a number of iterative cycles. This can take a long period of time. Once the solution is deemed satisfactory, it is implemented.

The Leveraging\Learning phase focuses on learning from what has been done and determining what goals and objectives have been met.   It also provides the opportunity for learning from the work undertaken and incorporating that knowledge into continued process improvement as further areas are identified and implemented during future iterations of the IDEAL cycle.

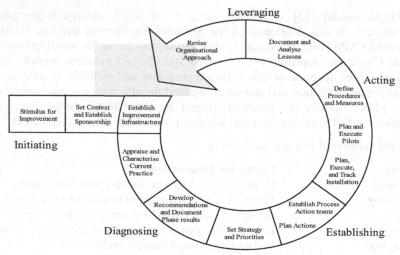

Fig. 1. The IDEAL Model [13]

6   Using the IDEAL Model

The IDEAL model was accepted as the life cycle paradigm for the initiative at a preliminary stage, its suitability was now reviewed in detail. It was determined that in general it provided comprehensive guidelines and direction to manage the change process. It was noted that it particularly addressed initial areas of concern in the key stages of the improvement project.   Management in Software Future Technologies agreed that it should be utilised in the development of the initiative's mission statement, initial project plan and as a framework for reference as the initiative developed. It was also agreed that it provided a good basis for continued improvement during future iterations of the process improvement cycle.

6.1 The Initiating Phase

Utilizing the IDEAL model as the basis for the process improvement initiative, the assessor and a senior manager held their first meeting. The first item to be addressed was to determine the stimulus for change. The business reasons for change had to be defined and articulated. The importance of this step cannot be understated. Without a clear understanding of why an improvement initiative is undertaken, it will in most circumstances be doomed to failure, given the level of commitment required by all concerned for its successful conclusion.

Two important questions were asked:

- Why are we initiating these changes?
- What are our business reasons for this undertaking?

The stimulus for change and business reasons identified included increased profitability, better levels of service to existing customers, and the development of new business. It was also realised that this initiative offered the opportunity for the development of a CMM-based development process. This would tie in with any future quality initiatives that might be undertaken by the parent organization. To address each business reason clear objectives were defined and agreed

Having determined the stimulus for change it was now time to set the SPI initiative in the context of Software Futures Technology's business strategy. It was determined that the initiative would assist with future development and expansion of business with new and existing customers by increasing customer satisfaction and enhancing the organization's reputation. It would allow the development of a repeatable, effective and efficient production process, which would underscore that expansion. It would help to ensure product delivery was on time and within budget. It would also allow management more visibility into the process at all stages of development, which was recognised as being essential for the successful maintenance and development of quality software.

Having determined what the business reasons were and how they fitted into the company's overall business strategy it was time to build sponsorship. The level of commitment required through managerial support and the availability of resources were outlined. The constraints that would have to be imposed on the effort were also defined and discussed. Management clearly understood what those constraints were and how they would impact on the level of achievable goals and objectives. This provided an excellent first step, which greatly assisted with the building of management sponsorship. A clear understanding of why the initiative was being undertaken, what goals it was going to achieve and how they fitted into the overall business strategy of the organization was invaluable in presenting and winning the required level of approval and commitment from senior management. As a result a senior manager was appointed sponsor and a long-term commitment to the initiative was made.

Sponsorship being established, it was essential to develop a mechanism to manage the implementation of the initiative. The need for the establishment of a Management Steering Group (MSG) was addressed and its role and responsibilities were defined. They included the strategic and tactical direction of the initiative. This necessitated the establishment of clear goals, setting direction, priorities and monitoring the effort.

A Software Engineering Process Group (SEPG) had been established in December 1997, but had been abandoned when the CMM initiative was cancelled. The SEPG was reconstituted and was made up of the assessor and the local outsourcing centre Project Manager. The role of the SEPG was to facilitate the definition, maintenance, and improvement of the software process. This included maintaining the motivation and the enthusiasm for process improvement within the organization.

To complete chartering the infrastructure the need for the establishment of Technical Working Groups (TWG) was identified. The role and responsibility of the TWG was defined and included dealing with specific element of process improvement as the initiative progressed. This incorporated the documenting, and assessment of current processes. It was also required to make a meaningful contribution in implementing process improvement.

It was decided after discussions with the sponsor that a mission statement would not be formulated. It was also agreed that the assessor would develop a project plan for the initiative in consultation with the MSG and the SEPG. The assessor would also be responsible for the development of a modified CMM-based appraisal method.

The project plan formally recognised the current and desired states for process improvement in the company. It set priorities for change and it formally outlined the business reasons for the initiative. It laid out a timeframe and highlighted key activities that would have to be carried out to implement the tailored process in keeping with the IDEAL model.

6.2   The Diagnosing Phase

Before meaningful process improvement can take place a company must determine its current level of maturity. „If you don't know where you are, a map won't help" [15]. To that end a CMM-based process assessment was undertaken [1]. As an initial step information was provided to the teams whose process was being assessed describing what the CMM was about and what was involved in a CMM assessment. There was no official rollout meeting for the initiative as the sponsor felt it was unnecessary. This was something the assessor disagreed with, as this offered an ideal opportunity to demonstrate visible management support for the effort.

A Project Manager, two team leaders and three software engineers completed the full CMM maturity questionnaire. Given the complexity of the questionnaire full support was provided to those who required clarification on any of the questionnaires content. On completion of all questionnaires a comprehensive report was complied detailing the results. This report was analyzed and areas highlighted for further research. A document review was undertaken and some queries were answered while others were raised.

Interviews were held to clarify outstanding issues. Seven people were interviewed, a Project Manager, two team leaders and four software engineers. Four of people interviewed had completed the questionnaire. The interviews followed a structured approach and while dealing with outstanding issues also endeavored to define the existing process culture. This broadened the assessment to include areas outside the definition of the CMM, but which directly impacted on the existing process. On completion an interview report was compiled

Each CMM Key Process Area was reviewed in the light of the questionnaire, document review and interview report. A maturity audit report was prepared and a maturity level determined. The outsourcing process was rated at a CMM Maturity Level 1. It was clear that two process cultures existed side by side in the teams reviewed. These cultures were a formal disciplined approach to the process and a more ad hoc, Rapid Application Development (RAD) approach. This was due to the background of the teams involved. The maturity audit report with its specific recommendations was incorporated into the assessment report. The findings were presented to management and the teams to ensure that they were aware of what had been achieved and to prepare them for the next phase.

6.3   The Establishing Phase

Having reviewed the assessment report and analyzed pressing business requirements the Management Steering Group prioritised the establishment of a defect tracking system as an urgent requirement. The template provided by the CMM Level 5 Defect Prevention Key Process Area (KPA) provided guidance on what was required. An implementation plan was prepared which outlined the schedule, roles, milestones, and metrics, tracking and reporting procedures for the initiative.

The Software Engineering Process Group met and undertook the management of the implementation of the Defect Prevention KPA. This was purely a supportive role. The assessor prepared a non-technical translation of the KPA's key practices for presentation to the Technical Working Group (TWG). The SEPG also took responsibility for informing management and staff on a regular basis on the status of the initiative.

The next step was the selection of the TWG. It was agreed that the initial group would be made up of four members, the assessor and three software engineers. Membership of the TWG was to be on a part time position. This would ensure that the TWG members were not divorced from the rest of the organization.

The initial role of the TWG would be to examine the requirements of the KPA. When they had established a clear understanding of them, they would tailor the KPA to meet the specific requirements of the company. When this was complete the group would take responsibility for introducing new procedures, roles, documentation, organize training and ensure the availability of essential infrastructure and resources. Feedback on the progress of the initiative would be presented to the rest of teams on a regular basis through the SEPG.

6.4   The Acting Phase

At the first 4 meeting of the TWG the goals of the initiative were outlined and the need for the establishment of a Defect Prevention Group presented. A presentation was made on the Defect Prevention KPA (CMM Level 5) and the introduction of a Defect Tracking System. Using the Defect Prevention KPA as guide a detailed action plan was drawn up; this included the identification of resources, responsibilities, tasks, and milestones. Measurements to assess the success of the initiative were discussed and agreed, these incorporated the metrics outlined in the implementation plan.

Having a clear understanding of what was required and utilizing the CMM as a template, an effective solution was created. There was no time and more importantly no need, for the development of a best guess solution, cyclical pilot testing and refining. The CMM outlined an effective approach and the knowledge and experience of the TWG confirmed that prior to its implementation. The tailored key practices of the Key Process Area were implemented on a project-by-project basis over a three-month period.

A problem-centred approach was applied in this initiative. If all the activities outlined for the Acting phase had been carried out the time scale required would have had a serious impact on the success of the program. Curtis [16] states, „*Most successful improvement programs begin working with projects to make improvements very early*". This ensures that preliminary positive results are available to management and staff and this encourages support and enthusiasm for continued process improvement. This is particularly important in a SME with limited resources.

Using a software process improvement model like the CMM, which outlines and addresses the achievement of the goals of a mature software organization ensures that a cyclical best guess approach is not required. Tailoring of the IDEAL model to meet the needs of the organization implementing process improvement is strongly recommended [12].

6.5   The Leveraging Phase

Having successfully introduced a Defect Tracking System based on the CMM Defect Prevention KPA it was time to validate and analyze what had been done. The criteria agreed to monitor the performance of the Defect Tracking System was evaluated and reviewed. The level of success achieved in all aspects of the improvement program was assessed. It was determined that the effort had been an overall success and had led to a quantifiable improvement in the operation of the software development process. The MSG, SEPG and TWG had all worked well together and having achieved an initial success it helped to reinforce the value of team effort and support.

While the Sponsor had been committed to the initiative, it became clear that there was a lack of overall senior management support for further process improvement in general. This was hard to understand given the success of the initiative and the minimal cost it incurred. There had been a positive effect on all aspect of the process as a result of the undertaking. The goals of the effort had been closely tied to the overall business strategy and objectives of the organization. Better software was being produced as defects were reduced and tracked back to source allowing preventive and effective action to be taken to stop reoccurrence. As a result of the re-evaluation of management sponsorship further process improvement was put on hold. To leverage from the exercise undertaken, as much material and experience gained was documented and stored. This valuable resource is available to be utilized in future process improvement activities.

7   Conclusion

The unorthodox approach to the CMM undertaken in this project is not ideal but practical. The problem with the Defect Prevention being a Level 5 Key Process Area has been used to criticise the CMM „*Why is defect prevention a Level 5 practice? Defects impact all organisations and their prevention and tracking is an important and necessary task for all organisations to be involved in regardless of their maturity level.*" Bach [17]. Taking this into consideration the implementation of the CMM presented in this project was based on the approach outlined by Bamberger [18].

The use of the IDEAL model made a substantial contribution to the success of the process improvement initiative outlined in this research. The only full time person employed on the initiative was the assessor. The Management Steering Group consisted of only two members, as did the Software Engineering Process Group. Membership of both groups was on a part time basis. The roles that both groups fulfilled provided a substantial contribution to the overall success achieved. When applying the IDEAL model in small to medium sized companies the temptation is to ignore roles like the Management Steering Group. Our research demonstrates that this group is vital and that its inclusion has direct benefits.

The Initiating phase addressed the need for a clear understanding of the initiative. Once that had been determined goals and objectives were defined and put in context with the objectives and business strategy of the organization. The clarity provided by this exercise allowed senior management to make an informed commitment to provide the necessary leadership and resources required for effective process improvement to take place. It also provided senior management with the opportunity to decide at an early stage if the effort would be worthwhile, or if it should be abandoned. The appointment of a committed sponsor ensured that the required resources would be provided and the resistance to change that is encountered in all organizations could be addressed and successfully overcome. The commitment of senior management is key to any successful process improvement initiative and cannot be underestimated.

The Diagnosing phase allowed a baseline to be established of the existing process. It allowed a maturity level to be determined and the strengths and weaknesses of the process were highlighted. This facilitated the development of clear recommendations for current and future improvements. During the Establishing phase changes were outlined and the need for a Defect Tracking System prioritized.   The Defect Prevention Key Process Area was utilized as a template for process improvement based on the business needs of the organization.   An implementation plan was prepared and the Technical Working Group was established.

In the Acting phase the Technical Working Group's approach and available time scale did not allow or require the development of a best guess solution. Neither did it require the use of pilot testing and further refinement prior to implementing the improvement strategy.   The CMM provided an excellent solution. The Technical Working Group did not divorce itself from the rest of the organization. Membership was a part-time role and change was introduced on a project-by-project basis. Based on the Defect Prevention KPA the Technical Working Group determined the requirements of the organization. The implementation of the Key Process Area was tailored to meet those defined requirements. If all the activities outlined in the Acting phases had been implemented it would have had a negative impact on the process improvement effort. This fact was identified at an early stage and the implementation of IDEAL model modified accordingly.

In his workshop presentation at the ICSE 2000 Curtis [5] outlined the problems encountered utilizing the IDEAL model. The problem as he defined it is what he termed „*the action teams separation from development work*". It takes too long to set priorities, develop and pilot its approach and implement process improvements. When improvements are finally implemented it is too late, both management and staff have lost faith in the improvement program. This paper concurs with those findings and has been researched independently of his work. We would not suggest that there should be a quick fix approach, but the CMM offers clear guidelines where and how improvements can be made. The CMM template should be utilized to ensure timely and effective process improvement takes place.

The Leveraging phase provides an excellent opportunity to evaluate what has been achieved and opportunity to learn from work, which has been completed. The activities of the initiative, which has been undertaken, are reviewed and analyzed. The achievement of goals and objectives are assessed. Lessons learned are recorded for future reference. The evaluation of continued sponsorship is very important. The IDEAL model quite rightly stresses the importance of continued sponsorship and support of senior management for effective process improvement to be undertaken in further iterations of the model.

In summary the IDEAL model provided a good framework for process improvement to take place within the SME we researched. That stated, we would stress that the model should be tailored to fit the needs of the organization utilizing it [19]. The need for tailoring is clearly understood and recommended by McFeely [12] who states, when referring to the IDEAL model „*One Size Does Not Fit All!*" and „*SPI managers must tailor the guide to their particular situation*".

The layers of management, supervision and support provided by the IDEAL model encouraged effective process change and improvement. The model did not require the establishment of a bureaucratic system to be effective and offered a clear path for continuous process improvement to take place. We conclude that the modified IDEAL model worked.

The Defect Tracking System introduced as a result of this effort led to a large reduction in the number of defects produced. Defects that do arise are logged, corrected, tracked back to source and discussed. Preventive action is taken to ensure that where possible such defects do not arise again, or are identified at an earlier stage in the process. The level of rework has been reduced; milestone and deadlines have been met on a more consistent basis. Both teams are much more aware of quality as each team member spends time working as part of the Defect Tracking Team. These improvements have been achieved with the support and guidance of the IDEAL model. The CMM provided the template while the modified IDEAL model provided the framework to implement it.

In our view the tailored IDEAL model is a useful framework for software companies who wish to implement process improvement. The Initiating, Diagnosing, Establishing and Learning phases are of particular value. If the activities of the Acting phase are adapted to the needs of the organization then required results can be achieved.

References

1. Casey Valentine B., The Application of a CMM Based Process Improvement Initiative to a Remotely Located Tool Based Software Development Environment, University of Limerick, Ireland, (October 2000)
2. Richardson Ita, SPI Model: What Characteristics Are Required for Small Software Development Companies?, Software Quality – ECSQ 2002 Quality Connection – 7th European Conference on Software Quality Helsinki, Finland 2002 Proceedings, Springer (2002)
3. Susman G. & Evered R., An Assessment of the Scientific Merits of Action Research, The Administrative Science Quarterly, Vol. 23, Issue 4. Pages: 582 - 603 (1978)
4. Baskerville Richard L., Distinguishing Action Research from Participative Case Studies, Journal of Systems and Information Technology, Volume 1, Issue 1, Pages 25 - 45 (March 1997)
5. Curtis Bill, T11 Software Process Improvement: Best Practices and Lesson Learned. Tutorial Notes, Pages: 4 –11, ICSE 2000, Limerick, Ireland, (June 2000)
6. Jalote Pankaj, CMM in Practice, Addision-Wesley, (2000)
7. Paulk Mark C., A Comparison of ISO 9001 and the Capability Maturity Model for Software, Technical Report CMU/SEI-94-TR-12 ESC-TR-94-12, SEI, (July 1994)
8. O'Tinney Michael, Comparing ISO 9000, Malcom Baldrige and the SEI CMM for Software, Prentice Hall, (1997)
9. Zahran Sami, Software Process Improvement, Practical Guidelines for Business Success, Addison- Wesley, (1998)
10. Varkoi T. K. & Mäkinen T. K., Case Study of CMM and SPICE Comparison in Software Process Assessment, Engineering and Technology Management, 1998. Pioneering New Technologies: Management Issues and Challenges in the Third Millennium. IEMC '98 Proceedings, International Conference, Pages: 477 – 482, (11-13 Oct. 1998)
11. Dunaway Donna K., CMM Based Appraisal for Internal Process Improvement (CBA-IPI) Team Members Handbook, CUM/SEI-96-HB-005, (May 1996)
12. McFeeley Bob, IDEAL: A Users Guide for Software Process Improvement, Handbook, CMU/SEI-96-HB-001, (February 1996)
13. Paulk Mark C., Charles Webber, V., Curtis Bill, Chrissis Mary Beth, The Capability Maturity Model, Guidelines for Improving the Software Process Addison, Wesley (1995) (8th Reprint November 1997)
14. Gremba Jennifer, Myers Chuck, The IDEAL Model: A practical guide for Improvement, Bridge, Issue 3, (1997)
15. Humphrey Watt S., Managing the Software Process, Addison Wesley, (1989)
16. Curtis Bill, From MCC to CMM: Technology Transfer Bright and Dim, Proceedings of the 22nd International Conference on Software Engineering, Pages: 521 – 530, (June 2000)
17. Bach James, The Immaturity of the CMM, American Programmer, September, (1994)

18. Judy Bamberger, Software Realities, Essence of the Capability Maturity Model, Computer Volume 30 Issue 6, Pages 112-114, June (1997)
19. Kautz Karlheinz, Hansen Henrik Westergaard, Thaysen Kim, Applying and Adjusting a Software Process Improvement Model in Practice: The Use of the IDEAL Model in Small Software Enterprise, ICSE 2000, Limerick, Ireland, Pages: 626 - 633 (June 2000)

On Software Maintenance Process Improvement
Based on Code Clone Analysis

Yoshiki Higo[1], Yasushi Ueda[1], Toshihro Kamiya[2],
Shinji Kusumoto[1], and Katsuro Inoue[1]

[1] Graduate School of Information Science and Technology, Osaka University
Toyonaka, Osaka 560-8531, Japan
Phone: +81-6-6850-6571, Fax: +81-6-6850-6574
{y-higo,y-ueda,kusumoto,inoue}@ist.osaka-u.ac.jp
[2] PRESTO, Japan Science and Technology Corp.
Current Address: Graduate School of Information Science and Technology
Osaka University
Toyonaka, Osaka 560-8531, Japan
Phone: +81-6-6850-6571, Fax: +81-6-6850-6574
kamiya@ist.osaka-u.ac.jp

Abstract. Maintaining software systems is getting more complex and difficult task. Code clone is one of the factors that make software maintenance more difficult. A code clone is a code portion in source files that is identical or similar to another. If some faults are found in a code clone, it is necessary to correct the faults in its all code clones. We have developed a maintenance support environment, Gemini, which provides the user with the useful functions to analyze the code clones and modify them. However, through case studies, several problems were reported. That is, the clones provided by Gemini were not appropriate to merge into one module. In this paper, we intend to extend the functionality of Gemini to cope with the problems. Finally, we apply the extended Gemini to several software and evaluate the applicability of the new functions.

1   Introduction

As the size and the complexity of software increase, it becomes important to develop high-quality software cost-effectively within a specified period. Software process improvement is one of the promising methods to attain it.

Recently, it is pointed out that maintenance phase is the most expensive one in the entire software development process. Many research studies have reported that large software companies spent a lot of cost to maintaining the existing systems. Maintenance of software system is defined as modification of a software product after delivery to correct faults, to improve performance or other attributes, or to adapt the products to a modified environment [20].

M. Oivo and S. Komi-Sirviö (Eds.): PROFES 2002, LNCS 2559, pp. 185-197, 2002.
© Springer-Verlag Berlin Heidelberg 2002

Code clone is one of the factors that make software maintenance more difficult [8]. A code clone is a code portion in source files that is identical or similar to another. Clones are introduced because of various reasons such as reusing code by `copy-and-paste' and so on. Code clones make the source files very hard to modify consistently. For example, when a fault is found in one clone, it must be carefully modified all the clones. So, effective code clone detection will support the improvement of software maintenance process. In order to detect the code clones effectively, various clone detection methods have been proposed.

We have developed a maintenance support environment, Gemini, which provides the user with the useful functions to analyze the code clones and modify them [22]. CCFinder [13] is one of the components of Gemini and used to detect code clones. Gemini primarily provides two diagrams: scatter plot and metrics graph. The scatter plot graphically shows the locations of code clones among source codes. The metrics graph shows metric value of each clone and has a feature to identify the distinctive code clones. Using the diagrams, we expected that maintenance process can be improved.

We have delivered Gemini to several software companies and evaluated it through case studies. In the case studies, we have received several practical problems. First, one has been appeared in applying Gemini to refactoring activities [8]. Usually, code clones are merged into one module (procedure, function, macro etc). The clones detected by Gemini were not appropriate to be merged, since it detects the maximal code clones that often include excessive tokens that should be omitted in merging the clones into one routine. Second is one how to identify the modified code portions as clone. As described above, code clone is introduced copy-and-paste programming. However, in most case, the copied-and-pasted code portion is not used as it was. Usually, some statements are inserted to the code portion or deleted from it. The practitioners in the company want to extract such modified code clones (called gapped clone) but Gemini cannot find them.

In this paper, we intend to solve the above issues to extend the functionality of Gemini. For the former issue, we have added the new function to extract the part of code clone that is easy to merge one module. For the latter issue, we propose a method to show all the candidates of gapped code clones. As spaces are limited, we mainly explain the first topics. Finally, we apply Gemini to several software and evaluate the applicability of the proposed method.

2   Code Clone Analysis

2.1   Definitions on Code Clone

A clone relation is defined as an equivalence relation (i.e., reflexive, transitive, and symmetric relation) on code portions [13]. A clone relation holds between two code portions if (and only if) they are the same sequences (Sequences are sometimes original character strings, strings without white spaces, sequences of token type, and transformed token sequences.). For a given clone relation, a pair of code portions is called clone pair if the clone relation holds between the portions. An equivalence class of clone relation is called clone class. That is, a clone class is a maximal set of code portions in which a clone relation holds between any pair of code portions.

A code portion in a clone class of a program is called a code clone or simply a clone.

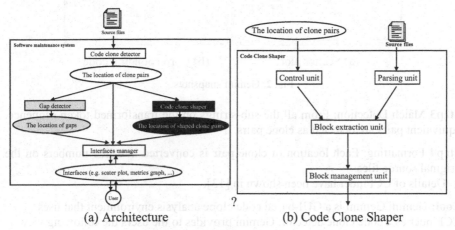

(a) Architecture   (b) Code Clone Shaper

Fig. 1. Overview of Gemini

2.2   Maintenance Support Environment: Gemini

In [21], we have developed a maintenance support environment based on code clone analysis (called Gemini). Figure 1(a) shows the system architecture. In Figure 1(a), the gray parts (a gray quadrilateral and ellipse) have been proposed in [22] and the black parts (, which is enlarged in Figure 1(b).) will be proposed in Section 3 in this paper. Basically, Gemini delivers the source files to the code clone detector, CCFinder [13], and then shows the information of the detected code clones to the user through various GUIs.

In this Section, we briefly explain the characteristic of CCFinder and Gemini.

Tool: CCFinder CCFinder detects code clones from programs and outputs the locations of the clone pairs on the programs. The length of minimum clone is set by user before.

Clone detection of CCFinder is a process in which the input is source files and the output is clone pairs. The process consists of four steps:

Step1 Lexical analysis: Each line of source files is divided into tokens corresponding to a lexical rule of the programming language. The tokens of all source files are concatenated into a single token sequence, so that finding clones in multiple files is performed in the same way as single file analysis.

Step2 Transformation: The token sequence is transformed, i.e., tokens are added, removed, or changed based on the transformation rules that aims at regularization of identifiers and identification of structures.   Then, each identifier related to types, variables, and constants is replaced with a special token. This replacement makes code portions with different variable names clone pairs.

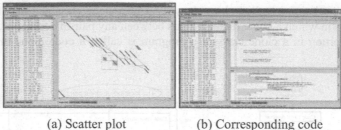

(a) Scatter plot   (b) Corresponding code

Fig. 2. Gemini snapshots

Step3 Match Detection: From all the sub-strings on the transformed token sequence, equivalent pairs are detected as clone pairs.

Step4 Formatting: Each location of clone pair is converted into line numbers on the original source files.

Details of CCFinder have been shown in [13].

Tool: Gemini Gemini is a GUI-based code clone analysis environment that uses CCFinder as a code clone detector. Gemini provides to the users the following view windows that enable an interactive code clone analysis:

- Scatter plot view,
- Metric graph view, and
- Source code view.

Scatter plot view shows visually where clone pairs exist in source files. It is very effective mechanism in early phase of code clone analysis since the state of distribution of code clone can be grasped at a glance. In the view, user can select clone pairs by mouse dragging. Figure 2(a) shows an example of scatter plot view. The detail of scatter plot will be described later.

Metric graph view is designed for enabling the users to select clones by the quantitative characteristics of them. In metric graph view, user can select clone pairs or classes by the values of metric for each clone class to easily select the distinctive ones.

The source code view works cooperating the scatter plot view on the metric graph view. The user can obtain the actual source code corresponding to clones selected in the other views. Figure 2(b) shows an example of source code view.

Scatter plot Figure 3 shows examples of scatter plot. Both the vertical and horizontal axes represent code portions of source files. The following two sequences are used as sample code portions in the scatter plot.

code portion X: ``ABCEFBCDEBCD'',
code portion Y: ``ABCEFBCDEBCD''

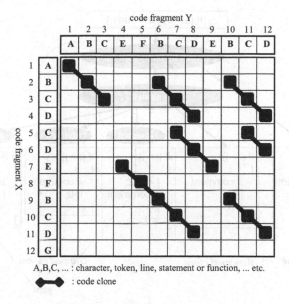

A,B,C, ... : character, token, line, statement or function, ... etc.

◆━━◆ : code clone

Fig. 3. Scatter plot of code clones

Here, symbols "A", "B", "C", ... are code portions in a unit such as character, token, line, statement, function, etc (In Gemini, it is token). In Figure 3, each small black square means that corresponding two elements on the two axes are the same. So, a clone pair is shown as a diagonal line segment. If the same code portions are arranged on the two axes, naturally, a diagonal line from the upper left to the lower right is drawn since such dot means comparison of token with itself, and the dots are symmetrical with a diagonal line.

The state of distribution of code clone can be grasped at a glance. However, as for large-scale software in which there are many code clones, it is very difficult to decide which plot (that is code clone) in the huge scatter plot should be kept our eyes on. That is, if many files are located on the axis of coordinate in naive order, such as alphabetical order with file name, the distribution of code clones is occasionally spread widely without conspicuous deviation. So, Gemini has the function to sort the order of files on the two axes. It causes code clones not to distribute all over a scatter plot as much as possible. As a basic idea, the more code clones exist among two source files, the nearer the files are to be located in each axis. The details are described in [21].

3 Proposed Method

3.1 Problems Found in Case Studies

We have applied Gemini (and CCFinder) to several commercial software products. In the case studies, the users reported some problems as feedback. Among them, the following two problems are repeatedly reported and serious ones.

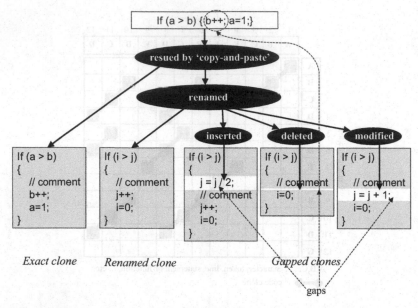

Fig. 4. Gapped Clone

As for the first one, in the case of `copy-and-paste' reuse, the developers usually do not reuse the code portion as it was but partially modifies and then reuse it. Moreover, in the modification, they do not only replace the user-defined identifiers in the code portion but also modify it. For example, additional statements would be inserted into it. Thus, some differences exist between the original code portion and the copied-and-pasted one. Here, we call the each difference ``gap" and such code clone as ``gapped clone". From a viewpoint of how to reuse code, we classify code clone into five categories shown in Figure 4. Then, CCFinder can only detect exact clones and renamed clones.

In such case, the developers can subjectively identify the code clones even if they include some gaps among them. On the other hand, CCFinder detects the clone as several short code clones separately. Or,? since the minimum length of a code clone must be set in CCFinder beforehand, if the code portion is too short, CCFinder does not identify it as a code clone. Conversely, if we set a small value to the minimum length, then many code clones are detected and the information is practically useless.

In [22], we proposed the solution of this problem. In the paper, we could refer to a certain set of gapped clones by representing visually exact/renamed clones and gaps themselves on scatter plot. In fact, the complexity of detecting all gapped clones one by one is massive (square of number of exact/renamed clones). So, we took the alternative solution.

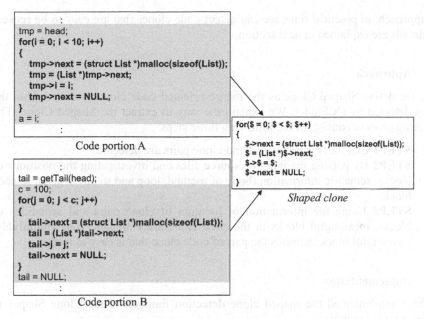

```
tmp = head;
for(i = 0; i < 10; i++)
{
    tmp->next = (struct List *)malloc(sizeof(List));
    tmp = (List *)tmp->next;
    tmp->i = i;
    tmp->next = NULL;
}
a = i;
        :
```
Code portion A

```
for($ = 0; $ < $; $++)
{
    $->next = (struct List *)malloc(sizeof(List));
    $ = (List *)$->next;
    $->$ = $;
    $->next = NULL;
}
```
Shaped clone

```
        :
tail = getTail(head);
c = 100;
for(j = 0; j < c; j++)
{
    tail->next = (struct List *)malloc(sizeof(List));
    tail = (List *)tail->next;
    tail->j = j;
    tail->next = NULL;
}
tail = NULL;
        :
```
Code portion B

Fig. 5. Example of merging two code portions

Next, as for the second problem, if we detect code clones for refactoring [8], sometimes semantically cohesive ones has more important meaning than maximal (just longest in local) ones although the former may be shorter than the latter. In our experiments, we found many clones that have not only primary logic statements but also the other coincidental clone statements before (and/or behind) them, since simple statements, such as assignment or variable declaration, tend to become clones coincidentally. Figure 5 shows an example. In Figure 5, there are two code portions A and B from a program, and the code portions with hatching are maximal clones among them. In code portion A, some data are substituted to list data structure from the head successively. In code portion B, they are done so from the tail successively. There is a common logic between these two processes that is code portions handling list data structure (in for block). However, before and behind for block there are sentences that are identified as a part of code clones coincidentally. It can be said that such blocks without coincidental portions are preferred to whole portions with hatching in the figure in the viewpoint of refactoring.

In [14] and [15], they detect semantically cohesive code clones using program dependence graph (PDG) for the purpose of procedure extraction and so on. However, currently, there are no examples of the application of their approaches to large-scale software since the cost to create PDG is very high. On the other hand, the clone detection process of CCFinder is very fast but only lexical analysis is performed. So, the detected clones are just maximal and not always semantically cohesive. Hence, it is necessary for the user of CCFinder to extract semantically cohesive portions manually from the maximal.

To solve this problem, we take a two-step approach in which we firstly detect maximal clones and secondly extract semantically cohesive ones from the results. By this approach, in practical time, we can detect code clones that are easy to be reused. The details are explained in next section.

3.2   Approach

Here, we define Shaped Clone as the merge-oriented code clone extracted from the clones detected by CCFinder. We explain the way to extract the Shaped Clone. The extracting process consists of the following three steps:

> **STEP1** CCFinder is performed and clone pairs are detected.
> **STEP2** By parsing the inputted source files and investigating the positions of blocks, semantic information (body of method, loop and so on) is given to each block.
> **STEP3** Using the information of location of clone pairs and semantics of blocks, meaningful blocks in the code clone are extracted. Here, intuitively, meaningful block indicates the part of code clone that is easy to merge.

3.3   Implementation

We have implemented the shaped clone detection function (Code Clone Shaper in Figure 1(a)) in Gemini.

The size of the function is about 10KLOC and implemented in Java. The target source files are also Java programs.

We explain the implementation of the proposed shaped clone detection method. The implementation includes the following units shown in Figure 1(b):

- Control unit
- Parsing unit
- Block extraction unit
- Block management unit

Control unit Control unit invokes the Parsing unit, Block extraction unit, and Block management unit through reading the code clone information (output from CCFinder).

Parsing unit Parsing unit conducts lexical and syntax analysis for the inputted source files. Here, we define **Block** as code portion enclosed by a pair of brackets. So we use only the result of lexical analysis in this paper and the information about syntax will be taken into the consideration in our future research. Then, the location information of the extracted token is stored. It is implemented using JavaCC [11].

Block extraction unit Block extraction unit extracts the block from the code clones detected by CCFinder using the stored data and analysis results from CCFinder.

Block management unit Block management unit puts the blocks extracted by Block extraction unit in an appropriate order. It is necessary to obtain the consistency of the data used in Gemini.

4   Case Study

In order to evaluate the usefulness of the proposed shaped clone detection method, we have applied it to famous Java software: ANTLR [2] and Ant [1].

ANTLR (ANother Tool for Language Recognition,) is a language tool that provides a framework for constructing recognizers, compilers, and translators from grammatical descriptions containing C++ or Java actions.

Ant is another Java based build tool. Instead of a model where Ant is extended with shell-based commands, it is extended using Java classes. Instead of writing shell commands, the configuration files are XML based calling out a target tree where various tasks get executed. Each task is run by an object, which implements a particular task interface.

In the evaluation, we have applied Gemini without using Code Clone Shaper and Gemini with it to the data, independently. Then, we compare the results. In this case study, we have set the minimum length of a code clone as 50 tokens.

4.1   ANTLR

ANTLR includes 239 files and the size is about 44KLOC (see in Table 1). Figure 6(a) shows the results of applying the Gemini without Code Clone Shaper. You can see that there are many clones in ANTLR. Here, we can find 338574 clone pairs and 1072 clone classes. So, it is very difficult to extract the clones that can be merged into one module.

On the other hand, Figure 6(b) shows the results of applying the Gemini with Code Clone Shaper. You can see that non-meaningful clones are omitted. Here, we can find 972 clone pairs and 142 clone classes. The reduction rate of the number of clone pairs and clone classes are about 1/350 and 1/8, respectively (see in Figure 6(c)).

Then, we checked the part labeled A in Figure 6(b) and found distinctive code clones. There are 28 clones and each of them includes 82 tokens. We can easily merge the clones to one method by adding two parameters shown in Figure 7. Code portions on the left side are clones provided by Gemini with Code Clone Shaper. If they are merge into one method, it will be like the code portion on the right side.

4.2   Ant

Next, we applied Gemini to Ant. Ant includes 508 files and the size is 141KLOC (see in Table 1). Figure 8(a) shows the results of applying the Gemini without Code Clone Shaper. You can see that code clones spread over the scatter plot. Here, 12033 clone pairs and 856 clone classes were detected. On the other hand, Figure 8(b) shows the results of applying the Gemini with Code Clone Shaper. Here, 103 clone pairs and 53 clone classes were detected.

Table 1. Source code size

	Number of files	Lines of code	Number of tokens
ANTLR	239	43548	140802
Ant	508	141254	221203

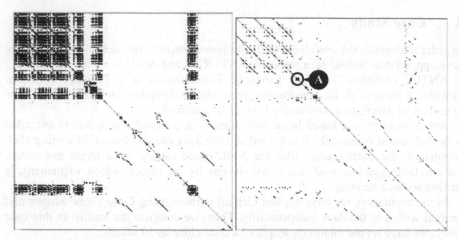

(a) Result without Code Clone Shaper   (b) Result with Code Clone Shaper

	Without code clone shaper	With code clone shaper
Number of clone pairs	338574	972
Number of clone classes	1072	142

(c) Number of clones

Fig. 6. Result of ANTLR analysis

You can see that most of the clones are omitted and the part labeled B stands out. Figure 8(d) shows the actual code clones of it. We found seven separate methods in the several files. Since the methods inherit the same super class, we can remove the clones easily by moving the method to the super class.

Also, the reduction rate of the number of clone pairs and clone classes are about 1/120 and 1/16, respectively (see in Figure 8(c)).

5   Conclusion

In this paper, we have extended the functionality of a maintenance support environment Gemini to easily merge code clones into one code portion. We have applied Gemini with Code Clone Shaper to two practical Java software ANTLR and Ant. By using Code Clone Shaper, we can dramatically reduce the number of clone pairs and clone classes. The clones removed by Code Clone Shaper have no meaningful block (not including the pair of brackets) and are difficult to merge as one method. Moreover, as shown in Figures 7 and 8(d), the selected clones are easy to merge into one code portion. So, we consider that Gemini achieves the evolution to support the maintenance activity more efficiently.

Of course, we have to continue applying Gemini to actual software maintenance process and improving/refining the functionality.

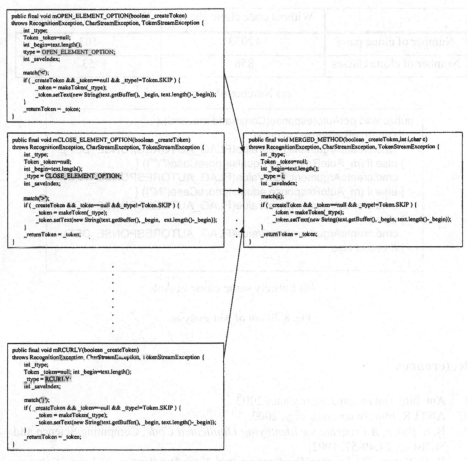

```
public final void mOPEN_ELEMENT_OPTION(boolean _createToken)
throws RecognitionException, CharStreamException, TokenStreamException {
    int _ttype;
    Token _token=null;
    int _begin=text.length();
    _ttype = OPEN_ELEMENT_OPTION;
    int _saveIndex;

    match('<');
    if ( _createToken && _token==null && _ttype!=Token.SKIP ) {
        _token = makeToken(_ttype);
        _token.setText(new String(text.getBuffer(), _begin, text.length()-_begin));
    }
    _returnToken = _token;
}
```

```
public final void mCLOSE_ELEMENT_OPTION(boolean _createToken)
throws RecognitionException, CharStreamException, TokenStreamException {
    int _ttype;
    Token _token=null;
    int _begin=text.length();
    _ttype = CLOSE_ELEMENT_OPTION;
    int _saveIndex;

    match('>');
    if ( _createToken && _token==null && _ttype!=Token.SKIP ) {
        _token = makeToken(_ttype);
        _token.setText(new String(text.getBuffer(), _begin, ext.length()-_begin));
    }
    _returnToken = _token;
}
```

```
public final void MERGED_METHOD(boolean _createToken,int i,char c)
throws RecognitionException, CharStreamException, TokenStreamException {
    int _ttype;
    Token _token=null;
    int _begin=text.length();
    _ttype = i;
    int _saveIndex;

    match(c);
    if ( _createToken && _token==null && _ttype!=Token.SKIP ) {
        _token = makeToken(_ttype);
        _token.setText(new String(text.getBuffer(), _begin, text.length()-_begin));
    }
    _returnToken = _token;
}
```

```
public final void mRCURLY(boolean _createToken)
throws RecognitionException, CharStreamException, TokenStreamException {
    int _ttype;
    Token _token=null; int _begin=text.length();
    _ttype = RCURLY;
    int _saveIndex;

    match('}');
    if ( _createToken && _token==null && _ttype!=Token.SKIP ) {
        _token = makeToken(_ttype);
        _token.setText(new String(text.getBuffer(), _begin, text.length()-_begin));
    }
    _returnToken = _token;
}
```

Fig. 7. Merged clone sample in ANTLR

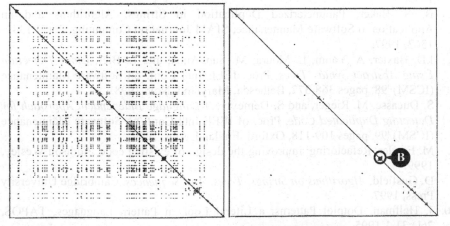

(a) Result without Code Clone Shaper   (b) Result with Code Clone Shaper

	Without code clone shaper	With code clone shaper
Number of clone pairs	12033	103
Number of clone classes	856	53

(c) Number of clones

```
public void getAutoresponse(Commandline cmd) {
    if (m_AutoResponse == null) {
        cmd.createArgument().setValue(FLAG_AUTORESPONSE_DEF);
    } else if (m_AutoResponse.equalsIgnoreCase("Y")) {
        cmd.createArgument().setValue(FLAG_AUTORESPONSE_YES);
    } else if (m_AutoResponse.equalsIgnoreCase("N")) {
        cmd.createArgument().setValue(FLAG_AUTORESPONSE_NO);
    } else {
        cmd.createArgument().setValue(FLAG_AUTORESPONSE_DEF);
    } // end of else
}
```

(d) Entirely same clone in Ant

Fig. 8. Result of Ant analysis

References

1. Ant, http://jakarta.apache.org/ant/, 2002.
2. ANTLR, http://www.antlr.org/, 2000.
3. B. S. Baker, *A Program for Identifying Duplicated Code*, Computing Science and Statistics, 24:49-57, 1992.
4. B. S. Baker, *On Finding Duplication and Near-Duplication in Large Software Systems*, Proc. IEEE Working Conf. on Reverse Engineering, pages 86-95, July 1995.
5. B. S. Baker, Parameterized Duplication in Strings: Algorithms and an Application to Software Maintenance, SIAM Journal on Computing, 26(5):1343-1362, 1997.
6. I.D. Baxter, A. Yahin, L. Moura, M. Sant'Anna, and L. Bier, *Clone Detection Using Abstract Syntax Trees*, Proc. IEEE Int'l Conf. on Software Maintenance (ICSM) '98, pages 368-377, Bethesda, Maryland, Nov. 1998.
7. S. Ducasse, M. Rieger, and S. Demeyer, *A Language Independent Approach for Detecting Duplicated Code*, Proc. of IEEE Int'l Conf. on Software Maintenance (ICSM) '99, pages 109-118, Oxford, England, Aug. 1999.
8. M. Fowler, Refactoring: improving the design of existing code, Addison Wesley, 1999.
9. D. Gusfield, *Algorithms on Strings, Trees, And Sequences*, Cambridge University Press, 1997.
10. J. Helfman, Dotplot Patterns: a Literal Look at Pattern Languages, TAPOS, 2(1):31-1,1995.

11. JavaCC, http://www.webgain.com/products/java_cc/, 2000.
12. J. H. Johnson, *Identifying Redundancy in Source Code using Fingerprints*, Proc. of CASCON '93, pages 171-183, Toronto, Ontario, 1993.
13. T. Kamiya, S. Kusumoto, and K. Inoue, *CCFinder: A multi-linguistic token-based code clone detection system for large scale source code*, IEEE Transactions on Software Engineering, 28(7):654-670, 2002.
14. R. Komondoor and S. Horwitz, *Using slicing to identify duplication in source code*, Proc. of the 8th International Symposium on Static Analysis, Paris, France, July 16-18, 2001.
15. Jens Krinke, *Identifying Similar Code with Program Dependence Graphs*, Proc. of the 8th Working Conference on Reverse Engineering, 2001.
16. J. Mayland, C. Leblanc, and E. M. Merlo, *Experiment on the Automatic Detection of Function Clones in a Software System Using Metrics*, Proc. of IEEE Int'l Conf. on Software Maintenance (ICSM) '96, pages 244-253, Monterey, California, Nov. 1996.
17. L. Prechelt, G. Malpohl, M. Philippsen, *Finding plagiarisms among a set of programs with JPlag, submitted to Journal of Universal Computer Science*, Nov. 2001, taken from http://wwwipd.ira.uka.de/~prechelt/Biblio/.
18. M. Rieger, S. Ducasse, Visual Detection of Duplicated Code, 1998.
19. Duploc, http://www.iam.unibe.ch/~rieger/duploc/, 1999.
20. Pigoski T. M, Maintenance, *Encyclopedia of Software Engineering*, 1, John Wiley & Sons, 1994.
21. Y. Ueda, T. Kamiya, S. Kusumoto, K. Inoue, *Gemini: Maintenance Support Environment Based on Code Clone Analysis*, 8th International Symposium on Software Metrics, pages 67-76, June 4-7, 2002.
22. Y. Ueda, T. Kamiya, S. Kusumoto, K. Inoue, *On Detection of Gapped Code Clones using Gap Locations*, 9th Asia-Pacific Software Engineering Conference, 2002, (to appear).
23. S. W. L. Yip and T. Lam, *A software maintenance survey*, Proc. of APSEC '94, pages 70-79, 1994.

Is Your Project Ready for Time-to-Market Focus?

Janne Järvinen[1] and Jouni Jartti[2]

[1] Solid Information Technology
Merimiehenkatu 36 D, Helsinki, FIN-00150, Finland
janne.jarvinen@solidtech.com
[2] Nokia Research Center
Itämerenkatu 11-13, FIN-00180, Finland
jouni.jartti@nokia.com

Abstract. There are many factors affecting the Time-To-Market (TTM) of a software project. A panel of experienced Finnish software professionals has produced an Excel-based questionnaire to gauge TTM-readiness of a software project. This paper studies not only the questionnaire but also the process of its construction, i.e. the means to capture expert knowledge in an intercompany cooperation network. The work has been based on the work done in the Esprit/PROFES project on Product-Process Dependencies. The emerging ISO 15504 standard was used as the framework for the questionnaire.

1 Introduction

Software intensive systems increasingly provide the competitive edge for companies. Therefore, business often mounts pressure on software projects to finish faster and faster. Few projects, however, systematically chart the potential impact and requirements of a Time-To-Market (TTM) critical project. According to our findings there are factors that can influence the outcome of the project. These include not only theoretical and technical aspects of the software development work but also practical aspects relating to work environment and team dynamics. There are probably many other factors as well but our decidedly limited scope prevented us from spending too much time in all facets of TTM. The focus was to find the most noteworthy TTM – related factors as seen by the expert members of the KOTEL TR12 team representing a limited sample of the embedded software industry in Finland.

The paper is structured as follows: Chapter 2 clarifies the background for this work and introduces the various standards, methods and organizations related to this study. Chapter 3 describes the actual work done to discover factors that were considered relevant for TTM. Chapter 4 records the main findings along with experiences and lessons learned, and Chapter 5 summarizes the paper.

M. Oivo and S. Komi-Sirviö (Eds.): PROFES 2002, LNCS 2559, pp. 198-206, 2002.
© Springer-Verlag Berlin Heidelberg 2002

2   Background

This chapter introduces the main concepts related to this study. In addition, a brief background of the KOTEL TR 12 working group is attached.

2.1   Product-Process Dependencies (PPD)

There are dependencies between product and the process that is used to create the product. These relationships are not often acknowledged nor systematically collected. Industrial experiences from the PROFES project [4] indicate that process improvement can be better focused by explicitly modelling these dependencies. Figure 1 describes an example PPD from the PROFES User Manual [10]. The example claims that software design inspections can influence product reliability.

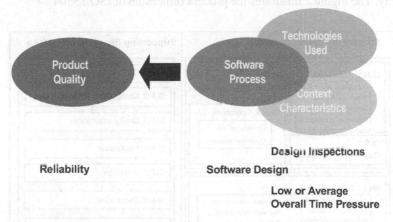

Reliability   **Software Design**

Design Inspections

Low or Average
Overall Time Pressure

Fig. 1. An example of Product-Process Dependency

The three main aspects of PPDs shown on the right side of Figure 1 can be characterized as follows [11]:

- *Process impact on product quality*
  The most high-level information contained in a PPD model is the impact of a process on a product quality. An example is that the software architecture design phase is particularly relevant for assuring high product reliability.
- *Technology impact on product quality*
  More detailed information is provided, when the PPD model also refers to a technology such as software inspections. For instance, it can express that software inspections are a good candidate technology for software architecture design, if high reliability of the software product is to be assured.
- *Context impact on technology application*
  The most comprehensive information is provided, when the PPD model also contains a context model. It describes in which context situations a technology can be expected to have particular impact on a certain product quality.

This division of PPD views was used to understand and classify the TTM -related factors found in this study, which actually spanned all three main PPD views. No actual PPD models were constructed but the findings as a set of TTM –related factors give a basis for defining explicit PPD models. See more information on PPDs from the following references ([9], [10], [11]). Read also the most recent developments in Product-Process Dependencies [3], which were scoped out from this study for practical purposes.

2.2   ISO 15504

ISO 15504 is a framework for software process assessment. The reference model in Part 2 of the proposed standard [7] contains a process dimension with best-practice definitions of software processes and a capability dimension with six levels of process capability. The Figure 2 illustrates the process dimension of ISO 15504:

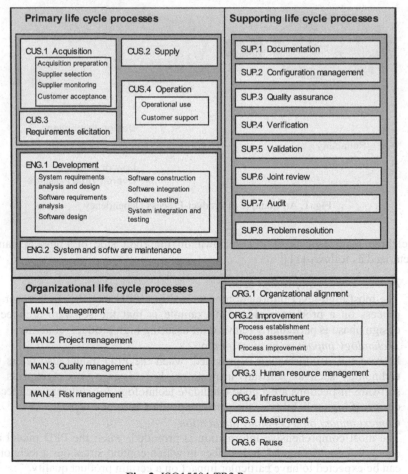

Fig. 2. ISO15504-TR2 Processes

For the interest of the KOTEL TR12 TTM study only the process dimension of ISO 15504 is of interest as the definitions of the ISO 15504 processes were used to classify TTM –related factors. Process capability was left outside of the scope of the study but it seems obvious that process capability has an impact to TTM as this is one of the fundamental assertions of the process capability movement (see e.g. [5]), so a further investigation of TTM and process capability is necessary.

2.3   Time-to-Market

Number of studies exists to understand factors that influence Time-To-Market. A DoD funded state-of-the-art report [12] on SPI strategies defines PSP [6] as the most significant factor for reducing cycle time. Benguria et al. [2] depend on surveys done at Insead and draw on experiences from European VASIE repository and MEPROS project to distill the most significant TTM factors:

- Requirements non-volatility
- Preventive actions
- Problem resolution management
- Software configuration management
- Project management & track

These are to a good degree consistent with the PROFES findings [11], where the following processes were found to be most significant for TTM:

- Software Implementation and Testing
- Software Integration and Testing
- System Integration and Testing
- Project Management
- Risk Management
- Configuration Management

The KOTEL TR 12 study on TTM –factors decided to adopt the same framework as PROFES for classifying the processes, and approach the subject from the perspective of an individual software project related to embedded systems development having TTM as the primary project goal. Time-to-Market was characterized as the capability of a software project to meet an aggressive (but realistic) development time estimate. No specific information on previous TTM analyses was given to the expert group of software professionals involved in this study.

2.4   KOTEL TR 12 Working Group

KOTEL (Association for Cooperation for Research and Development of Electronics) is a cooperation network of Finnish companies related to the development of electronics and software intensive products. The aim of KOTEL is to promote quality, reliability and economy in the design, manufacture, acquisition and maintenance of electronic components, equipment, systems and software. TR 12 is a KOTEL working group specializing on software engineering. The cooperation of TR 12 bases on voluntary work of the member companies on mutually interesting topics. According to TR 12 members Time-To-Market focus has emerged as a hot topic in software intensive product development in the industry. Hence, TR 12 undertook the work to investigate factors affecting software development under tight time constraints.

3   Group Work for PPD Discovery

The KOTEL TR 12 group was interested in gaining a better understanding of what does it mean in practice to have a Time-To-Market (TTM) focus for a software project, and what factors contribute to the successful attainment of a TTM goal. After an introduction of PROFES and PPD principles the TR12 team decided to do a study on the factors affecting TTM. The intention was to formulate findings in a form of a questionnaire so that the results of the study could be re-used easily. The following general steps were traversed during the study:

- Introduction
- Brainstorming
- Refining
- Packaging (including piloting of the questionnaire)
- Distribution

The first task was to share the insights and practical experiences among the expert group using a simple structured brainstorming technique. The plan was to uncover as many thoughts as possible without much screening at that stage. Each member of the group wrote their thoughts on post-it labels and fastened them on the meeting room walls. Everybody could see what others posted but any verbal communication was forbidden. After there were about twenty or thirty recorded thoughts on TTM factors by everybody in the team it was time to refine the findings that were divided into several categories. All thoughts and ideas were discussed by the team in detail and overlapping and non-significant factors were weeded out in the refining process. The ISO 15504 framework was very useful here but there were also other aspects to consider. For example, it was considered important that the project team works physically close to each other. Factors like this are not captured in ISO 15504 or other standards, so it was decided that there is a category for general TTM factors. In total the team ended up with 55 TTM –related factors distributed over six categories, namely General, Customer, Engineering, Management, Support and Organization. The findings are discussed in more detail in the following chapter.

As for packaging of the TTM factors, after some iteration it was decided that a questionnaire is perhaps easiest for the users of the KOTEL TR12 TTM factors to gauge their projects. This questionnaire was piloted several times in the TR12 member companies during the packaging step to find a suitable format. As a result an Excel –based questionnaire was drafted with the intention that a novice user of the questionnaire could complete it relatively quickly without external help. This meant that the TTM factors needed to be described in adequate detail in the questionnaire. Another aspect in the packaging of the TTM factors was to suggest that some TTM factors are more important than others. After some experimentation a simple weighing system was proposed, which was integrated in a straightforward results counting formula. Each factor can have a value (1, 2 or 3) and a weight (1, 3 or 9). Hence, most important factors have a weight of nine (9). After filling the questionnaire a probability estimate (between 0% and 100%) is calculated for the project to achieve its TTM goals. The questionnaire can also be filled only for one or more categories of particular interest. Naturally this estimate should be considered only as guidance in assessing project risk rather than an absolute value. Moreover, the results calculation formula presents only one baseline in time and should be calibrated to respond optimally in specific environments.

Traditionally the KOTEL documents have been distributed in paper format. Now KOTEL is breaking new grounds to as the KOTEL TR12 TTM questionnaire is in electronic format and is even freely available from the KOTEL web site *www.kotel.fi*.

4   Findings and Experiences

The TTM group work uncovered a total of 55 different factors distributed over six categories, namely General, Customer, Engineering, Management, Support and Organization. The analysis of the different factors was done by the experts in the KOTEL TR12 team. After piloting the questionnaire in actual projects in the KOTEL TR12 team member organizations the factors were refined and weights were set. The most important factors affecting TTM in this study were:

- New technology
- Project personnel skills and experience
- Project personnel relationships – „chemistry"
- Understanding customers business/Intensive customer participation
- Validity of Market/Customer research/Management of requirements
- Development tools/environments and lifecycle model
- System/software architecture/structure
- Product/Project management and decision making
- Support for Testing/Quality assurance
- Project/team size

For example, a project with experienced personnel having well-defined requirements and using proven technology, methods and tools most likely has a good chance in meeting their TTM target. As it can be seen many of these factors are similar to earlier findings (e.g. [2],[11]), but there were also some new factors that were seen as crucial, such as Project personnel relationships. The factor New technology probably speaks about the special interest of the KOTEL TR12 team, which is embedded software engineering. Some of the factors, such as Intensive customer participation, relate well to the recently popular extreme programming concepts. Finally some factors, such as Project personnel skills and experience or Understanding customers business, seem obvious but are perhaps at times neglected in real life. In general, novelty or scientific validity was not the focus for the factors identified in this study. Instead, the KOTEL TR12 team attempted to find a consensus on the TTM factors and their relative importance, and package the results in an easy-to-use questionnaire.

There are a number of experiences and lessons learned from the KOTEL TR12 TTM group work. Concerning extracting new knowledge it was found out that expert knowledge can be gathered quickly. The few brainstorming sessions gave ample material to digest. One advantage of the KOTEL TR12 team was that people have roughly similar background even if they are working in different companies working in different domains of embedded software engineering. Communication is at least initially more difficult if people do not share common conceptual background, vocabulary, etc. (see discussion in Järvinen et al [8]). Among other lessons learned from the group work it became clear that focusing is essential. It is often the most important and difficult task to confine a concise and useful center of attention for a group work, especially if the motivation and goals of participants often differ in a loosely coupled cooperation network such as KOTEL working groups. What made focusing easier in the KOTEL TR12 TTM group work was not only that there was a common overall goal, i.e. to understand factors affecting TTM, but that there were frameworks and standards that could be used for support and guidance. While the brainstorming sessions were regarded useful as such for the participants, the packaging of the findings was considered to be mandatory. Otherwise the many factors would have been very difficult for others to understand even individually let alone to be used as a whole for project risk evaluation. However, packaging knowledge requires work and expertise. Professional help for packaging would probably have resulted in a more usable result but even as such the KOTEL TR12 TTM questionnaire was considered to be useful among those who piloted the questionnaire in their actual projects.

5   Conclusions

Expert panel meetings provide a good mechanism for gathering expert knowledge quickly in the form of heuristics. In the constantly changing workplace it is often necessary to be able to process new demands and package results for immediate use even if the results are not always fully validated. Heavy methods, such as Experience Factory [1], do not respond well to these needs. The KOTEL TR12 TTM question-naire provides a light way for fast evaluation of a software project. Particularly if TTM is the primary project goal it is important to understand the factors affecting TTM. Looking beyond individual project needs the KOTELTR12 TTM questionnaire forms a set of TTM –related factors that can be translated to specific PPD models that may yield even better understanding of the domain parameters. However, this is a subject for future studies. Another example of future work is to better understand how the process capability of a project influences the TTM factors. Lastly, KOTEL TR12 welcomes any feedback for the content, structure or usability of the questionnaire as the TTM questionnaire is produced with relatively little effort with limited user scope. Please visit the KOTEL web site *www.kotel.fi* for further information and feedback.

Acknowledgements

The authors would like to thank all members of the KOTEL TR 12 team and especially Bert Bjarland of Nokia, Hannu Harju of VTT, Raimo Laitinen of Helvar, Kari Laukka of Vaisala and Antti Turtola of VTT. Many thanks also to everybody in the PROFES team, and especially Fraunhofer IESE - home of the PPD concepts.

References

1. Basili, Victor, Caldiera, Gianluigi and Rombach, H. Dieter. „Experience Factory". In John J. Marciniak, editor, Encyclopaedia of Software Engineering, Volume 1, John Wiley & Sons, pp. 469-476, 1994.
2. Benguria, Gorka, Escalante, Luisa, Elisa, Gallo, Ostolaza, Elixabete and Vergara, Mikel. „Staged Model for SPICE: how to reduce Time to Market (TTM)". In the Proceedings of QWE'98, 1998.
3. Birk, Andreas. "A Knowledge Management Infrastructure for Systematic Improvement in Software Engineering". PhD Theses in Experimental Software Engineering, Vol. 3, Fraunhofer IESE , Kaiserslautern, Germany. 246 p., 2000.
4. Birk, Andreas, Derks, Pieter, Hamann, Dirk, Hirvensalo, Jorma, Oivo, Markku, Rodenbach, Erik, Solingen, Rini van and Taramaa, Jorma. „Applications of Measurement in Product-Focused Process Improvement: A Comparative Industrial Case study". In the Proceedings of METRICS'98, 1999.
5. CMMI. „CMMI-SE/SW, V1.0 Capability Maturity Model ® – Integrated for Systems Engineering/Software Engineering, Version 1.0 Continuous Representation". Pittsburgh, PA. Software Engineering Institute. CMU/SEI-2000-TR-019. 618 p., 2000.
6. Humphrey, W. S. „Introduction to the personal software process". Reading, MA, Addison-Wesley, 1997.
7. ISO/IEC TR 15504-2. „Information Technology - Software Process Assessment - Part 2: A Reference Model for Processes and Process Capability". Technical Report type 2, International Organisation for Standardisation (Ed.), Case Postale 56, CH-1211 Geneva, Switzerland, 1998.
8. Järvinen, Janne, Komi-Sirviö, Seija. "The PROFES improvement methodology - enabling technologies and methodology design". Springer Lecture Notes in Computer Science 1840. PROFES, 2nd International Conference on Product Focused Software Process Improvement. Oulu, FI, 20 - 22 June 2000. Springer, 257 – 270, 2000.
9. Oivo, Markku, Birk, Andreas, Komi-Sirviö, Seija, Kuvaja, Pasi, Solingen, Rini van. „Establishing product process dependencies in SPI". In the Proceedings of European Software Engineering Process Group Conference 1999 - European SEPG99, 1999.
10. PROFES-ConsortiumA. „The PROFES User Manual". Stuttgart, Fraunhofer IRB Verlag, Germany, 400 p., 2000. Available online from: http://www.vtt.fi/ele/profes/PUMv10.pdf

11. PROFES-ConsortiumB. „The PROFES PPD Repository". 2000. Available online from:
http://www.iese.fhg.de/projects/profes/PPDRepository/PPDRepository.html
12. Rico, David. „Using Cost Benefit Analyses to Develop Software Process Improvement (SPI) Strategies". SP0700-98-D-4000, DACS (Data&Analysis Center for Software), Rome, NY. 2000. Available online from:
http://www.dacs.dtic.mil/techs/RICO/rico.pdf

Daibutsu-den: A Component-Based Framework for Organizational Process Asset Utilization

Hajimu Iida[1], Yasushi Tanaka[1,2], and Ken'ichi Matsumoto[1]

[1]Nara Institute of Science and Technology
Takayamacho 8916-5, Ikoma, Nara, 6300101 Japan
iida@ieee.org
matumoto@is.aist-nara.ac.jp
[2]Sony Corporation, Network & Software Technology Center
Software Process Solutions Department
Kitashinagawa 6-7-35, Shinagawa-ku, Tokyo, 1410001 Japan
yasushi.tanaka@jp.sony.com

Abstract. This paper describes our project to create (design) a reuse-oriented process/project planning support framework (codename: Daibutsu-den) using process component technology and pattern oriented process model. This framework addresses many aspects of CMM/CMMI key process area such as PP (CMM Lv.2), ISM (CMM Lv.3 / IPM CMMI ML3), PTO (CMM Lv.2 / PMC, CMMI ML2), QPM (CMM Lv.4), and OPD (CMM Lv.3). Key features of our framework are 1) Component-based and pattern-oriented support for process reuse and 2) Polymorphic representation of process description for various support tools.

1 Introduction

One of the major topics of CMM/CMMI is the utilization of Organizational Process Assets (OPA). Organizational Process Assets mainly archives the organization standard software processes (OSSP), which are developed, managed, and maintained by the software organization at CMM level3. The project's defined software processes (PDSPs) are tailored from the organization standard software processes. At CMM level3, the organization standard software process is repeatedly reused under different (but similar) contexts, and also improved through statistical measurement of actual process performance at level 4. This means that CMM aims to establish improved quality and higher productivity by employing the current optimal process, which is continuously maintained, managed and improved. Therefore, repeatedly employing the organization standard software process and its continuous improvement is the key issue for this approach.

However, in many of today's software development organizations, actual processes are not so stable for repeated reuse and improvement. The requirements for the development project are changed so frequently. One of the reasons is that product life

M. Oivo and S. Komi-Sirviö (Eds.): PROFES 2002, LNCS 2559, pp. 207-219, 2002.

cycle is becoming shorter and the new businesses are born so frequently. Another reason is that today's many companies are so heterogeneous as to have various product categories. Thus, we realize that the techniques for flexible reformation of development process are becoming much more important.

In order to make organization's standard-based project's defined software processes work properly in a situation like this, supplementing the following features are very important:

- Variants and alternatives of the process (=process assets) according to changing situations
- Pre-project tailoring mechanisms for project managers at end-user (non-Software Engineering Process Group (SEPG)) level
- Postmortem modification/annotation mechanisms for project managers and members for future improvement.

These features are often discussed as a low-level reuse and customization of the software process. However, specific changes in the product requirements usually affect the whole project. Therefore, requirement changes should be handled at the project level abstraction. This implies that process architecture and process patterns (design patterns for software process) will play very important roles for process asset utilization.

In this paper, we show the overview of our project „Daibutsu-den" (Japanese word which means the Great Buddha Hall) to create (design) a reuse-oriented process/project planning support framework using process component technology and pattern oriented process model. This framework addresses many aspects of CMM/CMMI key process area such as CMM/CMMI key process area such as PP (Project Planning: CMM Lv.2), ISM (Integrated Software Management, CMM Lv.3 / IPM Integrated Project Management CMMI ML3), PTO (Project Tracking and Oversight, CMM Lv.2 / PMC Project Monitoring and Control, CMMI ML2), QPM (Quantitative Process Management and Measurement, CMM Lv.4), and OPD (Organization Process Definition, CMM Lv.3).

One of the major problem for reusing process in the organizational process asset is the granularity of the process elements. Due to the diversity of the product categories, heterogeneous organizations have much difficulty in reusing coarse grained (=specific) process elements without large modification, while fine grained (=generic) process elements has to be organized as project's defined process by project leaders. We propose a framework using flexible process components (=fine elements), which can be organized by process patterns (=coarse elements), to solve this problem. This framework provides additional advantages in enabling multiple (polymorphic) representations of the process descriptions. Key features of our framework are:

- Component-based and pattern-oriented support for process reuse
- Postmortem description support for easy tailoring and improvements
- Metric-flow model embedded in each process component
- Polymorphic representation of process description for various support tools.

There is another characteristic of our approach. Some times, features of existing process support system don't sufficiently reflect the requirements of process improvement activities in the real field. Especially for CMM compliance, more

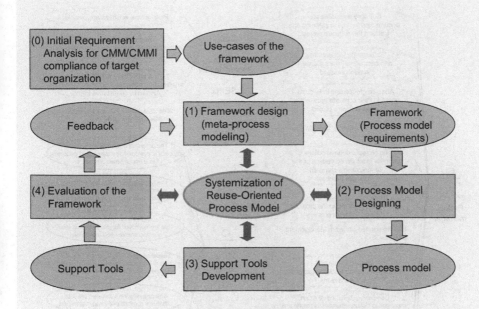

Fig. 1. Meta-framework of the Daibutsu-den Project

insightful assessment for the requirement of the supporting technologies is needed. In this paper, we carefully made a requirement analysis of supporting framework for CMM compliance.

In Section 2, we describe the scope and overview of our project and the framework. In Section3, the underlying process model and architecture are described. In Section 4, we describe the current design of support tools for process asset utilization. Finally, in section 5, we briefly discuss our project and show the future plan.

2   Project Scope and Overview

The main target user of our framework is a project leader who knows well his/her process but is a non-process engineering expert, who happens to be involved in software process improvement (SPI) activities such as CMM. The SEPG (Software Engineering Process Group) experts, of course, are also considered a target user who will use our framework for postmortem process improvement.

2.1   Meta-Framework

Fig. 1. shows the overview of the „meta-framework" of our project. Meta-framework includes the following steps:

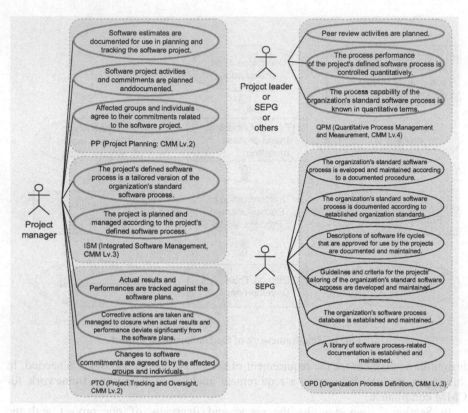

Fig. 2. Overview of Use-cases for Daibutsu-den Framework Derived from CMM KPAs

Initial Requirement Analysis: Investigate the requirements for the CMM/CMMI compliance of the target organization. The use-cases for our framework (Daibutsu-den) are derived.

The actual framework is designed according to the requirement use-cases.

The actual process model in compliance to the derived framework is developed

Support mechanisms and tools are developed based on the framework and the process model

Evaluate the whole framework (partially by using developed tools)

Step (1)~(4) will be repeated several times until the project is completed. During this cycle, Systemization of Reuse-Oriented Process Model is continuously updated.

2.2   Assumptions for the Context of the Organization

As we explained in the previous section, we assume that our target organizations have variety of the products with relatively short lifecycles and the requirements for the development project are changed so frequently. We also consider following situations in organizational process improvement activities:

- The Organization follows (or plans to follow) CMM/CMMI guidelines for process reuse
- OPA (Organizational Process Assets) are maintained in several different levels of granularity.
- SEPG mainly defines the organization's standard software process assets and defines their base-line, but end users such as project leaders are also expected to do the same job.
- OPA elements are reused and refined by end users (project leaders) as well as by SEPG
- OPA elements are reused by project leaders to construct each project process.
- Project leaders may modify OPA elements to fit tangible project constraints.
- Project leaders may make annotation to OPA elements to point out some notes for modifications, complements, deviations and such or, just for claim, during/after project for further improvement of the process asset.

2.3   Key Use-Cases of the Framework

Based on the assumptions given above, we first conducted a preliminary requirement analysis of our process framework for CMMI compliance activities. Use-cases in Fig. 2 show some of the results of our requirement analysis. For example, project leaders usually are expected to implement project plans at CMMI level2. At level 3, the project's defined software process implementation is included in the project leader's overhead work. If project leaders are not familiar with software process concepts and the detail of the process asset elements, this overhead seriously degrades the project leader's performance in creating a project plan document.

According to derived use-cases, we set two major objectives for our framework as follow:

Establish the technique to define the development process which can adapt to dynamic changes and various project characteristics
Save the project leader's overhead in project planning and project's defined software process implementation.

3   Component-Based Software Process Framework

In order to accomplish our objectives, we employ component-based process model as a key technique. In this section, we first describe the conceptual issues of the software project, which is the main target of our framework. Then, we describe our component-based software process model and related sub-models.

3.1   Component-Oriented Process Model

Since we consider that rapid and strong support to end-user's process design is essential to the purpose of the framework, we assume that the most important feature of the process model is the support for modularity and adaptability, just as plug-and-play mechanisms. Self-configurable software process component is a key technique of this feature.

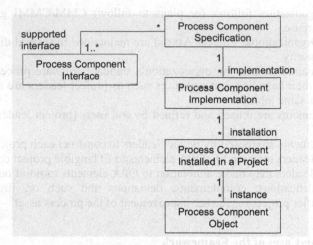

Fig. 4a. Process Component Model

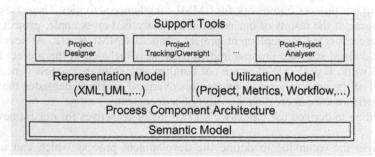

Fig. 4b. Sub-Models of Component-Based Process Model

In the area of the software component (componentware), there are several major component architectures such as Microsoft's COM family[13] and Sun's Java Beans families[14]. In this paper, we use the term „component" as „self-configurable component." This feature is mainly established by representing I/O interfaces which can be inspected from external components in a uniformed way.

Software Process Component also employs similar mechanisms. Each process component encapsulates a series of autonomous process activities. Every process component has the following characteristics:

- Process component has explicitly defined interface,
- Process component takes objects (artifacts/products) as input and output, and
- Process component has explicitly specified goal and the responsible.

For example, activities such as „requirement analysis", „spec documentation", „coding", „unit test", and „integration test" are typically considered to be process components.

Fig. 4. shows a conceptual model of software process components. There is a Process Component Specification, which is supported by multiple Process

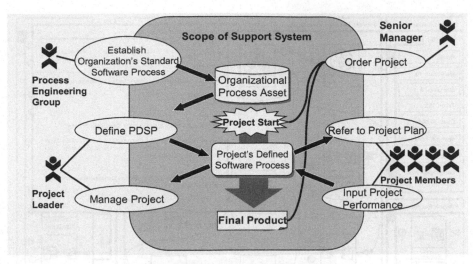

Fig. 5. Overview of the System Scope

Component Interfaces. Interfaces can be inspected externally so that external process modules can determine how to access the component. A Process Component is implemented based on the Component Specification, and then installed in an actual environment (i.e. in the organization's standard processes and process assets). Finally, each instance created in an actual context (i.e. in a software project) from installed Process Component is called Process Component Object.□Other Conceptual Issues for PDSP implementation support

Semantic model of the process component is a core model of the Daibutsu-den framework. The entire framework is composed of several sub-models such as representation models and a utilization model. Fig. 4 shows a rough structure of conceptual models of Daibutsu-den framework.

Representation models provide various views of process components according to the purpose of support tools. XML-based component documentation schema and UML-based graphical design language are typical elements of Representation Models. Utilization model provides the basic discipline for the feature of support tools. For example, a workflow model specifies structure and control flow of a project, and it provides guideline for tools such as project tracking/oversight tool.

In this paper, we take the stand point of product focused process management. That is, we assume that every project corresponds to its target product (=program/software). In other words, every instance in the product creation requires its own project, and the major characteristics of the project should be dominated by the characteristics of the target software. The characteristics of a project (e.g. objective, environment, resources, process assets, I/Os) reflect that of the target software (e.g. feature, environment, resources, I/Os, language).

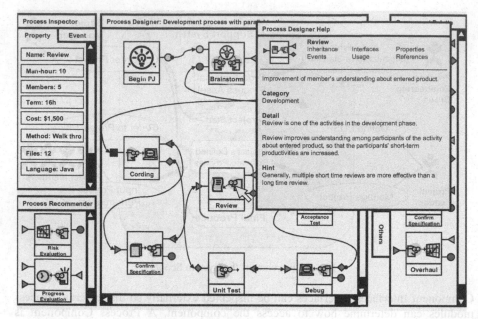

Fig. 6. Process Composition Tool

4   Support Toolset Design

4.1   System Scope

Fig. 5 shows the overview of the scope the Daibutsu-den process support tools cover. Current version of Daibutsu-den framework covers 6 use-cases of organizational process asset utilization described in Section2, and four of them (Define Project's defined software process, Manage Project, Refer to Project Plan, and Input PJ Performance) are actually supported by current version of Daibutsu-den support toolset.

4.2   Overviews of Support Tools

Based on the framework and the models explained in Section 3, the Daibutsu-den's software process support toolset prototype is now under development for the evaluation of the framework. In this section, we explain the architecture and the function of our support tool.

First, we describe the outline (our support tool's concept, and the system mounting form) of our support tool. Then, some features of our support tool set are explained using the example screen image.

System Overview

The fundamental concept of our support tool system is to represent a software development process as instances and combinations of the process components

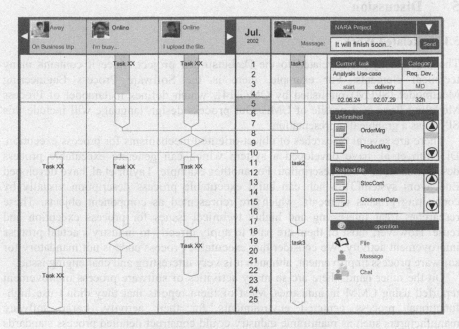

Fig. 7. Project Tracking and Oversight Tool

described in Sec. 3. By using the process description, management and a knowledge share of a software process which can be reused are realized.

Since a process component and its instance can be used in a system, description of document form needs to exist. In our system, XML based document form was used for fundamental process description.

Process *Composition* Tool
This tool supports project leaders in project's defined software process implementation work. The process definition is composed as a set of process components, which are graphically drawn on the window (see Fig. 6.) Project templates are also provided as process components. Each component provides its interfaces to connect with each other, but there are types of interfaces that only allow the valid combinations of the components. User can browse each component's description, which is fundamentally documented in XML.

Project Tracking & Collaboration Support Tool
This tool supports software project tracking and oversight. Each member of a project can report his/her progress through this system. The member of a project can check progress of other members, who are related to the member's work. A project leader can check progress of the entire project. In Fig. 7, the main window shows swim-lanes of project members. Simple messages can be exchanged using this tool.

5   Discussion

5.1   Related Work

There are many work related to the Daibutsu-den project, since it contains many technical elements. For example, there is the Software Process Engineering Metamodel (SPEM) published by OMG[14], which defines metamodel of Process Modeling Parts as a profile of UML. Our process design language will include this SPEM as a graphical representation.

There are several researches of object-oriented mechanisms for process execution. Di Nitto et al. have developed a system which can generate executable process description from UML description. For another example, Taylor et al. have developed Endeavors system[3] which can build executable process description visually by connecting process elements, which are represented as component objects. These researches treat interesting and highly technical issues for process execution and reuse. However, most of them are hard to apply directly to industry's actual process improvement activity. We consider that executable process code is not mandatory for software process improvement, although it is very interesting and challenging issue.

On the other hand, there are so many activities of software process improvement reported using CMM in industries. Most of them reports that they didn't use high-functional process centered environments for their activity. Large software manufacturers such as mainframe industry could construct detailed process standards and process asset, which are shared and reused in entire of the company. Smaller organizations having narrow product area may not be able to take the same approach due to high cost for huge standard process, but they may take anyhow simplified approach for process definition and reuse. In some cases, simply semi-formal documents such as Microsoft Word or Excel files are used as templates of process descriptions. They use these documents mainly because end-users can easily view/edit them.

However, it is very hard to share such process documents as it is in heterogeneous organizations manufacturing various kinds of products containing some software, for example, PC, video camera and mobile phone. Still, they also have motivation to establish process assets shareable and reusable in entire of the company. In this case, developing huge standard process documents or using just simple template documents of process may not work either. They need to store fine grained generic process elements, which can be reused in each division by re-organizing them into the project specific process definition.

In other words, they need powerful process documentation assistance using various project specific templates. In this sense, our approach is similar to that of the Spearmint/EPG system[1], which is developed by Fraunhofer IESE. Spearmint/EPG is a process modeling and documentation tool that eases process description work by supporting multiple representational views such as E-R diagram like product flow view, tree-formed structural view, and „electronic guidebook" style HTML view. Spearmint is a process modeling tool for process engineers. Although Spearmint's process models are stored in an object-oriented database, there is no explicit support for reuse of process elements. Our focus is process modeling/authoring support for end-users (non-SEPG project leaders), and we introduce component and pattern handling mechanism into our framework in order to explicitly support the reuse of process assets.

Process pattern is another key issue of our framework. There are several works on software process patterns[2],[7],[8],[9],[10],[11], For example, Gnats et. al. tries to represent process patterns as a kind of component, which can adapt to changing context.[8]. However, too much complex semantic seems to be exposed to users. Our approach aims additional mechanism for end-users' utilization.

5.2   Concepts to Be Investigated in the Daibutsu-den Framework

Fig. 8 shows the conceptual issues of the Daibutsu-den framework. This figure is composed of two parts, the Process Semantic Model part and the System Model part. The System Model includes various features and functions to be implemented. The Process Semantic Model provides the semantic basis for the process descriptions and it is implemented in the System.This figure is not fully completed and validated, and many relational links are omitted for the simplicity's sake. However, this diagram still provides a direct view of our interests and also issues that are currently not covered. For example, we are also interested in process simulation feature of the system as a part of project's defined software process implementation, but it is not covered at this time.

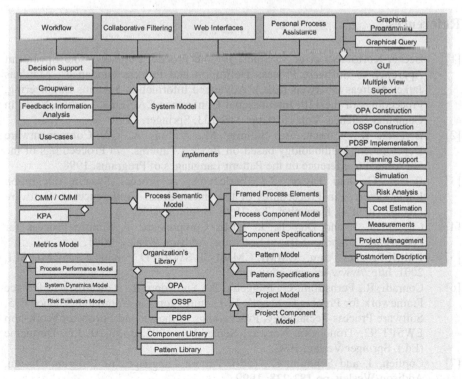

Fig. 8. Conceptual Issues of *Daibutsu-den* Framework

6   Conclusion

In this paper, we have described the overview of our component-based organizational process asset (OPA) modeling project. We have shown meta-framework of our project, scope of our project, framework of our process asset utilization, and plans for support tools. This project has started as a closed joint-research with NAIST and Sony. Currently we are developing process component architecture and data model. We are also developing the pilot implementation of support tools. The Daibutsu-den framework will be evaluated through the use of developed support toolset.

Acknowledgements

Many direct contributions to this paper were made by NAIST's Daibutsu-den project members, Mr. Hiroshi Igaki, Mr. Teppei Gotoh, Mr. Takero Kasubuchi, Mr. Naoki Ohsugi, and Mr. Hiroki Okai.

We would also like to thank Mr. Koji Kondo, project manager, Sony Corporation, for his support.

References

[1]   Becker-Kornstaedt et al. "Support for the Process Engineer: The Spearmint Approach to Software Process Definition and Process Guidance". Matthias Jarke, Andreas Oberweis (Eds.): Advanced Information Systems Engineering, Proceedings of the 11th International Conference CAiSE'99, Lecture Notes in Computer Science, Vol. 1626, pp. 119-133. Springer, 1999.

[2]   Bergner, K., Rausch, A., Sihling, M., Vilbig, A., „A Componentware Development Methodology based on Process Patterns." in Proceedings of the 5th Annual Conference on the Pattern Languages of Programs. 1998.

[3]   Bolcer, G., and Taylor, R., „Endeavors: A Process System Integration Infrastructure," in Proceedings of the International Conference on Software Process (ICSP4), December, 2-6, 1996, Brighton, U.K.

[4]   Cheesman, J. and Daniels, J., UML Components: A Simple Process for Specifying Component-Based Software, Addison Wesley, 2001.

[5]   CMMI Product Team, „CMMI: CMMI-SE/SW/IPPD Version 1.1," CMU/SEI, 2001. http://www.sei.cmu.edu/cmmi/

[6]   Conradi, R., Fernström, C., Fuggetta, A., Snowdon, R.: Towards a Reference Framework for Process Concepts. In Lecture Notes in Computer Science 635, Software Process Technology, Proceedings of the second European Workshop EWSPT'92, Trondheim, Norway, September, 1992, pp. 3-20, J.C. Derniame (Ed.), Springer Verlag, 1992.

[7]   Coplien, J. and Schmidt, D., (ed.). Pattern Languages of Program Design, Addison-Wesley, pp.183-238, 1999.

[8]   Finkelstein, A., Kramer, J., Nuseibeh B. „Software Process Modelling and Technology." Research Studies Press Ltd, JohnWiley & Sons Inc, Taunton, England,1994.

[9]   Gary, K., Derniame, J.C., Lindquist, T., and Koehnemann, H. „Component-Based Software Process Support", in Proceedings of the 13th Conference on Automated Software Engineering (ASE'98), Honolulu, Hawaii, October, 1998.

[10]   Gnatz, M., Marschall, F. Popp, G. Rausch, A. and Schwerin, W., „Towards a Living Software Development Process based on Process Patterns," In Proceedings of PROFES2001.

[11]   Iida, H., „Pattern-Oriented Approach to Software Process Evolution," in Proceedings of IWPSE'99, pp.55-59, 1999.

[12]   Kellner, M.I., „Connecting reusable software process elements and components," in Proceedings of the 10th International Software Process Workshop (ISPW '96), IEEE press, 1996.

[13]   Di Nitto et al., „Deriving executable process descriptions from UML," in Proceedings of the 24th International Conference on Software Engineering (ICSE2002), pp.155-165, ACM, 2002.

[14]   Open Management Group, The Software Process Engineering Metamodel (SPEM), OMG document number: ad/2001-03-08, 2001.

[15]   Paulk, M. et. al., „CMM: Key Practice of the Capability Maturity Model, Version 1.1," CMU/SEI-93-TR-25, CMU/SEI, 1993.

[16]   Rogerson, D., Inside COM, Microsoft Press, 1997.

[17]   Sun Microsystems, JavaBeans Documentations, http://java.sun.com/products/javabeans/

Extracting Initial UML Domain Models from Daml+OIL Encoded Ontologies

Ludwik Kuzniarz and Miroslaw Staron

Department of Software Engineering and Computer Science
Blekinge Institute of Technology
Box 520, Soft Center, SE-372-25 Ronneby, Sweden
{lku,mst}@bth.se

Abstract. The paper presents and elaborates on an automatic method for creating initial domain model using part of the knowledge contained in ontologies. It describes the method of how the initial domain model expressed in Unified Modeling Language (UML) can be obtained in an automated way from ontologies encoded in DAML+OIL. The solution is presented in the context of Unified Software Development Process, which uses UML as a modelling language. The elements necessary for construction of domain models are identified; a procedure for finding them in DAML+OIL encoded ontologies is described followed by suggestions for incorporation of the automatic domain model construction into software development process.

1   Introduction

One of the main artefacts constructed during the process of development of a software system is a domain model. Construction of the model requires an expert knowledge about the domain and in many cases system analyst responsible for the task has to put considerable time and effort in appropriate investigation of the domain and consulting domain experts. But the required knowledge may already exist expressed in the form of ontologies describing the domain under investigation and can be used to construct the initial domain model.

The paper explores this idea and presents what knowledge from the existing ontologies can be extracted for construction of the initial domain model and how the domain construction process can be automated.

The following assumptions concerning the representation of the information and processing technology were made: ontologies are expressed in DAML+OIL (DARPA Agent Markup Language and Ontology Interchange Language) [26], domain model is expressed in UML (Unified Modelling Language) [28], transformations are made using XSLT (Extensible Stylesheet Language for Transformations) [13]. They are discussed and justified in more details later - the main reasons for choosing UML and DAML+OIL were their expressive power and the fact that they are accepted standards.

M. Oivo and S. Komi-Sirviö (Eds.): PROFES 2002, LNCS 2559, pp. 220-231, 2002.

2   Basic Notions

Software development process describes an approach to building software systems. It is usually based on a certain technology and describes activities to be performed and artefacts to be produced and is structured into development phases. In the paper the following characteristics of the process are assumed:

1. it includes a phase (usually called analysis) during which an abstract view or model of the domain is constructed,
2. it uses object-oriented technology meaning that the model of the domain is expressed in terms of classes and their attributes relationships,
3. it is UML based that is all the artefacts produced are expressed in the UML modelling language.

An example of such a process is the Unified Software Development Process [5], which is object-oriented and UML based and the conceptual a basic artefact produced during the inception phase.

2.1   Domain Model

Domain model contains concepts that exist in real world and are important from the analysed domain perspective to understand the problem, formulate the requirements and establish a basis for a software solution. The concepts are abstractions of real-world phenomenons, which analysts and developers should take into consideration when analyzing the domain and later designing the software [21]. Domain models in UML based software development processes are expressed as UML class diagrams. Abstractions for a real world phenomenons are called concepts and are expressed as classes. The concepts can have certain properties described as class attributes and relationships between classes.

Domain models are used to provide a common understanding for the analyzed problem domain, the part of reality that significant for the system. The model allows to identify the important concepts and relationships between them, which exist in the real world. The detailed discussion of elements of domain models and their relevance in context of the acquisition process are discussed in [30].

2.2   Ontology

An ontology is a specification of conceptualization or an abstract model for some phenomenons in the real world [11]. Ontologies are widely used in the mobile agent systems, where they provide a definition of knowledge which is used across heterogeneous agents to enable them interpret the same knowledge in the same way. Recently ontologies are used to describe the resources in the Semantic Web [1,2]. This resulted in a development of a constantly growing number of ontologies, which cover a number of domains.

Information contained in ontologies represent a knowledge about a part of reality relevant to a certain domain. Even though there are ontologies that comprise knowledge across many domains, the majority contains knowledge specific for a certain domain. The ontologies are structured into two independent parts. The first, initial part contains information about the structure of knowledge and the second part contains the actual knowledge. The structure is defined by ontology classes describing concepts in the real world, properties of the classes, relationships between the classes and semantically information which together describe the instances of classes (objects) placed in the second part.

Classes can have class properties, which are properties that are expressed by another class and simple properties, which are the properties that can be expressed without referring to other classes. They are equivalent to concepts, attributes of the concepts and associations between concepts, which are used in domain modelling in software development process.

What is important, information contained in ontologies is already defined, widely used and machine processable. So deriving the domain model in an automated way can be desired and will provides a mean to ensure the consistency of the already used knowledge with the information that is used to build domain model. Moreover, the knowledge in ontologies is also used in the certain systems, which also means that it has been tailored to the specific domain.

The ontologies can be expressed in a spectrum of languages [6,9,12,14], however, the emerging standard is the DAML+OIL, which is a dialect of XML and is defined in [26]. The language is designed to be tool independent and able to express all elements which constitute an ontology while some of the other formats based on XML were found to be insufficient to express all information to be contained ontologies [12,15].

3   Domain Model Construction Process

Typically domain models are constructed manually. The construction process involves such activities as finding candidate concepts and their validation: The process demands from an analyst both an expert knowledge about the domain under investigation what may also require an extra time spent consulting domain experts as well as a considerable time needed for constructing the model itself.

Several techniques aimed to help in domain model construction have been suggested such as finding noun phrase candidates, category lists checking or CRC cards [4,5] all having a disadvantage of being time consuming as well as requiring expert knowledge and validation.

An alternative could be to search for a source on the required information which is already classified, structured and validated and can be automatically processed in order to obtain information required in the domain model. And it seems that a such a good candidate for the source of domain information is an ontology.

3.1   Domain Model Acquisition Process

The process of constructing domain model as it is performed manually is depicted on figure 1 represented by a dashed line. The system analyst investigates the real world domain and produces the domain model. But to be able to perform this activity, the analyst must possess domain specific knowledge or to consult a domain expert [5]. In many cases the description of the domain does already exist in different form - an ontology. It is produced by knowledge engineers, who defined an ontology describing this part of real world for other purposes. This knowledge can be used by software analyst to produce the desired domain model. To be able to use knowledge from ontologies, the software analyst must also be able to understand the structure of the knowledge in ontologies, and the elements used to define it. Thus the analyst must also be a knowledge engineer, which is not usually the case. Therefore assistance is required to discharge the system analyst from managing the ontology and the knowledge contained in it - what is depicted on fig. 1.

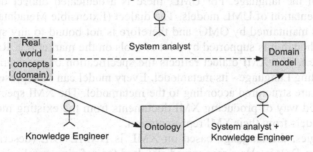

Fig. 1. Manual domain model construction from Ontology

The assistance can be performed by an automatic model acquisition procedure. Its placement in the context of domain model production from ontologies is presented on fig 2. It is depicted as a rectangular actor at the bottom of the figure.

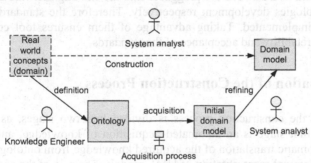

Fig. 2. Automatic initial domain model construction in the context of domain modelling

The advantage of the acquisition process is that it releases the system analysts from understanding formats used for definition of ontologies and at the same time providing a way of creating an initial version of the domain model, which is consistent with the knowledge analyzed by the knowledge engineers. This initial version of domain model must be refined by the analyst to tailor it to the specific requirements for the developed software system. Therefore the presented schema allows performing the activity showed as dashed arrow in a more formal and easier way, which introduces consistency and reuses the existing knowledge and at the same time not demanding new skills from analyst.

3.2   Characteristics of the Acquisition Process

An important characteristic of a good acquisition process is that it should not be bounded to any specific tool used for domain modeling or ontology engineering. The process should be tool independent. The independence should be supported by using technologies that are open and unbounded, but at the same time supported by more than one tool.

Furthermore, the acquisition process should be based on technologies, which are not restricted by proprietary laws. An industrial standard for a language that fulfills this requirement is Extensible Markup Language (XML) and a set of technologies built on top of the language. For UML, there is a dedicated dialect developed for internal representation of UML models. The dialect (Extensible Metadata Interchange - XMI) [29] is maintained by OMG, and therefore is not bound to any specific UML tool vendor. Though it is supported by a lot of tools on the market (i.e. Rational Rose, ArgoUML, etc.). The XMI dialect reflects the specification of an abstract syntax of Unified Modeling Language - its metamodel. Every model can be represented by a set of tags, which are structured according to the metamodel. The XMI specification also provides unified way of producing XMI documents from the existing models as well as creating models from their XMI representation.

For ontologies, the language based on XML is DAML+OIL (described in more detail in section 4). It is also a recognized standard for defining ontologies. It provides a necessary set of tags to encode the ontologies. It is also designed to be interpreted by autonomous mobile agents as well as tools for Semantic Web. DAML+OIL provides a mechanism to encode both the structure of the knowledge and the actual knowledge in a unified way in the same documents.

Both XMI and DAML+OIL are pluggable into the existing software developed for UML and ontologies development respectively. Therefore the standards are widely accepted and implemented. Taking advantage of them ensures tool consistency in terms of interpretability and acceptance of the standards.

4   Realisation of the Construction Process

Realization of the construction process is divided into two stages, as depicted on figure 3. The first stage is an automated acquisition of knowledge, and the second stage is an automatic translation of the acquired knowledge from ontology description language into internal representation of UML models. The role of the acquisition is to extract the elements of the ontology, that are of interest during domain analysis. In particular it leaves the structural information contained in the original ontology such as classes, class relationships and properties. This information is still expressed in the form of DAML+OIL encoded ontology which is then translated into the initial domain model. The role of the translation process is to change the representation of the acquired knowledge from ontology definition language to the UML representation language. It is defined by a mapping between the corresponding concepts in domain models and ontologies. The semantic information is intentionally not included. Including it in domain modeling requires some extensions of the language used for domain modeling to express it. The extensions should involve such elements as stereotyped dependencies, unnamed collection classes, etc. [3,7,8].

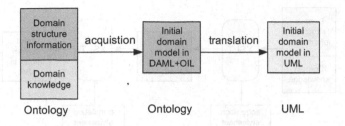

Fig. 3. Schema of construction of initial domain model

Given the two representation languages - XMI and DAML+OIL, the process can be performed by Extensible Stylesheet Language for Transformations (XSLT) [13] which is a technology dedicated for transformations of XML based languages. The XSLT technology is primarily designed for transforming the structure of XML document [13]. It is a high level declarative language, which describes rules how to transform the XML documents. The details of the implementation of how these XSLT transformations work are hidden behind the XSLT processors, which are responsible and designed for interpreting and realising XSLT stylesheets (definitions of XSLT transformation rules). With the use of this technology both acquisition, which is a transformation from DAML+OIL to DAML+OIL and translation, which is a transformation from DAML+OIL to XMI are performed both described by XSLT stylesheets as depicted on fig.4.

The dark gray rectangles depict ontologies. The left-hand ontology is the original one, and the ontology in the middle, which is the result of the acquisition process and contains only information about domain structure (domain model, but defined as DAML+OIL encoded ontology and so are gray shaded). The light gray colour designates elements that belong to the XSLT technology and which take part in transformations. Stylesheets are constant for every ontology and are bound to the process of domain model construction. The details and the specification of the stylesheets can be found in [18]. The resulting domain model (white rectangle) contains the information about the structure of the domain (encoded in XMI), which can be imported to the UML tool used. The advantage of the proposed acquisition process is that to execute it no prior knowledge is needed about the XSLT technologies it is only necessary to run a standard XSLT application with the supplied stylesheets and DAML+OIL encoded ontology. What is more the stylesheets are written once and there is no need to alter them unless the conversion rules ere changed.

The representation of information in DAML+OIL and XMI differs significantly, and thus the translation is much more complicated than in the case of the acquisition. XMI reflects the structure of the metamodel and therefore the translation not only maps corresponding concepts from DAML+OIL to the equivalents in XMI, but also adds some properties to the resulting elements. The properties are introduced with regard to the semantics of DAML+OIL elements and according to the XMI specification. The detailed description of mappings and introduced properties for elements previously described can be found in [18].

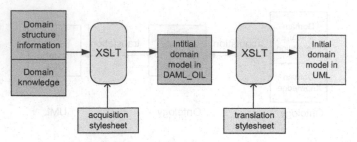

Fig. 4. XSLT transformations for domain model construction

The acquisition is not only the process of removing unnecessary information but it makes necessary adjustments to the original ontology. The adjustments do not change the semantics of the ontology, but make the translation to XMI easier. The changes are aimed to group elements concerning the same concept, or change equivalent elements (like restrictions on „Cardinality", which are changed to restrictions on both „minCardinality" and „maxCardinality"). Grouping elements concerning the same concept allows to translate the ontology in a more structured manner, and makes the realisation of translation straighforward.

5   Including the Construction Process into a Software Development Process

The right place in software development process, where the schema should be introduced is the initial construction of the domain model. This activity is performed at the beginning of transition from requirements to use cases. It usually takes place (depending on an individual variation of USDP) during the inception or early elaboration phase. Since prior to the knowledge acquisition, the search for the required ontology need to be performed, this activity should be performed during inception phase, in parallel to the activity of finalising requirements capture. Such a placement of ontology search has two main advantages. The first one is that at the end of requirements gathering activity, the analysts know what is the domain of system, so the proper ontology can be found. The second advantage is that if the search results in multiple ontologies, they can be evaluated according to the requirements for the built system. A helpful resource to search for ontologies is [27], where a rich set of ontologies is catalogued.

Resources in sense of time need to be devoted for seeking the proper ontology, but the resources are compensated by time that is saved for analysis of the domain and construction of the initial domain model. Nevertheless, the manual refinement of the initial version of this version of conceptual model cannot be eliminated since as every software deals with different matters so not all elements should be kept in the domain model.

Some concepts identified in the initial domain model should be included only as terms in the glossary document, and some should be removed from the documentation at all. What is more, some concepts are missing in the ontology, and they must also be added manually. Furthermore, for software which is meant to work on a verge of two domains, the manual merge of two domain models may be required.

A proper construction of the initial domain model is important for the subsequent activities, which are based on domain model and result in artefacts, which again are crucial for some activities. However, domain modelling is crucial, because it forms a „vocabulary" of the system, which is used throughout the development process [19,21]. The automated acquisition process helps to produce domain models, which are consistent with the existing knowledge about the domain, and what is more, the knowledge which is used, so it has been informally proved by others to be useful and properly defined.

6   Example

The practical usage of a method can be presented on the example of a small banking system. The example shows how the usage of this method can result in generating an initial version of a domain model, which can later be adjusted according to the specific software. The problem solved in this example is the banking system which allows to manage customer accounts and provide a possibility to withdraw and deposit money on the accounts.

One of the first activities performed during the development of this software is to analyse the domain of a bank. However, instead of using one of manual techniques presented in section 2, we try to use the ontology, which has been designed for use with mobile agents. For simplicity of the example, the knowledge that is contained in the ontology is not shown, and the ontology is abridged and visualized.

The ontology consists of two parts. The first one (at the upper side of fig 5) defines the knowledge about domain structure. It contains concepts (classes) and relationships between concepts. The second part (the lower part of the figure) contains the knowledge about objects in this domain. In case of this example, the knowledge is an instance of class Customer, and its connection to the instances of classes Account and Loan. The domain describes simple relationships between accounts, loans and customers of the bank. The properties are omitted for the sake of simplicity and because the discussion on the way to include them is summarized in [6].

From the original ontology, the acquisition process produced the ontology presented on fig. 6. Concepts that have been omitted are:

- existing objects within the domain:
  - instance of a customer (John Doe),
  - instance of an account (12345),
  - instance of a loan (12345-L01)
- semantic information (relationship sameClassAs between classes Client and Customer, relationship disjointWith between classes Saving and Normal)

The filtration also omits other information, but for the sake of simplicity of this example, it is not presented in the paper, but included in report [18]. The translation process, which has been performed on the acquired ontology produced an initial version of the conceptual model for the modelled banking system.

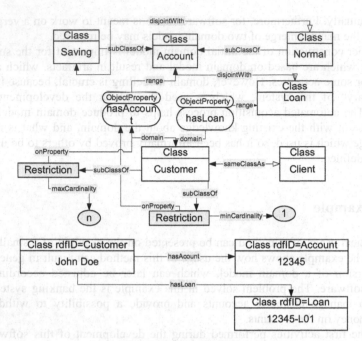

Fig. 5. Banking ontology

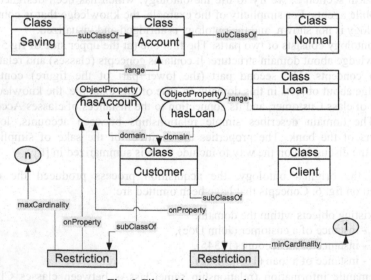

Fig. 6. Filtered banking ontology

The domain model as UML class diagram is presented on fig. 7. This domain model can later be changed by the analyst, who reifies the initial version produced so far. The reification can involve adding some concepts, which were not included in the ontology, but are crucial for the banking system which we build. What is more, the ontology contained no such concept as our modelled system.

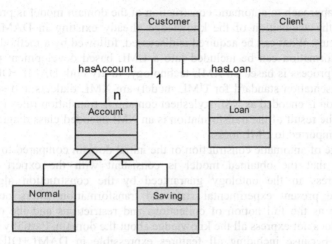

Fig. 7. Initial domain model for banking ontology

Therefore, this concept must also be added. The resulting domain model (after multiple alterations) can be used in the later stages of software development. It is presented on figure 8.

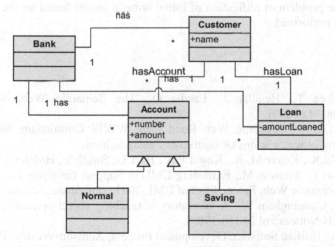

Fig. 8. Refined domain model for banking system

The analyst removed concepts that were redundant (class Client) and introduced some attributes that were not shown in the ontology.

7   Conclusions and Further Work

In the paper an approach to automatic construction of the domain model is presented. It is based on the acquisition of the knowledge already existing in DAML+-OIL encoded ontologies. What can be acquired is discussed, followed by a method of how the acquired information can be included into a UML based development process. The acquisition process is based on XML technology: firstly both DAML+OIL itself and XMI (representation standard for UML model) are XML dialects and secondly the transformation is encoded as XSL stylesheet containing translation rules for XML encoded data. The result of the transformation is an XMI encoded class diagram so it can be directly imported to UML tools.

The advantage of automatic construction of the initial domain compared to manual construction is that the obtained model is consistent with the expert domain knowledge express in the ontology guaranteed by the construction algorithm. However at the present experimental state the transformation filters out some knowledge such as the full notion of collections and restrictions and the obtained domain model does not express all the knowledge about the domain. Partially this is a desired feature because including all features expressible in DAML+OIL would require extending the UML metamodel [3] or using OCL and some of them were just omitted for technical reasons and are the subject of current research on the transformation tool. The current research is also focused on incorporation of the transformation into the UML tool so that it would be possible to import DAML+OIL encoded ontologies to obtain a class diagram expressing a domain model. A further research into the problem of reification of initial domain model based on the domain of the system is performed.

References

[1]   Barners-Lee T., Hendler J., Lasilla O., The Semantic Web, Scientific American, May 2001,

[2]   Barners-Lee T., Semantic Web Road map, WWW Consortium September 1998, http://www.w3c.org/DesignIssues/Semantic.html,

[3]   Baclawski K., Kokar M. K., Kogut P.A., Hart L., Smith J., Holmes III W. S., Letkowski J., Aronson M., Extending UML to Support Ontology Engineering for the Semantic Web, Proceedings of UML 2001 conference, Toronto 2001,

[4]   Beck K., Cunningham W., A laboratory of teaching object-oriented thinking, SIGPLAN Notices vol 24 (10/1989),

[5]   Booch G., Unified Software Development Process, Addison-Wesley, 1998,

[6]   Chang W. W., A Discussion of the Relationship Between RDF-Schema and UML, W3C note, document http://www.w3.org/TR/1998/NOTE-rdf-uml-19980804,

[7]   CraneField S., UML and the Semantic Web, In the Preceedings of SWWS 2001 Symposium, Stanford 2001,

[8]   Cranefield S., Purvis M., UML as an Ontology modelling language, in Proceedings of the Workshop on Intelligent Information Integration, 16th International Joint Conference on Artificial Intelligence (IJCAI-99), 1999,

[9]   Fenzel D., The Semantic Web and its languages, IEEE Inteligent Systems, November/December 2000,

[10]   Fensel D., Horrocks I., Van Harmelen F., Decker S., Erdmann M., Klein M., OIL in a nutshell, Proceedings of the 12th International Conference on Knowledge Engineering and Knowledge Management (EKAW 2000), volume 1937 of Lecture Notes in Artificial Intelligence, Springer Verlag 2000,

[11]   Gruber T. R., A Translation approach to portable ontology specification, Knowledge acquision 5(2), October 2000,

[12]   Hjelm J., Creating Semantic Web with RDF, Wiley 2001,

[13]   Kay M., XSLT, Programmer's reference, Wrox Press, 2000,

[14]   Klein M., Fensel D., Van Harmelen F., Horrocks I., The Relation between Ontologies and Schema-languages: Translating OIL-specifications in XML-Schema,Proceedings of the Workshop on Applications of Ontologies and Problem-solving Methods, 14th European Conference on Artificial Intelligence ECAI-00, Berlin, Germany August 20-25, 2000,

[15]   Klein M., Broekstra J., Decker S., Fensel D., Harmelen F., Horrocks I., Enabling knowledge representation on the Web by extending RDF Schema, http://www.ontoknowledge.org/

[16]   Klempe A., Warmer J., Object Constraint Language: Precise modeling with UML, Addison-Wesley, 1999,

[17]   Kruchten P. The Rational Unified Process, An Introduction, Addison-Wesley, 2000,

[18]   Kuzniarz L., Staron M., Hellman E. Extracting information about domain structure from DAML+OIL encoded Ontologies into UML Domain Models, Blekinge Institute of Technology Research Report 2002:02, ISSN 1103-1581, 2002,

[19]   Larman C., Applying UML and Patterns, An introduction to Object-Oriented Analisys and design and The Unified Process 2nd edition, Prentice Hall, 2001,

[20]   Rational Corporation website, www.rational.com,

[21]   Rational Unified Process User Guide, Rational Corp, www.rational.com,

[22]   Resource Description Framework (RDF) Schema Specification 1.0, WWW Consortium, 2000, document http://www.w3c.org/TR/2000/CR-rdf-schema-20000327,

[23]   RDF Model Theory, W3C Working Draft, WWW Consortium, September 2001, http://www.w3c.org/TR/2001/WD-rdf-mt-20010925,

[24]   Resource Description Framework (RDF) Model and Syntax Specification, WWW Consortium, 1999, http://www.w3c.org/TR/1999/REC-rdf-syntax-19990222,

[25]   Schwartz A., The Semantic Web In Breadth, http://logicerror.com semanticWeb-long,

[26]   Annotated DAML+OIL (March 2001) Ontology Markup, http://www.daml.org/2001/03/daml+oil-walkthru.html,

[27]   DARPA Agent Markup Language Web site, http://www.daml.org

[28]   UML Specification version 1.4, OMG 2001, www.omg.org,

[29]   XMI Specification version 1.1, OMG 2000, www.omg.org,

[30]   Kuzniarz L., Staron M., Generating Domain Models from Ontologies, In the proceedings of OOIS 2002, Springer-Verlag LNCS vol. 2425, 2002.

Assessment of User-Centred Design Processes – Lessons Learnt and Conclusions

Timo Jokela

University of Oulu
P.O. Box 3000, 90014 University of Oulu, Finland
timo.jokela@oulu.fi

Abstract. We carried out a series of case studies in industrial settings to learn how to perform effective assessments of user-centred design (UCD) processes. Our research strategy was to gather qualitative feedback from the organisations assessed, to understand how the different stakeholders perceive the assessments. We started with SPICE process assessment and a related UCD process model. Our observation was that the companies did not find traditional process assessment very useful. The approach and the related models were perceived difficult to understand, and not addressing 'the right issues'. During further case studies, the assessment style evolved towards a different assessment approach. We conclude that there are different assessment situations where different approaches are needed. In the category of our focus – process performance assessment as a basis for process improvement – the focus should be on the substance of UCD rather than on the management of processes, and making the results make sense is more important than formal process capability ratings.

1 Introduction

Usability is recognised as one of the most important quality characteristics of software intensive systems and products. Usability gives many benefits that can include "increased productivity, enhanced quality of work, improved user satisfaction, reductions in support and training costs and improved user satisfaction" [1].

The prevailing paradigm of developing usable products and systems is user-centred design[1], UCD: usable products are created through processes of user-centred design. There exist literature on UCD, e.g. books such as [2], [3], [4], [5], and the standard ISO 13407 [1]. All of them incorporate the same basic principles for developing usable products and system, such as user involvement, iterative design and multidisciplinary teamwork. A typical set of UCD processes is defined in ISO 13407. The standard identifies four processes of UCD as illustrated in Fig. 1.

---

[1] Called also human-centred design and usability engineering

M. Oivo and S. Komi-Sirviö (Eds.): PROFES 2002, LNCS 2559, pp. 232–246, 2002.
© Springer-Verlag Berlin Heidelberg 2002

The processes can be briefly described as follows:

- *Understand and specify context of use.* Know the user, the environment of use, and what are the tasks that he or she uses the product for.
- *Specify the user and organisational requirements.* Determine the success criteria of usability for the product in terms of user tasks, e.g. how quickly a typical user should be able to complete a task with the product. Determine the design guidelines and constraints.
- *Produce design solutions.* Incorporate HCI knowledge (of visual design, interaction design, usability) into design solutions.
- *Evaluate designs against requirements.* The designs are evaluated against user use requirements.

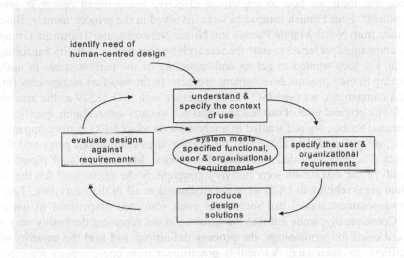

Fig. 1. Processes of user-centred design, UCD (ISO 13407)

UCD processes, however, are not typically largely present in software development projects. Or if there are some, their strategic impact in development projects is often invisible. Many products that are today in the market - or systems that are in use - represent poor level of usability. The challenge to improve the position of UCD in development organisations has been recognised in many presentations and panels in HCI conferences and seminars. There have been papers [6], tutorials [7], panels [8] and interviews [9] at CHI conferences. A European TRUMP project also recently addressed this topic [10].

A typical approach to start organisational improvement effort in any domain is to carry out *current state analysis*. Through current state analysis, one can identify the strengths and weaknesses of an organisation, and thus get a good basis for planning and implementing process improvements. In software engineering, current state analysis is a widely used practice in the form of *process assessment*. Well-known approaches for software process assessment are *CMM* [11], *Bootstrap* [12], and *ISO 15504 [13]*, also known as *SPICE*. A number of different approaches have been proposed for the current state analysis of UCD, or as we call, *usability capability assess-*

ment (UCA), too [14]. The first UCA approaches were introduced in the first half of 90's. A remarkable achievement in this area was the publication of ISO 18529 [15] in 2000, which defines the UCD processes in the format that complies with the requirements of ISO 15504. The UCD substance of the ISO 18529 model is mainly from ISO 13407.

In spite of the many approaches, usability capability assessments are not yet a very widely performed activity. According to a study of Rosenbaum & al [6], 16 organisations out of 134 (12%) reported using 'organisational audits' as a means for enhancing 'strategic usability'. In the same study, audits were ranked to be one of the least effective approaches in promoting strategic usability.

The target of our research project *(KESSU)* is „to develop practical and viable guidance and tools for how to implement effective user-centred design in product development". Four Finnish companies were involved in the project: namely, Buscom, some units from Nokia Mobile Phones and Nokia Networks, and Teamware Group.

The companies preferred to start the research project with a usability capability assessment; i.e. they wanted to get an understanding of the current status in usability engineering in their product development projects. In the two first assessments (in two different companies), we used ISO 15504 together with ISO 18529 as the assessment method. The original goal of our research was not to carry out research specifically on assessments. Rather, we just wanted to analyse the level of UCD in the companies. In any case, we gathered data about how the staff in the organisations perceived the assessments. The data indicated a number of problems. Many of the staff reported that the results of the assessment were not very concrete. Some of the staff felt that many important areas relating to UCD were not discussed at all in the interviews. They felt that the assessment model had sometimes even restricted discussions to irrelevant topics. Consequently, some felt that the results did not represent the reality very well. Some criticised the terminology, the process definitions and said the maturity scales were difficult to understand. A usability practitioner from one company reported that some of the staff had stated that the assessment was „academic stuff driven by the interests of the university". The members of the assessment team found difficult to interpret and agree on the process definitions. Some members of the assessment team felt that they did not get a good picture of the essential practices of the company.

Our conclusion from these two assessments was that some changes in the assessment method are needed for the next assessments. Thus, we had a research problem that was not foreseen when originally planning our research project: *What kind of assessment of UCD processes is useful in the context of our industrial settings?* (Stakeholder = a participant in an assessment).

We carried out six further case studies where the assessment approach evolved towards a different approach: *KESSU process performance assessment.* The evolvement of the assessment approach and the features of the approach are reported in [16], [17] and [18]. The focus of this paper is to summarise our conclusion on what we learned in the assessment we carried out.

We first briefly describe the KESSU assessment approach. Thereafter, we present our conclusions about different assessment categories. Then we discuss the category of our focus, process performance assessment for process improvement. In the next section, we contrast our case studies with the ones of SPICE trials, and finally summarise and discuss the results.

2   The KESSU Assessment Approach

As a result of the case studies, our approach for the assessment of UCD processes evolved to have the following main characteristics (for a more detailed description, see [19]):

-   A new UCD process model (Fig. 2) with three process performance dimensions
-   An assessment method where the assessment is implemented as a workshop and which includes always the assessment of all UCD processes

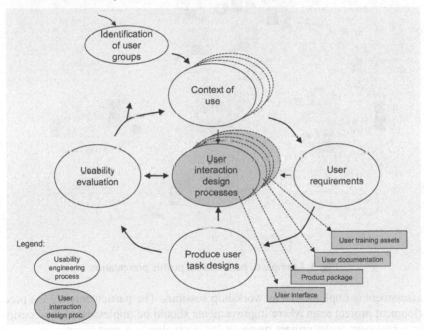

Fig. 2. The KESSU UCD Process model (compare with Fig. 1)

We identify six main processes: Identification of user groups process, Context of use process (multiple instances), User requirements process, User tasks design process, Produce user interaction solutions process, and Usability evaluation process. Each process is defined through a purpose statement and a list of outcomes.

We identify three process performance dimensions: *quantity*, *quality*, and *integration*:

-   The *quantity* of outcomes of the process. The more extensively an outcome exists, the higher performance score it gets.
-   The *quality* of the outcomes. With this dimension, we examine the quality and validity of the outcomes. For example, we want to make a difference whether an

outcome is based on someone's opinions or derived by using recognised user centred methods and techniques.

- The *integration* of outcomes with other processes. The more extensively the outcomes are communicated and incorporated in other relevant processes, the higher rating is given to integration.

The different process and performance models mean a different way of presenting the results. We use different symbols to denote the different dimensions. We present the performance profile in one visual picture. We use the process diagram of user-centred design as a background picture as illustrated in Fig. 3.

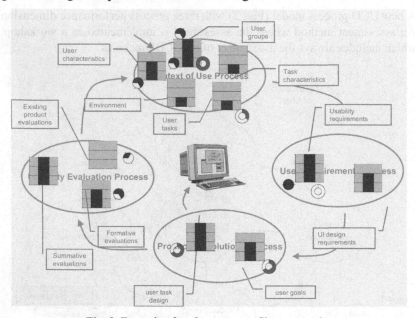

Fig. 3. Example of performance profile presentation

An assessment is implemented as workshop sessions. The participants are the product development project team where improvements should be implemented. The customer of the assessment is the project manager (or equivalent). A past project (or a project that is close to its end) is selected as the object for the assessment. The previous project should be such that is found as a relevant and representative project for the key persons of the customer project. In an ideal case, the past project is carried out with the same management and staff as the new one.

At high level, we apply the guidelines and requirements that are given for planning and carrying out software process assessment in [20] and [21]. The main steps are illustrated in Fig. 4. Before starting the planning of the assessment, the customer and baseline projects of the assessment should be chosen. This should be done on a voluntary basis. The key persons of the customer project should sponsor the assessment, and be committed to participate the assessment. The baseline project should be a meaningful project from the perspective of the customer project. As a basis for the assessment, the organisational infrastructure for the management of the assessment should be set up.

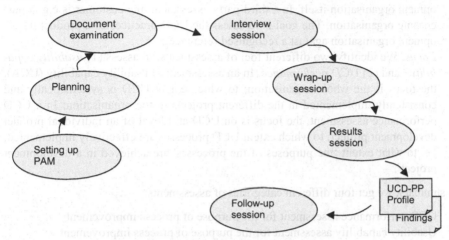

Fig. 4. Phases of carrying out an assessment

In the interview session, the baseline project is discussed thoroughly from the viewpoint of user-centred design activities. All the relevant issues should be revealed so that the rating of the outcomes of the processes is possible. Note. The assessment incorporates examination of all the processes of the KESSU UCD Process model. This is different from 15504-style assessments where a subset of processes is selected.

The purpose of the wrap-up session is to form a preliminary understanding of the results and to plan the results session. Only the assessment team participates this session. The main purpose of the results session is to agree on the results of the assessment together with the project team. To make the results sensible to the audience, the session has also another important purpose: the basics of UCD should be communicated to the audience. Although the assessment team has given the ratings in the wrap-up session, they are not launched to the project team. Instead, we propose that the project team agrees on the ratings. Finally, a separate session is organised for planning the UCD activities for the customer project.

3   Assessment Categories

One of our conclusions of our case studies is that the KESSU approach represents a different category of assessments, as does the SPICE process assessment approach. Our focus is assessing the process performance, not process capability. Moreover, our purpose is to provide a basis for improvement action, not to benchmark the level of performance.

We categorise assessments using two dimensions: *purpose* and *focus*.

- *Purpose*: We identify two different purposes of assessments: (1) *providing a basis for process improvement* and (2) *third-party certification*. In an assessment for process improvement, the goal is to make an organisational change towards improved user-centred design. The customer of the assessment is the product development organisation itself. In a third-party assessment, the customer is e.g. a purchasing organisation. The goal is to assess the UCD practices of a product development organisation against a recognised reference.

- *Focus*: We identify two different foci of assessments: to assess (1) *usability capability* [2] and (2) *UCD performance*. In an assessment of usability capability (UCA), the focus is the whole organisation: to which extent UCD is systematically and consistently implemented in the different projects in the organisation. In a UCD performance assessment, the focus is on UCD at a level of an individual product development project: to which extent UCD processes are effectively implemented, i.e. to what extent 'the purposes of the processes' are achieved in a development project[3].

In summary, we get four different categories of assessments:

- UCD performance assessment for the purpose of process improvement
- Usability capability assessment for the purpose of process improvement
- UCD performance assessment for the purpose of third-party certification
- Usability capability assessment for the purpose of third-party certification

3.1   Characteristics of The Different Assessment Categories

In an assessment for third-party certification, it is important that an assessment approach is based on recognised reference models (e.g. standards). On the other hand, we found usefulness and utility to be more important factors than a recognised, standard reference model in our case studies. For example, the usability practitioners of the companies gave their support to our different approach. Our conclusion is that an assessment approach for providing a basis for improvement action may be subject to ongoing improvement if some problems are found in its usefulness or utility. We have refined the assessment approach a number of times, based on what works and what does not work in the assessments.

In UCD performance assessments, an assessment approach should reveal those potential problems that are specific to the substance of UCD processes in an individual product development project. The basic issue to be examined is whether a UCD activity is performed at all. If an activity is performed (i.e. an outcome is produced), there are two other aspects to be examined: quality and integration. Quality reveals whether an activity is performed in a credible, efficient and professional way. Integration reveals whether an outcome truly has impact on designs.

Usability capability assessments should examine management of UCD processes, as well as performance aspects. According to the definition, usability capability is a characteristic of an organisation's ability 'to consistently develop usable products'. Consistent development, throughout the different projects, is a management issue. Ideally, one should also assess other relevant aspects that have impact on usability

---

[2] or user-centred design process capability

[3] This corresponds to the 0 – 1 level of capability of ISO 15504-process assessment.

capability aside from processes: usability in the business strategy and in the culture of the organisation, UCD infrastructure, etc.

The characteristics of assessment approaches in different categories are summarised in Fig. 7.

		Purpose	
		Process improvement	Third-party certification
Focus	UCD performance	Main requirement: usefulness Changes possible in reference models Addresses the substance of UCD processes	Main requirement: recognised reference models Stable reference models Addresses the substance of UCD processes
	Usability capability	Main requirement: usefulness Changes possible in reference models Addresses the management of UCD processes	Main requirement: recognised reference models Stable reference models Addresses the management of UCD processes

Fig. 5. Characteristics of assessment approaches in different categories

The category 'Assessment of UCD performance for third-party certification' – i.e. assessment of an individual project without examining organisation level aspects – is meaningful e.g. for a follow-up of the success of process improvement (i.e. for measuring whether improvements in the performance of UCD have truly happened). In this case, a 'third-party' could be, for example senior management in a product development organisation. The 'recognised reference model' refers here to the recognition of the models within the product development organisation. This kind of assessment could also be used to examine the relationship between product and process quality: in other words, to what extent the performance of UCD processes corresponds to the usability of the product.

3.2   Allocation of Assessment Approaches into Different Categories

The KESSU assessment approach falls into the category of 'UCD performance assessment for process improvement'. It may be used also for the follow-up of process improvement in the category 'UCD performance assessment for the purpose of third-party certification'. In this case, however, one needs to use the same version of the UCD process and performance models – the one that was used in the first assessment.

Traditional process assessment (ISO 15504 & ISO 18529) is used for both purposes – third-party certification and providing a basis for process improvement. It also incorporates two foci: UCD performance and usability capability. We find that it is effective in the category 'Usability capability assessment for third-party certification'. This is quite natural – the roots of process assessment (CMM) are there. It is also effective in covering management aspects. It is also potentially effective in 'Usability capability assessment for process improvement' when there are problems in management issues. We find this kind of assessment applicable e.g. in process-oriented organisations where UCD is at a relatively mature stage.

The breakdown of the assessment approaches into different assessments is illustrated in Fig. 6.

		Purpose	
		Process improvement	Third-party certification
Focus	UCD performance	**KESSU UPA** Traditional process assessment	**KESSU UPA** Traditional process assessment
	Usability capability	Traditional process assessment	Traditional process assessment

Fig. 6. Breakdown of assessment approaches into different categories. The bigger font, the better performance

4   UCD Performance Assessments

Our focus in the case studies was on 'UCD performance assessment for process improvement'. We approached the case studies as a cumulative process of learning about the criteria for successful assessments, parallel to developing an assessment artefacts approach.

4.1   User Requirements

The focus of this type of an assessment is to reveal the problems in the performance of UCD processes, and the main success criterion is 'usefulness', Fig. 5. The basic requirement for a successful assessment is naturally that the relevant potential problems in the process performance are identified. Our conclusion is that for that, one should examine the quantity, quality and integration of the outcomes of processes.

We found it challenging to understand what other requirements there are for a 'useful' assessment. Our general conclusion is that an assessment should be a meaningful experience, and 'make sense' to the project personnel. This was a clear requirement from the usability practitioners and management. The feedback from the staff supported this conclusion (see Introduction). At a more detailed level, we identify success criteria such as:

- An assessment should be an effective and efficient training session about the essence of UCD.
- During an assessment, the participants should understand by themselves where the weaknesses and strengths in the performance of UCD are.
- The staff should become interested and committed to UCD, and it should motivate people to learn more about UCD and to integrate it into their work. An academic flavour in assessments should be avoided.
- Concrete improvement action should follow spontaneously.

- Participants should feel that an assessment does not take much time; and the time spent in the assessment is perceived to be worthwhile. The assessment should be conducted in a way that does not unnecessarily burden the organisation being assessed.

Assessment should be meaningful also to the assessors. Our first assessments were rather tiring and frustrating for the assessors. From the assessors' point of view, an assessment should have the following features:

- Gathering findings and rating the performance against the reference models should be logical and easy.
- Assessments should provide a credible picture of UCD in the organisation.
- It should be possible to report essential results.
- An assessment should be motivating and interesting.

4.2   Requirements for an Assessment Approach

These success criteria for assessments in this category lead to identification of requirements for an assessment approach. We use the framework of March & Smith [22] to describe the different elements of an assessment approach:

- *Constructs* form the vocabulary of the domain. E.g. terms such as capability dimensions, processes, practices, capability levels, indicators, usability, UCA, UCD, etc
- A *model* is set of propositions or statements expressing relationships among constructs. For example, a model is a description of the results of usability capability assessment.
- A *method* describes a set of steps (an algorithm or guideline) used to perform a task: guidelines and algorithms for performing an assessment.
- An *instantiation* is the realisation of an artefact in its environment: techniques to gather data, supporting tools, interviewing styles, templates etc.

Constructs

- The basic requirement is naturally that the reference models effectively enable an identification of the potential problems in the process performance (in quantity, quality and integration).
- The concepts used in assessment should be understandable. The assessors need to understand the concepts for identification of the findings and to rate the processes. Staff in the product development organisation needs to understand the concepts in order to become interested and find the assessment useful.
- Identifying the findings and rating the performance should be logical and easy against the reference models.
- One should be able to explain the problems (and strengths) in the performance of UCD processes elegantly against the reference models. The reference models need to make sense to people, and 'explanation power'.
- The reference models should provide a mechanism for focusing on different problems and different levels of abstraction, to match and adapt to different or-

ganisational situations. For example, in one organisation a problem may be that some UCD activities do not exist, while in another the problem may lie in the use of inappropriate methods. In the former case, it should be possible to focus on the quantity aspects of the process performance, while in the latter case on quality aspects.

Models

- One should be able to communicate the results of the assessment clearly, specifically, and in an interesting way. The staff should understand the results so that they can compare them with their own judgement.
- The results of an assessment should depict the performance realistically.

Methods

- The method should focus on the substance of UCD processes (rather than on management aspects)
- A large part of the organisation under assessment should participate. It should support teamwork and decision-making.
- The assessment should be organised in a convenient way that makes sense to people.
- The assessment method should be able to take personal differences in the people into account, e.g. in terms of education and attitude.
- The assessment process must not be too resource-costly – applying it should be perceived as a good use of time.
- The method should guide to tailoring the assessment appropriately.

Instantiations

- The assessment team should be able to report and present the results online.

Our conclusion is that if an assessment approach meets these kinds of requirements, the assessment will prove to be a 'useful'. If an assessment approach fails to meet these kinds of objectives, it might be best to revise it. In this light, an assessment should always be regarded as a research project. On the one hand, an attempt should always be made to improve the assessment approach. On the other hand, one should strive for a better understanding of what makes an assessment a success.

5   Findings of our Case Studies vs. SPICE Trials

KESSU has a different strategy for defining processes and determining whether a process achieves level 1 of capability, compared with traditional ISO 15504-style process assessment (SPICE). We did not find the SPICE approach – specifically the base practices - work very well in our context. On the other hand, base practices have been rated as very useful in SPICE trials [23]. In the following paragraphs, we try to find some explanations for this kind of difference between our experience and the ones in the SPICE trials.

One possibility is that there is some substantial difference in the processes of UCD compared with many other processes. One specific characteristic of the UCD processes is that they solely exist for one quality feature, usability. This kind of specific nature of a process may have impact on how the process should be assessed.

Perhaps a key to the difference might lie in the background and purpose of the different approaches. The main interest for traditional process assessment is the management of a software development project: whether it is carried out on schedule and within the budget. Our concern, on the other hand, came from the practical experience of usability practitioners: UCD processes may be carried out with poor quality, or the results may not have any impact on product designs. We found that these kinds of aspects should be very clearly addressed in an assessment. Our concern was in the substance of UCD, not whether the UCD processes are managed well or not.

Another explanation may be in the training aspect of KESSU assessments. We wanted to explain clearly to the project staff what exactly was wrong (or right) with their project. In this respect, we find KESSU to be more precise than one using base practices: that is because we examine the quantity, quality and integration of *each* outcome. The SPICE approach includes also very specific issues (i.e. work products). At that level of detail, however, the model becomes quite complicated, with the disadvantage that it is not so easy to communicate to staff without prior process assessment training.

We find as a strong feature in our research that we gathered feedback from the organisational unit, and not only from the assessors. This feedback had a major impact on the development of our assessment approach. In the SPICE trials, on the other hand, feedback was gathered mainly from the assessors. The report from the second phase of the SPICE trials [23], does not mention any feedback from the organisation unit assessed.

6   Discussion

We carried out a series of case studies in industrial settings to learn how to perform effective assessments of user-centred design (UCD) processes. Our research strategy was to gather qualitative feedback from the organisations assessed, to understand how the different stakeholders perceive the assessments. We started with SPICE process assessment and a related UCD process model. Our observation was that the companies did not find traditional process assessment very useful. The approach and the related models were perceived difficult to understand, and not addressing 'the right issues'. During further case studies, the assessment style evolved towards a different assessment approach (KESSU). We conclude that there are different assessment situations where different approaches are needed. In the category of our focus – 'Process performance assessment as a basis for process improvement' - the focus should be on the substance of UCD rather than on the management of processes, and making the results make sense is more important than formal process capability ratings. An example of a different category is 'Usability capability assessment for third-party certification'. Here one should use an established assessment approach with recognised reference models, such as ISO 15504 together with ISO 18529. The focus is on the management of UCD processes.

One limitation of our research is that the history of UCD was rather short in some of those industrial organisations where the case studies were carried out. If user-centred design has a longer and more established position, traditional process assessments could make sense. On the other hand, our understanding is that UCD is generally not well established in most companies.

Our hypothesis in the beginning of the research was that an assessment – 'current state analysis' - is the way to start an effort to improve UCD. We still have the opinion that assessments are useful in many situations. An assessment can be a very positive intervention, culminating in improvements. Our case studies indicate that an assessment may be an effective and efficient training instrument. Providing the members of a project team with an opportunity to compare its past performance with what it should be seems to be very instructive and one that encourages improvement.

We can add a footnote, however, that assessments should be used carefully and sensitively. If they are carried out in an inappropriate way, the consequences can even be counter-productive. The danger is that people associate 'usability' with issues they do not find meaningful.

In some cases, it may not be wise to carry out a formal assessment at all. Such a case is, for example, when the customer of the assessment is a project team with no or only very limited experience of UCD. In some of our last case studies, we decided that it would not be wise to report the results of assessment at all. The interviews revealed that there had been only very few UCD activities in the past projects of the organisation, and we felt that it would not be 'nice' to report 'bad' results. (Instead of presenting the results, we gave a hands-on training on UCD to the project team in the session planned for results reporting.)

Whenever an assessment is carried out for the purpose of providing a basis for improvement action – no matter which assessment approach is used - one should consider it as research into the area of assessment, and not only as an attempt to understand the status of UCD processes. One should document how it was carried out and gather feedback on its success. Activities should be allocated carefully in the planning of the assessment; observations should then be made and feedback gathered during and after the assessment.

References

[1]   ISO/IEC, 13407 Human-Centred Design Processes for Interactive Systems. 1999: ISO/IEC 13407: 1999 (E).
[2]   Nielsen, J., Usability Engineering. 1993, San Diego: Academic Press, Inc. 358.
[3]   Hix and Hartson, Developing User Interfaces: Ensuring Usability Through Product & Process. 1993: John Wiley & Sons. 416.
[4]   Beyer, H. and K. Holtzblatt, Contextual Design: Defining Customer-Centered Systems. 1998, San Francisco: Morgan Kaufmann Publishers. 472.

[5]   Mayhew, D.J., The Usability Engineering Lifecycle. 1999, San Fancisco: Morgan Kaufman.

[6]   Rosenbaum, S., J.A. Rohn, and J. Humburg. A Toolkit for Strategic Usability: Results from Workshops, Panels, and Surveys. in CHI 2000 Conference Proceedings. 2000. The Hague: ACM, New York.

[7]   Bloomer, S. and S. Wolf. Successful Strategies for Selling Usability into Organizations. Tutorial 8. in CHI 99. 1999. Pittsburgh, USA.

[8]   Rosenbaum, S., J. Rohn, J. Humburg, S. Bloomer, K. Dye, J. Nielsen, D. Rinehart, and D. Wixon. What Makes Strategic Usability Fail? Lessons Learned from the Field. A panel. in CHI 99 Extended Abstracts. 1999. Pittsburgh, USA: ACM, New York.

[9]   Anderson, R., Organisational Limits to HCI. Interview session. Conversations with Don Norman and Janice Rohn. Interactions, 2000. 7(2): p. 36-60.

[10]   Bevan, N. and J. Earthy. Usability process improvement and maturity assessment. in IHM-HCI 2001. 2001. Lille, France: Cépaduès-Editions, Toulouse.

[11]   Paulk, M., C. Weber, S. Carcia, M. Chrissis, and M. Bush, The Capability Maturity Model: Guidelines for Improving the Software Process. 1995: Addison-Wesley.

[12]   Kuvaja, P., J. Similä, L. Kranik, A. Bicego, S. Saukkonen, and G. Koch, Software Process Assessment and Improvement - The BOOTSTRAP Approach. 1994, Cambridge, MA: Blackwell Publishers.

[13]   ISO/IEC, 15504-2 Software Process Assessment - Part 2: A reference model for processes and process capability. 1998: ISO/IEC TR 15504-2: 1998 (E)

[14]   Jokela, T. Usability Capability Models - Review and Analysis. in People and Computers XIV - Usability or Else! Proceedings of HCI 2000. 2000. Sunderland, UK: Springer, London.

[15]   ISO/IEC, 18529 Human-centred Lifecycle Process Descriptions. 2000: ISO/IEC TR 18529: 2000 (E).

[16]   Jokela, T., N. Iivari, M. Nieminen, and K. Nevakivi. Developing A Usability Capability Assessment Approach through Experiments in Industrial Settings. in Joint Proceedings of HCI 2001 and IHM 2001. 2001: Springer, London.

[17]   Jokela, T. An Assessment Approach for User-Centred Design Processes. in Proceedings of EuroSPI 2001. 2001. Limerick: Limerick Institute of Technology Press.

[18]   Jokela, T., Assessment of user-centred design processes as a basis for improvement action. An experimental study in industrial settings. Acta Universitatis Ouluensis, ed. J. Jokisaari. 2001, Oulu: Oulu University Press. 168.

[19]   Jokela, T. Making User-Centred Design Common Sense: Striving for An Unambiguous and Communicative UCD Process Model. in NordiCHI 2002. 2002. Aarhus, Denmark.

[20]   ISO/TR15504-3, Software process assessment - Part 3: Performing an assessment. 1998, International Organization for Standardization, Genève, Switzerland.

[21]   ISO/TR15504-4, Software process assessment - Part 4: Guide to performing assessments. 1998, International Organization for Standardization, Genève, Switzerland.

[22]   March, S.T. and G.F. Smith, Design and Natural Science Research on Information Technology. Decision Support Systems, 1995. 15(4): p. 251-266.

SPICE, SPICE Phase 2 Trials Interim Report, Version 1.00. 1998, Available at http://www-sqi.cit.gu.edu.au/spice/. p. 172.

Characteristics of Process Improvement of Hardware-Related SW

Jussi Ronkainen[1], Jorma Taramaa[2], and Arto Savuoja[2]

[1] VTT Technical Research Centre of Finland
Kaitoväylä 1, PL 1100, 90570 Oulu, Finland
jussi.ronkainen@vtt.fi
[2] Nokia Networks/IP Mobility Network
Kaapelitie 4, PL 319, 90651 Oulu, Finland
{jorma.taramaa,arto.savuoja}@nokia.com

Abstract. High-speed digital signal processing requires sophisticated solutions for both software and hardware. Enabling software support and control over hardware functionality is a problem that will be emphasised as systems become more complex. Developing hardware-bound software is not, however, application development, and the related requirements cannot be covered in full by traditional software development processes. This paper describes experiences from the development of hardware-related software development processes at Nokia Networks. As most important characteristics of hardware-related software development, hard real-time requirements, experimental nature of work, documentation requirements, and the role of testing are presented. Characteristics of software process improvement in a hardware-dependent software environment are reported. As a result, a current-state analysis of hardware-related software development was made. Better understanding of the development processes was gained, facilitating further process improvement activities.

1 Introduction

This paper describes experiences from performing Software Process Improvement (SPI) at Nokia Networks in an environment with tight hardware couplings. The environment is involved in providing infrastructure solutions for mobile communications, data communications and Internet, where radio transmission has been tailored for GSM (Global System for Mobile Communications), EDGE (Enhanced Data rates for Global Evolution) and WCDMA (Wideband Code Division Multiple Access) based cellular base stations[1].

---

[1] For more information, see Nokia Systems and Solutions, GSM/Basestation Subsystem http://www.nokia.com/networks/systems_and_solutions/.

M. Oivo and S. Komi-Sirviö (Eds.): PROFES 2002, LNCS 2559, pp. 247–257, 2002.

The initiative for the SPI work was the fact that planning software projects in the environment, involving both software and hardware, was known to be difficult. The reasons were mainly seen to be caused by the unique nature of software development in that area. This unique nature had not been thoroughly examined from a software process improvement point of view, and needed clarifying to support further SPI activities. Therefore, the starting point for the work described in this paper was in performing current state analysis.

The method for conducting the work was mostly to attend weekly development meetings of one group at Nokia Networks that developed hardware-coupled software, and other meetings where the software architecture, testing etc. issues were discussed. Therefore, the viewpoint of this paper is very much that of DSP (digital signal processing) software development.

Most of the current state analysis was about finding and describing those factors that differentiate the development of this software from the rest. Most of the factors were dictated by hardware design that was being done in parallel with the software development. Our findings on the characteristics of hardware-bound software development are described in Chapter 2.

Recent years have shown a vast increase in the amount of software in cellular base stations. By 1999, the amount of software in Nokia's products was up to 30000 KLOC [1]. At the same time, the flexibility software offers over hardware has caused an increase in the complexity of tasks done in software.

Traditional software development methods that work well in most areas of development tend to fall short in the turbulent hardware-software boundary. A direct cause from the lack of well-defined software processes is that project planning and measuring project progress are difficult. Software Process Improvement in the hardware boundary is discussed in Chapter 3.

Chapter 4 discusses the results we have gained from the work so far, illustrating the hardware-related software processes. Comments on the future direction of our work are also provided.

2   Embedded System Development in Signal Processing Applications

Embedded systems are application-specific computing devices that consist of standard and custom hardware and software components. Standard hardware usually consists of commercial microprocessors or microcontrollers whereas custom hardware is implemented as an application-specific integrated circuit (ASIC).

Wireless applications, such as cellular base stations, use digital signal processors, a special variant of microprocessor, for their realisation. During the last ten years, digital signal processing has been a facilitator of emerging technology, especially in audio and communication systems [2]. With increasing data rates and more sophisticated use of data (for example, streaming video), the role of signal processing grows from one telecommunication system generation to another [3]. As signal processing requirements grow, the role of hardware-software co-design becomes increasingly important in system design [4]. Fig. 1 illustrates this concept.

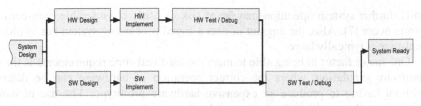

Fig. 1. A typical HW-SW project timeline

The partitioning between hardware and software is difficult to make; off-the-shelf digital signal processors offer flexibility in terms of software functionality, and updatability, but high performance requirements necessitate implementing the most time-critical parts of the signal processing chain in hardware [5]. Furthermore, as fast time-to-market cycles are important in embedded system development, both software and hardware have to be designed simultaneously [6].

Because a significant part of the functionality of the system is done in purpose-built hardware, a great deal of software has to be written merely to make the hardware-software co-operation possible. And, because of the complex control and testing support required over hardware, co-design increases in complexity, as illustrated in Fig. 2.

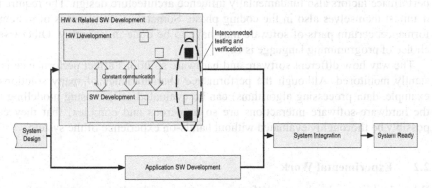

Fig. 2. The timeline of a DSP-ASIC co-design project

Contrary to many other embedded systems, in digital signal processing the hardware components that are controlled with software are not simple or passive (such as fans or temperature gauges), but elements that perform complicated mathematical tasks. This is demanding for the software that controls the hardware, and generates unique needs for the development process. In our work, four characteristics of hardware-bound software development were seen to rise above others. These characteristics – hard real-time requirements, experimental work, documentation requirements, and the role of testing – are described in the following.

2.1   Hard Real-Time Requirements

One labelling characteristic of HW-coupled SW is that the real-time requirements are strict. This means that if the software fails to meet the requirements (for example, by providing insufficient data throughput or by taking too much time processing a system call), further system operation may be at risk or other considerable, non-correctable errors occur [7]. Also, the amount of data a signal processing system has to process in real-time is typically large.

One major factor in being able to meet the hard real-time requirements is the use of hardware simulation, where the correct operation of hardware can be determined without having to produce an expensive hardware prototype. The use of hardware simulation also enables the testing of hardware-software co-operation, making the simulation environment an indispensable co-design tool.

The hardware simulators require, however, a lot of effort to set up and maintain. Furthermore, the required expertise to operate a hardware simulator is often available only through hardware (i.e. ASIC) specialists. Therefore, as hardware-related software has to be tested and verified in a simulator, software developers have to schedule their projects so that the required expertise is available. In practice, this means that software units that correspond to a certain hardware unit have to be tested and verified directly after the hardware unit, before the simulation environment is modified to support the testing of another hardware unit.

In hardware-related software development, real-time requirements such as data throughput rates, function call latencies, cycle counts, interrupt congestion and other performace factors also fundamentally influence architecture design. The requirements manifest themselves also in the coding phase. Sometimes, for reasons of system performance, certain parts of software may have to be done in assembly. Otherwise, the choice of programming language is C.

The way how different software and hardware solutions affect performance is constantly monitored. Although the performance characteristics of many solutions (for example, data processing algorithms) can be evaluated offline using modelling tools, the hardware-software interactions are so numerous and complex, that they cannot possibly be thoroughly evaluated without hands-on experience of the system.

2.2   Experimental Work

When building a hardware platform, consisting of hardware and the software that drives it, the initial learning curve for software developers is steep. Furthermore, as the hardware itself is still under development, the SW developers have to understand the impact of changes in hardware to their code, and therefore to have a solid understanding of the system. While the high level requirements are usually well understood and clear (as defined, for example, by the international 3GPP consortium[2]), implementation details are initially hazy. Each new generation of telecommunication devices tends to be much more complicated than the previous ones, and new technical solutions emerge.

An additional cause for non-determinism to the development is the fact that the other counterpart of HW-bound software, the telecommunication application, is not fully available until at a later stage of development. Hence, the early stages of HW-bound software development could be dramatised as building software that serves non-existent software, using non-existent hardware.

---

[2] The 3rd Generation Partnership Project, see http://www.3gpp.org/

Generally, software developers are taught some variation of the waterfall method, and their conception of how a software project should be carried out relies on that background. As the number of unknown quantities rises, however, the waterfall method becomes unmanageable.

It is no surprise that hardware-oriented software development is particularly experimental in nature. In order to gain understanding of the system, and to cope with changing requirements, software developers tend towards an iterative approach. Typically, a developer writes draft design documentation, and comes up against an uncertainty that blocks his progress. He then makes experiments with code, examining system characteristics and behavior, until he understands the particular problem well enough to proceed with design. An iterative approach is good in that it acknowledges the fact that every requirement cannot be known and every design decision cannot be made before writing software. Thus, the initially often overwhelming surge of unknowns can effectively be tackled, one issue at a time.

A problem caused by the impossibility to make complete designs in one go is that software developers, most having an engineering background that emphasises accuracy and exactness, tend to keep their incomplete design drafts to themselves. What is not commonly understood is that if half a page of documentation is all that can be made at some point, it is the documentation, and should be given to the people who need it.

2.3   Documentation Requirements

In order to be able to implement the software-hardware interface efficiently, communication between hardware and software designers has to work. DSP driver developers have to inform the hardware designers exactly how they intend to access the external hardware, and the hardware designers need to tell the SW developers how to operate the ASIC. By nature, both information are bit-specific, and have to be communicated in an exact fashion. Thus, writing hardware drivers and other software that directly accesses hardware relies particularly heavily on documentation.

The problem is that SW and HW designers come from very different backgrounds, and have different vocabularies and notations. Furthermore, the documentation both do have separate purposes and viewpoints. This results in communication overhead, with the many different notations confusing the developers on both sides.

One factor introduced by hardware-software co-design is change. Since the amount of software that is not directly related to hardware is great (most of the software that implements the telecommunication functionality), and the hardware-related software is done significantly ahead of that software, every performance etc. requirement cannot be accurately stated in early stages of development. Recent advances in hardware design and simulation technologies allow late freezing of hardware, enabling extensive experimentation in both hardware and related software development.

Because of the experimental development style, documentation is also subject to change. Therefore, colossal documentation of either code or designs is not feasible until very late stages of development. Early on in development, the level of documentation is largely up to the individual developer. Since code and design are likely to change, documentation is usually kept very light. Practices for reviewing and approving the documents also have to be efficient and fast, because the dependence on the changing hardware environment requires that software development can quickly change course. Extensive documentation is not produced until at a later phase, when they are needed in other SW development.

However, the iterative development method depends on timely and accurate information exchange between HW and SW developers; otherwise, the benefits of short development cycles may be lost in consecutive software iterations based on outdated HW documentation. The level of and the notation for the documentation has to be constantly balanced between extensiveness and having just the right information, in the right format, at the right time. In our case, Use Cases [8] and corresponding UML notations have been seen as a means of describing the relevant parts of hardware, software, and their interconnections in a coherent way.

2.4   The Role of Testing

Due to reliability and device autonomy requirements, testing is paramount in embedded, high-speed digital signal processing systems [6]. The role of testing is further emphasised by the parallel HW and SW development, where regression tests are commonly used to ensure that changes have been handled properly, and the parallel development lines are not allowed to drift too far apart.

In embedded system development, the range of testing is widespread. In addition to the traditional software test types (unit, integration, and system tests, for example), there are many specific testing types. The normal software tests are not quite conventional, either, as often the counterpart for testing is not another piece of software, but hardware. There is independent software and hardware testing, but testing the correct interaction between hardware and software is a crucial factor in determining whether the system works as expected. This stage of embedded system development, known as co-verification, often requires a significant part of the overall system development effort [9].

Co-verification is a major cause to the many test types specific to embedded system development. Since control is running on a DSP processor, Built-in Self-Tests (BISTs) implemented in DSP SW are currently considered as the most suitable technique for obtaining specific information about the HW to ensure proper device boot or to determine device status in case of malfunction. The BISTs are also used in production and maintenance phases.

The need to test against hardware models causes additional burden to testing, as extensive test harnesses are not available. In the end, the system under test has to work real-time. Because of this, typical software testing and debugging techniques, such as halting program execution and examining program state are not always possible.

In addition to the preplanned tests, software designers commonly write ad hoc tests to address acute development problems. Consequently, the overall amount of test software in a digital signal processing system is great, more than many developers of desktop software (or telecom application software, for that matter) often realise.

The amount and complexity of hardware-bound software are rapidly increasing. Furthermore, as hardware-bound software does not directly implement, for example, a function of WCDMA, it has not been regarded as „proper" telecommunication software. For this reason, SPI issues in hardware-bound software have been overlooked in the past.

3   Software Process Improvement

The trend in wireless communication is to move functionality from dedicated radio frequency hardware to digital signal processing in order to gain more flexibility in signal transmission / reception solutions. A system, where radio functionalities are largely replaced by signal processing, is often referred to as a software defined radio, or SW radio [10]. While the advent of a true software radio is yet to come, the amount of software that functions in the hardware boundary will steadily increase, as more signal processing functionality is required. In addition, some of current hardware functionality will in the future be replaced by DSP software, while the amount of hardware functionality will also rise. This development trend is illustrated in **Fig. 3**. The implementation technology in telecommunication applications is a mix of digital signal processor software and purpose-built hardware, and the roles of each technology have to be rethought for every product generation (for example, from GSM to EDGE to WCDMA), as the performance requirements grow. Typically, software functionality is increased until performance requirements necessitate the use of new hardware solutions (ASICs), forcing the software-hardware interface to be redesigned.

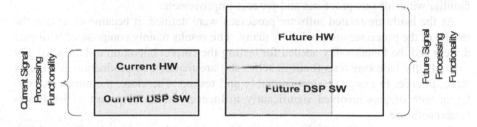

Fig. 3. The roles of software and hardware in current and future digital signal processing

Process improvement in the context of digital signal processing software has been a subject of research before (e.g., in [11]), but the specific effects of close hardware interconnections have not been addressed. Because of the increasing complexity of software, software process improvement will inevitably become crucial in the development of hardware-related software as well.

In our case it was initially known that the development of hardware-related software would differ from the development of telecommunication software. The software processes, mainly targeted at creating telecommunication application software, would not cover all the phases that are present in HW-related software development, causing difficulties in planning hardware-bound software projects. Most importantly, the estimates of required work and schedule could not be made accurately enough.

In order to support project planning, and to enhance the visibility of the hardware-related software activities, it was decided to determine how the hardware-bound software processes differ from the software processes used in producing other software. This would form a baseline for further process improvement.

The method for defining the baseline was to follow-up the development practices, and to document them. Great attention was given to the input and output documents, and recognising the various development phases. Concurrently, the specific features of hardware-related software development were identified and documented.

The documented practices were combined into a specifically tailored process description. A hardware-related software process typically consists of several concurrent development lines. For example, hardware tests, elementary drivers and driver interfaces for higher software layers are developed simultaneously. As the development lines depend largely on one another, each process phase is performed in an iterative fashion. Many process phases are labelled by their input documents, many of which are often produced by the concurrent hardware development. In fact, often there are more input documents from hardware development than there are from other software development. Also very characteristic of hardware-related software development is the continuous testing, which often depends largely on hardware development.

Interfaces that are purely software (for example, driver interfaces to higher software layers) are not particularly problematic as regards software processes. The people who design and implement the interfaces have software backgrounds, making co-operation simple. Both the hardware-related and the telecommunication software developers are familiar with software processes and process improvement.

As the hardware-related software processes were defined, it became clear that the results of the processes are needed by many. The results mainly comprise of hardware drivers and the functionality needed for testing the correct operation of hardware. For example, the hardware tests (built-in self-tests) are required by production at an early stage, in order to design product assembly and testing. Therefore, the number of different technologies involved significantly influences the development of hardware-bound software.

As a consequence, one of the major problems in hardware-related software development is in achieving efficient communication between all associated parties. Traditionally, there has not been such a great need for early communication between hardware and software developers; not much more than a decade ago, most of the functionality in telecommunication devices was done in hardware.

4   Results and Future Work

We observed and documented the processes of developing hardware-bound software at Nokia IMN for approximately one year. The most important results we got from that work were explicit process descriptions that describe the current development practices for HW-bound software, and an explicit definition of the specific document templates that are needed. The processes and their interrelationships are outlined in Fig. 4, along with their most significant external interfaces.

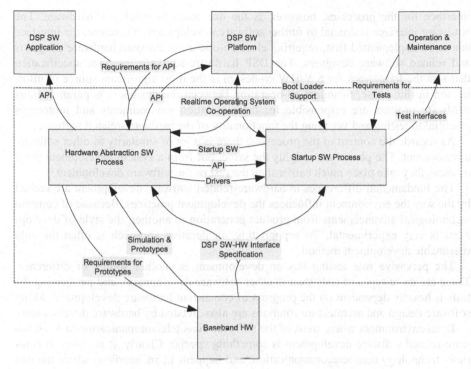

Fig. 4. The hardware-related software processes

The main processes covered by our work were the hardware abstraction software process and the startup software process (bounded by a dashed line in Fig. 4). These processes are responsible for creating hardware access functions along with a suitable abstraction layer (API, or application programming interface), and the software required to check that the hardware is running properly. The latter plays an important part in system boot and during the assembly of each device, as well as in after-delivery system maintenance. Both processes are tightly interconnected, as the tests require hardware access, and the hardware abstraction software eventually requires the startup functionality. The drivers are required by the startup software, as the system tests may call for a higher level of control over the system than the API offers to the higher layers of software.

The processes are a part of the DSP software platform that deals with all software-controlled, hardware-related functionality in a given product. The platform also offers common functionality that makes use of the real-time operating system running on the DSP. Incorporating the real-time operating system is a task that requires close co-operation with the designers of the drivers and the startup software, which hands the system boot over to the real-time operating system after initial boot tests.

The application programming interface and the test interfaces are what the hardware-related software processes offer to higher layers of software, and the corresponding requirements are important inputs for the processes. The most significant interface for the processes, however, is the one towards baseband[3] hardware. The hardware interface is crucial to further software development. Therefore, the interface has to be implemented first, requiring close co-operation between hardware designers and related software designers. The DSP hardware-software interface specification that sets the framework for SW-HW co-design is the most significant source of information in this phase. Seamless co-operation between the designers is paramount, as hardware projects are responsible for the simulation environments and prototypes essential to testing and verifying the functionality of the hardware-related software.

As regards the content of the processes, there is a lot of similarity to other software development. The phases are roughly the same, but from a system development point of view, they take place much earlier than the rest of the software development.

The fundamental differences in hardware-related software development are caused by the way the environment influences the development practices. Because of constant technological advancements from product generation to another, the style of development is very experimental. To support this, an iterative approach is often the only reasonable development method.

The pervasive role testing has on development is another source of difference. There are more types of tests than in other software development, and performing the tests is heavily dependent on the progress of concurrent hardware development. Many software design and architecture solutions are also dictated by hardware development.

In an environment where most of the software runs telecommunication tasks, hardware-related software development is something special. Clearly, it is closer to computer technology than telecommunication, and happens in an interface, where the two disciplines of hardware and software overlap.

Now that the process of writing HW-related software has been charted, corresponding project schedule estimates can be made more accurately. The amount of work required is now better known, as the process has become more visible. SPI-wise, more accurate project control methods can be applied, as the input and output documents, process phases etc. have been written down.

The process descriptions done during this work have been used in developing hardware-related software for a new generation cellular base station. The software developers' day-to-day work has also been made simpler by recognising the need for non-standard document and code templates, and providing them.

As the hardware-related software processes are more visible, and documented in more detail than before, it is now also possible to improve estimates and process control by introducing specialized metrics to measure them. Defining and piloting the metrics to further enhance the visibility of the processes is a prospective future task.

Our next task, however, will likely be to explore a bit deeper into the corresponding processes in hardware development. ASIC developers have their own work culture and processes, and their needs for documentation are different from those of software developers. The need for seamless co-operation between the two disciplines requires efficient harmonisation in those sections, where hardware and software co-operate. This will include more unified project planning and scheduling between hardware and

---

[3] The term „baseband" refers to signal processing at a signal's actual rate, before being modulated to a radio frequency.

software development, and more formal practices in the overlapping regions. Process improvement on the hardware-software boundary cannot be done by improving both technologies individually, but rather has to be done in close co-operation.

Acknowledgements

The authors wish to thank the Nokia Networks' experts who provided their input to this paper.

References

[1]   Känsälä, K.: Practices for Managing a Corporate-wide SPI Programme. In: European SEPG Conference. Amsterdam, The Netherlands. (1999)

[2]   Maliniak, L.: Will DSPs Blaze the Trail to 3G Wireless? Wireless Systems Design, Vol. 6(3) (2001) 37-40

[3]   Ajluni, C.: 3G Drives Base-Station Challenges. Wireless Systems Design, Vol. 2(11) (2000) 38-39

[4]   Kostic, Z., Seetharaman, S.: Digital signal processors in cellular radio communications. IEEE Communications Magazine, Vol. 35(12) (1997) 22-35

[5]   Gatherer, A., et al.: DSP-Based Architectures for Mobile Communications: Past, Present and Future. IEEE Communications Magazine, Vol. 38(1) (2000) 84-90

[6]   Kuvaja, P., et al.: Specific Requirements for Assessing Embedded Product Development. In: International Conference on Product Focused Software Process Improvement. Oulu, Finland. Technical Research Centre of Finland (1999) 68-85

[7]   Stankovic, J. A.: Real-Time and Embedded Systems. ACM Computing Surveys, Vol. 28(1) (1996) 205-208

[8]   Jacobsen, I., et al.: Object-Oriented Software Engineering: A Use-Case-Driven Approach. 4th edn. Addison-Wesley (1994)

[9]   Hopes, T.: Hardware/software co-verification, an IP vendors viewpoint. In: International conference on computer design: VLSI in Computers and Processors. (1998) 242-246

[10]   Buracchini, E.: The software radio concept. IEEE Communications Magazine, Vol. 38(9) (2000) 138-143

[11]   Vierimaa, M., et al.: Experiences of practical process improvement. Embedded Systems Programming Europe, Vol. 2(13) (1998) 10-20

Evaluating Evolutionary Software Systems

Teade Punter, Adam Trendowicz, and Peter Kaiser

Fraunhofer IESE
Sauerwiesen 6, D-67661 Kaiserslautern, Germany
{punter,trend,kaiser}@iese.fhg.de

Abstract. non-functional requirements (NFRs) of software-intensive systems that are under continuous evolution should be evaluated during early development phases in order to be able to improve those systems and achieve 'time-to-market'. However, current evaluations are often done during late stages, like coding and testing. In this paper we propose an approach to evaluate NFRs earlier. The requirements for this approach are the use of flexible and reusable quality models, which can deal with little data, that are transparent and measurement-based. Our approach, called Prometheus, is a way of modeling NFRs that should cope with those requirements. Prometheus applies the quality modeling concept from the SQUID approach, the probability concept of Bayesian Belief Nets (BBNs) and the specification concepts of the Goal Question Metric (GQM) approach.

1 Introduction

With the complexity of the software that is developed nowadays, also the attention for non-functional requirements has increased. Non-functional requirements concern the reliability, maintainability, efficiency or portability of a software-intensive system. Especially in complex systems where software is embedded, like automotive systems or medical devices, non-functional requirements have great influence on user-performance. For instance, rebooting a control panel in a car that takes one minute is unacceptable.

Especially in market-driven software development, where embedded software is developed the necessity of paying attention to non-functional requirements is already known. Market-driven software development focuses on markets instead of particular customer or (group of) user(s). An example is the TV-market. Dealing with software of TV-tuners requires considerable attention for Reliability issues. Putting the software once in a TV does not allow future improvement of the software after it has been sold. Of course, 'maintenance on the fly' is a possibility [1], but economical approaches for this, that have wide user-acceptance too, have not been proved yet.

A typical feature of these kind of software-intensive systems is their evolution context. *Evolution* is hereby considered as the evolution of requirements, systems and system families, system architectures, individual components, resource constraints

M. Oivo and S. Komi-Sirviö (Eds.): PROFES 2002, LNCS 2559, pp. 258–272, 2002.

(concerning timing & memory requirements) and underlying hardware. The existence of evolution in software systems is already known from the 1970's [2]. The increasing pressure of time to market, combined with the production of complex software in an evolution context pushes industry in estimating non-functional requirements as early as possible in the development process. Correcting or improving the software in an early phase is better than in front of the acceptance test. Instead evaluation of software intensive systems during their whole life cycle is necessary. This is derived from the requirements applied when generally designing reliable products in cost and time driven market, namely [3]:

- risks and potential problems are identified and resolved as much as possible in the early phases of the development process;
- actual capabilities of products, in terms of its functionality and non-functional quality are validated as soon as possible in the development process;
- where a mismatch between prediction and actual capability exist this mismatch is investigated on root-cause level and this information is deployed to the relevant actors.

This paper deals about the evaluation of NFRs in software-intensive system by focusing on the possibilities for early predicting system's quality. Section 2 identifies the problems in evaluating NFRs in software-intensive systems. We will argue that specific requirements for quality models should be set. These requirements are presented in section 3. The sections 4 and 5 define the Prometheus approach that should fulfill these requirements.

The presented research is a reflection of the work that the authors conduct for the ITEA Empress project[1]. The project aims at developing a methodology and process for real-time embedded software development that supports management of evolution in a flexible and dynamic way. The project has started in January 2002 and will run till December 2003.

2   Evaluating Non-functional Requirements

This section identifies the problems in evaluating NFRs in software-intensive systems. This is done by paying attention to the „why", „what", „how" and „when" questions regarding evaluating NFRs.

Why – it has already been stated in previous section that the increasing pressure of time to market, combined with the production of complex software in an evolution context pushes industry in estimating non-functional requirements as early as possible in the development process. Evaluation NFRs is required to control the development process as well as the complete systems´ lifecycle to produce real time and embedded software systems that meet the customer's expectations.

What is evaluation of NFRs? – it is the systematic examination of to which extent the non-functional requirements are fulfilled by (parts of) the software intensive sys-

---

[1] Empress stands for: Evolution Management and Process for Real-time Embedded Software System; http://www.empress-itea.org/index.html

tem. Evaluation NFRs has to do with verifying requirements [4], which is the examination, analysis, test, or demonstration that proves whether a requirement has been satisfied, however it is also related to validating the requirements to ensure that the set of requirements will be consistent and that a real-world solution can be built that satisfies the requirements, as well as that it can be proven that such a system satisfies its requirements.

How is evaluation conducted? – code metrics assessment is a major approach to evaluate NFRs. It is the Static analysis tools like QAC/++ or Logiscope are used for this code measurement. These tools are able to identify files of source code that are not conformant to the specified quality characteristics. Attributes that are often dealt in code metric assessments are: cohesion, and maintainability, fault proneness [5]. The tools can also be used to baseline the current state of the software.

When to evaluate? – code metric assessment is one of the evaluation approaches. Another approach is architecture assessment that is applied during the design phase when architecture is constructed. Major approaches for architecture assessment are SAAM and ATAM [6], which will prove whether software architecture is modifiable, what kind of modifications the system is likely to undergo and how the architecture can manage with this changes. Other approaches to evaluate NFRs exist as well, e.g., reliability modeling or the automatic requirement analysis tool [7].

The challenge for evaluating non-functional requirements during early development phases is to evaluate the product, process and/or resources during early phases in order to be able to give an accurate prediction of end-systems quality. On the one side the software cannot properly evaluated unless the requirements are at least known (what will be our product?) and also stable. Therefore evaluation is normally done on end products or at least on intermediate product components that have a certain maturity degree. On the other side market pressure urges companies to do earlier evaluation, as the introduction has shown already. Figure 1 depicts this dilemma of when to evaluate: starting an evaluation having enough data and criteria to judge or starting earlier to be in time to change the process and improve the product.

Looking at the evaluation approaches presented before, it is obvious that not all approaches are able to cover evaluation during the complete life cycle of the software system. For example the code metric approach can only be used when code is available. So during the requirements analysis and design phase the approach is not applicable. Meanwhile, architecture assessment is restricted to design and cannot be used later on in the development process. This means that the development phase determines the evaluation approach that is to be applied. This has to do with our ability to define criteria during the phases of a product.

The critical issue for successful evaluation is to have insight in the criteria and being able with this reference to judge about what is good and wrong about the evaluation object or at least to determine if the thing that is being evaluated is acceptable or not. Such criteria are available for development processes; think about the base practices stated in ISO 15504 or the key process areas defined in the CMM. Based upon these reference models, process assessments, like BOOTSTRAP can be done. These assessments focus on the process and resource issues.

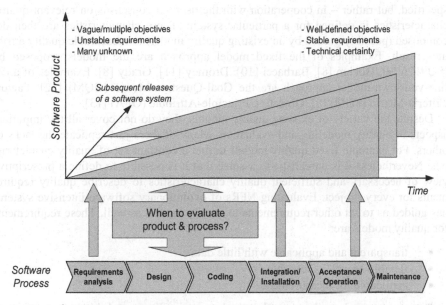

Fig. 1. The trade-off between having information to ground the evaluation and being in time to change the process and improve the product

We are less optimistic when looking at the criteria or reference models for product quality. Often these criteria are context dependent and not as that stable. This is illustrated in figure 1 with the transfer from the situation where we should deal with unstable requirements and where there are many unknowns to the situation where requirements are stable, with technical certainty. Of course we can partially rely on process assessment, because of the assumption that process quality determines product quality. However, for reliable and mature evaluation of NFRs this approach is too weak. Therefore we need an approach that specifically addresses our needs for evaluating NFRs and that covers process, product as well as the subcontractor perspective on the criteria that are set for the software intensive system. Quality models – that contain these criteria and that are in fact the reference model- plays a crucial role in our approach.

3   Quality Models to Evaluate Non-functional Requirements

This section defines requirements, which quality models should fulfill in order to be able to evaluate NFRs of software-intensive systems successful.

According to [8] there are two kinds of approaches to modeling product quality presented by researchers: fixed-model and define-your-own-model. The fixed-model approach assumes that all important quality characteristics are a subset of those in a published model. To control and measure each quality attribute, the models associated internal quality characteristics, measures, and relationships are used. This contrasts a define-your-own-model approach where not a specific set of quality characteristics is specified, but rather – in cooperation with the user - a consensus on relevant quality characteristics is defined for a particular system. These characteristics are then decomposed (possibly guided by an existing quality model) to measurable quality attributes result. Examples of the fixed model approach are the models proposed by ISO9126 [9], Boehm [8], Barbacci [10], Dromey [11], Grady [8]. Examples of a define-your-own-model approach are the Goal-Question-Metric (GQM) [12], Factor-Criteria-Metric (FCM) [8], Objective-Principle-Attribute (OPA) [13].

Despite the variety of existing quality models, they do not cover all the important aspects of quality modeling and evaluation. Many of them just replicate the lacks of others. For example fixed quality models define a constant set of quality characteristics. Nevertheless it is unrealistic to assume that it is possible to define a prescriptive view of necessary and sufficient quality characteristics to describe quality requirements for every project. Evaluating NFRs of evolutionary software-intensive systems has guided us to set other requirements to quality models as well. These requirements for quality models are:

- transparent and applicable with little data
- flexible as well as reusable
- applicable for measurement

Transparent and applicable with little data - A quality model should be transparent to know the rationale of how certain attributes are related to others and how to subdivide them into sub attributes. For example, the model presented by Barbacci [10] does include software safety aspects while the ISO 9126 [9] does not. Both models do lack a rationale for deciding which quality attributes relate to each other or how to refine an attribute into sub-attributes. As a consequence, selection of attributes, sub-attributes and metrics can be seen arbitrary. Transparency of a quality model does also mean that the meaning of the attributes and their interrelations are clearly (unambiguously) defined. In many models, the distinction between certain quality characteristics according to their definitions is not clear. For example, the average developer will not be able to distinguish between attributes like interoperability, adaptability, and configurability, e.g., in [9], as they might regard them as being identical. Transparency of a quality model requires also insight in interrelationships between the attributes to detect conflicts, trade-offs and redundancies. Those interrelationships are especially important as far as the model accuracy and its predictive capabilities are concerned.

Because of the lack of transparency such approaches as artificial intelligence (e.g., neural networks) and regression modeling –see e.g., [5]- are not suitable for our work on evaluating NFRs. They are in fact „black-box" approaches that do not provide insight into the quality model as well as that their creation cannot be influenced. Another reason why these approaches are excluded is their incapability to cope with little, imperfect data. Artificial intelligence and regression modelling require normally a lot of quantitative data that are often not available in NFR evaluation practice.

Flexible as well as reusable - A quality model should be flexible because of the context dependency of software quality. Normally this is denoted by the famous sentence 'quality is in the eyes of its beholders', which stresses that different stakeholders involved in the system development have different perspectives on the quality that should be the result. It is widely accepted that stakeholder views – like quality assurance, (sub) contractor or engineer- should take into account to specify quality successfully; see e.g., [14]. The need for flexibility in quality models is also given by software system's domain and the phase in the life cycle during which the system is evaluated. A project domain considers the different types of software systems, like embedded systems or web applications, which each has their own requirements. The life cycle phase during which a system is evaluated is another dimension that requires flexible quality models. This was already addressed in section 2 where it was made clear that not all evaluation approaches are able to cover evaluation during the complete life cycle of the software system. Methods like ATAM are applied in early stages of systems and software development. The methods as such do not deliver a set of criteria like quality models intend to do. So dependent on the data available during those phases, we can specify the required approach for such phases.

Flexibility of a quality models implies that such models have to be tailored to organization-specific characteristics; therefore the models should be transparent. In addition a quality model should reflect project individual characteristics, namely the stakeholders and lifecycle. At the same time it should be applicable in evolutionary environments and allow learning across similar projects. Fixed quality frameworks – as we referred to in the beginning of this section – do not provide guidance for this tailoring. Despite, define-your-own-models allow an organization custom-tailoring a quality model. Especially the GQM approach is suitable to specify a quality model that matches company-specific needs. However, as such approaches have the disadvantage that they each time start their new measurement program from scratch. Thus they are often not feasible when evaluating evolutionary software-intensive systems, because evaluation requires a considerable amount of effort, time and expertise that requires avoiding this 'reinventing of wheels'. Therefore quality models should be flexible as well as that they should reuse existing experiences that are stored in existing quality models.

Applicable for measurement - The term 'systematic examination' that was used to define evaluation in section 2 implies that evaluation should be measurement-based. Measurement is defined as the assigning of values (which may be a number or category) from a scale to an attribute of an entity [9]. Especially in a context of evaluation software-intensive systems it is important that quality models express the entities as well as their attributes. Quality models are inadequate for measurement when they only denote the attributes - the 'ilities'- of the system and abstract too much from the entities that relate to those attributes. For example, analyzability of documentation might require another evaluation than analyzability of the source code in programmable logic controllers (PLCs).

Some of the quality models; e.g., [9], have restricted accuracy due to fact that they do not explicitly map quality attributes to metrics. There is often no description of how the lowest-level metrics are composed into an overall assessment of higher-level NFRs. Then there is no means to verify how a chosen metric affects the observed behaviour of a quality attribute.

Different distinctions to identify software measurement, like direct versus indirect measurement and internal versus external quality, have their impact on the way attribute relationships should be constructed and the way how the associated metrics, that measure the value of the attributes, should be derived; see [9]. Two opposite types of metrics can be distinguished in evaluation [16], namely: 'hard' metrics (like code metrics, see section 2) versus 'soft' metrics (like for example applied in a expert judgement or a process assessment). Between those opposites, intermediary forms exist. Next table provides an overview of the factors that determine those two types of metrics.

Table 1. Identification of hard and soft metrics [16]

	'Hard' metrics	'Soft' metrics
Value (on a scale)	Quantitative	Qualitative
Value assignment	Direct, indirect	Indirect
Attributes	Intern	Extern, Quality-in-use
Measurement procedure	Objective	Subjective

Hard metrics are often preferred above the soft ones because the hard ones are considered as more objective and therefore better. The specific problem with soft metrics is the variance that is generated when doing qualitative measurement. For example, Andersen and Kyster report in [7] about a 40% variance between two expert ratings of the same software product. It is often addressed as ´subjective´ and therefore avoided. Determining opinions in a systematic way e.g., by using structured questionnaires and closed answer options − a fixed set of response possibilities for each question − can reduce variance. Other possibilities are to apply control questions, repeating questions by formulating them in another way or repeating questions by repeating the response possibilities; see e.g., [17].

An advantage of soft metrics is that they normally are able to measure attributes on a higher abstraction level and that it is often easier to implement them quickly than for example code metrics which face several problems e.g., they are dependent on the programming language. Soft metrics are also often more suitable to measure process as well as resource issues. This makes it necessary to try to apply hard and soft metrics in combination in order to be able to address (intermediate) products (e.g., size, reliability, maintainability) as well as process (e.g., effectiveness, efficiency) and resource issues (e.g., capability, capacity).

4   Prometheus: A Probabilistic Quality Model

This section presents the Prometheus approach. Prometheus stands for Probabilistic Method for early evaluation of NFRs. Prometheus develops quality models, which fulfill the requirements that were discussed in previous section. In order to achieve this we have combined three existing methodologies to modeling and evaluating quality of software product: Software Quality in Development (SQUID), Bayesian Belief Networks (BBN) and Goal-Question-Metric (GQM).

We apply concepts of the *SQUID approach* [15] to specify quality attributes and their dependencies in a measurement-based way. It also addresses the transparency, reusability and flexibility requirements for a quality model.

A structure quality model is drawn that allows us either adopting one (or more) of the existing quality models or developing from scratch the new model that best suits organization's characteristics. The basic elements of the structure model are: entity, attribute, value, unit and measurement instrument.

An *entity* can be any (intermediate) product or artefact, like document or module source code. It might be also a process (like requirements engineering or configuration management) or a resource (like a review technique, supporting tool or the development team). An entity possesses one or many *attributes* while an attribute can quantify one or many different entities. During an evaluation we want to determine the value of the attributes. Therefore, measurement is conducted during which values are assigned to the attributes. The *value* is than what is obtained by applying a specific measurement *unit* to a particular entity and attribute.

The metrics that are used for such measurement are represented in the structure model by unit. A *metric* is the unit (or scale) with the procedure to determine the value. The use of units is extended beyond the ratio and interval scales in order to allow for the definition of the scale points for the ordinal scale measures and categories used for nominal scale measures. This supports distinguishing between soft and hard metrics.

The technique that helps us with doing measurement is defined in the structure model as *measurement instrument*. This might be the shell to determine the value of the code metrics to be able to start a code analysis. With representing the element measurement instrument in the structure model, it is possible to distinguish between the measurement level (represented by unit and value) that is needed for the logical description of metrics and the technique level that we need for implementing those metrics during an evaluation.

We propose to add the elements stakeholder and phase to the existing SQUID model. The relevance of stakeholder has been discussed in the previous section. By modeling stakeholder in a relation to the element attribute, different views on quality could be reflected in different structure and content of a quality model. The importance of *phase* in the software life cycle is already elaborated in section 2 and 3. The phase is related to entity because different product artefacts become available during the development life cycles as well as different processes are conducted and different resources are applied during subsequent phases. With acknowledging phase in the structure model is will be possible to determine which entities are possible to evaluate at which point of time.

Another change that we propose in addition to SQUID concerns the decomposition of attributes. The SQUID approach distinguishes two types of decomposition, namely: the decomposition from quality attributes into sub-characteristics that refines different aspects of the original characteristics (like ISO 9126) as well as decomposition into criteria related to properties that are believed to influence achievement of quality attributes requirements (like the McCall model). Both relationships are important, but we think that it is better, to express the elements 'internal software property', 'quality characteristic' and 'quality sub-characteristic' not separately like SQUID does. The problem with this way of representing is that it will be often difficult to reuse such abstractions made in particular context for another context, because of their specific meanings. Therefore we propose a simpler representation approach and define only the element attribute with two additional relationships, namely: decompose and influence. Below our structure model – which is an adaptation of the SQUID structure model – is presented as an Entity Relationship diagram.

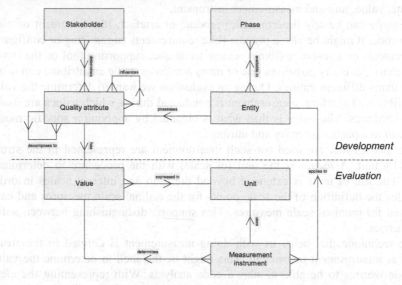

Fig. 2. Prometheus: the structure model

This structure model is used to derive actual decomposition trees, see the example in figure 3. In section 5 we will show that GQM-techniques like the goal measurement templates and abstraction sheets can support us in achieving the decompositions trees.

The *BBN approach* [18] is applied in addition to the structure in order to be able to model the decomposition and influence relationship among quality attributes and to reason (basis on those relationships and measurement data) about NFRs. With applying the BBN we address the following requirements for quality models: their transparency, reusability, dealing with missing data and different views (flexibility).

A BBN is a graphical network, which has a similar structure as the quality model (structure as well as content), contains a set of probability tables, which together represent probabilistic relationships among variables (attributes). The BBN graph consists of nodes and arcs where the nodes represent uncertain variables (discrete or continuous) and the arcs the influence relationships between the variables. Each node is described with a Node Probability Table (NPT), which cover conditional probabilities of the node's state basis on the states of nodes that influence this node.

An example of how to apply BNN in combination with the quality model is provided below given. The quality model that is presented in figure 3 is an example of a BBN for „reliability prediction" problem, which includes also the NPTs. The nodes represent attributes (discrete or continuous), for example, the node „Experience" is discrete and can have three values „low", „medium" and „high" whereas the node „size" might be continuous (such as LOC). Dependent of the organizations capabilities and needs it is of course possible to represent as discrete the variables which are in principle continuous.

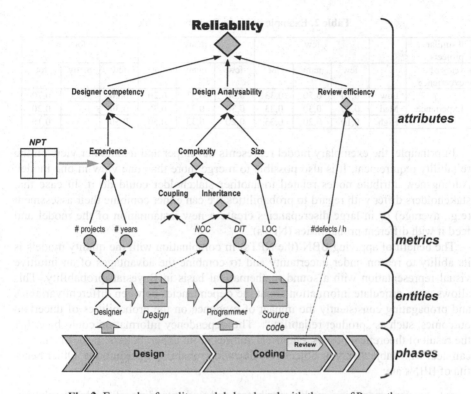

Fig. 3. Example of quality model developed with the use of Prometheus

For example we might represent size of code as „small", „medium" and „large". The arcs represent influential relationships between attributes. The number of similar projects he/she participated in and years of experience define designer experience. The exemplary node probability table (NPT) for „Experience" node might look the one shown in table 2. For the simplicity of the example we have made all considered in NPT nodes discrete so that each of them take on just three discrete values. The NPTs capture the conditional probabilities of a „Experience" node based on given the state of its parent nodes.

As we already mentioned there may be several ways of determining the probabilities for the NPTs. One of the benefits of BBNs stems from the fact that we are able to accommodate both subjective probabilities (elicited from domain experts) and probabilities based on objective data.

Having entered the probabilities we can use Bayesian probabilities to do various types of analysis. The most interesting is the propagation i.e. updating the actual probabilities after filling the model with evidence (fact). For example measured actual values of „# of similar projects" and „years of experience" are facts, and could be propagated in order to update the probabilities of „Designer level of experience". For detailed look at how BBN perform propagation we refer to the BBN-related literature e.g., [20].

Table 2. Example of Node Probability Table

# similar projects		few			many			lot		
years of experience		few	many	lot	few	many	lot	few	many	lot
	Low	0,70	0,50	0,33	0,50	0,33	0,20	0,20	0,33	0,70
Experience	Med	0,20	0,30	0,33	0,30	0,33	0,30	0,30	0,33	0,20
	High	0,10	0,20	0,33	0,20	0,33	0,50	0,50	0,33	0,10

In principle, the exemplary model represents developer and maintainer view on the reliability requirement. It is also possible to merge more than one view in one model. Adding new attribute nodes related to another stakeholder could do it. In case that stakeholders differ with regard to probabilities we can either combine their assessment (e.g., average) or in large discrepancies create a new instantiation of the model and feed it with different probabilities (NPTs).

The benefit of applying BBN (the NPTs) in combination with the quality models is its ability to reason under uncertainty and to combine the advantages of an intuitive visual representation with a sound mathematical basis in Bayesian probability. This allows us to articulate information about the dependencies between different variables and propagating consistently the impact of evidence on the probabilities of uncertain outcomes, such as „product reliability". The dependency information could be either the result of theoretical proves, empirical studies or jut expert beliefs. It means that we can deal with subjectively or objectively derived probability distributions. Other benefits of BBNs are:

- (easier) specifying quality attributes and understanding of modeled relationships among them (contradictions, redundancies) via transparent, graphical format;
- refining probabilities (across subsequent development phases or projects) in order to increase the accuracy of prediction;
- predicting with missing data;
- automatic tool support [18].

5   Specifying an Evaluation

Previous section has described the Prometheus approach to store information necessary to define transparent, flexible and reusable as well measurement quality models. This section focuses how to store the information in quality models and how to get information out of it during the evaluation process.

Based upon the general process for doing software product assessments [21] and the Quality Improvement Paradigm [22] the following phases for an evaluation process are distinguished:

- specify the evaluation of NFRs – this is to specify the non-functional requirements about a particular software-intensive system into measurable terms. The result of the specification phase will be an evaluation plan;

- execute the evaluation – this is the actual evaluation to determine the fulfillment of the system to its specified NFRs. This phase is conducted according
  to the evaluation plan and applies the evaluation techniques;
- define actions – this is definition of the actions to improve the product or process based upon the results from the execution of the evaluation. The actual
  execution of these actions, like e.g., starting reviews or component-based development is very important for using the evaluation results, but is not part of
  the evaluation. The definition of those actions should be considered as a phase
  in the evaluation;
- package evaluation experiences – this phase is important from an evaluator's
  perspective because it should provide the evaluator with information about
  criteria, techniques that might be applicable for future evaluations.

The remainder of this paragraph focuses on the first phase mainly. When specifying
the evaluation we are concerned about how to reuse existing quality models. In fact, a
match has to be made between the specific NFRs of the system that is under evaluation and the attributes (plus associated metrics and measurement instruments) proposed by the quality model. The goal measurement template and the abstraction sheet
are both techniques that facilitate this matching. Both techniques originate from the
Goal Question Metric (GQM) method [12]. The goal measurement template helps in
specifying the expectations about the evaluation. The template addresses five elements, namely:

- object – what will be analyzed? (e.g., processes, products or resource);
- purpose – why will the object be analyzed? (e.g., characterization, evaluation,
  monitoring);
  prediction, control, improvement [12]
- quality focus – what property of the object will be analyzed? (e.g., cost, correctness, defect removal, changes, reliability, user friendliness, maintainability);
- viewpoint – Who will use the data collected? (e.g., user, senior manager, project manager, developer, system tester, quality assurance manager);
- context – In which environment does the analysis take place? (e.g., organization, project, problem, processes, etcetera).

All elements of the template are equally important in the process to specify a specific evaluation plan, but especially the object and quality focus are relevant for reuse,
because they refer to entity and attribute in the quality model respectively. Having
defined the object and the quality focus for a particular evaluation, it specifies what
we need from the quality model. The viewpoint in the measurement goal template
defines which stakeholders should be taken into account during the evaluation. This
matches to the element Stakeholder in Prometheus.

Abstraction sheet is an additional technique that will help in further specifying what
is to be reused from the quality model. An *abstraction sheet* summarizes the main
issues and dependencies of an evaluation goal on four quadrants in a page, namely:

- quality model – the quality factors: what are the measured properties of the object in the goal?
- baseline hypothesis – what is the current knowledge with respect to the measured properties? The level of knowledge is expressed by baseline hypotheses.
- variation factors – which factors are expected to have an impact on quality models?
- impact on baseline hypothesis – how do these variation factors influence the quality model? What kind of dependence is assumed?

The abstraction sheets might already contain information from the quality model. When doing this it will be feasible to propose quality factors to the stakeholders so that a discussion can start on their relevance for the systems that has to be evaluated.

The goal measurement templates and abstraction sheets can also by applied to package the experience into a new quality model. The factors depicted in the abstraction sheets and the quality focus in the templates will transfer into the attributes, while the viewpoints and objects of the template are associated with the stakeholder and entity respectively.

Having specified the attributes and metrics for the evaluation the information the evaluation techniques have to be selected and assembled. The selection concerns the choice of appropriate techniques that can evaluate the stated attribute and that can cope as well with the output that results from the specified life cycle phases. General descriptions are needed that define the expected outputs per life cycle phase, for example that the requirements analysis phase is related to e.g., requirements, change requests, problem reports. Similar information should be gathered for the respective evaluation techniques, so that they can be selected.

The technique assembly is about putting the set of techniques in an order so that they can be applied for efficient and effective data collection. For example, in case of applying different assessment questionnaires the assembly will deal about when and how to consult the engineers to avoid too much disturbances. The assembly is also about passing the results of a technique to its successors, e.g., to be able to trace the same attribute during several phases of the life cycle. How to set up a taxonomy for information necessary for selection and assembly is subject of further research.

The selected evaluation techniques are to be assembled (constructed) into an integrated approach. The integrated approach makes it possible to collect information from the software process as it become available during the software engineering work and makes evaluation possible at selected intervals, such as project milestones.

6   Conclusions

In this paper we have argued that insufficient applicable criteria are available to evaluate non-functional requirements (NFRs) of evolutionary software-intensive systems during their early development phases. Therefore we need quality models that are transparent (for their rationale as well as the meaning of the attributes), able to deal with little data, flexible (being able to be tailored), reusable and measurement-based (which implies the application of hard as well as soft metrics).

An approach, called Prometheus, was introduced to cope with these requirements. It is basically a way of modeling quality that is measurement-based, that links the attributes to the evaluation objects, which might be processes, intermediate products as well as resources. The relationships between the attributes are modeled with probability tables. The quality models will be applied during a goal-oriented specification of an evaluation. The results of particular evaluation should be packaged in the quality models.

Our approach is particularly interesting for projects and organizations that want to perform measurement-based evaluation in a context of evolutionary systems. Prometheus enables them to learn effectively over several product variances/releases and will refine the proposed quality model through subsequent projects. The approach is meant to be applied during demonstrator projects in the ITEA EMPRESS project.

References

[1] Elixmann, M. and St. Hauptmann, Software Maintenance on the fly, in: Philips Res. Bull. On Software and Systems, no.14, November 1994.

[2] Belady, L.A., M.M. Lehman, A model of large program development, IBM Systems Journal, no. 3, pp.225-251, 1976.

[3] Minderhoud, S., Quality and reliability in product creation – extending the traditional approach, in: Quality and Reliability Engineering International, December 1999.

[4] Bahill, A.T. and Dean, F., "Discovering system requirements", Chapter 4 in the Handbook of Systems Engineering and Management, A.P. Sage and W.B. Rouse (Eds), John Wiley & Sons, 175-220, 1999.

[5] Briand, L., J. Wuest, "Empirical Studies of Quality Models in Object-Oriented Systems", to be published in Advances in Computers, Academic Press, updated Feb. 18, 2002.

[6] Kazman, R., e.a., The Architecture Tradeoff Analysis Method, in: 4th International Conference on Engineering of Complex Computer Systems, augustus 1998.

[7] N.E. Fenton S.LO.Pfleeger, "Software Metrics: A Rigorous and Practical Approach", PWS ISBN (0534-95429-1), 1998 (originally published by International Thomson Computer Press, 1996).

[8] Bache and Bazzana, Software metrics for product assessment, London, McGraw-Hill Book Company, 1994.

[9] ISO/IEC 9126 International Standard, Software engineering – Product quality, Part 1: Quality model, 2001.

[10] M. R. Barbacci, M. H. Klein, T. Longstaff and C. Weinstock, C. "Quality Attributes", Technical Report CMU/SEI-95-TR-021, ADA307888. Pittsburgh, PA, Software Engineering Institute, Carnegie Mellon University, December 1995.

[11] Dromey, G., Cornering the Chimera, in: IEEE Software, January, pp.33-43, 1996.

[12]   Solingen, R. van, E. Berghout, The Goal/Question/Metric method – a practical guide for quality improvement of software development, London, McGraw-Hill, 1999.

[13]   R.E. Nance, J.D. Arthur, „Managing Software Quality, A Measurement Framework for Assessment and Prediction", Springer 2002.

[14]   Kusters, R., R. van Solingen, J. Trienckens, H. Wijnands, 'User-perceptions Of Embedded Software Reliability', Proceedings of the 3rd ENCRESS Conference 1997, Chapman and Hall, ISBN 0412802805, 1997.

[15]   Kitchenham, B., S. Linkman, A. Paquini, V. Nanni, The SQUID approach to defining a quality model, in: Software Quality Journal, Vol.6, pp.211-233, 1997.

[16]   Punter, T. , Goal-oriented evaluation of software products (in Dutch), PhD thesis, Eindhoven University of Technology, 2001.

[17]   Xenos, M., D. Stavrinoudis, D. Christostodoulakis, *The correlation between developer-oriented and user-oriented software quality measurements*, in: Proceedings of International Conference on Software Quality, Dublin, pp.267-275, 1996.

[18]   Fenton NE, Krause P, Neil M, "A Probabilistic Model for Software Defect Prediction", accepted for publication IEEE Trans Software Eng, Sept 2001.

[19]   J. Pearl, „Probabilistic Reasoning in Intelligent Systems: networks of plausible inference", Morgan Kaufman 1988.

[20]   http://www.hugin.com/Products_Services/

[21]   ISO 14598-1, Information technology – Software product evaluation, Part 1 – General overview, Genève, ISO/IEC, 1999.

[22]   Basili, V.R., C. Caldiera, H.D. Rombach, Experience factory, in: Encyclopedia of Software Engineering, J. Marcianiak (ed), Vol.1, John Wiley and Sonns, pp. 469-476, 1994.

Improving the Reuse Process is Based on Understanding the Business and the Products: Four Case Studies

Jarmo J. Ahonen*, Heikki Lintinen, and Sanna-Kaisa Taskinen

Information Technology Research Institute
P.O.Box 35 (Agora), FIN-40014 University of Jyväskylä, Finland
{jarmo.ahonen,heikki.lintinen}@titu.jyu.fi
sanna-kaisa.taskinen@titu.jyu.fi

Abstract. The reuse of software engineering assets has been proposed as the most promising alternative for improving productivity and software quality. The improvement of reuse requires understanding of suitable reuse strategies and the software process. In four industrial cases the reuse process is analyzed for the purpose of its improvement and remarkable differences between successful processes are found. Those differences are due to differences in the products and businesses of the analyzed companies. In some cases the product line approach fits the business very well and high level of reuse can be achieved by using it. In other cases the black-box approach to reuse has turned out to suit the business better.

1 Introduction

The lack of talented personnel, overrun budgets, inadequate quality and timetables that do not hold are common problems in software engineering. Software companies are constantly fighting against those perils of software engineering and it seems obvious that there are no „silver bullets" for those problems (Brooks 1987). The problems are, however, very severe ones and some solutions, at least partial ones, must be found.

As one of the most promising solutions for at least some of the problems the reuse of software engineering assets has been proposed. Software reuse has quite widely been accepted as one of the most promising methods to improve the productivity of software engineering. Actually achieving software reuse has not, however, been easy. The reasons for that seem to be related to our insufficient understanding of the reuse process in general and possible reuse strategies. This may be changing because some interesting and promising frameworks for organizing the reuse have been lately proposed, see e.g. (Bosch 2000), (Jacobsen et al 1997), and (Lim 1998). In addition to that, some of the current software engineering methodologies have been evaluated in

---

* Corresponding author.

M. Oivo and S. Komi-Sirviö (Eds.): PROFES 2002, LNCS 2559, pp. 273–290, 2002.

the light of their support for software reuse (Forsell et al 2000)(Forsell et al 1999) and general guidelines for improving the software engineering process have been proposed (Zahran 1998).

The frameworks and approaches are, however, quite often based on ideal models or limited empirical studies. The amount of empirical data is, of course, always limited and the number of the cases on which the evidence is based will remain limited. It is, however important to broaden the types of software engineering businesses analyzed because a limited scope tends to gear research and development in directions which may not be beneficial outside the original scope. The importance of different types of software engineering businesses to be analyzed has been shown in an interesting way in an industry-cooperation project, in which we studied, analyzed and improved the reuse processes of the participating companies.

In the research reported in this article, the different types of businesses of the participating companies had evolved in ways which had created very different reuse strategies for the companies. Those strategies were based either on the product-line approach or on the black-box approach to reuse. The risks and problems of both strategies in the cases were analyzed and the problems turned out to be quite different and the strategies useful for different types of business.

2   Understanding the Reuse Process and Its Improvement

In order to evaluate and improve existing reuse processes one must have an ideal model of reuse, or at least some ideas on how reuse could be organized and performed. In addition to that the improvement of a process requires some context in which the improvements and the approach used for the improvement oriented interventions is justified. In the research reported in this article the selected reuse model is the one proposed by Lim (1998) and slightly modified in (Forsell 2002). The process improvement model is based on the gradual improvement approach proposed in (Humphrey 1989) and used in (Ahonen et al 2002).

The used model for reuse-oriented software development is shown in Fig. 1 (the figure is from (Forsell 2002)). In the model the essential features of reuse processes are tied up to the software development process.

The reasons why we selected Lim's model over other possible models are the following:

1. Lim's model had been previously used when cooperating with the companies and there were no factual reasons to change the framework;
2. Lim's model is process-oriented and the basic aim of the industry-cooperation project in which the data was collected, was to improve the software processes of the companies; and
3. Lim's model can be considered in connection with very different software engineering methodologies, which is important because every company had its own methodology and process model.

A model of the reuse process is not enough by itself in order to improve the actual reuse processes of the companies. In order to enable real changes in a consistent and

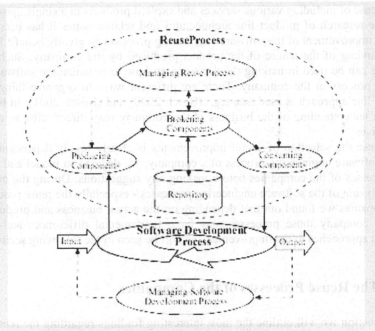

Fig. 1. A Model for reuse-oriented software development

measurable way there must be a systematic approach to the understanding and improvement. The main steps to the improvement were:

1. increase the knowledge of the real software process of the participating companies;
2. model the current software process;
3. identify the strong and weak points of the process; and
4. propose improvements, i.e. interventions to the existing practices.

In other words, the main objective of the research reported in this article was to improve the software reuse processes of the participating companies through modeling, understanding and intervention. The role of the intervention is to be the actual means of improvement.

In order to understand the software process of a company it must be modeled and analysed. The modeling technique used in this research is presented in (Ahonen et al 2002). The analysis of the process may be based on experience or on a specific model - preferably both. In this research the reuse model proposed by Lim was used as the ideal model, as noted earlier. The understanding of the software process requires understanding of the business of the company in question. The business of an IT company may be product oriented or service oriented. In addition to that, there may be differences in the number of products and the types of services provided. One of the interesting features of current IT businesses is that several types of products and services can be packaged in ways that are very different from to the traditional approaches to selling services or products. Individual packaging may be very different in the sense of including various services and explicit products in a single „product".

In the research of product line architectures and related issues it has been shown that the improvement of the software engineering process can greatly benefit from the understanding of the nature of the product produced by the company. Such understanding can be used in making the decisions on how to organize the software engineering process of the company. There are different ways to organize things if the product line approach is used, see e.g. (Bosch 2000) and (Bosch 2001). In the same way the understanding of the business of the company may direct reuse to different alternatives.

Because the selection of useful improvements is clearly highly dependent on the actual software engineering process of a company, we decided to model and analyze the processes of the companies before making any suggestions. During the modeling and analyzing of the software engineering processes - especially the reuse process - of the companies we found out that depending on the actual business and products of a specific company those processes may have fundamental differences and require different approaches to the improvement, as will be seen in the following sections.

3   The Reuse Processes of the Companies

In this section we will outline the most interesting findings regarding the reuse processes of the companies. The collection of empirical data was done in three phases, which were:

1.   process modeling;
2.   structured interviews; and
3.   workshops.

The process modeling was performed by using the process modeling technique presented in (Ahonen et al 2002). The number of modeling sessions per company varied from four to five and the modeling sessions were performed as described in (Ahonen et al 2002). The significant feature of the used approach is that the modeling sessions precede interviews, which are based on the results of the modeling sessions and the ideal model. The number of interviews per company varied from two to four and followed Lim's model. The workshop was used in order to get the company-specific analysis results and improvement recommendations approved by the company.

The companies which participated in the research will be denoted by acronyms AA, BB, CC, and DD, because the results are fairly sensitive. This is unfortunate, but necessary in order to make the results publishable. The findings and comments presented in the following tables are based on the actual comments of the representatives of the companies. Some comments may appear in several tables, but that is on purpose due to the interesting nature of those comments and the fact that the representatives of the companies thought those comments to be related to all those subprocesses of reuse. The cases in which the opinions are ours are marked by *emphasis*.

3.1   Managing the Reuse

In general it was surprising that in every company the actual amount of reuse was fairly high and at least some pieces of almost every reuse process could be found. In Tab. 1 the most important positive comments on the management of reuse are outlined and in Tab. 2 the most negative comments on the management of reuse are outlined.

Table 1. Positive findings and opinions on the management of reuse

AA	• The creation of components is performed as the normal software engineering process is performed. • Before a component is created, the need for it is separately evaluated. • Reuse is a fundamental part of the quality system of the company. The quality system includes various inspections in order to enable quality. • Participating in software reuse is everybody's responsibility. • When it is recognized that a component may be needed, a specific component implementation project is created (if the component is analyzed to be important enough). • There is no need to include component creation in the normal software engineering process.
BB	• One of the most interesting benefits of reuse was seen to be the possibility of making new employees productive faster than earlier. This would require, however, very good manuals and guidelines. • The resources required by the improvement of the reuse process will be available when needed. • There was no specific component production process.
CC	• The amount of actual reuse is high. (The amount was very likely the highest one of the cases - authors.) • Practically everything was considered reusable: product requirements, market researches, sales documents, different ideas and many other artifacts. • The product management process manages as much knowledge of implemented and considered and even rejected ideas as possible. • The idea was that reuse should be formalized and designed in a way that would make it possible for average project managers and analysts to achieve useful level of reuse. • The aim was to produce reusable components during individual product creation or enhancement processes, not with a specific process.
DD	• When a new product was under consideration, as many old plans were considered as possible. The aim of the consideration was to rip off and reuse as big parts of the previously created products as possible. • One of the methods of reuse was the intention to distribute experienced personnel to projects that had similar features as the earlier projects in which those people had participated.

Table 2. Negative findings and opinions on the management of reuse

AA	• * It seems to be the case that in order to enable reuse of existing components in a new project the aspects of reuse must be considered as early as possible in the process. That is mainly due to the fact that components tend to require changes in the specifications.
BB	• The guidelines for reuse were thought to be too vague. • There were practically no experiences on the reuse of requirements. • Possible reusable components were found by asking more experienced members of the staff. Experience played a bigger role than it should. • If reuse was considered too late in the process, then there tended to be no real possibilities for reuse. Reuse was considered to be most beneficial during the analysis and design phases. • * The identification of reusable parts of the outcome of a project required new phases to the software engineering process. Such phases were required for both the beginning of the process and the end of the process.
CC	• There were no guidelines or procedures for reuse. • The role of experienced members of the staff was very relevant. • Reusable assets were not collected in any specific way, they were scattered amongst other artifacts. Finding reusable assets required thorough knowledge and understanding of the products. • One of the most important hindrances for reuse was seen to be different licensing practices of commercial components. • It was estimated that introducing formal reuse to the process will not be without problems due to the fact that it will require changes in the ways people work. *(This was strange when considering the actual amount of reuse in the company - authors.)* • The benefits of reuse were seen to be quite difficult to be sold to employees because those benefits will materialize after a fairly long period.
DD	• The experience of employees was a necessary part of reuse. • Components that were regularly reused had not been collected into any specific place. They were found by experience. • The reuse of program code was very common, but there existed no guidelines nor rules for that.

One of the most outstanding findings is that although the level of reuse was fairly high, the guidelines and process models for managing reuse were very vague in companies CC and DD. The guidelines were much more precise in AA and BB.

3.2   Production of Components

The comments regarding the production of components are outlined in Tab. 3 and Tab. 4. Those findings outlined in the tables are very interesting.

Table 3. Positive findings and opinions on the production of reusable components

AA	• Components are produced in separate component creation projects.
	• Sometimes components are created in a customer case in which there has been a specific agreement on such creation.
	• The creation of components is performed as the normal software engineering process is performed.
	• Before a component is created, the need for it is separately evaluated.
	• The components include technical components and sometimes problem solving patterns.
	• Technical components are considered to be the most usable assets in real cases.
	• In the analysis phase the aim is to find patterns.
	• *One part of the analysis phase is „the design of reuse".
	• When it is recognized that a component may be needed, a specific component implementation project is created (if the component is analyzed to be important enough to require a real component).
	• The creation of components does not normally tax the resources of a project because components are created in separately funded and allocated projects.
BB	• Reuse of program code was very common. Most of the algorithms tend to be so complex that nobody wanted to be adventurous enough to design and implement them himself/herself.
	• The most promising assets for reuse were seen to be problem solving patterns, program code and document templates.
	• There was no specific component production process, but that alternative was under evaluation.
CC	• The opinion inside the organization was that the most natural way to develop components and other reusable assets was the actual software engineering process. No separate component engineering process was considered.
DD	• No need was seen for a separate component creation process. The opinion was that all actually reusable components will be created during the creation of the products.

A very interesting feature considering the creation of reusable assets in the companies is that the companies AA and BB had implemented or were considering the definition and implementation of a special process in order to create reusable assets. On the contrary, the companies CC and DD did not see any reason for a specific process for the creation of reusable assets.

Table 4. Negative findings and opinions on the production of reusable components

AA	<ul><li>The contract practices hinder the creation of components in customer cases.</li><li>The identification of potential components is considered to be a very demanding and difficult task, which depends on the experience and personal skills of the personnel.</li><li>The architects of the company were familiar with the concept of product lines, and their opinion was that the concept of product lines did not fit the business of the company very well.</li><li>The components tended to be fairly large and complex because the company produces complete information systems, not specific products.</li></ul>
BB	<ul><li>Architectural designs were considered to be too specific and difficult to be used. (This was in contrast to the fact that the use of problem solving patterns was clearly identifiable. Patterns were not documented in any particular way and their use was, therefore, based on personal experience. - Authors.)</li><li>Reuse of program code was based on ``copy and replace'' or the use of complete subsystems or systems; no formal tools were in use.</li><li>Customers were not seen promoting reuse because they normally wanted to own the results exclusively. That was, however, changing due to the pressures on project duration.</li><li>The opinion of the experienced personnel was that the identification of reusable parts of the outcome of a project required new phases to the software engineering process. Such phases were required for both the beginning of the process and the end of the process.</li><li>The obvious threat was that it might be tempting for the project manager to leave a component in an incomplete state due to lack of time.</li><li>The opinion was that the identification of components requires remarkable personal talents and good experience.</li></ul>
CC	<ul><li>Realizing the possibility of creating a component was considered a very demanding task. Therefore it required long and extensive experience on the products of the company.</li></ul>
DD	<ul><li>The number of ad hoc solutions and bad architectural designs made reuse much more difficult than it should have been.</li><li>It was not clear how to organize a product engineering project which aimed to produce reusable assets also.</li><li>The creation of new reusable components and finding reusable components were thought to require thorough understanding of the products. Therefore only a handful of the personnel was considered experienced enough to have the responsibility of those tasks.</li><li>The budget and timetable pressures were considered to work against the creation of reusable assets.</li></ul>

3.3   Brokering the Components

The findings considering the brokering of components are outlined in Tab. 5 and in Tab. 6. The most notable feature of brokering reusable assets in the companies is that there was no official brokering process in the companies CC and DD. In the company CC the brokering was performed as a by-product of the product management process - the actual brokering of reusable assets was not anyone's responsibility in itself. In the company DD no brokering process existed in any explicit form.

Table 5. Positive findings and comments on brokering components

AA	• When a component is finished it will be evaluated by its usability and completeness.
	• The company has a specific component repository for saving and distributing components.
	• The trust in existing components is created by implying strict classification and quality criteria to components included in the component repository.
BB	• The most promising assets for reuse were seen to be problem solving patterns, program code and document templates.
CC	• Practically everything was considered reusable: product requirements, market researches, sales documents, different ideas and many other artefacts.
	• Some specific parts of knowledge were managed and collected by the product and configuration management personnel as a part of their own process.
	• The product management -process manages as much knowledge of implemented and considered and even rejected ideas as possible.
	• The evaluation of product specifications is based on international standards, customer's standards and requirements and internal standards.
	• It was not considered necessary to introduce new technologies and tools to the process in order to enable reuse. The number of components and the structure of the products was seen reuse supporting. Therefore no reason to use a component repository or similar technologies was seen.
DD	• When a new product was under consideration, as many old plans were considered as possible. The aim of the consideration was to rip off and reuse as big parts of the previously created products as possible.
	• After a careful consideration the company decided not to implement a component repository. The main reason for that was the limited number of potential components and the clear nature of existing and planned product families.

Table 6. Negative findings and comments on brokering components

AA	• Many features of the process have to be adapted to the component repository used. In that sense the repository reduces the number of alternatives.
BB	• The design of databases should include many possibilities for reuse, but no practical cases were found.
	• Possible reusable components were found by asking more experienced members of the staff. Experience played a bigger role than it should.
	• Reuse of program code was based on „copy and replace" no formal tools or guidelines were in use.
	• It was noted that higher quality is not an automatic result of reuse: garbage in means garbage out.
	• The current resources were insufficient to manage a company-wide component brokering process.
CC	• The main obstacle of reuse was insufficient documentation of existing assets.
DD	• The experience of employees was a necessary part of reuse.
	• Components that were regularly reused had not been collected into any specific place. They were found by experience.
	• Program code included practically no comments at all. Other types of documentation were also quite rare.
	• It had turned out to be very difficult to reuse design patterns and analysis documents because they very neglected in the earlier projects.
	• Finding reusable assets was considered to require good understanding of the products.
	• Brokering the reusable assets was not anybody's responsibility.

More formal definitions of brokering existed in AA and BB. In the company AA an explicit brokering process was implemented and a specific repository used. In BB the idea of an explicit brokering process was considered and the implementation of a repository was thought to be an option although resources were lacking.

Considering the brokering process, the companies were thus divided into two pairs which had a quite different attitudes. We will come back to the possible reasons in the analysis.

3.4   Consuming the Components

The findings and opinions regarding the consumption of reusable assets are outlined in Tab. 7 and in Tab. 8. The differences between companies are remarkable.

The characteristics of process of consuming reusable assets are, again, in two quite different pairs. The companies AA and BB were quite similar and the companies CC and DD were relatively similar. The experts from the companies AA and BB considered the understanding of reuse opportunities a very demanding task in which experience and intellectual skills are very important. The companies CC and DD were happily reusing existing assets and the representatives of those companies were much more concerned with the lacking documentation.

Table 7. Positive findings and comments on consuming components

AA	• Participating in software reuse is everybody's responsibility. • The components include technical components like subsystems, complete systems, code components and problem solving patterns. • Technical components are considered to be the most usable assets in real cases..
BB	• Software and systems modernization provides many possibilities for the reuse of requirements due to the fact that most of the features do not change in the semantical sense. • Reuse of program code and systems was very common. Most of the algorithms and subsystems tend to be so complex that nobody wants to be adventurous enough to design and implement them himself/herself. Document templates were also widely reused. • Testing plans and tools were reused in a routine way.
CC	• Practically everything was considered reusable: product requirements, market researches, sales documents, different ideas and many other artefacts. • Architectural patterns and design patterns were reused on a daily basis. That reuse was not formalized, it was based on personal experience and knowledge of existing products. • Architectural plans are mostly based on existing plans and designs. Completely new designs are required in the case of new product families. • Old architectures, modules, program codes and documents were regularly used as the basis of new projects. Knowledge of those artifacts was, however, informal and required active participation of the experienced members of the staff. • Testing plans and even test cases were regularly reused inside a product family. • All documentation was based on existing templates and content descriptions. • The benefits of reuse were considered to be: faster implementation, lower cost, and fewer problems during the design (due to the fact that many design problems are not unique).
DD	• When a new product was under consideration, as many old plans were considered as possible. The aim of the consideration was to rip off and reuse as big parts of the previously created products as possible.

Table 8. Negative findings and comments on consuming components

AA	<ul><li>The definition of the reuse strategy was not specific enough.</li><li>The identification of potential components is considered to be a very demanding and difficult task.</li><li>It seems to be the case that in order to enable reuse of existing components in a new project the aspects of reuse must be considered as early as possible in the project.</li><li>Although the creation of components is performed in a specific process, the use of components was considered somewhat vague. It seems that the guidelines on how to maximize the benefits of existing components were too vague and had too much confidence on individual skills.</li><li>The components tend to be fairly large and complex.</li></ul>
BB	<ul><li>Previously designed interfaces are very rarely reused although they may not change.</li><li>Actual architectural designs were considered to be too specific and difficult to be reused.</li><li>If reuse was considered too late in the process, then there tended to be no real possibilites for reuse. The best phases were analysis and design.</li><li>The guidelines and process descriptions for reuse were too vague and they were considered to be amongst the first steps to be taken in order to improve reuse.</li></ul>
CC	<ul><li>Reusable parts and components were not collected in any specific way, they were scattered amongst other artifacts. Finding possibly reusable parts was a remarkable achievement and required thorough knowledge and understanding of the products.</li><li>The main obstacle of reuse was insufficient documentation of existing assets.</li><li>The process of finding and consuming components was considered to require remarkable understanding of the operational domain and of the products of the company.</li></ul>
DD	<ul><li>Knowledge of existing products was a necessary part of reuse.</li><li>Components that were regularly reused had not been collected into any specific place. They were found by experience.</li><li>Program code included practically no comments at all. Other types of documentation were also quite rare.</li><li>It had turned out to be very difficult to reuse design patterns and analysis documents because they very neglected in the earlier projects.</li><li>The number of ad hoc solutions with bad architectural designs made reuse difficult.</li></ul>

4   The Analysis and Improvement Suggestions for the Companies

The cases are analyzed in the light of the reuse model. We will briefly analyze the reuse processes of the companies and outline the suggested improvements.

4.1   The Reuse Strategies of the Companies

The management of reuse (specific features are outlined in Tab. 1 and in Tab. 2) was done in different ways in different companies. For example in the company AA reuse was strictly coordinated and written into the quality process of the company. In AA a separate component creation process was used and the creation of components had a quite bureaucratic feeling and required a fairly large organization with strict coordination and mature processes. The concept of a separate component engineering process had shown itself effective and useful. We assume that one of the reasons for using a separate component creation process is the difficulty of creating a working bonus system for the software engineering process. A working bonus system would be required in order to make reuse attractive to the employees participating in a successful software engineering project. One aspect of such success would be the level or reuse. That would require a predefined and fair set of metrics for all aspects of reuse and that was considered very difficult.

It seems that there were two separate concepts of reuse in the companies. The companies AA and BB considered reusable assets to be modular, well-defined and separate entities. The companies CC and DD viewed reusable assets to be entities which may be quite large and modified before the actual reuse.

The reusable assets in which the companies AA and BB were most interested could be called „building blocks". Those companies had been very successful in creating and reusing such assets. The assets varied from strictly defined code components (like EJB components or subsystems written in e.g. COBOL or C) and problem solving patterns to complete information system building blocks.

The concept of building blocks was very important for the company AA. The reuse process of AA considered a GUI module and a short routine used for checking the social security number to be components. They did, however, consider also a complete warehouse management system a component, which communicated with other parts of the customer's company-wide information system by using e.g. a persistent messaging system. In the company AA the concept of a component as a building block was very dominant, and in most cases the creation of reusable assets aimed to create well-defined black-box components which could be stored in the repository and reused as-is by the company or its customer companies.

In the company BB the concept of reuse was very similar to the concept of reuse in AA. The majority of the reusable entities in the company BB had the black-box nature. For example complex algorithms and subsystems were packaged as separate entities and used without any changes. In addition to that, as many types of artifacts as possible were reused as-is. The reuse process of the company clearly aimed to produce, broker and consume components which could be reused without changing them. In that sense the companies BB and AA both aimed for „building-block" -type of reuse. The companies CC and DD had a very different approach to reuse. The attitude was much more like the attitude of scavengers: in those companies the aim of reuse was to rip-off as big parts of existing products and related artefacts as possible and use those parts with or without modifications in order to create new products.

The key difference between the reuse strategies is in the nature of business of the companies. Both AA and BB are selling information systems related projects, which may implement a customer specific system, or a subsystem of a larger system, or an extension to an already existing system. Almost every customer-case in their business is somehow different from the others and therefore the „building-block" approach is a natural one. The companies CC and DD are clearly product-oriented, in which case the reuse process tries to enable faster creation of new versions of existing products or new products. Both the companies CC and DD seem to have more-or-less deliberately selected the product-line oriented reuse strategy described in (Bosch 2000).

The company CC produces complete systems which include hardware and software embedded into that hardware. Therefore the business of the company CC seems to be quite ideal in order to benefit from implementing the technical and organizational changes required by a full-scale implementation of the product line -oriented approach (see e.g. (Niemelä and Ihme 2001)). Similar features can be found in the products of the company DD. Those products are included as parts of larger systems, in which case only a relatively small number of licences are sold in a completely similar configuration.

4.2   The Problems in Different Reuse Strategies

It seems to be the case that different types of reuse have different problems. The problems associated with „building block" -reuse are different when compared with product-line oriented reuse.

In the building-block reuse the most important challenges seem to be in the identification of reusable entities early enough. That is because in many cases the reusable asset is so complex and large that its use causes remarkable changes to the design of the final system. That requires good experience and excellent intellectual skills from the achitects and designers of the system. That phase can be made less demanding by introducing techniques and methodologies which make the identification of possible reusable entities easier (see e.g. (Forsell 2001a)(Forsell 2001b)).

One of the problems with the building-block approach is that the organizational resources required in order to manage the reuse process are quite remarkable. This seems to suggest that the building-block approach to reuse is a very resource and skill intensive approach. In addition to that, it is not clear how actual products can be incorporated into the building-block model, which seems to suit project oriented businesses that make large numbers of tailored systems.

The problems with the product-oriented approach are quite different. One of the most striking problems outlined by the personnel of the companies is that the product-line approach is very vulnerable to problems caused by bad designs. The identification of reusable assets was seen as a demanding task, but the required skills were not thought to be as rare as in the building-block approach, which seems to be extremely demanding. In addition to that, with the product-line approach a much higher level or reuse can be achieved with less resources and in a shorter time.

Common problems were the lack of skilled and experienced people and timetables. In every case it was thought that normal project timetables and budgets do not support reuse. That problem was at least partially solved in the company AA by using specific component creation projects. In the companies CC and DD the problems did not exist with the same severity due to their very different approach to reuse.

4.3   The Proposed Improvements

We proposed several improvements to the companies. The final outcomes of the implementations of those improvements are not yet known due to the fact that the implementation of such improvements generally takes at least a year. The improvements for every company are outlined in this subsection.

For the company AA the most obvious improvements deal with the roles of employees and with guidelines. Because the reuse strategy selected by the company is very demanding and requires extensive skills from the personnel, the education of the personnel and the identification of skilled architects should be paid serious attention. In addition to that, as specific guidelines as possible should be created in order to make the selection and employment of reusable assets as formal as possible. The bonus system of the company was also thought to require some enhancements in order to make reuse more tempting and rewarding.

The most problematic issue to be solved in the case of the company AA is the definition of formal steps by which problem solving patterns are used to solve individual problems by using existing black-box components and gluing them together. The approach has shown to be effective, but it is very demanding and the required meta-level instructions which could have made the task easy for average project managers and analysts were not defined in a sufficient way during the research. The formal definition of the process with necessary tools was our highest priority improvement proposal.

In the case of the company BB the software engineering process required new phases. The alternative of new reuse oriented phases would have been the design and implementation of a specific component engineering process. A specific process was not, however, yet implemented, and therefore the identification and implementation of reusable assets was incorporated into the normal software engineering process. The new process required new roles specified for reuse. The guidelines and process descriptions for reuse were required and they were amongst the first steps to be taken in order to improve reuse. Another proposed high-priority improvement was the introduction of a repository for reusable assets and their management. In addition to those steps, the importance of educating the personnel was stressed because the reuse strategy of the company was very demanding.

The most important suggestions for the company CC were related to formalizing the architectural designs and related documentation. Because the company CC had a very high level of actual reuse, the most important improvements were aimed for institutionalizing and formalizing the reuse by defining new roles and phases in the processes. This was especially important because the company was growing quite fast during the time of the research. In order to maintain the high level of effective reuse, the reuse process had to be formalized as a normal part of the product management and software engineering processes. Most of the formalizing effort was directed to maintaining and developing the architectural descriptions of the existing product families, which actually were product lines in the sense of (Bosch 2000).

The most interesting feature of the design and management of product families in the company CC was that the organizational model spontaneously selected by the company conceptually resembles the hierarchical domain engineering model presented in (Bosch 2001). This is surprising because the number of employees of the company is much smaller than the practical limits proposed in (Bosch 2001). That could have been a result from the fact that the company had several distinct product families which did not share very much technology, although all those families were sold to different subdomains of the same larger domain. Therefore the organization of the company was considered mature enough and effective enough in order to enable the formalization of the product line architectures and the estimated growth of the company.

The company DD resembled the company CC in the sense that it had clear product families. The proposed improvements for the company DD were related to better definition of the product line and the creation of necessary roles required by that. The organizational structure of the company DD was proposed to be organized according to the domain engineering unit model outlined in (Bosch 2001). In that model a specific team of talented people would define and develop the main architecture and technology used in the products and various groups defined by the product type or the type of business would create the actual products based on the general architecture and implemented reusable technical components.

5   Discussion and Conclusion

In order to improve the software process of a company, it is necessary to understand the actual software engineering process of the company and its specific characteristics. One of the first questions is the actual nature of the business of the company and its products.

The improvement of reuse is fairly straightforward if the business of a company is based on products. In that case the product line approach seems to be the natural choice. The nature of product engineering seems to gear the reuse process and the management of products towards the implementation of product lines and product line architectures. The implementation of product lines and product line architectures make it straightforward to achieve a relatively high level of reuse. The product line architectures are, however, very vulnerable to bad decisions made during the design of the architecture. Hence the architectural aspects require further research in order to make the possibility of mistakes smaller.

If the company produces large numbers of „single-shot" systems and acts as a system integrator, it may be very difficult to introduce the concept of product-lines and product-line architectures to the company-wide software process. Such companies do not have many choices available in order to improve their reuse process. This is the case especially if the main business of a company is to add new parts or additional functionality to enterprise level information systems which may have very different architectures and technologies even in a single enterprise. In those cases the additional functionality may be provided by a combination of new code and subsystems.

For a system integrator the working solution seems to be the implementation of the black-box reuse strategy. Real-world cases have shown that the black-box approach to reuse can be successful in both achieving a relatively high level of reuse and being cost-effective in the large scale. The black-box approach to reuse is, however, a resource and skill intensive approach, which requires a reasonably large, mature and strictly coordinated organization in order to be successfully implemented. Special attention should be paid to the avoidance of common reuse antipatterns (see e.g. (Long 2001)) and the availability of required skills.

The borderline between the cases in which the product line approach is the natural one and the cases in which the natural approach to reuse is based on the black-box approach is not clear. In addition to that, it is not clear how to manage the development and engineering of the components used in the black-box approach. That requires, however, further research and empirical results in order to find working solutions.

References

[1]   Ahonen, J. J., Forsell, M. and Taskinen, S-K. (2002). A Modest but Practical Software Process Modeling Technique for Software Process Improvement. *Software Process Improvement and Practice*, 7(1). 33-44.

[2]   Bosch, J. (2001). Software Product Lines: Organizational Alternatives. In *Proceedings of the 23rd International Conference on Software Engineering, ICSE 2001*. 91-100.

[3]   Bosch, J. (2000): *Design and Use of Software Architectures*. Addison-Wesley. London.

[4]   Brooks, F. (1987). No Silver Bullet - Essence and Accidents of Software Engineering. *Computer*, April 1987. 10-19.

[5]   Forsell, M. (2002). *Improving Component Reuse in Software Development*. PhD Thesis. Jyväskylä Studies in Computing 16. Jyväskylä University Printing House. Jyväskylä.

[6]   Forsell, M. (2001a). Adding Domain Analysis to Software Development Method. *In Proceedings of the 10th International Conference on Information Systems Development, ISD2001}*. September 4-6, 2001. London. To be published by Kluwer Academic/Plenum Publishers. New York.

[7]   Forsell, M. (2001b). Using Hierarchies to Adapt Domain Analysis to Software Development. In *Proceedings of the 9th International Conference on Information Systems Development, ISD2000*. August 14-16, 2000. Kluwer Academic/Plenum Publishers. New York. 105-118.

[8]   Forsell, M., Halttunen, V. and Ahonen, J. (2000). Use and Identification of Components in Componen Based Software Development Methods. In *Proceedings of 6th International Conference on Software Reuse, ICSR-6, Lecture Notes in Computer Science 1844*. Springer-Verlag, Heidelberg. 284-301.

[9]   Forsell, M., Halttunen, V. and Ahonen, J. (1999). Evaluation of Component-based Software Development Methodologies. In: Penjam J. (Ed.). *Fenno-Ugric Symposium FUSST'99. Software technology*. Technical Report CS 104/99. Institute of Cybernetics at Tallinn Technical University. August 19-21, 1999. 53-64.

[10]   Humphrey, W. (1989). *Managing the Software Process*. Addison-Wesley, New York.

[11]   Jacobsen, I., Griss, M. and Jönssön, P. (1997). Software Reuse - Architecture, Process and Organization for Business Success. Addison-Wesley, New York.

[12]   Lim, W. C. (1998). Managing Software Reuse - A Comprehensive Guide to Strategically Reengineering the Organization for Reusable Components. Prentice Hall. New Jersey.

[13]   Long, J. (2001). Software Reuse Antipatterns. *ACM SIGSOFT Software Engineering Notes*, Vol 26, no 4. 68-76.

[14]   Niemelä, E. and Ihme, T. (2001). Product Line Software Engineering of Embedded Systems. In *Proceedings of SSR '01 Symposium on Software Reusability*. 118-125.

[15]   Zahran, S. (1998). *Software Process Improvement*. Addison-Wesley, London.

„Leave the Programmers Alone" – A Case Study

Hans Westerheim[1] and Espen Frimann Koren[2]

[1] SINTEF Telecom and Informatics
SP Andersens veg 15B, N-7465 Trondheim, Norway
hans.westerheim@sintef.no
[2] Simula Research Laboratory
PO Box 134, N-1325 Lysaker, Norway
espen.koren@simula.no

Abstract. There has been much focus on the development process in the Software Process Improvement community. This paper describes software process improvement work done within a product division in a medium-sized Norwegian software company. The division has the main responsibility for the market activities, development, implementation, maintenance and support of their software products. We identified three main problem areas related to the overall process for management of the software product. None of the problem areas were directly concerned with the development process itself. The problem areas were addressed by the division's management. Despite the lack of focus on the programmers and the development process, the programmers' attitude changed into a more positive one. One reason might be that the new overall product handling process „protected" the programmers from the market activities, and also clarified responsibility for the core development and the maintenance development. This paper discusses the findings in the case-study, and concludes that maybe the best software process improvement initiative would be to simply leave the programmers alone.

1 Introduction

Traditionally, research on Software Process Improvement (SPI) has had a strong focus on the development process. SPI has been closely related to development tools, project management, quality systems, methodology, inspections and test procedures [1], [2], [3], [4], [5]. The focus on development and maintenance of a software product, in environments with customers, sales managers, product managers, support functions and competitors, has been weaker, especially in engineering organisations. Product Lines is now being introduced more and more as a way of organising the software, and the development of the software [6], [7]. The architectural principles seem to be the dominating approach.

M. Oivo and S. Komi-Sirviö (Eds.): PROFES 2002, LNCS 2559, pp. 291-299, 2002.

When an organisation starts the improvement work, we can at least imagine two different approaches; using a normative process model, and improving the existing process bottom-up.

1.1   Normative Process Models

The first approach is to select a normative process model, like the CMM [2] or the ISO 9000 series of standards [8]. These models give advices, or guidelines, on how to design processes. Taking this normative model, the next step will be to design and document the desired software process, and completing the documentation with a milestone plan for the implementation of the new process in the organisation.

The most known normative process model is the Capability Maturity Model, CMM [2]. The model focuses on Key Point Areas, KPA, and the developing organisation's ability to perform according to these areas is used as a basis for the assessment of the maturity of the organisation. None of the Key Point Areas covers the overall product handling process.

Using normative process models can be viewed as a „top-down" approach to process improvement.

1.2   Improving the Existing Process Bottom-Up

Another approach is to analyse the present software process in the organisation. This analyse would include documenting the process' strength and weaknesses. The documentation could then be analysed to identify improvement initiatives.

When studying an overall process, and identifying improvement areas, it is not necessarily important to study the different sub-process, from which the overall process is composed. The most obvious „points" to study might be the initial input to the overall process, the final output and the transitions between the different sub-processes.

This approach can be viewed as a „bottom-up" approach to process improvement.
We have sympathy for the bottom-up approach, and this approach might be the right one when seeking support in the organisation [9].

1.3   Software Process Improvement in a Product Division

There are some differences between developing software on a consulting basis, where the customer, requirements, technical environment and staffing are different for each project. In these cases the development is often conducted in projects. This type of development has many challenges for the developing organisation.

A product owner is in a different situation. The development is concentrated on the same product, or products. There is not the same finite situation as in a consulting development organisation.

A product owner has to take into consideration the desired technical strategy for the products, market strategy, customer care, maintenance and support, and the funding of the development. An organisation like this is in need for an overall management function, this function is often given to a *product manager*.

Where the consulting organisation may concentrate the improvement effort on the development process, the product owner has to take these other aspects into consideration as well.

1.4   The Case-Study

The work described in this paper took place during the winter 2001/2002. The work was conducted within the PROFIT-project.

The overall aim of the SPI-initiative in the company was to be more prepared to a forthcoming certification according to the ISO standards. In parallel the company wanted to document the processes used in the development. The main focus was intended to be put on design and development.

1.4.1   The Company

The work described in this paper took place within a division within a medium-sized Norwegian company. The company develops information systems for the telecom industry. The company is divided into four main divisions.

This case-study is based on the software process improvement initiative within one of the product divisions developing software for customer care and billing. This software operates in the fulfilment segment within the telecom companies, which means that the software is critical in the operation for the telecom companies. The software covers both order management and product management. This division has departments in several locations, both within Norway and also in Europe and the US.

The researches have in this case worked together with the part of the division managing the software for order management, and this paper covers the work in this part of the division only.

During this work, the organisation of the division was changed. The number of departments was reduced from five to four.

There are two product managers in the division; one responsible for the order manager software, the other has the responsible for the product manager software.

We interviewed four developers, the two product managers, the division's head of office, the responsible for maintenance and support, and the project manager for the implementation of the software product by the main customer. The programmers interviewed in this case all had 15-20 years experience as programmers.

2   Research Method

Researchers within the field 'Informatics' often choose the engineering approach into the research, with use of quantitative research methods [10]. Another approach would be the qualitative research methods, whereas action research is among the latest approach.

2.1   Action Research

When working within companies on common improvement goals, with developers, action research is a well-used approach.

Action research associates the research and practice in such a way that both the researchers and the practitioners gain value of the cooperation [11], [10]. Using this research approach means that the researchers often have two types of goals. One type is the research goal. The other type is related to the work done in the organisation, in our case, the process improvement itself.

Using action research requires that both types of goals are stated and communicated [11].

2.2   PROFIT

PROFIT is a Norwegian initiative within Software Process Improvement. All research activity take place within real development projects in different Norwegian companies. PROFIT is a successor of the SPIQ project [12]. SPIQ promoted the pragmatic approach to software process improvement, an approach that is followed up by PROFIT.

The research in PROFIT covers among other things, use of the Rational Unified Process (RUP) as basis for the development processes, use of Extreme Programming (XP) in development of software and use of Experience Databases.

Researches from The Norwegian University of Science and Technology (NTNU), SIMULA Research Laboratory and SINTEF Telecom and Informatics participate in the PROFIT project.

2.3   Data Collection; Semi Structured Interviews

The work within different companies in the PROFIT-project has shown that the use of Post-Mortem Analysis is a valuable way to gain information [13]. However, the use of this type of data collection has been closely related to software development projects, where the activities are finite. In this case we were following a continuous production of software and the finite nature of a project was not present.

The researchers therefore chose *semi structured interviews* as a method for collecting information regarding the sub processes and the overall process in the product division. The idea was to bring people together in the interviews, instead of interviewing single persons. The interviews focused on strengths and weaknesses in the product development and handling, and the transactions between the different departments.

The interviews were conducted with two researchers present; one had the main responsibility to run the interviews. The other researcher had the main responsibility to document the interviews. In the first round of interviews seven interviews were conducted. Most of the interviews had 3-4 participants in addition to the researchers. In the second round of interviews we conducted three interviews. The interviews lasted 2-4 hours.

An important issue was to document as close to the real course of the interview as possible. As tool for the documentation the researchers used MindManager, a mind-map drawing tool[1].

The data collection method is more closely described in [14].

---

[1] www.mindjet.com

2.4   Analysis

We did not use any specific analysis method when analysing the information from the interviews.

Shortly after the last interview in the first round we compared all the transcriptions from the interviews. We marked all the negative points that were made during the interviews. These points were then grouped. In this case it was easy to relate the negative points to three main problem areas.

The interviews in the second round were not really analysed. We could easy state that the negative points were not an issue anymore. During the interviews we asked the participants if the three problem areas from the first round were handled. When the answer was positive, we asked if there have been any other main changes in the organisation or in the environments.

The interviews were summarised in two internal reports.

3   Results

3.1   Findings in the First Round of Interviews

During the first round of interviews the division was formed by five departments; Business Development, Product Design, Product Development, Product Implementation and Maintenance and Support.

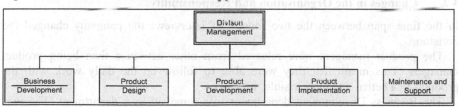

The main intention was to uncover and analyse improvement areas for the whole division.

What we found interesting was the programmer's views on developing processes. During their long experience as programmers, some of them had been using a lot of rather strict and formal processes. The attitude to such written and formal processes was negative. What they felt, was that the improvement potential was in the overall product management process. If the improved overall process enabled the programmers to concentrate on developing the core versions, that would be the most valuable improvement for them.

Two overall steering documents were produced, the Road Map and the Scope. The Road Map is the long-term, strategic steering document. The Road Map covers 2-3 versions of the software, while the Scope covers the next version.

The business development function and the product design function both had responsibility for these documents, though the responsibility was not clarified. This led to a situation where the programmers did not have „faith" in these documents.

Three main problem areas were identified; P1) Product Management P2) A unified and continuous scope P3) Organisation.

P1) Product Management

The developers were not able to point out one single person, or department, that had the overall responsibility for the software products. As part of this they could not identify where the software product where controlled.

Another aspect was that the priority between development of the software's core, maintenance development and customer adjustment of the software had to be done by the developers themselves.

P2) A Unified and Continuous Scope

The strategy of the software development were stated in two different documents; the Road Map prepared by Business Development and The Scope prepared by Product Design.

P3) Organization

This problem area is behind P2. The product managers were located in Product Design; whereas the „start" of a new version was located in Business Development. This fact made the product managers invisible to the rest of the organization, and they did loose power as managers of the products.

3.2   Changes in the Organisation and Responsibility

In the time span between the two rounds of interviews the company changed the division.

The product managers were released from other activities than being product managers. This meant that they were able to follow up the daily work with the products in a better, and more visible, way.

The Business Development department was removed as a department. The pre-sales function in this department was moved to the sales and marketing division. The work with the road map was moved to the product design department.

The development process itself was not changed.

3.3   Findings in the Second Round of Interviews

During the second round of interviews the division consisted of four departments; Product Design, Product Development, Product Implementation and Maintenance and Support.

The product managers were now more visible to the whole division. The responsibility for both the road map and the scope was located within the product design department, managed by the product managers.

There was a clearer distinction between the development of the core functionality and the bug-fix, maintenance and customer-specific development. This distinction was controlled by the product managers. The developers felt that the „noise" was reduced, and that the product managers worked as buffers against the market.

The programmer's attitude and willingness to do a good job both seemed to be increased a lot.

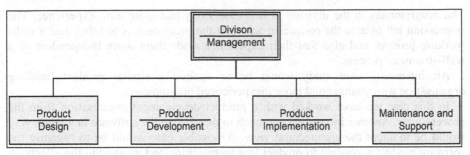

4   Discussion and Conclusions

4.1   Using Semi-Structured Interviews

The data collection in the first round of interviews made the researchers able to uncover three main problem areas. The division did handle the problem areas uncovered. When we conducted the second round of interviews, it was clear that the developers felt that the division handled the correct problem areas.

Therefore, in this case the data collection method was working well since handling the areas uncovered really did lead to a better overall process.

4.2   Software Process Improvement Has to Cover More Than the Development Process Itself

The work in this case study unveiled a situation where improvements in the overall process, forming the development environment, did improve the programmer's ability to produce quality software.

When working with Software Process Improvement initiatives in product organisations like this one, the initiative should have focus also on the overall process. In this case this was important since others than the developers were responsible for the overall process. The developers felt that these persons, the product managers, had the responsibility for controlling the environment in which the development process was working. Addressing this responsibility and management outside the development process did also improve the development process itself.

4.3   Leave the Programmers Alone

The results from this case study indicate that a software organisation managing a software product, should leave the programmers alone when running software improvement initiatives. This case study has shown that this is the case when an organisation is initiating such an initiative.

If the initiatives address environmental processes and managing issues, the programmers will benefit from this.

5   Further Work

The programmers in the division in this case study had quite long experience. The impression left over to the researcher said that the programmers felt they had a well-working process, and also that their experience made them more independent of a well-structured process.

An interesting case study would be to analyse a similar product handling organisation with younger and more inexperienced programmers.

In this case we have worked with a product development organisation from the process view. Another interesting approach to developing the software in a better way would be to adopt the architectural view. A possible case would be to organise the software product according to product line architecture, and measuring the effects on the software process.

Acknowledgements

We would like to thank M. Sc. Geir Kjetil Hanssen and Dr. Torgeir Dingsøyr, SINTEF Informatics for valuable review.

The work is sponsored by The Norwegian Research Council via the PROFIT project NFR-number 137901/221.

References

[1]   Barry Boehm, „Anchoring the Software Process," *IEEE Software*, vol. 13, pp. 73-82, 1996.

[2]   Watts S. Humphrey, *Managing The Software Process*: Addison-Wesley Publishing Company, 1989, 0-201-18095-2.

[3]   Fran O'Hara, „Irish Experiences with Software Process Improvement," EuroSPI 2001, Limerick, 2001.

[4]   Kim Man Lui and Keith CC Chan, „Managing Inexperienced Programmers by Better Managing Design-Coding," EuroSPI 2000, Copenhagen, Denmark, 2000.

[5]   Patrica A. McQuaid, „Managing Projects in a Rapid Application Development (RAD) Environment," EuroSPI 2001, Limerick, Ireland, 2001.

[6]   John D. McGregor, Linda M. Northrop, Salah Jarad, and Klaus Pohl, „Initiating Software Product Lines," *IEEE Software*, vol. 19, pp. 24-27, 2002.

[7]   Klaus Schmid and Martin Verlage, „The Economic Impact of Product Line Adaption and Evolution," *IEEE Software*, vol. 19, pp. 50-57, 2002.

[8]   Philip Wain, „ISO 9001 as a process improvement tool; Is 9000:2000 the last chance for the standard?," EuroSPI 2001, Limerick, Ireland, 2001.

[9]   Reidar Conradi and Alfonso Fuggetta, „Improving Software Process Improvement," *IEEE Software*, pp. 92-99, 2002.

[10]   Richard L. Baskerville and A. Trevor Wood-Harper, „A Critical Perspective on Action Research as a Method for Information Systems Research," *Journal of Information Technology*, pp. 235-246, 1996.

[11]   David Avison, Francis Lau, Micheal Myers, and Peter Axel Nielsen, „Action Research," *Communications of the ACM*, vol. 42, pp. 94-97, 1999.

[12]   Tore Dybå, *Software Process Improvement for better Quality: Methodology Handbook*. Trondheim: Norwegian University of Technology and Science, 2000.

[13]   Andreas Birk, Torgeir Dingsøyr, and Tor Stålhane, „Postmortem: Never leave a Project without It," *IEEE Software*, vol. 19, pp. 43-45, 2002.

[14]   Hans Westerheim Espen F. Koren, „Techniques for Gathering Information about an Organisation and its Needs for Software Process Improvement,", University of Keele, 2002.

Software Configuration Management Principles and Best Practices

Ronald Kirk Kandt[*]

Jet Propulsion Laboratory, California Institute of Technology
4800 Oak Grove Dr., Pasadena, CA 91109, USA
ronald.k.kandt@jpl.nasa.gov

Abstract. This paper identifies fundamental principles and practices essential to the successful performance of a configuration management system. Practices are grouped into four categories that govern the management process, ensure product quality, protect software artifacts, and guide tool use. In addition, the practices are prioritized according to their effect on software products and processes and the coverage of the identified principles. When these practices should be applied in the software development lifecycle is discussed, as is the potential for automating and validating practices.

1 Introduction

A configuration management system establishes and maintains the integrity of software artifacts throughout the software lifecycle [1]. A configuration management system identifies the managed artifacts and their configuration at various points in time, as well as controlling the changes to software configurations. In addition, a configuration management system maintains the sequence of derivations of each configuration and individual artifacts throughout the software development lifecycle. The products managed by a configuration management system include the products delivered to an end user or customer and other artifacts produced or used that assist in their development. In sum, a configuration management system includes the set of policies, practices, and tools that help an organization maintain software configurations.

To support configuration management, several configuration management tools have been developed over the years. Some examples include SCCS [2], RCS [3], and CVS [4]. These systems are freely available, delivered with some operating systems, and still used today. Several newer systems provide much greater functionality (e.g., ClearCase [5], Perforce [6]). However, no configuration management tool widely available today provides all of the capabilities that support the practices identified in this paper, although it is probable that some will within the next five to ten years.

---

[*] The research described in this publication was carried out at the Jet Propulsion Laboratory, California Institute of Technology, under a contract with the National Aeronautics and Space Administration.

M. Oivo and S. Komi-Sirviö (Eds.): PROFES 2002, LNCS 2559, pp. 300–313, 2002.

The primary purpose of this paper is to identify principles fundamental to successfully managing the configuration of developed software and to identify those practices that best embody them. This information will later be used to develop a new software configuration management tool. The practices described in this paper resulted from introspection and by examining explicitly defined best practices ([1], [7], [8]) and other practices implicitly defined by configuration management processes and procedures ([9], [10], [11], [12]) and tool evaluations [13]. Therefore, many of these practices are well known, whereas others are infrequently or newly discussed.

There are three secondary purposes for identifying the configuration management principles and practices. First, organizations can use these principles and practices to train configuration management specialists and evaluate the configuration management practices they use. Second, these principles and practices can be used to define a core set of configuration management practices as a baseline for a software process improvement effort. Third, the identification of these principles and practices can motivate others to explore opportunities for automating these practices, as well as automating their verification.

2   Principles

There are ten basic principles that support configuration management activities.

Principle 1: Protect critical data and other resources. The process of developing software produces many artifacts. Some of these artifacts include the definition of requirements, design specifications, work breakdown structures, test plans, and code. All of these artifacts generally undergo numerous revisions as they are created. The loss of such artifacts and their revisions can cause great harm (e.g., financial loss, schedule slip) to an organization. Thus, it is vital that these artifacts and their interrelationships be reliably maintained. This implies that these artifacts are always accessible to consumers or quickly recoverable when failure does occur.

Principle 2: Monitor and control software development procedures and processes [1]. An organization should define the processes and procedures that it uses to produce artifacts. Such definition will provide a basis for measuring the quality of the processes and procedures. However, to produce meaningful measures of the processes and procedures, the organization must follow them. Consequently, the organization must monitor its practitioners to ensure that they follow the software development processes and procedures.

Principle 3: Automate processes and procedures [1] when cost effective. The automation of processes and procedures has two primary benefits. First, it guarantees that an organization consistently applies them, which means that it is more likely to produce quality products. Second, automation improves the productivity of the people that must execute the processes and procedures because such automation reduces the tasks that they must perform, which permits them to perform more work.

Principle 4: Provide value to customers. Three issues ultimately affect the success of a product. The first one is that a product must reliably meet the needs of its customers. That is, it must provide the desired functionality and do it in a consistent and reliable manner. Second, a product should be easy to use. Third, an organization must address user concerns and issues in a timely manner. All three of these issues affect customer value, and a configuration management tool should automate those practices that provide the greatest value to its user community.

Principle 5: Software artifacts should have high quality. There are many measures of product quality. Such measures attempt to identify several qualities of a product, such as its adaptability, efficiency, generality, maintainability, reliability, reusability, simplicity, and understandability. Adaptable products are easy to add new features or extend existing ones. Efficient products run faster and consume fewer resources. General products solve larger classes of problems. Maintainable products are easier to fix. Reliable products perform their intended tasks in a manner consistent with user expectations. Reusable products fulfill the needs of many tasks. Simple products are easier to understand, adapt, and maintain. Furthermore, simple products are often elegant and efficient. Understandable products permit developers to easily alter them. That is, products that are difficult to understand tend to be poorly designed, implemented, and documented. Consequently, they generally are less reliable. In sum, quality is not simply a measure of the number of defects that a product has. Instead, quality is a broad characterization of several qualities, characteristics, or attributes that people value. Thus, several quality measures of software artifacts must be continuously taken.

Principle 6: Software systems should be reliable. Software systems should work as their users expect them to function. They also should have no significant defects, which means that software systems should never cause significant loss of data or otherwise cause significant harm. Thus, these systems should be highly accessible and require little maintenance.

Principle 7: Products should provide only necessary features, or those having high value. Products should only provide the required features and capabilities desired by their users. The addition of nonessential features and capabilities that provide little, if any, value to the users tends to lower product quality. Besides, an organization can better use the expended funds in another manner.

Principle 8: Software systems should be maintainable. Maintainable software systems are generally simple, highly modular, and well designed and documented. They also tend to exhibit low coupling. Since most software is used for many years, maintenance costs for large software systems generally exceed original development costs.

Principle 9: Use critical resources efficiently. Numerous resources are used or consumed to develop software, as well as by the software products themselves. Such resources are generally scarce and an organization should use them as efficiently as possible.

Principle 10: Minimize development effort. Human effort is a critical resource, but one that is useful to distinguish from those that do not involve personnel. The primary motivation to efficiently use human resources is to minimize development costs. In addition, the benefits of minimizing the number of personnel used to develop software increases at a greater than linear rate.

3   Practices

Twenty-three fundamental configuration management practices support these ten principles. These practices fall into four primary groups: those that govern the management process, those that affect product quality, those that protect the primary work products, and those that guide how people should use a configuration management tool.

3.1   Management Practices

Seven key management practices enhance the success of a configuration management system.

Practice 1: Maintain a unique read-only copy of each release. After each release, the configuration manager should label the entire code base with an identifier that helps to uniquely identify it. Alternatively, a configuration management tool can automatically name each release using one of many defined schemes. By protecting critical information in this manner, software engineers can easily identify artifacts that an organization used to produce a release. It also prevents software engineers from altering source artifacts and derived work products specific to a release after deployment.

Auditors should verify that an organization has labeled its releases and made them read-only, although it may be difficult to verify that the organization properly captures the correct version of each required artifact. Further, recreating a build and successfully executing a regression test suite does not guarantee that the build is identical to the original build. On the other hand, a configuration management tool can maintain a unique copy of each release and track subsequent changes to it or prevent such change from occurring.

Practice 2: Control the creation, modification, and deletion of software artifacts following a defined procedure [1]. A defined procedure should identify every item that an organization uses to make every work product (e.g., compilers), regardless of the type of work product – code or documentation. Control procedures should also identify who can create, alter, and delete a software artifact and under what conditions. Further, each transaction involving a software artifact should be recorded. During each transaction, metrics should be collected for each type of artifact. These metrics should attempt to measure all quality attributes of Principle 5. For example, an organization should record the number of changes to each component and how many of those changes are related to defects.

A defined procedure for controlling software changes has several benefits. First, it helps to eliminate rework. In a poorly managed organization, programmers often create multiple versions of the same artifact in a disorganized manner and have difficulty recovering desired versions of artifacts. Second, it improves the predictability of performing successful software builds and deliveries by focusing development efforts on planned changes. Third, it encourages the production of software having the greatest return on investment. That is, only feature additions and defect repairs that best satisfy user needs should be approved. Fourth, a controlled procedure provides management insight into the progress of a project team.

Auditors should identify that a defined procedure exists and that personnel follow it. In addition, auditors should verify that reports are generated on a periodic basis and that management examines and acts on the reports in a prudent manner. An organization should use automated methods to generate such reports, define software processes, and validate adherence to them.

Practice 3: Create a formal approval process for requesting and approving changes [1]. A formal approval process should identify who has responsibility for accepting a change request and allocating the work. It should also identify the evaluation criteria that determine the requests that an organization will perform, as well as how it prioritizes them. The approval process should require the requestor to produce documentation that the development or maintenance team may need, the reason for the change, and a contingency plan.

Controlling the process of requesting and approving change requests is the primary way to inject stability into software development efforts. The benefits of controlling change are that an organization can ensure that it adds only necessary or beneficial features to a system. It also allows the organization to prioritize changes and schedule change in the most efficient or practical manner.

Auditors can examine the configuration management plan of an organization to detect that an organization defines a change management procedure. A configuration management tool may also embody such a plan, model the process, and partially automate it.

Practice 4: Use change packages. A change package defines a unit of work, whether it is the repair of a defect, the addition of a new feature or capability to a system, or an original development activity [13]. Consequently, a change package should be traceable to a planned activity of a work plan or schedule. If it is not, the schedule is not an accurate reflection of the work a team is performing or when the team is performing it. The benefit of using change packages is that they aggregate collections of individual, yet related, changes, which helps to control the instability within a software system.

Change packages can be used with or without automated support. Auditors can verify the manual use of change packages by examining the documents that describe such change packages. However, such manual use is doubtful to occur since it is not practical. Instead, support for change packages will almost surely be provided by a configuration management tool. Auditors can easily verify whether a configuration management tool provides such a capability by examining its documentation and an organization's use of it.

Practice 5: Use shared build processes and tools [14]. It is rare that individual members of a project team use different build processes or tools. When they do, the results are often inconsistent and difficult to debug. Thus, an organization should avoid such an approach. By controlling the build processes and tools, an organization encourages all its members to produce the same work products in the same manner. An additional benefit is that members can assist one another in tool use, which helps to reduce training costs.

Auditors can easily identify if an organization follows this practice with or without an automated aid. However, the use of a full-function configuration management tool using standard build specifications will ensure that an organization follows this practice.

Practice 6: A version manifest should describe each software release. A version manifest should identify all components that comprise a release, all open and closed problems, the differences between versions, relevant notes and assumptions, and build instructions. Since a version manifest explicitly identifies the specific version of each artifact that makes up a release, it permits a software development organization to better maintain and deploy systems.

Auditors can verify that a version manifest exists for and accurately reflects each release. The verification of whether a manifest accompanies each release is trivial, but validating its accuracy is not. Thus, it is best to permit a configuration management tool to generate manifests and use auditors to validate their generation or the underlying generation process. Verifying a manual process, on the other hand, is an extraordinarily tedious process.

Practice 7: Segregate derived artifacts from source artifacts [14]. Source artifacts are works created by an author. Derived artifacts are those artifacts that result from processing source artifacts. For example, a binary object file is the result of compiling a source file written in a programming language. Work products, on the other hand, may be source artifacts, but they may also be derived objects. Work products are those products that an organization delivers to a customer or some end user or uses to develop a product. Delivered work products are those work products actually delivered to a customer, whether they are source or derived objects. If possible, an organization should separate these different categories of artifacts to ease their management.

A configuration management tool does not necessarily have to maintain derived artifacts using version control because it can reconstruct the derived artifacts from the source artifacts. The main reason for maintaining derived objects is to reuse their intermediate results computed by one user for another. For example, some configuration management tools use smart compilation, which greatly reduces compilation efforts by not recompiling object files when suitable ones (i.e., ones equivalent to the ones that a compiler would reproduce for the given environment) already exist.

Segregation of artifacts allows an organization to limit the scope of software management activities if it chooses not to manage derived artifacts that are not delivered work products. Segregation also isolates artifacts that tend to be large or expendable, which simplifies storage management functions and allows them to be efficiently used.

Auditors can easily verify the segregation of source and derived artifacts by various means, but a configuration management tool should automate this practice.

3.2   Quality Practices

Seven key practices ensure quality of the configuration items of a configuration management system.

Practice 8: All source artifacts should be under configuration control [14]. The quality of delivered work products derived from source artifacts not under configuration control is suspect. Further, such a situation does not permit traceability within a configuration management system, which means that impact analysis cannot be reliably performed. The benefit of placing all source artifacts under configuration control is that an organization can better control the development process, as well as better maintain traceability between artifacts.

Auditors can verify the artifacts that an organization maintains under configuration control and it can identify those artifacts not maintained under configuration control by examining how releases are built and generated.

Practice 9: Use a change control board [1]. Feature additions are generally expensive to implement. Thus, projects must add functionality that end-users or the marketplace determines to be essential or have high value. A change control board controls the features of a system by considering explicitly and consistently the performance, quality, schedule costs, and benefits of each proposed change. Thus, a change control board reviews suggested changes, determines the ones to accept, prioritizes the accepted requests, and assigns the implementation of each one to a specific software release. To make the best decisions, the change control board should represent a cross-section of people from the client, development, and user communities. For example, project management, marketing, development, quality assurance, documentation, and user support personnel should participate on change control boards.

Auditors can verify the adherence to this practice by verifying the existence of a change control board and assessing whether it follows the guidance described in a configuration management plan. It is possible for a configuration management tool to record the decisions of a change control board, as well as the rationale for each one. A configuration management tool could even help formalize the decision process.

Practice 10: Build software on a regular, preferably daily, basis, followed by immediate invocations of regression test suites ([14], [15]). Increasing the frequency of software builds reduces the number of changed artifacts between builds, which reduces the number of potential flaws, or unwanted interactions, of each build. Consequently, by increasing the frequency of software builds, an organization reduces the effort to find such incompatibilities since fewer artifacts are likely to have changed.

This simple process produces two significant benefits. First, it minimizes integration risk by keeping integration errors small and manageable. Second, it improves quality by preventing a system to deteriorate to the point where time-consuming quality problems can occur. When an organization builds and tests a product every day, it is easier to identify new defects in a product, which helps to minimize the debugging effort.

Each software build should produce a version manifest including the time of a build. Both people and programs can inspect the sequences of manifests to determine that an organization is performing regular software builds. Even better, a configuration management tool could automate the execution of daily builds and regression test suites.

Practice 11: Document identified software defects [1]. An organization can categorize software defects in many ways: by type, source, and severity of failure, by the source of detection, and so on. The documentation of identified software defects helps to identify the quality of a product. It also permits an organization to identify the artifacts that may be inherently flawed and it may need to replace.

Auditors can verify that an organization documents software defects, although it may have difficulty identifying that it consistently does so. Similarly, a configuration management tool can report the defects that an organization has added to it, but it cannot guarantee that its contents are complete.

Practice 12: Software artifacts that comprise a release should adhere to defined acceptance criteria [14]. Typical acceptance criteria should include various metrics. For example, code metrics may include the use of code coverage criteria, various complexity metrics, and various sizing metrics. Most artifacts will have acceptance criteria that include a review or test process, if not both of them. Adoption of this practice will ensure that all artifacts adhere to a defined level of quality.

Both people and automated methods can determine that artifacts meet acceptability criteria. However, without automated aid, it will be difficult for auditors to do this. Therefore, a configuration management tool should automate the execution of acceptance criteria.

Practice 13: Each software release should be regression tested before the test organization receives it. A regression test suite should strive to achieve complete code coverage, complete testing of exception conditions for each software component, and thorough testing of boundary conditions for all actual parameters of each function, and conduct complete functional tests derived from system requirements. Adhering to this practice helps to ensure that old code works roughly as well as before, enhancing quality and reliability.

If the regression test suite produces a record for each test case then both people and programs can verify that an organization executes a regression test suite. Examining the test records for correctness, without a standard protocol, can be extremely challenging for humans and impossible for a program.

Practice 14: Apply defect repairs to every applicable release or ongoing development effort. Many software development organizations have various releases in use by their end users. These releases may be necessary to operate within various different environments composed of varying operating systems, database systems, windowing system, or other utilities. Additionally, some releases may update older releases but in the same operating environment. Regardless, each of these releases and internal development efforts may contain the same defect and the person repairing the defect should ensure that each release and internal development effort either does not have the defect or receives the repair. Alternatively, a change control board or another entity may decide which releases and internal development efforts should receive the repair. This practice simultaneously eliminates defects in multiple releases, yielding customer benefit. It also benefits ongoing development efforts, which improves personnel productivity and future product quality.

Auditors can verify that an organization follows this practice by examining several change requests and determining whether developers modified multiple releases and internal developments. If not, it can examine the organization's change management procedures. Alternatively, a configuration management tool could support such an activity by assisting the person or group who authorized the work related to a reported defect.

3.3   Protection Practices

Four key practices enhance the reliability of the configuration management activity.

Practice 15: Use a software system to perform configuration management functions. By definition, a configuration management tool provides several basic features. First, it maintains a history of each software artifact (i.e., version control). Second, it maintains configurations of larger aggregations of these artifacts (i.e., configuration management). Third, it generally provides a utility to build derived artifacts, which are usually executable programs (i.e., build management). In combination, these three features permit an organization to capture a snapshot of each release, whether major or minor, as long as it needs, which ensures that releases can be built and modified to satisfy future needs. Fourth, a configuration management tool sometimes provides a mechanism to manage software changes. Such changes may be to correct software defects or to enhance software systems. Fifth, a configuration management tool can automate the deployment of software by maintaining an accurate record of its customers operating environments and the software they are entitled to use. This last capability has yet to become commercially available.

Furthermore, a configuration management tool should manage various kinds of artifacts and interrelationships among the artifacts. Examples of such artifacts include requirements, specifications (e.g., architectural), plans (e.g., test), user documentation, and training materials. Maintenance of artifact interrelationships makes it easy to perform impact analysis.

The use of a configuration management tool to control software development activities is beneficial for three reasons. First, it provides permanence for each software release, as well as a recovery mechanism for software artifacts. Thus, it helps to protect critical information. Second, it can enforce institutional policies, procedures, and processes. Third, it can automate the deployment of software, and ensure the validity of such deployment. Auditors can easily verify the use of a configuration management tool, but may have more difficulty identifying whether the organization effectively uses it in daily operations.

Practice 16: Repositories should exist on reliable physical storage elements. An organization can enhance the reliability of a repository by using mirrored disk drives, RAID-5 drives, redundant networks, and clustered servers. Adoption of this practice will yield highly available solutions and reduce the potential for significant loss of work products, which requires time and energy to replace. Auditors can verify this practice by examining an organization's configuration management plan and verifying its implementation.

Practice 17: Configuration management repositories should be periodically backed-up to non-volatile storage and purged of redundant or useless information. Several types of backups are possible (e.g., full and incremental). A configuration management plan must define the types of backups a software team will use, when an operator will perform each type of backup, the tape naming conventions for each one, and the manner of storing each backup. Backups may be stored remotely or locally and protected in various ways (e.g., fireproof vaults). Regular backups ensure the reproducibility of software guarding against data and program loss. In addition, removing information no longer needed uses less computer storage and makes it easier to find information.

Auditors can verify that reliable media, such as magnetic tapes, contain software backups and that the software backups are properly managed. In addition, both auditors and programs can detect the existence of backup logs, as well as examine them.

Practice 18: Test and confirm the backup process. Most organizations backup their repositories, but seldom restore them. Thus, they have faith that the repositories will be accurately restored, but seldom validate that they are correctly saved and restored. This is a critical flaw in most configuration management processes. The benefit of performing this practice is to ensure that backups accurately capture the contents of repositories and that the restoration process can fully and accurately restore them.

Auditors can validate this process by conducting interviews with development team members. However, a configuration management tool could more effectively validate the capture and restoration of repositories.

3.4   Tool Practices

Five key practices support the practical use of configuration management tools.

Practice 19: Check code in often [14]. This practice should be constrained when checking in code on the primary development branch. That is, developers should only check in working versions of code to a development branch. The frequent check in of code helps to eliminate the loss of a large change. That is, this practice ensures that software losses, if they should occur, will be small. This practice also permits individuals to synchronize their work with the most recent incarnation of the work of others.

People and programs can trivially verify this practice. However, a configuration management tool can automate it following the specifications that a project manager provides.

Practice 20: Configuration management tools should provide patch utilities. A patch facility deploys the equivalent of a new release by modifying an existing release. The benefit of a patch mechanism is that incremental releases can by deployed using telecommunications equipment much quicker. This is especially beneficial to users that use slow communication mechanisms, such as dial-up modems. The importance of this is that by providing such a patch mechanism, an organization will provide better service to its customers.

Auditors can verify the development of patch releases, although they will have difficulty verifying the correctness of such releases. Consequently, an organization should use an automated method for generating release patches, and an audit team should verify the automated process.

Practice 21: Do not work outside of managed workspaces [14]. A configuration management tool can only manage artifacts within managed workspaces. In addition, configuration management tools generally use workspaces to facilitate communication among developers working on related tasks. That is, each developer can examine what is happening in the workspaces of others.

Thus, by working outside of managed workspaces, several problems can arise. People that develop artifacts outside the workspace cannot easily share them with others. People that develop artifacts outside the workspace also do not have access to the automation functions provided by a configuration management tool, such as the automated generation of reports. Consequently, working within a managed workspace eliminates many problems, which reduces development effort.

Auditors could have difficulty verifying that a software organization adheres to this practice, although it can interview software engineers to verify it. Unfortunately, no program can verify this practice.

Practice 22: Do not share workspaces [14]. A workspace should have a single purpose, such as providing a build and test area for a single developer or for a product release. When sharing a workspace, the actions of one person may adversely interact with those of another. By not sharing workspaces, an organization can avoid such development problems, which reduces development effort.

Auditors could have difficulty verifying that a software organization adheres to this practice, although it could conclude one way or the other based on interviews of software engineers. On the other hand, a configuration management tool could enforce, and verify, this practice.

Practice 23: When developing software on a branch other than the primary development branch, regularly synchronize development with the development branch [14]. A person's work in a team environment depends on the artifacts that others develop. Consequently, programmers should integrate the mainline changes of others into their workspaces on a periodic basis. Infrequent integration will lead to integration difficulties.

Adoption of this practice ensures that the development efforts of the entire team will be compatible with one another on a periodic basis. This has the effect of reducing the effort required to fix incompatibilities to manageable units of work. In addition, it prevents the surprise of having unanticipated, large integration efforts from occurring immediately before a software release. In other words, it permits managers to manage the development process by making several small schedule changes, if needed, instead of creating a few large, possibly unpredictable, perturbations.

Verification of this process is very easy to achieve by an auditor, although a configuration management tool could provide such functionality.

4   Relationships between Principles, Practices, and the Software Lifecycle

Of the ten configuration management principles, Principles 1 through 6 are the ones of primary importance. Of these, Principle 1 is by far the most important because it guarantees that the artifacts that products are derived from remain intact. Principles 2 through 6, on the other hand, help to keep customers because these principles focus on product quality and customer satisfaction. Consequently, the practices associated with Principles 1 through 6 are of primary importance, whereas the practices associated with Principles 7 through 10 are of secondary importance.

The following discussion identifies when an organization should perform each primary practice, as well as how it should perform each one. If existing technology already exists that supports a practice then selected supporting products are discussed. Finally, if new technology is needed to perform a practice, or can be developed to aid it, then such technology is identified.

During the project planning phase, an organization should perform three important tasks. First, it should acquire highly reliable and redundant physical storage and processing elements for the software repository. Second, it should acquire a configuration management tool that is able to document identified software defects and produce release patches. Several such systems exist today, although few, if any, commercial versions support the production of release patches. Third, it should establish a change control board that will define a configuration management process and rules for approving changes to artifacts.

During all development and test phases of the lifecycle, an organization should perform five critical tasks. First, it should control the creation, modification, and deletion of all source artifacts using the configuration management tool and defined procedures and rules identified during the project planning phase. Second, it should regularly back-up configuration management repositories to non-volatile storage and periodically purge them of redundant or useless data. Such backups can be automatically performed by writing a trivial program or script. Third, it should periodically verify that the backup process functions properly. This is easily achieved by writing a simple program, but seldom, if ever, done. Fourth, it should document artifact defects using the configuration management tool. Fifth, it should produce read-only copies of each release.

During the programming phase, an organization should follow four practices. First, it should build and test software on a regular and frequent basis. A configuration management tool should automate such a process, although none currently does. Second, an organization should use change packages to define collections of related changes. Third, its software engineers should frequently save incremental, working code changes in the repository. Fourth, when its software engineers fix one version of a software system, they should fix all other released versions, including the one undergoing development.

Note that most of the primary practices can be achieved using existing configuration management tools. In situations where existing configuration tools do not directly support these practices, there are generally mechanisms for an organization to easily add them through the augmentation of simple programs.

All secondary practices should be exercised during the programming phase and enforced, when possible, during software audits. These practices ask programmers to synchronize development, work within managed workspaces, separate source artifacts from derived ones, include a manifest with each software release, and not share workspaces. A configuration management tool could automate the process of separating artifacts and creating release manifests.

5   Summary and Conclusions

This paper identified ten fundamental principles and twenty-three best practices that a software configuration management system should embody. In addition, it identified principles and practices that largely differ from most software process advice, such as that given by the Capability Maturity Model for Software [1]. This paper, for instance, gives very detailed recommendations about what an organization needs to do, and about what capabilities an organization should expect from a tool. Many of these ideas are new, or at least not widely discussed.

Although existing configuration management tools provide several valuable benefits, they still suffer from several limitations. Two specific examples of this follow. First, most configuration management tools are file-based and do not capture artifacts at the level of granularity that is truly useful – individual requirements, design concepts, classes, functions, test cases, and so on. Second, most configuration management systems do not interoperate within an enterprise – the industry needs a configuration management tool that operates in every environment in the same manner. Thus, the development of a new configuration management tool is the goal of the author. Its development will be driven by the principles and practices identified in this paper and will enforce and automate many of these practices.

Acknowledgments

The author would like to acknowledge the competent and comprehensive comments made on an early draft of this paper by Bill Pardee. The author also appreciates the constructive criticisms made by the reviewers of this paper.

References

[1]   Paulk, M. C., Weber, C. V., Curtis, B., Chrissis, M. B.: The Capability Maturity Model: Guidelines for Improving the Software Process, Addison-Wesley (1994).

[2]   Rochkind, M. J.: The Source Code Control System. IEEE Transactions on Software Engineering SE-1 (1975) 364-370.

[3]   Tichy, W. F.: Design, implementation, and evaluation of a Revision Control System. Proceedings of the Sixth International Conference on Software Engineering (1982) 58-67.

[4]   Krause, R.: CVS: an introduction. Linux Journal 2001 (2001).

[5]   White, B. A.: Software Configuration Management Strategies and Rational
        ClearCase: A Practical Introduction. Addison-Wesley (2000).

[6]   Perforce 2002.1 User's Guide. Perforce Software (2002).

[7]   Babich, W. A.: Software configuration management: coordination for team
        productivity. Addison-Wesley (1986).

[8]   Jones, C.: Software Assessments, Benchmarks, and Best Practices. Addison-
        Wesley (2000).

[9]   Bersoff, E. H.: Software configuration management, an investment in product
        integrity. Prentice-Hall (1980).

[10]   Whitgift, D.: Methods and Tools for Software Configuration Management.
        Wiley (1991).

[11]   Berlack, H. R.: Software configuration management. Wiley (1992).

[12]   Buckley, F. J.: Implementing configuration management: hardware, software,
        and firmware, 2nd ed. IEEE Computer Society Press (1996).

[13]   Rigg, W., Burrows, C., and Ingram, P.: Ovum Evaluates: Configuration
        Management Tools. Ovum Limited (1995).

[14]   Wingerd, L. and Seiwald, C.: High-level Best Practices in Software
        Configuration Management. Proceedings of the Eighth International Workshop
        on Software Configuration Management (1998).

[15]   McConnell, S.: Rapid Development: Taming Wild Software Schedules.
        Microsoft Press (1996).

Benefits Resulting from the Combined Use of ISO/IEC 15504 with the Information Technology Infrastructure Library (ITIL)

Béatrix Barafort, Bernard Di Renzo, and Olivier Merlan

Centre for IT Innovation, Centre de Recherche Public Henri Tudor
6 rue Coudenhove-Kalergi, L-1359 Luxembourg-Kirchberg, Luxembourg
www.citi.tudor.lu

Abstract. This paper relates how different thoughts and experiences with ISO/IEC 15504 standard and the Information Technology Infrastructure Library (ITIL) lead to a R&D project definition for a combined use of both standards, in a SMEs adapted way. The idea is born from empirical findings emanating from several IT process improvement projects taking place in the Centre de Recherche Public Henri Tudor (Luxembourg). After underlining several facts such as disconnection between IT service management and IT development, IT quality standards not adapted to SMEs, and the more and more frequent implementation of ITIL and ISO/IEC 15504 within companies, the paper describes the links that can be established between both standards and the resulting R&D project aiming at building an integrated assessment and improvement approach combining their use, and dedicated to SMEs.

1 Introduction

Nowadays, organisations are highly dependent on their Information Technology (IT) services and expect they not only support them but also bring new possibilities to fulfil the objectives of the organisation.

Used ontrary to the past when many IT organisations were centred on internal technical matters, today's businesses have high requirements regarding the quality of services and these needs are quickly evolving with time. IT organisations have to meet these requirements and must pay attention to service quality and develop a more customer-oriented approach: cost issues are now high on the agenda as is the development of a more businesslike attitude to provision of service.

In that context, the IT Infrastructure Library (ITIL), produced by the CCTA (Central Computer and Telecommunications Agency in UK) in the late '80s, is probably the most comprehensive structured approach publicly available on providing IT services[1]. The ITIL rapidly became a worldwide de facto standard for Service Management. Since 2000, the UK Office of Government Commerce (OGC) has incorporated the CCCA that no longer operates as a separate agency. ITIL focuses on

M. Oivo and S. Komi-Sirviö (Eds.): PROFES 2002, LNCS 2559, pp. 314-325, 2002.
© Springer-Verlag Berlin Heidelberg 2002

providing high quality services with a particular focus on customer relationships. Its success can be explained by the fact that ITIL is able to include existing methods and activities without major difficulty and can be easily set in existing structures context.

Besides, a relatively new standard like ISO/IEC 15504:1998[2], resulting from the SPICE (Software Process Improvement and Capability dEtermination) major international initiative, is coming in the area and also plays an important role. The foundation of the ISO/IEC 15504 model is that organizations assess themselves against a range of 'best practices' (such as development, project management, etc...) in order to improve their processes or to determine suppliers capability for the assessed processes (in order to select the supplier which demonstrates the best capability). The main topic that interests us is the use of ISO/IEC 15504 standard in the sole context of process assessment and process improvement. The targeted processes are then selected according to companies' business objectives. This is made available by the flexible use of the model (available set of processes).

The origin of this paper takes place within the projects owned by the CITI (Centre for IT and Innovation) in the Information and Communication Technology field in Luxembourg. The CITI department belongs to the Centre de Recherche Public Henri Tudor, founded in 1987 as a public research centre and was created to promote innovation and technological development in Luxembourg. The Centre's goal is to improve the innovation capabilities of the private and public sectors by providing support services across the main technology-critical areas: information and communication technologies, industrial and environmental technologies.

The CITI carried out several assessments and reviews of software processes by making use of IEC/ISO15504[3][4]. For the last two years, we noticed several times that assessed organisations were also using ITIL as the standard for service management. Beyond the comparison that can be made between both standards, it has been a precious experience to analyse and collect information coming directly from day-to-day users of the standards.

It is important to notice that due to the CITI's mission and to the economical context of the Grand Duchy of Luxembourg, SMEs are *de facto* targets of research and development activities. Contrary to what is often alleged, both standards can suit the needs of small organisations (with „SMEs" we refer to organisations of up to 50 IT employees). CITI's management always encouraged initiatives to develop the use of world-class standards into small companies in Luxembourg and their interest in applying the standards is continuously growing.

Once this significant practical knowledge acquired, CITI's quality specialists logically raised the following matter as a subject of research: „Does the combined use of ITIL and IEC/ISO 15504 truly increases effectiveness and efficiency and can be adapted to the need of flexibility of today's organizations? ". Right from the start, it has been obvious that CITI's familiarity with companies using both standards concomitantly would be of great help in that respect and will almost certainly lead to valuable results. This paper describes how all these thoughts are organised in a new research project.

2   Empirical Findings Emanating from CITI's Projects

Facilitating the quality management of IT services and of the technical IT infrastructure in the organisation is becoming a true challenge. In that context, organisations managers are expecting from ITIL and IEC/ISO 15504 to assist organisations to provide high quality IT scrvices in the face of budgetary constraints, skill shortages, system complexity, rapid change, current and future user requirements and growing user expectations. One of our goals has been to search for the common denominators between our different experiences: most of the time, organisations have common types of benefits and problems that are every so often emanating directly from the use of the standards. The below list can be considered as reasonably comprehensive regarding our accumulated experiences:

-    Every IT organization we met wants to keep full control of any kind of change to their environment: it is the case for technology changes and is also true for process changes. According to that, they have chosen the standards for the pragmatic benefits they can expect from their use as well as their flexibility.
-    Most organizations begin their quality and business capability improvements by using the standards as guidelines and don't directly aspire to be comprehensive in their approach. In fact, they are taking in standards what they are considering as relevant for their day-to-day activities. This lack of comprehensiveness in the approach leads several organisations to experience maturity inconsistency in some of their processes.
-    A major nuisance for process owners is the terminology. The major advantage of a recognized method is the use of a common language which describes a large number of terms that, when used correctly, can help people to understand each other within IT organisations. An important part of ITIL and IEC/ISO15504 duty is getting people to speak that common language. That is why training on standards is the essential basis of an improvement program implementation. Regrettably, there is no common language or mapping between ITIL and IEC/ISO 15504 and it is one of the perceptible problems encountered by the companies implementing the bilateral approach. However, as the area of use of both standards is different it strongly helps to decrease terminological problems. Moreover, the combination of standards is always associated to the combination of participants coming from disparate sub disciplines: it provides an excellent blend of appropriate talents to address the multi-faceted problems and encourage the creation of a proprietary terminological standardization using ITIL and IEC/ISO 15504 as a basis.
-    Another terminological problem comes from the appropriation-time needed for the organisations to understand the content of the standards. Understanding the most evolved concepts of the standards can take time. An external help as for instance consultancy assistance is often needed to speed up the learning process.
-    Using the ITIL and/or ISO/IEC 15504 increases reliably the level of maturity of the processes deployed across the organization but the way of implementing improvements depends on the size of the organisation. For large organisations with high-risk projects, serious management is required and a formalized

approach is necessary. For small organisations, a more ad-hoc process is used and usually depends on the type of customers and projects, and on team leaders or managers. By implementing appropriate ISO/IEC 15504 and ITIL processes slowly over time, using consensus to reach agreement on processes and adjusting as the organisation grows and matures, productivity is improved. At the same time, attempts are made to keep processes simple and efficient, minimize paperwork, promote computer-based processes and automated tracking and reporting, minimize time required in meetings and promote training.

Companies	Period	Processes assessed (ISO/IEC 15504 assessment)	Use of standards
6 companies (3 banks, 1 research centre, 1 administra-tion)	From 1996 to 1998	Project Management, Require-ments Engineering, Development, Tests, Joint Review, Documen-tation, Organisation alignement	ISO/IEC 15504 only
6 companies (3 financial organisa-tions, 1 insurance company, 1 distribu-tion company, 1 research centre)	From 1999 to 2002	Project Management, Require-ments elicitation, Contract Mana-gement, Operational Support, Supply, Distribution, Configuration Management	5 out of 6 companies use ISO/IEC 15504 and ITIL standards

Fig. 1. This table sums up data coming from experiences within CITI projects and shows the evolution of standard use and for quality actions performed with companies of the Grand-Duchy of Luxembourg, and of the French speaking area around

Most big companies have separate departments for IT services and IT developments. When such companies adopt a structured approach for improving their current practices in one or the other department, the selection and implementation of such practices are performed independently, according to the respective budget allowed. Contrary, in most SMEs, IT services and development activities are gathered in one IT team but are performed by dedicated skilled staff. The standards help to create a solid environment for all of these organizations that encounter recurrent problems and have similar concerns. In that context it is interesting to note that CITI's specialists used as a methodological background several international initiatives that particularly address these points and are shortly mentioned below:

- the new version of the ISO 9001:2000[5] standard has been build according to a process approach and can be implemented by all kinds of companies (all kinds of sizes and activities);
- the EFQM (European Foundation for Quality Management) has developed a dedicated model for SMEs (the European Model for Small and Medium sized Enterprises), with an associated award (the European Quality Award for SME's) [6] [7];
- concerning the CMM (Capability Maturity Model)[8], a company named LOGOS has worked out a lightened approach for small businesses, small organisations and small projects[9];
- the European Commission has brought out programs which aimed at developing SME's dedicated approaches, such as the SPIRE project (SPIRE

stands for *Software Process Improvement in Regions of Europe* and helped small companies apply SPI to develop software. About 70 case studies describe SPI activities performed and a SPI handbook has been formalised) [10];

- ITIL for SME's[11] : while ITL was not specifically written for large-scale, data-centre-type operations, it was certainly written with such installations in mind, since they represent the approach to IT within UK government. ITIL practices for small units have been described in a specific book of the library, focusing on the nature of these environments and how ITIL techniques apply.

This baseline of findings and experiences leads us going through a theoretical analysis of the combined use of the ITIL and ISO/IEC 15504 standards.

3   ITIL and SPICE Used together: The Way to Improve Efficiency in It Processes?

Before considering the complementary aspects of the ITIL and IEC/ISO 15504, it is essential to understand the historical and methodological background and the content of each of them.

3.1   ITIL Overview

The ITIL was created in the late 1980s and originally consisted of ten core books covering the two main areas of Service Support and Service Delivery; subsequently 30 complementary books covering a large range of issues have been added to support these core books.

Nowadays, the ITIL is going to be reorganized in order to make simpler the access to the information needed to manage services.The new ITIL will consist of six sets: Service Support; Service Delivery; Planning to Implement Service Management; ICT Infrastructure Management; Applications Management; The Business Perspective. At the moment only Service Delivery and Service Support have been made available by the OGC, the four others sets do not yet exist.

Although the ITIL covers a number of areas, its main focus is on IT Service Management (ITSM). By the mid-1990s, ITIL was recognised as the world *de facto* standard for Service Management and provided the foundation for quality IT service management. The widespread acceptance of the ITIL guidance joined to its public availability has encouraged international organisations, most of the time commercial and non-proprietary, to develop supporting products as part of a shared 'ITIL Philosophy'.

The two available areas of IT Service Management (ITSM) are Service Support and Service Delivery and consist of 10 disciplines that are responsible for the provision and management of effective IT services.

The method clearly claims that using ITIL does not signify a completely new way of thinking and acting and prefers focusing on best practice that can be used in diverse ways according to need: placing existing methods and activities in a structured context as well as having a strong relationship between the processes avoid the lack of communication and co-operation between various IT functions.

3.2   SPICE Overview

An international collaborative effort to develop a standard had been underway (unofficially) since 1990 and officially since June of 1993. IT was known as the SPICE (Software Process Improvement and capability determination) project. The prospective standard was intended to, among other things, establish a common framework for expressing the process capability ratings resulting from a SPICE-conformant assessment and to provide a migration path for existing assessment models and methods wishing to become SPICE-conformant.

The effort was being carried out under the auspices of a joint technical committee of the International Standardization Organization and the International Electrotechnical Commission. The SPICE project culminated in a new international standard referred to as ISO/IEC 15504, as a set of Technical Reports in February 1998.

ISO/IEC 15504 provides a framework for the assessment of software processes. This framework can be used by organizations involved in planning, managing, monitoring, controlling, and improving the acquisition, supply, development, operation, evolution and support of software.

The major benefits of a standardised approach to process assessment are that it provides a public, shared approach for process assessment and leads to a common understanding of the use of process assessment for process improvement and capability evaluation. It also facilitates capability evaluation in procurement. It is controlled and regularly reviewed in the light of experience of use, and is changed only by international consensus. Finally it encourages harmonization of existing schemes.

Process assessment has two principal contexts for its use: process improvement and process capability determination.

Within a process improvement context, process assessment provides the means of characterizing the current practice within an organizational unit in terms of the capability of the selected processes. Analysis of the results in the light of the organization's business needs identifies strengths, weaknesses, opportunities and risks inherent in the processes. This, in turn, leads to the ability to determine whether the processes are effective in achieving their goals, and to identify significant causes of poor quality, or overruns in time or cost. These provide the drivers for prioritising improvements to processes.

Process capability determination is concerned with analysing the proposed capability of selected processes against a target process capability profile in order to identify the risks involved in undertaking a project using the selected processes. The proposed capability may be based on the results of relevant previous process assessments, or may be based on an assessment carried out for the purpose of establishing the proposed capability.

ISO/IEC 15504 has been designed to satisfy the needs of acquirers, suppliers and assessors, and their individual requirements from within a single source. To conclude and sum up briefly this overview, we can say that the overall objective of IEC/ISO 15504 is to help the software industry to make noteworthy gains in efficiency and quality and deals with software processes such as development, management, customer support and quality.

3.3   Key Links between ITIL and ISO/IEC 15504

Used separately, ITIL and ISO/IEC 15504 standards are an undeniable help for today's organisations: let's see where the connection can be made between them.

As it was explained above, the ITIL framework of proven best practices can be easily used within organisations with previously existing methods and activities in Service Management. Relationship with quality systems such as ISO 9000 and a total quality framework such as European Foundation for Quality Management (EFQM) is clearly mentioned by the standard. ITIL supports these quality systems by providing defined processes and best practice for the management of IT Services, enabling in some cases a fast track towards ISO certification.

ISO/IEC 15504 is complementary to several other International Standards and other models for evaluating the capability and effectiveness of organizations and processes. ISO/IEC 15504 incorporates the intent of the ISO 9000 series to provide confidence in a supplier's quality management whilst providing acquirers with a framework for assessing whether potential suppliers have the capability to meet their needs. Process assessment provides users with the ability to evaluate process capability on a continuous scale in a comparable and repeatable way, rather than using the pass/fail characteristic of quality audits based on ISO 9001. In addition, the framework described in ISO/IEC 15504 provides the opportunity to adjust the scope of assessment to cover specific processes of interest and that are aligned to business goals of an organisational unit, rather than all of the used processes. ISO/IEC 15504, and particularly part 2, is also directly aligned to ISO/IEC12207 :1995, Information technology:-Software life cycle processes. This standard provides an overall contextual framework for software life cycle processes, and the process dimension of the reference model is closely mapped to this framework.

Contrary to EFQM and ISO9000, ISO/IEC 15504 is not mentioned in the „quality management appendix" of ITIL. The ISO/IEC 15504 standard does not mention either the ITIL standard.

Nevertheless the link can be easily made: ITIL uses an adapted process model as base for process control and execution. All processes have an input as well as an output and process control is under the responsibility of the process owner who verifies the process goal using quality parameters and performance indicators. For each process ITIL also describes the resources and the roles necessary to execute the activities and sub-processes. For the input and the output of the process ITIL describes the specifications necessary to bring the process to a good end. If we look at the ISO/IEC 15504 standard, we find a similar process description approach: process definition with process goals, outcomes, inputs, outputs, and base practices. Beyond the process model, an international standard like ISO/IEC 15504 has a major role to play to support the Process Assessment. Obviously, the key relationship between both standards is the process approach.

By developing furthermore this idea, it becomes evident that measuring the current level of maturity of IT organizations by using the ITIL processes as reference for IT services, the ISO/IEC 15504 processes for IT development, and specifically ISO/IEC 15504 as the assessment tool can provide the organization with clear-cut and extended information. Besides the process measurement, the companies have their organizational, management, service and technology/tool aspects measured.

Organizations have already intuitively understood the possibilities offered by this combination even if they are not properly using them on a combined way today.

At this point, it is important to mention that OGC recently published two questionnaires that allow ITIL's users to assess Service Management processes based on a ten-levels-scale of maturity. However, the questionnaires cannot be compared to a comprehensive methodology, they can be considered as a good quality basis on which is possible to develop first-rate assessment if concomitantly used with IEC/ISO 15504. They are not a solution to replace the use of ISO/IEC 15504 but a complementary tool valuable in that respect.

By going more in depth through the study, we found another attention-grabbing characteristic of the combined use of IEC/ISO 15504 and ITIL. Their concomitant use can help organisations making the link between their development and service management processes. One of the main explanations is the fact that Configuration Management is an additional irrefutable connection between the standards: it is the common basis on which it is possible to build software development, operation, maintenance, and enhancement. Without Configuration Management, considerable time and effort would be required to control the products of Software Development Life-cycle projects or systems in production. As a key transversal process it must be considered as a necessity to unify the interrelated system of processes. Problem management is also treated in both standards but at a less distinguishing level: ISO /IEC 15504 doesn't make a distinction between incident and problems as ITIL does. Operation use, customer support and infrastructure are mentioned as IEC/ISO 15504 processes although the relationship is not easy to create with the ITIL's processes.

To sum up the above scheme, we can assert the following: as the main objective of ITIL is to facilitate the quality management of IT services and of the IT technical infrastructure in the organisation it can be considered as a service management-oriented standard.

On the IEC/ISO 15504 side, it was intended from its beginning, that the framework would be suitable for use in the primary context of process assessment, process improvement and capability determination: it covers contract, development, project management, etc. but the less-developed topic of ISO 15504 is undeniably service management. SPICE is considered as a development-oriented standard.

Consequently, using IEC/ISO 15504 combined with ITIL then becomes a true benefit for any organisation that wants to perfectly master the entire value chain of processes.

To bring to a close this chapter it is interesting to note that another way to make use of notions emanating from ISO/IEC 15504 is to implement service delivery using ISO 15504's project management principles; this allows to monitor and control ITIL service management implementation projects. The ITIL provides explanation on what is needed in terms of activities to conduct the execution of service management processes while ISO/IEC 15504 provides a dedicated management process and the methodological assessment tool to verify the maturity.

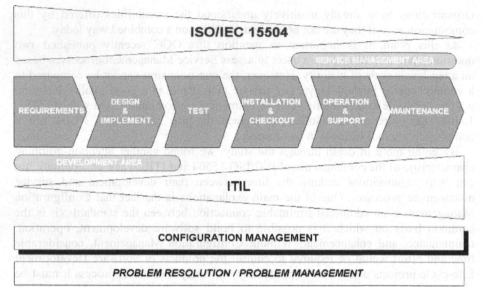

Fig. 2. The above scheme gives a representation of the area covered by the standards as well as the key processes .Two different types of processes can be considered: some of them are needed throughout the life cycle of the project and are well described by the both standards (typically configuration management) and the others are more specifically in the area of development (i.e. ISO/IEC 15504) or service management (i.e. ITIL)

4   CITI's Suggested Approach to Implement the Standards

After having analysed empirical findings collected during the various missions in the local business area and finalized the theoretical analysis on it, CITI's specialists came up with a method that could be considered as a toolbox intended to be used by organisations needing guidelines on how to implement ITIL and IEC/ISO 15504. The following gives a quick overview of what is the planned implementation project for developing this methodology.

A first plan of a research project named AIDA (Integrated Approach for Improvement) has been recently drafted: more than enhancing the current approach with new features, it is also supposed to downsize it to be applied by SMEs.

4.1   Process Selection

The scope must be chosen and based on the nature of the organisation and its critical processes. Appropriate processes must be selected into both standards; it is clearly required to obtain an unambiguous agreement on what is suitable for improving organization's vital everyday tasks. Processes selection can be simplified by conducting pre-assessment of the organization, this is especially helpful in terms of discovering what and where are its strengths and weaknesses.

To support these thoughts, we have already experimented that using the value chain diagram helps identifying the most critical core processes and IT key processes[12]. With that approach, the selected IT processes for assessment and improvement are directly connected to IT objectives and key success factors of the company, and are then automatically connected to its general objectives.

According to the SPICE standard and to the CITI's experience with SMEs, we noticed that a set of processes, even if they are partially implemented, have to be established in a systematic way. They always contribute to the value chain activities. We suggest a list of generic activities that are often present and applicable to the software context: product specification, product selection and/or product development, product maintenance, technology management and management of activities.

Considering the ISO/IEC 15504 process model, the following list of processes that contribute to the core activities of most companies and IT organisational units has been established: acquisition, supply, project management, risk management, problem resolution, configuration management, infrastructure, development, maintenance.

These processes will then have to be combined with service support and service delivery ITIL processes.

4.2   Development of an "Integrated Assessment Approach"

The integrated assessment approach consists of a set of activities that are conducted during the whole project to verify that the processes are executed according to the standards specifications and in a mature manner. It also verifies that the means set up by the management are correctly and fully applied.

CITI's internal and external project owners have developed this approach by building, using and gathering miscellaneous questionnaires, audit trails, micro-assessment tools, and also ISO/IEC 15504 assessment technique in order to be able to provide SMEs with a full package of assessment services. There are mainly three reasons for recommending the use of an integrated assessment approach:

- First of all, to establish objectively, consistently, and reliably the presence or absence of maturity in the chosen IT processes.
- Secondly, to deal with problems associated with resistance to the introduction and adherence to new approach.
- And thirdly, to prepare workforce to an external assessment.

4.3   Performance of an Integrated Assessment

As explained previously, the external assessment is based on the IEC/ISO 15504 methodology even to evaluate emblematic ITIL processes. A first compulsory assessment is the trigger event of the overall improvement program in a company. CITI strongly recommends that the time between assessments not exceed a 12-month period. More frequent assessment may be recommended if the organization has a serious difficulty to improve processes. Based on CITI's experience, it is imperative to mention that without an effective integrated assessment approach the process implementation will probably be analysed as incomplete during the external assessment.

One of the primary purposes of the external assessment is to determine whether management with executive responsibility ensures that an adequate and effective process improvement has been established as well as the appliance of the standards at the workforce level. External assessment must consist of a formal, planned check of all selected processes. However, re-assessment of deficient matters is not always required, it is frequently more efficient to help company by leading them to adopt an outsourced approach that could smooth the progress into processes improvement. In fact, it often permits to reveal irregularities and to indicate possible improvements more clearly than with the use of internal employee.

4.4 Development and Implementation of an "Integrated Improvement Approach"

Based on the assessment results, improvement actions have to be implemented by the companies. In order to support and monitor them, an integrated improvement approach will be developed by the CITI. As for the integrated assessment approach, ITIL and SPICE previous research project experiences will be used in order to build a methodological toolbox. This toolbox will provide methodological tools and services combining the use of SPICE and ITIL, on a particular adapted way for SMEs.

As previously said, the approach suggested to implement the standards must be considered as a toolbox where it is possible to choose what are the most relevant tools: CITI's purpose is clearly to provide SMEs with a flexible methodology allowing them to improve and assess their processes by integrating IT development and service management, and in a near future security management in a continual improvement approach.

The CITI will provide monitoring services in order to assist organisations implementing their improvement actions, and to adjust the methodological toolbox. These case studies will enable to validate the toolbox in its own improvement cycle.

4.5 Promotion, Awareness and Dissemination Activities

Management with executive responsibility (i.e. has the authority to establish and make changes to the company quality policy) must assure the objectives are understood at all levels of the organisation. It can be done with the help of knowledgeable internal or external resources: seminars, training sessions, workshops, dissemination of white papers and miscellaneous relevant information can be considered as good techniques to plainly involve organisation's workforce. This part of the method must be conducted throughout the lifecycle of the implementation: as always, communication remains a crucial factor to reach success in such activities.

5   Conclusion

The combined use of ISO/IEC 15504 and ITIL can be considered as coming from the need of the organizations to develop a quality improvement framework including development and service management aspects. With both standards used together, almost all processes specifically related to development and service management are fully available to the organizations and it definitively helps them to improve service quality.

CITI's projects results have shown that introduced parts of both standards often had beneficial results into different organizations even if sometimes some problematic issues remain (terminology, lack of a comprehensive approach). It is also clear that both standards used concomitantly lead to attain good quality results in terms of increasing maturity of IT processes.

It allows us to think that a growing number of organizations will probably adopt both standards in a near future. It is realistically possible that the introduction of the ITIL four „missing" sets will reinforce the relationship and the need for using the best of each standard. The actual evolution of the ISO/IEC 15504 standard is also bringing new bricks in the process improvement building, by providing a process assessment technique that can be implemented for all types of processes in all kind of organisations (not only software ones), and by providing requirements for defining process reference models. All these statements and thoughts are contributing to the definition of this research project that will enable companies of the Grand-Duchy of Luxembourg, and the close French speaking regions such as the Walloon area in Belgium and Lorraine in France, to take profit of a combined use of ITIL and ISO/IEC 15504 standards.

References

[1]   IT Infrastructure Library – Service Support, Service Delivery, The Stationery Office Edition, 2000
[2]   ISO/IEC JTC 1/SC 7, ISO/IEC TR 15504, 1998
[3]   Barafort B., Hendrick A., A SME dedicated framework to evaluate the internal usage of IT, in: Proceedings of the International Conference Software Process Improvement, SPI'98, Monte-Carlo, Principauté de Monaco, 1998
[4]   Barafort B., SPIRAL Network development results, in: Proceedings of the International Conference EuroSPI'2001, Limerick, Ireland, 2001
[5]   NF EN ISO 9001:Décembre 2000
[6]   The EFQM Excellence Model – Small and Medium sized Enterprises, EFQM publications, 1999-2001
[7]   Moving from the SME Model to the EFQM Excellence Model – SMEs Version, EFQM Publications, 2001
[8]   Mark C. Paulk, Bill Curtis, Mary Beth Chrissis and Charles Weber, Capability Maturity Model for Software, Version 1., SEI, CMU/SEI-93-TR-24, Pittsburgh, Pa, Feb. 1993
[9]   Brodman G. J., Johnson L. D., The LOGOS Tailored CMM for Small Businesses, Small Organisations, and Small Projects, LOGOS International, Inc., Needham, UK, September 1997
[10]   SPIRE Project Information Pack - ESSI Project 23873 – April 1997
[11]   IT Infrastructure Library practices in small IT units, Central Computer and Telecommunications Agency, 1995
[12]   Porter Michael E., Millar Victor E., How information gives you competitive advantage, in: Harvard Business Review Article, July 1985

Enabling Comprehensive Use of Metrics

Outi Salo, Maarit Tihinen, and Matias Vierimaa

VTT Technical Research Centre of Finland
P.O. Box 1100, FIN-90571, Oulu, Finland
{outi.salo,maarit.tihinen,matias.vierimaa}@vtt.fi
http://www.vtt.fi/ele/indexe.htm
fax: +358 8 551 2320

Abstract. Although software measurements have been used in industry for several decades, it is still difficult for companies to make the most of them. An efficient use of measurements is a fundamental issue – without it, measurement is waste of time and effort. In this paper we present an approach to supporting and boosting the utilisation of measurements at both project and organisational levels. The underlying idea behind the approach is to create a practical measurement utilisation plan. We present how the utilisation plan can be developed and how this approach can motivate software developers and managers to collect and utilise metrics. We also describe the experiences and feedback gained from a case study. We consider our approach as a vital enhancement to existing measurement methods, one to be adopted when aiming at a comprehensive utilisation of measurements. Moreover, our approach prepares the ground for packaging the measurement results in an organisation.

1   Introduction

Software development has a great role in the total development costs of embedded products. Due to hard competition in the market of embedded products (such as mobile phones), software has a significant selling impact. The size and complexity of software development has increased, and the software development for an embedded product is often done in parallel in several sites and also by several companies. For an attempt of gaining an understanding and improving software development practices in such an environment, measurable and reliable information about software development is called for. Although software measurement has been used for several decades (e.g. [1]) for improving software development and for gaining a better understanding of it, it has proven difficult to implement measurement programs in companies [2].

VTT (Technical Research Centre of Finland) is the largest independent R&D organisation in the Nordic countries. VTT Electronics, one of the six units of VTT, has been applying software measurements in several process improvement projects

M. Oivo and S. Komi-Sirviö (Eds.): PROFES 2002, LNCS 2559, pp. 326-336, 2002.

with national and international companies operating in the field of embedded software, see for example [3], [4] and [5]. According to our researches, most companies developing software today have a lot of data available about software processes and products. Although the data is available, the effort to analyse and to learn from it is often seen too time consuming, due to time-to-market pressure or changes in the environment. The measurement paradigms, for example GQM [6], "stop at the point at which measurement concepts or specific metrics are identified" [7]. They do not define how such measures could be analysed or utilised through the software processes. Therefore, it is pointed out in this article that the use of measurements should be planned carefully, and a systematic utilisation of measurements should be regarded as one of the main goals of software measurement.

A number of problems can be seen in the utilisation of software metrics related data beyond a single project. Kitchenham [8] points out the problems concerning the definition of comparable product or process measures, stating that "the project differences can be as large as company differences". This issue pertains to the utilisation of data between multiple projects, which can be rather complicated even in a single company. We claim that measurements should not be used as a stand-alone mechanism for comparing projects. Instead, measurements should always be analysed and utilised together with project personnel, making use of their valuable knowledge of, e.g., interpreting measurement data.

The focus of this paper lies on describing how to create a utilisation plan to support measurement utilisation, and on presenting the experiences and feedback gained from its implementation in a case study. For one, creating a utilisation plan serves as an opportunity for motivating and guiding the people involved within the organisation to use metrics in a more comprehensive way. Therefore, focusing on utilisation and finding out why individuals want to collect or use measurements in everyday work will lead to a higher degree of commitment.

In section 2, the background for the perspective of this paper is given by introducing the idea and its relevance to some existing methods. In section 3, the process of creating a utilisation plan is described, and its benefits and aims are explained. Section 4 summarises the experiences and observations gained whilst creating the utilisation plan in the case study conducted.

2   Background

Software measurement can be seen simply as an information obtaining process: Fenton & Pfleeger [9] have divided software measurement into three basic activities 1) understanding, 2) controlling, and 3) improving. The following activities provide the key reasons for software measurement [10]:

-    understand and model software engineering process and products
-    aid in the management of software projects
-    guide improvements in software engineering processes

Although any of the causes given above could offer a strong enough motivation for implementing a software measurement program, projects are – based on the experience gained at VTT Electronics – often carried out in such a hectic and quickly changing environment that measurement implementation may be difficult. Often, even if some measurement programs are implemented, practices are likely to remain the same in the everyday life of these organisations. Furthermore, a measurement program that focuses on the collection process, or one that does not have a clear plan for the utilisation of measurements, seems most likely to fail [10].

The IEEE Standard [11] presents a format for metrics definition, data item documentation, examples of their use, along with related guides and templates. While the standard offers a useful method for developing software measurement practices, it provides no guidance for determining utilisation issues, e.g., at which level – that of project or organisation - the metrics should be utilised, or by whom, when and how. Furthermore, although the standard recommends documenting the factors related to metrics and the interpretation of measurement results, utilisation issues such as applied analysing and interpretation methods, timetables or responsibilities are not discussed.

The Goal/Question/Metric (GQM) paradigm [12], [6] provides a method for planning measurements based on selected goals. The GQM approach is an effective way of defining the metrics and striving for the goal itself. On the basis of some industrial cases in which GQM has been applied, it can, however, be stated that this method produces a lot of metrics, and that it may still be difficult to define good ones [13]. Another problem is that the measurements derived from defined goals may not directly meet the everyday needs of the people actually collecting the metrics, which may cause a serious lack of motivation towards the measurements.

A number of paradigms and methods, such as the Quality Improvement Paradigm (QIP) [12] and Experience Factory (EF) [14] suggest that measurement data and experience should be packaged to be reused at project and organisational levels. The data, information, knowledge and experience gained by collecting metrics from a project should benefit not only the project itself, but other projects and higher organisational levels as well.

EF introduces an organisation structure for processing the information provided by projects, enabling to give feedback to them. It is also capable of producing some more generalised information for the projects and for the organisational level, such as baselines and lessons learned [14]. EF can thus be seen as an organisation structure that significantly supports the utilisation of project level results gained from, for example, measurement processes. It supplies the analysed and synthesised experiences on demand to projects and to the organisational level, while it is left up to the projects and the organisational level to know what their own utilisation needs are, i.e., what they should provide the EF with in order to request the processed data that fits their needs. In other words, the project and organisational levels should clearly plan their needs for measurement utilisation in advance, and the appropriate phase to do this is in connection with measurement planning.

3   How to Create an Efficient Utilisation Plan

In this section, the process of creating a utilisation plan is described (Fig. 1.) as conducted in our case study.

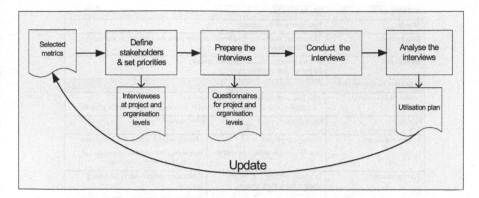

Fig. 1. The process of creating a utilisation plan

The starting point for the utilisation plan was provided by the previously selected metrics in our case study organisation. The detailed phases of the utilisation plan creation are described in 3.1. Also, the ideas and aims of the plan are presented, along with the benefits, experiences and feedback gained from the process.

3.1   Utilisation Plan Creation

During the case study, the semi-structured personal interview [15] was considered the most suitable method for fulfilling the various information needs of creating a utilisation plan. This technique was well suited to utilisation plan interviewing due to the different roles and organisational levels of the interviewees and, thus, their different perspectives on the subject under survey. Also, the method enabled new questions to arise during the interview, depending on the responses of the interviewee, which allowed obtaining additional details about the subject.

The various utilisation needs were detected by conducting interviews with people working in different roles within the organisation, operating at both project and organisational levels, who were likely to benefit in some way from utilising the information provided by the selected metrics (Fig. 1.). Separate questionnaires were prepared for project and organisational level interviews. The preparation of interviews (i.e. questions, schedule, interviewees) is an essential task and should be carried out with great care, because the implementation of the interviews has a significant effect on the results.

Finally, the utilisation plan was produced by analysing and interpreting the interviews (Fig. 1.). The utilisation plan contained information about who utilised or who could or should benefit from utilising each of the selected metrics at different organisational levels, including the aspect of utilisation between projects. In addition, the details about how and when the metrics were utilised, along with the different factors to be considered when doing so, were included in the utilisation plan. A template of the utilisation plan was developed during the case study and is presented in [16]. In Fig. 2. the template is filled with some example data.

METRIC SET:	RELIABILITY		
Metric:	Found defects by severity		
Description:	This metric shows the number of defects - and their severity - during the predefined period.		
Data items:	Defect severity (minor, medium, major) Reported date (dd.mm.yyyy)		
Utilisation in the project			
Project characteristics	- the phase of the project (in the lifecycle) - the project is a continuum to a similar, previous project / a new project		
Who utilises (role in the project)	When utilised		How utilised
Project manager	During the project (e.g. biweekly in project meetings)		Making release schedule estimations Estimating the number of remaining defects (for effort estimation)
Testing manager	In testing phases: e.g. in the integration testing phase		Evaluating the efficiency of testing process Evaluating the maturity (readiness) of software
Utilisation between projects			
Project characteristics	- used programming language - size of the project		
Comparison requirements	Project type, e.g. distributed or non-distributed project People factors: project size or project members' experience Code: e.g. used programming language, size, percentage of reused code or development tools		
Who utilises (role in the project)	Metric	When utilised	How utilised
Project manager	Synthesis metric: Average of found defects by severity from selected projects (see comparison req.)	During the project After the project	Evaluation if the project's defects are within normal limits compared with other similar projects Comparing the testing efficiency of the project with other projects Looking for improvement areas and causes for abnormalities
Utilisation in the organisation			
Comparison requirements	Group criteria, e.g. departments, products, sites		
Who utilises (role in the project)	Metric	When utilised	How utilised
Upper management in the organisation	Synthesis metric: Average of found defects by severity regarding selected group criteria (see comparison req.)	Twice a year or quarterly.	Comparing the values of departments /sites /products with others Looking for improvement areas (e.g. process quality or efficiently)
Marketing department	Related metric: Updated release estimations from project managers	The end phase of the product lifecycle	Evaluating the time to market for specific products

Fig. 2. Filled utilisation plan template

After the utilisation plan has been created, the chosen metrics should be evaluated and updated if necessary. This may involve removing any metrics that have no real use. Also, if any new improvement needs are discovered during the utilisation planning process, these have to be considered too.

Although the metrics collection should be carried out on a continuous basis, the goals, metrics, and utilisation needs may change over time at both project and organisational levels. For these reasons, the utilisation plan should be reviewed and updated regularly along with the goals, metrics and utilisation needs involved.

3.2   Aims, Benefits and Problems of Utilisation Planning

There are a number of environment-related and other aspects that have to be taken into consideration when planning the utilisation of measurements. Figure 3 describes how measurement data is collected in projects, and how it is analysed and synthesised for different utilisation needs in an organisation. Some metrics are used only within a single project, and some metrics may only be used at the organisational level. The 'filter level' (Fig. 3.) can be used for preventing a direct comparison of single projects. However, a single project is allowed to obtain synthesised data from other projects.

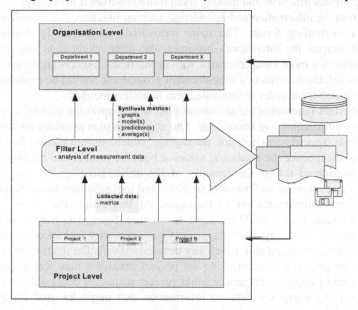

Fig. 3. The environment of measurement utilisation

Utilisation interviews can serve a number of purposes. Both project-related and organisational aspects of utilising project-level metrics data should be considered. Although the metrics collected in a project might be chosen on the basis of project-level goals, there is always, or at least there should always be, an organisational level goal in the background. According to Florac et al. [17], one of the basic principles of successful process measurement is that process measures are driven by business goals, which ensures that a sufficient degree of commitment is achieved at the organisational level and that software measurement is generally accepted.

One of the tasks of the interviews is to analyse current and possible future utilisation needs. This is done by fathoming out the short-term and, if possible, also the long-term utilisation needs of "key utilisers" acting in different roles within the organisation. While the main emphasis should lie on the selected metrics, the possibility of finding new important needs should also be considered. Valuable information is obtained by analysing how metrics data is used in the project, between projects, and also at higher organisational levels. Also the tools and practices used for analysing, storing and viewing collected measurements can be included in the utilisation interviews in order to further the implementation and development of organisation specific tool solutions.

Another important purpose of utilisation interviews is to define the environmental and project characteristics [14] affecting the comparison of metrics between projects. It is a matter of fact that there will never be two similar projects allowing to be compared without any need to consider characteristics such as size, experience, tools and project practices. Comparing project measurements can yield valuable information also about different practices, and it can thus be used as a mechanism for optimising project practices and making them more coherent if necessary.

Apart from the information and knowledge seeking function, the interview can also serve as a motivating forum. The more motivated and knowledgeable about the benefits of metrics the interviewee becomes, the more likely it is that he/she will utilise metrics in a more comprehensive way in the future. According to van Solingen & Berghout [6], the benefits of a measurement programme should be promoted among the project members in order to motivate them to collect metrics.

One important function of the utilisation plan is to support the packaging of metrics related data, information and knowledge. The utilisation plan provides for the building of a company specific solution for packaging, which, unfortunately, has been left undone too often. Since the needs and views at both the project and the organisational level are considered during the creation of the utilisation plan, it also guides the planning of measurement environment (Fig. 3.) and tool solutions for packaging along with the actual implementation of packages. At this point, the issues related to information hiding [18] should be taken into account. Some data may be preferred to be kept at project level only, since the project personnel may feel uncomfortable about the idea of managers being able to see any detailed information that might be used for evaluating the project personnel. Also the project managers may feel uncomfortable about the idea of higher managers or other project managers being able to survey, to compare and to modify any detailed information that might be used for evaluating their project. The organisational structure presented in EF is one way of solving this problem.

The creation of utilisation plan aims at developing a comprehensive view on the environment of measurement utilisation in organisations (Fig. 3.) and matching the measurements with the needs for utilising them. This is done by observing and clarifying the various factors, needs and activities related to measurements from different viewpoints: within and between projects and, at the organisational level, from the personal viewpoints of measurement users. If the different viewpoints, advantages, reasons and needs for measurement utilisation are clearly understood and accepted at all organisational levels, there is a better chance of attaining a continuous, effective and long-term measurement culture.

3.3   Applying Utilisation Planning with Existing Methods

Without a comprehensive utilisation of measurements, only part of the benefits of collecting metrics can be gained, if any at all, and software measurement can be a waste of time and effort. Our suggestion is to include the planning of utilisation, i.e. creating a utilisation plan, in the existing measurement practises.

The utilisation aspect can be embedded into the existing methods related to measuring software processes. The IEEE standard [11] can be supplemented with a utilisation plan: the goals and usage at project and organisation levels (including utilisation between projects) should be planned, and the analysis and interpretation of results should be determined and documented in a scheduled manner along with the responsibilities at each utilisation level.

Regarding the GQM method, utilisation planning can be implemented, for example, in the GQM interviews, after the measurement goals have been defined. However, GQM interviews lack the organisational level viewpoint and this should be added to the interviews. Also, a separate interview session concerned with utilisation planning should be arranged if seen appropriate. A utilisation plan document [16] should be created, and the metrics-related issues found should also be included in the GQM plan document.

The utilisation plan approach could provide an extremely valuable input also for the Experience Factory organisation, giving extensive insight into what measurement data should be packaged and how it should be packaged to be reused in an organisation.

4   Empirical Experiences of Utilisation Plan Creation

In the environment of our case study, two organisational level interviews and seven project level interviews were considered sufficient. The project members were acting in different roles and in several projects. Although the metric sets had been defined and chosen before creating the utilisation plan, new viewpoints could be gained and added to the metric sets through the utilisation plan creation. The interviews made it possible to map the responsibilities and tasks related to the measurements in the respective organisation and it also revealed problems related to these. In addition, the utilisation aspect of measurements proved a highly motivating viewpoint, making the project members interested and willing to take part in the interviews - and thus to make the effort necessary for creating the utilisation plan. One of the comments received from the interviews stated that it was encouraging that someone was finally interested in the real everyday measurement needs: *"It is nice to notice that someone is enquiring our needs. I believe that if someone really investigated our needs and demands, the metrics would be far more useful and more efficiently used".*

An active participation of the interviewees in the interviews, in itself, is not, however, any guarantee of their effort in the tasks of collecting or utilising the metrics, not to mention those of providing other projects and organisation levels with project measurement data. The reasons for and advantages of comparing data between projects at organisational and project levels should be well motivated to the management of the projects producing the data and, furthermore, their motivation and encouragement for measurement utilisation should remain strong and constant. The interviews in our case study clearly indicated that the project level was interested in the possibility of being able to compare their metrics and practices with other projects. However, some 'filter level' (Fig. 3.) was seen important for hiding specific information of single projects. In addition, an enhanced feedback concerning the organisational level synthesis of measurements was considered necessary at the project level. These factors speak for the implementation of specific structures for packaging the measurement results.

In our case study, several interesting project-related and environmental issues were found which clearly showed that some of the metrics were disparate between projects and that no generalisations with them should be made before standardising the practices in the projects to some degree, e.g. concerning the classification or collection processes of certain metrics. From this viewpoint, the creation of utilisation plan helped us also to clarify both the dissimilarities and differing practices in the projects compared. At the organisational level, it is important to be aware of different practices – or even divergent processes – because these may give a boost to improving or standardising the processes and practices used.

On the other hand, the utilisation plan makes any special needs for measurement data more easily recognised, thanks to the different perspectives offered by it within the organisation. The project members will also gain a better understanding of what kind of measurement data the organisation level is interested in, and why, and vice versa. For example, during the case study it was realised that the feedback from the organisation level to the project level was all too often omitted. At the project level, it was not always clear why some specific data had to be collected or who actually needed some specific metrics and how it was to be utilised. One project level interviewee commented: *"Great! All at once somebody is interested in our wishes and hopes ... and measurement needs .... Look at what kind of metrics we have to collect: I don't know why ...".* Usually this was the case when the measurements were to be provided for the organisational level. This kind of absence of organisational feedback proved to cause a lack of motivation for collecting valid and verified data for organisational usage. One interviewee stated: *"We don't get any feedback on the data collected by us ... maybe our project manager does ...".* In addition, some of the collected metrics were found unused in the organisation and thus their necessity was suggested to be reconsidered.

The interviews gave us necessary background information for planning and suggesting an organisational structure and a tool solution to be used for packaging the metrics related data in an organisation. In this case, our suggestion was a WWW-based tool, which was also implemented. It is to be noted, however, that in another case study conducted by us a database tool was preferred as a packaging tool. The tool selection is highly dependent on the tools and practices used in the target organisation.

5   Conclusions and Further Work

The goal of this research was to develop an approach that would support and boost the utilisation of measurements within target organisations. The starting point was the recognition that the needs concerning measurements were different at the organisation and project levels. These two levels needed to be taken into consideration early on when planning the measurements, so as to guarantee an efficient use of the metrics. The aim of our case study was, rather than measuring the success of the utilisation plan in the target organisation or comparing it with other methods, to experiment the idea of utilisation plan and to fathom out the potential in it. Our experiences and the feedback gained from the case interviewees have been thoroughly positive, which has encouraged us to further develop and experiment the developed method as a potential enhancement to the existing measurement approaches such as GQM.

The target case indicates that the creation of a utilisation plan facilitates the establishing of measurement practises at both project and organisational levels. It also improves the visibility of measuring needs and purposes within the whole organisation. In addition, it serves as a strong motivating agent for continuous measuring and comprehensive utilisation of measurements. To be successful, however, measurement utilisation requires a firm support from the organisation management.

The utilisation plan constitutes the basis for the packaging of measurements. The building of packages should be based on the needs presented in the utilisation plan. This perspective of packaging and measurement reuse shall be further studied within the Knots-Q project[1] (Knowledge-centered Tools and Methods for Software Production Quality) also carried out at VTT Electronics.

Acknowledgements

This work has been done within the MIKKO project, funded by TEKES and further processed in the Knots-Q project partially funded by the Academy of Finland. The goal of the MIKKO project was to study the measurement aspects related to a comprehensive collection and utilisation of measurement data in the software process. In the Knots-Q project, the ideas evolved during the MIKKO project are further processed from a knowledge-centred viewpoint. The authors would like to thank the case companies, the funding organisations and persons at VTT Electronics involved in the MIKKO and Knots-Q projects. Special thanks to Seija Komi-Sirviö for giving valuable comments during our writing process.

References

[1]   Basili, V., Weiss, D.: A Methodology for Collecting Valid Software Engineering Data. IEEE Transactions on Software Engineering, Vol SE-10, no. 6, November 1984, 728-738

[2]   Rifkin, S.: What Makes Measuring Software So Hard? IEEE Software, May/June 2001, 41-45

[3]   Järvinen, J.: Measurement based continuous assessment of software engineering processes. Doctoral thesis, 2000. VTT Electronics, Espoo. 97 p. + app. 90 p. VTT Publications: 426 ISBN 951-38-5592-9; 951-38-5593-7

[4]   Komi-Sirviö, S., Parviainen, P., Ronkainen, J.: Measurement automation: methodological background and practical solutions - a multiple case study. Proceedings of the 7th International Software Metrics Symposium, METRICS 2001. London, GB, 4 - 6 April 2001. IEEE Computer Society. Los Alamitos (2001), 306 - 316

---

[1] http://knots-q.vtt.fi/

[5]   Vierimaa, M., Kaikkonen, T., Oivo, M., Moberg, M.: Experiences of practical process improvement. Embedded Systems Programming Europe. Vol. 2 (1998) No: 13, 10 - 20

[6]   van Solingen, R., Berghout, E.: The Goal Question Metric Method: A Practical Guide for Quality Improvement of Software Development, The McGraw-Hill Companies, London (1999)

[7]   Kitchenham, B., Hughes, R.: Modeling Software Measurement Data. IEEE Transactions on Software Engineering, vol.27, no. 9, September 2001

[8]   Kitchenham, B.: The Case Against Software Benchmarking. Fesma-Dasma 2001, Heidelberg, Germany (2001)

[9]   Fenton, N.E., Pfleeger, S.L.: Software Metrics: A Rigorous and Practical Approach. International Thomson Publishing CO, Boston (1997)

[10]   Software engineering laboratory series: Software Measurement Guidebook, revision 1, NASA-GB-001-94, SEL-94-102, Greenbelt Maryland (1995)

[11]   IEEE Standard for a Software Quality Metrics Methodology (IEEE Std 1061-1992)

[12]   Basili, V., Caldiera, G., Rombach, H.: Goal Question Metric Paradigm. In John J. Marciniak, editor, Encyclopaedia of Software Engineering, Vol 1. John Wiley & Sons (1994) 528–532

[13]   Mäkäräinen, M., Vierimaa, M.: Evaluating the process - experiences from three methods on the improvement of the DSP SW process. Proceeding the European Conference on Software Process Improvement. SPI '98, 1 - 4 Dec. Society of Plastic Industry SPI, Monaco (1998)

[14]   Basili, V., Caldiera, G., Rombach, H.: Experience Factory. In John J. Marciniak, editor, Encyclopaedia of Software Engineering, Vol 1. John Wiley & Sons, (1994) 469–476

[15]   Judd, C.M., Smith, E.R., Kidder, L.H.: Research Methods in Social Relations, Harcourt Brace Jovanovich College Publishers, United States of America (1991)

[16]   Vierimaa, M., Ronkainen, J., Salo, O., Sandelin, T., Tihinen M., Freimut, B., Parviainen, P.: MIKKO Handbook: Comprehensive Collection and Utilisation of Software Measurement Data. VTT Publications, Espoo (2001)

[17]   Florac, W., Park, R., Carleton, A.: Practical Software Measurement: Measuring for Process Management and Improvement. SEI Software Engineering Institute, Carnegie Mellon University, CMU/SEI-97-HB-003, Pittsburgh (1997)

[18]   Grady, R.B.: Practical Software Metrics for Project Management and Process Improvement. Prentice Hall, Englewood Cliffs New Jersey (1992)

Product and Process Metrics:
A Software Engineering Measurement Expert System

Yingxu Wang, Qing He, Chris Kliewer, Tony Khoo, Vincent Chiew,
Wendy Nikoforuk, and Lian Chen

Theoretical and Empirical Software Engineering Research Centre (TESERC)
Dept. of Electrical and Computer Engineering, University of Calgary
2500 Univ. Dr., NW, Calgary, AB, Canada T2N 1N4
wangyx@enel.ucalgary.ca
Tel: +1 403 220 6141, Fax: (403) 282 6855

Abstract. Software engineering measurement and metrics are key technologies toward quantitative software engineering. However, software measurement is so complicated that practitioners in software engineering might not be able to adopt and use a comprehensive measurement system. To address this problem, a software engineering measurement expert system tool (SEMEST) is developed based on the software engineering measurement system (SEMS) established by TESERC [8, 9]. SEMEST provides an expert environment for supporting and implementing software engineering measurement, metrical analysis, and benchmarking in the software industry.

Keywords: Software engineering, measurement, metrics, SEMS, expert system, SEMEST

1 Introduction

Measurement and metrical analysis in software engineering are recognized as complicated system activities that consist of a large number of measures and require intensive mathematical and statistical analysis [2 - 6]. A comprehensive software engineering measurement system (SEMS) is developed [8, 9] to put existing and innovative software engineering measures into a unified framework.

However, it is found that practitioners in the industry may not be able to carry out a formal measurement and analysis manually in software engineering. As a solution, a software engineering measurement expert system tool (SEMEST) is developed by the authors as a supporting environment for quantitative software engineering measurement and analysis. Based on SEMEST, software engineering measurement practitioners, such as project managers and quality engineers, can manipulate the complex measurement procedures and their analysis based on the support of the expert tool. SEMEST can be used by industrial practitioners to gain insight into quantitative soft-

M. Oivo and S. Komi-Sirviö (Eds.): PROFES 2002, LNCS 2559, pp. 337-350, 2002.
© Springer-Verlag Berlin Heidelberg 2002

ware engineering through software measurements, and can be used by students to learn more about a comprehensive and unified software engineering measurement system.

This paper describes the structure and configuration of the software engineering measurement system (SEMS). Then, the design and implementation of the SEMS-based measurement expert system tool (SEMEST) are presented. Applications of SEMS and SEMEST are discussed, and future work on emigrating SEMEST onto a web-based platform is overviewed.

2   The Software Engineering Measurement System (SEMS)

This section describes the architecture of the software engineering measurement system (SEMS) framework and the schema that is used to model all measures and metrics in SEMS.

2.1   Structure of the SEMS Framework

Software engineering measurement is a systematic activity rather than separated individual activities [8, 9]. Conventional work on software metrics was focused on software products. However, important measurements, such as software engineering processes, quality, defects, testing, and project estimation, were rarely addressed in existing metrics.

SEMS consists of software product measurement, software engineering process measurement, and software engineering project predictive and estimative measurement. The architecture of the SEMS measurement framework is shown in Table 1.

As shown in Table 1, SEMS models a comprehensive set of software engineering measures with more than 300 meta and derived measures for software engineering measurement. Generally, more than half of the measures in SEMS are newly developed in almost all categories, such as the equivalent functional size, coding efficiency, architecture, complexity, defect, test, quality, early-phase processes, benchmarking, project estimation, etc.

2.2   Implementation of SEMS

All software engineering measures identified in SEMS are formally and rigorously described by formulae. A formal schema for each SEMS measure is defined as follows:

$$
\begin{aligned}
\text{SEMS ? Category} \\
\text{| Measure} \\
\text{| Symbol} \\
\text{| Definition} \\
\text{| Unit} \\
\text{| Scale} \\
\text{| Property} \\
\text{| Remark}
\end{aligned}
\tag{1}
$$

Table 1. The Structure of the Software Engineering Measurement System (SEMS)

Category Number	Category of Measurement	Subcategory of Measurement
1	Software product measurement	
1.1	Sizes	
1.1.1		Physical source size
1.1.2		Code memory size
1.1.3		Equivalent functional size
1.1.4		Function-point size
1.2	Coding efficiency	
1.3	Managerial attributes	
1.3.1		Time
1.3.2		Effort
1.3.3		Productivity
1.3.4		Costs
1.3.5		Cost-benefit ratio
1.4	Architecture	
1.4.1		Component-based architecture
1.4.2		OO architecture
1.5	Complexity	
1.6	Defects	
1.7	Test	
1.7.1		Test coverages
1.7.2		Testability
1.7.3		Residual defects
1.8	Reliability	
1.9	Quality	
	External quality	
1.9.1		Reliability
1.9.2		Usability
1.9.3		Availability
1.9.4		Maintainability
1.9.5		Exception handling capability
1.9.6		Fault-tolerant capability
1.9.7		Safety and security
	Internal quality	
1.9.8		Test quality and defects
1.9.9		Implementation efficiency
1.9.10		Process capability
2	SE process measurement	
2.1	Process attributes	
2.2	Process capability	
2.3	Requirements analysis process	
2.4	Specification process	
2.5	System design process	
2.6	SE process benchmarking	
2.6.1		Benchmarks description
2.6.2		Benchmarking analysis
3	Software project predictive and estimative measurement	
3.1	Project planning and estimations	
3.2	Defect estimation	

For example, the 5 measures for software sizes can be formally defined in Table 2, where each measure is referred to by a category number and symbol with a mathematical definition of measurement method, inputs and output(s), as well as the unit and measurement scale of the metric. For a complete set of definitions of the SEMS measurement system, see [9].

Table 2. Software Product Measurement – Sizes

Category	Measure	Symbol	Definition	Unit	Scale	Property	Remark
1.1 Sizes							
1.1.1	Physical source size	S_p	# (source lines of code)	LOC	$\aleph$	**Meta**	
1.1.2	Source memory size	S_s	# (information value of a source file)	Byte	$\aleph$	**Meta**	
1.1.3	Object memory size	S_o	# (information value of an object file)	Byte	$\aleph$	**Meta**	
1.1.4	Equivalent functional size	S_f	$S_f = N_i * N_{bcs} * N_o$	EFU	$\aleph$	Derived	EFU: equivalent functional unit
1.1.5	Function-point size	S_{fp}	$S_{fp} = f(N_i, N_o, N_q, N_{lf}, N_{if}, TCF)$ $= UFP * TCF$ $= (\sum_{k=1}^{5} w_k * N_k)$ $* (0.65 + 0.01 \sum_{j=1}^{14} d_j)$	FP	$\Re, \Re > 0$	Derived	

SEMS categorizes software architectural measurement into component-based and OO architectures as shown in Fig. 1. New measures introduced in this category are: equivalent functional size of component ($s_f(c_k)$ [EFU]) and of system (S_f [EFU]), cohesion (CH [%]), coupling (CP [%]), and level of test reuse ($L_{t\text{-reuse}}$ [%]).

As a comprehensive software engineering measurement system, SEMS is designed to support current approach to software engineering measurement, such as the goal-oriented [1], process-oriented [7], and project-oriented [2, 7, 9] measurement as shown in Fig. 2.

#Inputes (N$_i$) →	SEMS	1.4.1 Component-based architecture
#Outputs (N$_o$) →		→ The unit size of a component (s$_u$ [EFU])
#Base control		→ Equivalent functional size of a component
structures (N$_{bcs}$) →	1.4	(s$_i$(c$_i$) [EFU])
	Architecture	→ Equivalent functional size of a system
Class fan-out		(S$_i$ [EFU])
(FO$_{cl}$ [#]) →		→ Component cohesion (CH(c$_i$) [%])
Depth of inheritance		→ System cohesion (CH [%])
(DP$_h$ [#]) →		→ Component coupling (CP(c$_i$) [%])
		→ Coupling (CP [%])
		1.4.2 OO architecture
		→ Level of code reuse (L$_{creuse}$ [%])
		→ Level of test reuse (L$_{treuse}$ [%])

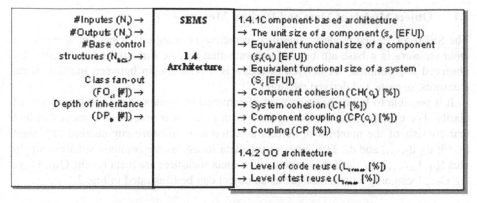

Fig. 1. SEMS category 1.4 – Architecture measurement

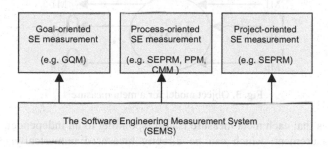

Fig. 2. Usage of SEMS

3   Design of the SEMEST Tool

As presented in Section 2, it can be seen that SEMS is a complicated measurement and metrics system. To support practitioners in software engineering to understand and apply the measurement system, a software engineering measurement expert system tool (SEMEST) is developed based on the SEMS model.

The SEMEST tool consists of three subsystems. They are the SEMEST graphical user interface (GUI), the SEMS methods, and the SEMEST engine.

SEMEST GUI: This is the system interface for user to interact with SEMEST for measurement selection and data entry. It also enables users to access SEMEST definitions, explanations, and references.

SEMS methods: This is a comprehensive set of software engineering measures with mathematical definitions and descriptions of relationships with other measures.

SEMEST engine: This is the inference engine of the tool that automatically extracts the appropriate measurement inputs, calculates measurement result according to a specific formula, and generates measurement outputs and illustrations.

3.1   Object Models of Meta and Derived Measures

The SEMEST engine models a *measure* or metric as being either *meta* or *derived*. A *meta measure* is a base attribute of software that can be directly and independently observed and counted. A *derived measure* is a relationship between multiple meta measures, or meta and derived measures.

It is possible to logically group a set of common meta measures for the purposes of clarity. For example, the *number of defects injected in a process* is a meta measure that consists of the numbers of defects detected in 6 software engineering processes [8, 9]: d_1, d_2, ..., and d_6. The inputs of the meta measures are common software attributes I_{M1}, I_{M2}, ..., I_{Mn}; and the outputs of the meta measures are meta results O_{M1}, O_{M2}, ..., O_{Mn}. Designing a meta measure as an object can be illustrated in Fig. 3.

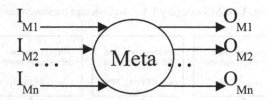

Fig. 3. Object model for a meta measure

Fig.3 shows that each meta measure is corresponding to an independent attribute in software measurement, which can be directly measured numerically. Since meta-measures possess scalar units, the object representation has its outputs correspond to the input attributes.

Derived measures are a relationship between meta measures, or meta measures and derived measures, defined by a formula. Derived objects can be modeled in Fig.4, with inputs from the outputs of meta and/or derived objects.

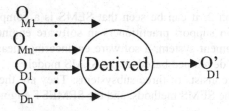

Fig. 4. Object model for a derived measure

Based on the definition of meta and derived measures, the class architecture of the SEMEST engine becomes a tree-like structure that supports part/whole hierarchies as shown in Fig. 5. Derived measures (whole) may have a branch of meta measures (part) and other derived measures (whole). A modified composite pattern allows the definition of each derived and meta measure with its dependencies resolved at the beginning to reduce overhead in constructing and maintaining these relationships during runtime.

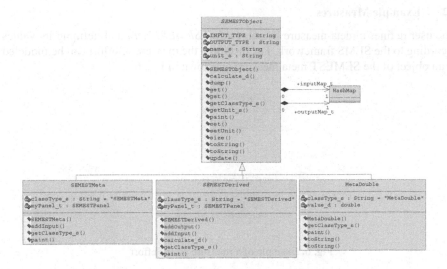

Fig. 5. Generic object for meta and derived measures

For the system-level design, we adopt an OO design approach and make it easy to be expanded. Based on the open architecture, if we want to add new measures we don't need to change the architecture of the system. For implementing this design, special class hierarchies are considered as follows:

- SEMESTObject;
- SEMETMeta and SEMEST Derived
- Metameasure and Derived Measure

The *SEMESTObject* is the superclass of the system. It contains two hash tables that defines the input and output attributes for a measure. Input attributes are stored as a key pairs in input hash table. In one record, measure name is considered as a key, an object which is composed of measure name, value and unit is defined as a value. In the same way, output attributes are stored in output hash table. Sub-class *SEMESTMeta* and *SEMESTDerived* allows all meta measure classes and Derived measure classes to be stored in container classes accordingly. Thus, the system has 3 levels of class hierarchy. In the case of meta measure, the input attributes are strictly scalar double representations of *MetaDouble* type. The output hash table is simply a reference to the input attributes. Derived measures may rely on inputs from both meta and derived and must store it accordingly. Currently, there is only one output but can be expanded to multiple outputs.

Classes in the first two hierarchies are less change prone. They are reused through inheritance more often and some changes may be happened via subclasses or by adding new participant classes rather than modifying present classes. This is because of the difficulty of modifying a class with many descendants and subclasses – any change to a superclass potentially affects a descendent.

3.2   Example Measures

The user defines a meta-measure by sub-typing *SEMESTMeta* and defining its values according to the SEMS framework. For instance, the measure of effort can be modeled as an object of the SEMEST meta measure as shown in Fig. 6.

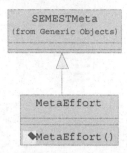

Fig. 6. Example of a measure on the effort

The *MetaEffort* defines, in its constructor, the units, range, definition, symbol, and value for the effort attribute. Once created, this meta-measure is referenced by related derived measures as an input to its calculation.

Derived measures are sub-typed from *SEMESTDerived* to allow the user to define the particular formula for the measure. For example, *DerivedSourceCodeProductivity* and *DerivedObjectCodeProductivity*, as shown in Fig.7, are defined with their own formulae, which are called by executing `calculate_d()`.

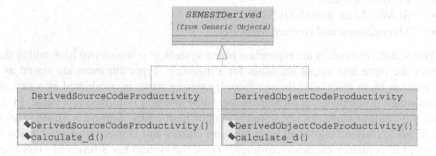

Fig. 7. Example source and object code productivity

3.3   Object Models of Frames and Panels

The *frame* partitions its windows into smaller manageable sections called panels, as shown in Fig. 8. Each *panel* contains control boxes (i.e. label, text box, combo-box, scroll bar, etc.) that is populated with information from the frame.

By adopting an OO design approach, the SEMEST engine decomposes measure contents and painting with them into two components. It allows the updating of the panel's contents within a frame without any of the measures knowing about the frame and how it is painting it. Conversely, the frame does not know how a particular measure manipulates its interface. There is maximum abstraction between the measures that furnish the information and frame that paints itself with the information. This is accomplished by modifying the decorator pattern to allow the frame properties to be extended by objects, which modify the frame by introducing a layer of indirection in the panel. Meta and derived measures are objects that have information about their selves in the hash table. Updating the screen results in individual measures to define what needs to be painted and the frame to define how to paint. As shown in Fig. 8, the class *SEMESTPanel* extends super class *BevelPanel,* which has frame properties. By obtaining information from hash table, its object *panelMeasure_t* is used to painting measure information within the frame.

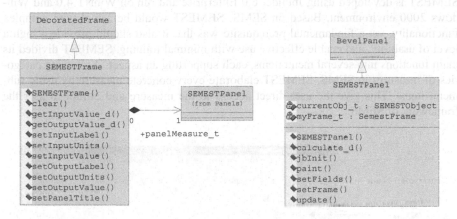

Fig. 8. Frames and panels

3.4   The Object Model of the GUI

The design of the SEMEST GUI uses several frames as described below.

SemestFrame1: This is the main frame of the application as shown in Fig.9. It is this frame from which all work in the application takes place. When this frame is closed the program is terminated. The frame contains the main menu and two panes. All measurement names and their beacons are placed in main menu and its submenu.

The right hand panel is *jPanel* and this pane is used to display a picture label. The picture label will contain a graphic of the measure that has currently been selected. The left hand pane is *panelMeasure_t* and it is used to display the inputs and outputs of the selected measure. The left panel shows the heading of the measurement specifics and at the bottom of the panel it contains a calculate button for calculating the measures when derived measures are selected.

SemestFrame2: This is the frame for the file browser: The *browser* is used to view files written in HTML. This makes it simple for the programmers to add new information to the program in the form of HTML files that can then be called from menu selections in the application.

SemestFrame1_AboutBox: This is the frame for the about box. The *about box* is accessed under the HELP main menu. It displays information about the SEMEST program.

SEMESTOpeningSplashScreen: This is used as an introductory screen for the program. It is a modal dialogue box that can only be closed by pressing the OK button.

4   Implementation of the SEMEST Tool

SEMEST is developed using Jbuilder 6.0 Enterprise and run on WinNT 4.0 and Windows 2000 environment. Based on SEMS, SEMEST would be a tool with complex functionality, yet a fundamental prerequisite was that it also should provide a high a level of usability, and enable effective use with minimal training. SEMEST divided its main functions into several menu items, each supporting an aspect. Following categories of measures in SEMS, SEMEST elaborate every concrete measure by using submenu items. This give the user direct access to the measure and introduce user the framework of SEMS.

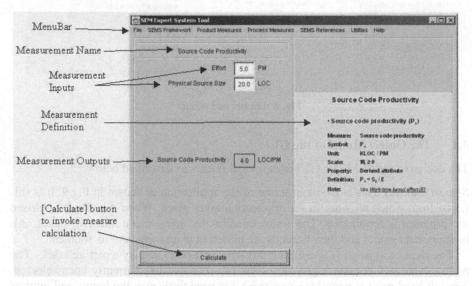

Fig. 9. The main application screen of SEMEST

Figure 9 shows the General page. User chooses the measure included by SEMS. Once user enters necessary parameters, SEMEST engine will automatically diagnoses the type of measurement model and give results accordingly.

The SEMEST menubar as shown in Fig. 9 consists of 7 submenus that are described in Table 3.

The *help* menu item contains submenus to reference materials that users of SEMEST will find beneficial for further studies in SEMS by referring to related

URLs, books, papers, and software metrics tools. The URLs menu item provides users some websites related to software metrics and software measurement. The Books menu item points to reference books on software metrics and measurement theories and applications. The Papers menu item refers users to the literature related to software metrics and software measurement.

Table 3. Design of Menubars of SEMEST

Submenu	Description
File	This submenu contains an [EXIT] menu item that will allow the user to exit the program when clicked
SEMS Framework	This submenu contains an introduction to the SEMEST program, explanations of meta and derived measurements, and the framework of the SEMS
Product Measures	This submenu contains the SEMS product measures
Process Measures	This submenu contains the SEMS process measures
SEMS References	This submenu contains references and information that pertain to the SEMS
Utilities	This submenu is for future implementation
Help	This submenu provides SEMEST reference database and URLs

There are currently 200 measures supported by SEMEST engine. Details on each type of measure are presented in the following sections.

- **SEMS Product Measurement**

This menu (Fig. 10) contains all the product measures broken down by topic. Each of these menu items contains a submenu of the actual product measures for that topic.

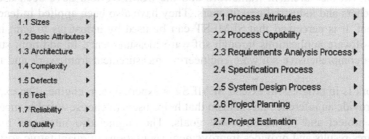

1.1 Sizes ▶
1.2 Basic Attributes ▶
1.3 Architecture ▶
1.4 Complexity ▶
1.5 Defects ▶
1.6 Test ▶
1.7 Reliability ▶
1.8 Quality ▶

2.1 Process Attributes ▶
2.2 Process Capability ▶
2.3 Requirements Analysis Process ▶
2.4 Specification Process ▶
2.5 System Design Process ▶
2.6 Project Planning ▶
2.7 Project Estimation ▶

Fig. 10. SEMS product measures menu   **Fig. 11.** Process measurement menu

- **SEMS Process Measurement**

This menu, as shown in Fig. 11, consists of the process measures broken down by topic. Each of these menu items contains a sub-menu of the actual process measures for that topic.

SEMEST runs by the interaction between system frame, panel, meta and derived measures, as shown in Fig. 12. By using the SEMEST tool, complicated software engineering measurement activities are simplified by menu-based selection, data entry, and measurement results interpretation. Therefore, ordinary software engineers with short training will be able to use the tool in software engineering project measurement and analysis.

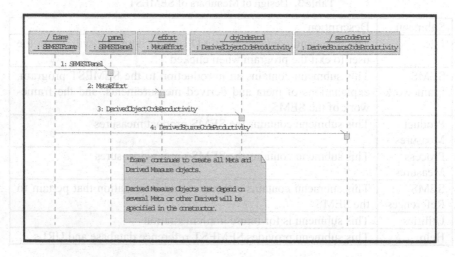

Fig. 12. MSC description of the initialization of SEMEST

5   Applications of SEMEST and Future Work

The SEMS measurement framework and the SEMEST tool have been used by both researchers and industrial practitioners. They have also been applied in teaching environment. It is perceived that SEMEST can be used by industries to gain insight into their software applications through software measurements. In addition, students can learn a comprehensive software engineering measurement framework and its applications.

Work is in progress to extend SEMEST's expert system engine. The expert engine will provide an inference mechanism that helps users to choose suitable measures for a given project and its measurement goals. The engine also interprets meanings of measures results and provides improvement suggestions in quantitative software engineering.

Other planned enhancements of SEMEST include the following:

- A web–based version of SEMEST, which provides software engineering measurement services for the software industry.
- Automatic measurement report generation, which enables users to obtain an analysis report for a specific project measured.

6 Conclusions

Because of the complexity of software product and process measurement, a software engineering measurement expert system tool (SEMEST) is needed in software engineering. This paper has described the structure and configuration of the software engineering measurement system (SEMS), which is the theoretical foundation of SEMEST. The design and implementation of the SEMS-based expert tool, SEMEST, have been developed as a supporting environment for practical software engineering measurement and analysis. SEMEST has been found useful in a wide range of applications in the software industry towards quantitative software engineering. SEMEST has also been found beneficial to students in software engineering education in the university environment.

Acknowledgement

This work is partially supported by the research fund of the Natural Sciences and Engineering Research Council of Canada (NSERC).

References

[1]   Basili, V.R., C. Caldiera, H.D. Rombach (1994), Goal Question Metric Paradigm, in J.J. Marciniak ed., Encyclopedia of Software Engineering, Vol. 1, John Wiley & Sons, pp. 528-532.

[2]   Fenton, N.E. and S.L. Pfleeger, ed. (1998), *Software Metrics: A Rigorous and Practical Approach* (2nd ed.), Brooks/Cole Pub Co, ISBN: 0534954251.

[3]   Grady, R.B. (1992), Practical Software Metrics for Project Management and Process Improvement, Prentice-Hall, Inc., Englewood Cliffs, NJ.

[4]   Lorenz, M. and J. Kidd (1993), *Object-Oriented Software Metrics: A Practical Guide*, ISBN: 013179292X.

[5]   Melton, A. ed., (1996), *Software Measurement*, International Thomson Computer Press, ISBN: 1-85032-7178-7.

[6]   Solingen, V.R. and E. Berghout (1999), *The Goal/Question/Metric Method: A Practical Guide* Y. (2001), Formal Description of Object-Oriented Software Measurement and Metrics in SEMS, *for Quality Improvement of Software Development*, McGraw-Hill Co., London.

[7]   Wang, Y. and G. King (2000), *Software Engineering Processes: Principles and Applications*, CRC Press, USA, ISBN: 0-8493-2366-5, 752pp.

[8]   Wang, Proceedings of the 7th International Conference on Information Systems (OOIS'01), Springer-Verlag, London, August, ISBN: 1-85233-546-7, pp. 123-132.

[9]   Wang, Y. (2003), Software Engineering Measurement: An Applied Framework of Software Metrics, CRC Press, USA, to appear.

[10]   Wang, Y. (2002), *Component-Based Software Measurement*, Chapter 14 in F. Barbier ed. Business *Component-Based Software Engineering*, Kluwer Academic Publishers, UK, 2002.

[11]   Wang, Y. (2001), *A Software Engineering Measurement Framework (SEMF) for Teaching Quantitative Software Engineering*, Proceedings of the Canadian Conference on Computer Engineering Education (CCCEE'01), IEEE and Univ. of New Brunswick, NB, Canada, May, pp.88-101.

Empirically Driven Design of Software Development Processes for Wireless Internet Services

Ulrike Becker-Kornstaedt[1], Daniela Boggio[2], Jürgen Münch[1],
Alexis Ocampo[1], and Gino Palladino[3]

[1] Fraunhofer Institute Experimental Software Engineering
Sauerwiesen 6, 67661 Kaiserslautern, Germany
{becker,muench,ocampo}@iese.fhg.de
[2] Motorola GSG-Italy, Via Cardinal Massaia 83, Torino, Italy
adb005@email.mot.com
[3] Investnet, Via Fava 20, Milan, Italy
g.palladino@investbv.com

Abstract. The development of software for wireless services on the Internet is a challenging task due to the extreme time-to-market pressure, the newness of the application domain, and the quick evolution of the technical infrastructure. Nevertheless, developing software of a predetermined quality in a predictable fashion can only be achieved with systematic development processes and the use of engineering principles. Thus, systematic development processes for this domain are needed urgently. This article presents a method for the design of an adaptable software development process based on existing practices from related domains, industrial piloting, and expert knowledge. First results of the application of the method for the wireless Internet services domain are described. The benefit for the reader is twofold: the article describes a validated method on how to gain process knowledge for an upcoming field fast and incrementally. Furthermore, first results of the process design for the wireless Internet services domain are given.

1 Introduction

Experience indicates that developing software with high quality requirements can only be done successfully if an explicitly defined process is followed. Furthermore, a lack of a development process makes accurate planning very difficult and in many cases impossible. Experience from progressive software development organizations like the NASA Software Engineering Laboratory (SEL) [11], for instance, has shown that one essential precondition for developing software of a predetermined quality in a predictable fashion is the design, establishment, and use of systematic software development processes.

Process deployment can fail especially if an organization does not put enough emphasis into the design and promotion of process models and the infrastructure needed

M. Oivo and S. Komi-Sirviö (Eds.): PROFES 2002, LNCS 2559, pp. 351-366, 2002.

for process deployment. Early results from a multi-case study conducted at Nokia Mobile Phones clearly show the importance of a stable and well implemented infrastructure for process deployment [24]. A prerequisite for this are explicitly defined process models for the application domain that are tailorable to specific project contexts.

Usually, for new and therefore unknown application domains, no explicitly defined software development processes are available yet. Furthermore, the design and introduction of such processes is very risky, because typically there exists no previous experience on which processes or process fragments are suitable and executable in the environment of the developing organization. An application domain that has to deal especially with such problems is the wireless Internet services domain because its development cycles are very short. In order to produce software of sufficient quality and thus remain competitive in the market, an appropriate and piloted development process is needed very quickly. This is valid in general for a new domain, but it is especially valid for the wireless Internet domain: If a specific process for wireless Internet services is not defined, the risk exists that the process followed in Internet services development will also be inherited for wireless services. As the wireless Internet gets popular, the Internet service providers will try to provide the same services over the wireless Internet as well, and they may easily try to follow the same development process they use for Internet services. This is very risky because the wireless world is different from the fixed world and additional issues must be considered during the implementation of services in order to get a final product with a certain level of quality, which can be competitive on the market.

This article describes a method for the empirical design of development processes for new domains. The overall method can be applied to unknown new domains in general, but as the focus of this work is the wireless Internet domain, special emphasis is placed on the particularities of this domain. First results of the application of the method in this specific domain are discussed. The goal of the method is to rapidly come up with a process that considers existing experience. The process is subsequently evaluated in pilot projects. As a consequence, drastic risk reductions in developing applications for the new domain are expected. The method was applied in the wireless Internet services domain in the context of the WISE project, which involves several European industrial and research organizations.

The two key ingredients for the method are the set-up of selected pilot projects and the creation of descriptive process models from the pilot projects. The pilot projects ought to rely as much as possible on practices already in place in the development organization. For instance, new domains may require new practices or adaptations of existing practices. Variations and commonalities of processes need to be identified. Commonalities may indicate typical process steps and can lead to abstractions of the process in the model; variations are indicators for possible factors impacting the process and may lead to specializations of the process. Finally, the process models are integrated to form a comprehensive process model.

The article is structured as follows: Section 2 gives background information on the problem of process modeling for new domains, introduces the wireless Internet services domain and sketches the WISE project in which this work was done. Section 3 describes the method for designing processes for new domains. First results of the application of this method for the wireless Internet services domain are described in Section 4. A process sketch and an overview of processes and practices from related fields are given. Section 5 briefly surveys existing approaches for designing software development processes. Finally, Section 6 summarizes the article and discusses experiences and open issues.

2   Background

An explicit process model is a key requirement for high productivity and software quality. Since software development projects are unique regarding their combination of specific goals and characteristics, providing 'ideal' and at the same time universal development processes is no solution for real life [9]. Instead, effective and efficient software development processes custom-tailored to the particularities of the application domain and project constraints are required. The design of processes for unknown domains implicates several difficulties: 1) Whereas for conventional software development, several standards exist, for new domains no such standards are available that could be used as reference. 2) New domains lack specific experience on particular techniques, their applicability and constraints. 3) The variations of the applications and, as a consequence possible variations of the development processes are not sufficiently understood. 4) The impact of the variation of the enabling technology on the developed service is not always known and this may affect the development process. There are several ways towards solving this problem: one widely accepted idea in the software engineering community is descriptive modeling of development processes, which leads to the explicit definition of process models, product models, and resource models [26]. Descriptive software process modeling attempts to determine processes as they take place in development. Adapting practices and processes from related domains can be a means for getting initial process models.

For establishing baselines (e.g., an effort baseline), collecting and using measurement data may further enhance the understanding and control of software development processes and products, and relationships between them [4]. This leads to the development of empirical quantitative models, which is not the focus of this article.

An upcoming new application domain is the wireless Internet services domain, which can be characterized as follows: rapid disposability of software for wireless Internet services with reasonable quality and high usability has an outstanding importance for the marketability of such services. Wireless Internet services can be characterized by quickly evolving technology, upcoming new devices, new communication protocols, support for new different media types, varying and limited communication bandwidth, together with the need for new business models that will fit in with the completely new services portfolio. Examples of new wireless Internet services can be expected in the domain of mobile entertainment, telemedicine, travel services, tracking and monitoring services, or mobile trading services. At the moment, there is very little experience on developing software for such services systematically. From the viewpoint of a Process Engineer, the following questions arise: How can we quickly adapt software development processes from other domains for the development of wireless Internet services? How can processes be sped up by perpetuating acceptable quality? Which existing techniques, methods and tools can be used? How should these be selected, adapted, and integrated into the process? What are typical variations of the processes in this domain? What are the impact factors on the effects of the processes? What kind of documentation is required?

If a specific process for wireless Internet services development is not soon identified and advertised, the risk exists that experienced developers and content and service providers will apply the same process they succeeded with in developing services for the fixed Internet. This will lead most of them to fail or to produce services that do not fit in with the wireless world requests and cannot turn out to be competitive on the market.

The described work was conducted in the context of the WISE project (Wireless Internet Software Engineering), which was started in 2001 and will run until 2004. The project aims at delivering methodologies and technologies to develop services on the wireless Internet. The methodology part comprises an overall process to drive the engineering of mobile services, a business model to specify roles and skills of involved parties, and guidelines to handle heterogeneous clients (e.g., handhelds, laptops). The technology part comprises a high level architecture for mobile services, a service management component, a data replication and synchronization component, and software agents to support negotiation functions in components. WISE follows an underlying experimental paradigm: Experimenting methodology and technology in real life applications is seen as the key to understanding, validating and improving methodology and technology. Therefore, several pilot developments have already been performed or are planned in the near future. This article describes the results with respect to the software process for the first iteration of two pilot projects. Industrial partners responsible for the pilot development and the underlying infrastructure are Motorola Global Software Group - Italy (Motorola GSG-Italy), Investnet, Sodalia, and Solid. The industrial partners identified several success factors for wireless Internet services, especially time-to-market, the ability to quickly deliver functionality with simultaneous fulfillment of high quality requirements and high usability requirements in terms of service performance. These quality requirements vary with different services. For example, wireless trading services require particularly high reliability, functional correctness, scalability, and redundancy. On the other hand, wireless entertainment has no strict reliability requirements but it has even stricter requirements in terms of usability and performances of the designed service architecture. Research partners responsible for developing processes, methods and tools are the Fraunhofer Institute for Experimental Software Engineering (IESE) in Germany, Politechnico de Torino (Italy), and VTT Electronics (Finland).

3   Method

The overall method, its steps along with the major input and output products is depicted in Figure 1. The method consists of the following steps: In the first step, *set-up pilots*, suitable pilot projects have to be determined and organized. Pilot projects are to be determined by market demands in such a way that the pilots are representative for the new application domain. In the step *perform pilots*, the pilot projects are conducted. In the step *elicit and model processes*, the processes as performed in the pilot projects are observed and modeled, resulting in a set of descriptive process models. A first version of the process models can be obtained based on similar past projects. The corresponding information is obtained through interviews with involved persons and other information sources, such as project plans or process artifacts.

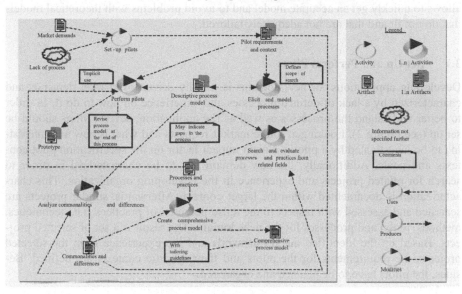

Fig. 1. Top level activities of the method

In parallel to these three steps, a step *search and evaluate processes and practices from related fields* is performed: The Process Engineer looks for processes and practices from related areas. This information will be used to fill the process model where it is incomplete and to introduce new practices into the process where old practices were seen as inefficient or are no longer adequate. In the step *analyze commonalities and differences*, commonalities and differences between the different process models have to be analyzed in order to identify process variants and justifications for them. This must recognize differences in the application domain as well as goals and contexts of the pilot developments. In the final step, create *comprehensive process model*, the descriptive models for the pilots, practices and processes from related fields are integrated into a comprehensive process model. Accompanying these steps, continuous improvement of the process during the pilot development with continuous flow of feedback will help to tailor the process during development and identify necessary changes early. The different steps will be detailed in the following sections.

This approach has several benefits: first, performing pilot projects and modeling their processes reveals the strengths and weaknesses of the processes early on. This can be seen as process prototyping. For an organization that introduces a process designed in such a descriptive manner, this reduces potential risks related to the introduction of a newly designed process. Second, introducing a new process based on existing practices typically requires a smaller shift in work procedures and is therefore more likely to be accepted by the Process Performers. Third, this concept allows for an incremental approach, which is more manageable than introducing a process in one shot. An additional benefit of this approach is that Process Performers of the domain are directly involved and can contribute to the development of the new process. Therefore the process is more likely to be accepted and adapted. A bottom-up approach allows to quickly get an accurate model and to avoid problems with theoretical models that do not fit and that are not adequately tailored.

3.1   Set Up and Perform Pilots

Developing applications for new domains is usually driven by market demands and characterized by a lack of defined processes and experience on how to do it. In order to better understand the processes as well as the application, several pilots should be set up (see Figure 2). Looking at future market requests and what is new and interesting to be investigated by a pilot is a main impact factor on the specification pilot contexts and goals. Additionally, the new domain has to be characterized in order to search for related projects and experience in the developing organization. This characterization is documented within the target context. Afterwards, similar projects are searched and assessed with respect to the reuse potential of practices (i.e., techniques, methods, tools) and processes for the new domain. The result is a set of selected projects. Based on the identified market demands and the experience from the selected projects, the requirements for the pilots and their specific contexts are defined. Besides, the pilots have to be planned and organized.

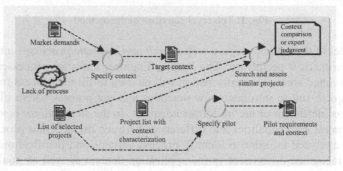

Fig. 2. Refinement of *set up pilots*

In the step *perform pilots* the pilot projects are conducted. Pilot performance is both, product and process prototyping. It combines the benefits of product prototyping (early validation of requirements, understanding the technology, experiencing the architecture etc.) with the benefits of process prototyping (evaluating procedures and practices, understanding the effects of processes, identifying organizational problems etc.).

3.2   Elicit and Model Process

For each pilot project, a descriptive process model is developed. Figure 3 details the elicitation and modeling activity. For the identification of existing processes, we recommend the Prospect [7] approach to descriptive process modeling: The main information sources used are interviews with Process Performers and analysis of documents used or produced in the process. The identification of existing processes consists of two stages, *orientation* and *detailed elicitation*. During the orientation phase a process outline is developed. The process outline provides an overview of the process and facilitates further elicitation activities. For example, process information can be described with the help of the process modeling schema [29] implemented in the Spearmint [6] tool. The outline will help sample interviewees and select information sources in the second stage, *detailed elicitation*. If weaknesses in the current process are already known, they should be eliminated. Thus, during the interviews Process Performers should already be asked which practices in the current process they consider inefficient.

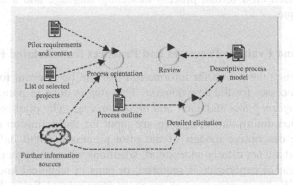

Fig. 3. Refinement of *elicit and model process*

Subsequently, the process model is reviewed: People who provided information for the model are asked to review the model to make sure that all information captured was correctly transformed into the model. The result is a description of pilot processes as they actually are being performed in the respective environment. One further benefit of this method is that involving Process Performers early increases process awareness among them. Moreover, involving Process Performers in the definition/tailoring of the process can lead them to more strictly follow a process that they somehow have helped to define, rather that a process that is externally defined and imposed.

3.3   Analyze Models and Create Comprehensive Process Model

The different process models are integrated to form a comprehensive model. To develop a comprehensive process model, commonalities and differences among and between the different process models have to be analyzed. Commonalities between the pilot processes may indicate typical process steps and can lead to abstractions of the pilot process models. Variations of the pilot processes may lead to specializations of the comprehensive process model. In this case, different context characteristics (such as developers' experience, system type) of the pilots may indicate the reasons for process variations. If processes differ and no context deviations can be identified, the context is probably not characterized completely and there is at least one influence factor on the process that has not been identified yet. The comprehensive model comprises guidelines or rules on how to adapt the generic parts of the comprehensive model to project-specific goals and characteristics.

As a prerequisite, an appropriate representation of the comprehensive process model and tailoring mechanisms is required. Identification of specific conditions and effective adaptations can be done based on process designer experience, on continuous feedback from process performers during service implementation, and on available literature and historical data on similar project. Several software reuse approaches (e.g., templates, generation, composition, transformation) can be applied to express the comprehensive process model and the tailoring mechanism. One example approach for describing and tailoring comprehensive models is the ProTail approach [5], which is based on a formal process modeling language and a transformational tailoring technique.

3.4   Search and Evaluate Processes and Practices from Related Fields

This step comprises the search for information that can be relevant for the design of development processes for the new domain. This step is done in parallel to the steps *set-up pilots*, *perform pilots* and *elicit and model process*. The pilot requirements and contexts identified during the set-up step are input for the definition of the scope of the survey. The descriptive models of the pilot processes might indicate gaps, i.e. process steps that are not clearly understood, situations where the procedure on how to proceed is unclear or experience is required, or gaps in technical knowledge. These gaps might be filled with processes or practices from related fields. During the performance of the pilots, identified practices and processes for gaps are used implicitly. Afterwards, they should be explicitly integrated into the comprehensive model, if their performance was successful.

4   Application and First Results

This section describes the application of the method for two pilots. In the WISE project, pilots are a means for designing processes and understanding the technology and methodology to engineer and operate with wireless Internet services in realistic contexts and different application domains. Based on market demands (such as the need to adapt existing services for the Internet towards wireless Internet services or to create new services) and companies' interests, initially two target contexts for the two pilots were defined: the development of a wireless Internet service for mobile online trading (Pilot 1) and the development of a service for mobile entertainment (Pilot 2). An excerpt of the description of the pilot contexts is shown in Table 1.

Table 1. Context description for the pilots

Characteristics	Pilot 1	Pilot 2
Application domain	Service development/mobile online trading	Service development / mobile entertainment
Project type	System adaptation	Creation from scratch
System type / component type	Application software	Application software
Experience of developers	Professional developers	8 professional developers, 1 student
Domain analysis technique	Informal	Informal (provided by domain experts)
Requirements technique	List in natural language, intended screen masks, forms, and outputs	Structured text / UML use cases
Design technique	UML state diagrams, UML sequence diagrams, UML package diagrams, WISE-specific component diagrams	UML state diagrams, UML sequence diagrams, UML package diagrams, UML class diagrams, WISE-specific component diagrams
Implementation technique	WML	Java on both client side (J2ME) and server side (J2EE)
Validation technique	Black-box testing	White-box unit testing with JUnit tool, different integration testing techniques, feature testing directly on the target terminal
Organizational context	Investnet	Motorola GSG-Italy and Sodalia

The goal of Pilot1 is to provide a service for the management of a virtual portfolio. For Pilot 1, similar projects could be identified that are concerned with the development of Internet trading services (i.e., development of a market informational and trading simulator site). Pilot 1 is an adaptation of this service to the wireless domain. The requirements for Pilot 1 comprise very high availability, correctness of data, and stringent reliability of customer identification and authorization as well as instantaneous response time in terms of quick data provision.

The goal of Pilot 2 is the development of a multiplayer online game operated from mobile terminals. The requirements for Pilot 2 comprise the ability for user interaction on a shared environment, short response times and the portability on different platforms. For Pilot 2, no similar projects with regard to the application domain were identified because the intention is to develop a completely new service. Nevertheless, existing similar projects concerned with the development of server and client software could be identified.

First results of the descriptive process modeling, the analysis of commonalities and differences, and the search and evaluation of processes and practices from related fields are described in the subsequent sections. The creation of a comprehensive pro cess model can be based on these results. The results are based on the first iteration of the pilot projects. It is planned to have three iterations of each pilot: In the first itera tion, the pilots are built with a very sketchy version of methodology and technology. A second iteration uses enhanced methodology and technology as well as an enhanced underlying standard (such as UMTS). The third iteration uses a consolidated version of technology and methodology. In order to gain experience, the pilots are performed with an accompanying goal-oriented measurement program that provides information feedback to all parties and helps in controlling and understanding processes and prod ucts and identifying cause-effect relations between them.

4.1   Process Sketch

This section sketches the initial process models for each pilot, and lists most striking commonalities and differences found between the pilots. Specifics of the pilot process can be found on the refined level: For example, the development phase of Pilot 1 contains the following list of activities: develop prototype, create preliminary system, release system preliminary, rework. These activities seem to be strongly related with the requirements of the wireless Internet services domain. The development of a pro totype and preliminary system helps to achieve and demonstrate part of the applica tion's functionality early in a project. Also, it will be useful to reduce risks with new technical requirements. Furthermore, appropriate network infrastructure has to be established and a friendly customer needs to be involved in the validation of the pre liminary system. The product flow of the process model for Pilot 2 (mobile entertain ment) is shown in Figure 4. The Figure does not include the description of the control flow, i.e., the performance sequence.

Activities, artifacts, roles, and tools from every pilot are analyzed to obtain valu able information for the comprehensive process model. Some very striking com monalities detected between the two pilot processes are the following: Both pilots have very close involvement by the customers and the providers of technical infra structure. Market demands need to be carefully examined and understood. In both processes, a design document is produced as input for the implementation phase. Commonalities can be especially recognized in the structure of the architecture, which is described in the design document. For instance, logical architecture components for user authentication, billing, accounting, and user profiling can be found in both archi tectures of the pilots. This has implications on the processes, e.g., the development of respective interfaces has to be considered by the processes. There is at least one activ ity for explicitly setting up the test environment in both pilots. In both pilots, there are internal tests as well as external tests with a provisional technical infrastructure. Fi nally, both pilot processes include an acceptance test in the customer environment.

Some of the differences that were encountered are the following: Pilot 2 is a new development oriented to a wider market spectrum, which implies to cover more platforms, while Pilot 1 is an adaptation of an existing service towards the wireless domain. The main adaptation tasks in Pilot 1 are downscaling of functionality and interface adaptations. Therefore, the focus of testing in Pilot 1 is more on the interface and less on testing single units. Furthermore, Pilot 1 uses WAP browsers on the client side, whereas Pilot 2 has to develop a dedicated client. Other process differences result from different user interface requirements (developing multimedia interfaces requires other procedures than developing pure textual interfaces) and different nonfunctional requirements (e.g., mobile online trading requires much higher reliability, which can be supported by implementing redundancies on the server side, for instance). This results, for example, in different validation tests for the final product: Pilot 1 shall be reliable and guarantee highly secure transactions, Pilot 2 shall guarantee high performances and usability features, therefore different test suites shall be designed to verify that the final products fulfill specific requirements.

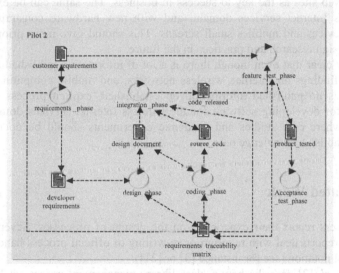

Fig. 4. Top-level product flow for Pilot 2

4.2   Existing Processes and Practices from Related Fields

This section sketches the search for information that can be relevant for the design of new software development processes for wireless Internet services. There was no literature available that describes software development process models as a result of case studies, surveys or experiments for the wireless Internet services domain as a whole. This emphasizes the importance of the WISE project goal.

The process models in related domains found (Adamopoulos *et al.* [1]), (Karlsson [16]), (Gutowsky [12]), (Zettel *et al.* [30]), (Nilsson *et al.* [23]) are based on an incremental development software process model. Whether the application is for the Internet or the telecommunications domain, it should be delivered as soon as possible, and increments are suggested to maintain control. Therefore, it is probable that for the wireless Internet services domain an incremental development approach is important.

Industrial key players in the telecommunications domain (Gutowski [12]), (Nilsson *et al.* [23]), and (Tapani [19]) have developed process models as part of a software process improvement program. The use of metrics was essential to control, observe and publish the progress on the models. Therefore, a metrics program becomes a priority for any process model to be established.

Two process models (Adamopoulos *et al.* [1]) and (Zettel *et al.* [30]) use as explicit notation UML and Spearmint respectively, to describe activities, inputs, roles and outputs. The need of a simple, generic, understandable notation will be relevant for easily describing the process model for wireless Internet services.

There exist guidelines and practices for web site content development and layout design (Taylor *et al.* [27]). They range from simple ones like a navigation chart, to more sophisticated ones like 'usage-centered design'. The papers found (Nerurkar [22]), (Hammar [13]), (Roe *et al.* [25]), (Constantine *et al.* [10]) point out the 'usability' of the web sites as the key to success in business. The same can be expected for the wireless Internet services domain, and with new hardware constraints for the handheld devices and mobiles small screens. This should give more priority to user interface design research and practices in the future.

It is very clear that even though there is a lot of information published about tools and recent findings on Internet, wireless networks, and mobile computing technologies, there is no published information on established, explicit process models, or guidelines for developing software for the wireless Internet services domain. It is a new field where case studies and academic experiments should be documented in order to establish a knowledge base.

5   Related Work

Several papers report their experience on the design of processes. Several of these experience reports deal with redesign or re-writing of official process handbooks in a more formal notation (see for instance [3] or [21]).

Arlow *et al.* [2] describe how a class library management process at British Airways was modeled at a very fine-grained level. In this organization a complete picture of the overall process was missing. Thus, the goal of the modeling task was to develop a comprehensive process model. From the official process documentation, information regarding roles, responsibilities, and library structure could be elicited. From this information, process models using state transition diagrams – a notation Process Performers were familiar with – were developed. The diagrams were discussed in interviews with Process Performers.

Kellner and Humphrey created a process description based on existing practices [15]. They used information gained from interviews with the people directly involved in process execution. This information was supplemented with information gained from people involved in managing the process, and with regulations on the process.

Henry and Blasewitz [14] describe their experience in developing a common process at General Electric Aerospace. As the process involves several organizations, and different groups within these organizations, the main goal here was to obtain a common and consistent overall picture of the process. Each of these groups was tasked to define their process phase. The different models were then validated to ensure consistency. Then a series of meetings with representatives of each group was conducted to review and finalize phase definitions.

In general, it can be said that none of these approaches developed a process for a new application domain, but all of the experience reports listed above focus on the formalization or description of processes that are already in place and have been around for a while. Thus, the steps described in these experience reports can be compared to the step *elicit and model processes*. However, none of these describes how to design a process for a new and unknown domain.

6   Summary and Discussion

This article presented a method on how to gain process knowledge for an upcoming application domain and surveyed first results of the process design for the wireless Internet services domain. Several experiences with the approach have been made: The performance of pilots helps to avoid later problems with respect to process and product. The time spent on the pilots is probably much less than the time needed for fixing problems in the process - had the process not been piloted. The process elicitation approach used has been proven effective. Descriptive modeling helped recognize and react on weaknesses in the process very early. Additionally, recommendations for process improvements from the developers could be considered. The review of the process models was difficult, because the developers were located in different geographical locations. An electronic process guide (EPG) helped improve the review. Coupling an EPG with an off-line commentation system would improve the review procedure further. During pilot performance it is necessary to verify that the descriptive process and the process actually performed do not deviate. It is recommended to perform a measurement program in addition to the pilots. This will allow to get initial effort and defect baselines as well as a deeper understanding of the success factors (such as time-to-market) and their influences (such as requirements stability). Guidelines for such a measurement program are, for example, provided in [8].

Summarizing the experience with the wireless Internet services domain, it can be said that the main impact factors on process design are the necessity to understand varying market demands and technology changes, as well as a set of specific nonfunctional requirements for wireless Internet services. Other important characteristics of the domain are that user interface design plays an important role and that it is difficult to set up an appropriate test environment. These specifics have to be considered in the process design.

Future work will be the performance of pilot iterations and the creation of a comprehensive process model. A third pilot project for a wireless content downloading service is starting at this moment at Solid and Sonera. The presented process design approach should be evaluated further in other new domains. Nevertheless, the initial results for the wireless Internet services domain show that the presented process design approach helps to rapidly come up with an approved process model that drastically reduces development risks.

Acknowledgements

The work has been funded by the European Commission in the context of the WISE project (No. IST-2000-30028). We would like to thank the WISE consortium, especially the coordinator Maurizio Morisio, for the fruitful cooperation. Additionally, we would like to thank Filippo Forchino from Motorola GSG-Italy for the valuable comments to this article, and Sonnhild Namingha from the Fraunhofer Institute for Experimental Software Engineering (IESE) for reviewing the first version of the article.

References

[1]   Adamopoulos, D.X., Pavlou, G., Papandreou, C.A.: An Integrated and Systematic Approach for the Development of Telematic Services in Heterogeneus Distributed Platforms. Computer Communications, vol. 24, pp. 294-315 (2001)

[2]   Arlow, J., Bandinelli, S., Emmerich, W., Lavazza, L.: A Fine-grained Process Modelling Experiment at British Airways. Software Process–Improvement and Practice, vol. 3, No 3., pp. 105-131 (1997)

[3]   Aumaitre, J.M., Dowson, M., Harjani, D.R.: Lessons Learned from Formalizing and Implementing a Large Process Model. In: Warboys, Brian., (ed.): Proceedings of the Third European Workshop on Software Process Technology, pp 228-240. Lecture Notes in Computer Science vol. 772. Springer–Verlag, Berlin Heidelberg New York (1994)

[4]   Basili, V.R., Rombach, H.D.: The TAME Project: Towards Improvement-Oriented Software Environments. IEEE Transactions on Software Engineering, vol. 14, No. 6, pp. 758-773 (1988)

[5]   Becker-Kornstaedt, U., Hamann, D., Münch, J., Verlage, M.: MVP-E: A Process Modeling Environment. IEEE Software Process Newsletter vol. 10, pp. 10-15 (1997)

[6]   Becker-Kornstaedt, U., Hamann, D., Kempkens, R., Rösch, P., Verlage, M., Webby, R., Zettel, J.: Support for the Process Engineer: The Spearmint Approach to Software Process Definition and Process Guidance. Proceedings of the Eleventh Conference on Advanced Information Systems Engineering (CAISE '99), pp. 119-133. Lecture Notes in Computer Science, Springer-Verlag. Berlin Heidelberg New York (1999)

[7]   Becker-Kornstaedt, U.: Towards Systematic Knowledge Elicitation for Descriptive Software Process Modeling. In: Bomarius, F., Komi-Sirviö, S., (eds.): Proceedings of the Third International Conference on Product-Focused Software Processes Improvement (PROFES). Lecture Notes in Computer Science, vol. 2188, pp. 312-325. Springer-Verlag. Berlin Heidelberg New York (2001)

[8]   Briand, L.C., Differding, C., Rombach, H.D.: Practical Guidelines for Measurement-Based Process Improvement. Software Process. Improvement and Practice, vol. 2, No. 4, pp. 253-280 (1996)

[9]   Brooks, F.P. Jr.: The Mythical Man-Month. Essays on Software Engineering, Anniversary edition. Addison Wesley. Reading MA (1995)

[10]   Constantine, L., Lockwood, L.: Usage-Centered Engineering for Web Applica-
        tions. IEEE Software, vol. 19, No. 2, pp.42-50 (2002)
[11]   McGarry, F., Pajerski, R., Page, G., Waligora, S., Basili, V.R., Zelkowitz,
        M.V.: An Overview of the Software Engineering Laboratory. Software Engi-
        neering Laboratory Series Report, SEL-94-005, Greenbelt MD USA (1994)
[12]   Gutowski, N.: An Integrated Software Audit Process Model to Drive Continu-
        ous Improvement. Proceedings of the 8th international conference on software
        quality, pp. 403-415. Portland USA (1998)
[13]   Hammar, M.: Designing User-Centered Web Applications in Web Time. IEEE
        Software, vol. 18, No. 1, pp. 62-69 (2001)
[14]   Henry, J., Blasewitz, B.: Process Definition: Theory and Reality. IEEE Soft-
        ware, vol 9, pp. 103-105 (1992)
[15]   Kellner, M., Hansen, G.: Software Process Modeling: A Case Study. In: Pro-
        ceedings of the 22nd Annual Hawaii International Conference on System Sci-
        ences, vol. II, pp. 175-188 (1989)
[16]   Karlsson, E.: A Construction Planning Process. Q-Labs, LD/QLS 96:0381,
        Lund Sweden (1999)
[17]   Karlsson, E., Vivaldi, N., Urfjell, T.: Guidelines for Step-Wise Design. Q-
        Labs, LD/QLS, 95:0520, Lund Sweden (1999)
[18]   Karlsson, E., Taxen, L.: Incremental Development for AXE 10. ACM
        SIGSOFT Software Engineering Notes, vol. 22, No. 6 (1997)
[19]   Kilpi, T.: Implementing a software metrics program at Nokia. IEEE Software,
        vol. 18, No. 6, pp. 72-77 (2001)
[20]   Kovari, P., Acker, B., Marino, A., Ryan, J., Tang, K., Weiss, C.: Mobile Ap-
        plications with Websphere Everyplace Access Design and Development. IBM
        SG24-6259-00 (2001)
[21]   Krasner, H., Terrel, J., Linehan, A., Arnold, P., William, H.: Lessons Learned
        from a Software Process Modeling System. Communications of the ACM,
        vol.35, No. 9, pp. 91-100 (1992)
[22]   Nerurkar, U.: Web User Interface Design: Forgotten Lessons. IEEE Software,
        vol. 18, No. 6, pp. 69-71 (2001)
[23]   Nilsson, A., Anselmsson, M., Olsson, K., Johansson, Erik.: Impacts of Meas-
        urement on an SPI Program. Q-Labs
        (http://www.q-labs.com/files/Papers/SPI99_Imp_of_Meas_on_SPI.pdf)
[24]   Raffo, D., Kaltio, T., Partridge, D., Phalp, K., Ramil, J.F.: Empirical Studies
        Applied to Software Process Models. In: International Journal on Empirical
        Software Engineering, vol. 4, No. 4 (1999)
[25]   Roe, C., Gonik, S.: Server-Side Design Principles for Scalable Internet Sys-
        tems. IEEE Software, vol.19, No. 2, pp. 34-41 (2002)
[26]   Rombach, H.D., Verlage, M: Directions in Software Process Research. Ad-
        vances in Computers, vol. 41, pp. 1-63 (1995)
[27]   Taylor, M.J., McWilliam, J., Forsyth, H., Wade, S.: Methodologies and Web-
        site Development: A Survey of Practice. Information and Software Technol-
        ogy, pp. 381-391 (2002)
[28]   Upchurch, L., Rugg, G., Kitchenham, B.: Using Card Sorts to Elicit Web Page
        Quality Attributes. IEEE Software, vol. 18, No. 4, pp. 84-89 (2002)

[29]   Webby, R., Becker, U.: Towards a Logical Schema Integrating Software Proc-ess Mod-eling and Software Measurement. In: Harrison, R. (ed.): Proceedings of the Nineteenth International Conference on Software Engineering Work-shop. Process Modeling and Empirical Studies of Software Evaluation, pp. 84-88 Boston USA (1997)

[30]   Zettel, J., Maurer, M., Münch, J., Wong, L.: LIPE: A Lightweight Process for E-Business Startup Companies based on Extreme Programming. Proceedings of the Third International Conference on Product-Focused Software Processes Improvement (PROFES), pp. 255-270, (2001)

The WISE Approach to Architect Wireless Services

Patricia Lago[1] and Mari Matinlassi[2]

[1] Dipartimento di Automatica e Informatica, Politecnico di Torino, Italy
patricia.lago@polito.it
[2] VTT Technical Research Centre of Finland
90571 Oulu, Finland
mari.matinlassi@vtt.fi

Abstract. The Internet is quickly evolving towards the wireless Internet that will be based upon wirelines and devices from the traditional Internet, and will reuse some of its techniques and protocols. However, the wireless Internet will not be a simple add-on to the wireline Internet. From the technical point of view, new challenging problems arise from the handling of mobility, handsets with reduced screens and varying bandwidth. As a result, developing and operating new mobile services will be a challenging software engineering problem. The WISE (Wireless Internet Service Engineering) Project aims at producing integrated methods and tools to engineer services on the wireless Internet. In particular, this paper introduces the WISE approach to service engineering, describes how it is applied to a real world Pilot service and reports initial feedback from project partners when applying the approach.

1   Introduction[1]

The demand for wireless Internet services is growing quickly, partly because 3G mobile phones are entering the market. The development of wireless services faces challenges, like handling to support mobility with continuous communication, handsets with reduced screens and varying bandwidth. This also causes new business models to emerge.

In this changing evolving scenario, the WISE (Wireless Internet Service Engineering) project aims at anticipating the problems of wireless Internet service engineering by producing integrated methods and tools to engineer services on the wireless Internet, capable of reducing costs and time to market. In detail, the WISE Project has the following objectives:

- Deliver methodology and technology to develop services on the wireless Internet.
- Experiment with methodology and technology in real life applications.
- Prepare tools and metrics to evaluate the effect of methodology and technology.
- Disseminate results to the broadest possible audience.

[1] This work has been partially supported by IST Project 30028 WISE (Wireless Internet Service Engineering). URL http://www.wwwise.org

M. Oivo and S. Komi-Sirviö (Eds.): PROFES 2002, LNCS 2559, pp. 367-382, 2002.

In this paper we introduce the WISE approach, a methodology to be applied to wireless services. The WISE approach is based on the QADA method defined in [1]. The Quality-driven software Architecture and Quality Analysis (QADA) method includes three viewpoints at two levels of abstraction: structural, behavior and deployment. The WISE approach extends the modeling requirements with a definition of the fourth viewpoint, the development viewpoint [2]. According to IEEE Std-1471-2000 [3], „an architectural view is a representation of a whole system from the perspective of a related set of concerns". In the literature, there are several approaches to the design of software architecture that concentrate on different views of architecture. The first of these view-oriented design approaches was the 4+1 approach, developed by Krutchen [4]. After this, several others have approached the jungle of architectural viewpoints. For instance, Jaaksi et al. introduced their 3+1 method in 1999 [5] and Hofmeister et al. used four views to describe architecture [6].

Among these approaches there is no agreement on a common set of views or on ways to describe the architectural documentation. This disagreement arises from the fact that the need for different architectural views and architectural documents is dependent on two issues: system size and software domain e.g. the application domain, middleware service domain and infrastructure service domain. Again, both the system size and domain have an impact on the amount of different stakeholders. Therefore, it is obvious that none of these methods alone is comprehensive enough to cover the design of software architectures for systems of a different size on various domains, or provide an explicit means to create architectural descriptions for all the systems. We are neither trying to cover all the domains, nor to define a catchall set of architectural viewpoints. Instead, we concentrate on the wireless service architectures and the viewpoints needed in wireless service architecture modeling.

WISE Pilots are demonstration environments to experiment with the methodology and technology. Moreover, to simulate the evolution of a Pilot through successive developments, each Pilot undertakes three iterations in which experience gained during previous iteration is taken into the current one. In particular, the Project is now in its first iteration, in the „architecture definition phase". The next step will be to define the reference architecture and reiterate; the final Project goal is the consolidation of a reference architecture for wireless services, refined at each iteration.

The paper is structured as follows. After an introduction to the WISE approach and its architectural viewpoints, we present one of the WISE Pilot services and explain the WISE viewpoints and modeling notation through examples taken from the Pilot. Finally, we draw some initial considerations, and report feedback from industrial partners, when applying the WISE approach to service engineering.

2   The Approach

WISE approach (Fig. 1) starts with „pre-studies & analysis" that define the driving requirements for the system and identifies possible constraints for service engineering. Driving requirements are the main requirements for the whole system, i.e. the main quality and/or functional goals the system has to provide. Constraints may e.g. be related to rules set by laws, enabling technologies or hardware device manufacturers [1].

The next step is made up of three tasks that can be carried out in parallel, prior to successive steps. In particular, the aim of the task „survey architectural styles & patterns" [7] is to identify the applicable styles and patterns for the system under development. In addition to requirements engineering, the task „define service taxonomy" assists in the design of the conceptual architecture by identifying the functional domains to which services belong. For instance for the wireless domain, the adopted service taxonomy classifies wireless Internet services into four preliminary domain categories:

- End-user services that are provided directly for the end-users (customers).
- Technology platform services that provide basic functions on which end-user services rely (even though usually not directly used by the end-user as such). Third party service developers can provide these services.
- Application Domain Support Services that are not as generic as technology platform services but specific for the application domain and, on which end-user services also rely. For instance, the domain of multi-user arcade games requires at least a service enabling multi-user communication.
- Management services that are needed to make service available and linked to business processes, even though they are not specific to end-user services.

However, other categories as the mentioned may be used. These categories are used as guidelines defining the structure of the conceptual architecture, and they assist in grouping services into reasonable blocks. Next, the features of the services in those domains are grouped. The features are related to requirements categories of services. The features provided by each domain guide for selecting the general requirements and constraints for service development.

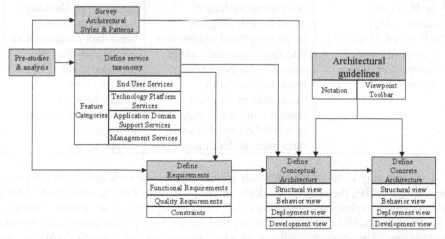

Fig. 1. The main steps of the approach for wireless service engineering

Before development of Pilot architecture, the task „architectural guidelines" defines a set of viewpoints modeling the conceptual and concrete architecture: each viewpoint represents a specific architectural aspect as described below. Guidelines also define each viewpoint's notation [8].

Conceptual and concrete architectures are both organized into four views, which are: the structural view, the behavioral view, the deployment view, and the development view [3, 4, 5, 6]. The *conceptual* structural view maps functional and quality responsibilities on a conceptual structure, whereas the *concrete* structural view illustrates the component decomposition at the lower aggregation level and extends component and relationship descriptions into inner details. That is, both the aggregation and abstraction levels are affected while moving from conceptual architecture to the concrete one.

The *conceptual* behavioral view defines dynamic actions of and within a system. The *concrete* behavioral view aims to illustrate the behavior of individual components and interactions between component instances. The modeling notation for these views is based on Object Management Group (OMG) Unified Modeling Language (UML) [9]. Diagramming constructs for the first two views are described in Table 1.

Table 1. Modeling notations for the structure and behavior viewpoints

	Structural view	Behavioral view
Conceptual architectural methodology - It yields an architectural, specification-oriented perspective of the system	Entities and logical associations - Guidelines	Interactions among entities - Collaboration diagram
Concrete architectural methodology - It yields a technical, design-oriented perspective of the system	- Class diagram (detailed component structure) - Component diagram (shows exported component interfaces, interface usage and each component as a black-box module) - Component diagram (shows complex components as white-box modules with their internal decomposition)	- Sequence diagram (gross level, showing interactions among black-box components) - Sequence diagram (detailed level, showing how interactions are implemented internally to white-box components)

The remaining views of the approach are the *deployment view* and the *development view*. In particular, the *conceptual* deployment view describes the allocation of units of deployment to physical computing units. Units of deployment are atomic units (e.g. a group of components working together) that cannot be deployed across a distributed environment. The *concrete* deployment view focuses on the concrete hardware and software components and their relationships.

The *conceptual development view* describes the components to be developed and acquired. In addition, it figures out who is responsible for each service and which standards and enabling technologies do the services use. The *concrete* development view illustrates the realization of software components and their interrelationships. Table 2 summarizes the modeling notations for the deployment and development views described above.

Table 2. Modeling notations for the deployment and development views

	Deployment view	Development view
Conceptual architectural methodology (methods + notation) - It yields an architectural, specification-oriented perspective on the system	Deployment diagram (service development + communication links)	On top of structural VP - Assorting components according to the level of completeness - Allocating development responsibilities
Concrete architectural methodology - It yields a technical, design-oriented perspective on the system	Networked structure Mapping of black-box components on top of the networked structure Business model and service provisioning	Technology details Hardware, software, external resources Templates Guidelines Implementation, configuration, usage procedure

The four views at two levels of abstraction cover the main aspects of a distributed service architecture, from static structure to dynamic behavior, and represent a complete set of views on a system under development. Of course, for simple systems, some views might be omitted because they are trivial or missing: it is up to the architects to identify which views are necessary, and omit the others. In other words, these views can be considered as a view toolbar, or a set of views at disposal for describing all and only those views relevant for the system under development.

3   An Initial Experiment

The WISE approach is applied to develop pilot wireless services (or Pilots). For each Pilot, both conceptual and concrete architectural views are described. For the sake of simplicity, the following shows just some views of the Pilot 2: the wireless interactive gaming service. The complete architecture can be requested on [10] and for the complete Pilot description refer to [11].

3.1   The Problem

The focus of the experiment is on architecting a wireless interactive gaming service, i.e. an arcade game supporting multiple players executing a mission in a dungeon labyrinth. This wireless entertainment service is composed of several smaller services, which together provide the functionality and qualities described below.

Table 3. Non-functional requirements

Quality attribute	Requirement definition	Scope/How
Scalability	The number of concurrent players in the game is 2 – n.	Client-Server architecture style Component Game Server at server side
Portability	The game can be played with devices supporting either GPRS or UMTS connection. End-user devices support: PalmOS, EPOC, WinCE.	Client application. This requirement is realized by component Communication Manager Layered architecture style Client application includes a virtual machine layer
Extendibility	Features can be enriched, hence ensuring service evolution (in the WISE project, evolution is simulated by carrying out three development iterations).	Extension points in the architecture and code. - On the Server side e.g. quest sending, fights & attacks, manage high score list - On the Client side e.g. quest receiving and handling, fights/attacks/defending, buy/sell items
Modifiability	Services should be easily modified under the evolution of mobile terminals' hardware capabilities.	Client application. By separating communication manipulation and game management, and by splitting logically related functionality, modification is easier. Of course any modification is isolated if interfaces are not influenced.

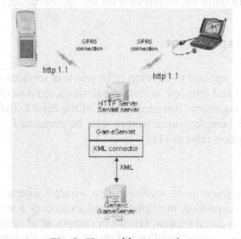

Fig. 2. The problem overview

Players participate in the game using mobile devices (Fig. 2), with limited processing power and memory and therefore, it is obvious to delegate the common, shared playing environment to the server. This, in addition to a capability to manage several wireless network connections at the same time, results in the server to be a robust, thick server, whereas terminals are thin clients only hosting the user applications. This allocation of software conforms to the traditional client-server architectural style [12] with services centralized on a server and clients located across the network.

Non-functional requirements for our problem are described in Table 3. Each non-functional requirement is associated with a quality attribute refined with requirement definition and scope. That means refining what are the semantics of each quality attribute in this specific system, and where is the requirement context [13]. Non-functional quality requirements drive the definition of service architecture, which again drives the scoping of quality requirements.Concerning development constraints, of particular relevance are the capabilities offered by mobile terminals, which usually put strict limitations on the provided service features. In particular, for wireless terminals we analyzed (for each service) the impact of both the terminal generation (2.0, 2.5 3.0, etc.) and the terminal equipment class (e.g. 10 Lines' screen, video resolution, memory, etc.). As an example, the Pilot service used in our experiment is not limited by terminal generation but it requires support for J2ME technology.

3.2   Applying the WISE Approach

After this short introduction to requirements, we now turn to the illustration and discussion of how the approach was applied in architecting a wireless service.

Conceptual Architecture. For the Pilot we present two main conceptual views, the structural view and the deployment view. The first view (Fig. 3) identifies the main elements and their relationships at the conceptual level. These elements are specified out of required macro-functions, defined during requirement engineering and carried out through interviews of industrial partners, and provide the initial functional-to-structural mapping of the service under development.

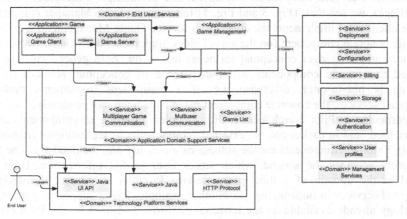

Fig. 3. Pilot conceptual structural view

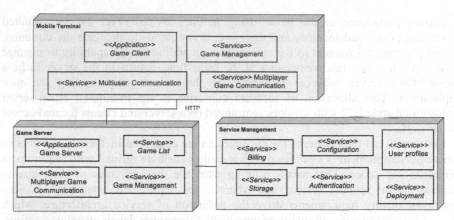

Fig. 4. Pilot conceptual deployment view

In particular, we can observe how this view presents the first draft of required domains (e.g. End-User Services, Technology Platform Services), distribution of elements on domains, and, particularly relevant for wireless services, roles in communication across domains (e.g. usage, data exchange, control).

The next step is to classify structural elements and their communication links. This is provided by the conceptual deployment view (Fig. 4).

On the conceptual level, the conceptual elements are treated as services. In this Pilot service, examples of services are Game Management, Game Server and Multiplayer Game Communication.

Concrete Architecture. For the Pilot, we present the concrete structural, behavioral and deployment views, as follows.

Structural View. The structural view shows the modules (classes and components) making up the service. In distributed architectures, these views provide the structure of distributed components and their interconnections.

On the concrete level, the *conceptual* services will be mapped on *concrete* components. Concrete components implement one or multiple conceptual services. Accordingly, we see that, (Fig. 3 and Fig. 5) the concrete GameManager component (on the client side) implements the conceptual service Game Management, the Game Manager concrete component (on the server side) implements both Game Server and Communication Manager conceptual services, and so on. As a general rule, names assigned to concrete components will match those of conceptual services (if the mapping is one-to-one); otherwise, i.e. if a component implements multiple conceptual services, the concrete component name is decided independently.

In particular, in Pilot 2 architecture, Fig. 5 depicts in white all components to be implemented, and in darker colors „external" components or technologies (reused or bought). External components are the authentication center and the database. The first component accesses the second, which stores User profile information. Both are located in the domain of a third party Service Provider in charge of managing orthogonal services in outsourcing. As another example, Kjava support is part of the technology already available on the terminal platform, and used by the Pilot client-side.

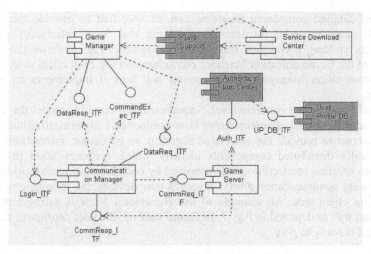

Fig. 5. Concrete structural view: System-level component diagram

In the domain of the Service Provider, two components implement service-specific functionality: the Game Server component implements the game and the coordination of each game session. The Service Download Center component is a service-common component, providing support for the end-user to choose and download (on the client side) the application implementing the GUI of the game. In particular, the end-user can in principle first choose a game from an Application Provider (e.g. a game center), and only afterwards decide to play on-line game sessions supported by a Service Provider.

Finally, on the client side there are two components providing service-specific functionality: the Game Manager component implements the GUI and the processing of data related to an on-going game session. It interacts locally with the Communication Manager component that supports distributed communication with the remote Service Provider. Together, these two components implement the game, and are downloaded from a Service Download Center.

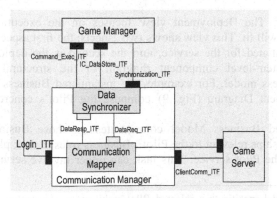

Fig. 6. Concrete structural view: Detailed component diagram for the Communication Manager component

Further, detailed component diagrams can be specified to provide the detailed structural view (in terms of internal elements and local interfaces) of those components yielding a complex structure. For example, Fig. 6 shows the detailed structure of the Communication Manager component on the Pilot client side, i.e. how the Communication Manager is decomposed and how it implements its external interfaces.

Behavioral View. At the concrete level, Sequence Diagrams [14] model the concrete behavior scenarios: each diagram shows how components implementing the gaming service interact to provide the associated scenario. In particular, interactions among geographically distributed components identify which communication protocol is required on wireless connections, and supported by component implementation.

As wireless communication always involves user devices, the following will focus on the Pilot client side. An example of the Behavioral View is a fragment of the „Game start up" as depicted in Fig. 7. In Game start up, the user configures the game session and is ready to play.

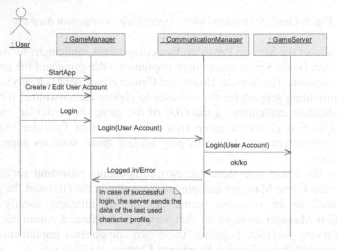

Fig. 7. Concrete Behavioral view: Start Application, create/edit user account, and login

Deployment View. The Deployment view focuses on the execution environment where the service will fit. This view shows two aspects: the first aspect is the business model [15] instantiated for the service, and the second is the deployment diagram mapping the system-level component diagram of the structural view, on the instantiated business model. For example, the instantiated Business Model (Fig. 8) and the Deployment Diagram (Fig. 9) compose the Pilot's concrete Deployment View.

The instantiated Business Model concentrates on those Business Roles and Business Relationships relevant to the Pilot[2]. Business roles in dark play some task in the operation of the Pilot service. This task can either involve service provisioning

---

[2] The business model specific to a selected Pilot architecture is instantiated from a generic business model (called the WISE Business Model [16]) defined for the wireless service domain. Project iterations aim at refining this along with the generic WISE architecture.

(see those roles inside the dashed box) if there will be some software components deployed in a networked structure, or not involve service provisioning (see roles outside the dashed box) if they have a business relationship prior to service provisioning (e.g. Technology provider). The latter seems particularly relevant for customers, who need to represent the complete service business chain.

In particular, two issues need special attention:

- **The business relationship of Application provider to Service user/provider (ApplicProv):** it models „game download" prior to game provisioning. Game download supports the acquisition from the end-user of the application needed to play the game (i.e. client components). Download can be carried out from both a fixed node (e.g. using any Internet browser) and a mobile node. This aspect is under refinement, representing wired-wireless inter-operation.
- **The business relationship between Service providers (Peer):** the Pilot considers authentication and user profile storage as management services supported by a third party service provider. This aspect will be detailed during current Project iteration.

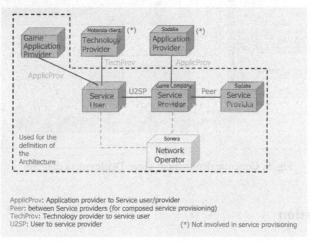

ApplicProv: Application provider to Service user/provider
Peer: between Service providers (for composed service provisioning)
TechProv: Technology provider to service user
U2SP: User to service provider   (*) Not involved in service provisioning

Fig. 8. Concrete deployment view: The WISE business model instantiated for the Pilot

The second part of the concrete Deployment View is the Deployment Diagram (Fig. 9): once defined, our instantiated business model, the Deployment Diagram maps the component diagram on top.

In particular, the diagram proves the following important issues:

1. The domain associated with role Service User, can be deployed on a fixed node (e.g. a PC connected to Internet) for game download[3], or on a mobile node (e.g. a 3G cellular phone or a 4G mobile device).

---

[3] Game execution can be also carried out on a fixed node. This scenario along with the analysis of QoS and development differences will be possibly investigated later in the Project.

2. On the Service Provider side, there are two types of nodes mapped on two
   different domains playing the same role: The service node provides the game
   control, and service core components are deployed on the service node.
   Management service node provides the outsourced management services, on
   which service-common components are located. In particular, these components
   implement orthogonal services, like user profile access and storage, and
   authentication.

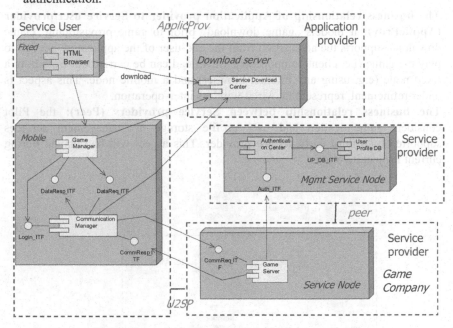

Fig. 9. Concrete deployment view: Deployment diagram

4   Discussion

As introduced in the first part of the paper, the WISE Project is still in its first
iteration that concludes in the end of year 2002. At the moment of writing this paper,
industrial partners are working on the Pilot implementation phase. Therefore, we do
not yet have the final results for the complete development of wireless service Pilot
architectures. Nonetheless, we can already draw some initial conclusions, and report
feedback from these industrial partners, in particular when applying the WISE
approach to service engineering.

4.1   Learning Curve

At the beginning of the first iteration, the WISE approach has been designed and
explained in a document stating definitions of terms, guidelines for applying it, and
the semantics and notation of viewpoints. The whole approach has been explained to
industrial partners in special meeting sessions especially conceived for training. This,

in consideration of the well-known fact that one of the most critical steps in introducing new working procedures is people resistance to changes.

In addition, flexibility in learning new concepts decreases with time. Nonetheless, in this scenario, the use of examples of toy wireless services has been of great help, as has the fact that the approach viewpoints are based on OMG UML, which is familiar to all industrial partners, hence providing a common initial background.

After the „training phase", service engineering started with interview sessions in which specialists in the proposed approach elicited requirement and design information from people in charge of service implementation. This kind of „tutored architecting phase" has been fundamental as a starting point for overcoming people resistance and learning how to proceed. Afterwards, developers continued the work on their own, with some sporadic off-line consultancy. Finally, we could observe that technical people already used to innovation are more receptive than business-oriented people accustomed to settled working methods.

4.2   Tool Support

We said that previous knowledge of UML among people has been of great help in overcoming resistance to a new working approach. In this respect, the use of a software tool for requirements engineering and design, has been particularly helpful in the learning process. After an analysis of available tools and their potentialities, as well as familiarity of tools, we decided to adopt a commercial UML tool that is familiar to most of them and widely available, and to adapt the tool to support viewpoint diagrams in addition to pure UML diagrams. In spite of the difficulties in drawing, developers applied the approach to their work (not without any difficulties). We can say that current state of Pilots' wireless service architecture is maturing fast. Even industrial partners not used to service engineering at all, are now using the approach effectively.

4.3   Market- and Business-Related Issues

Among industrial partners, business people found that business views focusing on market analysis are missing. Used to industrial service engineering in which market-driven motivation is necessary, they experienced a gap between the four viewpoints defined by the WISE approach, and „real world" aspects like market analysis and revenues. It must be underlined that the approach is meant for technical purposes only (i.e. to engineer the software architecture of services), and business issues are supposed to be worked out and solved in advance. Nevertheless, diagrams like the business model provide a natural interface from service architecture to market analysis and business-related issues.

4.4   Network Viewpoint

During requirements analysis, industrial partners made use of informal drawings to depict the networked structure of devices, machines and terminals involved in service provisioning. This informal network diagram seems to be very effective in understanding the execution environment of the service under development, and in spite of its informality, it provides a valuable common communication mean. This aspect should be included in the development view (it is under investigation if at the conceptual or at the concrete level). Its role will be mainly to identify hardware technologies, network configuration, communication protocols and external software components.

4.5   Development Viewpoints

Another ongoing work in the WISE Project is the definition of the contents and the border between concrete and conceptual development viewpoints. We can agree that this viewpoint provides (at the concrete level) service documentation when service development concludes or at least is ongoing (examples of development documentation are installation and release notes, usage instructions, hardware and software pre-requisites, etc.). Nonetheless, also at the conceptual level technology adoption or hardware/software limitations must be considered in the development process as early as possible. An important issue then, is to decide what belongs to which level, and to avoid overlapping.

5   Conclusions

The aim of this paper was to introduce an approach to architect wireless services. In addition, it was to illustrate the adoption of this approach with an example. The example was wireless interactive gaming service under development in the WISE Project. This paper also presented the initial experiences gained during the first development iteration.

The WISE approach identifies development steps, and a set of architectural viewpoints and associated visual notation. The main steps are to survey architectural styles and patterns, to define service taxonomy, and to define service requirements. These are grouped into functional and quality requirements and constraints. With the influence of these initial steps, we define the conceptual architecture. Conceptual architecture is described with up to four architectural views: structural, behavioral, deployment and development. Conceptual architecture is then refined into the design-oriented concrete architecture, which describes the similarly named four views at more technical level with specific details and lower-level decomposition. This paper represented selected views and diagrams, as examples.

In the WISE Project, these steps will be processed iteratively three times. The first development iteration is described here, and it comprises only the basic features of the game; these basic features will be enriched in the two future iterations.

We are currently adopting the WISE approach in the industry and results have been encouraging. The resistance to change is already overcome with successful help of training, consulting and example toy services. In addition, the UML-based notation has been easy to learn and also there is also tool support by adapting familiar commercial UML tools.

Except for already achieved good results, we have few issues to solve or improve, especially in relationship to the network viewpoint and the development viewpoint as explained in the previous section.

Acknowledgements

We would like to thank all partner members of the WISE project, especially Mr. Kalaoja, Mr. Tikkala, professor Niemelä and Mr. Boggio who are the co-authors of the architecture guidelines and the game service architecture.

References

[1] Matinlassi, M. Niemelä, E. and Dobrica, L: Quality-driven architecture design and quality analysis method. A revolutionary initiation approach to a product line architecture, VTT Publications 456, Technical Research Center of Finland, Espoo, FI, 2002.

[2] Purhonen, A., Niemelä, E., Matinlassi, M.: Views of DSP Software and Service Architectures. Submitted to Journal of Systems and Software. 30 p.

[3] IEEE Std-1471-2000: IEEE Recommended Practice for Architectural Descriptions of Software-Intensive Systems. IEEE Computer Society.

[4] Krutchen, P. B: The 4+1 View Model of Architecture, IEEE Software Vol. 12(6), 1995.

[5] Jaaksi, A., Aalto, J-M, Aalto, A. and Vättö K..: Tried & True Object Development. Industry-Proven Approaches with UML, Cambridge University Press, New York, 1999.

[6] Hofmeister, C., Nord, R. and Soni, D.: Applied Software Architecture, Addison-Wesley, Reading, MA, 2000.

[7] Gamma, E.: Design Patterns: Elements of Reusable Object-oriented Software, Addison-Wesley, Reading, MA, 1994.

[8] Niemelä, E., Kalaoja, J., Lago, P., Tikkala, A.. and Matinlassi, M.: Conceptual Architecture and Guidelines to Use It, V. 1.0, IST 30028 WISE Project, Deliverable D4, April 2002.

[9] OMG: The Unified Modeling Language (UML) Resource Page. On-line at http://www.omg.org/uml

[10] WISE: The „IST WISE Project home page". On-line at http://www.wwwise.org

[11] Lago, P., Boggio, D., Tikkala, A. and Forchino, F.: Architecture for Pilot 2, V. 1.2, IST 30028 WISE Project, Deliverable D11, June 2002.

[12] Bass, L., Clement, P. and Kazman, R.: Software Architecture in Practice, Addison-Wesley, Reading, MA, 1998.

[13] Matinlassi, M. and Niemelä, E.: Designing High Quality Architectures, International Conference on Software Engineering, Workshop on Software Quality, Orlando, FL, May 2002.

[14]   Lago, P.: Rendering distributed systems in UML, In: Siau K. and Halping D. (Eds.): Unified Modeling Language: Systems analysis, design and development issues, Idea Group Publishing, 2001.
[15]   TINA-C: „TINA Business Model and reference Points", TINA-C Baseline, v4.0, May 1997. On-line at TINA Consortium (Telecommunications Information Networking Architecture) Web site, http://www.tinac.com
[16]   Kallio, P.: Business Models in Wireless Internet, V. 1.0, IST 30028 WISE Project, Deliverable D11, May 2002.

Improving Estimation Practices by Applying Use Case Models

Bente Anda[1], Endre Angelvik[2], and Kirsten Ribu[1]

[1]Simula Research Laboratory
P.O. Box 134, NO–1325 Lysaker, Norway
{bentea,kribu}@simula.no
[2]Mogul Norway
Drammensveien 134; NO-0277 Oslo, Norway
endre.angelvik@mogul.com

Abstract. An estimation method based on use cases, *the use case points method*, has given promising results. However, more knowledge is needed about the contexts in which the method can be applied and how it should be adapted to local environments to improve the estimation process. We applied the use case points method to several projects in a Scandinavian software development company as the first activity in a software process improvement project on improving estimation. The second activity of the improvement project was to conduct interviews with project managers and senior developers about how to obtain continued and more widespread use of the method in the company. Based on the interviews, we propose a tailored, potentially improved version of the method and suggest how estimation practices can be improved by applying it. We believe that these experiences may be of interest to other companies that consider applying use case models as part of their estimation practices.

1 Introduction

A use case model describes the functional requirements of a system to be constructed, and use case models are frequently used as input to the process of estimating software development effort. An estimation method based on use cases, the use case points method, was introduced by Karner [9]. This estimation method has been evaluated in several software development projects with promising results [2,3,12]; it was considered easy to use and performed similar to or better than teams of very experienced software developers. Nevertheless, more knowledge is needed about how to apply the method and tailor it to a specific organization.

We evaluated the use case points method on three projects as the first activity in a software process improvement project on improving estimation in a Scandinavian

M. Oivo and S. Komi-Sirviö (Eds.): PROFES 2002, LNCS 2559, pp. 383-397, 2002.
© Springer-Verlag Berlin Heidelberg 2002

software development company, Mogul [3]. Since then, the company has also applied the method on a couple of other projects with success.

The improvement project is conducted as part of a Norwegian software process improvement project, PROFIT, with the Universities of Oslo and Trondheim, SINTEF and 12 software development companies as partners. The goal of Mogul's improvement project is to develop an estimation method based on use case models that is simple to use and that is supplementary to expert estimates.

The second activity in the project was to conduct interviews with project managers and senior developers to

1.   understand the ordinary estimation process in the company,
2.   find out how the method for estimation based on use cases can be tailored to the company, and
3.   establish the necessary context for applying the method successfully.

It is often difficult to sustain software process improvement projects beyond the initial phase, so the interviewees were also asked about how a supplementary method could obtain continued and widespread use in Mogul.

This paper describes Mogul's ordinary estimation process and its current practices for use case modeling. Then, contrasting the ordinary estimation process with evaluated best practices for estimation [8], areas of Mogul's estimation process are identified that may be improved by applying the use case points method. The paper also discusses requirements on the use case model that must be fulfilled for the use case points method to be applicable.

Context information is often missing when new or improved estimation methods are reported. The work described in this paper may provide a background for other companies that wish to improve their estimation practices applying use case models.

A major result of the interviews is a proposed modification of the use case points method, which includes, for example, an alternative way of measuring the size of a use case and modified adjustment factors.

The remainder of this paper is organized as follows. The use case points method is described in Section 2. Section 3 describes the context of the study. Section 4 describes estimation practices in Mogul and how they can be improved. Section 5 describes current practices for use case modeling. Section 6 suggests how the use case points method can be tailored to the company. Section 7 concludes and suggests future work.

2   The Use Case Points Method

The use case points method was initially developed by Gustav Karner [9]. It is based on the function points method [1], and the aim was to provide a simple estimation method adapted to object-oriented projects. This section gives the steps of the method as described in [13]. The method requires that it should be possible to count the number of transactions in each use case. A transaction is an event occurring between an actor and the system, the event being performed entirely or not at all.

1. The actors in the use case model are categorized as *simple, average* or *complex* depending on assumed complexity. A weight is assigned to each actor category:
    *   Simple actor – another system with a defined API: weight = 1
    *   Average actor – another system interacting through a protocol: weight = 2
    *   Complex actor – a person interacting through a graphical user interface or web-page: weight = 3

The total *unadjusted actor weight (UAW)* is calculated counting the number of actors in each category, multiplying each total by its specified weight, and then adding the products.

2. The use cases are correspondingly categorized as *simple, average* or *complex,* depending on the number of transactions, including the transactions in alternative flows. A weight factor is assigned to each use case category:
    *   Simple use case – 3 or fewer transactions: weight = 5
    *   Average use case – 4 to 7 transactions: weight 10
    *   Complex use case – more than 7 transactions: weight 15

The *unadjusted use case weights (UUCW)* is calculated counting the number of use cases in each category, multiplying each category of use case with its weight and adding the products. The UAW is added to the UUCW to get the *unadjusted use case points (UUPC).*

3. The use case points are adjusted based on the values assigned to a number of technical factors (Table 1) and environmental factors (Table 2). These factors are meant to account for effort that is not related to the size of the task. Each factor is assigned a value between 0 and 5 depending on its assumed influence on the project. A rating of 0 means that the factor is irrelevant for this project; 5 means that it is essential.

The technical complexity factor (TCF) is calculated multiplying the value of each factor in Table 1 by its weight and then adding all these numbers to get the sum called the *TFactor.* Finally, the following formula is applied:

$$TCF = 0.6 + (.01 * TFactor)$$

The environmental factor (EF) is calculated accordingly by multiplying the value of each factor in Table 2 by its weight and adding all the products to get the sum called the *Efactor.* The following formula is applied:

$$EF = 1.4 + (-0.03 * EFactor)$$

The *adjusted use case points (UCP)* are calculated as follows:

$$UCP = UUCP * TCF * EF$$

4. The number of person hours per use case point for a project estimate is determined by the environmental factors because these are considered to have a large impact on the actual effort [13]. The number of factors in F1 through F6 that are below 3 are counted and added to the number of factors in F7 through F8 that are above 3. If the total is 2 or less, 20 person hours per UCP is used; if the

total is 3 or 4, 28 person hours per UCP is used. If the number exceeds 4, it is recommended that changes should be made to the project so the number can be adjusted, or alternatively that the number of person hours should be increased to 36 per use case point.

Table 2. Technical complexity factors

Factor	Description	Wght
T1	Distributed system	2
T2	Response or throughput performance objectives	2
T3	End-user efficiency	1
T4	Complex internal processing	1
T5	Reusable code	1
T6	Easy to install	0.5
T7	Easy to use	0.5
T8	Portable	2
T9	Easy to change	1
T10	Concurrent	1
T11	Includes Security features	1
T12	Provides access for third parties	1
T13	Special user training facilities are required	1

Table 1. Environmental factors

Factor	Description	Wght
F1	Familiar with Rational Unified Process	1.5
F2	Application experience	0.5
F3	Object-oriented experience	1
F4	Lead analyst capability	0.5
F5	Motivation	1
F6	Stable requirements	2
F7	Part-time workers	-1
F8	Difficult programming language	-1

A spreadsheet is used to implement the method and produce an estimate. The method provides an estimate in total number of person hours.

The use case points method can be criticized from a theoretical point of view as has the function points method. The addition and subsequent multiplication of ordinal values, for example, is theoretically invalid [10]. However, the function points method has shown to predict effort reasonably well for many types of systems.

There are several other methods for use case based estimation. The methods differ in that size and complexity of the use cases are measured differently, and in that different technical and environmental factors are considered. Two alternative methods for estimation based on use cases are described in [6,14]. The method described in [6] maps attributes of the use case model into function points. In [14] a certain number of lines of code is assumed for each use case, and the total number of lines of code is used as a basis for the estimate. *Tassc:Estimator* is a commercial tool for estimation based on use cases [17]. A metric suite for use case models, which can be used for estimation, is suggested in [11], but a complete estimation method is not presented.

3   Context of Study

This section gives some characteristics of the company we studied, presents the results from the former case studies conducted to evaluate the use case points method, and describes the interviews with senior personnel of the company.

3.1   The Company

Mogul is a medium sized Scandinavian software development company located in Norway, Sweden and Finland. In Norway there are approximately 180 employees. The business area is software development for public and private sector, in particular banking and finance. Mogul's projects can roughly be divided into two types: traditional software development projects based on a three-layer architecture and web-projects, that is, intranet, internet or extranet solutions. The web-projects often consist in adapting existing systems to a web-environment. The company takes responsibility for complete projects or sell hours as consultants or mentors on methods and architecture. Mogul gives courses on the Rational Unified Process (RUP), which is also used in their own projects whenever possible.

Table 3. Characteristics of three software development projects

Characteristic	Project A	Project B	Project C
Size	7 months elapsed time, 4000 staff hours	3 months elapsed time, 3000 staff hours	4 months elapsed time, 3000 staff hours
Software architecture	Three-tier, established before the project	Three-tier, known, but not established in advance	As project B
Programming environment	Java (Visual Café and JBuilder), Web Logic	MS Visual Studio	Java (Jbuilder), Web Logic
Project members	6 developers with 0 to 17 years experience	6 developers with 0 to 12 years experience	5 developers with 2 to 10 years experience, 4 consultants were involved part time.
Application domain	Finance	CRM (Customer relationship manage-ment within banking), part of a larger solution	Banking (support for sale of credit cards)

3.2   Results from Case Studies

The use case points method has been evaluated in 3 development projects in Mogul. The estimates produced with the use case points method were compared with expert estimates and actual effort. The results were promising in that the estimates provided by the method were as accurate as the average estimates of the projects in the company. Table 3 shows some characteristics of the case studies. Table 4 gives the results.

3.3   The Interviews

The interviewees, 1 administrative manager, 7 project managers and 3 senior developers, had from 6 to 26 years experience with software development, and were chosen because they were very experienced estimators.

The interviews were semi-structured with open-ended questions to allow the respondents to speak more freely of issues they felt were important. They were conducted by one or two interviewers, lasted from 45 – 60 minutes and were tape recorded.

Table 4. Expert estimate, use case estimate and effort (in hours)

Project	Expert estimate	Use case estimate		Actual effort
A	2730	2550		3670
B	2340	3320	2730[1]	2860
C	2100	2080		2740

4   Estimation Practices and Possible Improvements

This section describes current practices for estimation in Mogul based on the information from the interviews. The estimation practices are compared with best practices for estimation described in the literature to identify particular areas that may benefit from applying use case based estimation.

The two types of projects in the company are estimated differently, and are therefore treated separately below.

4.1   Estimating Traditional Software Development Projects

A project manager is responsible for producing a first estimate early in the inception phase. He/she may gather a team for the estimation process, but the actual developers are usually not allocated at this stage. The estimate indicates the need for resources, often together with a completion date. RUP gives generally good opportunities for negotiating with the client about functionality; specified functionality is frequently changed and given new priorities along the way. It is also often possible to get more resources if necessary. The completion date, however, is often critical.

---

[1] The first estimate for project B, 3320 hours, was produced based on information about actors and use cases given by the project manager. In the second estimate, 2730 hours, several actors with a very similar user interface were generalized into one super actor, and included and extending use cases were omitted.

The estimate is typically based on a requirements specification from the client, possibly with a solution outline and some use cases. Several of the interviewees also develop a high-level use case model, based on the available information, which in turn is also used in the estimation process.

Some estimates are made in offer situations where Mogul is bidding to get a project. In such situations only the client's description of the functionality is available; and it is difficult to get more information. The company therefore depends on the clients' ability to describe what they actually want.

If the project mainly involves new development, Mogul's policy is to conduct a pre-project to clarify the requirements and construct a detailed use case model before committing to an estimate. However, the client often wants to know what kind of solution can be had for the price they can afford without paying for a pre-project, and it may therefore be difficult to avoid giving an early estimate based on insufficient information. One of the interviewees describes this situation using the analogy of buying a car: „You have all sorts of requirements for your new car, but you only have € 5000, so you wish to know what you can get for that amount of money".

The estimation process is bottom-up because the project is broken down into activities that are estimated separately, perhaps by different people. Sometimes two people are involved in estimating the same activity, either discussing to reach an estimate, or by letting an independent person go through the estimate afterwards. Mostly, however, estimation is done individually, and estimates for different parts are added to form the complete estimate. Several of the interviewees had their own methods or spreadsheets to help them in the estimation process.

The ability to identify risks is an important part of estimation. The interviewees claimed to be good at identifying technological risks, but believed themselves to be less good at identifying organizational risk.

The time for project management, in the order of 5-15%, is added to the estimate. The estimate must also take into account that much of the developers' time is spent on other activities such as meetings. The percentage of the developers' time believed to be available for development varied among the interviewees from 50% to 80%.

It may also be sensible to consider whether the client is in public or private sector. This may impact effort because more people tend to be involved in the decision process in the public sector. Expected lifetime for the system should also be considered because this has implications for the documentation and subsequently for the effort.

New estimates are usually produced in the elaboration phase, typically after the first iteration. The developers re-estimate their bits, for example, screens or modules and assess how much time is needed for completion.

Mogul does not keep track of the accuracy of its estimates, so it is impossible to assess the typical precision of their estimates. The interviewees stated, however, that the estimates are usually overrun.

1.2   Estimating Web-Projects

The web-projects differ from the traditional development projects in that they are smaller, they more often build on an existing solution, and the functionality is less complicated. The most important part of these projects is establishing the information structure. According to the interviewees, 40% of the resources are typically used on this activity. An outline of a graphical design is a prerequisite for an estimate. The effort put into the graphical design will vary based on how much the client is willing to pay. A solution will also include a number of templates into which the users will fill in information. Each template typically takes one day to develop.

At present, estimating these projects is not difficult, but some of the interviewees expected the two types of projects to merge as traditional software projects start include advanced web interfaces.

1.3   Improving Estimation Practices

We have compared the ordinary estimation practices in Mogul with best practice principles for estimation [8] to identify how the use case points method can improve the estimation practices and thereby the accuracy of the estimates. Below we describe the best practice principles that are relevant in our context and how they can be fulfilled:

1.   „Ask the estimators to justify and criticize their estimates."
    A supplementary use case based estimate may, if it differs from the expert estimate, provide a basis for criticizing the expert estimate.
2.   „Estimate top-down and bottom-up, independently of each other."
    The company's expert estimates are made bottom-up. The use case points method, on the other hand, provides a top-down estimate. A top-down estimate is produced identifying some characteristics of the development project and using those as input to a complete estimate.
3.   „Combine estimates from different experts and estimation strategies."
    It has been shown sensible to combine models and human judgment [5], but more work is needed on how to best combine expert estimates and estimates produced with the use case points method.
4.   „Assess the uncertainty of the estimate."
    The spreadsheet used to produce an estimate with the use case points method makes it possible to vary the input both with regards to the number and size of the use cases and with regards to the different technical and environmental factors. This may help assess uncertainty due to unknown factors in the development project.

The use of an estimation method in combination with expert estimates can also lead to the avoidance of biases and large overruns, and estimation methods have been shown to perform better than expert estimators with little domain experience [7,8]. Therefore, the support given by an estimation method may make more people competent to take part in estimation.

5   Practices for Use Case Modeling

To be suitable as a basis for estimation, a use case model should be correct and described at an appropriate level of detail. This section gives a brief overview of how use case modeling is done in Mogul, and discusses challenges relating to correctness and level of detail of the use cases.

In Mogul, use case modeling is applied in traditional software development projects to identify and describe business logic. Use case modeling is usually not applied in web-projects because use cases lack the possibility to describe functionality where a web interface lets the user perform a function by switching among different web pages or where it is necessary to save current work and later resume it. Another problem is that the terminology in RUP is unfamiliar to several of the participants that typically take part in web-projects, for example, graphical designers.

Moreover, the use cases are perceived as belonging to and driving development projects; they are seldom maintained in the elaboration phase and never when the system has become operational. Therefore, the original use cases are often outdated and unsuitable as a basis for specifying modified functionality in maintenance projects.

5.1   Use Case Modeling Process

The use case modeling process in Mogul is as follows. In the inception phase, use case models may just be described at a high level without details. It may supplement the client's requirements specification or be derived from it.

A detailed use case model is usually constructed as part of a pre-project together with representatives of the client. The use case modeling process is a breadth-first process where the first activity is to identify actors and use cases, and then construct a use case diagram. Subsequently, the use cases are detailed out, possibly in several iterations. The participants from Mogul set up the structure, while the participants from the client fill in the details. The participants work individually on the different use cases and meet regularly to discuss them. The use cases may also be constructed solely by the clients. The use cases are often supplemented by screens and a domain model.

Pen and paper are often used to construct the use cases, and then Rational Rose is used to document the use case diagram and different templates, depending on the project, are used to document the use case descriptions. Some of the interviewees also use the add-on tools to Rational Rose, Requisite Pro or SODA, to document the use cases.

When the use case model is completed, the project participants, in particular those from the client, often read through the use case model to verify that the requirements are covered.

5.2   Correctness of the Use Case Model

A use case model should be correct in that the functional requirements of all user groups are included. The interviewees found the use case modeling useful because it helps focus on functionality from the point of view of the user and helps assure that the requirements of all the user groups are included. They also found the technique useful for obtaining a common understanding of the requirements and for reaching agreement with the client.

The use case modeling process can often be a maturity process for the clients; they are forced to think through what they actually want. One of the interviewees described it like this: „The clients' domain expert thought she had a good overview of the requirements, but because of the use case modeling process we found out that not everybody agreed with her about what should be the functionality of the system."

It may, however, be difficult to find end-users with sufficient competence and interest to participate in use case modeling. Some of the interviewees meant that use cases were too abstract for end-users. End-users may also be confused by the sequential description of the steps of the individual use cases and believe that the sequence must be followed strictly. They may also find it difficult to understand from the use case model how the individual use cases relate.

5.3   Level of Detail of the Use Cases

A balanced level of detail in the use cases is important when the use case model is to be used as a basis for estimation. If the use cases are unbalanced, there may be difficulties when measuring the size of the use cases with the use case points method. The interviewees found it difficult to balance the use cases. In their opinion, use case descriptions tend to include too much detail. One of the interviewees described the problem in the following way: „The use cases tend to expand infinitely because to get complete descriptions we keep discussing unimportant details for a long time." The proposed solution to this problem is to have good examples of use case models available, and to use tabular descriptions of the use cases to avoid too much text. Another solution may be to use specific guidelines in the use case modeling process as proposed in [4].

Since use cases describe functionality from the point of view of the end-users, they seldom provide sufficient architectural information, and the descriptions may hide complex business logic. These issues are described further in the next section.

6   Adapting the Use Case Points Method

The interviewees had experience from estimation based on use cases, and had suggestions for tailoring the use case points method, both with regards to measuring size (Section 6.1) and with regards to which technical and environmental factors were relevant in this particular company (Section 6.2). Section 6.3 discusses how to estimate architecture when the use case points method is applied. Section 6.4 suggests how the use case points method can be more widespread in Mogul.

6.1   Assessing Size of the Use Cases

The use case points method takes the size of each use case as input. Size is measured in number of transactions in the use case descriptions. According to the interviewees, there are some problems with this measure:

- It is desirable to estimate with the use case points method in the inception phase, but at this stage the use cases may not sufficiently detailed out to show the individual transactions.
- When the use case descriptions are detailed out, they may be described at an unbalanced level of detail, which in turn may lead to skewed results due to inaccurate measure of size.
- The size measure does not capture complexity in the business logic and the architecture that may be hidden in the use case descriptions.

As a response to these difficulties, the interviewees suggested alternative ways of measuring size, for example, that weights could be assigned to each use case based on the intuition of the estimator or that the use cases could be used as a basis for identifying components to be estimated. However, these suggestions may contradict our goal of developing a method that requires little expert knowledge.

The following method was suggested by one of the interviewees as a supplement to counting transactions.

Consider for each use case what has to be done in the presentation layer, the persistence layer and the business layer:

1. The effort in the presentation layer will depend on the number of new screens, the number of transfers from one screen to another, the number of forms in the screens and the number of places where dynamic content must be generated.
2. The effort in the persistence layer will depend on the impact on the data model and persistent data, that is, on the number of new tables, the number of changes to table definitions, and the number of queries and updates on the tables.
3. The effort in the business layer is difficult to quantify as it may be anything from input to a database to complicated data processing, possibly also access to different back-systems. One of the interviewees described it this way: „The business logic may just be about transferring data, but you may find that you need a lorry to actually do it". Our advice is, therefore, that the estimators should break down each use case sufficiently to form an opinion about the complexity of the business logic necessary for realizing it. If this is impossible, alternative estimates could be made for the most likely and the most pessimistic size of the use cases.

6.2   Adjustments Factors

In the use case points method, the estimate based on the size of the use cases is adjusted based on a number of technical and environmental factors. The method is inspired by the function points method, particularly the MkII function point analysis (MKII FPA) [15]. The two methods use several of the same technical factors. The technical factors of MkII FPA, however, have since been discarded [16]. They may be relevant early in a project's life-cycle when the requirements are stated in a general form, but when the requirements are detailed out, many of them will have influenced the functional requirements, so that adjusting the effort using the technical factors may lead to double counting. In [10] evidence is also presented that the adjustment factors applied in the function point method are unnecessary, particularly when the method is used in a single organization. In a case study, the use case points estimates for five projects were on average more accurate when the technical factors where omitted [12]. We therefore propose that the technical factors be omitted when the use case points method is applied to detailed use cases.

The environmental factors are not taken into account by the detailed use case descriptions and should therefore be considered. Some environmental factors may, however, be irrelevant to this particular company, and it may be necessary to consider other factors. The environmental factors regarding the development team, F1 – F6, were all considered relevant by the interviewees. Nevertheless, they stated that it would be beneficial to specify productivity and availability for each team member, instead of having to calculate an average, because there are large differences in productivity among developers. The interviewees also felt that they were usually too optimistic about the productivity of the team members. Regarding availability, many of the company's projects are located at the clients, which means that they are „at the mercy of the clients" regarding their ability to provide people with necessary knowledge about the application domain and technological infrastructure. The environmental factors may also be useful to show the client the consequences of uncertainties and risks in the project.

Requirements stability, F7, was considered irrelevant when using RUP, because one of the primary motivations for using RUP is that it gives the possibility to continually change the requirements.

Difficulty of the programming language, F8, was considered difficult to assess and therefore irrelevant because the development projects now require that the developers have knowledge about the technology used at each layer in the architecture.

6.3   Functionality versus Architecture

The interviewees meant that architecture mostly should be estimated separately from functionality: „The whole project can be estimated based on use cases only if you know the customer and the architecture well from previous projects, but if there is much uncertainty, the architecture should definitely be estimated separately."

Our goal is to develop a method that can provide a complete estimate, which requires that it can estimate a new or modified architecture. We therefore propose that if an architecture already exists, the impact on the architecture should be considered for each use case and be used to adjust the size measures based on number of transactions.

We also propose, as did one of the interviewees, that the environmental factor F7, could be used to assess the architecture. A value of 5 (meaning new architecture or major changes to existing architecture) assigned to F7 increases the estimate by approximately 60% compared with the estimate produced when the value of F7 is 0 (meaning existing and stable architecture). One problem with this solution is, however, that the percentage of effort added for architecture is the same independently of the size of the project. In the interviewees' opinion, the proportion of the effort required for the architecture compared with the effort required for the functionality varies with the size of the project; the larger the project, the smaller is the proportion of effort needed to establish the architecture. One of the interviewees explained that many of the activities to establish the architecture must be done whether there are 5 or 50 use cases. He also mentioned as an example a project that took 8 months, and where 1/3 of the effort was on architecture and 2/3 on functionality. In a smaller project that took 3 months, 1/2 of the effort was spent on architecture and 1/2 on functionality.

6.4   Widespread Use of the Use Case Points Method in Mogul

The use case points method has been applied to several projects in Mogul. Nevertheless, obtaining continued and more widespread use of the method remains a challenge. We therefore wanted the interviewees' opinion about the prerequisites for a successful use of the use case points method in a larger scale. Our interviewees tended to use various tools for use case modeling, and they also used various tools and spreadsheets in estimation. This may indicate that there is a culture for applying tools and methods in an ad-hoc way in the company. Some of the interviewees stressed that they wanted a tool to be applied when they themselves found it useful, not methods that they were forced to apply. Hence, it may be difficult to get the whole company to agree on applying the use case points method.

Nevertheless, the interviewees were positive towards applying the use case points method; they found it desirable to apply the use case models in more activities in the development projects because of the effort that is often put into making it. A method to supplement expert estimates was considered particularly useful in projects with much uncertainty.

Although we agree that the use of the use case points method should be voluntary in Mogul, more experience with the method is needed to make it generally applicable.

7   Conclusions and Future Work

As part of a former software process improvement work in the software development company Mogul, an estimation method based on use cases, the use case points method, was evaluated with promising results. This paper described a follow-up software process improvement work that included interviews with senior personnel of Mogul to establish how the use case points method could improve the company's estimation practices, the prerequisites for applying the method and how to tailor it to this particular company.

We found that the use case points method can improve estimation practices in Mogul in that it provides a supplementary estimate in addition to the expert estimate. Combining estimates from different estimation strategies, particularly combining bottom-up estimates with top-down estimates, is an evaluated principle for improving estimates. In addition, applying an estimation method may help avoid estimation biases and thereby large overruns.

We also found that even though Mogul has good knowledge of RUP and use case modeling, it is challenging to construct a use case model that forms a good basis for estimation in that it correctly describes the functionality of the system and that the use cases are balanced. In particular, it is difficult to find end-users with sufficient competence and interest to take part in use case modeling. Nevertheless, the interviewees found use case models superior to old, unstructured requirements specifications.

The use case points method requires that the use cases should be detailed out, that is, each event between the system and the actor should be described, but this is not always done. We therefore proposed how the assessment of size of each use case could be refined, and made some suggestions for how the technical and environmental factors in the use case points method can be applied successfully to estimate the company's projects.

Nevertheless, more work is needed on how to tailor the use case points method. The following activities are planned:

• Establishing a scheme for measuring improvement to the estimation process. The most obvious success criterion is the accuracy of the estimates. Another criterion may be the number of people in the company who are competent estimators.
• Conducting a follow-up study to evaluate the proposed modifications to the use case points method.
• Investigating further how estimates produced with the use case points method can be combined with expert estimates.
• Investigating how use case modeling can be applied in web-projects.
• Investigating how to measure the size of a change to a use case, enabling the use case points method to be used in maintenance projects.

Acknowledgements

We gratefully acknowledge the employees of Mogul who took part in the interviews. We also acknowledge Dag Sjøberg for valuable comments on this paper. This research is funded by The Research Council of Norway through the industry-project PROFIT (PROcess improvement For the IT industry).

References

[1]   Albrecht, A.J. Measuring Application Development Productivity. Proceedings of joint SHARE, GUIDE and IBM Application Development Symposium. 1979.

[2]   Anda, B. Comparing Use Case based Estimates with Expert Estimates. Proceedings of the 2002 Conference on Empirical Assessment in Software Engineering (EASE 2002), Keele, United Kingdom, April 8-10, 2002.

[3]   Anda, B., Dreiem, H., Sjøberg, D.I.K., and Jørgensen, M. Estimating Software Development Effort Based on Use Cases – Experiences from Industry. UML'2001 - 4th Int. Conference on the Unified Modeling Language, Concepts, and Tools, Toronto, Canada, October 1-5, 2001, LNCS 2185, Springer-Verlag, pp. 487-502.

[4]   Anda, B., Sjøberg, D.I.K. and Jørgensen, M. Quality and Understandability in Use Case Models. ECOOP'2001, June 18-22, 2001, LNCS 2072 Springer-Verlag, pp. 402-428.

[5]   Blattberg, R.C. and Hoch, S.J. Database models and managerial intuition: 50% model + 50% manager, *Management Science*, Vol. 36, No. 8, pp. 887-899. 1990.

[6]   Fetcke, T., Abran, A. & Nguyen, T-H. Mapping the OO-Jacobson Approach into Function Point Analysis. Technology of Object-Oriented Languages and Systems, TOOLS-23. IEEE Comput. Soc, Los Alamitos, CA, USA, pp. 192-202. 1998.

[7]   Jørgensen, M. An empirical evaluation of the MK II FPA estimation model, Norwegian Informatics Conference, Voss, Norway. 1997.

[8]   Jørgensen, M. Reviews of Studies on Expert Estimation of Software Development Effort. Submitted to Journal of Systems and Software.

[9]   Karner, G. Metrics for Objectory. Diploma thesis, University of Linköping, Sweden. No. LiTH-IDA-Ex-9344:21. December 1993.

[10]   Kitchenham, B. A. Software Metrics: Measurement for Software Process Improvement. Blackwell Publishers. 1996.

[11]   Marchesi, M. OOA Metrics for the Unified Modeling Language. In Proc. of the Second Euromicro Conference on Software Maintenance and Reengineering, IEEE Comput. Soc, Los Alamitos, CA, USA, pp. 67-73. 1998.

[12]   Ribu, K. Estimating Object-Oriented Software Projects with Use Cases. Masters' Thesis, University of Oslo. November 2001.

[13]   Schneider, G. & Winters, J. *Applying Use Cases – A Practical Guide*. Addison Wesley. 1998.

[14]   Smith, J. The Estimation of Effort Based on Use Cases. Rational Software, White paper. 1999.

[15]   Symons C.R. *Software Sizing and Estimating, MKII FPA*. John Wiley and Sons, 1991.

[16]   Symons, C. Come back function point analysis (modernized) – all is forgiven! Software Measurement Services Ltd. 2001.

[17]   http://www.tassc-solutions.com/

Software Process Improvement through Use Cases: Building Quality from the Very Beginning

Andrea Valerio and Massimo Fenaroli

Thera S.p.A., 25100 Brescia, Italy
andrea.valerio@coclea.it, massimo.fenaroli@thera.it

Abstract. This paper describes an experiment we are conducting in an industrial setting concerning the introduction of use cases inside the software process with the goal to enhance the process in its very early phases. The process improvement action, named PIUC, is being conducted inside an Italian software development company named Thera S.p.A, and it is a best practice action the firm decided to undertake with the objective to better capture and formalize evolving customer expectations and requirements. In this paper we describe the work performed until now (the experiment will finish at the end of the year) and we present some quantitative data collected during the project and a preliminary qualitative evaluation of the project, highlighting the positive aspects we observed and some reflections about the impact of use cases.

1   Introduction

This paper presents an industry best practice experience that is currently undergoing inside an Italian software development company.

The goal of the Process Improvement through Use cases project (PIUC) is to improve the software development process of Thera S.p.A. by introducing the use cases method in order to better capture and formalize evolving customer expectations and requirements. Use cases, firstly proposed by Ivar Jacobson [1], are a rather well-known technique to collect and formalise user needs and initial requirements, but they are not so widespread in the software industry. They should allow to define a user-centred view of a system, represented by an object-oriented model containing the definition of the system's behaviours and actors who interact with the system in different ways. Being user-centred, they are an efficient means of communicating with customers about expectations and requirements; being object models, they facilitate subsequent analysis, design and implementation phases by having already structured the system in a coherent way.

Use cases should bring, in the framework of an object oriented approach, a relevant benefit in the development process by enhancing the very first phases of it that are still mainly based on expertise and personal skills of the analysts. The promise is to introduce a structured, well-formalised and controlled approach that should directly

M. Oivo and S. Komi-Sirviö (Eds.): PROFES 2002, LNCS 2559, pp. 398-406, 2002.

support and feed up the successive analysis and design steps. Besides, use cases should provide a description of software systems in such a way that can be immediately understood and validated by the user since the very early phases of the development process. The introduction of use cases should also improve working conditions of personnel involved in the software process, because it provides a better organization and support of the initial phases of the software life cycle. This should help domain experts and analysts in their daily job, lead to an improved interpersonal communication and team-work, gain a better organization of the working activities and reduce the stress and pressure associated with these activities.

But there is still a general need of empirical and experimental data that show the real impact that use cases can lead to a software firm adopting them. This represents an issue for firms that require improving the very early steps of the software process and that are planning to adopt use cases. Besides, we have to consider that the impact of use cases embraces the whole software life cycle and this complicates the activity of verification and assessment of their usefulness and benefits due to the time frame required to perform a reasonable validation. The PIUC project has been designed in order to perform a focused and time-effective empirical evaluation of the impact that use cases have in the development process, considering a well defined experimental setting in order to minimize side effects and to better control external variables influence. The PIUC project aims at demonstrating the feasibility and the impact that a technology transfer action could have in an industrial firm, but, as we already put into evidence, the goal of the project is also to provide a case study on the effectiveness and efficiency of use cases. In this perspective, the project is being conducted as an exercise of empirical software engineering: the execution of each activity is monitored and during the experiment quantitative and qualitative measures are collected. This data will allow at the end of the experiment to assess if the expected results have been achieved and to quantitatively analyse the effectiveness of use cases in the early stage of the software process.

The PIUC project aims to achieve inside a real industrial setting several benefits:

- it defines a formal and structured process for capturing customer expectations and requirements, replacing the ad-hoc and informal process currently used;
- it fosters the domain-scoping activity, through early detection of common aspects, variants and possible evolution of a domain;
- it defines a precise (unambiguous), formal (because of the use of standard templates) and accountable (because the use cases will act as a contract between the customers and the developers) way of representing user requirements;
- it improves the software quality by identifying the customer implicit exceptions earlier in the development process;
- it obtains a better traceability between requirements and correlated modules throughout the following development phases;
- it facilitates the organization of the system test providing concrete „scenarios" to check;
- it helps technical writers in structuring the overall work on the user manuals at an early stage of the development process.

At a technical level, PIUC aims to better the capability to model complex and evolving software systems, to improve the capturing of functional and non-functional requirements, to enhance the description and representation of its static structure and the dynamic interactions among sub-systems, to achieve a better integration between analysis and design.

From a business perspective, use cases introduction should contribute to decrease time-to-market and development costs and to increase customer satisfaction. The project aims to improve product quality, to decrease time-to-market and development costs and to stimulate the entrance of the firm into the market of software components. The project is also driven by the business needs to increase productivity and efficiency, gaining competitive advantage over competitors through quality, establishing better relations with clients, enlarging the presence in the software market and improve the organisation of the production process.

The experimentation of use cases is a concrete step in the direction to better structure the early phases of the software process, contributing to the set up of a controlled and effective component factory inside the organisation. This project has the objective to assess the effective benefits that use cases could take inside a software organisation from an empirical and very practical point of view.

2   The PIUC Project

Thera S.p.A. is an IT company for which one of the main business goals is to develop software products for rational management of firms and their resources. With the conviction that product quality and customer satisfaction are key elements for consolidating and enlarging the market presence, Thera is pursuing the improvement of the software development process and practices, combining the request for flexible iterative short-cycle processes with the need of continuous monitoring and control over the projects. This led to the definition of a series of actions aiming to enhance the development environment, in particular moving from traditional development models (like the waterfall process) to more flexible and iterative ones that allow refinement and incremental production, shortening the life cycle also with the introduction of the object oriented methodology.

Within this context, building on current object-oriented practices and on previous improvement steps (like the experimentation of domain analysis methodologies in order to better understand reuse potential and domain specific characteristics), the PIUC project focus on improving the collection of the user expectations and needs and their translation into structured and formal requirements. The introduction of the use cases method should lead to an improvement of the first phase of the software development process, reducing effort and production costs and increasing the quality of the identified requirements. This should enhance the current situation that could be defined somehow „creative", because of the lack of standardized practices and methodologies. Use cases should spread its benefits over the whole development process [3], because the increased quality of collected requirements reflects in the improvement of the subsequent phases, performed with object oriented methods (previously the Booch method and now the UML method) within a wider Domain Analysis context scheme, which has been drawn from PROTEUS and FODA methods.

The PIUC project was organised into four main phases:

1. training and education of personnel, in order to provide the technical notions needed to use the new method and useful motivations to people;
2. adaptation of use cases method to the software development environment of the firm, in order to adjust and integrate it with the other methodologies and tools currently use in its software process;
3. application of the use cases to the baseline project, translating customer expectations in structured requirements by a formalized process, following the guidelines defined in the previous step; the experimentation is executed inside a baseline real project of the firm named „Claim management".
4. data collection, analysis, comparison and final evaluation of results, in order to assess the outcomes of the process and the impact it will have had on the software process and environment.

2.1   Baseline Project

The PIUC project is based on the experimentation in a real baseline project of the improvement action. The baseline project that has been chosen deals with the development of a software product named "Claim Management". It is a new proprietary Web application, whose main goal is to help an insurance company to manage accidents, from the communication of the accident report to the final paying off, in an integrated manner (regarding both branch offices and call-centers and the headquarter).

The Claim Management product is multi-company, multi-currency and multi-language and it is constituted by different applicative subsystems:

- Accident administrative management
- Accident handling
- Accident paying
- Reserve funds management
- case management
- Statistical data production
- Management of branch and central offices

The Claim Management product is built in Java within J2EE Web architecture, adopting the object-oriented methodology, and UML as modelling language, and using the Rational ROSE tool.

The baseline project is carried out through the following development phases:

- environment set-up;
- requirements definition and formalisation;
- analysis and design of the modules;
- development and unit test;
- system test;
- preparation of user and marketing documentation;
- beta test at a pilot customer site.

The experimentation of the PIUC project will overlap with the second and third phases of the baseline project. The Claim Management project has been chosen as a test-bed for the experimentation of use cases because:

- it is a typical Thera project for the development of a software system in a domain pretty stable for the firm operations;
- the Claim Management application is strongly correlated to a correct capture of customer requirements and, therefore, it is highly sensitive to improvements in this phase;
- the experimentation of a new development practice in this project is a very good test-case but it does not present high risks.

2.2   Current Status

After the successful execution of the first two phases, i.e. training of personnel and use cases method adaptation, we are today experimenting the use cases method in the context of the baseline project, in particular collecting and analysing the customer needs and requirements, writing the use cases and exploiting them in the object-oriented analysis.

Training and education of personnel was the first action developed. The impact on personnel determined by the introduction of a new methodology assumes a great importance in a project (and even more in an improvement action) and it is one of the most important factors conditioning the success of such a methodology. This first phase aimed to prepare and train the people directly involved in the project on the methodology and technique that was introduced, building the necessary competencies and skills to carry out the planned activities. Moreover, this phase was a very important moment for exchanging opinions and ideas in order to better understand the aspects necessary for the customisation of the method and for the integration in the development process of the firm. Another important achievement of this phase was the motivation of the personnel, because it showed the (potential) benefits, also from a personal point of view, that the new methodology should have on the development process and on their work.

Adaptation of use cases method to the development environment of the firms was the second activity performed. It focused on the definition of the method to be experimented and its customisation to the specific needs of the firm in order to make it effective [2]. Use cases propose an object-oriented approach in the requirement elicitation phase, introducing a simple graphic notation and a structured textual description of user's requirements and needs. In this phase we produced the methodology guidelines that defines how to adopt use cases in the software development process of Thera, integrating use cases with the successive analysis and design phases.

In this phase we also defined the monitoring program, i.e. the set of measures and metric to be used during the experiment phase in order both to control its execution and for assessing the project achievements and the impact it had on the development process. We focused on two main types of measures:

- process-oriented measures, applied in order to keep track of the effort spent to perform specific production and support activities (adopting the Activity Based

Costing method), in particular the effort spent for capturing and formalising customer requirements with use cases;

- product-oriented measures, devoted to the evaluation of the use cases and the related requirement documentation from the point of view of stability, understandability of requirements and linking with the following development phases.

We decided to consider both quantitative and qualitative measures, being the latter devoted to assess several aspects such as structure and understandability of use cases and documentation produced, impact of the use cases both in the requirements elicitation and analysis phase and in the next development process activities.

The experiment of the use cases in the context of the baseline project started on February 2002. It includes two partially overlapped activities: the first is the collection of user requirements and expectations and the definition of the use cases modelling this information, the second phase consist of the application of the released use cases as the main input information source driving the object-oriented modelling and design phases of the baseline project. The collection of the user needs and expectations was performed through direct interviews of the users by the analysts; the same analysts then wrote the use cases with an iterative process (interviewing users, writing the use cases, checking the information with users and then refining and updating the use cases until the users validate them). In the second phase, use cases feed up the analysis and modelling activity, exploiting the object-driven specifications depicted by the use cases and in linking such usage „scenarios" with the object-oriented modelling activities of the system to develop. This process in two phases should guarantee that requirements are defined in a formal way and the whole process of collecting and formalizing them doesn't depend any more on the skill and experience of the analysts who conducted the interviews to the customer.

At the date of this paper, most of the use case collection and writing process has been performed (it will end in September) and the object oriented modelling and design phase has already been started (we are about in the middle).

3   Preliminary Results

In this section we provide some initial quantitative data collected during the monitoring and measuring program and we illustrate some preliminary considerations about the project and the experiment phase.

3.1   Quantitative Data

During the execution of the experiment several measures are collected in order to monitor the status of the work and with the goal to collect sufficient data for the analysis and final evaluation of the project. We measure both process metrics, in particular time spent and effort consumption, and product metrics. This information will be used in order to assess the impact that the introduction of use cases has on the baseline project, focusing on benefits and possible drawbacks in the use of the methodology.

At the date of this report, we are finishing writing the use cases and almost all of the user requirements and expectations have been collected. We have already started the analysis of the use cases and the modelling and design activity.

The number of use cases produced till now is 111. This number includes significant use cases and not very simple and straight 'use case-like' information (such as particular data or situation definition). In order to provide an indication on the 'size' of these use cases, we considered the effort spent to produce them (in man-days) and we defined the following classification:

- simple use cases, when the effort was less of 1 man-day;
- medium use cases, when the effort was less than 3 man-days and bigger than 1;
- complex use cases, when the effort was larger than 3 man-days.

Adopting this classification for the use cases produced, we have that 22,5% of the use cases are simple, 36,9% are medium and 40,5% are complex.

Considering the time and the effort spent in the definition of the use cases (considering the interviews, writing the use cases and reworking them until the customer finally validates them), we have the following figures (related to the total estimated effort for the project):

- Effort spent for the interviews with the customer: 4%
- Effort spent for writing the first version of the use cases: 10%
- Effort spent in reworking and refining the use cases until the final validation from the customer: 3%
- Effort spent for the definition of the test cases: 2,5%.

If we consider only the initial phase of the experiment, i.e. from requirements collection to the definition of the use cases, we have the following figures:

- Effort spent for the interviews with the customer: 23,5%
- Effort spent for writing the first version of the use cases: 59,0%
- Effort spent in reworking and refining the use cases until the final validation from the customer: 17,5%

We also recorded how many cycles we made in order to achieve the final validation from the customer of the use cases. The average value is 1,4. This indicator represents the number of times we reworked the use cases and it represents the efficacy of the requirement collection and analysis phase.

The information we presented in this section has to be considered as preliminary. When the project will be completed (we plan at the end of the year), we will be able to calculate precise final figures.

3.2   Qualitative Evaluation

The information collected till now allow to draw some positive qualitative considerations:

1. It seems that the collection of the use cases (that is done starting from interviews with the customers) introduces a well-structured approach that helps personnel in performing initial elicitation of requirements, and this turns into a more efficient

process. Having a structured document that guides the collection of information is very helpful and gives a homogeneous approach to all the people involved in the activity. On the other hand, the capability to properly conduct an interview, in particular considering the ability to create a positive and proactive situation with the customer, seems to remain a personal characteristic. In a similar way, the abstraction capacity of interviewers is affected and improved only partially by use cases: the ability to reveal and capture the significant aspects (considering also implicit information) while leaving unnecessary details seems to be directly related to each person's experience and ability.

2. Use cases seems to help and support the adoption of an effective iterative process in capturing and detailing user requirements: the graphic notation and the structured textual description allow to approach interviews and elicitation starting from the main scenarios (where most important aspects are usually described) and then moving in successive steps toward the refinement of the requirements. We revealed that in this process it is important to trace the historical evolution of the documentation, avoiding unnecessary particulars but recording specific constraints or aspects that could be important also in successive steps.

3. Another interesting aspects that seems to emerge is that the adoption of use cases helps in the planning of the interviews and it simplify the organisation of the requirement collection when more resources are working in parallel. The reason is that use cases stimulate a very clear structuring of the work and of the information that has to be gathered, combining an initial top-down approach with successive refinements (also bottom-up) and deeper investigation of each scenario and use case.

Considering the feedbacks we collected till now, we have also to highlight some specific points:

One of the promised benefits of use cases we can found cited in the scientific literature is the improvement of the relationship with the customers. During the collection of the user requirements, the adoption of use cases and the documentation produced should be easily understood by the customers and this shuold help the verification and refinement of the information collected, speeding-up the activity and augmenting the confidence (and satisfaction) of the customers. In our experience, the customer experienced several difficulties in understanding the use cases documentation. We verified during validation interviews that customers were not able to properly read and understand the plain use case notation, at least without the continuous support of the analyst. This observation has to be further investigated in order to understand the reasons behind it, but during the experiment we overcome this difficulty providing the customers some draft interfaces associated to the flow of events described in the use case. With the sketch of the user interfaces it seems that the comprehension and understanding really improved.

A second observation regards the empirical evaluation of the experiment. The definition of the metrics and measures that could be adopted to monitor the experiment and to analyse the results are not straightforward. At a first look at the literature it is possible to find many contributions and proposal, but it seems there is a lack of real and sound indicators. An example: how can we measure the complexity of a use case? We will deep this argument in order to understand if there are industrial experiences or best practices that can be considered. But, perhaps a most important question is to relate measures and metrics with project management and impact analysis. And again this is an argument for a deeper investigation.

As we indicated in the previous section, we expect to have sufficient data to draw a quantitative evaluation at the end of the summer. These data will allow assessing the impact that use cases had on the software process in a real industrial setting. We expect to achieve positive results and to provide clear evidence of how technology transfer can help software firms in improving both the internal process and the external satisfaction perceived by customers. The dissemination of this experience to a European audience will permit to share empirical data on technology transfer and adoption by software firms.

Conclusions and Future Work

In this paper we presented the experience we are conducting with a software process improvement action in a real industrial setting. We described the project, the core ideas and the current status of the experiment we are conducting inside a baseline project in order to collect empirical data for assessing the improvement action.

Use cases, the idea underlying the improvement action, can improve the software process in the initial phases in order to enhance the quality of the software product from the very beginning. The initial analysis we made of the experiment (we have finished the collection of the use cases and we are now conducting the software modelling and design activity) seems to give positive feedbacks, but we also highlight some points and aspects that (at a first analysis) should be further investigated. The experiment will be completed in October and with all the information about it we will be able to complete a full and detailed analysis of the experience we made and of the results achieved.

Acknowledgments

The PIUC project is a Best Practice action carried out in the context of the IST Take-up Actions – Accompanying Measures (PIUC - Process Improvement through Use Cases - IST-1999-20097). It is financially supported by the European Commission.

References

[1]   Ivar Jacobson and others, Object-Oriented Software Engineering: A use case Driven Approach, Addison-Wesley, 1992.
[2]   Alistair Cockburn, Writing effective use cases, Addison-Wesley, 2001.
[3]   Larry L. Constantine and Lucy Lockwood, Software for Use: A Practical Guide to Models and Methods for Usage Centered Design, Addison-Wesley, 1999.

From Knowledge Management Concepts toward Software Engineering Practices

Gerardo Canfora, Aniello Cimitile, and Corrado Aaron Visaggio

RCOST – Research Centre on Software Technology
Department of Engineering, University of Sannio
Palazzo ex Poste, via Traiano, 82100, Benevento, Italy
{canfora,cimitile,visaggio}@unisannio.it
http://rcost.unisannio.it

Abstract. Knowledge Management spans on three abstraction layers: the first one is concerned with organisations, the second one regards engineering practices, and the third one is about tools. The organisation level encloses concepts strongly tied with strategies and resources management; the engineering level regards processes, methods and heuristics, tested or empirically validated, that support effective processes design, management and enactment; the third level comprehends software tools for storing and operating with knowledge. Currently, a major concern is a gap between the first and the second level in order to properly exploit theory and to cope with the nowadays turmoil of the marketplace. In this paper we propose a map linking a significant set of selected theories in knowledge management with a set of appropriate engineering practices able to realise them; furthermore we wish to determine the components from the third layer that are effective in making the selected engineering practices working in real contexts.

1 Introduction

Many definitions for knowledge management enriched the literature, especially in the business and software engineering areas. According to the *business vision* in reference [1] the main target of Knowledge Management (KM) theories is to strategically use information in order to successfully provide for: a clear and deep understanding of the organisation's market scope; innovations and new capabilities; institutionalised processes to externalise tacit knowledge, and to combine diverse pieces of explicit knowledge in order to build a knowledge base for problem solving that is sharable through the organisation's individuals and departments.

Referring to KM as a set of knowledge extraction processes, authors in [9] claim that 'Knowledge Management [...] focuses on the individual as an expert and as the bearer of important knowledge that he or she can systematically share with an organisation. KM supports not only the know-how of a company, but also the know-where, know-what, know-when, know-why. [...]'

M. Oivo and S. Komi-Sirviö (Eds.): PROFES 2002, LNCS 2559, pp. 407-422, 2002.
© Springer-Verlag Berlin Heidelberg 2002

KM means basically *creating knowledge* by appropriate technologies; reference [22] states: 'Knowledge management (KM) refers to the methods and tools for capturing, storing, organising, and making accessible knowledge and expertise within and across communities. At the individual or team level, the KM flow is a cycle in which solving a problem leads to new knowledge, initially tacit (that is, known but unexpressed), and then made explicit when experiences are documented, distributed, and shared (via databases, e-mail, or presentations). Once explicit, the knowledge is used by others for solving new problems. The application of the explicit knowledge to a new problem creates new tacit knowledge, with the potential of initiating a new KM cycle.'

These definitions highlight that interest in knowledge management is not framed within well defined boundaries, but it spreads on different research areas, generating multi-disciplinary issues. In this paper we focus on KM applied in software organisations, an area that has raised a growing attention in the last decade [9]. According to [21] knowledge management activities should include:

- *Strategy:* which goals the organisation wish to achieve? Which plans must be established?
- *Processes:* which are the procedures, technologies, and methods to be used?
- *Tools:* which are the tools to enhance the processes?

In this perspective it makes sense to consider knowledge management as a three-layer structure of abstraction, where each layer yields a well defined type of knowledge assets and identifies a degree of abstraction. A primary goal of knowledge management is to put organisations in a position of successful planning strategies for mastering effectively changes in the marketplace: such a consideration leads straight toward the management's scope. The first layer in the structure is formed by *Knowledge Management Concepts* and is basically concerned with organisation and human resource management. This is the most abstract layer and is characterised by a rich set of theories that need to be linked with well defined processes ready to work in actual contexts. Because knowledge management regards collecting, extracting, combining, converting, and relating information from diverse sources of diverse nature, *Software Engineering Practices* constitutes the second layer of the structure and its main contribution stays in process models, methods, and heuristics in order to define, institutionalise, and apply successful knowledge management strategies.

For manipulating and producing knowledge [2][1] in the real world with respect to KM goals, it is needed that both humans and machines be able to properly handle information. Thus, developing tools for storing, retrieving, combining, and widely working with knowledge's objects becomes necessary. This defines the third layer, named *Knowledge Management Tools,* which lies at the lowest level of abstraction. KM tools' development requires systems for supporting: communication, cooperative work, databases management, and document management. Moreover the layer should include also *knowledge based systems* such as inferential engines, descriptive logic, and domain analysers and should involve outcomes from disciplines like ontology [3][4][10], machine learning [7][8], and data mining [5][6][16].

Before stepping forward we point out a distinction between two close but different concepts: *methodologies for knowledge based systems development* and *knowledge management.* The former regards topics like abstract problem solving, domain modelling, inference engines, machine learning, and knowledge elicitation and focuses on the processes for making *abstract* a certain kind of knowledge –conceptual relationships between data, heuristics, rules for problem solving – in order to automatically re-apply it in different contexts. Knowledge Management focuses on *extracting* personal and embedded – tacit – knowledge from the experts in order to *distributing, combining, linking* it and *creating* new knowledge that has never been explicitly acquired by any human being. The latter is ampler and exploits the former in many ways.

In an ideal state the three layers should be integrated in a comprehensive body of knowledge: the first layer provides for the principles and laws, and for explained goals; the second one provides for the methods and practices to realise the outcomes from the first layer; the third one provides for technological solutions to act on the raw *chunks* of knowledge in order to turn the results coming from the second layer in *actual* projects and activities. However the literature shows a deep gap, especially between the first and the second level.

With this work we aim to draw a three-layered map for connecting some of the most widely trusted theories of knowledge management with existing software engineering practices and methods able to implement them; furthermore each practice or method will be connected with a suitable set of third layer's technologies and tools in order to provide for a technical support. This linkage can be useful in several contexts, for example: to drive the investments of knowledge management tools producers; to help software organisations to select the most appropriate set of methods and tools based on their goals, and; to the research community, to frame existing work and identify open issues.

In Section 2 theories of basic relevance are considered in order to be implemented, while Section 3 shows valid cases or proposals of application of knowledge management in the branch of software engineering. Section 4 provides considerations about third layer's elements currently present on the marketplace or in research. Finally, Section 5 discusses next steps in approaching knowledge management with software engineering techniques and methods.

2   Candidate Knowledge Management Concepts

In this section the basic and most trusted concepts of knowledge management will be presented in order to select the candidates to be associated with software engineering practices. Knowledge is tightly related with three further terms: data, information and experience. '*Data* consists of discrete, objective facts about events. [...] Data is raw material for creating information. *Information* is data that is organized to make it useful for end-users who perform tasks and make decisions. *Knowledge* is not only contained in information, but also in the relationships among information items, their classification, and metadata. *Experience* is applied knowledge.'[13]

Knowledge can be classified in three categories: *tacit, explicit, and cultural* [18].

Tacit knowledge	It is the implicit knowledge used by organisation members to performing their jobs. It can be learned through observation and imitation and often it is not expressible in symbols and schemes. That's the reason why it is diffused in communities by using analogies, metaphors, stories and models.
Explicit knowledge	It is knowledge codified in systems or symbols and it is easy to diffuse and share. It may be **object-based** or **rule-based.** In the first case it is represented by strings of symbols or it is embodied in physical entities and characterises artefacts, such as products, patents, software code. In the second case it is codified in rules, laws and practices, easily transferable to others. This kind of knowledge could be shared and diffused inside the organisation and could be recorded in documents of various format and nature.
Cultural knowledge	It is a body of beliefs and assumptions letting organisation members describe and explain reality, that are used in recognising the saliency of new information and in evaluating alternative interpretations and actions. Cultural knowledge is expressed in the form of conventions, expectations, and norms.

Coupled with Knowledge and the status of *knowing* is the *process of learning.* Learning is the process of transferring knowledge between people and it is becoming very popular especially paired with the word 'organisation'. *Learning Organisation* differs from individual learning in two respects [17]: first, it occurs through shared insight, knowledge and shared models. Second: it is not only based on the memory of the participants in the organisation, but also on „institutional mechanisms" like policies, strategies, explicit models and defined processes (we call this the „culture" of the organisation).

There are three basic approaches for learning inside an organisation [21]:

Learning through Participation	It occurs when 'teachers' try to isolate knowledge and transfer it to 'students' in environments free of context. This behaviour characterises the *community of practices* that can be recognised in any kind of work group: learning through participation leads to establish private 'practices, routines, rituals, artefacts, symbols, conventions, stories, and histories.'[19]
Learning from experience	It relies on the Kolb's model [20], named 'Four Modes of learning'. According to this model experience relates to learning throughout four modes ordered in two dimensions: the first dimension concerns how people take hold of experience, called the *grasping* dimension, the second regards how people convert experience, called the *transformation* dimension. The grasping dimension comprehends two modes: *apprehension* (producing tangible, felt qualities of immediate experience) and *comprehension* (producing symbolic representations). The transformation dimension comprehends two further modes: via *intension* (throughout internal reflection) and via *extension* (throughout manipulation of the external world).
Learning as conversion process between tacit and explicit knowledge	According to Nonaka and Takeuchi [26], knowledge passes through different modes of conversion in a spiral that makes the knowledge more refined, and also spreads it across different layers in an organisation.

Nonaka and Takeuchi [26] prepared a *model of learning* describing the processes in which knowledge passes through the four combinations originated by the tacit and explicit states.

		To	
		TACIT	**EXPLICIT**
From	**TACIT**	Socialisation	Externalisation
	EXPLICIT	Internalisation	Combination

Fig. 1. Nonaka and Takeuchi model

The model, depicted in figure 1, includes four types of learning processes:

Socialisation	It defines a learning mode based on '*story telling* ' and sharing of knowledge by putting together experts and practitioners in a room where they can exchange their own experiences about specific problems encountered.
Internalisation	It consists of repetitively applying principles and procedures till they are absorbed as tacit knowledge of the individual's style and habit.
Externalisation	It is a fundamental target of knowledge management research. It means turning tacit knowledge in a form universally understandable and sharable. The hurdles to overcome constitute the hardest work in this research field. Not all the knowledge can be described in terms of rules, laws, patterns, and cause-effect relationships. In fact the largest part of personal knowledge is built with mental models that do not follow structured frameworks and often feelings and personal sensations make up them as essential components.
Combination	It consists of relating explicit knowledge to *create* further explicit knowledge and to derive new knowledge. This is the highest peek in the evolution of knowledge management and should determine the maturity of a *learning organisation*. Combination of knowledge arises by obtaining experience from previously extracted knowledge.

A basic KM theory is the *theory of action* [27], according to which organisational actions arise from the proper combination of *norms* –norms for corporate performance-, *strategies* –strategies for achieving norms-, *assumptions* –assumptions to apply strategies- (NAS). Organisational Knowledge is a repository of validated NAS relationships spanning the entire lifecycle of products. *Organisational actions* enclose procedures to be enacted in order to apply NAS in the processes of the product's lifecycle. Organisational learning consists of correcting errors occurring in decision making by properly adjusting either NAS relationships or organisational actions.

Learning can happen in two feedback loop modes: *single loop learning,* when the correction of errors regards adjusting actions, and *double loop learning* when error correction entails adjusting NAS relationships. By associating strategies of NAS to process models, a learning process is a feedback loop that is started by the outcomes of an enacted process and that modifies the original process model according to single or double loop. This theory is very close to Lehman's FEAST approach in applying feedback actions on process models, due to process management decisions [28].

The concepts upon which we will concentrate our attention are: *learning through participation, learning as theory of action, combination, externalisation, and socialisation.* In the next section we will link these concepts to practices and methods by using software engineering technologies.

3   Candidate Software Engineering Practices

In this section we will discuss cases in which policies and systems for knowledge management have been implemented both *in* software engineering environments and *with* software engineering technologies. The aim of this brief overview is to identify directions that may be taken to actually realise knowledge management theories by exploiting software engineering *practices*.

An argument of interest for next discussion is the *Experience Factory* (EF) [12], an infrastructure aiming at capitalising and reusing lifecycle experience and products. EF is a logical and physical organisation, whose activities are independent from the ones of the development organisation, and provides organisations for building software competencies and supplying them to projects according to the Quality Improvement Paradigm (QIP) [25].

Reference [11] focuses on the reuse of knowledge from previous projects as a variant of knowledge management. Experience is basically *applied* knowledge [13]: with respect to EF concepts, the knowledge can be made explicit by the use of *cost-process-resource models, algorithms, lessons learned, formulas, diagrams,* and other forms for formally representing information gathered during project [12].

The strongest limit of the quoted work is that it is restricted to software process improvement, where the useful knowledge can be made explicit relying on the richness of studies around EF. It should be possible to extend the findings on knowledge management's methodologies and practices also to processes in which relevant knowledge is not always easy to extract in explicit form.

The SEC (Software Engineering Center) project at DaimlerChrysler aims '*to investigate experience reuse and apply insights and collected experiences to SPI [Software Process Improvement].*'[11] Relying on the classical experience factory, two knowledge management goals are targeted: *sharing knowledge* by using intranets and hypertext to connect several documents like materials, checklists, frequently asked questions; *knowledge explicitation,* by involving interviews and feedback forms.

In turning SEC in a *learning organisation* three major challenges must be kept in account:

1. disseminating best practices to govern the *behaviour of stakeholders* to adequately cope with changes;
2. promoting the use of experience-based checklists to individuate common risks and related solutions;
3. constituting packages to anticipate user needs and to understand what actually project is requested to offer.

The problem of finding the proper sources of information, especially without wasting precious and scarce resources, such as time and energy, becomes a priority. Connecting in a uniform net the elements building a corporate knowledge is suggested to be a solution [14]: it is named *knowledge network*. Inside the organisation, knowledge network allows identifying what is needed, and knowing where and how it can be founded. Needed capabilities are:

Categorizing	It consists of classifying unstructured data automatically, in order to gather documents enclosing potential useful knowledge.
Hyperlinking	Knowledge is information about information, better defined as meta-information. Identifying and expressing relationships among information items helps in building knowledge.
Alerting	The automatic notification to users and agents of new information that might be of interest to them. For knowledge management producing added value, the knowledge itself should reach the user, in order to cope with network's growth.
Profiling	Defining diverse categories of knowledge for diverse categories of users.

Forming a Knowledge Management team in order to institutionalise Knowledge management policies [14] is becoming popular among the government agencies in US, as cases at US Navy, Federal Aviation Administration prove.

The NASA Goddard Space Flight Center (GSFC) has several initiatives under way, and has formed the knowledge Management Working Group to provide knowledge stewardship roles. The current ongoing phase is to select the best videos about critical stories and lessons learned involving software engineering area and project management; this can support the socialisation process. Additionally the GSFC is attempting to develop metrics to determine the value added benefits of using knowledge management.

The work being carried out at NASA suggests some software engineering practices:

1. Capturing key stories putting in evidence success factors, isolating side effects or noise, relating failure causes, risk exposure, resulted losses.
2. Exploiting a lesson learned management facilities, including functions for pushing them toward the appropriate person or department;
3. Conducting sharing knowledge forums;
4. Capturing knowledge via exit interview packets, to glean lessons learned from individuals before they leave the organisation.

Wei, Hu, and Chen [15] have developed a system for supporting organisations in knowledge creation, update, sharing, and reuse. Basically, the system includes:

1. Lessons-learned repository that contains basically validated experiences.
2. Case repository, containing previously disapproved cases, or those undergoing validation, where a case comprehends: a problem's or phenomenon's description, analyses, comments, and recommendations for treatment, as well as the contributors' contract information.
3. Organisational directory, containing organisational structure, individuals' profiles and contract information, and the names of domain experts in various areas. The system supports a set of common functions: knowledge creation, maintenance, search and usage analysis.

The system pushes the created knowledge via e-mail to the potential users, the person who proposed the problem, and the solicited experts.

Authors in [9] focus on the role knowledge management might play in the software development processes and industry. They classify three core activities:

Document management	Software development processes are centred on documents and related activities, such as authoring, reviewing, editing, and obviously using them; on the other hand documents are the assets retaining the most validated and used explicit knowledge of the organisation.
Competence management systems	Create own people profiles and competence descriptions or automatically generate them by people's emails and documents.
Software reuse	It requires appropriate knowledge on specific features and parameters of the code to be reused, the environment in which the code must be operative and the requirements this code should satisfy.

In reference [22] the rationale to build a *knowledge portal* is presented. Document must be automatically gathered by the system, registered, managed, and analysed; in the features must be included also functions such as text analysis for clustering, categorisation, searching, navigation, and visualisation of documents. Text features must be extracted for handling the conceptual content of written assets.

Knowledge work involves solving problems. This definition implies human analysis of information, synthesis of new information expressing implications and solutions, and authoring of new artifacts to communicate solutions to colleagues. An important feature is supporting collaborative authoring. It is needed to keep track of multiple contributions, annotate contributions of coauthors, and merge multiple edits. Collaborative annotation allows annotation by readers at large, enriching documents with comments and additional perspectives. Knowledge portals help disseminating knowledge captured in electronic form. Portals support sharing of documents and collaboration by giving users access to summaries of persons' resumes and areas of expertise and by publishing documents.

In reference [23] authors focus on the following two processes: 'Using knowledge acquisition processes to capture structured knowledge systematically; Using knowledge representation technology to store knowledge, preserving important relationships that are far richer than those possible in conventional databases'.

The work tests the usefulness of these processes by a case study in which the drilling optimisation group of a large oil and gas service company uses knowledge-engineering practices to support three knowledge management tasks: *knowledge capture, knowledge storage, knowledge deployment*. In this work the authors show some basic components that should make up a knowledge management system:

Document management system	This kind of functionality is discussed previously in the paper.
Discussion forums	For gaining advantage from socialisation.
Capability management system	Similar to competence management previously discussed.
Lesson-learned knowledge base system	A repository for experience.

In order to maintain high level of competence upon edge technology Microsoft founded the SPUD [24] project, which addressed two goals:

1. To use *competence model* to better matching employees to jobs and work teams;
2. To create a *competence inventory* for being used across Microsoft and to relate each worker to specific courses inside and outside Microsoft or specific projects.

An example of a system distributing experience through the web is *Dipnet* [39], realized by an Italian company called Network Services. It is an experience (experiments, software processes, frameworks, quality models and plans, and others) repository that can deliver the assets at different levels of detail, according with the part of experience the customer needs to apply in his operative context.

After the previous overview on knowledge management's implementation with software engineering techniques or within software engineering initiatives, now we wish to draw a starting map showing which SE practices could support the implementation of the key KM concepts identified in the previous section. The selected SE practices are illustrated in table 1 together with the rationale.

Table 1. KM concepts- SE practices map

KMConcepts	Software Engineering Practices
Learning as theory of action [ToA]	**Best practices management** [b.p. could support the loop enactment] **Forums** [Analysing forum can help to identify hot themes and the best solutions to associate with them.] **Lessons learned management** [represents a formalisation of which behaviour fits for which context]
Learning through participation [LtP]	**Alerting** [agents can push knowledge to appropriate users, supporting the knowledge's growth of the community] **Profiling/competence management** [it can formalise each role in the community] **Lessons learned management** [sharing the knowledge among community's members] **Case repository** [the same of 'Lessons Learned Management'] **Organisational directory** [the community can 'know' the exact form of the Organisation] **Workplace support** [support for the community at work]
Combination [Com]	**Categorising unstructured data** [connecting meaningful documents together results in further explicit knowledge] **Hyperlinking** [the same of the previous] **Alerting** [the same of the previous but among people] **Profiling/competence management** [the same of the previous but concerning job, people, skills, competencies] **Lessons learned management** [expliciting a lesson learned needs to make explicit a set of elements such as context, tasks, side effects and relate them] **Organisational directory** [the same as categorising unstructured data but which organisation's elements]
Socialisation [Soc]	**Storytelling** [telling stories is the most directed and unstructured way to share experiences and knowledge] **Forums**[Analysing forum can help to identify hot themes and the best solutions to associate with them.
Externalisation [Ex]	**Interviews and feedback**[helps extract personal knowledge]; **Best practices management**[formalising knowledge about procedures]; **Categorising unstructured data**[attributing information to unstructured data]; **Profiling/competence management**[formalising the skills of employees]; **Forums** [*when properly managed they can make explicit the relationship problem-solution*] **Lessons learned management**[formalising experience in order to accomplish reuse]; **Organisational directory**[formalising the actual structure of the organisation]; **Automatic reasoning**[extract general rules from specific cases];

4 Knowledge Management Tools

In this section we will briefly analyse some knowledge management tools present on the marketplace. The purpose is to extract features from the tools and connect them with the SE practice they can support. The elements treated here will be related with the software engineering practices selected in the previous section, for going straight to the final (but not definitive) map of *KM concepts- SE practices- KM tools*.

This census cannot be considered exhaustive, as it has been limited by the following factors: we have explored a limited slice of the existing marketplace, although supported by some dedicate websites such as KMWorld.com; the analysis of each tool should deserve a more accurate detection that we plan to accomplish in future work.

A classification of tools to manage knowledge inside organisations is provided by [21] as follows:

Knowledge repositories and libraries	Tools for handling repositories of knowledge in the form of documents.
Communities of knowledge workers	Tools to support communities of practise in work; like organising workspaces for communities for online discussions and distributed work.
Knowledge cartography	Tools or mapping and categorising knowledge, from core competence in a company to individual expertise; what we can refer to as meta-knowledge.
The flow of knowledge	Here we find tools for supporting the interaction between tacit knowledge, explicit knowledge and meta-knowledge.

According to this taxonomy, we have extracted a further sub-set of functions, shown in Table 2, and classified a group of tools to build a cross-reference matrix, shown in figure 2, that indicates which tools include which functions. Finally, table 3 shows a map linking KM concepts, SE practices, and KM tools; note that the tools' feature Document Management System, Customisable taxonomy and Web Interfacing, can be considered common to all SE practices.

Sometimes the words '*govern*' and '*management*' refers to the same SE practice, but the former is included in the tool's features column, the latter in the software engineering practices column (i.e. best practices management and best practices govern). When occurring be aware that '*govern*' refers to a set of functions specific of the tool supporting the SE practice, whereas '*management*' refers to the methods for realising the related SE practice that are independent from the specific tool. In addition to the features listed above, the following list presents a group of features that our census has not revealed but that should be considered when working with knowledge:

Inference engine	It can help in the elicitation of an abstract rule from a specific context in the form: problem-solution.
Ontology support system	Ontology can be used in defining knowledge objects, give them a semantics in order to migrate or manipulate them on diverse platforms and contexts.
Domain modelling	Description of the application domain in order to handle domain entities separately from the context.
Automatic reasoning	It defines the kind of action to accomplish relating with a kind of context: it applies a rule problem-solution.

These features help creating, deriving, combining and representing knowledge, and therefore they should be employed in a KM project; however, the census results indicate a very weak diffusion in KM industry.

		Repositories and Libraries						Community of Practices						Cartography					Flow of Knowledge		
	Tool's features	tg	bp	dm	ac	mg	dc	fs	cs	ct	lb	ws	pi	n	wi	d/sm	rep	ep	tv	a	rwr
	Soffront KM[31]		x					x				x					x		x		
	Hyperwave Eknowledge suite [32]		x	x	x			x	x			x					x			x	
	Thebrain EKP[33]		x					x													x
	Knowledge Mail[34]														x	x	x				
T o o l s	Stratify Discovery System[35]		x	x	x	x			x												
	Partecipate Enterprise 2[36]							x	x			x						x	x		
	IT Factory[37]	x		x				x		x							x			x	
	Intraspect 5.5[38]	x	x	x				x	x			x	x		x					x	x

Fig. 2. KM tools- Tools'features

5 Conclusions

Knowledge Management has developed as a multi-disciplinary field of research. Knowledge Management can be considered as structured in three layers and each of them expresses a certain level of abstraction, from the theory to the software tools. Given the increasing attention of the Software Engineering community to these themes and the fitness of some SE practices in implementing certain KM policies, we have drawn a map between KM concepts, SE practices, and KM tools; this aims to create connections among the layers in order to implement KM theories with processes being able to work in real contexts. The work done produced some observations we have grouped according to the three layers structure.

5.1 Software Engineering Practices

Referring to [27], learning inside organisations should be a process that can be activated when bias from expected outcomes occur either when enacting the entire process or when realising a single process' activity. In particular, to accomplish *single and double loop learning* means that *during* each process and activity running in the organisation, the *possible* bias must be detected, registered, analysed and, by executing the proper feedback loop, knowledge database must be properly modified in order to identify the right combination of norms-assumptions-strategies or the right set of organisational actions to realise. Formally speaking NAS should be process models or algorithms whereas Organisational Actions should be, respectively, activity's procedures and code. Thus double loop entails changing process definitions or algorithms, whereas single loop entails changing procedures definition or codes.

In the light of these considerations, SE practices seem to be *static* methodologies to be used when needed and can be useful as a *support* for a *learning process* that can be instantiated when a bias from expected outcomes appears.

Table 2. KM tools' features

Repositories and libraries	*Template govern (Tg)*	Functions included in this category can span all the lifecycle of templates: creation, modification, elimination, distribution throughout different project sites and machines.
	Best practices Govern (Bp)	Best practices enclose previous experience upon critical or problematic situations to be reused. The functions regard: definition according to company standards, storage and retrieval.
	Document Management System(Dm)	Supporting all the lifecycle of documents: version controlling, authoring, editing, and publishing.
	Automatic Characterisation (Ac)	These functions serve automatically building clusters or organising ordered collections of documents that can be explored and scanned for search's ends. In this category similarity operations should be included in order to determine how far two documents present similar *semantic and structural* characteristics.
	Document crawler (Dc)	Capability of selecting a document among a huge set based on a precise set of characteristics.
	Metadata govern (Mg)	Metadata provide information about author, format, history, ownership, content, structure, support, size, and other properties of the document.
Flow of knowledge	*Topics voting (Tv)*	Functions relieving the most central topics for the communities by automatic ranking in order to realise collections of FAQs or solutions ready for use.
	Agents (A)	The use of agents can be oriented to bring notifications, controlling the occurrence of a query or any other activity involved with the control of states on particular database.
	Structures that Reflects real world relationships (Rwr)	These functions serve to create logical relationships between entities forming the knowledge field treated.
Cartography	*Dynamic/static mode(D/Sm)*	Cartography can be designed as *one for all* by a centralised committee of the organisation, allowing different views with respect to the role and the operative needs of the employee or it can be dynamic, in the sense that every worker can create and modify a personal organisation map.
	Relating employee-problems (Rep)	Functions for relating the employee with a specific category of problems. In the class statistics operations and algorithms for rating the most recurrent problems and who has successfully solved them can be included.
	Navigation inside the maps (N)	Maps can be very large and tangled so to make difficult a fast retrieval of wished information. Search functions and navigate functions can turn it in a fitful support to understand organisation competency distribution.
	Web interfacing (Wi)	This function allows the access via web to the overall services of knowledge management.
	Expertise profiling (Ep)	Profiles can help assign the right employee to the project or hire the employee the company needed.
Community of practice	*Forum support (Fs)*	Functions to realise forums. Forums need to be governed and moderated in order to extract the relevant themes of discussion..
	Communication support (Cs)	Devices to cope with distributed projects.
	Customisable taxonomy(Ct)	Functions to define terms and attribute specific for a specific domain.
	Load balance (Lb)	Distribute work load among parties in order to effectively and timely realise tasks
	Workplace support system(Ws)	Management of documents, templates, tools to be used for accomplishing the cue of assigned tasks.
	Personalised intranet interfaces (Pi)	Highlighting relevant links, tools, contacts, documents, web-pages, and handbooks, useful to work.

Table 3. KM Concepts- SE Practices-KM Tools map

Document management Ex	*Automatic reasoning; Metadata govern; Document crawler;*	*Document management system; Customisable taxonomy; Web interfacing; Cntology support*
Interviews and feedback forms Ex	*Template govern; Inference engine; Communication support;*	
Storytelling Soc	*Template govern; Communication support; Domain modelling;*	
Hyperlinking Com	*Automatic characterisation; Metadata govern ;Automatic reasoning; Inference engine;*	
Best practices management ToA, Ex	*Template govern; Best practices govern; Topics voting; Automatic reasoning; Inference engine;Domain modelling; Document crawler; Automatic characterisation;*	
Categorising unstructured data Com, Ex	*Automatic characterisation; Metadata govern; Automatic reasoning; Inference engine; Domain modelling; Document crawler;*	
Profiling/competence management LtP, Com,Ex	*Navigation inside maps; Dynamic/static mode; Relating employeeproblems; Expertise profiling; Structure that reflects real world relationships; Automatic reasoning; Domain modelling;*	
Forums ToA, Soc,Ex	*Forum support; Topics voting; Automatic reasoning; Inference engine; communication support;*	
Lessons learned management ToA, LtP,Com,Ex	*Automatic characterisation; Template govern; Automatic reasoning; Inference engine; Domain modelling; Document crawler; Automatic characterisation;*	
Alerting LtP	*Agents; Inference engine; Automatic reasoning;*	
Case repository LtP	*Structure that reflects real world relationships; Template govern; Domain modelling;*	
Organisational directory LtP,Com,Ex	*Structure that reflects real world relationships; Template govern; Relating employee problem;*	
Workplace support LtP	*Communication support; Load balance; Workplace support system; Personalised intranet interfaces;*	

For *learning through participation (LTP)* it is important a continuous assessment of the community evolution. If we consider the set of business goals, competencies maps, organisation procedures, policies and practices as the *state* of the organisation, the purpose of LTP is to mutate the state of the organisation according to the variation occurring in the real context. Although there is not a consolidate model to describe the evolution of Communities of Practice (CoPs), some proprietary models have been proposed in the literature. For example, the US Navy [30] and IBM [29] propose a CoPs assessment model based on 5 states. While the states are different, it is possible to draw equivalences among the models, as demonstrated in table 4.

For properly realising LtP, CoP's evolution should be ever monitored during all the community's operation and causes of regression should be timely identified and removed. That purpose may be reached by using the listed SE practices, but organised in a systematic process that helps keep under control CoP's state and that specifies the procedures to make changes in CoP when needed. This process should be defined and metrics to evaluate its capability should be established.

Table 4. CoP's Evolution states

[29]	[30]
Potential	Potential
Coalescing	Building
Active	Engaged
	Active
	Adaptative
Dispersed	-
Memorable	-

5.2   Knowledge Management Tools

The current market landscape seems to ignore the contribute coming from knowledge based systems. All the past experience in research and industry on these themes are scarcely integrated in available tools. In the view of knowledge management theories the capability of defining a domain model at a high abstraction level, the elicitation of rules by automatic reasoning for determining the pairs problem-solution, the exploitation of a inference engine to determine generic descriptions of a context to be reused in similar ones constitute the grounded features.

There is no a kind of standardisation about what is a knowledge management function. Some key functions of knowledge management theory are scarcely implemented, such as: expertise profiling, template govern, best practices, and customisable taxonomy.

Currently, it seems that communities of practice have a stead support from industry, especially with regard to communication means such as forums, e-mails, bulletin boards, FAQs and chats. However, it is not clear how the process of *obtaining* explicit knowledge from all these means can be supported.

5.3   Future Works

Starting from previous considerations we are planning controlled experiments in order validate two indicators, an economic one and a strategic one to measure the degree of learning within learning organisations.

Considering that learning can be accomplished basing on QIP methodologies and exploiting the technology of Experience Factory, the two indicators are inserted in a mathematical model, aiming at monitoring the degree of learning corresponding to the efficiency of the Organisational Experience Factory. The economic indicator provides for evaluation of the return of Investment of the Experience Factory. The strategic one helps defining improvement initiatives for the Experience Base in order to put organisation in position of effectively learning. The research program may be a starting point to give knowledge inside organization a measurable value in order to hook first layer theories with a formal control and validation tool.

References

[1]   Choo, C., W.: The Knowing Organization. How organizations use information to construct meaning, create knowledge, and make decision. Oxford University Press (1998).

[2]   Choo, C., W.: Sensemaking, Knowledge Creation, and Decision Making: Organisational knowing as emergent strategy. In: Choo, C.,W., Bontis, N. (eds.): Strategic Management of Intellectual Capital and Organisational Knowledge. Oxford Univ Press (2001).

[3]   Staab, S., Studer, R., Schnurr, H. P., Sure, Y.: Knowledge Processes and Ontologies. IEEE Intelligent Systems Vol.16 N°1 (2001) 26-34.

[4]   Guarino, N., Welty, C.: Evaluating Ontological Decisions with OntoClean. Communications of the ACM Vol.45 N°2 (2002) 61-65.

[5]   Chung, H.,M., Gray, P., Mannino, M.: Introduction to Data Mining and Knowledge discovery. Proceedings of Thirty-First Annual Hawaii International Conference on System Sciences (1998) 244-247.

[6]   Yen, S.,J., Chen, A.,L.,P.: An Efficient Data Mining Technique for Discovering Interesting Association Rules. 8th International Workshop on Database and Expert Systems Applications (1997) 664-670.

[7]   Cybenko, G.: Machine Learning. Computing in Science and Engineering Vol.3 N°3 (2001) 95-96.

[8]   Bischof, F., W., Caelli, T.: Scene Understanding by Rule Evaluation. IEEE Transactions on Pattern Analysis and Machine Intelligence Vol.19 N°11(1997) 1284-1288.

[9]   Rus, I., Lindvall M,: Knowledge Management in Software Engineering. IEEE Software Vol.19 N°3 (2002) 26-38.

[10]   Holsapple C., W., Joshi, K., D.: A Collaborative Approach to Ontology Design. Communications of the ACM Vol.45 N°2 (2002) 42-47.

[11]   Basili, V., R., Schneider, K., von Hunnius, J., P.: Experience in Implementing a Learning Software Organisation. IEEE Software Vol.19 N°3 (2002) 46-49.

[12]   Basili, V., R., Caldiera, G., Rombach, D., H.: The Experience Factory. In: Encyclopedia of Software Engineering. John and Wiley & Sons, New York (1994) 469-476.

[13]   Rus, I., Lindvall, M., Sinha, S., S.: Knowledge Management in Software Engineering. A State-of-the-Art-Report. Fraunhofer Center for Experimental Software Engineering Maryland and the University of Maryland for Data and Analysis Center for Software, Department of Defence, USA (2001): http://www.isr.umd.edu/~sachinss/KMSE_Sachin.pdf

[14]   Liebowitz, J.: A Look at NASA Goddard Space Flight Center's Knowledge Management Initiatives. IEEE Software Vol.19 N°3 (2002) 40-42.

[15]   Wei, C., P., Hu, P., J., H., Chen, H., H.: Design and Evaluation of Knowledge Management System. IEEE Software Vol.19 N°3 (2002) 56-59.

[16]   Karypis, G.: Data Mining. IEEE Computing in Science and Engineering Vol.4 N°4 (2002) 12-13.

[17]   Stata, R.: Organizational learning: The Key to Management Innovation. In: Starkey, K.(ed): How organizations learn. Thomson Business Press, London (1996) 316–334.

[18]   Choo C.W.: Working with Knowledge: How Information Professionals Help Organisations Manage What They Know. Library Management Vol.21 N°8 (2000).

[19]   Wenger, E.(ed.): Communities of Practise: Learning, Meaning and Identity. Cambridge University Press, New Jork (1998).

[20]   Kolb, D.: Experiential Learning: Experiences as the Source of Learning and Development. Prentice Hall, Englcwood Cliffs, NJ (1984).

[21]   Dingsøyr, T.: Knowledge Management in Medium-Sized Software Consulting Companies. An investigation of Intranet-Based Knowledge Management Tools for Knowledge Cartography and Knowledge Repositories for Learning Software Organisations. Tapir Trykkeri, Trondheim (2002).

[22]   Mack, R., Ravin, Y., Byrd, R.,J.: Knowledge Portals and the Engineering Digital Knowledge Workplace. IBM Systems Journal Vol.40 N°4 (2001).

[23]   Preece, A., Flett, A., Sleeman, D., Curry, D., Meany, N., Perry, P.: Better Knowledge Management through Knowledge Engineering. IEEE Intelligent Systems Vol.16 N°1 (2001) 36-43.

[24]   Davenport, T., H.: Knowledge Management Case Study. Knowledge Management at Miscrosoft. (1997).
        http://www.bus.utexas.edu/kman/miscrosoft.htm.

[25]   Basili, V., R.: Quantitative Evaluation of Software Engineering Methodology. Proceedings of the First Pan Pacific Computer Conference (1985).

[26]   Nonaka, I., Takeuchi, H.: The Knowledge-Creating Company: How Japanese Companies Create the Dynamics of Innovation. Oxford University Press, New York, NY (1995).

[27]   Argyris, C., Schön, D.,A.: Organisational Learning: a Theory of Action Perspective. Addison-Wesley, Reading, MA (1978).

[28]   Lehman, M., M.: FEAST/2 Final report- Grant Number GR/M44101. (2001).
        http://www.doc.ic.ac.uk/~mml/feast2/papers/pdf/683.pdf

[29]   Congla, P. Rizzuto, C.,R.: Evolving Communities of Practice: IBM Global Experience. IBM Systems Journal Vol.40 N°4 (2001).

[30]   Community of Practice Practioner's Guide. Version 1.0a. (2001).
        http://www.km.gov/documents/DoN_CoP_Practitioner's_Guide_ver_1.doc

[31]   http://www.soffront.com
[32]   http://www.hyperwave.com/
[33]   http://www.thebrain.com/
[34]   http://www.stiknowledge.com/
[35]   http://www.stratify.com/
[36]   http://www.participate.com/
[37]   http://www.itfactory.com/
[38]   http://www.intraspect.com/
[39]   http://www.dipnet.it/

What Are the Knowledge Needs during the Project Lifecycle in an Expert Organisation?

Susanna Peltola, Maarit Tihinen, and Päivi Parviainen

VTT Technical Research Centre of Finland
P.O.Box 1100, FIN-90571 Oulu, Finland
{susanna.peltola,maarit.tihinen}@vtt.fi
paivi.parviainen@vtt.fi
http://www.vtt.fi/ele/indexe.htm
fax: +358 8 551 2320

Abstract. Every organisation has to acquire, create, store, distribute and use knowledge in order to operate effectively, or simply to be able to operate in the first place. Knowledge is needed during projects and tools can be used for supporting projects' knowledge management. However, it has proven to be difficult to find the best suitable tool for a specific project and to determine the requirements for a knowledge management tool that would enable supporting projects in an efficient way. This paper describes how knowledge needs for supporting the project lifecycle have been defined in an expert organisation and what the knowledge needs are in the different roles of the organisation. It was found that the main knowledge needs were the experiences and the main results from ongoing and closed projects, along with project specific information like used tools and methods.

1   Introduction

One of the largest problems facing companies today is the management of software development: it is estimated that only 18 % of completed software projects are within budget or on time [1]. Examples of causes for these problems are [1] insufficient project planning, and inexperienced or poorly trained project managers. Experienced project managers will know, e.g., if the estimations are unrealistic or if the project is creeping. To do that they combine their experience with the information of the project, that is, they use their knowledge. Thus, project management, and project work in general, should be supported with the right knowledge during the project lifecycle. One way to do that is to collect and to share the knowledge created during the project work.

Knowledge management (KM) has been widely researched [2], [3], [4] during the past years, thus at present there's plenty of knowledge available of its nature, concerns and its meaning for organisations. Knowledge is considered an important immaterial asset for expert organisations [5] and thus KM is understood to be

M. Oivo and S. Komi-Sirviö (Eds.): PROFES 2002, LNCS 2559, pp. 423-435, 2002.

necessary for spreading knowledge in an organisation. However, not much research has been conducted on the knowledge needs during projects or on the KM tools supporting those needs. It is true that discussion or face-to face meetings, for example, are the best ways to transfer knowledge, but a KM tool can add value to knowledge transfer if an expert is not available at a certain time. A KM tool also supports the storing and spreading of knowledge in an organisation. KM tools alone cannot make KM successful [6], [7] but with the right knowledge content and with an appropriate KM tool projects can be supported [8].

An experience factory [9] can be used to collect and share knowledge between individuals in an organisation, but creating, building and maintaining the experience factory needs resources and time. In addition, experience repositories are often focused on project management, collecting lessons learned at the end of the projects and enabling their use for planning and estimating project effort [9], [11]. Instead of analyzing project planning or estimation this paper focuses on investigating knowledge needs to support projects throughout the project lifecycle. Thus, the right knowledge content in a KM tool is seen as an important aspect in motivating to use the tool.

The research described in this paper was carried out at the Technical Research Center of Finland (VTT). VTT is an independent and impartial expert organisation that carries out technical and techno-economic research and development work. VTT consists of research areas, each containing several research groups with different research foci. The motivation for defining the knowledge management needs in one particular research area was given by the results of a staff survey, which showed that knowledge sharing between research groups was not efficient enough.

Our main research problem was to find out the knowledge needs of the experts during the project lifecycle. A secondary aim was to clarify what kind of KM tool support would benefit the experts most. A plentiful supply of various KM tools [18] exists, but the aim was not to introduce a new tool, but rather to make as much use of the existing KM solutions in place at VTT as possible.

The research method was a survey for gathering the knowledge needs and essential requirements for using KM tools, and a case study for implementing a KM tool to fulfil the requirements not covered by the existing tools. The results show that the knowledge needs of the experts vary depending on their respective roles in the expert organisation.

This paper has been structured as follows: in section two, the research background and a number of concepts and definitions central to this paper are introduced. Section three presents the results of our case study, and the results are discussed and generalised in section four. Finally, in section five the conclusions and some ideas for further work are presented.

2   Background

Knowledge is neither data nor information, although it is related to both; knowledge includes both data and information. Data is facts about events, and it describes what has happened, but it doesn't include any interpretation about the event. Information can describe a message that has a sender and a receiver. The purpose of information is to change the way the receiver perceives something and to make an impact to her/his judgement and behaviour. Knowledge is more; it is a dynamic blend of experience, values, contextual information and expert insight. This kind of knowledge provides a framework for evaluating and incorporating new experiences and information. [2].

One of the aims of KM is to bring information in its many forms effectively into action [12]. KM is the process of managing the processes of acquiring, creating, storing and sharing knowledge [14]. Knowledge acquisition is the collection and codification of new knowledge. Knowledge creation is the creation of new knowledge from the ground of the previous knowledge. Knowledge storing is the storing of the collected knowledge for further use. Knowledge sharing is spreading the knowledge in organisation from one individual to another.

Strictly speaking, only individuals can create knowledge, thus suitable circumstances must be built for knowledge creation in the organisation. Knowledge can be divided into two general categories: tacit and explicit. Tacit knowledge is of personal and context-specific kind, and it is hard to formalise and share with others, while explicit knowledge is transmittable in formal, systematic language. Individuals possess created knowledge and their knowledge should be made visible to others in the organisation. This means that the organisational knowledge creation process should be understood as a process of amplifying individual knowledge and generalising knowledge into the knowledge network of the organisation. [3]

The work and results in this paper are based on work done in an expert organisation. Generally, expert organisation is understood as an organisation producing immaterial services, which are usually largely dependent on individual experts' knowledge and skills. This expert knowledge is needed, for example, if the customer is not able to demand the kind of service that would be the most beneficial to her/him. In that case, the experts must be able to offer the service that will fulfil the customer's immediate needs, but that will also consider long-term customer needs. These kinds of expert services depend largely on individuals: different experts gain different experiences and information about the customers and other issues. Thus, experts are unique. [15]

2.1   The Role of Tool Support in KM

The purpose of a KM tool is to support the KM processes: acquiring, storing and sharing knowledge in an organisation. The relationship between tools and KM can be described as a synergy: tools can help the individuals within the organisation when the existing knowledge is stored somewhere and there is an opportunity to efficiently search from this storage [16]. On the other hand, although information technology makes connections to storage possible, it does not make it actually happen [4].

Organisational activities can be made more effective by improving the knowledge sharing process within an organisation [4]. Also, the value of products offered by an organisation can be increased with enhanced KM [5]. Knowledge can be stored at various storage places, which constitutes an organisational memory. Thus knowledge can be searched from this storage rather than from sources outside of organisation. Although a number of tools have been developed to support the managing of knowledge [17], [18], it is not tool support alone that will make KM efficient – changes are also required in behaviour, culture and organisation [2]. Knowledge acquiring, sharing, and storing must be connected to the work practices of the organisation.

Different tools can be used to support the KM processes of creating, acquiring, storing and sharing knowledge. The role of the tools varies depending on the specific KM process. Knowledge acquiring, storing and sharing can be directly supported with tools, but for knowledge creation the tool support is of indirect nature. Tool support is essential for knowledge acquisition and it often can also ease and speed up the knowledge sharing activities. Figure 1 presents the support tools as used in the different KM processes.

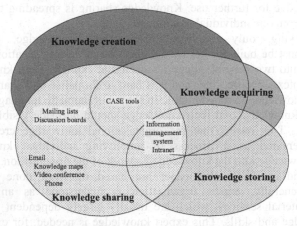

Fig. 1. Tool support for KM processes

Tools cannot make knowledge creation happen, but they can provide vital support by making acquired and codified knowledge available to all in an organisation [3]. Created knowledge should be collected and stored for further use, since knowledge that is created but not collected can disappear from the organisation when, for example, an expert leaves. An information management system forms a good basis for this purpose, since teamwork requires everybody to have access to the information and knowledge storage of the organisation [12]. Tacit and explicit knowledge sharing set different requirements for the tools. For example, while videoconference tools and ordinary phones can be regarded as good tools for sharing tacit knowledge [2], explicit knowledge sharing can, at its best, be supported with tools such as information management systems, Intranets, discussion boards, mailing lists, email, and CASE tools [4].

Knowledge creation, acquiring, storing and sharing can be supported with tools and thus support project work. Accordingly, the knowledge produced in one project can be made visible in that project and be shared with other projects as well. This requires that the knowledge needs of the project and the importance of these needs to project members or managers be clarified in order to include the right information in the tool.

2.2   Prerequisites for Using a KM Tool

Besides appropriate KM support tools and organisation culture, it is very important for effective KM to get a picture of the knowledge dealt with in the projects [19]. This can be done by finding the answers to the following questions: What knowledge is needed? Who needs the knowledge? Where is the knowledge needed? When is the knowledge needed? What process activity provides this knowledge? [19]. Providing answers to these questions will facilitate future knowledge acquisition.

Knowledge can be stored in a knowledge storage, and the specific needs of the organisation should guide what knowledge is worth acquiring and saving in the storage [6]. Knowledge can become information or even data if the volume of knowledge in storage is too high [2]. The knowledge worth acquiring and storing should be chosen so that it helps the organisation, projects and experts to better achieve their goals. Too much information and knowledge can cause an information glut for the employees [12].

Before the tools supporting KM exist in the organisation, it is difficult to predict how willing the individuals are to use the tools. This can be found out only after the tools have been implemented. [2]. The use of new tools is easily opposed, because at first they are likely to cause some extra workload and training needs [4]. KM tools are capable of supporting KM only when they meet the actual knowledge needs of the individuals and the organisation. Adjusting the tool properties to the needs of the experts working with the tool provides an effective means of promoting tool use within the organisation. In short, the qualities and features of the tool have to meet the requirements of the respective organisation.

3   Defining Knowledge Needs and Tool Requirements for Expert Organisations

The following results are gained from a survey that was conducted in the Embedded Software research area at VTT Electronics, including 80 employees. The research area contains several research groups with different research foci. The motivation for this work was given by the results of a staff survey made at VTT, which showed that knowledge sharing between research groups was not efficient enough. This study has been reported in more detail in a master's thesis [8].

The data for this survey was collected with a semi-structured questionnaire, which was delivered to all employees. The questionnaire comprised open questions and structured ones. The questions were prepared so that the knowledge needs, the organisation culture and the technical requirements for the tool could be clarified. The questionnaire also fathomed out the respondent's role, the knowledge needs of the different roles, and the importance of the knowledge needs of the various roles. In addition, the willingness for tool use and any prohibitive or restrictive factors for using the tool were considered.

The response rate was 57%, thus the amount of answers can be considered large enough, so that one respondent's answer does not have too great an effect on the results. Seeing that the percentage of return was so high, it can be concluded that the employees mainly perceive finding the knowledge needs and tool support for KM as an important matter.

3.1   Roles and Knowledge Needs

Figure 2 presents the importance of knowledge needs for all respondents. The knowledge needs have been arranged according to the total amount of responses. The figure also shows the relative importance of specific knowledge needs to the respondents (first, second or third).

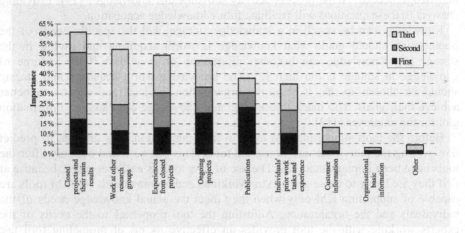

Fig. 2. Importance of knowledge needs for all respondents

The results were further elaborated and the knowledge needs - and their relative importance – in relation to each role of the organisation were analysed, as presented in Figure 3. The human figures represent the roles and the numbers with lines show the importance of specific knowledge needs to this role. The knowledge needs and their contents are presented in respective boxes.

In the role of line manager the person occupying the position is superior to project managers and other personnel. The project manager, again, is responsible for managing a project. Research scientists, for their part, are members of a project and perform executive work within this project. In the expert research organisation of our study, project managers are typically research scientists, but in the role of project manager their knowledge needs differ from those of research scientists. Line managers include group managers and the research manager.

The knowledge needs of line managers are directed towards ongoing and closed projects. They have a need to track the progress of ongoing projects. As their tasks involve preparing future projects, the information and experiences from closed and on-going projects will help them in this work. The information about other groups' projects will also facilitate building co-operative projects, in which groups can combine their competence.

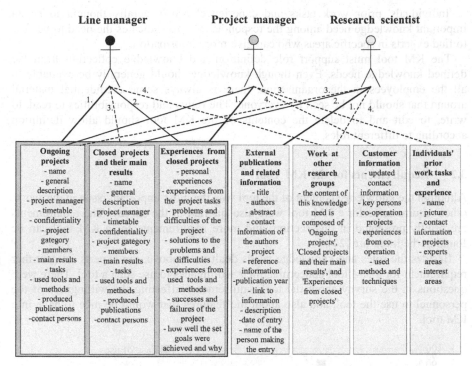

Fig. 3. Knowledge needs of different roles and content of knowledge needs

Project managers need information about closed projects, their results and experiences. This information will help them to make detailed plans for new projects. The need for individual expert areas and customer information is related to project planning, too. The individual information will help project managers to select project members, while customer information will facilitate co-operation with the project customer.

Research scientists are in charge of the executive work of the project and according to the survey one of their main knowledge needs is the one concerning publications - publications produced by both projects and externally produced publications. Research scientists also need to have access to knowledge about the ongoing and closed projects of all groups. The results and publications of these projects may be useful to research scientists in their work within the project at hand.

At further analysis of 'Ongoing projects' and 'Closed projects and their main results' revealed that the contents of these are relatively similar. As also the 'Experiences from closed projects' were related to project information, all these three knowledge needs were combined into a single knowledge need. This new knowledge need was named 'Project'. The knowledge need 'Project' is marked in Figure 3 with an extra box. Also the knowledge need 'Work at other research groups' has a similar content to the combined knowledge need 'Project'. Yet this need has been marked separately in the figure, since it contains the knowledge about the projects at other groups. The large amount of attributes needs to be considered when tool requirements are defined.

'Individuals' prior work tasks and experience' was generally thought to be an important knowledge need among the respondents. This indicates the need to be able to find experts in specific areas who can give more information.

The KM tool must support role definition and knowledge collection from the defined knowledge needs. Even though knowledge should generally be available to all the employees in the organisation, there is always some confidential material around that should not be seen by everyone. The rights and responsibilities to read, to write, to edit and to delete the contents of the KM tool should allow definition according to different roles.

3.2   Requirements for the KM Tool

Although the knowledge content of the tool was the most important issue in our work, other requirements for a KM tool were also queried in the survey. The requirements are briefly presented in this section, and more requirements for a KM tool can be found in the literature [20].

Besides the roles and knowledge needs dealt with above, the experts set a further requirement for a KM tool concerning their willingness to use such a tool. There were questions in the survey about the tool requirements affecting the willingness of the personnel to use the tool, and also about the features that would be nice to have in a KM tool.

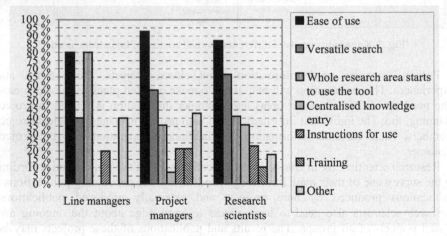

Fig. 4. Requirements affecting the willingness to use the tool

The most important requirements that were set for a KM tool were ease of use, versatile search and that everyone should use the tool. These requirements were considered more important than training or instructions of use. Those respondents that had chosen the 'Other' option, cited requirements like 'rich, relevant and updated content', 'tool must be connected to present work practices', 'tool must be so easy to use that no training is needed', and 'tool must contain a help function' (Figure 4).

The most popular 'nice to have requirements' for a KM tool were 'announcement when new knowledge has been added to tool according to user profile', 'browser user interface', 'guided knowledge addition', and 'user profile with the possibility of editing it.

The survey provided information also about factors that would restrict the use of a KM tool. The most important reason for not using a KM tool was that the content of the KM tool was outdated. Another factor undermining the readiness to use the tool cited by the respondents was irrelevant tool content.

On the basis of the requirements worked out, a KM tool is being implemented at VTT Electronics. The tool will support knowledge acquisition, sharing and storing about projects, project experiences, publications, project related information, and individual experiences. The tool will enter into a piloting phase next autumn.

4   Generalisation of Requirements

The outcome of our requirement definition process is that the knowledge needs – thus also the requirements for the content of a KM tool - vary a lot depending on both the roles in the target organisation and the phase of the target project life cycle. Figure 5 presents the knowledge needs of the various roles in the different project lifecycle phases.

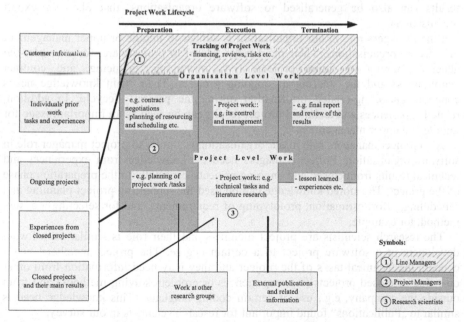

Fig. 5. Knowledge needs supporting project work

In Figure 5, the lifecycle of project is divided into three main phases: preparation, execution and termination. The colours represent the roles (research scientists, project managers, or line managers) marked with numbers 1 to 3 in the figure. Project phases have been coloured according to which role is emphasised in the respective phase.

The boxes represent the knowledge needs. They have been connected with actual project phases with lines, the thickness of which shows the relative importance of each individual knowledge need.

The importance of the KM processes - creating, acquiring, storing, sharing - can be seen to vary during the project life cycle according to the defined knowledge needs. The knowledge sharing process can be regarded to have an important role during project preparation, while the exact content of knowledge also needs to be investigated and defined. Only this way can the right content of knowledge needs be implemented for a KM tool, and the knowledge sharing process be supported during the project life cycle.

In the execution phase of the project lifecycle, the knowledge creation and acquiring process is emphasised. The last phase of the project lifecycle is focused on the knowledge collection and storing process. Final reviews are held and final reports are prepared in this project phase. For example, the lessons learned and experiences of the project should be gathered and stored for further use based on the defined knowledge needs of the organisation.

4.1   Roles and Knowledge Needs

Although this research was targeted at and carried out in a research organisation, the results can also be generalised to software organisations, that also are expert organisations.

Line managers role in our organisation is similar to middle or upper management in software organisations. Their main tasks related to projects are, for example, the general planning of future projects (e.g. resourcing, financing, and contract negotiations) and the steering of ongoing projects. Their main knowledge needs concern controlling-related information during the project lifecycle. In addition, related experiences and technical project results can be seen as an important issue for middle and upper management.

Also project managers role in our organisation is similar to project manager role in software organisation. Project managers need the knowledge from experiences and technical results from closed and ongoing projects, especially in the preparation phase of the project. The stored knowledge can be used for supporting project planning and scheduling, effort estimation, prototyping of requirements, and for selecting a design method, for example.

The research scientists are project members and their role is similar to software developers in a software project to a certain degree. The project members' needs concern the technical tasks of the project and they may need information from other on-going or closed projects (e.g. experiences or problem solving methods) and from outside the company, e.g., use of certain coding language. This knowledge need is similar to „Publications" found important for research scientists in our survey.

4.2   General Requirements for a KM Tool

The right content of a KM tool is one of the most motivating aspects for its deployment. The content of the stored knowledge should be based on the knowledge needs of project work: the knowledge needs of each role can be considered 'content' requirements for a KM tool. There can be several other tools (e.g. electronic news boards, program libraries or knowledge maps) supporting project execution in the organisation. Therefore, the specification of the knowledge content should be done carefully also taking existing tools into consideration to avoid overlaps.

To benefit most of a KM tool, it should be taken into use in the whole organisation. We, therefore, suggest that the use of the tool is connected with project activities through a quality assurance process. The use of KM tools should be made part of standard work practices. Also, the organisational culture should be supportive to knowledge sharing process. In addition, the deployment of a KM tool could be supported, for example, by introducing bonuses, because at first tool use is likely to demand some extra effort, as knowledge needs to be stored into the tool.

5   Conclusions and Further Work

Project management and project work should be supported with the right knowledge during the whole project lifecycle. However, not much research has been conducted on the knowledge needs of the individuals during projects or on the KM tools supporting those needs.

We found that the knowledge needs – thus also the requirements for the KM tool content – vary a lot depending on both the roles and the phase of the target project life cycle. The right content of a KM tool is one of the most motivating aspects for the deployment of the tool. Although this research was targeted at and carried out in a research organisation, the results can also be generalised to software organisations, since they also are expert organisations.

As the result of our research, it was found that the most important knowledge needs were the experiences and the main results (e.g., publications) from ongoing or closed projects, along with project specific information (e.g., used tools and methods), which could be searched later when information is needed. Further, it can be stated that successful tool support requires that the knowledge needs - the content of a KM tool - are specified in the organisation. The tool should also address other requirements – such as versatile search, or user-friendliness.

The trial version of the KM tool will be piloted and further developed on the basis of the experiences gained from piloting. Our future research will be concerned with a further investigation into how useful the developed tool is for the different roles and how well the knowledge needs could be defined within this study.

Acknowledgement

The research has been carried out within TOTEM2001, the strategic research project at VTT Electronics, and the results have been further processed within the Knots-Q project[1], partially funded by the Academy of Finland. The authors would like to thank the founding organisations, and the employees of VTT for answering the survey and

---

[1] http://knots-q.vtt.fi/

giving their valuable input for the requirement specification process. Special thanks are due to Seija Komi-Sirviö for her valuable comments during the writing process.

References

1. Dufner, D., Kwon, O., Doty, A.: Improving software development project team performance: a Web-based expert support system for project control. Proceedings of the 32nd Annual Hawaii International Conference on Systems Sciences: HICSS-32 Hawaii (1999)
2. Davenport, T.H., Prusak, L.: Working Knowledge. Harvard Business School Press, Boston (1998)
3. Nonaka, I., Takeuchi, H.: The Knowledge-Creating Company. Oxford University Press, New York (1995)
4. O'Dell, C., Grayson, C. J. Jr.: If only we knew what we know: the transfer of internal knowledge and best practice. The Free Press, New York (1998)
5. Brooking, A.: Corporate Memory: Strategies for KM. International Thomson Business Press, London (1999)
6. Komi-Sirviö, S., Mäntyniemi, A., Seppänen, V. Toward a Practical Solution for Capturing Knowledge for Software Projects. IEEE Computer Society. IEEE Software May/June 2002. Pp. 60-62
7. Kuzca, T., Komi-Sirviö, S.: Utilising KM in Software Process Improvement - The Creation of a KM Process Model. Proceedings of the 7th International Conference on Concurrent Enterprising: ICE 2001. University of Nottingham - Centre for Concurrent Enterprising, Nottigham (2001)
8. Peltola, S.: Master's thesis: Tool Support for Knowledge Management in an Expert Organisation. University of Oulu (2002) (in finnish)
9. Basili, V.R.:The Experience Factory and its Relationship to Other Improvement Paradigms. Proceedings of the 4th European Software Engineering Conference: ESEC '93. Garmisch-Partenkirchen, Germany (1993)
10. Engelkamp, S., Hartkopf, S., Brössler, P.: Project Experience Database: A Report Based on First Practical Experience. Proceedings of the Second International Conference on Product Focused Software Process Improvement. Oulu, Finland (2000)
11. Tautz, C.: PhD thesis: Customizing Software Engineering Experience Management Systems to Organisational Needs. University of Kaiserslautern (2000)
12. Van den Hoven, J.: Information Resource Management: Foundation for KM. http://www.brint.com/members/01060524/irmkm/irmkm_1.html   (9.7.2001) (2001)
13. Allweyer, T. A.: Framework for Re-Designing and Managing Knowledge Processes. http://www.processworld.com/content/docs/8.doc (12.6.2000) (1997)
14. Kuzca, T.: KM Process Model. VTT Publications 455. VTT Electronics, Espoo (2001)
15. Sipilä, J.: Asiantuntijapalveluiden markkinointi. Weilin+Göös, Porvoo (1996) (in finnish)

16. Newman, B., Conrad, K.: A Framework for Characterizing KM Methods, Practices, and Technologies. http://www.metakm.com/article.php?sid=117 (9.7.2001) (1999)
17. Kucza, T., Nättinen, M., Peltola, S. Tools and Techniques for Knowledge Management. Internal report. VTT Electronics, Oulu (2001)
18. Rus, I., Lindvall, M., Sinha, S. S. Knowledge Management in Software Engineering A State-of-the-Art-Report. Fraunhofer Center for Experimental Software Engineering Maryland and The University of Maryland http://www.cebase.org/umd/dacs_reports/kmse_-_nicholls_final_edit_11-16-01.pdf (12.8.2002) (2001)
19. Wiig, K.-E., de Hoog, R., van der Spek, R.: Supporting KM: A Selection of Methods and Techniques. Expert Systems With Applications, Vol. 13, No. 1. (1997) 15-27
20. Senge, P.M.: The Fifth Discipline: The Art & Practice of Learning Organisation. Century Business, London (1993)

Consensus Building when Comparing Software Architectures

Mikael Svahnberg and Claes Wohlin

Department of Software Engineering and Computer Science
Blekinge Institute of Technology, PO Box 520, S-372 25 Ronneby, Sweden
{mikael.svahnberg,claes.wohlin}@bth.se
http://www.ipd.bth.se/serl

Abstract. When designing a software system it is beneficial to study and use architectural styles from literature, to ensure certain quality attributes. However, as the interpretation of literature may differ depending on the background and area of expertise of the person reading the literature, we suggest that structured discussions about different architecture candidates provides more valuable insight not only in the architectures themselves, but in peoples' opinions of the architectures' benefits and liabilities. In this paper, we propose a method to elicit the views of individuals concerning architecture candidates for a software system and pinpoint where discussions are needed to come to a consensus view of the architectures.

1   Introduction

When developing software, it is important to have an appropriate architecture for the system, or sub-systems comprising the full system. The choice of, or evolution into, an appropriate architecture is not only governed by functional requirements, but to a large extent by quality attributes [2][2][4][2][4][6].

However, knowing this, it is still a non-trivial task to discern between architecture candidates. There are usually more than one quality attribute involved in a system, and the knowledge of the benefits and drawbacks of different architecture structures with respect to different quality attributes is not yet an exact science. Decisions are often taken on intuition, relying on the experience of senior software developers.

Moreover, because decisions are taken in this ad-hoc manner, there may be perspectives and issues that are not brought to attention before a decision is taken. Different software engineers may have different experiences with similar software systems and similar quality attributes, and it is important that these differing views are also heard before a decision is taken.

To alleviate the identification of these differing opinions and to base the decisions on a firmer ground than mere intuition it is important, we believe, to be able to compare software architecture structures based on quantified data. Likewise, it is important to be able to compare the strengths and weaknesses of a single software

M. Oivo and S. Komi-Sirviö (Eds.): PROFES 2002, LNCS 2559, pp. 436–452, 2002.

architecture structure based on quantified data. If this is not done, there will always be subjective judgements involved when selecting between architecture structures.

What is even more important is that everyone involved in designing a software architecture share the same view of what benefits and drawbacks different architecture structures have. To do this, it is important that the views of different persons are extracted in a quantified way that enables comparisons between the views, and a synthesis of the different views into a unified consensus view. If this is not done, misunderstandings caused by the differing views are likely to emerge later during development, and may introduce severe problems.

We propose that the understanding of architectures starts with eliciting the knowledge of individuals and that structured discussions should be held to reach a further understanding and learn from others during the process of building consensus around the benefits and liabilities of different architecture candidates. After this is done, the senior software architect is able to take a more informed decision based on the collective experiences from the entire software design team.

It should be noted that we use the term „software system" rather loosely in this paper. We use it to mean any software entity, be it an entire product suite, a single product, a subsystem within a product, a software module, or a software component.

1.1   Scope and Goal of Paper

In this paper, we describe a process for capturing knowledge from individuals into a framework that enables analysis of and comparison between software architectures with respect to quality attributes. In the process of synthesizing this framework, the views of the individuals participating in the process are extracted and presented in a way that enables and facilitates discussion where the participants are in disagreement. The purpose of these discussions is to create a joint understanding of the benefits and liabilities of the different software architectures.

Illustration. Throughout this paper we illustrate each step with data and experiences from conducting the step with the participation of colleagues, who have also participated in creating the initial data sets in a previously conducted experiment, described in further detail in [17].

We would like to stress the fact that even if we in this experiment used generic architecture structures and quality attributes one would, if using the method in a company, develop architecture candidates and elicit quality requirements for a particular system rather than using generic architectures and quality attributes. The method would thus operate on architectures that can be used in the particular system. Likewise, the quality attributes used would be elicited for the particular system, and would hence be expressed in terms pertinent to the system's problem domain.

Moreover, the focus of this paper is mainly on the process described and the discussion of this rather than on the example, which is mostly included to illustrate the different steps.

We would like to mention that we have also recently applied the ideas in this paper in a case study together with an industry partner with the purpose of validating the described method. Without going into details of this study, the results are mostly positive and the final analysis of the data from the study is progressing rapidly.

Paper Outline. The remainder of this paper is organized as follows. In Section 1.2 we present an outline of the process proposed in this paper. In Section 2 we present how to create individual views, discuss these and combine them to a unified framework. In Section 3 we present how to evaluate this unified framework, and in Section 4 we present how to analyse it. Finally, the paper is concluded in Section 5.

1.2   Outline of Process

The process we describe in this paper consists of the following five steps (also illustrated in Figure 1), each of which we go through in further detail in this paper:

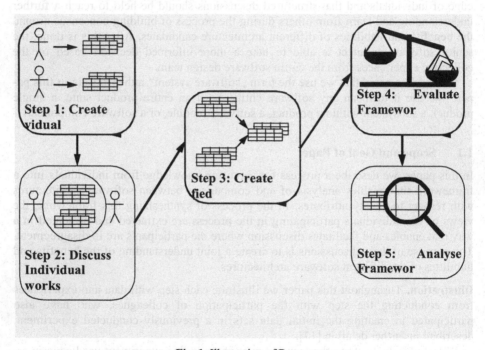

Fig. 1. Illustration of Process

1. Create individual frameworks, as outlined in Section 2.1. The individual frameworks consists of two tables per participant, where one table describes the participant's ranking of the support for different quality attributes for each of the architecture structures, and the other ranks the architecture structures for each quality attribute.
2. Discuss the individual frameworks and decide upon a strategy for combining them into a unified consensus framework, which we go through in Section 2.2 in this paper.
3. Create the unified framework as presented in Section 2.3.
4. Evaluate Framework, as presented in Section 3.
5. Analyse the framework. This step is described in Section 4.

As presented by Johansson et al. [9], it is expected that stakeholders have different views of the importance of different quality attributes, and we also expect developers with different backgrounds to have different views of different architecture structures. The purpose of steps 1 and 2 of the process in this paper is hence to elicit the views of different stakeholders and use these as a basis for further discussions where the causes for the different views are investigated.

These discussions serve as one important input to the architecture design process and the development process, but it is also important to analyse the framework to understand the benefits of different architecture structures. This is not only useful if the architectures represent initial designs for a system, but is even more important if the purpose of the evaluation is to see whether the current architecture of an evolving system is still the most appropriate alternative given the (potentially also evolved) domain and quality requirements of the software system. By regularly re-evaluating the choice of software architecture phenomena such as software aging [13] may be, if not stopped, so at least slowed down. This analysis consists of steps 4 and 5, where the framework are first evaluated to measure the amount of uncertainty it contains (step 4) and then each architecture candidate analysed in further detail compared to the other architecture candidates (step 5).

2   Creating the Framework

The framework we intend to create consists of two tables, which we refer to as the *FQA (Framework for Quality Attributes)* and the *FAS (Framework for Architecture Structures)*. These two tables consist of a set of vectors, normalized so that the values in each vector sum up to 1, and the tables describe the architecture structures with respect to quality attributes in two ways: the FQA describes a ranking of architecture structures with respect to a certain quality attribute, and the FAS describe the ranking of different quality attributes within a particular architecture structure.

We create these two tables by first acquiring the individual views of a number of participants, as described in Section 2.1 and then discussing these views in a meeting, which we describe in Section 2.2. The last step is to combine all individual views into a unified framework, as described in Section 2.3.

However, before the framework can be created, it must be known which quality aspects are relevant to consider, and a set of architecture structures must be developed for the system to design. We do not describe this further, as it is done using traditional requirements engineering (e.g. [5][5][12]) and architecture design methods (e.g. [4][4][6][4][6][8]). The input for the method is thus highly context dependent, as the architecture structures and the quality attributes are designed and elicited for a particular software system, in a particular domain and for a particular software company with a certain software development culture.

The elicited relevant quality aspects and the architecture structure candidates are used as input to the first step of the process, as described below.

2.1   Creation of Individual Frameworks

The first step after the architecture structures are created is to understand how different individuals, potentially with different backgrounds, perceive the strengths and weaknesses of the architecture structures with respect to a set of quality attributes.

One can choose whether to elicit the views, in terms of the FAS and FQA, of each individual or whether to obtain a collective framework in a group meeting. If the participants create the framework collectively, there is a risk that opinions are suppressed, wherefore we suggest that it is better if each participant create an individual framework that becomes the basis for discussions, e.g. as presented in Section 2.2. Each of these individual frameworks should then describe the strengths and weaknesses of the architecture structures in a comparable way, so that differences between participants can be identified and discussed.

However, to explain in comparable terms what the strengths and weaknesses of a particular architecture structure are, is not a trivial task. To facilitate this, we propose the use of methods available from the management science literature, for example in Anderson et al. [1]. The methods are often denoted multi-criteria decision processes.

One such method is the Analytic Hierarchy Process (AHP for short), which was originally proposed by Saaty [14] (and also described in a later publication [15]). This approach has been applied in software engineering by other researchers addressing, for example, requirements engineering [10] and project estimation [16]. The Analytic Hierarchy Process can be used to prioritize different items or aspects. The result is a priority vector with relative weights on the different items or aspects being prioritized.

In order to create the individual frameworks, what needs to be done is to complete two AHP questionnaires, with questions pertaining to the following two issues:

- A comparison of different quality attributes for each software architecture structure.
- A comparison of different software architecture structures for each software quality attribute.

AHP is a method that uses pair-wise comparisons on a nine-point scale in favour of either element compared to create a matrix, from which a prioritized vector is calculated. The values in this vector are normalized so that they together sums up to 1. In our usage of AHP we obtain data for, and create one vector for each architecture structure and each quality attribute. Hence, this result in two tables per participant, related to the FAS and the FQA as earlier described.

Illustration of Creating Individual Frameworks. In a previous study [17], we present an experiment where we conduct the type of AHP ranking as mentioned above, i.e. we describe and apply a method for assessing the support different architectural structures have for different quality attributes, and also which architectural structures best fulfil certain quality attributes.

The outcome of this experiment is a series of vectors for each participant in the study. In our study each of the eight participant produced six vectors ranking architectural structures for each quality attribute and five vectors ranking the quality attribute potential within each architecture structure. These vectors are grouped into two tables per participant, corresponding to the FAS and the FQA as described above.

The quality attributes used were those from the ISO 9126 standard [7], namely: Efficiency, Functionality, Usability, Reliability, Maintainability and Portability, and the architecture structures used were a selection from Buschmann et al. [3], namely: Microkernel, Blackboard, Layered, Model-View-Controller and Pipes and Filters. It should however be noted that the method is not bound to these attributes and structures in particular. Any other set would have worked just as well.

The individual frameworks can be studied separately, but the real use comes if they can be combined into a single, comparable view of the architecture structures and quality attributes, e.g. as described in the next sections.

2.2   Discussing the Individual Frameworks

The purpose of discussing and comparing the individual frameworks is to create a further understanding of where the software engineers disagree in their judgements of the architecture candidates, and to elicit the reasons why this disagreement occurs. We expect to find disagreements, as it is rare that all software engineers have the exact same background and experience, and these differences will be manifested in the individual frameworks created in the previous step.

In order to identify the discrepancies that are most relevant to discuss, we propose to use the sum of the squared distance to the mean value, described by the following formulae:

$$\sum_{i=1}^{N} (x_i - \bar{x})^2$$

where N is the number of participants. This formulae is applied over all participants for each vector in the FAS and FQA (in effect, for each quality attribute and each architecture structure), and hence produce a value for each vector that describes the amount of disagreement between the participants. After this, a suitable threshold value is selected to discern which of the vectors are worthy of further examination.

Although it is up to the user of our method to set a suitable threshold value and it is depending on the number of discussion points one wish to identify, we suggest that the threshold value is set to the 75th percentile, thus pinpointing the upper 25% of the data set. However, this also needs to be augmented by visually inspecting graphs of the individual answers and identifying places where there are interesting outliers even though the spread of the answers do not exceed the threshold value.

During a meeting, each of the identified data points are discussed, and participants with a differing opinion from the rest get a chance to explain why their values differ.

Embracing Disagreement. That different persons have different backgrounds is not an uncommon situation, neither in academia nor in industry. Thus, any formed group will consist of persons with different backgrounds, which is partly what makes a group successful. As all group members form their interpretations of the situation at hand based on their background, one cannot expect all participants to have the same interpretation. We believe that the key to success is to acknowledge this and to find ways to cope with the differing interpretations.

If participants disagree on the meaning of a certain quality attribute, or of a certain architecture structure, this is a disagreement that would manifest itself later during the development process and, in a worst case, be the source of flaws in the delivered product.

The major contribution of the meeting presented in this section is that the participants get to present their rationale, and this creates a better joint understanding of how to interpret the quality attributes and architecture structures.

Another goal of the discussions is that the individual vectors should be combined into vectors that everyone can agree upon. There are several ways to combine the vectors, e.g.:

- Use the mean value.
- Remove outliers and use the mean value.
- Use the median value.
- Let the participants, with the gained knowledge from the discussion, re-do the AHP questionnaire for the vector in question and hold a second meeting to discuss the new vector.
- Let the participants jointly complete an AHP questionnaire for the vector in question.

Which method to use can be decided during the meeting for every vector, but we suggest that in most cases using the median value is sufficient. It is less time-consuming than the other choices, while still giving a more accurate image than just using the mean value. The mean value would be unduly influenced by extreme values, whereas the median value indicates where the bulk of the participants are located without biasing towards outliers.

Illustration of a Consensus Discussion Meeting. With the goal of creating a unified view of the eight different opinions (stemming from the eight different participants in the previous study [17]), we conducted a follow-up meeting. During this meeting, the 11 calculated vectors (one vector for each architecture structure and quality attribute used: 5 architecture structures + 6 quality attributes) per participant based on the AHP study was presented and then discussed from the perspective of a smaller set of data points which was deemed worthy of further examination. These data points include those where there is a large spread among the answers of the participants, and those where the participants' opinions form two, or in some cases three distinct groups.

As a guideline for finding these data points, we used the sum over all participants of the squared distance to the mean value, with a threshold value of 0.10, which roughly corresponds to the 70th percentile. Hence, any data point where the sum over all participants of the squared distance to the mean value was larger than 0.10 was deemed interesting enough to warrant further discussion.

Using this simple technique, we identified 20 data points out of 60 (Five architecture structure vectors with 6 values each, and six quality attribute vectors with 5 values each equals 60 data points per participant, and we are looking across all of the participants) that warranted discussion. Of these, 6 data points were only marginally over the threshold value and were not discussed in as great a detail. Even though the set threshold value roughly corresponds to the 70th percentile, we thus only held detailed discussions about the data points above the 75th percentile.

In addition to the data points identified by the threshold value described above we also noticed, while studying graphs of the data sets, that in some cases one or two participants disagreed largely with the rest of the group. We included these data points as discussion points as well, as it is important that all arguments are heard, and the disagreeing person or persons may have very compelling reasons for disagreeing with the rest of the participants.

As stated, the intention of the discussion meeting is to find out the specific reasons for why the participants may have differing opinions in the identified data points. In our case, it soon became apparent that all disagreements could be put down to the same factor, namely that the interpretation and application of architecture structures are dependent on the background of the participants. This led people with different backgrounds from different disciplines to interpret the architecture structures differently. As the architecture structures in themselves are rather abstract, many of the participants envisioned a typical system in which the architecture is used, to put a context to the question. These envisioned systems differed depending on the background of the participants.

If the framework were created and the discussions were held in an industry case this would, however, not be an issue, as the context in that case is given by the software system in focus, and the architecture structures and quality attributes directly relatable to this system. Moreover, this difference in the systems envisioned is of minor importance to this paper, as the focus is on the presented process for eliciting and analysing peoples' opinions of different architecture candidates, and to study the problems surrounding the creation of a consensus view of the strengths and weaknesses of the different alternatives.

2.3   A Unified Framework

After conducting the meeting described above, where the disagreements are discussed, a unified Framework for Architecture Structures (FAS) and a unified Framework for Quality Attributes (FQA) is constructed of the participants' views using the method decided upon to unite the individual views. Most often, the median value will be sufficient, unless arguments are brought forward to use another method (e.g. the ones mentioned in the previous section) for uniting the individual frameworks.

By using the median value, these unified frameworks are no longer normalized as the individual tables were, i.e. the columns in the FAS and the rows in the FQA no longer sum up to 1. Because of this, a step is added where the data is re-normalized so that the columns in the FAS and the rows in the FQA sum up to 1.

Illustration of Unified Framework. The FAS and FQA constructed from our study after the consensus discussion meeting are presented in Table 1 and Table 2.

The FAS (Table 1) presents the ranking of quality attributes for each architecture structure. This table should be read column-wise. For example, it ranks microkernel as being best at portability (0.309), followed by maintainability (0.183), efficiency (0.161), reliability (0.122), functionality (0.119) and usability (0.106), in that order. Moreover, the figures indicate that for example microkernel is almost twice as good at portability as it is at efficiency (the value for microkernel is 0.309 compared to the value for efficiency which is 0.161).

The FQA (Table 2) presents the ranking of architecture structures for each quality attribute, and should be read row-wise. For example, the FQA ranks pipes and filters as the best choice for efficiency (0.360), followed by microkernel (0.264), blackboard (0.175), model-view-controller (0.113) and layered (0.0868), in that order. As with the FAS, the figures indicate how much better a choice for example pipes and filters is compared to the other architecture structures. It is, for example, twice as good a choice as blackboard (with a value of 0.360 compared to the 0.175 that blackboard scores).

Table 1. Framework for Architecture Structures (FAS)

	Microkernel	Blackboard	Layered	Model-View-Controller	Pipes and Filters
Efficiency	0.161	0.145	0.0565	0.0557	0.218
Functionalit	0.119	0.321	0.237	0.115	0.151
Usability	0.106	0.127	0.255	0.104	0.0818
Reliability	0.122	0.0732	0.0930	0.105	0.144
Maintainabilit	0.183	0.273	0.221	0.300	0.271
Portabilit	0.309	0.0597	0.138	0.320	0.135

Table 2. Framework for Quality Attributes

	Microkernel	Blackboard	Layered	Model-View-Controller	Pipes and Filters
Efficiency	0.264	0.175	0.0868	0.113	0.360
Functionalit	0.205	0.252	0.199	0.206	0.139
Usability	0.0914	0.113	0.250	0.408	0.137
Reliability	0.126	0.142	0.318	0.190	0.224
Maintainabilit	0.191	0.0921	0.285	0.239	0.193
Portabilit	0.112	0.0689	0.426	0.139	0.255

3   Evaluation of Unified Framework

Previously we discussed the importance of embracing disagreement. This is not only done by venting peoples opinion in a meeting, as earlier described. For each value in the FAS and FQA, a value can be added to indicate the amount of disagreement between the participants. Such disagreement indicators can be used to judge the accuracy of decisions or statements based on data from the framework.

Disagreement indicators can be constructed in a number of ways, but we suggest that the same measure as earlier is used, i.e. the squared distance to the mean, and count the number of participants with a larger value than a certain threshold.

As before, the idea is to set the threshold such that it identifies where the partici-pants actually are in disagreement, which means that if the threshold is too high too much disagreement is allowed, and if it is too low there is too little tolerance for variations in the answers.

However, it is not feasible to set the threshold value to identify a particular percentile as we did to identify data points that warrants discussion. Instead, we need a value that correctly depicts the amount of disagreement found and not a value that identifies a particular group of data points. To this end, we recommend that points where the squared distance to the mean is larger than two standard deviations (of all the squared distances to the mean) are deemed to be in disagreement with the rest of the participants. As before, what value to use as a threshold value is up to the user of the method, but we find that two standard deviations give a fair picture of the amount of disagreement.

This measure of disagreement is only one in a series of uncertainty indicators. For every step of the way, we have indicators of uncertainty, and these should be considered so that, if the uncertainty becomes too large, it should be possible to backtrack and re-do steps to get more certainty in the data sets and hence in the accuracy and usability of the framework:

The uncertainty indicators available hitherto are:

1. Individual consistency ratio for each of the produced vectors. If a method such as AHP [14][14][15] is used, this is obtained as part of the results from the method, otherwise these may need to be calculated separately.
2. Differences between individuals, as discussed in Section 2.2 and using the measure introduced there.
3. Differences between the unified FAS and FQA. In [18] we describe a way to measure and compensate for these differences. Briefly, we compensate for inconsistencies between the FAS and FQA using one of the frameworks to improve the quality of the other, which is then used in the subsequent steps of the method.

In every step of the way, the goal has been to quantify the knowledge about architecture structures, while still retaining a qualitative rationale. Every step of the way helps in removing ambiguity and increasing the clarity and the understanding of the architecture structures. This will, in a development process, ensure that architecture design decisions can be taken with more certainty.

The uncertainty indicators on all levels and during all steps of the creating of the framework can be used to ascertain that the uncertainty, and hence the risk involved, is reasonably low, but also to identify factors upon which people have different opinions and where further discussions are needed to avoid problems further on in the development process.

Illustration of Disagreement Measure. In our example, the standard deviation of all squared distances to the mean value is 0.0166, and hence the threshold value is set to the double, i.e. 0.0332. By confirming against a plotting of all the participants, we are able to determine that this threshold value gives a fair representation of where participants disagree with the majority.

Counting the occurrences where the participants in the study diverge more than this threshold number, we find that there are 43 places where participants disagree, out of the total 480 data points (6 vectors with 5 values plus 5 vectors with 6 values, and all this times 8 participants). The persons in disagreement are distributed over the different vectors as shown in Table 3 and Table 4.

Table 3. Disagreement in FAS

	Microkernel	Blackboard	Layered	Model-View-Controller	Pipes and Filters
Efficiency	1	1			1
Functionality		1			
Usability	1				
Reliability				1	
Maintainability		1	1		1
Portability	4	1			1

Table 4. Disagreement in FQA

	Microkernel	Blackboard	Layered	Model-View-Controller	Pipes and Filters
Efficiency	2			2	
Functionality	1	4		1	
Usability	1	1		2	
Reliability	1		2	1	1
Maintainability		1	4	1	1
Portability	2				

In these tables, we see for example in Table 3 that for Microkernel one person had a different opinion to that of the majority regarding its efficiency value, one person regarding its usability value and as many as four persons disagreed on Microkernel's abilities regarding portability. Studying a graph with all the participants' individual frameworks, it becomes clear that the participants form two distinct groups with respect to this issue (although the points identified by the disagreement measure come from both of these two groups).

Moreover, we see that in general the architecture structures Microkernel and Blackboard contribute with more than half of the disagreement issues, which indicates that for these two architecture structures much discussion is needed in order to fully understand them, and the consequences of using them in a software system.

In Table 3 and Table 4, we see that there are a total of eight places where two or more participants disagree with the majority. While these places certainly need further discussions to elicit the reasons for the disagreement, we can also conclude that the unified framework seems to be constructed by persons who are mostly in agreement, and the framework can thus be used with reasonable accuracy.

4   Analysis of Framework

In this section, we describe the logical next step after the framework is evaluated for consistency, which is to analyse the framework internally, i.e. to discern how the different architecture structures relate to each other and how each of the architecture structures support different quality attributes.

This is important in order to really understand the relations between the architecture structures and the quality attributes. Moreover, to analyse the framework instead of simply using it creates a learning effect, in that by understanding the qualities of one software architecture, it may be easier to understand the qualities of the next architecture, i.e. the next time software architectures are designed and when evolving the software architectures, the designers will have an increased understanding from the start of the strengths and weaknesses of different design alternatives.

Furthermore, if the purpose of creating the framework is to re-evaluate the architecture of an existing software product, it becomes even more vital to analyse the architecture alternatives in the created framework to understand for which quality attributes there is an improvement potential in the current software architecture of the system.

The analysis is based on the two tables, i.e. the FAS and the FQA. We have attempted several ways to integrate these two tables into a single table, but have come to the conclusion that it is better to keep the two tables separate.

There are two dimensions to the analysis: (a) a comparison between different archi-tecture structures, for which the FQA is used, and (b) a comparison of the software qualities within a particular architecture structure, for which the FAS is used. As before, the FQA is read row-wise, and the FAS is read column-wise.

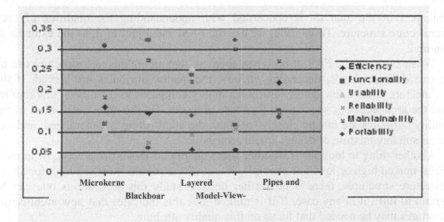

Fig. 2. Plotting of FAS

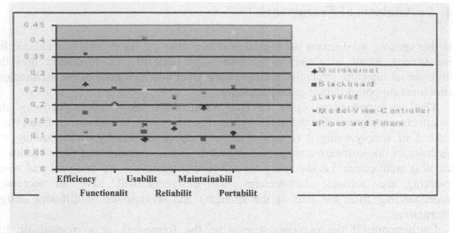

Fig. 3. Plotting of FQA

Rather than studying the mere numbers, which can be difficult to compare, we suggest that the data is plotted into graphs. Examples of such graphs, based on the FAS in Table 1 and the FQA in Table 2, can be found in Figure 2 and in Figure 3.

The graph in Figure 2 is read column-wise, i.e. one column in the FAS correspond to one column, or rather a vertical line, of dots. Figure 3 corresponds to the FQA, which is read row-wise, but as there is no meaningful interpretation of comparing the quality attributes with each other in this table, we choose to plot this table so that its graph is also read column-wise.

4.1   Analysis of Architecture Structures (FAS)

This part of the analysis is concerned with understanding the qualities of each architecture structure. To this end, we use the FAS, and a plot of it, as the example in Figure 2.

When studying the FAS, it becomes apparent that an architecture structure can be of two different kinds, depending on how the quality attributes are spread. If the architecture ranks a few quality attributes highly compared to the others, this implies that the architecture is specialized for these purposes. On the other hand, if all of the quality attributes are ranked closely together, the architecture is generalized, and can better suit any mixture of desired quality attributes.

Another thing to look for is whether some quality attributes are always, or in most cases, ranked high or low. For example, if a quality attribute is ranked high for all architecture structures, there is no further need to study this attribute as one can be certain to fulfil it in any case. If it is ranked low, this indicates that new architecture structures may be needed that focus on this quality attribute.

The purpose of this analysis is to understand the strengths and weaknesses of each architecture structure, which may help the next time an architecture is to be designed. As stated, it may also help in pointing out the need for new architecture structures that either favours a particular quality attribute, or is equally good at a number of quality attributes.

Illustration. In Table 1 (and in Figure 2) all of the architecture structures, except for possibly the pipes and filters structure, are specialized for certain purposes. For example, microkernel is specialized for portability. Portability scores a value of 0.309 compared to the second largest, which is maintainability with 0.183. The relative distance between portability and maintainability is thus 0.126, whereas the relative distance between maintainability and the quality attribute with the lowest score is 0.0770, which is considerably smaller than between portability and maintainability. Another example of a specialized architecture structure is model-view-controller which is specialized on portability and maintainability, with values of 0.320 and 0.300, respectively. The distance to the third best quality attribute is more than 0.185, as compared to the distance between the third best and the last quality attribute, which is 0.0593.

Another thing that the FAS from our experiment seems to indicate is that there are some quality attributes that no architecture structure is really good at. For example, all architecture structures except for pipes and filters have a fairly low value on efficiency. What this implies is that there is room for specialized architecture structures with emphasis on this quality attribute.

Similar situations can be found with usability, where only the layered architecture structure ranks it highly, and reliability, which no architecture structure in our study seems to focus on, or is capable of.

Since no architecture structures in our study focus on reliability, one can ask the question whether reliability is at all a quality attribute that affects the software architecture or whether it is an attribute that mainly manifests itself in the software development process. This, in turn, may be depending on the interpretation of reliability.

Maintainability, on the other hand, seems to be a quality attribute that most, if not all, architecture structures seem to focus on. This manifests itself in the relatively high values for maintainability compared to the other quality attributes for all architecture structures.

4.2   Analysis of Ranking per Quality Attribute (FQA)

The other part of the analysis is to compare architecture structures with each other. To this end we use the FQA, and a plot of this, as is exemplified in Figure 3.

Patterns one can discern here are whether a particular architecture structure always gets better values than another, which of course would mean that this architecture structure is always to prefer over another. One can also see if there are certain quality attributes that favours the selection of a particular architecture structure. This may, in time, create an increased understanding of what traits of a software architecture it is that benefits a particular quality attribute.

Illustration. In the FQA in Table 2 (and the corresponding plot in Figure 3), the layered architecture is considerably better at most quality attributes than the other architecture structures, except for efficiency and functionality (and usability, where model-view-controller is extremely better than the rest of the architectures). Likewise, we see that blackboard is in general a bad choice, except when functionality is a desired quality. If a situation like this occurs when comparing architecture structure candidates for a system, this would indicate that the evaluation can be aborted and the high-ranking architecture (in our example the layered architecture structure) can be chosen directly, unless efficiency is a desired quality.

5   Conclusions

In this paper we present a way to build consensus around the benefits and liabilities of software architecture structures through the process of creating a unified, quantified and comparable view of architecture structures with respect to quality attributes.

Instead of just reading about the architecture structures in a book, we believe that the process of expressing ones own knowledge and experience of different architecture structures in a structured way creates a further understanding of how the architecture structures will work in the specific situation.

When this is compared to other peoples opinions as well, this creates a learning effect and allows differences of opinions to be identified and discussed to form a consensus before the development process continues.

Without this consensus, it is our belief that the differences of opinion will appear later during the development, and take the form of inconsistencies in the developed system, and an increased development time.

Unlike related literature (e.g. [3][3][4]), which only present benefits and liabilities by means of logical reasoning, a framework created using the process in this paper provides relative measures of the level of support for different quality attributes, thus enabling measurement of the importance or severity of different traits. Furthermore, we also provide a way to compare these traits over different architecture structures. This complements the work of e.g. Buschmann et al. [3] and Bosch [4] by providing an opportunity to quantitatively analyse architecture structures, and thus create a further insight into how these architecture structures work.

Moreover, the framework can be constructed for any set of architecture structures and quality attributes, which means that companies can perform their own analysis for architecture structures and quality attributes related to their business and the domain of their systems, and is hence not bound to the selection of architecture structures and the descriptions of these that can be found in mainstream literature.

The focus of the paper is on the different steps that assist in the process of building consensus among the participants while ensuring that all, or at least many, relevant aspects are covered before more time and effort is spent on further developing the software system at hand.

We illustrate these steps by reporting from a case study conducted according to the steps in this paper. Hence, we would again like to stress that the framework we present in the illustrations is only one example of using the proposed process. The created framework and the steps to discuss, evaluate and analyse it can be used on any set of architecture structures and quality attributes. Which sets to use is primarily determined by the context and the domain in which the process is being applied.

Moreover, we would also like to stress that albeit the framework is constructed by capturing the *perception* of architecture structures and quality attributes from professionals, it is our belief that the perception professionals have about architecture structures are also represented as actual qualities of the architecture structures themselves. Nevertheless the framework is only indirectly based on the actual qualities of the architecture structures. However, as the usage of the framework is mostly as an aid to identify where there are differing opinions it is in fact the individuals' perceptions that are sought, so this may not necessarily be a drawback of the method.

The process for consensus building in this paper has the following benefits:

- It can be used to create a better understanding of different architecture structures.
- It can be used to kindle a dialogue between software developers to iron out and understand discrepancies in interpretations of architecture structures.
- It can be used to identify the need for architecture structures specialized on certain quality attributes.
- It can be used as a sub-step in methods for comparing different architecture structures when selecting which architecture to use in a system to design, as in [18].
- It can be used to evaluate architectures against a „baseline" of common architecture structures.
- It can be used as a learning tool to allow software developers to share their experiences with each other in a structured way.
- It can be used to confirm or confute „myths" regarding software architectures. For example if all architecture structures rank performance and maintainability highly, this indicates that it is at least possible to create architecture structures where these are not in conflict, thus refuting the myth that this, in general, is not possible.

To summarize, the contribution of this paper is that we present a process for creating a data set around which discussions can be held to find out if and why there are disagreements in a group of software developers. Such a discussion is, we believe, vital to create a joint understanding of the architecture candidates for a system to design. Our advice is to acknowledge that there will be disagreement, and to use this disagreement to power discussions to create a better understanding of the architecture structures and quality attributes involved.

References

[1]   D.R. Anderson, D.J. Sweeney, T.A. Williams, „An Introduction to Management Science: Quantitative Approaches to Decision Making", South Western College Publishing, Cincinnati Ohio, 2000.

[2]   L. Bass, P. Clements, R. Kazman, „Software Architecture in Practice", Addison-Wesley Publishing Co., Reading MA, 1998.

[3]   F. Buschmann, C. Jäkel, R. Meunier, H. Rohnert, M. Stahl, „Pattern-Oriented Software Architecture - A System of Patterns,,, John Wiley & Sons, Chichester UK, 1996.

[4]   J. Bosch, „Design & Use of Software Architectures - Adopting and Evolving a Product Line Approach,,, Addison-Wesley, Harlow UK, 2000.

[5]   L. Chung, B.A. Nixon, E. Yu, J. Mylopoluos, „Non-Functional Requirements in Software Engineering", Kluwer Academic Publishers, Dordrecht, the Netherlands, 2000.
[6]   C. Hofmeister, R. Nord, D. Soni, „Applied Software Architecture", Addison-Wesley, Reading MA., 2000.
[7]   Software Qualities", ISO/IEC FDIS 9126-1:2000(E).
[8]   I. Jacobson, G. Booch, J. Rumbaugh, „The Unified Software Development Process", Addison-Wesley, Reading MA, 1999.
[9]   E. Johansson, M. Höst, A. Wesslén, L. Bratthall, „The Importance of Quality Requirements in Software Platform Development - A Survey", in Proceedings of HICSS-34, Maui Hawaii, January 2001.
[10]   J. Karlsson and K. Ryan, „A Cost-Value Approach for Prioritizing Requirements", in IEEE Software 14 (5):67–74, 1997.
[11]   J. Karlsson, C. Wohlin and B. Regnell, „An Evaluation of Methods for Prioritizing Software Requirements", in Information and Software Technology, 39(14-15):938-947, 1998.
[12]   G. Kotonya, I. Sommerville, „Requirements Engineering", John Wiley & Sons, Chichester UK, 1998.
[13]   D.L. Parnas, „Software Aging", in Proceedings of the 16th International Conference on Software Engineering, IEEE Computer Society Press, Los Alamitos CA, pp. 279-287, 1994.
[14]   T. Saaty, „The Analytic Hierarchy Process", McGraw-Hill, 1980.
[15]   T.L. Saaty, L.G. Vargas, „Models, Methods, Concepts & Applications of the Analytic Hierarchy Process", Kluwer Academic Publishers, Dordrecht, the Netherlands, 2001.
[16]   M. Shepperd, S. Barker, M. Aylett, „The Analytic Hierarchy Process and almost Dataless Prediction", in Project Control for Software Quality - Proceedings of ESCOM-SCOPE 99, R.J. Kusters, A. Cowderoy, F.J. Heemstra, E.P.W.M. van Weenendaal (eds), Shaker Publishing BV, Maastricht the Netherlands, 1999.
[17]   M. Svahnberg, C. Wohlin, „An Investigation of a Method for Evaluating Software Architectures with Respect to Quality Attributes", Submitted, 2002.
[18]   M. Svahnberg, C. Wohlin, L. Lundberg, M. Mattsson, „A Method for Understanding Quality Attributes in Software Architecture Structures", in Proceedings of the 14th International conference on Software Engineering and Knowledge Engineering (SEKE 2002), ACM Press, New York NY, pp.

Software Technologies for Embedded Systems: An Industry Inventory

Bas Graaf, Marco Lormans, and Hans Toetenel

Faculty of Information Technology and Systems, Delft University of Technology
The Netherlands
{b.s.graaf,m.lormans,w.j.toetenel}@its.tudelft.nl

Abstract. This paper addresses the ongoing inventory activities within the ITEA MOOSE project. The inventory result will be a complete view on the application of methods, techniques and tools for software production within some of the leading European industrial companies within the embedded system field, such as Philips, Océ, ASML and Nokia. The current results are remarkable, as they confirm the cautiousness of industry to adopt recent state of the art development technologies, even as the production of in-time reliable software products becomes more and more an unreachable target.

1 Introduction

Embedded systems are getting more and more complex. At the same time an increasingly bigger part of embedded systems is implemented through software. This results in big challenges for developing embedded software. As developing embedded software is fundamentally different from developing non-embedded software research specifically targeted at the embedded domain is required. With the ever-increasing penetration of embedded systems in society and the related increase in investments by industry to develop such systems, the investments in embedded software engineering technologies (methods, tools, techniques, processes) increase as well.

This paper presents some results of the MOOSE (software engineering MethOdOlogieS for Embedded systems) project [1]. MOOSE is an ITEA project [2] aimed at improving software quality and development productivity in the embedded systems domain. One of the goals of this project is to integrate systems and software engineering, requirements engineering, product architecture design and analysis, software development and testing, product quality and software process improvement methodologies into *one common framework and supporting tools for the embedded domain*.

In order to create a framework of embedded software development technologies, more insight is needed in currently available methods, tools, and techniques. The main focus of this paper is the embedded software development technologies used in industry or, more precisely, used in the industrial partners of the MOOSE-consortium.

M. Oivo and S. Komi-Sirviö (Eds.): PROFES 2002, LNCS 2559, pp. 453-465, 2002.
© Springer-Verlag Berlin Heidelberg 2002

The results of this inventory will be applied to classification schemes for embedded software product and projects that are to be developed. Finally these classification schemes must enable us to design the framework for embedded software development technologies. The framework can be seen as a structure of which methods, tools and techniques are the components. This industrial inventory cannot only contribute to the design of the framework but also can be used to add information to the framework.

Besides its use for creating the framework, the results of the inventory can also be used to determine the direction for additional research within the MOOSE project. For instance when it turns out that some technologies are missing or not completely applicable for development of embedded systems and software.

In this paper we will present the results of the inventory. The rest of this paper is organized as follows. Section two provides background on the essence of embedded systems. We define how we understand embedded systems and give a short survey of software methods, techniques and tools of today. Section three presents the main part of this paper. It describes the inventory process and the resulting product. Section four relates the work in MOOSE to other similar projects. Section five concludes the paper and presents future work.

2   Embedded Systems

2.1   What Are Embedded Systems?

As the MOOSE project is about methods, techniques and tools in the embedded systems domain, we need a definition of embedded system together with some characteristics of embedded systems. We can then decide whether a certain method, technique or tool is relevant for our project or not. Also we can use the definition to define embedded *software* as the software in an embedded system.

There is no general consensus about what an embedded system is nor is there a complete list of characteristic properties of such systems. What is generally agreed on is that an embedded system is a mixed hardware / software system dedicated to a specific application [3–7].

An embedded system is in general part of a larger system, i.e. it is a subsystem of another system. Mostly the relation with that supersystem is that the embedded system reacts on it. An embedded system is thus mostly a reactive system. This means that a car by itself is not an embedded system, nor is a mobile phone. However some subsystems of these systems possibly are (e.g. fuel injection system).

The supersystem has to be a system of a certain type before we can speak of an embedded system. For example a computer system that monitors stock rates can also be part of a larger system of a bank's trading department that involves procedures, people and stocks. We will not consider this to be an embedded system. We will only take into account systems that are embedded in other systems that are physical entities. Embedded means at least logically connected and maybe physically.

These are the most fundamental characteristics of embedded systems. Therefore we will use the following definition in this paper:

Definition 1. An embedded system is a mixed hardware / software system dedicated for a specific application and is part of and reactive to a larger, physical system to which it is at least logically connected.

Properties of embedded software can mostly be deduced from these characteristics. Besides that the product type also implies some specific characteristics for embedded software.

For example: controlling real world entities often implies that embedded software has real-time constraints. Also controlling real-world, physical entities means that physical damage can occur due to failure of such software. Other properties that are common and can be deduced from the fundamental characteristics or are specific for certain product types are:

- limited functionality
- hard to change
- safety / business critica
- limited resources (memory, power, time)
- long operation required
- mass produced
- short time-to-market

These characteristics, of which some are specific for embedded systems, make that developing software for such system differs from developing non-embedded software from an engineering point of view.

2.2   Embedded Software Methods, Techniques and Tools

The market for software engineering technologies is largely fragmented. There is no clear market leader, and there is no supplier present that fully supports the whole development chain of embedded products. There are different suppliers for requirements engineering technologies, different vendors for design tools, etc.... Most dominant is the sales of software tools. Tools imply to support or be supported by a method or technique. Some suppliers provide methodologies with their tools, while others support generic methodologies or techniques, such as UML (OMG's Unified Modeling Language) or MOF (OMG's Meta Object Facility).

Different suppliers are present in various areas of the software engineering domain. For example the most dominant vendors of analysis, modeling and design tools [8] are: Computer Associates, Oracle, Rational Software, Versata, and Sybase. While the most dominant vendors of Quality Tools [9] are: Mercury Interactive, Compuware, Rational, Empirix, IBM, Seque Software, Cyrano, Hewlett-Packard, McCabe & Associates, RadView Software, Computer Associates, and Telelogic. Another example are vendors of Configuration Management Tools [10]: Rational, MERANT, Computer Associates, SERENA Software, Telelogic, Microsoft, MKS/Mortice Kern Systems, StarBase, IBM, Technology Builders/TBI, and Hewlett-Packard. The above overview shows clearly how differentiated this market is. Furthermore, it shows a large dominance of US companies in this market domain: Europe is laying behind in this market. Close co-operation within Europe, providing solutions to integrate / connect existing technologies or construct additional technologies will enable more focused, effective and efficient, development of embedded systems.

Table 1. Dutch MOOSE partners

ASML	lithography systems for semiconductor industry
Philips	consumer electronics
Océ	document processing systems
CMG	IT services

The improvement management domain is still in its infancy. Main dominance has come from the US Software Engineering Institute's methods, of which the Capability Maturity Model is the most well-known. Experience has shown that such models always need to be customized and tailored to the respective company that applies it to improve its embedded software processes. New developments such as product assessments are not present in the market at all. Furthermore is there no commercial organization dominating the improvement management market. Most dominant players are the European IT consulting companies and tool vendors, but this is always different from country to country.

An other important technology for fast delivery of embedded systems comes from the COTS domain. Today's COTS market is rapidly changing, as the needs of companies increase. More and more components are appearing in the software market each day in order to fulfill the business demand. A quick look at COTS purchase market confirms that COTS sales are indeed getting bigger very fast every year. There exists a clear geographical distribution in software components sales (US and rest of the world). There is still a patent differentiation between the number of sales made in Europe and those reported in the US.

3   Inventory Results

3.1   Introduction

In this section we present the results of an inventory of (embedded) software engineering methods, tools and techniques used in industry. This inventory is performed as part of the MOOSE project. At the time of this writing it has been done at four Dutch industrial MOOSE partners.

It was carried out by doing interviews at different industrial MOOSE partners. First an inventory approach was made. It contained a list of topics and subtopics to be discussed. The primary focus was on the software development processes and the methods, techniques and tools used within these processes. This focus was roughly organized by the following subtopics: requirements, architecture design, modeling, coding, and testing. Besides the topics related to the software product, other items were added to get a general understanding of the type of products built. Finally there were some items about management aspects of embedded software development including items concerning project metrics and project organization.

A total of 16 respondents were interviewed at four Dutch industrial MOOSE partners. The results were processed individually, which yielded sixteen interview reports. All of the respondents were invited to provide feedback, which was processed afterwards in the results. Finally an inventory report was made per company (four reports) on which this section is based. The four partners and the products involved are mentioned in Table 1.

The embedded software products that are built at the participating companies are very diverse. The software products were embedded in systems ranging from consumer electronics to highly specialized industrial machines.

3.2   PROFES and BOOTSTRAP

To make it possible to place specific techniques, methods and tools in perspective we used a software process model based on the PROFES methodology [11]. This model is suited for characterizing the development processes of embedded systems and is based on the BOOTSTRAP methodology [12, 13] for software process assessment and improvement. However, in our approach it is only used to characterize the various applied technologies.

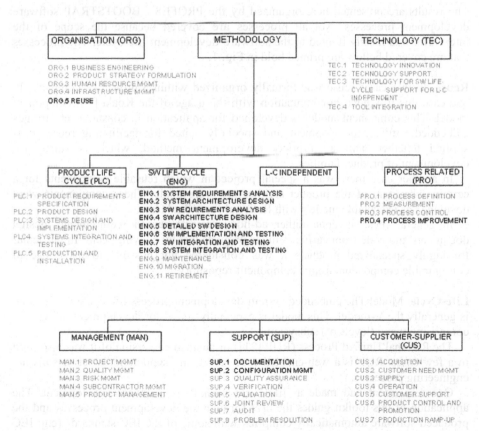

Fig. 1. BOOTSTRAP / PROFES processes

BOOTSTRAP is a methodology for software process assessment and improvement focused at the European industry. The BOOTSTRAP Consortium developed it during the years 1990-93. It is a methodology comparable with SPICE [14], CMM [15, 16] and ISO 9000 [17]. Compared with the other methodologies mentioned earlier, which are more management or organization oriented [18, 19], the software process model used in BOOTSTRAP is more oriented towards software engineering processes. This makes the BOOTSTRAP process model more suited for processing the results of the inventory, which is primary focused on the software engineering technologies.

The PROFES improvement methodology was developed in the PROFES Esprit project. During this project the BOOTSTRAP process model was enhanced to better suit the embedded systems domain. As some of the MOOSE project members also participated in the PROFES project, the usage of the PROFES process model for the inventory results seemed most appropriate. The PROFES / BOOTSTRAP processes are depicted in Fig. 1.

3.3   Results

The results are presented here organized by the PROFES / BOOTSTRAP software development processes. Not all processes are covered because the scope of the interviews was mostly limited to the software development life-cycle. The processes that are covered bellow are printed bold in Fig. 1.

Reuse. In two cases reuse was formally organized within a project or company. In one case this was done in combination with the usage of the Koala [20] component model. This component model is developed for application in consumer electronics embedded software development and specially suited for facilitating reuse. It is applied together with a propriety development method, which is suited for development of product families.

In another case there was a special project in which reusable components for a certain subsystem of the product architecture were made. These components were developed as executable models with Rational Rose RealTime.

In general reuse is done rather ad-hoc. Projects reused requirements, design documents and code from earlier, similar projects just by copying them. In particular for highly specialized products it was considered not possible to make use of configurable components from a component repository.

Life-Cycle. Model The embedded system development process life-cycle model used is generally the V-model. This model is especially suited for development of systems comprising many (levels of) subsystems.

The Rational Unified Process (RUP [21]) or an adapted version of it was also used in a few cases. RUP is a web-enabled tool facilitating support for a set of software engineering processes.

One respondent had made a 'life-cycle toolkit' for software development. The application of this toolkit guides the user through the development processes and the produced software automatically complies with some of the IEC standards (e.g. IEC 61508 for safety related systems). Also a propriety software development method called MG-R was used which enabled large-scale, multi-site and incremental software development.

System Requirements Analysis. System or product engineering is an activity typically performed when developing embedded systems. However in some cases system requirements and system architecture were already known in advance. This can be the case when the hardware is developed first or when the system architecture is stable for a specific product family. A feasibility study is often done in this phase. Also prototypes are built from a technical or customer perspective. This is done to establish technical feasibility or customer requirements respectively.

Sometimes use cases and UML [22] sequence diagrams are applied to express requirements on a system level. However, the meaning of UML notations has to be agreed on this level. Typical input for system requirements comes from customers or marketing, support, manufacturing, hard- and software suppliers and other stakeholders.

System Architecture Design. On the system level is decided what is built in software. While there are some basic guidelines for this, these decisions are often based on implicit criteria. Depending on the complexity of the product, the architecture is composed of multi- or mono-disciplinary subsystems. The subsystems are decomposed into mono-disciplinary components. This gives a tree of requirements and design documents. In this tree a design on one level is (input for) a requirement on a lower, more detailed level.

Software Requirements Analysis. Pre- and post conditions are a commonly used technique in specifying software requirements. This is mostly done in natural language or a semi-formal notation (e.g. pseudo code). Use cases are also used in OO-environments for specifying software requirements. In one case concerning a safety critical system, the formal notation Z [23] was used for specification.

Often Microsoft Word templates are used to introduce some general structure in requirements. However, there still is a lot of freedom for analysts to specify requirements. As a consequence requirements from different projects can look quite different.

Real-time constraints were sometimes expressed in a separate section in the requirements documents. However, these constraints were mostly not taken into account during design. Rate monotonic scheduling analysis [24] was tried in some cases, but techniques like these are typically not used. In some cases there is a separate real-time team in a project, which is responsible for real-time aspects. Often real-time constraints are implicit in the requirements. Only one tool used was specifically suited for developing real-time systems (Rational Rose RealTime).

Other constraints that are typical for embedded software, like power consumption and memory usage, were also mostly not explicitly addressed during requirements specification and design.

In some cases Rational RequisitePro was used for requirements management. However in general this was done rather ad hoc. Hand made tables were then used for tracking down requirements to design documents and test cases.

Software Architecture Design. Managing the complexity of the generated software is done by making use of layered (component) architectures with well-defined interfaces. In the case were the Koala component model was used the architecture was described with a special graphical notation. Koala also provides interface and component definition languages based on C syntax. In most cases however UML class diagrams are used for specifying the software architecture. Mostly this was done with Rational Rose.

The hardware architecture is often mirrored in the software architecture. This makes the impact of changes in hardware easier to determine. Because the hardware is developed before the software, the software often has to deal with a suboptimal hardware architecture. This is also true when dealing with third-party software that is used. Possible defects of this software have to be taken into account during design.

Detailed Software Design. The Unified Modeling Language (UML) is the most commonly used notation. UML is used as well in requirements as in design (architecture) documents. Even in system requirements and design it is used. In the last case however the meaning of notations has to be agreed on. For drawing UML diagrams only two tools are frequently mentioned: Microsoft Visio and Rational Rose (RealTime).

Other notations that are used for modeling are dataflow diagrams, entity-relationship diagrams, flowcharts, Hatley-Pirbhai diagrams [25] and the Koala notation for describing component architectures.

Third-party hard- and software have an impact on the requirements of an embedded system. This means that it also has to be taken into account during design of an embedded system and its software. An example of this is the use of third-party operating systems, such as Microsoft TV or OpenTV, for the development of set-top boxes. This forms a big challenge and is currently not handled well.

Software Implementation and Testing. Embedded software is mostly implemented using (ANSI) C. In one case C++ was used as target language for code generation. Rational Rose RealTime was used for generating the code. This is an UML software design tool in which a few concepts are added to the UML notation. With these extra concepts and class- and state diagrams it is possible to produce executable UML models. Only some code fragments have to be provided in the state diagrams. Because code is only inserted in the model itself the model and generated code are always synchronized. Traditional objections against the use of C++, such as its complexity and dynamic memory allocation, were overcome by visual development environments and instantiation of all objects during initialization.

In other cases C++ and in general OO-languages were often considered as resulting in too slow and too big programs. However sometimes the OO-paradigm is used in the design of some drivers.

Several tools are used to enhance the quality of the produced code: QA-C (QA-systems), SNiFF++ (WindRiver) and lint.

Software Integration and Testing. For testing different techniques are used. Test cases are mostly created manually based on the requirements specifications on different levels of the V-model. They are performed by dedicated test engineers. Only on the component level the developers do the tests themselves.

Code coverage can be measured with special tools, such as Rational Purify and Insure (Parasoft). In some case homemade tools for monitoring threads and throughput are used. Also test programs were made to automate testing, which can be implemented using scripting languages like Perl. Typically test programs can be reused.

Failures observed during testing can be examined with use of root cause analysis techniques.

Software stubs are often used as a replacement for the hardware or the rest of the system. In one case a complete simulation of some hardware components was built to use for testing. This can be a solution when time on a target machine is not always available.

Hand made tables were used to relate test cases to requirements. In this way it can be checked that all requirements are covered by at least one test case.

System Integration and Testing. On higher levels the software is more often tested on the target itself. Regression tests can be used in this phase. A subset of tests that is already executed is then re-executed to ensure that changes do not have unintended side effects. Random- or monkey testing is also used when testing on the target. In one case a device that generated random infrared signals to simulate a remote control.was used for this. This is an easy to use testing technique that can be fully automated.

After testing a test report is created with the results of the tests. This is also done on lower levels. These documents generally correspond to a requirements document on a certain level.

Measurements. In most cases not much is measured concerning process and product. Project duration and the number of change requests and problem reports are measured in most projects. Lines of code made and changed are measured using tools like QA-C.

Process Improvement. In one case a process improvement project was defined. It used the six key process areas of CMM level 2 as a blue print. Baseline measurements were taken and project leaders had to periodically report on estimated end date, effort spent and progress. It turned out that different groups of software developers (e.g. embedded vs. non-embedded) required a different approach to create commitment for such a project.

Documentation. Documentation is generally created using Microsoft Word. Not much automation was seen here. In one case LaTeX documentation containing requirements and design could be generated from a development environment based on SDW (BWise).

Configuration Management. Mostly all documents created during the development process and also other items, such as tools and platforms are subject to configuration management. However, in many cases documents are not updated properly. This leads to situations were only the code is up-to-date.

Various tools are used for configuration management: Rational Clearcase, Contineous CM Synergy (Telelogic) and propriety tooling.

For change management often an approach with change requests and problem reports is used, which can be managed through Rational ClearQuest.

4   Related Work

The MOOSE project complements the ongoing research IST projects PECOS, TOGETHER and DISCOMP by providing a comprehensive methodology deriving functional and quality requirements from the systems engineering to requirements engineering and architecting.

PECOS will provide a meta model for component and architecture specifications of embedded software, a component repository and interactive composition environment for assembling and testing embedded software of automation devices. Contrary to PECOS, MOOSE provides design and analysis methods for the development and validation of intermediate artifacts of embedded product lines, a set of different products that embody common functional and quality requirements and software architecture.

The TOGETHER project aims at formal specifications and higher quality of code by using code generation as a means of transferring formal CASE models of components to target embedded code. Product quality assessment and validation of the intermediate products of product lines are omitted in both cases, PECOS and TOGETHER.

Furthermore, MOOSE focuses on improvement management of products and processes of different types of embedded systems whereas DISCOMP focuses on process improvement and component based distributed design using object-orientation principles and tools for design and implementation of sensor based measurement software.

COTS evaluation and metrics of software development processes are also topics that are not covered by other research projects. Furthermore, are results from the already finalized IST projects PROFES, SCOPE and BOOTSTRAP applicable and will be used as input methodologies to some of the MOOSE work packages. Especially the PROFES project is a high potential in this, as the results are dedicated to the embedded domain, publicly available, and focused to establishing relationships between embedded product quality and the underlying software engineering processes.

5   Conclusions and Future Work

The preceding overview of our preliminary observations is only a high-level description of some of the methods, tools and techniques used for various software development processes. We conclude with some general remarks.

The used methods, tools and techniques do not only vary between the companies, but also within the companies themselves. Mostly there is a general high-level approach present, but not much is standardized on a more detailed level. So different projects often use different tools and notations. Many differences between companies and projects can be explained when looking at specific product characteristics. But still that is not always sufficient for explaining the differences.

Another remarkable observation was that the methods, tools and techniques used were rather common software engineering tools. We expected some more specialized tools were used in this area.

Finally real-time, power and memory constraints were far less prominent in software development as we expected. This could of course be related to our previous observation.

Comparing Sect. 2.2 and Sect. 3.3 we see that there is a relatively large gap between what is available and what is used in the companies we visited. The question: "Why?" is interesting in this context. However, it was not sufficiently answered during the interviews. Partly because this was not an objective when conducting the interviews. However, some things were mentioned about it. Sometimes techniques and tools were considered not mature enough for application in real-world situations (e.g. code-generation). Another explanation was the complexity, which made it too hard to apply specific tools or techniques (e.g. simulation, formal methods). Limited management support was also a success-factor in the case of SPI. Even sentimental reasons were suggested.

In literature some results can be found of the research on the (non-) usage of CASE (Computer-Aided Software/Systems Engineering) tools. We will assume that these results can be extended to the use of methods, techniques and tools in general.

In [26] a number of possible factors affecting usage and effectiveness of CASE are presented and their impact determined by regression analysis. One interesting result is the positive correlation between CASE usage and effectiveness. Even more interesting is the resulting self-reinforcing cycle of CASE usage: higher CASE usage implies higher CASE effectiveness, which implies higher perceived relative advantage. This higher-relative advantage has a positive correlation with CASE usage and thus the cycle is complete.

In [27] among others the following factors affecting CASE adoption were found: complexity, online help, ease of use and ease of learning.

Another aspect of this not covered in these articles is that it is hard to select the appropriate methods, tools and techniques in a specific situation. Especially when there is much available. This would clearly not have a stimulating effect on the use of modern technologies.

Assuming that the use of current methods, tools and techniques is a good practice it would be worthwhile to take away some of the preventing factors for adopting and using these technologies. A framework for embedded software development methods, tools and techniques can help in this. It could take away some of the preventing factors mentioned above.

Besides its main purpose, providing a means of selecting the appropriate methods tools and techniques in specific situations, it can also reduce the complexity these technologies. Of-course it cannot actually change the complexity of methods, tools and techniques. The perceived complexity however can be reduced by it. This by providing background information and case examples of application of the method, tool or technique involved. This is also related to ease of use and ease of learning.

Another factor mentioned in [26] is expectation realism. It is easily seen that a framework could have a good impact on expectation realism.

The inventory will be continued for MOOSE partners in Finland and Spain. Also a second series of inventory sessions will be done at the Dutch MOOSE-partners. These sessions will focus more on software process improvement, quality assurance and project management activities.

Besides that the shortcomings of the existing methods, tools and techniques will be discussed in more detail with people from the field. These discussions will focus on requirements and design. The results will be used to develop possible solutions for one or more problems encountered. Finally experiments will be defined to be carried out at one or more of the industrial partners to test the proposed solution in real-world situations.

References

1. MOOSE homepages. http://www.mooseproject.org, 2002.
2. ITEA. http://www.itea-office.org, 2002.
3. Michael Barr. *Programming Embedded Systems in C and C++*. O'Reilly, first edition, 1999.
4. Sanjaya Kumar, James H. Aylor, Barry W. Johnson, et al. *The Codesign of Embedded Systems: A Unified Hardware/Software Representation*. Kluwer Academic Publishers, 1996.
5. Juan Carlos López, Román Hermida, and Walter Geisselhardt. *Embedded Systems Design and Test*. Kluwer Academic Publishers, 1998.
6. Jean Paul Calvez. *Embedded Real-Time Systems: A Specification and Design Methodology*. Wiley Series in Software Engineering Practice. John Wiley & Sons, 1993.
7. Pasi Kuvaja, Jari Maansaari, Veikko Seppänen, et al. Specific requirements for assessing embedded product development. In *International Conference on Product Focused Software Process Improvement*, pages 68–85. VTT Electronics and University of Oulu, Finland, June 1999. http://www.inf.vtt.fi/pdf/symposiums/1999/S195.pdf.
8. Analysis, modeling and design tools market forecast and analysis, 2001–2005. International Data Corporation, report IDC #24809.
9. The distributed automated software quality tools market forecast and analysis, 2001–2005. International Data Corporation, report IDC #25176.
10. Software configuration management tools forecast and analysis, 2001–2005. International Data Corporation, report IDC #24811
11. Profes Home Page. http://www.ele.vtt.fi/profes, 2002.
12. Pasi Kuvaja, Jouni Similä, Lech Krzanik, et al. *Software Process Improvement: The BOOTSTRAP Approach*. Blackwell Publishers, 1994.
13. BOOTSTRAP Institute. http://www.bootstrap-institute.com, 2002.
14. ISO/IEC JTC 1/SC 7/WG 10. SPICE: Software Process Improvement and Capability dEtermination Website. http://www.sqi.gu.edu.au/spice, 2002.
15. Software Engineering Institute Carnegie Mellon University. *The Capability Maturity Model: Guidelines for Improving the Software Process*. Addison-Wesley Publishing Company, 1995
16. CMMI Production Team. Capability Maturity Model Integration, version 1.1. Technical Report CMU/SEI-2002-TR-012, Carnegie Mellon University, Software Engineering Institute, March 2002.
17. Östen Oskarsson and Robert L. Glass. *An ISO9000 Approach To Building Quality Software*. Prentice Hall PTR, 1996.

18. Y. Wang, I. Court, M. Ross, et al. Quantitative evaluation of the SPICE, CMM, ISO 9000 and BOOTSTRAP. In Proceedings of the Third IEEE International Software Engineering Standards Symposium and Forum (ISSES97): Emerging International Standards, pages 57–68. IEEE Computer Society, June 1997.
19. Yingxu Wang, Graham King, Hakan Wickberg, et al. What the software industry says about the practices modelled in current software process models? In *Proceedings of the 25ᵗʰ EUROMICRO Conference,* volume 2, pages 162–168. IEEE Computer Press, 1999
20. Rob van Ommering, Frank van der Linden, Jeff Kramer, et al. The Koala component model for consumer electronics software. *IEEE Computer,* 33(3):78–85, March 2000.
21. Rational   Software   Corporation.   Rational   Unified   Process. http://www.rational.com/products/rup, 2002.
22. OMG. OMG Unified Modeling Language Specification, version 1.4. http://www.omg.org/technology/documents/formal/uml.html, September 2001.
23. The Z notation. http://www.afm.fbu.ac.uk/z, 2002
24. C.L. Liu and James Layland. Scheduling algorithms for multiprogramming in a hard real-time environment. *Journal of the Association for Computing Machinery,* 20(1):46–61, January 1973
25. Derek J. Hatley and Imtiaz A. Pirbhai. *Strategies for Real-Time System Specification.* Dorset House Publishing, 1987.
26. Juhani Ivari. Why are CASE tools not used? *Communications of the ACM,* 39(10):94–103, October 1996
27. David Finnigan, Elizabeth A. Kemp, and Daniela Mehadjiska. Towards an ideal CASE tool. In *Proceedings of the International Conference on Software Methods and Tools (SMT2000),* pages 189 197. IEEE, November 2000.

Integrating Software Engineering Technologies
for Embedded Systems Development

Rini van Solingen

Project manager of the MOOSE project
CMG, The Netherlands
rini.van.solingen@cmg.com

Abstract. In order to solve the ever-increasing gap between required productivity and quality of embedded software on the one hand, and the industrial capabilities in fulfilling these requirements on the other hand, several European organisations decided to tackle this problem together. By forming the MOOSE consortium ("Software Engineering Methodologies for Embedded Systems"), they started an effort for integrating the available tools, techniques, methods and processes involved in embedded software development. The main starting point of MOOSE is that the available technologies for embedded software development are too fragmented; time, effort and money can be saved by supporting a better integration over development phases and between technologies. This paper presents the starting points of the MOOSE project and introduces some first concepts for achieving the ambitious goals set by the consortium.

1   Introduction

With the ever increasing penetration of embedded systems in society and the related increase in investments by industry to develop such systems, the investments in embedded software engineering technologies increases as well. Forecasts [2] predict continuing increase in embedded systems specific technologies. This paper uses the term 'technology' for any method, technique, process or tool that can be used to support a certain development activity.

The market for software engineering technologies is largely fragmented. There is no clear market leader, and there is no supplier present that fully supports the whole development chain of embedded products. There are different suppliers for requirements engineering technologies, different vendors for design technologies, etc. Most dominant is the sales of software tools. Tools imply to support or be supported with a methodology. Some suppliers provide methodologies with their tools, while others support generic methodologies, such as UML (OMG's Unified Modeling Language) or MOF (MOG's Meta Object Facility).

As the market of technologies is fragmented, so are the technologies themselves. Technologies in general are stand-alone solutions for specific problems. As embedded

M. Oivo and S. Komi-Sirviö (Eds.): PROFES 2002, LNCS 2559, pp. 466-474, 2002.

software development is collection of complex and technical problems, several technologies are applied in parallel [3]. It does not take very much time or experience to observe that this lack of integration is a cause for problems too. Technologies are used separately but depend on each other, interfaces are not defined, inconsistencies occur, etc. Despite this loss of quality due to lack of integration, there is moreover a loss of time, effort and money due to duplication, redundancy and cost of non-quality. As time pressure is prominent in many market domains where embedded systems are sold, this indicates a potential gain in time-to-market. Time-to-market gains in embedded systems development cause high potential revenue gains due to earlier market introduction and therefore deeper market penetration. Industrial companies therefore support initiatives for time-to-market reduction strongly. This is the starting point of the MOOSE project.

2   MOOSE

In 2001 several companies joined their efforts in establishing a consortium for increasing integration in embedded systems development. A project proposal has been set-up, which was rewarded with the ITEA label within the ITEA programme [4]. The MOOSE project runs from March 2002 until February 2004, consists of 13 organisations in 3 European countries, with a total effort of more than 100 person-years and a budget over 15 million Euro.

2.1   MOOSE Partners

The MOOSE partners in those three European countries are:

Finland:

Nokia	Application partner
Solid	Application partner
University of Oulu	Technology partner and exploitation partner
VTT Electronics	Technology partner and exploitation partner

Netherlands:

ASML	Application partner
CMG	Application partner and exploitation partner
Océ	Application partner
Philips	Technology partner and application partner
Technical University Delft	Technology partner

Spain:

Datapixel	Application partner
ESI	Technology partner and exploitation partner
SQS	Technology partner
Team Arteche	Application partner

Three roles are distinguished for the partners:

- Application partner: will use the results of the project within their organisation for embedded software development projects, and will provide input to the project by giving feedback on practicality and validity of project results. The application partners also aim to support the technology partners by providing requirements that help in optimising the industrial relevance of the project results.
- Technology partner: will bring knowledge and expertise on software engineering methodologies to the project and facilitate the validation activities at the industrial partners.
- Exploitation partner: will market and promote outcomes of the project after its finalisation.

2.2   MOOSE Objectives

The MOOSE project aims at increasing embedded software development productivity and product quality. By making development more productive and increasing product quality, development cycles become shorter and cost (and time) of non-quality drops, also causing shorter development cycles. Dependent on the specific market situation, embedded systems suppliers can decide to use the available time for earlier market introduction, additional development, or establishing cost reductions. Looking at the current situation in most embedded system markets, earlier market introduction will be the most frequently selected option.

In order to work towards this aim, the MOOSE project has a set of project goals. These goals are to:

- Integrate systems and software engineering, requirements engineering, product architecture design and analysis, software development and testing, product quality and software process improvement methodologies into one common framework and supporting tools for the embedded domain. This framework will enable the structuring, management and evaluation of embedded software projects in order to guarantee the attainment of its objectives.
- Develop new or enhance existing systems and software engineering methodologies to be integrated in this framework, with the aim to improve product quality and software development productivity through optimised integration and interfacing. Product quality (a) will be defined clearly and measurable and (b) has to be guaranteed by co-ordinated process adaptation, product architecture design and quality assuring measures.
- Validate the operational strength of the framework by extensive usage in different types of embedded software projects (e.g. automotive, telecom, consumer electronics).

2.3   MOOSE Project Structure

For project management purposes the project has been subdivided into four related but different workpackages. Each workpackage has a workpackage manager, and several partners in the consortium cooperate in several different tasks in these workpackages. The four workpackages of the MOOSE project are:

- Workpackage 1: Framework Development and Validation. In this work package a common framework for integrating several systems and software engineering methodologies for embedded systems will be developed and validated. The framework will provide a means for each embedded software development project to select the most beneficial set of software engineering methodologies in order to achieve its goals with respect to cost-effectiveness, time-to-market and product quality. As such it is used for self-evaluation of projects, or decision making for technology-update and improvement.
- Workpackage 2: Systems and Software Requirements Engineering. This workpackage focuses on tailoring, customising and combining existing systems and software requirements engineering and quality techniques, methods and tools to complex embedded systems and software development. The question „how systems requirements engineering relates to software requirements engineering and how these should co-operate over which kind of interface" is a central theme in this workpackage.
- Workpackage 3: Embedded Product Architectures. This work package focuses on tailoring, customising and combining existing product architecture definition, design and development methods and techniques into embedded systems development, and to interactions between systems and software requirements engineering and improvement management within the framework.
- Workpackage 4: Improvement Management. This work package focuses on customising and combining existing improvement methods and techniques to embedded systems development. Typical examples of these methods and techniques are: Software design or code measurement, Product quality assessment and Process capability assessment. Product and process assessments are basic tools for improvement management, which only makes sense when baselines exist to compare to. Measurement is needed to make these comparisons. Specific emphasis is put on the software implementation and testing tasks, as they are highly relevant for embedded systems development.

The project will focus on three main topics within the lifecycle of an embedded system: requirements engineering, product architecture, and improvement management. Testing is an integral part of all three work packages as testing of for example requirements is dealt with in WP2, while testing of architectures is dealt with in WP3. Software implementation (coding, commenting, etc.) is being addressed in WP4: improvement management. This work package focuses to improvement of development processes, and as coding is one of the most dominant processes within embedded software development, it is dealt with fully in WP4, together with the testing aspects of software implementation.

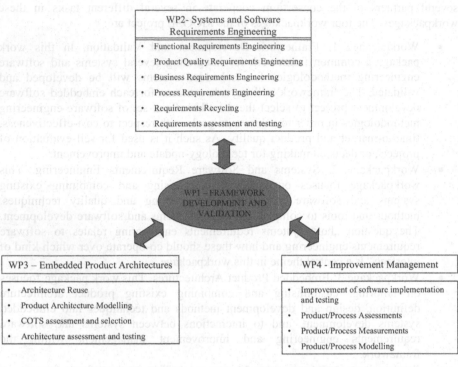

Fig. 1. Workpackage organisation of the MOOSE project

2.4   MOOS Output Results

The main visible results of the MOOSE project will be:

- The framework with defined component interfaces which guarantees an effective software development approach for a specific situation and which enables future innovation and expansion. This framework is supported with a decision model for selecting appropriate software engineering methods, techniques and tools, which will be publicly accessible through a web-based repository that is maintained and shared based on open-source principles.
- Experiences with applying the framework and its components in many industrial projects, within or maybe even outside the consortium, in order to validate its effectiveness and efficiency.
- A number of enhanced/new systems and software engineering methodologies and related tools that function as components in the framework (e.g. product assessment, process architecting, requirements engineering, etc.)

3   Embedded Domain Specific Requirements

Though many software product and process technologies are already available, the embedded software domain puts specific demands to the application of these technologies. Dedicated research results and products are present for software architecture development and assessment, requirements engineering and validation, software process improvement, and tools to support all these technologies. However the major disadvantages of these technologies are that they do not take into account the specific needs for embedded systems and that they are applied „stand alone", which in many cases is not very effective and leads to disappointing results.

The embedded systems industry puts specific demands to the usage of such methodologies, such as the large dependency on real-time features, limited memory storage, large impact of hardware platform technology and the related cost drivers of the hardware, etc. The existing software engineering methodologies do not distinguish the specific impacts or necessary customisation for the embedded domain, nor is it indicated how they should be used specifically for each specific area within this domain, i.e. automotive, telecom, consumer electronics, safety critical, etc. The embedded software domain puts dedicated pressure on these methodologies. Reasons for this are the high complexity of these products and the dependency in this domain on innovative highly technical solutions.

Furthermore, the embedded domain is much more driven by reliability, cost and time-to-market demands. This makes the embedded domain a specific area for which available generic methodologies need to be adapted.

4   Proposals for the MOOSE 'Integration Framework'

The integration of existing software engineering technologies into one framework is required, in order to achieve an effective overall approach, which is customisable to the needs of each specific software development of embedded systems. Application of these methodologies requires mutual information exchange and co-operation along specific interfaces. The framework will arrange these interfaces and will make it possible to exchange methodologies, depending on the specific needs of the product and the organisation, as if they are components.

The framework contains: processes, methods, techniques, tools and templates. The framework also contains classification of business situation, project area, etc. that supports the decision making model. The fact is that there are too many methods or approaches available and, therefore, there is a need to reduce uncertainty in the decision making in selecting the set of methods, techniques and tools for a certain use situation. That means that support for decision making in choosing the method for a certain situation is needed.

Quite typical situation where the framework is needed is a project aiming to choose the most effective and efficient way for the development of embedded systems. The framework integrates knowledge about processes, methods, techniques, tools and templates into a decision making model that operates as outlined in the following picture.

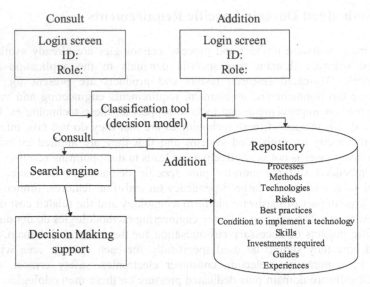

Fig. 2. First concept for MOOSE framework

4.1   Framework Directions

In several workshops in the MOOSE consortium a rough outline of the framework has recently been constructed and is included in figure 2.

The overall framework will be a web-repository including a decision model and filled with the findings from the inventory in the MOOSE project. The repository will be maintained based on open source concepts, guaranteeing knowledge from large variety of sources and continuous innovative expansion.

The web-repository is accessible in two modes: consulting (getting answers to questions) and adding (expanding the repository with results and experiences on technologies). The exact structure of the repository is currently designed but will contain commercial areas (for vendors) non-commercial areas for engineer experiences, best-practice areas, links, explanations, etc.

Furthermore there will be a classification tool included which supports in classifying embedded systems projects. The demands put on different embedded systems are varying largely, the structures of embedded software projects are also various. Grouping these projects together will have the effect that recommendations from the web-repository will be too general. Therefore, a classification mechanism will be constructed that subdivides the total set of embedded projects in several classes that share key-characteristics. A more specific focus can be provided, and projects and technologies can be better linked. There are several scenarios in which the web-repository will be used, for answering user questions such as:

- I want to know more about a certain technology. Tell me more about it.
- I have a certain 'problem'. Which technology solves this problem?
- Which project type do I have? Please classify my embedded project?
- Which project types are there anyway? Show me the options?

- What type of embedded product do I have? Please classify my product?
- Which embedded product types are there anyway? Show me the options?
- What typical technologies fit to my project type?
- What typical technologies fit to my product type?
- What best practices are known for a specific project/product type?
- Can I contact other practitioners that have more experiences with a certain technology?

4.2 Further Steps

In order to construct the framework as illustrated above, several steps are required. It would take too much time to present the full MOOSE project plan and steps in this paper. However, based on the current concepts for the framework there will be initiatives to:

- Construct a classification scheme for embedded software projects based on the inventory [1] in the companies of the industrial partners and in literature.
- Construct a list of important factors for embedded software to inventarise software engineering technologies, in order to list the most important issues for the known technologies (e.g. cost, learning time, support in multi-site development, etc.).
- Construct the web-repository based on the above concepts and fill the repository with knowledge on currently available and known technologies.
- Experiment in industrial projects with the usage of the framework during project construction

5   Conclusions

The MOOSE consortium has been formed in order to solve a challenging, complex, but highly relevant issue: integration between software engineering technologies for embedded systems. The project has started recently, but current intermediate results are promising. Especially the dominant position of industry in steering the output results of the project are expected to be a key-factor for success. Success of the project will be measured in the amount of support that can be provided to embedded software projects and that is experienced helpful by those projects.

The MOOSE project will continue to work on its objectives. If you want to keep in touch, please visit the MOOSE web-pages: http://www.mooseproject.org/

Acknowledgements

The author would like to thank all partners in the MOOSE consortium who have all provided their input to the construction of the concepts presented in this paper. Furthermore the national authorities in the three countries are thanked for their rewards in funding this project. Finally, regards go to the ITEA programme for enabling and supporting the MOOSE collaboration.

474   Rini van Solingen

References

1. Graaf, B., Lormans, M., Toetenel, H., „Software Methodologies for Embedded Systems: An Industry Inventory", submitted to PROFES 2002 conference.
2. IDC, IDC reports: 24809, 25176 and 24811, Http://www.idc.com/, 2001
3. Solingen, R. van, Product Focused Software Process Improvement: SPI in the embedded software domain, BETA Research Series, Nr. 32, Downloadable from: http://alexandria.tue.nl/extra2/200000702.pdf, Eindhoven University of Technology, 2000.
4. ITEA, Http://www.itea-office.org/

Experiences and Lessons Learned Using UML-RT to Develop Embedded Printer Software

L.A.J. Dohmen[1] and L.J. Somers[1,2]

[1] Océ Technologies BV, P.O. Box 101
NL-5900 MA Venlo, The Netherlands
{lajd,lsom}@oce.nl
[2] Eindhoven University of Technology, Dept. Math. & Comp.Sc.
P.O. Box 513, NL-5600 MB Eindhoven, The Netherlands
wsinlou@win.tue.nl

Abstract. From 1997 on Océ has used UML-RT (formerly ROOM) to develop its embedded printer software. This paper highlights our experiences in relation to a number of development process issues. Our conclusion is that UML-RT is well suited for developing embedded printer software, but still has a few shortcomings, mainly with respect to the specification and verification of hard real-time requirements.

1   Introduction

Embedded real-time software forms a continually increasing part of the development effort of a device like a printer or scanner.

Such a device has many actuators and sensors (like heating or engine control) that need to be controlled synchronously or asynchronously with the speed of the printing process. A sheet of paper travels with a speed of 0.5 meter per second though a printer and at the same time a toner image is produced through a photo-electric process. Both sheet and image should be synchronized when fusing the toner image on the sheet, requiring registration accuracy of tens of millimeters. At one moment in time more than 10 sheets may be traveling through the printer, each demanding attention from the embedded control software.

Among the typical characteristics of the embedded software is the fact that it has to control a physical environment that has non-deterministic and concurrent behavior. The software has to respond in time and is difficult to test because the target environment differs from the development environment. Last but not least, requirements are not specified at one moment in time, but gathered during the whole engineering phase. Often they are incomplete, ambiguous and subject to change.

Océ has set two main goals for the development of embedded software: the development should become more efficient (products should ship earlier and with less effort) and the quality level should be raised. As a consequence, the underlying technology basis for the development of embedded software should give ample and adequate support for issues like requirement specification, architecture description, reuse of

M. Oivo and S. Komi-Sirviö (Eds.): PROFES 2002, LNCS 2559, pp. 475-484, 2002.

components, and testing. Some important aspects to consider are concurrency, timeliness, and understandability.

In the remainder of this paper we outline the history of our use of methods for embedded software development (section 2) and focus on our experiences with UML-RT with respect to the criteria mentioned above (section 3 and 4). Section 3 deals with process-related issues, whereas section 4 treats the modeling aspects of UML-RT. Finally, section 5 summarizes our main conclusions.

2   Evolution

Before going into detail about UML-RT, we first give a short overview of the history of our use of software development methods for embedded printer software.

2.1   Early Experiences

In the past we have used Ward/Mellor [1] to model the behavior of the real-time embedded control software. This method uses a number of different views to describe a system: entity-relationship diagrams model the data of a system, data flow diagrams show a.o. the control flow, and state transition diagrams show the state changes. Although Ward/Mellor uses environmental modeling (mapping elements from the system's environment into the model by means of event-lists) instead of functional decomposition, the resulting model is still presented as a functional model.

In our case, the real-time embedded software of a typical printer has to cope with a very large number of internal and external events, which turn out to be difficult to manage in single level state transition diagrams. The number of diagrams soon explodes. Component reuse becomes difficult as soon as small changes have to be applied to a new instance. The main problem is the fact that the consistency between models and actual code has to be kept manually. Generated code amounts to at most 20% of the total code size.

2.2   Transition to UML-RT

Confronted with the problems sketched above and the promising emergence of object oriented methodologies, we decided in 1997 to use the ROOM modeling language [2] supported by the ObjecTime Developer tool for the development of embedded software. Currently, the ROOM diagrams have been merged into UML, giving rise to the UML-RT extensions [3],[4] supported by the Rational Rose RealTime tool (RoseRT). In the future, UML 2.0 will encompass these extensions.

Because the diagrams in UML-RT are related explicitly, the tool is able to generate fully executable code. If one also models parts of the environment, the model can be simulated.

The primary modeling element in UML-RT is a capsule (called actor in ROOM). A capsule is a concurrent, active class with a precisely defined responsibility and interface. The dynamic behavior of a capsule is expressed by a state-chart (based on the state-chart formalism of Harel [5]). The interfaces of a capsule are specified by protocol classes that define exactly the valid messages and message sequences. Sequence diagrams are used to visualize the message flows between objects.

2.3   Current Status

We have used UML-RT initially during the period 1997 – 2001 for the development of a print-engine (DPS400) able to print up to 100 pages per minute. This product has been released and shipped in May 2001.

The print-engine contains approximately 120 sensors and 100 actuators. The developed software contains 350 capsule (actor) classes and 170 protocol classes. The total size of the code is 520 Kloc (executable code), from which the main part (490 Kloc) has been generated from UML-RT. Code reused from previous projects involves only a small part of the total code base. All engineers have attended UML-RT, C++, and operating system training courses.

Motivated by the success of this project, UML-RT is currently being used for the software development in four other projects.

The following sections show our experiences based on the development of the DPS400 print-engine mentioned above.

3   Process Related Experiences

Together with the modeling language UML-RT we have used a development process based on three approaches: architectural driven, requirements driven and iterative / incremental. In the early phases of the software development the architecture of the software system is defined. This architecture guides the software engineers through the succeeding phases by defining the major structure, behavior and interfaces of the system.

The software requirement specifications are the basis for all other development activities. They are defined in the requirements analysis phase, they drive the model construction in the design and implementation phase, and finally they are used to verify („Have we build the system right?") and validate („Have we build the right system?") the system in the testing phase.

To better control the development process we apply iterative (not everything perfect at once, paying attention to learning) and incremental development (not all requirements at once).

Applying a new technology like UML-RT for software development also has its consequences for the development process that is being used. The issues that are most important in our opinion are listed below.

No Silver Bullet. A good modeling language like UML-RT contributes to a more efficient software development, but yet alone does not guarantee success. Most engineering practices learned in the past (like requirements engineering, testing, quality assurance, project management, etc.) are still absolutely necessary for success.

A lot of software developers may feel attracted to a new technology and may tend to forget about the most suitable way it has to be applied in the development process.

Development Effort Not Decreased. Mainly because of the learning curves of the software engineers (new modeling language, new programming paradigm, changed development process, new case-tool) the development effort has not been reduced compared to previous projects.

Due to such initial effects it may be difficult to justify the introduction of a new methodology. Anyhow, it is very important to make a planning that explicitly takes into account the learning curve. Also, if other projects are going to adopt the new methodology, one should try to „reuse" the experiences of the first project. Although very straightforward in theory, in practice a vast number of organizational problems may arise.

Because the introduction of new technologies is expensive, it is important to synchronize among the many projects that exist in a large R&D organization. An innovation management group should chart clear roadmaps for future technologies.

Another issue is whether one should use UML-RT also during prototyping activities. In our development, a lot of prototyping code has been written outside the case-tool domain. The use of two paradigms (plain C for prototyping code versus UML-RT for final code) had a negative effect on the ability of the software engineers to use UML-RT properly during the engineering phase.

Improved Understandability. The use of a highly visual modeling language greatly improves the understandability, resulting in a higher quality of the software. Peer reviews (which are commonly considered to be one of the most important practices to enhance the product quality) become much more efficient, because the software engineers quickly understand each other's models.

Importance of System Requirements Engineering. In our development process, requirements were written for all software modules, but no or poor requirements were written at system level. Because of the absence of such multi-disciplinary requirements, the software requirements lacked a stable basis and a lot of changes were caused by unclear system requirements.

4   UML-RT Modeling Experiences

In the previous section we concentrated on the implications of the introduction of UML-RT for the development process. This section shows the technical aspects we experienced with the usage of UML-RT in combination with the RoseRT development environment. Note that part of the actual experience already originates from the predecessors ROOM and ObjecTime Developer.

4.1   Strengths

First we highlight the positive points we experienced with the usage of UML-RT together with the RoseRT development environment. For each aspect, some concrete examples within the development of the DPS400 print-engine are given.

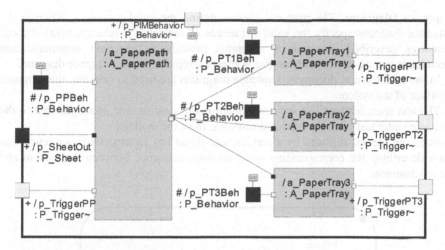

Fig. 1. Capsule of the Paper Input Module (PIM) with three paper trays

Modelling the Physical Environment with Capsules. The primary modeling element in UML-RT is a capsule (see for example Fig. 1). All capsules in a model will run concurrently and can respond to events in the physical environment.

Thanks to the use of parallel capsules, no complex software was necessary for task synchronization, e.g. no semaphores, message queues, task creation/deletion, etc. Because capsules are classes, physically identical functions can be controlled by just instantiating the particular capsule class twice.

Hierarchical State Charts. With multi-level state-charts it is possible to describe complex behavior within one class. It is not necessary to decompose the static structure by creating more and more classes. Multi-level state-charts enable the reuse of top-level behavior (e.g. abstract behavior).

The higher level states (idle, standby, running, low power, etc.) are implemented in an abstract superclass. Each module subclasses from this superclass and automatically inherits all status behavior. Fig. 2 shows this behavior. This abstract behavior is also mentioned in [2] and is called „internal control".

Communication Based Approach. UML-RT uses protocol classes for specifying the inter-capsule communication. The definition of protocol classes is vital for reusing components. Furthermore, it is a basis for polymorphism (different components can share the same interface), and necessary for separating the interface and the implementation.

The capsules within the DPS400 model can easily be replaced by new reusable components from the „reuse group". As long as the interface is identical, replacing a component is just plug-and-play (black-box approach).

A powerful usage of polymorphism is the use of the status protocol. Each module has the same status protocol and reacts to the same messages. Only the internal behavior with respect to these messages is module-specific. For example, all modules receive the „initiate" command, will do their specific initialization and will reply with „initiateDone".

480   L.A.J. Dohmen and L.J. Somers

Sequence Diagrams. The protocol classes define the valid messages, whereas the sequence diagrams specify the valid sequences of messages between several objects. Scenarios described in sequence diagrams provide an excellent communication mechanism among team members. Fig. 4 shows a representative sequence diagram.

In the architectural document sequence diagrams are used to describe the dynamic behavior of the system.

The test specifications use sequence diagrams to describe the messages sent to the „module under test" and the expected response from the module.

Each service test initiated by a service technician has an associated sequence diagram describing the corresponding valid message sequence between the system and the environment.

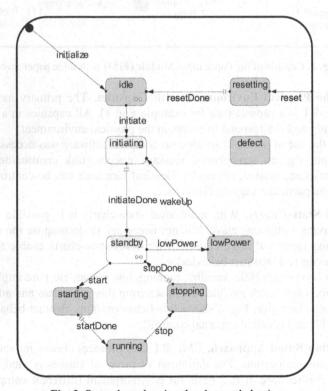

Fig. 2. State chart showing the abstract behavior

Inheritance. If a software component does not completely implement the desired behavior, inheritance allows the addition of the missing behavior in a derived subclass. Copy/paste actions (and thereby loosing the relation with the original component) can be replaced by inheritance.

The executors in the DPS400 model (responsible for generating the action triggers) are all derived from one superclass. This superclass specifies 70-80% of the functionality and the derived executor only adds the module specific behavior.

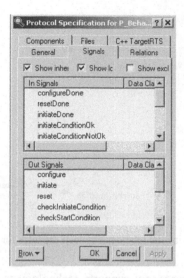

Fig. 3. Protocol class for controlling behavior

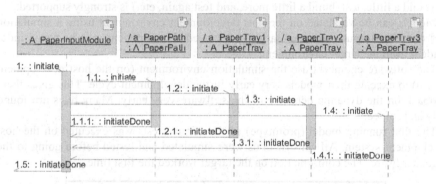

Fig. 4. Sequence diagram showing the initialization of the Paper Input Module

Class Diagrams. In ROOM it was difficult to see the relations between classes. However, UML-RT supports class diagrams to visualize class relationships.

The Model Is the Implementation. The typical separation between the design and implementation is eliminated. The model is always consistent with the implementation. The developers use the graphical interface to build the model and the tool set captures the structure, behavior, data and communication paths of the application. These models are automatically converted to C++ code.

All application code for the DPS400 has been generated from the graphical models. There is no translation from design to implementation. This means that all graphical models are consistent with the implementation.

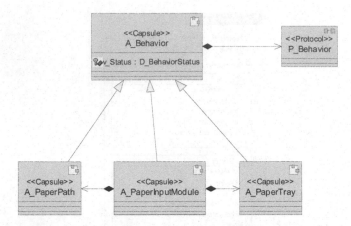

Fig. 5. Class diagram showing the relations between capsules for the Paper Input Module

Executable Models. The case-tool supports technology to execute the model and observe the running behavior. A popular „agile" work-style approach of the developers (build a little, test, build a little more, and test again, etc.) is strongly supported.

Models can be validated on the host development environment using a simulation environment. Because an actual target is not needed, components can be tested independent from the target environment.

The software engineers use the simulation environment (on the host development system) to execute their models very early in the development cycle. This gives them feedback on the dynamic behavior of the software very early. Many bugs are found early and solved.

The first running model (prototype) of the service tests was executed on the host development system. All constructions were simulated and tested before going to the target hardware. The confrontation on the target worked the first time.

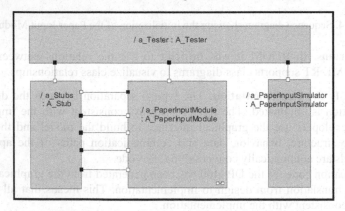

Fig. 6. Typical configuration of the simulation model

4.2   Weaknesses

Although our overall opinion about the usage of UML-RT is positive, some aspects still need improvement. This section gives an overview of the main problems we experienced.

Difficult to Realize Real-Time Requirements. UML-RT does not support the specification, implementation and verification of hard real-time constraints.

Due to this limitation of UML-RT, we had to write our own set of rules for dealing with real-time requirements. To facilitate the verification of the real-time behavior we have changed the RoseRT run time environment and added the logging of timestamps. The adapted run time system logs all messages in a file (including timestamps) and off-line this log file is translated into a sequence diagram (see Fig. 7). With this procedure we can verify the real-time behavior. But we cannot analyze the real-time behavior before implementing the complete software, nor can we prove the real-time correctness of the software.

No Formal Analysis. Although the tool-set supports early executing of models, it is not possible to perform any formal analysis like protocol deadlock or timing analysis. The latter is necessary to guarantee correctness, because a simulation or test will never execute all possible execution paths.

Timing analysis very early in the development phase can also guide the design choices where hard-real time requirements have to be met.

Weak Support for the Testing Phase. No tooling support is available for coverage testing like code-coverage or path-coverage. Tracing requirements and test case execution has to be done manually by the software engineer.

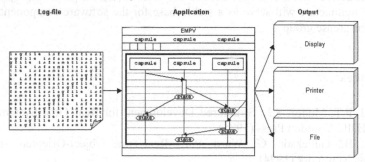

Fig. 7. Logging real-time behavior for verification purposes

Note that we did not use Quality Architect, which should be able to generate a test harness from a defined message sequence chart.

Bad Target Observability. It is very difficult to debug the software as soon as it has been downloaded to the target hardware. The offered tooling slows down the software execution and is therefore not usable.

It is hardly possible to view the performance and latency of the software running on the target hardware. Tuning the real-time behavior to meet all timing deadlines takes a lot of time.

5   Conclusions and Future Developments

Our two main goals for the development of embedded software, more efficient development and higher software quality, have only been met partially.

Although we have not seen a reduction in development effort, we believe that subsequent projects will benefit from the work achieved in this first project with UML-RT. The quality of the software increased duc to the use of a visual modeling language and code-generation („the model is the code").

The two main issues we still have to tackle are the timely availability of system level requirements (a software process issue) and a solution for protocol analysis together with the specification and verification of real-time constraints (a technical issue). For the second point, a model checking approach might help, but it is unclear whether it will scale sufficiently.

In retrospect, we first migrated from assembly to high-level languages to develop software. Now we experienced the transition to graphically oriented languages (like UML-RT). A graphical model is many times more expressive than any number of source files. This enables a higher level of abstraction while thinking about the „real" problems.

To benefit even more from the chosen technology, we have started a „reuse group" responsible for delivering software components to the projects using UML-RT. The strong encapsulation and the exact definition of interfaces in UML-RT potentially enable an easy reuse of components. The challenges of this group are more organizationally oriented and less technological.

A second initiative for the future is the definition of an Embedded Software Reference Architecture (ESRA). ESRA defines the architecture for all new projects. This reference architecture will serve as a stable base for the software components developed by the „reuse group".

References

1.   Ward, P.T, Mellor, S.J.: Structured Development for Real-Time Systems. Prentice-Hall / Yourdon Press (1985)
2.   Selic, B., Gullekson, G., Ward, P.T.: Real-Time Object-Oriented Modeling. Wiley, New York (1994)
3.   Selic, B.: Using UML for Modeling Complex Real-Time Systems. In: Mueller, F., Bestavros, A. (eds.): Languages, Compilers, and Tools for Embedded Systems. Lecture Notes in Computer Science, Vol. 1474. Springer-Verlag, Berlin Heidelberg New York (1998) 250-260
4.   Lyons, A.: UML for Real-Time Overview. Rational Software Corporation (1998). http://www.rational.com/media/whitepapers/umlrt_overvi ew.pdf
5.   Harel, D.: Statecharts: A Visual Formalism for Complex Systems. Science of Computer Programming 8 (1987) 231-274

COTS Evaluation Using Desmet Methodology & Analytic Hierarchy Process (AHP)

David Morera

European Software Institute, Technological Park of Zamudio
Building 204, 48170 Bilbao, Spain
david.morera@esi.es

Abstract. Diversity on COTS selection is causing that certain companies spend large amount of time and effort evaluating those COTS for integration within their custom made systems. This evaluation is most of the times based on de-facto rules and techniques that unfortunately may lead the company in choosing the worse or not the best component for its system. This research gives an interpretation on how to evaluate COTS making use of two different methodologies for software selection and decision making respectively. The purpose is to present how the DESMET methodology along with the AHP methodology can be combined in such a way that COTS selection would be easier and more accurate than before. This new evaluation approach will make COTS selection less human dependable and more straight forward, providing with the mean for ranking the different alternatives in a numerical way so deciding becomes more empirical base and less human base.

1 Introduction

As software development phase for any kind of system (including embedded systems) is becoming less artistic and more industrial, companies now realize that developing a whole system from scratch is completely worthless, and in most of the cases a black hole financially spoken. Software Industry as well as embedded systems industry are becoming customers of others software developers that build the software components for them.

Therefore, this new way of building systems arises another problem. Which component should I use? Which component will fit better into my system? Which component should I trust the most? Building component-based systems implies the integration of several commercial components named COTS (Commercial Off-The-Shelf) and make them work together as one unique system. Although, it may not seem a big trouble, the task of evaluating several COTS for a certain system may not be a trivial task, and should be treated seriously if we want to get a good result.

In response to this the European Software Institute under the MOOSE (Software engineering methodologies for embedded systems) project (ITEA) has studied several

M. Oivo and S. Komi-Sirviö (Eds.): PROFES 2002, LNCS 2559, pp. 485-493, 2002.
© Springer-Verlag Berlin Heidelberg 2002

evaluations models and decision making techniques in the market, and have come up with a new approach of COTS evaluation based on the DESMET and AHP methodologies.

2   COTS Evaluation Foundations

This new approach for COTS evaluation is based in two different methodologies that cover different objectives.

2.1   Desmet Methodology

The DESMET methodology was the result of a collaborative project in the United Kingdom in the last decade. This project identified a number of evaluation methods as well as formal experiments to evaluate software engineering methods and tools within a particular organization. The main steps are:

1. Define scope of evaluation
2. Select evaluation method & procedure
3. Set roles & responsibilities
4. Specify assumptions & constraints
5. Specify timescales & effort
6. Analyze & interpret results
7. Present results to decision makers

The main objective of the DESMET methodology is to help an organization to plan and execute an evaluation program in order to find the most suitable method or tool for its software development in each case.

2.2   Analytic Hierarchy Process (AHP)

The AHP is one of the best known decision making process to help people into the hard task of making the best decision out of a set of possible options. Therefore, AHP is considered a multi-criteria decision making process that balances both quantitative and qualitative aspects.

AHP was developed by Dr. Thomas L. Saaty in 1980 while he was a professor at the Wharton School of Business, and has been widely used since then by several companies such as the US Department of Defense, US Air Force, Boeing and several governments. The main steps are:

1. Identify final objectives
2. Identify alternatives
3. Evaluate key trade-offs among objectives & alternative solutions
4. Agree on final solutions.
5. An important note from these two methodologies is that they are not intended to use for COTS evaluation.

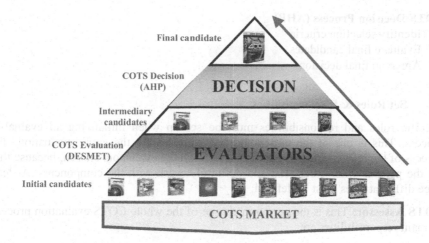

Fig. 1. Hierarchical COTS evaluation process

3   Process for Evaluating COTS in Depth

Although these two methodologies (DESMET & AHP) are not though to be used for COTS evaluation, we are going to demonstrate how they can be successfully combined and adapted to work with COTS components.

Figure 1 illustrates the combination of these two methodologies in a hierarchical pyramid.

As we can see from Fig. 1., two basic groups of people is involved in an evaluation process.

Technical group, involved mostly in the preliminary research, evaluation and selection of several candidates from the market. As a result of this research, we come up with the first set of possible candidates, which is a narrow group of COTS more oriented to our project requirements.

Business group, involved in the final decision making process. This group of people must evaluate the intermediary candidates proposed by the technical group and proposed a final candidate to the ultimate responsible for deciding.

The two big processes represented in Fig. 1. (COTS evaluation and COTS Decision) correspond directly to the DESMET and AHP processes and with each group of participants respectively. Therefore, the final COTS evaluation process presented in this paper is composed of seven different steps within two main processes:

COTS Evaluation Process (DESMET)

1. Set roles & responsibilities
2. Set time scale & effort
3. Define scope and candidates
4. Specify assumptions & constraints
5. Select an evaluation method
6. Evaluate and present results

COTS Decision Process (AHP)
7.   Identify selection criteria
8.   Evaluate final candidates
9.   Agree on final decision

3.1   Set Roles & Responsibilities

Specific roles and responsibilities must be set up when initializing an evaluation process. This is one of the most important steps within the entire evaluation. The success of the results obtained depends greatly on the evaluators chosen, because they are the persons who search, test and definitely work with the components. At least three different roles must be defined:

COTS Assessor: This is the person in charge of the whole COTS evaluation process. Its main responsibilities are:

- Lead COTS Evaluation
- Select evaluation team
- Specify system requirements
- Set time & effort needed
- Review evaluation report
- Chose final candidates

Evaluation Team: This team is formed by a group of technical people whose main objective is running the different sub-tasks of COTS evaluation:

- Collect COTS users requirements
- Define COTS features
- Chose initial alternatives
- Select evaluation method
- Carry out the evaluation
- Prepare evaluation report to the COTS Assessor.

COTS Users: These are the final users of the COTS. They are also called COTS integrators because their main task is to integrate the selected COTS into their own system. Although the evaluation team could be also the COTS users as well, it is recommended to have different groups of people within these two roles in order to be more objective when selecting the COTS. Their main tasks are:

- Identify COTS requirements
- Proposed initial alternatives/candidates
- Review COTS features
- Review evaluation report

3.2   Set Time Scale & Effort

One of the first tasks of the COTS assessor is to determine the time scale of the whole process and the effort we'll take us to perform the evaluation. One task earlier is to establish which actions should be taken, who should participate and the time limit for each of these tasks. Once we have all this information, then we can outline a preliminary planning which could be modified later on.

Some information the planning should have is:

- Tasks to perform
- Milestones
- Due dates
- Staff involved
- Effort required
- Final reports

3.3   Define Scope and Candidates

Here the COTS assessor along with the COTS users must define together the scope of the evaluation as well as the possible candidates we initially must take into account. One of the aspects that will influence in the final selection of the initial candidates is the type of COTS based system we are building:

- COTS integrated system: COTS plus self development code
- COTS solution system: System based only on COTS.

Another important issue within this step is to define the specific domain the COTS will have to cover and the characteristics of the required COTS. Finally we should to come up with a short list of possible candidates that will be examined and compared later on. Depending the domain and the requirements of the system, the initial candidate list might be too long to evaluate all COTS, so an initial screening selection could be performed in those cases. The final candidates list must contain the most representative list of COTS for the specified domain.

3.4   Specify Assumptions & Constraints

Specifying any special assumptions or constraints from either the system or the COTS candidates will help us to predict future drawbacks from the chosen solution. Therefore, it is essential to spend some time thinking on the types of things we should take into account when selecting the initial candidates such as:

- Limited budget assigned
- Required infrastructure & support
- Required training
- Required environment for validation
- Trial version availability
- IPR issues
- Open source.

3.5   Select an Evaluation Method

According to the DESMET Methodology we can select among three different types of evaluation that can be applied to COTS selection process. These types of evaluation are:

- Quantitative: Measure the benefits of using each COTS in a quantitative way.
- Qualitative: Assess features and characteristics of each COTS.
- Hybrid: This type of evaluation is a combination of the two, Quantitative and Qualitative

The DESMET Methodology also defines several ways of organizing the evaluation depending on the type and quantity of resources do we have. These ways of performing the organization are:

- Screening assessment: Initial pre-evaluation of the COTS through sources like Internet and COTS vendors profiles.
- Formal experiment: Set up an experiment in-situ to test several COTS.
- Case Study: Read related information from other people that have already implemented such COTS in their systems.
- Survey: Get different opinions from people that may have used the same COTS for integration.
- Expert Analysis: Get a formal opinion of either an internal or external expert in the pre-selected COTS.
- Benchmarking: Study and investigate other companies' best practices regarding COTS integration to adapt the same ideas and improve our performance.

3.6   Evaluate and Present Results

Finally we have to perform the evaluation throughout all the pre-selected COTS according to the timescale, roles, effort and evaluation type from the previous steps. As a main result of this task we will obtain the final group of candidates for the decision makers.

It is also convenient to write a report for each COTS evaluation performed for future reference.

3.7   Identify Selection Criteria

The initial COTS candidates proposed in step 6 are the input to this step in which the business group or decision makers are involved. The main objective of this step is to identify the major aspects that will influence in the final decision. These aspects are called selection criteria and might be for instance:

- Financial aspects (COTS cost, Maintenance cost, upgrading cost, ...)
- Technical aspects (Reliability, safety, performance, requirements, quality, ...)
- Business aspects (COTS vendor recognition, COTS vendor properties, Historical records, ...)
- Legal aspects (Type of contract, license agreement, escrow, ...)

Choosing the right selection criteria is crucial for the final decision. So if COTS vendor recognition is not important for us, then we will not chose it; otherwise, if COTS maintenance is essential in this project then we will selected as criteria. Select only the most significant aspects to avoid complicated selection trees.

3.8   Evaluate Final Candidates

The entire process of evaluating the final candidates for selecting the best COTS to this project is divided into 5 sub-steps represented in Table 1.

Table 1. Sub-steps in evaluating the COTS candidates

EVALUATE FINAL CANDIDATES	
1. Ranking selection criteria	In this step we have to rank each of the chosen selection criteria among each other within a 9 value scale: 1 – Equal 3 – Moderate 5 – Strong 7 – Very Strong 9 – Extreme The final result will be a table called Pair-Wise comparison in which the overall weight for each criteria respect to each other is also calculated. Therefore, what we know so far is the percentage of importance of each criteria respect to each other in a scale from 0 to 1.
2. Ranking different candidates	In this step we have to do basically the same as we did when ranking the selection criteria. However, this time we must rank each set of candidates regarding each criteria. The tasks are the same and the result that we obtain is the percentage of importance of each candidate respect to each other and selection criteria.
3. Draw ranked hierarchy tree	In order to have a clear view of the values we have obtained so far, we must draw the final ranked hierarchy tree where all the calculated values are represented respectively. This tree will give us an overall view of the weights of each candidate under each criteria, and will allow us to depict which could be the „winner". However, two more steps are needed to get to the final answer.
4. Final candidates ranking	In this step we do the product matrix between all the candidates weights found in sub-step 2 and the weights for each criteria from sub-step 1. The resulting values will represent the final ranking of all the candidates.
5. Cost / Benefits analysis	However, another further step is needed if we want to obtain a real and objective value of which candidate is most suitable for our system. To do this we must perform a cost / benefits analysis from the values obtained in sub-step 4 and the normalized cost of each COTS.

Finally, after several steps we know which COTS might be the most suitable and convenient for our purpose. Therefore, if we take a closest look into these previous 8 steps we see that there exist two main actions to perform in this kind of evaluations. The first action is to select a good candidate list by the technical group, and the second one is to define a good set of selection criteria by the business group. These two actions will influence greatly in the final results.

3.9   Agree on Final Decision

Now we arrive to the hardest part of the whole evaluation process. We have a nice list of COTS ranked in other of importance for our specific project. We also know which COTS is more suitable for our project and why, and we also have nice reports that describe is COTS in detailed. However, these are all numbers and business is more than numbers, it's human knowledge too.

Therefore, in this last step we must agree or disagree on the values we obtained before. COTS selection, as any other selection, is always human dependable. Numbers only help us to easily discard and select the best COTS to evaluate, and give us an idea of which ones are better; however, we cannot base our final decision only on numbers. We have to discuss all together the final results and come up with the selected COTS.

4   Conclusion

The objective of this paper has been to present how two different well-known methodologies for selection and decision making (DESMET & AHP) can be combined together to perform a COTS evaluation process. We all know COTS usage implies some benefits and also some risks when integrating within our system. Therefore, once we have decided to use COTS in our systems, then we skip to the next problem, how do I know which COTS to use. So COTS evaluation is not only a requirement, but also help us to mitigate risks during integration.

Another important key factor of COTS evaluation is that COTS evaluation is always context dependent. It means that, an evaluation process must be carried out for a specific project and not for several different projects with distinct characteristics. So a good COTS for a certain project might not be so good for another project. Different evaluation processes must be performed in these cases.

As we have seen during the entire process, people from all levels in the company must be involved in such process in order to get a most realistic answer. In fact the most important steps within the whole evaluation, the initial candidates list and COTS criteria selection, are carried out by two different groups of people, the technical group and the business group.

Money is always an important aspect for everybody when acquiring a product. Therefore, it must be also taken into account separately also in this type of acquisition. Cost / benefits analysis will provide us with a more realistic answer within our environment.

Last but least, COTS evaluation, as any other evaluation process is always human dependable, so numbers will only guide us to the final answer, but never will be used as a rule of thumb.

References

1. Barbara Ann Kitchenham: Evaluating Software Engineering Methods and Tool. National Computing Centre, Manchester, England
2. Michael A. Trick: Analytic Hierarchy Process. Carnegie Mellon University. Available online at: http://mat.gsia.cmu.edu/mstc/multiple/node4.html
3. Yan Jianyuan: Using Analytic Hierarchy process as the auxiliary decision of computer integrated system for library management (CISLM). Nankai University, Tianjin, China. Available online at: http://web.simmons.edu/~chen/nit/NIT'92/387-yan.htm

4. Les Frair: Student Peer Evaluations using the Analytic Hierarchy Process Method. University of Alabama Tuscaloosa, Department of Industrial Engineering. Available online at: http://fie.engrng.pitt.edu/fie95/4c3/4c31/4c31.htm

5. David Carney, Kurt Wallnau: COTS Evaluation. Software Engineering Institute, Carnegie Mellon University.

Black-Box Evaluation of COTS Components Using Aspects and Metadata*

Alejandra Cechich[1] and Macario Polo[2]

[1] Departamento de Informática y Estadística, Universidad Nacional del Comahue
Buenos Aires 1400, 8300 Neuquén, Argentina
acechich@uncoma.edu.ar
[2] Escuela Superior de Informática, Universidad de Castilla-La Mancha
Paseo de la Universidad 4, Ciudad Real, España
Macario.Polo@uclm.es

Abstract. Current approaches to automated black-box testing of components tend to focus on reducing the effort required to reveal component's properties by partially automating interface probing. This often leads to the development of test cases, which make too many assumptions about interfaces. Aspect-oriented component engineering uses the concept of different system capabilities to reason about component provided and required services. Aspect information is used to help implement better component interfaces and to encode knowledge of a component's capability. We describe and illustrate a proposal on the use of aspect-oriented component engineering techniques and notations to search for components inputs on which the component properties are revealed using a combination of existing test generation methods for black-box testing and a categorisation of component services.

1   Introduction

Black box testing techniques are characterised by focusing tests on the expected behaviour of a software component and ensuring that the resulting functionality is correct [1]. In many cases this behavioural testing is done without the aid of source code or design documents, and it is possible to provide input test cases and only test the outputs of the object for correctness. This type of black box testing does not require knowledge of the source code and so is possible to do with COTS components. Strategies for black box testing that may be effective for COTS components include test case generation by equivalence classes, error guessing and random tests. These

* This work is partially supported by the CYTED (Ciencia y Tecnología para el Desarrollo) project VII-J-RITOS2 (Red Iberoamericana de Tecnologías de Software para la década del 2000), and by the project TAMANSI (Técnicas avanzadas para la mantenibilidad de sistemas de información), Consejeria de Ciencia y Tecnología de la Junta de Comunidades de Castilla-La Mancha (PBC-02-001).

M. Oivo and S. Komi-Sirviö (Eds.): PROFES 2002, LNCS 2559, pp. 494-508, 2002.

three techniques rely only on some notion of the input space and expected functionality of the component being tested [1,2]. With COTS components, the user should know these facts and be able to create test cases around them. To guide test case selection, the operational profile of the COTS component can be used. The operational profile identifies the criticality of components and their duration and frequency of use. Both the operational profile of the COTS component and the whole system must be taken into account.

Most component-based black-box testing techniques focus on the identification of interfaces supporting functional decomposition [3,4]. Interface probing is a technique used in black-box understanding and it is mainly used to understand functionality and limitations of COTS components. However, one of the major disadvantages of this approach is that frequently a large number of test cases have to be created and analysed. In addition, developers may frequently miss major component limitations and incorrectly assume certain component functionality. This may lead to incorrect use of the component when it is integrated with a software system under development [4]. On the other hand, aspect-oriented component engineering uses the concept of different system capabilities to reason about component provided and required services. Aspect information is used to help implement better component interfaces and to encode knowledge of a component's capability [5,6]. Each component aspect has a number of aspect details that are used to more precisely describe component characteristics relating to the aspect. Some research groups [7] take advantage of reflection to implement aspect-oriented features where the aspect logic has the entire runtime state and control at its disposal. Another benefit is that the aspect code can make decisions based on actual runtime values. Computational reflection enables a program to access its internal structure and behaviour and this is beneficial for testing by automating the execution of tests through the creation of instances of classes and the execution of different sequences of methods [8]. Thus, in this way the aspect code can dynamically decide how to instrument the running application and evolve based on runtime data. Metadata are also used, in existing component models, to provide generic usage information about a component (e.g. the name of its class, the name of its methods) as well as information for testing [9,10] providing a general mechanism for aiding software engineering tasks. In the context of self-checking code, the metadata needed to accomplish a task consist of pre-conditions and post-conditions for the different functions provided by the component, and invariants for the component itself. This information is used to implement a checking mechanism for calls to the component.

In this paper, we present a preliminary approach that can be used in the process of black-box understanding in conjunction with interface probing. The major goal of our work is to reduce the effort required to determine component properties by automating a search process. In particular, when reasoning about provided and required services of components we analyse these in terms of its particular aspect details. In Section 2 of the paper we introduce the main characteristics of black-box testing for components. Section 3 then presents how aspect-oriented component engineering is used to analyse properties of components and we briefly present metadata in this context. Section 4 of the paper describes our approach for improving black-box component testing techniques by using aspects and metadata. Finally, we conclude with an overview and future research directions.

2   Black-Box Component Evaluation

Developers must have a good understanding of COTS components in order to evaluate them. As a result, developers have to identify many component properties (e.g., functionality, limitations, pre-conditions) recording which properties are in conflict with other expected properties. There are two major methods of black-box understanding: binary (object code) reverse engineering and interface probing. Binary reverse engineering is used to automatically derive a design structure of a component from its binary code. Interface probing is often used to understand functionality and limitations of COTS components. Using this technique a developer designs a set of test cases, executes a component on these test cases, and analyses outputs produced by the component.

Regarding to interface probing, there are a number of black-box methods for evaluating a component: manual evaluation, evaluation with a test suite, and automated interface probing. Typically, manual evaluation of COTS components consists of gathering information about the component's behaviour from available documentation, building an evaluation driver, and performing interface probing. On the other hand, evaluation with a test suite involves developing a test suite that contains an evaluation driver and a set of inputs together with expected outputs.

Automating the search process of test cases could reduce the effort required to determine properties of a component. In these approaches, assertions are used to describe properties of a component. After assertions are provided, the developer specifies the search, e.g., ranges of values for input parameters used in the search. After the search is specified, the search engine (an automated test case generator) performs the search to identify component inputs that exhibit the specified property. If such input is found, this indicates that the component has the specified property. In most cases the source code of COTS components is not available so only execution-oriented test generation methods may be used. In particular, a formal evaluation specification for components with multiple-interfaces consist of three different types that express component's properties related to: (1) individual interfaces, (2) interactions between interfaces, and (3) a state behaviour [3].

The interface specification is used to express stand-alone properties of individual interfaces. However, many components interfaces are related in such a way that interactions introduce new types of component properties. Therefore, the interaction evaluation specification describes the properties of interest and the relationships between the interfaces of a component. For many components, it may be very easy to create such tests, however for other components creation of "good" tests may be a difficult task.

A different approach can be followed to automatically create a system model from individual requirements and then automatically generate test cases related to these requirements [11]. From the requirements, a system model is automatically created with requirement information mapped to the model. The system model is used to automatically generate test cases related to individual requirements. Several test generation strategies are presented. For example, the tester chooses a testing strategy that should be used in selective testing from a list of various testing strategies: each state that has a marked incoming or outgoing transition is traversed at least once (state coverage); each marked transition is traversed at least once (transition coverage); etc. Computational reflection enables a program to access its internal structure and behaviour and also to pragmatically manipulate that structure, thereby modifying its behaviour. In testing, computational reflection has been used to load a class into a testing tool extracting some of the methods and invocating them with the appropriate parameters. Therefore, reflection is used to build test cases by extracting the needed characteristics of classes [8]. Moreover, as the execution of methods in a class can create and use instances of other different classes, the approach is also helpful to test the integration of classes.

Component developers can provide the component user with different kinds of information, depending on the specific context and needs. This information can be presented as metadata describing static and dynamic aspects of the component. A framework using metadata for components in such a way that there is a unique format for each kind of metadata has been proposed by [9]. Metadata is used in the context of testing and analysis of distributed-component systems. In this case, the metadata needed to accomplish a task consist of pre-conditions and post-conditions for the different functions provided by the component, and invariants for the component itself. The metadata-based technique has also been extended and applied to regression test selection for component-based applications [10].

In sum, the problem of testing component-based software is complicated by a number of characteristics of component-based software engineering. Distributed component-based systems of course exhibit all the well-known problems that make traditional testing difficult. But testing of component-based software is further complicated by the fact that different functionality is provided inside a component depending on its interfaces and state. Developing a foundation for testing component-based software is a complicated issue, even though a formal model of test adequacy for component-based software has been developed [12].

3   Aspect-Oriented Component Specification

Aspect-Oriented Component Engineering (AOCE) focuses on identifying various aspects of an overall system a component contributes (provides) services to, or services it uses (requires) from other components. Aspects typically affect many components identified by functional decomposition of common system characteristics such as user interfaces, persistency and distribution and collaborative work. Unlike most Aspect-Oriented Programming approaches, AOCE avoids the concepts of "code weaving" and the use of run-time reflection mechanisms [7,13,14]. Instead, AOCE focuses on developing components whose characteristics are factored into the component interfaces so that components can be run-time re-configured and dynamically composed [6].

The concept of component aspects allows a better categorisation of component capabilities according to a component's contribution to an overall component-based system's functions and helps organise non-functional constraints. A key feature of this categorisation of component characteristics is the idea that some components provide certain aspect-related services for other components (or end users) to use, while other components require certain aspect-related services from other components. Each component aspect has a number of aspect details that are used to describe component characteristics relating to the aspect. These details aim to increase developers and end users knowledge about components by providing a more effective categorisation and codification mechanism for the component services.

When reasoning about operations of components we analyse these in terms of particular aspects. For example, developers can describe interfaces in terms of a collaborative work aspect, persistency-related aspect, or user interface aspect. Note that some aspect categorisations may overlap (a service might be considered a user interface aspect as well as a collaborative work aspect). Figure 1 illustrates how some aspects map onto some services. The Accounting View component has only services described in terms of user interface aspects, meanwhile the Editing Balance component has services described in terms of one aspect as well as overlaps between the user interface aspect and the collaborative work aspect, and the collaborative work aspect and the persistency aspect.

Metadata lets the component developer provide information to make the component more usable. In particular, the following information could be provided [9]:

- Information to evaluate the component: for example, information on static and dynamic metrics computed on the components,
- Information to deploy the component: for example, additional information on the interface of the component,
- Information to test and debug the component: for example, a finite state machine representation of the component,
- Information to analyse the component: for example, summary data-flow information, control-flow graph representations of part of the component, etc.
- Information on how to customise or extend the component: for example, a list of properties of the component.

Therefore, metadata range from finite-state-machine models of the component to a general list of properties. In [9, 10] metadata have been used to implement a run-time checking mechanism for applications and to introduce some techniques for regression testing. In particular, an implementation of the metadata provides a generic way of adding information to, and retrieving information from, a component, and is not related to any specific component model.

Two separate issues are addressed: (1) what format to use for the metadata, and (2) how to attach metadata to the component. A metadatum is thus composed of a header, which contains a tag identifying its type and subtype (for example, the metadata type "analysis/data-dependence" could tell a component user the kind of metadata retrieved), and a body containing the actual information. The way a component developer can add metadata to his component can be accomplished by providing each component with two methods: one to query about the kinds of metadata available, and the other to retrieve a specific kind of metadata.

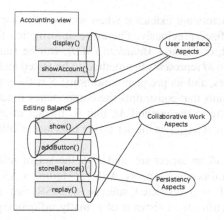

Fig. 1. Illustration of component aspects

In our approach, we have extended the notion of using metadata for testing COTS by classifying testing information using aspects. A number of meta-procedures for black-box testing are introduced in the following section to allow reasoning about completeness of data supplied for testing, and eventually facilitating the use of test cases along with automated tools for black-box testing.

4   Black-Box Component Testing Using Aspects and Metadata

One of the major steps towards achieving efficiency of COTS testing lies in using testing techniques which support the identification and creation of test cases that are relevant for the component. Another is building up a sufficiently large and well-documented data of these test cases. Using metadata and aspects can extend the documentation of a component to define and validate its test cases. For example, in our approach documentation for defining test cases is grouped into a meta-object used as a descriptor of a base-object. Documentation is extended to include an aspect-based analysis that allows reasoning about several properties of the test cases.

To introduce the approach, a number of concepts must be defined. We first define the notion of *aspect scope* of a method as the set of all aspects that influence a particular component's method. For the example we introduced in the previous section, the aspect scope of all the methods is the following:

ASc = {(show(), {User Interface, Collaborative Work}), (addButton(), {User Interface, Collaborative Work}), (storeBalance(), {Collaborative Work, Persistency}), (replay(), {Collaborative Work, Persistency})

Identifying and creating test cases relevant for a component involve analysing test cases for a single method as well as test cases for multiple-methods. Defining tests cases depends on several factors such as the component's state, the invariants on the functionality associated to the component, and preconditions and post conditions of each method. These factors are extended when we consider aspects by including the aspect scope as we defined previously. Therefore, information for defining test cases of a particular method, or *Method Metadata (MM)*, can be summarised as the tuple *(M, S, ASc$_M$, Inv)* where *M* represents the method to be tested and it implicitly includes its name and parameters, and its pre/post conditions; *S* is the state of the component, *Inv* is the set of invariants that constraints the component's functionality, and *ASc$_M$* is the aspect scope relating to the method *M*, that is, the set of aspects relevant to the method *M*. For example, *ASc$_{show()}$* is the set {User Interface, Collaborative Work}.

More formally, let *AS* an aspect set, and *ASR* the set of relations between a particular method and its influencing aspects, ASR = (Method x AS)-set, the aspect scope *ASc* can be expressed as a restricted subtype of ASR that satisfies the property *is_in_scope*, which certifies the existence of actually influencing aspects on the relationship:

ASc = {asc: ASR | is_in_scope(asc)}
is_in_scope: ASR → Bool
is_in_scope(asr) ≡ ∀ as: AS, m: Method • (m, as) ∈ asr ⇒ influence(as, m)

Hence, a meta-procedure for aspect-oriented generation of test cases can be enunciated based on the *MM* information as Figure 2 shows. For example, the method show() in Figure 1 is affected by two aspects: User Interface and Collaborative Work. We first select the pre/post conditions relevant to the aspect User Interface and find test cases by using traditional techniques for black-box testing. After that, we proceed doing the same for the aspect Collaborative Work. Once all aspects have been considered, we analyse all test cases to identify incompatibility or inconsistency among them generating a new set of test cases, where tests are compatible. That is, values are selected from a consistent range of possibilities for every test case. Finally, several analyses of properties of test cases can be done. In particular, a completeness analysis that checks that all aspects have been considered and hence all domains have been consolidated could be useful for identifying a wider spectrum of test cases.

```
For each M
    For each aspect in the set ASc_M
            Specialise the pre/post conditions of M ac-
            cording to the considered aspect
            Select test cases for M
    Analyse the compatibility of all test cases
    Select compatible test cases and constraint domains
    Analyse completeness of selected test cases with
    respect to a combined domain for all aspects in ASc_M
```

Fig.2: A meta-procedure (*MP1*) for aspect-oriented generation of test cases

Again, *MP1* can be expressed more formally as a function definition. We need to express the information of a method as a type variable containing the method's name, its parameters and its pre/post conditions - *Method* = (name, param, pre, post); and let *Test* a type variable containing information about a particular test case, such as its values passed as input, its expected results and its actual results - *Test* = (obj, expectedRes, actualRes) - and *TestCase* a type variable representing a set of Test, *MP1* is defined as:

$MP1$: ASc x Inv $\rightarrow$ TestCase
$MP1$ (asc, i) $\equiv$ { ts | $\forall$ as: AS, m: Method, a: Aspect $\bullet$
$\qquad$ (m, as) $\in$ asc $\wedge$ a $\in$ as $\wedge$ compatible(m.pre, m.pos, as) $\Rightarrow$
$\qquad\qquad\qquad\qquad$ $\exists$ t: Test $\bullet$ test_m(a, m, t) $\wedge$ is_adequate(t, i) $\wedge$ t $\in$ ts }
is_adequate: Test x Inv $\rightarrow$ Bool
is_adequate(t, i) $\equiv$ adequate(t.expectedRes, t.actualRes) $\wedge$
$\qquad\qquad\qquad$ satisfies_invariants(state(t.obj), i)

Functions *compatible, test_m, adequate*, and *satisfies_invariants* are abstract function definitions, which should implement previously mentioned constraints in several ways. Particularly, compatibility of pre/post conditions relevant to the aspect should be verified by defining the function *compatible*; consistency of test values should be verified for every test case by defining the function *test_m*; and adequacy of test cases should be verified by analysing its results and verifying the satisfaction of invariants previously stated.

It's widely recognised that black-box evaluation techniques are highly dependent of the characteristics of the artefact that is been tested. Hence, our procedure is broadly enough to allow analysing test cases using different techniques.

A more complete selection of test cases also involves analysing valid ranges from a combined view of methods so aspects affecting methods can be used as a way of partitioning the testing space. We define the notion of *relevant methods* (*RM*) as the set of all methods affected by a particular aspect. For the example in Section 3, relevant methods of all the aspects are defined as follows:

RM = {(User Interface, {show(), addButton()}), (Collaborative Work, {show(), addButton(), storeBalance(), replay()}, (Persistency, {storeBalance()})}

and RM_A is the relevant method set relating to the aspect A, that is, the set of all methods relevant to the aspect A. For example, $RM_{UserInterface}$ is the set {show(), addButton()}.

More formally, let *ME* a method set and *RMR* the set of relations between a particular aspect and the set of methods influenced by this aspect, that is RMR = (Aspect x ME)-set, the relevant methods *RM* can be expressed as a restricted subtype of RMR that satisfies the property *is_influenced_by*:

RM = {rmr: RMR | is_influenced_by(rmr)}
is_influenced_by: RMR $\rightarrow$ Bool
is_influenced_by(rmr) $\equiv$ $\forall$ me: ME, a: Aspect $\bullet$
$\qquad\qquad\qquad$ (a, me) $\in$ rmr $\Rightarrow$ is_influenced(me, a)

Hence, another meta-procedure for aspect-oriented generation of multi-method test cases can be enunciated as Figure 3 shows. For example, the method show() is related to the method addButton() by means of the aspect User Interface. After generating test cases for show(), we proceed selecting the aspect - User Interface - that we want to consider.

```
For each M
Select test cases for M          /* applying the meta-
procedure MP1 */
      For each aspect in the set RM
              For all other Mk  related by a particular as-
              pect in the set RMA
                    Specialise the pre/post conditions of Mk
                    according to the considered aspect
                    Select test cases for Mk   /* applying
                    the meta-procedure MP1  */
      Analyse the compatibility of all test cases  for
      {M, Mk1, Mk2, ....}
      Select compatible combined test cases and con-
      straint domains to the intersection
      Analyse completeness of selected test cases with
      respect to a combined domain for all interfaces in
      RMA
```

Fig. 3: A meta-procedure (*MP2*) for aspect-oriented generation of multi-method test cases

Then, the method addButton() is analysed and again we select the pre/post conditions relevant to the aspect User Interface and we find test cases by using traditional techniques for black-box testing. After that, we proceed analysing all test cases to identify incompatibility or inconsistency (between show()'s test cases and addButton()'s test cases). That is, values are selected from a consistent and common range of possibilities. Finally, a completeness analysis that checks that all ranges have been considered and hence all domains have been consolidated is done for all methods affected by the same aspect.

More formally:

$MP2$: RM x ASc x Inv $\rightarrow$ TestCase

$MP2$ (rm, asc, i) $\equiv$ { ts | $\forall$ me: ME, m_1,m_2: Method, a: Aspect, as_1, as_2: AS $\bullet$

$(m_1, as_1) \in$ asc $\wedge$ $(m_2, as_2) \in$ asc $\wedge$ a $\in as_1$ $\wedge$

(a, me) $\in$ rm $\wedge m_1 \in$ me $\wedge m_2 \in$ me $\wedge$

compatible_pre(m_1.pre, m_2.pre, a) $\wedge$

compatible_pos(m_1.pos, m_2.pos, a) $\Rightarrow$

$\exists t_1, t_2$, tc: Test $\bullet$ test_m(a, m_1, t_1) $\wedge$ test_m(a, m_2, t_2) $\wedge$

$t_1 \in$ MP1((m_1, as_1)) $\wedge t_2 \in$ MP1((m_2,as_2)) $\wedge$

is_combination(t_1, t_2, tc) $\wedge$

is_valid(tc, i) $\wedge$ tc $\in$ ts }

We should note that the procedure *MP2* doesn't explicitly mention the location of the methods M_k. This is particularly useful at this meta-level specification because the entire procedure can be adapted to black-box testing as well as integration testing among components too. If we consider the example detailed in the previous paragraph, the set of methods relevant to the aspect User Interface, is calculated inside the component `Editing Balance` focusing on black-box techniques. However, the same procedure could be applied if we consider all methods in the model related by the aspect User Interface, that is, methods in `Editing Balance` as well as methods in `Accounting View`. Therefore, focusing on integration testing is another possible implementation of procedure *MP2*.

Finally, methods are relating each other by shearing a set of aspects that influence their behaviour. This situation leads to an "aspect overlap" meaning that methods tested according to procedure *MP2* are also influenced by compatibility of common ranges. To clarify this point, just consider our example of Figure 1. Procedure *MP1* has produced test cases for show() from the point of view of User Interface, addButton() from the point of view of User Interface, show() from the point of view of Collaborative Work, and so on. Procedure *MP2* has continued evaluating methods from the same point of view, such as show() and addButton() from the point of view of User Interface. But show() and addButton() should also be analysed considering that both methods share different points of view or aspects (User Interface and Collaborative Work), which could constrain our test cases domain.

Therefore, we define the notion of *common aspects* (*CA*) as the set of relations between all methods affected by a particular set of aspects. That is, a set of aspects is affecting to a set of methods producing an intersection of relevant test cases for a particular domain. For the example in Section 3, common aspects are defined as follows:

$$CA = \{ (\{\text{User Interface, Collaborative Work}\}, \{\text{show}(), \text{addButton}()\}),$$
$$(\{\text{Persistency, Collaborative Work}\}, \{\text{storeBalance}()\}) \}$$

and CA_k denotes an element of the set *CA* as the pair *(a, m)* where *a* is a particular set of aspects influencing the particular set of methods *m*.

More formally, let *CAR* the set of relations between a set of aspects and its influenced methods, that is CAR = (AS x ME)-set, the common aspects *CA* can be expressed as a restricted subtype of CAR that satisfies the property *is_influenced_by*:

$$CA = \{\text{car: CAR} \mid \text{is\_influenced\_by(car)}\}$$
$$\text{is\_influenced\_by: CAR} \rightarrow \text{Bool}$$
$$\text{is\_influenced\_by(car)} \equiv \forall \text{ me: ME, as: AS} \bullet$$
$$(\text{as, me}) \in \text{car} \Rightarrow \text{is\_influenced(me, as)}$$

Hence, the last meta-procedure for aspect-oriented generation of test cases can be enunciated as Figure 4 shows. Every element of the set *CA* is evaluated to identify possible common test cases and/or inconsistency among previously selected cases.

```
For each CA_k = (a, m)
    For each method in the set CA.m
        Evaluate common ranges and compatibilities
        for test cases analysed in every CA.a      /*
        applying the meta-procedure MP2 */
```

Fig. 4: A meta-procedure (*MP3*) for aspect-oriented generation of overlapping test cases

More formally:

MP3: CA x Inv → TestCase

MP3 (ca, i) ≡ { ts | ∀ me: ME, m: Method, a: Aspect, as: AS •

(as, me) ∈ ca ∧ a ∈ as ∧

m ∈ me ⇒ ∃ t: Test •

t ∈ *MP2*((a,me),(as,m), i) ∧

compatible(t, as, me) ∧ t ∈ ts }

4.1   Test Selection Example

In this section, we introduce the example presented in [9] that will be used to motivate the need of aspects and metadata and to show a possible use of this information. A complete example is omitted for brevity.

```
public class BankingAccount {
    //@ invariant ( ((balance  > 0) || (status == OVERDRAWN)) && \
    //@                ((timeout < LIMIT) || (logged == false))   );

    public void open()  throws CantOpenException,
                                 InvalidPINException {
        //@  pre (true);
        //@  post (logged == true);
        //@  aspects (Collaborative Wok);
    }
    public float withdraw(float amount) {
        //@  pre   (logged == true)  && \
        //@          (amount < balance) ) ;
        //@  post ( (return == balance' ) && \\
        //@          (balance' == balance – amount) ) ;
        //@  aspects  (Collaborative Work, Persistency, User Interface);
    }
    public float deposit(float amount)  {
        //@  pre   (logged == true) ;
        //@  post ( (return == balance' ) && \\
        //@          (balance' == balance + amount) ) ;
        //@  aspects (Collaborative Work, Persistency, User Interface);
    }
}
```

Fig. 5. BankingAccount fragment of the component metadata

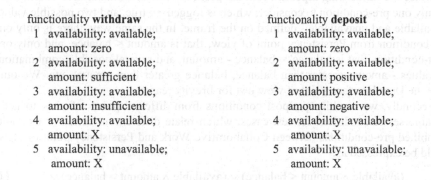

functionality **withdraw**
- Params:
    - zero
    - insufficient [amount > balance]
    - sufficient   [amount = < balance]
- Environment
    - available [logged == true]
    - unavailable [error]

functionality **deposit**
- Params:
    - zero
    - positive [amount > 0]
    - negative [amount < 0]
- Environment
    - available [logged == true]
    - unavailable [error]

Fig. 6: A possible set of categories, choices, and constraints for withdraw and deposit

functionality **withdraw**
1 availability: available;
   amount: zero
2 availability: available;
   amount: sufficient
3 availability: available;
   amount: insufficient
4 availability: available;
   amount: X
5 availability: unavailable;
   amount: X

functionality **deposit**
1 availability: available;
   amount: zero
2 availability: available;
   amount: positive
3 availability: available;
   amount: negative
4 availability: available;
   amount: X
5 availability: unavailable;
   amount: X

Fig. 7: Test frames for methods withdraw and deposit

The example consists of part of a distributed application for remote banking where one or more instances of an externally-developed component are used to access a remote database containing account-related information, for the sake of this example we assume that the source code of `Banking Account` is unavailable. We have extended the notation to include aspects as part of the component's metadata. Figure 5 shows a subset of the `BankingAccount` component interface and a fragment of the component specification for invariants, pre/post conditions and aspects.

Sets ASc, RM, and CA are easily calculated from metadata information. Particularly, ASc is part of the metadata, and RM and CA are extracted as:

RM = {(User Interface, {withdraw(float amount), deposit(float amount)}), (Collaborative Work, {open(), withdraw(float amount), deposit(float amount)}, (Persistency, {withdraw(float amount), deposit(float amount)})}

CA = { ({User Interface, Collaborative Work, Persistency}, {withdraw(float amount), deposit(float amount)})}

Black-box testing techniques develop test cases based on a functional description of the system. One such technique, the category-partition method, produces test frames that represent a test specification for the functional units in the system. As functional units, components can be analysed to produce a test frame based both on analysis of the component's interface and on its metadata. Figure 6 illustrates, for the methods withdraw and deposit, a possible set of categories, choices, and constraints on the choices derived by applying the category-partition method to the component BankingAccount. Figure 7 shows a set of test frames derived from the test specifications in Figure 6. Value "X" indicates any value. Note that overdrawn is not included in our analysis.

We can now select test cases by applying the meta-procedures *M1* and *M2*. First of all, we consider compatibility of pre/post conditions grouped into different aspect sets. When analysing the withdraw method, Collaborative Work, Persistency and User Interface are influencing aspects. From the point of view of Collaborative Work, there is only one pre-condition to consider, which is logged == true, and two possible values - available and unavailable - defined on the frame. In the same way, there is only one pre-condition from Persistency point of view, that is amount < balance, and only one post-condition, that is balance' = balance - amount, and several possible combinations of values - amount greater than balance, balance greater than amount, etc. We omit here the User Interface point of view just for brevity reasons.

Secondly, we combine pre/post conditions from different points of view to get a suitable set of conditions for test cases, which relate different aspects. For example, combined pre-conditions between Collaborative Work and Persistency point of views could be expressed as:

$$(\text{available} \wedge \text{amount} < \text{balance}) \vee (\text{available} \wedge \text{amount} > \text{balance}) \vee \qquad \textbf{(1)}$$
$$(\text{available} \wedge \text{amount} = 0) \vee \text{unavailable}$$

In the same way, an expression for combined pre-conditions of the deposit method is obtained as:

$$(\text{available} \wedge \text{amount} < 0) \vee (\text{available} \wedge \text{amount} > 0) \vee \qquad \textbf{(2)}$$
$$(\text{available} \wedge \text{amount} = 0) \vee \text{unavailable}$$

Finally, we need to combine pre-conditions according to every influencing aspect. To do that, we select compatible constraints and we analyse the completeness of the resulting expression. As a negative balance is not allowed, in our case, expressions (1) and (2) can be simplified as:

$$(\text{available} \wedge \text{amount} < 0) \vee (\text{available} \wedge \text{amount} < \text{balance}) \vee (\text{available} \qquad \textbf{(3)}$$
$$\wedge \text{amount} > \text{balance}) \vee (\text{available} \wedge \text{amount} = 0) \vee \text{unavailable}$$

Therefore, test cases can be associated to expression (3) that considers pre-conditions from two different aspects. Iteratively, we construct a combined expression for all influencing aspects on the component interface and define its associated test cases. After that, we proceed building an evaluation driver and performing interface probing.

5   Conclusion

We have introduced a procedure for black-box testing of component-based applications by using aspects and meta-data. The technique is based on packaging additional information together with a component. The presence of metadata allows component developers to provide information useful for black-box test selection. In particular, aspects allow classifying metadata information to improve the test selection activity by reducing complexity of analysis. In general, separation of concerns has been widely applied on software engineering tasks improving human capacity for dealing with abstractness and modelling. Splitting metadata according to aspects brings the possibility of applying separation of concerns, as a principle, on component testing selection. We have shown, by using a simple example, how this can be done.

We have presented a procedure that is defined in general way, so to allow for handling different kinds of black-box testing techniques. Our future work includes the identification and definition of different instantiations for the most common black-box testing techniques for components, and an actual application of the procedures. Different scenarios will be empirically analysed to investigate positive and negative effects from our approach.

References

1. Beizer B.: Black-Box Testing. Techniques for Functional Testing of Software and Systems, John Wiley & Sons (1995).
2. De Millo et al.: Software Testing and Evaluation, Menlo Park, CA: Benjamin/Cumming Publishing Co. (1987)
3. Mueller C. and Korel B.: Automated Black-Box Evaluation of COTS Components with Multiple-Interfaces. In Proceedings of the 2nd International Workshop on Automated Program Analysis, Testing, and Verification, ICSE 2001,Toronto, Canada (2001)
4. Korel B.: Black-Box Understanding of COTS Components. In Proceedings of the 7th International Workshop on Program Comprehension, IEEE Press. (1999) 92-99
5. Grundy J.: Aspect-Oriented requirement Engineering for Component-Based Software Systems. In Proceedings of the 4th IEEE International Symposium on Requirements Engineering, IEEE Press (1999) 84-91
6. Grundy J.: Multi-Perspective Specification, Design, and Implementation of Software Components using Aspects. International Journal of Software Engineering and Knowledge Engineering, Vol. 10 (6), World Scientific Publishing Co. (2000)
7. Sullivan G.: Aspect-Oriented Programming using Reflection and Metaobject Protocols. Communications of the ACM, Vol. 44(10) (2001) 95-97
8. Polo M. et al: Automating Testing of Java Programs using Reflection. In Proceedings of ICSE 2001 Workshop WAPATV, IEEE Press (2001)

9. Orso A. et al.: Component Metadata for Software Engineering Tasks. In Proceedings of EDO 2000, LNCS Vol. 1999, Springer Verlag. (2000)
10. Harrold M. et al.: Using Component Metadata to Support the Regression Testing of Component-Based Software. Technical Report GIT-CC-01-38, College of Computing, Georgia Institute of Technology. (2001)
11. Tahat L. et al.: Requirement-Based Automated Black-Box Test Generation. In Proceedings of the 25th Annual International Computer Software and Applications Conference (COMPSAC'01), IEEE Press. (2001) 489-495
12. Rosenblum D.: Adequate Testing of Component-Based Software. Technical Report 97-34, Department of Information and Computer Science, University of California, Irvine. (1997)
13. Pawlak R. et al: Distributed Separations of Concerns with Aspect Components. In Proceedings of the Technology of Object-Oriented Languages and Systems (TOOLS33), IEEE Press. (2000) 276-287
14. Pulvermüller E. et al.: Implementing Collaboration-based Designs Using Aspect-oriented Programming. In Proceedings of the Technology of Object-Oriented Languages and Systems (TOOLS34), IEEE Press. (2000) 95-104

The Dimensions of Embedded COTS and OSS Software Component Integration

Tuija Helokunnas

Tampere University of Technology, P.O.Box 541, 33101 Tampere, Finland
Nokia Research Center, P.O.Box 407, FIN-00045 Nokia Group, Finland
Tuija.Helokunnas@tut.fi

Abstract. This paper describes the dimensions of the integration of embedded Commercial-Off-The-Shelf (COTS) and Open Source Software (OSS) components in the telecommunication systems. The paper emphasizes a telecommunications system vendor view to COTS and OSS component integration. The paper is based on semi-structured interviews held both at component supplying and integrating companies in Finland. The following embedded COTS and OSS acquisition, integration and maintenance dimensions were identified: Vision and strategy, business and markets, software engineering processes, software engineering environments and collaboration approaches. The paper describes the main characteristics of each dimension. The paper focuses on the collaboration approaches and especially on the information and knowledge exchange between a system vendor and all of the component suppliers.

1   Introduction

The aim of this paper is to describe the dimensions of the integration of embedded Commercial-Off-The-Shelf (COTS) and Open Source Software (OSS) components in the telecommunication systems. Software component as a concept has attracted software community during the past thirty years. Principles of Component Based Software Engineering (CBSE) have been considered to provide the software product developing companies with means to manage complexity of the software systems. In addition to develop components in-house, the telecommunication system vendors have recently studied and deployed the acquisition, integration and delivery of the externally developed components, e.g., [1]. Currently an essential part of a telecommunications system planning is to perform make/buy/reuse decisions, i.e. select COTS, OSS and in-house developed components to be integrated into a system.

Meyers & Oberndorf [2] defined the COTS component as a product that is sold, leased or licensed to the general public in multiple, identical copies. It is offered by a vendor, which supports and evolves it and tries to profit from it. The COTS product is being used without internal modification from the customer. IEEE [3] defined Modified-Of-The-Self (MOTS) software to be similar to COTS software; however,

M. Oivo and S. Komi-Sirviö (Eds.): PROFES 2002, LNCS 2559, pp. 509-518, 2002.

the MOTS software is tailored to buyer-specific requirements by the component vendor. OSS software is different from COTS software in several ways including unlimited access to source code, free distribution of the software and its modifications without restrictions and not allowing discrimination based on users or usage [4]. This paper uses the term external component to cover COTS, MOTS and OSS software components.

Most of the embedded software development companies lack competent human resources. In addition, it is not feasible to develop all the needed software in-house. The main reason for companies to acquire external components is to speed up product development. Attempts to utilize external software components include the use of very small pieces of code such as a sorting algorithm implementation downloaded form the Internet to the integration of large subsystems like embedded database management systems and distribution management systems. However, the product processes and system architectures typically do not yet fully support the integration of external embedded component activities.

This paper emphasizes a telecommunication system vendor view to COTS and OSS component integration. The system vendor integrates in-house developed and external components into products and deliveries the products mainly to telecommunication operators. The paper is based on information gathered during the last year. Information gathering included interviewing of 22 people working for a global telecommunications system vendor in Finland. The interviewed people had at least two years experience in working with COTS and OSS components. The interviewed people had technical, commercial and legal background. The rough questionnaire followed during the interviews was:

-    How widely do you use COTS, MOTS and OSS components?
-    What is a feasible size of a COTS, MOTS and OSS component?
-    What are the changes caused by the use of COTS, MOTS and OSS components?

Typically the discussion originated by the third question was quite long. Several more detailed questions were presented during the discussion. The more detailed questions included:

-    What are the changes needed to software development processes?
-    What are the changes needed to software engineering environments?
-    What are the changes needed to software architecture design approaches?

Additional interviews were performed in three embedded software component vendor companies located in Finland. The interviewed people included the managing directors and R&D directors of the companies. The questions presented include:

-    What is your business logic model?
-    What are the legal requirements?
-    How is the collaboration and knowledge exchange with customers performed?

2   COTS and OSS Software Component Dimensions

The interviewed people at the system vendor side estimated that the amount of COTS, MOTS and OSS software in lines of code varies from nearly zero to about 75 % of a mobile network element subsystem. Typically, COTS, MOTS and OSS software had quite a minimal portion compared to 70 or even 80 % share that external software was identified to have in the most network management systems. Most of the COTS, MOTS and OSS software components were found from the reusable communication software platforms. Typical components were operating systems like Linux, database management systems and distribution management systems.

One of the interviewed people who had six years experience in the external component acquisition and management argued that the feasible size of an external component equals to 2 to 4 man years development effort. Otherwise the additional work caused by the acquisition of the component is typically not covered by the decreased development efforts. This is in line with the literature, e.g., Szyperski [5] felt that too small components with a variety to choose from, e.g. hundreds of different implementations of stacks and queues, are not likely to increase software development productivity.

2.1   Changes Caused by the External Component Integration

The interviewed people identified the following areas to be affected by the acquisition and maintenance of external components (Figure 1): Vision and strategy, business and markets, software engineering processes, software engineering environments and collaboration approaches. The identified areas are close to those mentioned by Lim [6] when describing areas related to software reuse.

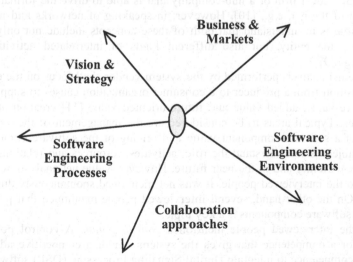

Fig. 1. Areas affected by the acquisition and maintenance of external components

Vision and Strategy give the fundamental reasons for the external component integration activities. Several interviewed people said that the acquisition and integration approaches of the external components should be supported by the strategy of the company. When a company replaces a part of in-house software development with the integration of external components, the nature of the company changes from a producer to a consumer organization [2]. The top management of the company shall be committed to this change. Strategy planning and communication provides the top management with means to lead the change. For example, instead of stating that the company shall be the best mobile software house in the next two years, the top management defines that the company shall become the best mobile software integrator.

Business and Markets include value net analysis, revenue logic analysis, market analysis, planning of control points and caring of stakeholders. A system vendor as well as a component supplier needs to describe and analyze *the value net* of products and services. According to a rather general view, the concept of value can be regarded as the trade-off between benefits and sacrifices [7]. Some authors define value purely in monetary terms, whereas others use a broader definition, which also includes such non-monetary revenues as competence, market position, and social rewards [8]. In this paper the broader definition of value is applied covering also the non-monetary aspect. The concept of „networks of organizations", i.e. networks, is understood as any group of organizations or actors that is interconnected with direct/indirect exchange relationships [9]. These business networks cannot be designed and managed by any single actor. The concept of „network organizations", i.e. *nets,* refers in here to a more narrow concept than the term network. In other words, whereas networks are viewed from macro-level, nets are viewed from the micro-level, usually from a view-point of a single actor. This kind of business net is characterized often by the importance of a focal firm or a hub-company that is able to drive the formation and management of the net, e.g., [10]. However, in speaking of networks and nets, the important issue is to understand that both of these concepts include not only actors that compose the entity, but also different kinds of interrelated activities and resources, e.g., [9].

The value net analysis performed by the system vendor shall focus on the changes that the transition from a producer to a consumer organization causes to supplier and customer core value, added value and future-oriented value [11] creation activities and resources. Typical areas to be considered are the management of the value net, measuring of a software component value and pricing of the software components. The main subject is to understand the role, activities, resources and relationships of the company currently and in the near future. However, value net analysis was quite unfamiliar to the interviewed people. It was not mentioned spontaneously during the interviews. On the other hand, several interviewed people mentioned that pricing of the external software components is a key topic.

One of the interviewed people mentioned *control points*. A control point is a technology or a competence that gives the system vendor a competitive advantage such as the competence to integrate Digital Signaling Processing (DSP) software into base station. The planning of the control points is based on the value net analysis. It provides the company means to manage the customer relationship.

A system vendor should evaluate and prioritize the *revenue logic* approaches of software component suppliers. The revenue logic evaluation is needed for the cost/revenue analysis of the end product. Especially, the maintenance costs of external component based products might be remarkably high. One way to minimize the maintenance costs is to acquire only those components that have a second source. Revenue logic analysis and especially having the second source was identified to be important by half of the interviewed people.

2.2   Processes and Architecture

COTS and OSS integration requires that the general in-house component development based **software engineering processes** are modified. The most important modifications are related to make/buy/reuse decision-making, agreement negotiations with component vendors, technical, commercial and legal evaluations and software architecture including the external component integration approaches.

The management of the end product shall make the *make/buy/reuse decisions*. The decision-making is based on the negotiations and evaluations results. The decision-making is supported by the decision criteria. Especially, the criteria include formula for the financial comparison of the integration of external components versus the development of in-house components. Most of the interviewed people considered the decision-making process to be quite demanding.

One of the interviewed people mentioned that *the technical, commercial and legal evaluations* shall be carried in parallel to reduce the duration of the evaluations. This idea was supported by all of the interviewed people. Before the evaluations shall be performed the requirements and the evaluation criteria of the components to be acquired shall be described and analyzed. The end product management shall accept the evaluation criteria including various aspects such as the maturity of the vendor, the price of the component, the applied pricing model, the partnership agreement conditions, the maintenance of the component and the required integration work with the component.

It is the **software architecture** of a system that defines the structure of a component based system. The architecture shall support the integration and especially the maintenance of the external components. One of the most comprehensive definitions of the term software architecture was given by Meyers & Oberndorf [2]: "Architecture is a representation of a system or a subsystem characterized by functionality, components, connectivity of components and mapping of functionality onto components". The software architecture shall define the COTS and OSS component interfaces. Especially, if the COTS or OSS component interface is not an industry or official standard, glue software in multiple layers shall be developed on the top of the component. The maintenance of the end product requires that the changes in the interface are minimized and strictly controlled. Often the integration of COTS components causes delays during the testing phases because the testing-correcting cycle duration is longer with an external component than with an in-house developed component. One of the interviewed people argued that „OSS components are superior to binary code COTS components during the testing and maintenance phases because if the integrator has access to the source code, the integrator is able to correct high priority errors when needed".

Software Engineering Environment shall support the distribution of acquired COTS components and related documentation inside the organization. Especially, the environments shall support external and internal OSS component development and maintenance. Internal OSS, i.e., corporate source management system provides the company with means for reusing source code. Controlling of the interface of internal OSS components is the main issue.

3   Collaboration Approaches

Schrage [12] defined that collaboration is the process of shared creation: two or more individuals with complementary skills interacting to create a shared understanding that none had previously possessed or could have come to on their own. Sonnenwald and Pierce [13] further emphasize that collaboration includes the completion of tasks with respect to a mutually-shared superordinate goal and takes place in a particular social or work setting. It is a primary mechanism to generate intellectual capital. The interviewed people were especially interested in finding out the practical requirements for successful collaboration. According to Marmolin et al. [14] collaboration consists of information sharing, knowledge integration, communication and co-working. These collaboration activities are conducted when a system vendor joins the OSS community or deals with a COTS vendor. A temporal joining of the OSS community for a software download, further development and upload or the acquisition of a widely used COTS component present a loosely coupled form of collaboration. On the other hand, a deep partnership relation with a COTS supplier is an advanced form of tightly coupled collaboration.

During the recent years the most common ways to collaborate with a supplier for a software product development have been body shopping and software project subcontracting. However, the future communication software development will be based on the Internet Protocol (IP). This means that the possibilities to use the general IT software components in the traditional communication software development field will increase. Therefore, the communication software field needs to learn new ways to collaborate with component suppliers. On the other hand, the previous software project vendors need to adopt new ways to approach the system vendors.

It is especially the management of the relationships with OSS and COTS sources where the system vendors need to focus on (Figure 2). Joining of the OSS community means that the integrator needs to actively not only download and further develop software but also upload the modified software for the others to use. Most of the interviewed people emphasized that a system vendor should avoid the making of software branches that are only further developed by the integrator itself. In addition, the system vendor whose aim is to produce reliable products has to very carefully evaluate the risks of using unknown source of software. In most cases the system vendor shall have a relationship with a reliable supplier. The supplier, i.e., a risk broker provides the system vendor with the external components that originally were free software, public domain software, shareware, OSS or COTS. It is the supplier that is responsible for the maintenance of the components. In addition, the supplier delivers the modified OSS components back to the OSS community.

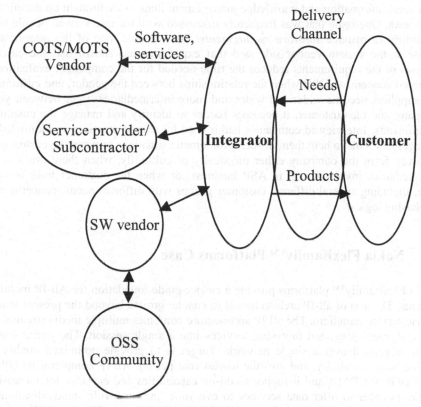

Fig. 2. Ways to acquire external software components to be integrated into communication software

One of the main drawbacks of the integration of external components has been identified to be the long-lasting negotiations and evaluations. One of the interviewed people said that the negotiations have lasted even longer than one year. While the negotiations have been ongoing, the technical requirements have often changed. Especially, this has been the case when the requirements have not been thoroughly analyzed and understood. In some cases when the commercial and legal negotiations were finally finished the component to be acquired was already outdated. Therefore, long-lasting and deep partnership relations with a few preferred COTS supplier are needed to speed up the negotiations. In addition, partnership relation is required for developing shared and feasible software component roadmaps.

Currently there are many software technology areas in the communication software field such as in the base station software development where there are only a few or even none software components available. A system vendor may launch horizontal component markets by ordering components as a subcontracted development work and allowing the vendor to sell the components on the markets. However, a supplier moving from a software project business to software product business faces a need for a change. Often it is more practical to establish a new company for the product business than to try to change the existing company operation mode.

Several information and knowledge management items were brought up during the interviews. One issue that was frequently discussed with the interviewed people was the ability to manage *software requirements*. For example, one of the interviewed people at the system vendor side said that experience has shown that the careful analysis of the requirements reduces the time needed for the component evaluations. A shared concern was that when the relationships between the vendor, end customers and suppliers become wider and wider and more intermediaries occur between your company and the customer, it becomes harder to identify and manage the customer requirements. Interviewed companies had a need for shared practices and knowledge management tools to help them in such problematic situations as when the customer is far away form the company either physically or culturally, when there are several intermediaries involved, e.g. in ASP business, or when the customer base is very wide, including several different customer groups with different needs, concerns and purchasing logics.

4   Nokia Flexifamily™ Platforms Case

Nokia Flexifamily™ platforms provide a carrier-grade foundation for All-IP mobility systems. The aim of all-IP architecture is to enable growth beyond the present voice-centric service paradigm. The all-IP architecture combines multiple media streams for rich call, messaging, and browsing services into a single session. The packet-based traffic is carried over a single network. Target is to provide optimized quality of service, total scalability, and thus the lowest cost per bit. All-IP complements GPRS and EDGE/WCDMA and it supports add-on capabilities and capacity for increasing traffic. In order to offer data services to everyone, industry-wide standardization of interfaces is required, through forums like 3GPP, WAP Forum, Wireless Village, and IPv6 Forum. [15]

The development of Nokia Flexifamily™ platforms included integration of external COTS and OSS components. For example, one part of the platforms is The Nokia FlexiServer™ in the network domain. FlexiServer is a carrier-grade server platform using the Linux® operating system. FlexiServer will be the foundation for core network products with functions such as session control and registers. In radio access, FlexiServer is used for managing the signaling plane of mobility control functions, including common radio resource management. [15] Experiences in FlexiServer development raised a need for COTS and OSS component related process development. Especially, the decision-making process for the evaluation and integration of an external component was further developed.

During the platforms development effort Nokia invited other industry players to share and standardize open specifications for interfaces of All-IP platforms. The Carrier Grade Linux Working Group under Open Source Development Lab [16] and Service Availability (SA) Forum industry initiatives [17] supports adoption of new technologies. Nokia contributes to standardization initiatives and implements them in products, using a "Networked Product Creation" product development processes and environments. The aim of Nokia is to create an ecosystem with economies of scale and leveraging capabilities - enabling industry innovation for all parties in the value net. Nokia argues that the use of a standards-based system, platforms, software components, and mainstream hardware reduces development, deployment, and operating costs to enable mobile data services to take off. The aim of Nokia is to focus on new key competence areas and leverage industry innovation by combining Nokia's own R&D with industry player partners. [15] This means that Nokia has had to develop and integrate collaboration processes into "Networked Product Creation" product development processes. This paper is strongly based on experiences gathered during the collaboration process development. Currently Nokia has agreed to follow the several collaboration issues covering processes such as a process for COTS and OSS component acquisition and maintenance and a process for glue software development.

5   Summary

This paper described dimensions of the development of COTS and OSS component based embedded software products. The following areas were identified to be related to the acquisition and maintenance of external components: Vision and strategy, business and markets, software engineering processes, software engineering environments and collaboration approaches. Business and markets include value net analysis and revenue logic analysis. The software component integrator needs to describe and analyse the value net of products and services. The value net description shall focus on the changes that the transition from a producer to a consumer organisation causes. Typical areas to be considered are the measuring of a software component value, pricing of software components and the management of the value net.

Collaboration activities shall be included in the value net management. Collaboration between the integrator and vendor is needed to minimize work effort and time spent on the technical, business and legal negotiations and evaluations. The lack of standardized software component interfaces makes the need for a well working relationship even more obvious. Software sourcing in the value net is a topic of a future research.

References

1. Helokunnas, T. & Nyby, M.: Collaboration between a COTS Integrator and Vendors. Proc. of the 7th European Conference on Software Quality. Helsinki, 2002
2. Meyers, B.C., Oberndorf, P.:Managing Software Acquisition. Open Systems and COTS Products. SEI Series in Software Engineering, Addison-Wesley (2001)
3. IEEE STD 1062-1993. IEEE Recommended Practice for Software Acquisition. USA (1998)
4. The Open Source Definition, version 1.9. http://www.opensource.org/docs/definition.html (2002), site visited 2002-08-03
5. Szyperski, C.: Component Software: Beyond Object-Oriented Programming. ACM Press & Addison-Wesley, 1997

518   Tuija Helokunnas

6.   Lim, W. Managing Software Reuse: A Comprehensive Guide to Strategically Reengineering the Organization for Reusable Components. Prentice-Hall, July 1998´
7.   Parolini, C.: The Value Net.A Tool for Competitive Strategy. John Wiley & Sons Ltd. (1999)
8.   Walter, A., Ritter, T., Gemünden, H.G.: „Value Creation in Buyer-Seller Relationships", Industrial Marketing Management, Vol. 30, Issue 4, May (2001) 365-377
9.   Axelson, B. and Easton, G., (eds.): Industrial Network. A New View of Reality. Routledge, London. (1992)
10. Doz, Y.L. and Hamel, G.: Alliance Advantage. The Art of Creating Value through Partnering. Boston, Massachusetts: Harvard Business School Press (1998)
11. Möller, K., Rajala, A.,Svahn, S.: „Strategic Business Nets – Their Types and Management", submitted to Journal of Business Research (2002)
12. Schrage,M.: No More Teams! Mastering the Dynamics of Creative Collaboration. Currency/Doubleday, 1995
13. Sonnenwald, D.,Pierce, L.:"Information behavior in dynamic work contexts: Interwoven situational awareness, dense social networks and contested collaboration in command and control". Information Processing & Management, 36(3) (2000) 461-479
14. Marmolin, H., Sundblad, Y. and Pehrson, B. : An Analysis of Design and Collaboration in a Distributed Environment, Proceedings of the Second European Conference on Computer-Supported Cooperative Work, ECSCW 91, Netherlands, 1991
15. Nokia (2002): Nokia Flexifamily™ platforms provide an open carrier-grade foundation for All-IP mobility systems. www.nokia.com, visited September 24, 2002
16. Open Source Development lab. http://www.osdlab.org/projects/cgl/, visited September 24, 2002
17. Service Availability Forum. http://www.saforum.org/, visited September 24, 2002

Software Engineering Process Benchmarking

Vincent Chiew and Yingxu Wang

Theoretical and Empirical Software Engineering Research Centre
University of Calgary, Calgary, Alberta, Canada
chiewv@shaw.ca
wangyx@enel.ucalgary.ca

Abstract. This paper proposes a Software Engineering Process (SEP) benchmarking methodology and a benchmark-gap analysis technique to assist industrial practitioners in quantitative software engineering. This work adopts the comprehensive SEP Assessment model (SEPRM), as a foundation to SEP benchmarking. In this approach, a number of conventional benchmarking challenges may be overcome. Case studies are presented to demonstrate the usage of the benchmarking technologies and supporting tools.

1 Introduction

A software organization can perform two kinds of benchmarking in software engineering: the internal and/or external benchmarking. The former is trying to improve a project based on internal benchmarks. The latter is intended to learn from common industrial benchmarks by analyzing own gaps against them. In addition, internal benchmarking provides the customer with an organization's competency information [13] and external benchmarking provides the customer with information if they are dealing with the best in the market place [5]. That is why it is necessary for any software organization to continuously strive on competency by software engineering benchmarking and improvement.

This paper is aimed to develop an SEP benchmarking methodology, which can be used by the software industry in an efficient and effective manner. The main objectives of this work are to explore the ways of SEP benchmarking, and to examine how the SEP benchmarking techniques can be effectively applied in software engineering. To achieve these objectives, a comprehensive SEP benchmarking methodology is proposed based on the unified SEP Assessment Model (SEPRM) [16].

This paper describes the development of new gap analysis techniques in software engineering benchmarking. Case studies are used to evaluate the effectiveness of the methodology. Additional information is provided on how the benchmarks may contribute to an organization's effort in goal-setting, cost management, process improvement, and knowledge assets allocation.

M. Oivo and S. Komi-Sirviö (Eds.): PROFES 2002, LNCS 2559, pp. 519-531, 2002.
© Springer-Verlag Berlin Heidelberg 2002

2   Software Engineering Process Benchmarking

In 1979, Xerox used benchmarking as the basis for its operation functional continuous process improvement, known as process benchmarking [4, 12]. Process benchmarking according to Xerox is a process of learning to become better. Ever since, benchmarking has been gaining recognition as an acceptable way to perform continuous process improvement. An International Quality Study [10] on over 900 management practices covering over 500 organizations concluded that an organization must look at all processes, then select those with the most impact on financial and/or marketplace result, and get lean. The study also pointed out that assessment is an important process in many high performance organizations that value quality, and must be coupled with external benchmarking to gain a competitive advantage. In 2001, a benchmarking firm in Australia [2] showed that assessment plus benchmarking methodologies have been proven beneficial to over 400 Australian enterprises and over 1300 corporate members.

Software Process Improvement (SPI) based on a reference model can be traced to IBM [Lehman M., Ramil J., 1999] during the development of their OS/360 systems. This paper uses a unified process model developed by the Theoretical and Empirical Software Engineering Research Centre (TESERC) at the University of Calgary, known as SEPRM [16, 17], which stands for Software Engineering Process Reference Model.

Most software engineering standard committees honestly believe the standards they promote represent industries best practices [15]. That is why it is common to see benchmarking reports based on only one standard or model. It is becoming common to find many organizations with multiple standards certifications or registrations. ISO 9001 is the most recognized standard and widely benchmarked along with other standards [11]. The new SEP benchmarking methodology presented here will hopefully make the task of compliance to multiple standards more manageable and effective.

The software engineering benchmarking framework is illustrated in Fig. 1. SEPRM is utilized to provide a comprehensive process capability assessment, which can be easily mapped to various software engineering standards and models. Using such multiple models can provide more added-value than any single model alone [1, 11, 14]. SEPRM is also helpful in maximizing assessment data collection efficiency by using its process mapping mechanisms and algorithms.

The SEPRM reference model based benchmarking provides efficiency for the software industry, because its mapping mechanisms to multiple process models and standards [16]. A conventional performance analysis would require 'n*(n-1)' number of benchmarking processes as shown in Fig. 2. The Benchmarked-based performance analysis only requires 'n' number of benchmarking processes. It has an advantage of nicely segregating internal and external projects by using the benchmarks as an interface. Upper management can use the benchmarks for strategic planning, and internal projects can use the benchmarks for tactical planning.

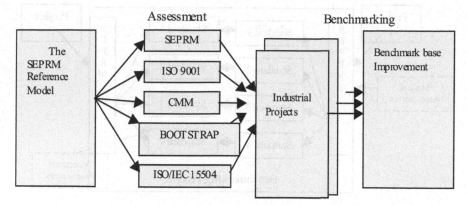

Fig. 1. The Framework on SEP Benchmarking

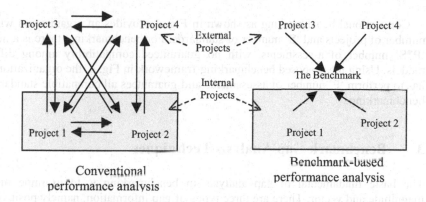

Fig. 2. Internal Best Practice Reference Model

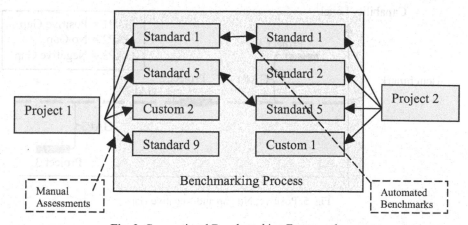

Fig. 3. Conventional Benchmarking Framework

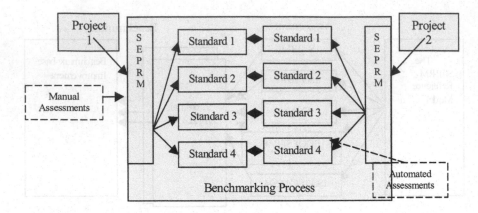

Fig. 4. Proposed Benchmarking Framework

Conventional benchmarking as shown in Fig. 3 provides an organization with 'P' number of projects and 'S' number of standards. For benchmarking, there is a need of 'P*S' number of assessments, with no guaranteed compatibility among different models. Using the proposed benchmarking framework in Fig. 4, the organization only has to perform 'P' number of assessments and guarantees all compatible standards for benchmarking.

3   Benchmark Gap Analysis Techniques

The basic fundamental of gap analysis in benchmarking is to examine the gap magnitude and vector. There are three types of gap information, namely positive gap, no gap, and negative gap. The three types of gaps are illustrated in Fig. 5.

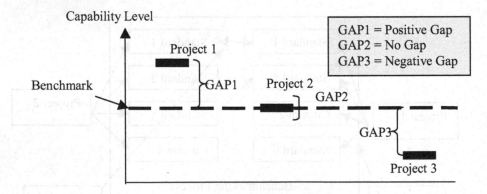

Fig. 5. Positive, No gap and Negative Gaps

The magnitude of the gap is the range of the gap. A range is defined as the magnitude between two Capability Levels (CLs). The range is between the Project CL and the Benchmark CL. The range is the simplest measure of dispersion utilizing two values [6]. Gap magnitude is the absolute value of the range, expressing as |Gap|, i.e.:

$$|Gap| = |Range| \tag{1}$$
$$= |Value\ 1 - Value\ 2|;$$
$$= |Project\ CL - Benchmark\ CL| \tag{2}$$

From Fig. 5. , we can further define the gap definition in rule or equation forms as follows:

Positive gap is when (Project CL - Benchmark CL) > 0   (Rule 1)
No gap is when (Project CL – Benchmark CL) = 0   (Rule 2)
Negative gap is when (Project CL - Benchmark CL) < 0   (Rule 3)

Where, Rule 1 indicates that the Project Capability Level (CL) is superior to the benchmark CL. Rule 2 indicates that the Project CL is at par with the benchmark. Rule 3 indicates that benchmark CL is superior to the project CL.

When looking at the various standards benchmarks that are of interest to gap analysis we need to know the following pieces of information.

1. The current Project CL
2. The competitor's strength (BM Max CL) and weakness (BM Min CL)
3. For an industry application, the average CL in the industry (BM Avg CL)
4. If we benchmark using a standard or model we need to know its maximum CL (Ultimate Max CL) and minimum CL (Ultimate Min CL)

These capability levels can be illustrated as follow:

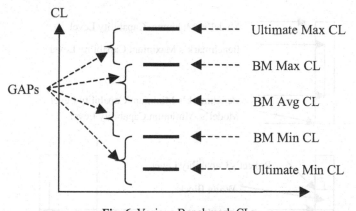

Fig. 6. Various Benchmark CLs

Various rules can be derived for the gaps from Fig. 6 that are applicable to current software process standards and models. The rules are as follow:

(Ultimate Max CL)	>=	(BM Max CL)	(Rule 4)
(BM Max CL)	>=	(BM Avg CL)	(Rule 5)
(BM Avg CL)	>=	(BM Min CL)	(Rule 6)
(BM Min CL)	>=	(Ultimate Min CL)	(Rule 7)
(Ultimate Max CL)	>	(Ultimate Min CL)	(Rule 8)

It is noteworthy that Rules 4 to 7 are not truly transitional because they are constrained by Rule 8. This implies that we should not have the case where,

| (Ultimate Max CL) | = | (Ultimate Min CL) | (Rule 9) |

Rule 9 means the model has no capability level hence cannot be assessed.

The next step is to examine the possible location of the project CL. The project CL can only lie between BM Max CL and BM Min CL exclusively as shown in 6. When the project CL is taken into consideration, more rules can be derived as follow:

(BM Max CL)	>=	(Project CL)	=<	(BM Min CL)	(Rule 10)
(Project CL)	>=	(BM Avg CL)			(Rule 11)
(BM Avg CL)	>=	(Project CL)			(Rule 12)
(Rule 11)	XOR	(Rule 12)			(Rule 13)

Note that Project CL is also bounded between Ultimate Max CL and Ultimate Min CL, according to Rules 4 to 10. Rule 13 indicates that Rule 11 and Rule 12 are exclusive to each other.

Understanding these rules enables users to better interpret the benchmark for effectiveness and help to develop an effective visualization of the benchmark for interpretation.

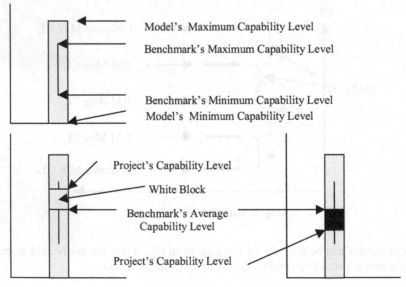

Fig. 7. Benchmark Legend

Table 1. Summary Benchmark Record in CMM

KPA	Description	Project	Model	BM Max	BM Avg	BM Min
1,1	Initial	0	0	0	0	0
2,1	Requirement management	3	3	3	2	0
2,2	Software project planning	15	15	15	12	2
2,3	Software project tracking and oversight	13	13	13	9	0
2,4	Software subcontract management	13	13	13	9	0
2,5	Software quality assurance	8	8	8	5	0
2,6	Software configuration management	10	10	10	8	1
3,1	Organization process focus	4	7	7	4	0
3,2	Organization process definition	6	6	6	3	0
3,3	Training program	6	6	6	5	0
3,4	Integrated software management	11	11	11	7	0
3,5	Software product engineering	10	10	10	7	1
3,6	Intergroup coordination	7	7	7	5	0
3,7	Peer reviews	3	3	3	2	0
4,1	Quantitative process management	7	7	7	3	0
4,2	Software quality management	5	5	5	3	0
5,1	Defect prevention	8	8	8	4	0
5,2	Technology change management	8	8	8	4	0
5,3	Process change management	4	10	10	4	0

The Benchmark Legend presented in Fig. 7 will be used to illustrate the benchmark information mentioned previously. The graph representation idea was based upon the *boxplot* in statistics, applied in [8, 9].

4   Industrial Case Studies

There were 16 case studies based on industrial self-assessments. A benchmarking case study is presented in this section based on an internal best practice project at organization X. This is not an actual project but a project based on the company's procedure, which reflects its current process practices.

4.1   Benchmarking

The SEPRM reference model enables multi-model-based assessment and benchmarking. A set of benchmarking results for the Capability Maturity Model (CMM) will be used as an example due to space limitation.

According to the CMM benchmark summary, see Table 1, ProjectX's practices are below average in the „Process Change Management (KPA 5.3)". The organization is not that much ahead of the competitors in the areas of „Requirement Management

(KPA 2.1)", „Organization process focus (KPA 3.1)", and „Peer reviews (KPA 3.7)". ProjectX has superior performance in areas such as „Software project planning (KPA 2.2)", „Software project tracking and oversight (KPA 2.3)", „Software subcontract management (KPA 2.4), „Software quality assurance (KPA 2.5), „Organization process definition (KPA 3.2)", „Integrated software management (KPA 3.4)", „ quantitative process management (KPA 4.1)", and „Defect prevention (KPA 5.1)".

Fig. 8 is a graphical representation of the data summarized in Table 1. This graph shows the benchmarked capability for each process at each capability level.

4.2   Comparative Analysis of the Benchmarking Results

This subsection provides the comparative analysis of the benchmarking results of all the benchmarked projects. Fig. 9 shows the distribution of all the projects according to CMM CL. It shows how many competitors are ahead or behind of the project of interest and the benchmark range.

The percentile ranking analysis in Fig. 10 provides an overall comparative analysis at the project level. It provided more information regarding the overall standing of ProjectX's practice standing and ranking among the benchmark projects. This chart is produced using the project level capability information to determine the ProjectX's practice standing among all the competitors for the given models.

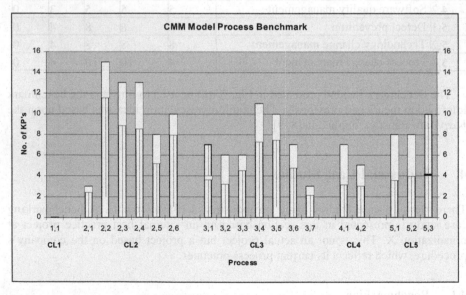

Fig. 8. CMM Model Process Benchmark

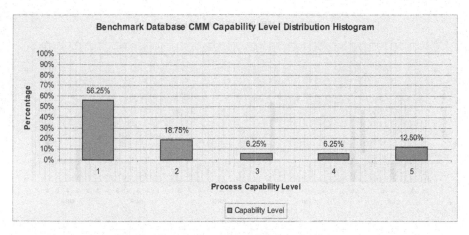

Fig. 9. CMM Projects Capability Level Histogram

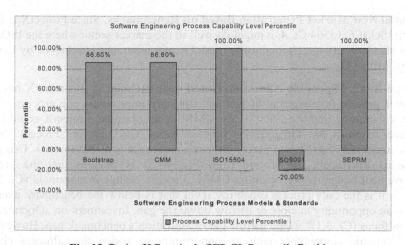

Fig. 10. ProjectX Practice's SEP CL Percentile Ranking

5   Benchmarking Analysis

Let us look at an example by picking a process in ProjectX that is relatively weak. Fig. 11. illustrates that ProjectX practice is the weakest in „Assess customer satisfaction (CUS 8)", based on the ISO/IEC 15504 model. According to the benchmark, the ProjectX practice is at capability level 0 while the competitors average capability level is at 2.5, with at least one competitor at capability level 5. Even though the ProjectX practice was ranked among the best according to Fig. 10, there were still potentially significant weaknesses within the organization's practices.

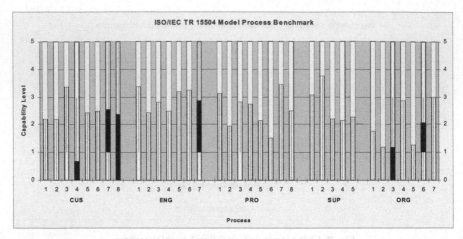

Fig. 11. ISO/IEC TR 15504 Model Process Benchmark

Potential New Market Penetration Based on Benchmarks. Since ProjectX is fairly well in ISO/IEC 15504 CL 4, it might do well in the market sector where the ISO/IEC 15504 standards are more prominently used. Greater assurance is achieved by looking at Figs. 11 to 13.

Limited Budget Spending Allocation Based on Benchmarks. If ProjectX has only a limited process improvement budget and can only improve on one process, which process should be improved first? Take CMM as an example, ProjectX could try to improve on either its „Organization process focus (CL 3.1)" or „Process change management (CL 5.3)" based purely on assessment results as shown in 3. Using the additional benchmark information from Fig. 8, it is obvious that the process improvement budget is best spent on CMM „Process change management (CL 5.3)" because it is the only process capability level that is below the benchmark average. This is an opportunity to close or narrow down the gap. Investment on „Organization process focus (CL 3.1)" would narrow the organization's benchmark gap. However, it would provide competitors with an opportunity to widen the „Process change management (CL 5.3)" gap.

Limited Budget Spending Allocation Based on Benchmarks. The organization can start by identifying all weak benchmark processes. Choosing the CMM process „Process change management (CL 5.3)" to work on all its related activities, the organization essentially improves the other models' processes as well. Using reverse mapping of the activities, the organization actually improves partially the CMM „Organization process focus (CL 3.1)" process, partial Bootstrap process (CL 2.1) and ISO/IEC 15504 process 5.3. From an assessment point of view, much was to gain from this investment, except for increasing CMM „Process change management (CL 5.3). From a benchmarking point of view, it also raises the SEPRM process 1.2's capability level closer to best practice and makes the most significant contribution to ISO/IEC 15504 „Improve the process (ORG 3)" by raising its capability maturity level from level 0. This is an example where benchmark could be both complement and supplement assessment results.

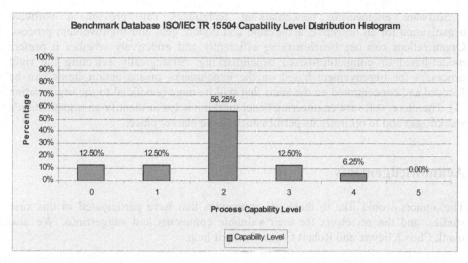

Fig. 12. ISO/IEC TR 15504 Projects Capability Level Histogram

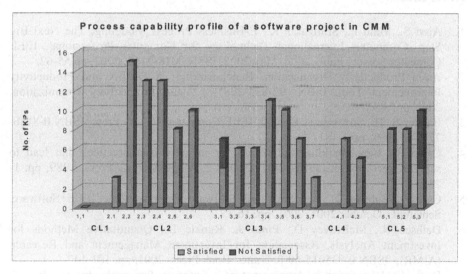

Fig. 13. Process capability profile of a software project in CMM

6   Conclusions

This paper has described how to implement software engineering benchmarking efficiently on the basis of SEPRM and the gap analysis techniques. Industrial case studies have shown that by using the comprehensive SEPRM, assessment and benchmarking efficiency can be increased. The visual presentation of benchmarking results has enabled information analysis at a glance. The case studies and benchmarking projects have received positive feedbacks from the industry.

Software engineering benchmarking techniques can provide a software organization for an objective, achievable and doable goal and improvement process. Organizations can use benchmarking efficiently and effectively whether it prefers model-based or competitor-based benchmarking. Strategically selecting the right processes for improvement based on the benchmarks means action items can be focused and concentrated on the areas that will be most beneficial to the organization [3]. Therefore, software engineering benchmarking helps to identify an organization's weaknesses and to optimize its performance in the market place.

Acknowledgements

The authors would like to thank all companies that have participated in this case studies, and the reviewers for their valuable comments and suggestions. We also thank Chris Kliewer and Robert Chiew for their help.

References

1. Aissi S., Malu P., Srinivasan K., E-Business Process Modeling; The Next Big Step, Computer: International Technology for Computer Professional, IEEE Computer Society Publication, May 2002, ISSN 0018-9162, 2002, pp 55-62.
2. Asian Productivity Organization, Benchmarking: A Quality and Productivity Improvement Tool, ISBN: 92-833-2287-8, Asian Productivity Organization, 2001, pp. 3-98
3. Baetjer Jr. H., Software as Capital, IEEE Computer Society Press, ISBN 0-8186-7779-1, 1998, pp 1-181.
4. Camp R., Benchmarking: the search for industry best practices that lead to superior performance, ISBN 0-87389-058-2, ASQC Quality Press, 1989, pp. 1-288.
5. Card D, Zubrow D, Benchmarking Software Organizations, IEEE Software, September/October 2001, 2001, pp. 16-17.
6. Defusco R., McLeavey D., Pinto J., Runkle D., Quantitative Methods for Investment Analysis, Association for Investment Management and Research (AIMR), ISBN 0-935015-69-8, United Book Press, 2001, pp. 101-147
7. Dyck, S., Experience in Assessment of a Software Project by Using Multiple Process Models, 7th International Conference on Object Oriented Information Systems, Springer-Verlag London Limited, ISBN 1852335467, 2001, pp. 405-414.
8. Emam K., Birk A., Validating the ISO/IEC 15504 measures of software development process capability, The Journal of Systems and Software, Volume 15, Number 2, 15 April 2000, ISSN 0164-1212, Elsevier Science Inc., 2000, pp. 119-150.
9. Emam K., Jung H., An empirical evaluation of the ISO/IEC 15504 assessment model, The Journal of Systems and Software, Volume 59, Number 1, 15 October 2001, ISSN 0164-1212, Elsevier Science Inc., 2001, pp. 23-41.

10. Ernst & Young, American Quality Foundation, The International Quality Study: Best Practices Report – An Analysis of Management Practices that Impact Performance, Ernst & Young, 1992, pp. 6-46.

11. Jung H, Hunter R., The relationship between ISO/IEC 15504 process capability levels, ISO 9001 certification and organization size: An empirical study, The Journal of Systems and Software, Volume 59, Number 1, 15 October 2001, ISSN 0164-1212, Elsevier Science Inc., 2001, pp. 43-55.

12. Kulmala J., Approaches to Benchmarking, Finnish Employers' Management Development Institute, FEMDI, Aavaranta, http://www.jyu.fi/economics/research/hankkeet/hankerekisteri/hanke5_benchmarking.htm, 2002.

13. Spence D., Ciaschi R., Mantineo A., The Certification of ESOC to ISO 9001, European Space Agency (ESA) bulletin, Number 101, February 2000, ESA Publications Division, ISSN 0376-4265, 2002, pp. 48-54.

14. Thayer R., Software System Engineering: A Tutorial, Computer: International Technology for Computer Professional, IEEE Computer Society Publication, April 2002, ISSN 0018-9162, 2002, pp 68-73.

15. Volcker C., Cass A., Winzer L., Carranza J., Dorling A., SPiCE for SPACE: A Process Assessment and Improvement Method for Space Software Development, European Space Agency (ESA) bulletin, Number 107, August, 2001, ESA Publications Division, ISSN 0376-4265, pp. 112-119.

16. Wang, Y. and King, G, Software Engineering Processes: Principles and Applications, CRC Press, USA, ISBN: 0-8493-2366-5, 2000, pp 1-708.

17. Wang, Y. , A Web-Based European Software Process Benchmarking Server, The 23rd IEEE International Conference on Software Engineering (ICSE'01), Poster paper, Toronto, May, 2001.

18. Lehman M., Ramil J., The Impact of Feedback in the Global Software Process, The Journal of Systems and Software, Volume 46, Number 2/3, 15 April 1999, ISSN 0164-1212, Elsevier Science Inc., 1999, pp. 123-134.

A Meta-model Framework
for Software Process Modeling*

Marcello Visconti[1] and Curtis R. Cook[2]

[1] Departamento de Informática, Universidad Técnica Federico Santa María
Valparaíso, Chile
visconti@inf.utfsm.cl
[2] Computer Science Department, Oregon State University
Corvallis, Oregon, USA
cook@cs.orst.edu

Abstract. We present a refined version of a meta-model process modeling framework that can be effectively used to identify key practices to initiate and sustain a software process improvement effort focused on a single process area. Our approach moves away from the overall software development process and computation of maturity levels and focuses on a particular process area or task and its key practices. In determining process key practices our framework considers process dimension, and quality and usability/costumer satisfaction of the products produced or services provided by the process. The refined version of the model gives suggested types of key practices and useful questions and hints for constructing these key practices. We show the completeness, flexibility and ease of using this proposed meta-model by applying it to two particular process areas, generating a set of key practices we believe adequately cover the key issues to properly drive a process improvement effort.

1   Introduction

Over the years, many software development efforts have produced low quality products that are late, often with reduced functionality, not reliable, and over budget. In an effort to improve this situation, one branch of software engineering research has focused on the process. It is based on the premise that software development is a process that can be controlled and improved. Hence improving the process should improve product quality and customer satisfaction [9].

Among the models for the process improvement cycle are the IDEAL[sm1] model [11] developed by the Software Engineering Institute (SEI) and those based on Deming's Plan/Do/Check/Act [9]. The IDEAL model is an excellent framework for understanding the cycle of ongoing process improvement and how the various activities fit together. See Figure 1. The five phases of the IDEAL model are:

---

* IDEAL[sm] is a service mark of Carnegie Mellon University.

M. Oivo and S. Komi-Sirviö (Eds.): PROFES 2002, LNCS 2559, pp. 532-545, 2002.

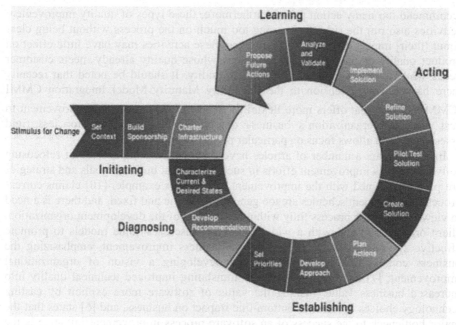

Fig. 1. The IDEAL Model

Initiating, Diagnosing, Establishing, Acting and Learning. Activities in the Initiating phase are stimulus for improvement, obtain sponsorship, and establish the infrastructure. In the Diagnosing phase the current process is assessed and recommendations for improvement generated. Activities in the Establishing phase are set strategies and priorities, establish process action teams, and construct action plans. The Acting phase activities are carrying out the plans formulated in the previous phase and defining processes and measures. In the final phase, Learning, what was learned from an analysis of the process measures from the previous phase is documented and used in the formulation of a revised organizational approach. It in turn forms the basis for iterating the entire IDEAL process again.

Many process models like SEI's Capability Maturity Model (CMM[sm2]) [12], [13] have been proposed to aid in the diagnosing stage of the IDEAL model. For example, CMM-based assessment and recommendations methods SPA (Software Process Assessment) and CBA IPI[sm] (CMM-Based Appraisal for Internal Process Improvement) [1] identify process strengths and weaknesses and attempt to foster a commitment of the personnel to process improvement. However, major limitations of basing software process improvement initiatives on CMM are that the appraisal is very expensive, disruptive and time consuming, especially for small organizations. Thus performing a CMM-based assessment may be impossible for some organizations and frequent assessments impossible for nearly all organizations. These types of assessments, being based mostly on process, have the risk of generating recommendations that may not be in line with organizational business goals, or just

---

[2] CMM[sm], CBA IPI[sm], CMMI[sm] are service marks of Carnegie Mellon University.

recommend too many action paths. Furthermore, these types of quality improvement activities also run the risk of „focusing too much on the process without being clear about [their] impact on quality" [15]. Hence these activities may have little effect on product quality or may affect product areas whose quality already meets customer needs while overlooking areas deficient in quality. It should be noted that recently there has been an extension to the Capability Maturity Model Integration CMMI (CMMI[sm]) [14] that offers more flexibility in the selection order of improvement to best meet the organization's business objectives, has provisions for less rigid assessments and allows focus on particular processes.

In recent years a number of articles have discussed the importance of refocusing software process improvement efforts in such a way that business goals and strategies are properly aligned with the improvement efforts. For example, [10] claims current process improvement schemes are too general, too static and fixed, and there is a need to view the software process fully within the context of the development organization, client organization and with a wider focus; [4] discusses some models to promote effective system change in the context of business improvement, emphasizing the business context and the desirability of developing a vision of organizational improvement; [7] addresses the issue of translating improved technical quality into increased business value, making the value of software more explicit by casting technology choices in terms of bottom-line impact on business, and [6] states that the major bottleneck to the success of an software process improvement initiative is the lack of business orientation in the way the program is run, stressing the need to link any software process improvement program to business goals and to follow it up closely with indicators related to the initial goals.

To better connect the process and product quality [15] proposed a product centric P-SPI (Product focused Software Process Improvement) approach. In P-SPI product quality needs have equal footing with product functionality. Product quality specifications are included in the requirements, process actions that effectively contribute to product quality are incorporated in the development process and measurements are used to evaluate conformance to product quality specifications and evaluate whether process actions are having their intended effects. They have reported the benefits of such an approach in [15].

One proposed approach to overcome or mitigate the limitations of CMM-based assessments is to limit the scope of the assessment. This is illustrated by models like the Documentation Process Maturity Model (DPMM) [5],[16], the Modular Mini-Assessment (MMA) [20], the Testing Maturity Model (TMM) [2], [3] as well as the CMMI and its Continuous Representation [14]. These process models focus on a particular process or task. These approaches have the benefit of providing a more in-depth assessment of the particular process and at a greatly reduced cost.

In our previous paper [17] we introduced the meta-model framework for constructing a process model for a particular process or task. Rather than focusing solely on the process dimension of the product or service, the model constructed from the framework integrates the process, quality, and usability/customer satisfaction dimensions. The process modeler applies the framework to develop key practices for each dimension for the particular product or service. These key practices will then drive the process assessment. In this paper we present a refined version of the meta-model and provide guidance for constructing the process model. The refinements take into account our experience in applying the earlier version of the meta-model framework. As part of the refined version of the meta-model we give suggested types of key practices and useful questions and hints for generating these key practices.

The next section presents the structure of the refined meta-model. The structure provides guidelines for constructing the key practices, including useful questions and hints for each of the key practice guidelines. Then in Section 3 we give two examples of the application of the framework. These examples demonstrate the construction of a process model for a particular application and the completeness of the process models constructed using the framework. Finally we present our conclusions and future work.

2   Meta-model Framework

The process meta-model [17] is a framework whose main purpose is to serve as a guide for the identification of key practices that will drive the process assessment and improvement. The meta-model was developed to overcome some of the assessments shortcomings explained in the previous section, and especially to help produce more useful information to proceed with planning for process improvement. The meta-model is designed for constructing models for single-focus process areas. In addition, rather than focusing entirely on process, the meta-model framework incorporates assuring the quality and usability of end products produced or customer satisfaction with the service provided by the process.

2.1   Refined Process Meta-model

The refined meta-model framework differs from the original in the phase distinction and guidance in constructing models. We distinguish Identify and Monitor phases from Measure and Feedback phases. In the first case (Identify and Monitor), we separately identify key practices for each of the three dimensions, namely core process, quality assurance and usability/costumer satisfaction; in the second case (Measure and Feedback) we don't distinguish practices for those three dimensions, because activities that support measurement and feedback are dimension-independent. Table 1 gives an overview of the framework. From Table 1 we see that the structure of the meta-model reflects not only the process itself, but also the quality and usability/customer satisfaction dimensions of the products or service produced by the process. It defines four major action phases (Identify, Monitor, Measure, Feedback) for the three dimensions: core process, quality assurance and usability/customer satisfaction. The Identify phase defines the product or service, its importance to the organization, the practices in the process and the components of the process. The Monitor phase checks for evidence of organizational support, and checks to see whether the practices and components of the Identity phase are being done. The Measure phase defines measures for each of the three dimensions, and activities to collect and analyze these measures. Finally, the Feedback phase generates recommendations for improvements from the measurements, evaluates and prioritizes them, and generates plans to incorporate them into the process.

The idea behind the development of the meta-model is to provide a framework for developing a model for a particular software process area or task. The process models developed using this framework are different from other process maturity models in several important ways. First, in the model developed using the meta-model there is equal focus on the process, quality assurance and usability/customer satisfaction dimensions. The CMM and other similar process models focus on the process and pay little attention to the quality of the resulting product or service and the usability/customer satisfaction. These models tacitly assume that a high quality or mature process will automatically produce a high quality and usable product or a high quality service that satisfies its customers. In [19], process-oriented methods are taken to task for their process preoccupation. The emphasis on assessing quality rather than achieving it is a major shortcoming of these methods. We believe, from the organization's viewpoint that the bottom line is the quality and usability of the product (quality of service and customer satisfaction) and not merely the assessment of the process. Hence we believe that the quality assurance and usability/customer satisfaction serve important roles in evaluating and improving the process.

Second, the framework is specifically geared for developing a model for a particular process or task rather than encompassing the entire development process. Such an approach has several advantages. Because of the focus on a single process or task the assessment procedure is less costly and time consuming. Another advantage is that it is easier to identify a small number of key practices to focus on. The assessment itself only produces knowledge, the actual benefits come with the follow-on activities such as action planning and actual practice improvement execution. Thus, a point in favor of the single-focus approach is that it provides a more in-depth evaluation of the particular process than that provided by comprehensive process models.

Table 1. Process Dimension of the Meta-Model

Phase	Meta Practices for each Dimension		
	Core Process	Quality Assurance	Usability/Customer Satisfaction
Identify	Define important practices of process for generating product or providing service	Define important quality assurance practices for product or service	Define important practices for product usability or customer satisfaction
Monitor	Monitor adherence to process	Monitor quality assurance activities	Monitor usability/customer satisfaction activities
Measure	Define, collect and analyze measures		
Feedback	Generate, evaluate, prioritize and incorporate recommendations		

Table 2. Suggested types of practices and hints for generating the key practices for Identify and Monitor phases - Quality Assurance dimension

Phase	Suggested types of practices for Quality Assurance	Useful questions and hints for generation of key practices
Identify	Define organizational policy for quality assurance of product (service)	• Why is important to generate/provide a high-quality product/service? • Who is responsible for product/service quality assurance? • How does product/service quality affect organization functions and business goals? • Written statement about product/service quality policy?
	Define factors that determine product (service) quality	• What are the main drivers/determinants of product/service quality?
	Define activities to verify product (service) quality	• What activities are executed to verify product/service quality?
Monitor	Monitor adherence to product (service) quality assurance policy	• Actions supporting product/service quality assurance policy: management practices, resources allocated, responsibilities assigned?
	Monitor verification of product (service) quality	• What mechanisms are used (e.g. checklists) to check that product/service quality verification activities are executed?

Third, because the meta-model is a framework it is flexible and the models developed using the framework can easily be tailored to the particular process and the particular organization. The user of the framework can choose the particular process or task and the particular aspects of the process or task to focus on. For example, if the organization is small and its product must be highly reliable, the framework can be used to construct a model of the testing process tailored to its product. As another example, if a group in an organization provides software configuration management support services to other parts of the organization, the framework can be used to construct a model tailored to the support services provided by the group. The key is that in both of these examples the organization does not have to use a general one size fits all process model that may not address their specific needs or issues.

2.2   Guidance in Applying the Meta-model Framework

Two questions that naturally arise because the framework is so flexible and general are:

1. How difficult is it to construct a process model using the meta-model framework?
2. How do process models geared for a particular process that have appeared in the literature compare with a process model constructed using the meta-model framework?

Table 3. Suggested types of practices and hints for generating the key practices for Measure and Feedback phases

Phase	Suggested types of practices	Useful questions and hints for generation of key practices
Measure	Define measures of process performance, product (service) quality, and product usability (customer satisfaction)	• What are the main drivers/determinants of process performance? product (service) quality? product usability (customer satisfaction)? • What attributes can show alignment with organization functions and business goals? • What attributes can be measured?
	Define activities to collect measures of process performance, product (service) quality, and product usability (customer satisfaction)	• Which activities are executed to collect measures?
	Define activities to analyze measures of process performance, product (service) quality, and product usability (customer satisfaction)	• Which activities are executed to analyze measures?
Feedback	Generate recommendations for process improvement based on analysis of measurements	• How are target/desired values compared with actual values? • How are recommendations for process improvement generated?
	Evaluate/prioritize recommendations for process improvement	• How are recommendations for process improvement evaluated and prioritized?
	Incorporate recommendations into process	• How are recommendations fed back into process?

To address the first question, as an aid in constructing the process model, for each of the core process, quality assurance, and usability/customer satisfaction dimensions, we provide both suggested types of key practices for each phase and useful questions and hints for each suggested practice. Tables 2 and 3 show the suggestions for the quality assurance dimension (Identify and Monitor phases) and Measure and Feedback phases. Full details for suggested practices are in [18]. In the next section we give an example illustrating the application of the meta-model framework to construct a process model for Configuration Management Support service within an actual organization.

To answer the second question, we have compared process models for a particular process or task that have appeared in the literature with process models constructed with our framework. The biggest difference we have found is that our models are more complete. The primary reason for this is the models in the literature are usually based on the CMM and hence focus on the process and pay little attention to quality assurance and usability/customer satisfaction. An example is given in the next section.

3   Meta-model Application

In this section we illustrate the application of the meta-model to two applications: Software Configuration Management Support and Software Testing. The first example illustrates the ease of constructing a process model (key practices) using the useful questions and hints. The second example compares the key practices of a model for a particular process (testing) that appeared in the literature with the key practices that would be developed using our framework. The comparison shows the testing model is quite complete for the process dimension but is weak in the quality assurance and usability/customer satisfaction dimensions. In presenting these examples our goal is to show that the meta-model is easy to use, flexible, and results in a more complete set of key practices.

3.1   Example 1: Software Configuration Management Support Process Model

The key practices shown in Tables 4 and 5 have been taken from [8], where the first version of the meta-model [17] was applied to the SCM Support Process to generate the key practices and the assessment questionnaire. They show the suggestions for the core process dimension (Identify and Monitor phases) and the usability/customer satisfaction dimension (Identify and Monitor phases). Full details for application of meta-model in this example are in [18]. It is interesting to note that the original meta-model did not include any hints or useful questions to help in the identification of key practices, yet only two of the suggested types of practices were not generated, and they are indicated with (*). A preliminary analysis of the key practices generated shows that they form a reasonably complete and coherent set that is a good starting point to launch a software process improvement effort.

Incidentally when the student applied the assessment questionnaire to a small pilot group he found the following: the process had only informal policies and little documentation of some of the activities; monitoring and measuring in selected areas with feedback informally incorporated into the process; there were some informal norms for quality assurance, ad hoc monitoring, few measurements, and negligible feedback for process improvement; informal guidelines for user satisfaction; monitoring only when a new team member is set up; only informal input from customers may lead to some changes in the process. Overall, the assessment highlighted areas that have caused problems in the past and need improvement.

Table 4. Suggested key practices for SCM Support Process – Identify and Monitor phases - Core Process dimension

Phase	Suggested types of practices for Core Process	SCM Support Process
Identify	Define product generated (service provided) by process	• Define what SCM Support Process produces for the software development process*
	Define importance of product (service) to organization	• Define policy for importance of SCM

	Define product (service) components	•	Define activities of SCM support group (define policy for providing change control mechanisms, define policy for providing status accounting mechanisms, define policy for providing audit mechanisms, define policy for customizing the SCM environment for individual group needs, define policy for managing SCM repositories, define a policy to identify development tools requirements, define resource management policy, define risk management policy)
	Define process to generate product (provide service)	•	Define SCM support process (define policy for determining support requirements, define policy for assessing resources to meet support requirements, define policy for SCM group training, define group communication policy)
Monitor	Organization support for importance of product (service)	•	Monitor practices to ensure SCM Support Process resources, etc*
	Monitor creation and completion of product (delivery of service) and components	•	Monitor completion of SCM support group activities (monitor change control mechanism availability and functioning, monitor status accounting mechanism availability and functioning, monitor audit mechanism availability and functioning, monitor SCM environment customization requests, monitor adherence to SCM repository management policies, monitor development tool usage and requests for new tools and versions, monitor resource usage, monitor compliance with risk assessment and management policy)
	Monitor adherence to defined process	•	Monitor adherence to SCM support process (monitor support requests and compliance to policies when handling them, monitor communications between the support group and its customers, monitor adequacy of head count in support group, monitor SCM support group member training)

Table 5. Suggested key practices for SCM Support Process – Identify and Monitor phases - Usability/Costumer Satisfaction dimension

Phase	Suggested types of practices for Usability/Customer Satisfaction SCM Support	Process
Identify	Define policy for product usability (customer satisfaction)	• Define policy for importance of user satisfaction with SCM support activities
	Define factors that determine product usability (customer satisfaction)	• Determine factors that determine user satisfaction with SCM support activities
	Define activities to verify usability of product (customer satisfaction)	• Define activities to verify user satisfaction with SCM support
Monitor	Monitor adherence to product usability (customer satisfaction) policy	• Monitor adherence to SCM support user satisfaction policy
	Monitor verification of product usability (customer satisfaction)	• Monitor user satisfaction with SCM support activities

A few brief comments about the amount of interaction between the student and the second author during the project is appropriate. The student completed the project in four months while employed full-time by the organization. That the student was a member of the SCM support group and hence familiar with its functioning certainly aided in the construction. However, the student was able to develop the process model and questionnaire with limited contact and interaction. The organization and student were located about 80 miles from the university. Initially the meetings were primarily by telephone and face-to-face to clarify aspects of the meta-model while the later contact was by e-mail and primarily about wording changes in the key practices and assessment questions. The assessment questionnaire was constructed by the student directly from the model and key practices and with little assistance. Overall, the model and questionnaire were constructed with less guidance and assistance than the student would receive if he had done the project working with people at the organization.

3.2 Example 2: Software Testing Process Model

Tables 6 and 7 show the key practices proposed in the Testing Maturity Model [2], [3] that are related to the quality assurance dimension (Identify and Monitor phases) and Measure and Feedback phases. Full details for application of meta-model in this example are in [18]. We have assigned each key practice to an appropriate category or categories using the useful questions and hints provided by our meta-model framework.

Table 6. Suggested key practices for Testing Process – Identify and Monitor phases – Quality Assurance dimension

Phase	Suggested types of practices for Quality Assurance	Testing Process
Identify	Define organizational policy for quality assurance of product (service)	• Establish an organization-wide review program (upper management must develop review policies, support the review process, and take responsibility for integrating them into the organizational culture) • Software quality evaluation (management and testing and software quality assurance groups must define quality-related policies, quality goals, and quality attributes for software products) • Quality control (software test group and SQA group must establish quality goals for software products such as product unit defectiveness, confidence levels, and trustworthiness, test managers must incorporate these quality goals into the test plans) • Application of process data for defect prevention (defect prevention team must be established with management support) • Quality control (test group must be trained in statistical methods) • Application of defect data for defect prevention (causal analysis mechanism must be established to identify the root causes of defects) • Test process optimization (effectiveness of testing process must be continually evaluated, and decisions on when to stop testing must be related to quality goals and made in a measurable and optimal manner)
	Define factors that determine product (service) quality	• Software quality evaluation (management and testing and software quality assurance groups must define quality-related policies, quality goals, and quality attributes for software products)
	Define activities to verify product (service) quality	• Establish an organization-wide review program (test group and software quality assurance group must develop and document goals, plans, follow-up procedures, and recording mechanisms for reviews throughout the software lifecycle, Items for review must be specified) • Software quality evaluation (testing process must be structured, measured, and evaluated to ensure the quality goals can be achieved) • Application of process data for defect prevention (defects injected or removed must be identified and recorded during each life cycle phase) • Control and monitor the testing process (set of corrective actions and contingency plans must

		be developed, recorded, and documented for use when testing deviates significantly from what is planned)
Monitor	Monitor adherence to product (service) quality assurance policy	
	Monitor verification of product (service) quality	

These tables show how the key process areas and their main practices, as prescribed by the Testing Maturity Model, match the set of suggested types of practices as prescribed by the meta-model. Considering that TMM is a process-based maturity model highly influenced by CMM, it is not surprising that nearly all of the core process key practices are covered while the suggested types of practices for the quality assurance dimension are partially covered and usability/customer satisfaction dimension are almost entirely uncovered. This example shows how the proposed meta-model can help generate a much more complete set of key practices to drive a process improvement effort.

Table 7. Suggested key practices for Testing Process – Measure and Feedback phases – all dimensions

Phase	Suggested types of practices	Testing Process
Measure	Define measures of process performance, product (service) quality, and usability (customer satisfaction)	• Establish a test measurement program (organizational-wide test measurements policies and goals must be defined) • Control and monitor the testing process (set of basic test process-related measurements must be defined, recorded, and distributed)
	Define activities to collect measures of process performance, product (service) quality, and product usability (customer satisfaction)	• Establish a test measurement program (test measurement plan must be developed with mechanisms for data collection, analysis, and application)
	Define activities to analyze measures of process performance, product (service) quality, and product usability (customer satisfaction)	• Establish a test measurement program (test measurement plan must be developed with mechanisms for data collection, analysis, and application)
Feedback	Generate recommendations for process improvement based on analysis of measurements	• Establish a test measurement program (action plans that apply measurements results to test process improvements must be developed and documented) • Test process optimization (mechanism must be in place to evaluate new tools and technologies that may improve the capability and maturity of the testing process)
	Evaluate/prioritize recommendations for process improvement	
	Incorporate recommendations into process	

4   Conclusions and Future Work

We have presented a revised meta-model framework for developing a process model of a particular process or task. The proposed framework moves away from focusing entirely on process and from computing maturity levels and concentrates on key practices for a particular process area or task taking into account the quality and usability/customer satisfaction of the actual products or services. The process models constructed from the framework focus on three dimensions (core process, quality assurance and usability/customer satisfaction) and differ from other process models that focus primarily on the process dimension and pay little attention to the other dimensions. For a particular software process or task, the set of key practices is directly generated from the meta practices identified in the meta-model taking advantage of the useful questions and hints that help identifying those key practices. This freedom and flexibility in generating key practices allows the process model to be tailored to the specific organization's need. We believe process models constructed using the meta-model framework effectively identify the key practices needed to initiate and sustain an improvement effort focused on a single process area or task. Furthermore, the meta-model framework supports and facilitates development of assessment techniques such as the generation of the questions associated with each key practice in an assessment questionnaire.

We have applied this meta-model framework to two different process areas or tasks (configuration management support process and testing process). While these are only two examples, they do demonstrate the flexibility, ease of application, and completeness of the key practices generated from applying the framework. We are very interested in working with organizations in applying the framework to processes they may want to evaluate and improve.

References

1. R. Basque. CBA IPI: How to build software process improvement success in the evaluation phase?, *IEEE Computer Society Software Process Newsletter*, **5** (Winter 1996).
2. I. Burnstein, T. Suwannasart and C. Carlson. Developing a testing maturity model: part I. *CrossTalk*, **9(8)** (1996) 21-24
3. I. Burnstein, T. Suwannasart and C. Carlson. Developing a testing maturity model: part II. *CrossTalk*, **9(9)** (1996) 19-26
4. D. Bustard, R. Oakes and Z. He. Models to promote effective system change, in *Proceedings of International Conference of Software Maintenance*, Oxford, UK, September 1999, pp. 297-304
5. C. Cook and M. Visconti. What to do after the assessment report?, in *Proceedings of the 17th Pacific Northwest Software Quality Conference*, Portland, Oregon, October 1999 (PNSQC, Portland, 1999), pp. 214-228
6. C. Debou and A. Kuntzmann-Combelles. Linking software process improvement to business strategies: experiences from industry. Software Process Improvement and Practice, 5(1) (2000) 55-64

7. J. Favaro and S.L. Pfleeger. Making software development investment decisions. ACM SIGSOFT Software Engineering Notes 23(5) (1998) 69-74

8. B.S. Ghotra. Software Configuration Management (SCM) Support Process Capability Maturity Model, Master's Project (Computer Science Department, Oregon State University, 2001)

9. R. Grady. Successful software process improvement (Prentice-Hall, Upper Saddle River, New Jersey, 1997)

10. E.M. Gray and W.L. Smith. On the limitations of software process assessments and the recognition of a required re-orientation for global process improvement. *Software Quality Journal* 7 (1998) 21-34

11. R. McFeely. IDEAL: a user's guide for software process improvement. Technical Report CMU/SEI-96-HB-001 (CMU/SEI, Pittsburgh, Pennsylvania, 1996)

12. M. Paulk, B. Curtis, M. Chrissis and C. Weber. Capability Maturity Model, version 1.1. IEEE Software, 10(4) (1993) 18-27

13. M. Paulk, C. Weber, S. Garcia, M. Chrissis and M. Bush. Key practices of the Capability Maturity Model version 1.1. *Technical Report CMU/SEI-93-TR-025* (CMU/SEI, Pittsburgh, Pennsylvania, 1993)

14. S. Shrum. Choosing a CMMI Model Representation. CrossTalk, 13(7) (2000) 6-7

15. J. Trienekens, R. Kusters and R. Van Solingen. Product Focused Software Process Improvement: Concepts and Experiences from Industry. *Software Quality Journal* 9 (2001), 269-281

16. M. Visconti and C. Cook. Evolution of a maturity model – critical evaluation and lessons learned. *Software Quality Journal* 7(3/4) (1998), 223-237

17. M. Visconti and C. Cook. A meta-model for software process maturity, in *Proceedings of FESMA-AEMES Software Measurement Conference 2000*, October 2000, Madrid, Spain

18. M. Visconti and C. Cook. A meta-model framework for software process modeling, Technical Report 02-60-02, Computer Science Department, Oregon State University, March 2002

19. J. Voas. Can clean pipes produce dirty water?. *IEEE Software*, 14(4) (1997) 93-95

20. K. Wiegers and D. Sturzenberger. A modular software process mini-assessment method. *IEEE Software*, 17(1) (2000) 62-69

An XMI-Based Repository
for Software Process Meta-modeling

Francisco Ruiz, Mario Piattini, Félix García, and Macario Polo

Alarcos Research Group, University of Castilla-La Mancha
13071 Ciudad Real, Spain
{Francisco.RuizG,Mario.Piattini,Felix.Garcia,
Macario.Polo}@uclm.es
http://alarcos.inf-cr.uclm.es/english/

Abstract. In order to be able to work correctly with all the concepts handled in software process improvement it is useful to establish different abstraction levels that help to manage the complexity. Correct use of all the data and metadata (models and meta-models) handled in the different abstraction levels is necessary. This paper proposes a tool, based on MOF (Meta-Object Facility) conceptual architecture, for the management of these models and meta-models, that are stored in a repository in the form of XMI (XML Metadata Interchange) documents. This tool can be used as an integrated vertical component in other horizontal tools oriented to software process improvement and management. As example, we present its vertical integration with MANTIS, an environment for software maintenance management.

1   Introduction

In the field of software engineering, achieving high quality products is a common objective. A factor which is fundamental to and greatly influences the final quality of a software product is precisely the process which has been followed in order to develop or maintain the product. As a result, in a Software Engineering Environment (SEE) it is important that all the software processes should be managed in an integrated fashion, taking into account both the way in which software processes are developed (defining the required methodologies and tools) and their execution (especially its control).

A software process consists of a set of concurrent and cooperative activities that are related to the development and maintenance of the software as well as to the management of the project and the quality of the product. Software processes are inherently complex as they involve a lot of people, with different responsibilities and skills, and they produce or modify a wide range of elements [1]. In order to manage and improve software processes, it is necessary to establish abstraction levels that enable us to reduce this complexity, dealing satisfactorily with all their different aspects. Metadata constitute the key element for the integration of all the concepts involved in software

M. Oivo and S. Komi-Sirviö (Eds.): PROFES 2002, LNCS 2559, pp. 546-558, 2002.

process management. Metadata are descriptive information about the structure and meaning of the data, and of the applications and processes that manipulate them [6]. When different abstraction levels are defined (multilevel conceptual architectures), correct management of the data and metadata and the relationship between these becomes an essential aspect. All the information carried by the data and metadata must be stored in repositories in order to deal with the diversity of the data sources.

The aim of this paper is to present RepManager, a software component for managing metadata repositories that deals with all the information necessary for the managing and improving of software processes. In the following paragraphs we will describe the functions carried out by the RepManager tool, and explain the importance of each of them. We will then look at a practical application of this component in its integration with MANTIS [16], a SEE oriented to software maintenance management. At last, we will comment some related works, which are the future lines of this work, and the main conclusions.

2   Description of the Repository Manager

The first consideration to be taken into account when designing a repository is in which format the data and metadata are going to be stored. In order to have an open format for the storage of the data and meta-data at our disposal, the RepManager tool uses *XML Metadata Interchange* (XMI), [9]. It is essential for the repository manager to guarantee the possibility of interchange between the models and meta-models defined, so that both the meta-models defined with the tool and the meta-models defined with other tools -that support XMI- are usable. The principal objective of XMI is to facilitate the interchange of metadata between modeling tools and between metadata tools and repositories in distributed heterogeneous environments. XMI constitutes the integrating element for metadata originating from different sources, as it represents a common specification. Therefore, to a great extent the RepManager component provides a tool with support enabling it to interchange metadata with other repositories or tools that support XMI.

Another important aspect that should be taken into consideration is that the information of the repository should be accessible to all those that need it. For this reason, the metadata repository manager is a specialized software component which is designed to provide the necessary infrastructure and support for the storage of interrelated information components [7]. Therefore the functions of RepManager are similar to those provided by a database management system, but with the special characteristic that the information is stored as XMI documents. These functions will be supported via a set of calls to the system and are basically (see figure 1):

1. *Storage* of models and meta-models defined in the tool in a local metadata repository represented in XMI (for exportation).
2. *Importation/exportation* of models and meta-models.

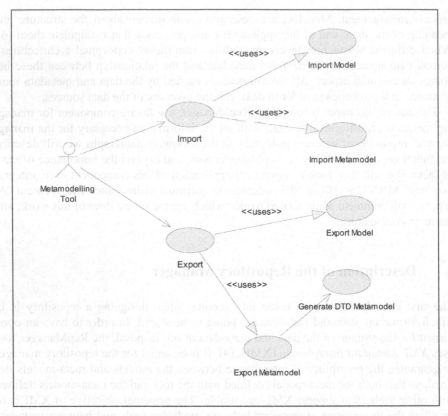

Fig. 1. RepManager imports/exports models and meta-models (UML use case diagram)

In order to gather the information on the models (at the different abstraction levels) that has been specified by the users or is contained in an XMI document, a class hierarchy has been defined that serves as a communication link between the control layer and the storage layer of RepManager. This class hierarchy is based on the specification of XMI, which establishes a series of production rules for the transformation of the meta-models into correct XML documents for the interchange. The storage function in the RepManager tool is supported by a specific service that generates the XMI document and the *Document Type Definition* (DTD) that represents it starting from a meta-model with its corresponding structure. When carrying out this operation the RepManager tool must guarantee that the updates are coherent with the syntax specified in the scheme associated with each type of XMI document.

As far as loading the meta-models is concerned RepManager provides another specific service which receives the document representing the meta-model as input and represents the information it contains according to the previously mentioned class hierarchy.

With the aim of managing the complexity, RepManager use 4 conceptual levels which are based on the MOF standard [8]. MOF is „a model for specifying, constructing, managing, interchanging and integrating metadata in software systems thus allowing the flexible integration of the systems" [8]. MOF describes an abstract modeling language aligned with the UML kernel. In table 1 we can see these four levels of the MOF architecture and their adaptation to RepManager.

Real specific software projects (with time, cost and resources restrictions) are found in level M0. The data dealt with at this level are instances of the concepts defined in the upper level M1. The specific models in level M1 represent the methods and techniques specific for each application domain. Level M2 corresponds to the software process (SP) generic meta-model. In M3, the last conceptual level, the SP meta-model of M2 level is represented as an MOF-model. An MOF-model basically comprises two types of objects: MOF-class and MOF-association (from our point of view these are the principal objects, although others do exist: packages for reuse purposes, types of data, etc.). Consequently, all the concepts represented in the level M2 are now considered examples of MOF-class and MOF-association. For example „Activity", „Resource" or „Artefact" are examples of MOF-class and „Activity uses Resource" or „Artefact is input of Activity" are examples of MOF-association.

In figure 2 we can see the basic operation scheme of the RepManager tool with its principal functions. As can be seen in this figure, RepManager provides the CASE tools for meta-modeling with two basic services: the storage and importation of meta-models. The CASE tool for meta-modeling calls up these services from its control layer and provides RepManager with all the necessary information (contained in a set of objects grouped in the specified class hierarchy) for the generation of the XMI documents that represent the correspondences between the different levels and the DTD that represent each type of XMI document generated. For the generation of XMI documents and their associated schemes the RepManager tool uses the generation rules specified in the XMI standard. Finally, the manipulation of the repository, that is to say, the storage and retrieval of information at document level, is carried out using the Document Object Model (DOM) [18]. This standard provides a collection of classes that represent the hierarchic structure on which all XML documents are based. The model provides classes that represent documents, nodes, list of nodes, etc., with the necessary properties and methods for the construction and editing of XML documents.

These services enable the CASE tools for meta-modeling to store the meta-models and models correctly by means of using a simple set of calls which constitute the repository interface.

Table 1. Correspondences between the conceptual levels of MOF and RepManager

Level	MOF	RepManager	Examples
M3	MOF-model (meta-meta-model)	MOF-model	MOF-class
M2	Meta-model	Generic SP meta-model	Activity
M1	Model	SP models (concrete methods and techniques)	Codification
M0	Data	SP instances	Codification of the PXB module

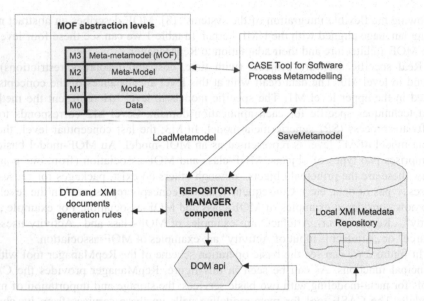

Fig. 2. RepManager interacts with other MOF-based tools

In the following sections we present a specific application of RepManager: the management of the repository of MANTIS, a SEE specially designed for the Software Maintenance Process (SMP) improvement and management.

3   One Use Case: MANTIS Environment

Software Maintenance (SM) represents the stage in the lifecycle of a software product that consumes most resources [11], and taking into account its special characteristics that clearly differentiate it from the development stage, it is very useful to have specific methods, techniques and tools at ones disposal. Moreover, to the improvement of this process, it is highly convenient to define and construct an environment for the integral management of the SM projects, due to the complex nature of this type of projects (as a result of the size and complexity of the product to be maintained and the difficulty of the task to be undertaken).

The MANTIS project aims to define and construct an integrated Environment for the management of SM projects [16]. By using the term Environment (with a capital „E") MANTIS is considered as a broader concept than the concepts of:

-    *methodology* (in the usual sense, meaning a series of related methods or techniques); and
-    *software engineering environment*, meaning a collection of software tools used to support software engineering activities [4].

MANTIS includes different aspects that must be taken into account when undertaking SM projects. For SMP management and improvement, MANTIS integrates the following:

-    the *personnel* (with specific skills and specific roles to carry out in the project).
-    the *techniques* (methodologies) used by these persons.
-    the *tools* (that help to comply with the standards).
-    the *activities* (in which the teams participate and which help important objectives to be reached).

The adaptation of the conceptual architecture showed in table 1 to this application domain is summarized next. In level M1, the MANTEMA methodology [12] and a set of techniques adapted to the special characteristics of SM (effort estimation, risk estimation, process improvement [13], audit [15], etc...) are proposed. Our generic SMP meta-model of M2 level is based on the informal ontology for SM proposed by Kitchenham et al [5], the „*Workflow Reference Model*" proposed by the Workflow Management Coalition [21], and the schema for software process modeling and software measurement proposed by Becker-Kornstaedt and Webby [1]. For example, the generic object type of „Maintenance Activity" used in M2 is instanced in the activity types "Analysis of the Modification Request" or „Urgent Corrective Intervention" in M1, and these in turn, in instances of level M0 as „Intervention n° 36 in the project PATON".

3.1   MANTIS-Metamod

MANTIS-Metamod is a tool for the meta-modeling of software processes in general, although constructed with the SM in mind (by means of its integration in the MANTIS environment) [16]. This tool can be integrated into horizontal tools based on the Meta Object Facility (MOF) standard. With MANTIS-Metamod the modeler can specify models and meta-models at the different levels of the MOF architecture.

The meta-models and models defined for the user by means of MANTIS-Metamod are validated and internally represented using the RepManager component. MANTIS-Metamod manages the correspondences between the levels M3-M2 and M2-M1. The correspondences between the levels M1 and M0 have not been included because they are related to the enactment of real projects instead of to process modeling.

The internal software architecture of this tool is based on a three layer model (presentation, control and storage) with the aim of reducing complexity and providing a certain degree of encapsulation. For the input of user data, the application comprises a meta-model administrator as its principal component and a windows system that permits a visual description of the classes that make up the models and meta-models (Package, Class, Data Type, Attribute, Operation, Reference, AssociationBegin, AssociationEnd and Constraint). In the meta-model administrator, as in the MOF model, the information is structured in a hierarchical fashion: a package contains classes and associations, a class contains attributes and operations, an association contains restrictions, etc. (see figure 3).

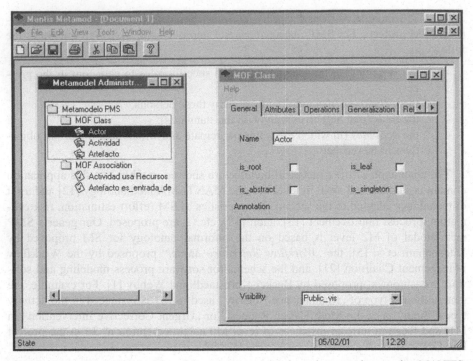

Fig. 3. Users can view and edit models and meta-models in an integrated way using MANTIS-Metamod

To complement this tool, other tools of visual modeling can be used. This functionality is possible owing to the fact, as already mentioned, that MANTIS-Metamod has the capacity to interchange meta-models and models in XMI format using the services of the RepManager tool. For example, you can use Rational Rose to draw the class diagrams of a model (level M1) and of a meta-model (level M2), and export both to MOF/XMI format. Using MANTIS-Metamod (and therefore, RepManager for the storage function) you will be able to edit both in a combined way; compare one with other, check the adaptation of the model to the meta-model, or visualize the model objects associated with a certain meta-model object.

We believe that the main utility of MANTIS-Metamod (and RepManager) is, in fact, to be able to manage and edit a model jointly with its associated meta-model.

4   Using RepManager in MANTIS

One of the objectives of MANTIS is the integration of the concepts on which it is based and more importantly the correct management of all the metadata and data at the different conceptual levels previously mentioned. In order to achieve this, the models and meta-models of the different levels can be stored in a repository -of XMI documents- managed by the RepManager tool. Each XMI document stored in the repository represents a correspondence between the M_i level and M_{i-1} level, as each XMI document will contain the metadata (level M_i) that describe the corresponding data (M_{i-1} level instances). As a result, and bearing in mind that we work with four conceptual levels in MANTIS, three types of XMI documents will be stored in the repository:

- XMI documents that represent the correspondences between the levels M2-M3, such as the correspondence between the MOF-model and the SMP meta-model. The DTD or scheme that will represent this type of XMI documents is unique and will be the DTD of the MOF-model (only the MOF-model is present at level M3 in order to integrate the possible meta-models of the lower level).
- XMI documents that represent the correspondences between the levels M2-M1, such as the correspondence between the SMP generic meta-model with the specific MANTEMA methodology. In this case the DTD represents the meta-model of level M2, for example, it would be necessary to store the DTD of the SMP generic meta-model.
- XMI documents that represent the correspondences between the levels M1-M0 such as the correspondence between MANTEMA methodology and a specific project enactment applied in a company that is using that methodology. In this case the DTD represents specific models of level M1. In the MANTIS environment case it would be necessary to store the DTD corresponding to the MANTEMA methodology.

In figure 4 we can see the document types stored in the repository which give support to MANTIS and the correspondences between them. As can be seen, the data of a level M_i are transformed into metadata of level M_{i-1} which is immediately below. In this way „Maintenance Activity", which is a piece of data (associated with the MOF-class M3 element) in the XMI document that represents the correspondence M3-M2, is converted into a label (metadata) in the XMI document that represents the correspondence between the levels M2 and M1. Two instances of „Maintenance Activity" are defined in this M2-M1 mapping document: „Urgent Corrective Intervention" and „Modification Request Analysis". In turn, in the M1-M0 mapping document, „Urgent Corrective Intervention" is a new element label with one new instance named „Intervention number 36" corresponding to one real task of real SM project enactment.

4.1 Applying to the Assessment Process

In MANTIS, an important application of the RepManager tool is to integrate the different concepts involved in the assessment and improvement of the SMP [23]. Given the importance of improvement, and hence of the assessment, of software processes, it finds important to be able to treat all the concepts involved in these processes in an integrated way. To achieve this integration, we have extended the already commented 4 level architecture of MANTIS with a concrete model of assessment. This way, at level M0 are represented the results of the application of an assessment process to a maintenance project. That is to say, at this level there would be the results of a process from which it would be possible to establish its strong and weak points. The specific model used at level M1 represents the assessment model proposed in part 5 of ISO 15504 standard [22]. In this level we focus on the guidance that ISO provides with regard to the assessment process.

The main activities that ISO 15504 identifies to assess a software process are Planning, Collecting Data, Validating Data, Process Rating and Reporting. The assessment process output is formed by the process profile which records all data related to the assessment of a process. In table 2 the main correspondences between the elements of the generic SMP meta-model and the main elements of the assessment process are summarized.

We can generate automatically the DTD associated to the assessment process model of ISO 15504 (level M1) using the RepManager tool. This way, the tools used to perform specific assessment processes (level M0) could exchange their data efficiently (in XML documents adapted to the previous DTD).

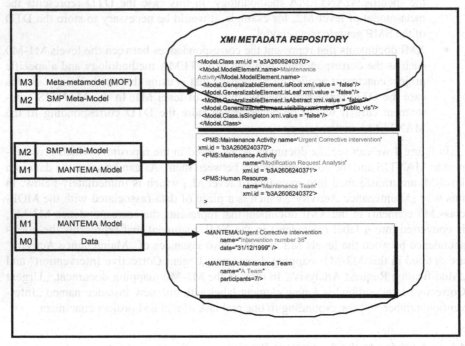

Fig. 4. Using RepManager with the three mapping layers of MANTIS

5   Related and Future Works

There are several examples of recent literature that demonstrate the advantages of MOF and XMI for the construction of CASE tool and SEE repositories. The project FAMOOS (Framework-based Approach for Mastering Object-Oriented Software Evolution) is a good example of this [2]. The goal of this project is to build a framework to support the evolution and reengineering of object-oriented software systems.

With this aim in mind, FAMIX, a language-independent meta-model (in M2 level of MOF) for describing object-oriented source codes at the program entity level, has been developed [17]. In this case RepManager could be used as a repository manager by storing the meta-model FAMIX (together with its associated DTD) and a model (in M1 level) for each of the programming languages used.

In [10], SPAIL (Software Process Assessment Interchange Language) is presented. It is a XML-based language oriented to representing and exchanging descriptions of process assessment results. SPAIL gives rise to a DTD that defines the grammar of this language, taking as its base a specific model of the assessment process, proposed in the standard SPICE [14]. An XML document based on the DTD of SPAIL, containing the results of a real-world process assessment, is an instance of correspondence M1-M0 (relationships between model objects and data objects). Using RepManager it is possible to store and manage this model along with any other model of the same or related processes. In fact, the DTD of SPAIL can be automatically generated by Rep-Manager. To achieve this, all you have to do is define the process meta-model (level M2) using an MOF-based meta-modeling tool (for example, with Mantis-Metamod, although another option would be to use a CASE tool that allows MOF to be exported e.g. Rational Rose for the graphic design of this meta-model) and invoke the GeneratedDTDMetamodel use case of RepManager. Although RepManager does not include a use case for generating DTD models, it is not in fact necessary, as by defining the model of the level M1 in the same way as the meta-model of the level M2, their DTDs will also be the same.

The main aim of the RepManager tool is to provide support in the form of a model and meta-model repository to any CASE tool that may need it. This functionality is particularly useful in the area of Process-centered Software Engineering Environments (PSEE), [3]. The MANTIS environment, which we have discussed previously, has an architecture of this type whose main feature is a central process concept. A basic aspect of software processes is that they are subject to changes both when being put into use in a specific real-world project and in relation to the associated process model. The improvement of a process also leads to both types of alterations. In order to manage these changes it is necessary to be able to represent the different models (a new version of a process model whilst similar to the original model is in reality a different process model) and associated meta-models. It would also be useful to enchance RepManager with support for facilitating the re-engineering of models using the common meta-model as an intermediate step.

A further improvement, of a technical type, is to facilitate partial access to the information contained in a model or meta-model by means of a query engine based on the use of the Xquery language [20], a standard proposal of the W3C for XML documents query. The use of XML schemas instead of DTD is also being studied in order to take advantage of their greater semantic capacity [19]. Moreover, XML schemas have XML syntax and as a result can be handled with DOM, the same API as that used for the XML documents themselves [18].

Table 2. Mapping between the generic SMP of MANTIS and the assessment process model of ISO 15504

M2 classes	M2 instances (M1 classes)
Activity	Defining the assessment input
	Perform the assessment process
	Planning
	Collect data
	Validate data
	Process rating
	Reporting
	Record the assessment output
Artifact	Process to assess
	Process profile
Activity contains Activity	„Perform ..." contains „Planning"
	„Perform ..." contains „Collect ..."
	„Perform ..." contains „Validate ..."
	„Perform ..." contains „Process ..."
	„Perform ..." contains „Reporting"
Activity consumes Artifact	„Perform ..." consumes „Process to assess"
Activity produces Artifact	„Perform ..." produces „Process profile"

6   Conclusions

In this document we have presented RepManager, a component tool for the management of repositories of software process models and meta-models stored in XMI documents, and its vertical integration with MANTIS, an integrated environment for software maintenance management and improvement.

Nowadays the development and maintenance of software have become inherently overly complex processes due to the distributed, heterogeneous character and the size of the applications. The solution for dealing with this complexity is to be found in a classic but valuable concept of information system terminology: modeling. Models provide the abstraction that is necessary for dealing with this complexity. However, due to the great complexity of the applications, modeling architectures have been proposed that allow the models themselves to be handled in different levels.

The correct management of data and metadata represents the key to dealing with these architectures. Data and metadata repositories have become a key element for the management of software processes. Metadata enable the construction of easy-to-maintain applications and moreover the efficient management and improvement of software development and maintenance processes.

The tool that we have presented allows the management of data and metadata defined for software process modeling. The Repository Manager facilitates working with the models and meta-models stored in the repository. Moreover it provides the user with transparency when handling the data as the system conceals the details related to the way in which the data and metadata are stored, thus allowing these to be efficiently managed.

Any other modeling tool that uses the abstract language provided by MOF and XMI for the definition and storage of meta-models will be able to collaborate with RepManager tool, and in so doing would increase the efficiency of the software process management. As an example of this functionality, we have presented the integration of RepManager with the MANTIS environment and, as demonstration of its generality, we have commented the integration of the assessment process.

Acknowledgements

This work has been partially funded by the TAMANSI project financed by „Consejería de Ciencia y Tecnología, Junta de Comunidades de Castilla-La Mancha" of Spain (project reference PBC-02-001).

References

1. Becker-Kornstaedt, U. and Webby, R.: A Comprehensive Schema Integrating Software Process Modelling and Software Measurement. Fraunhofer Institute, IESE report Nº 047.99/E., v. 1.2 (1999)
2. Ducasse, S. and Demeyer, S.: The FAMOOS Object-Oriented Reengineering Handbook. University of Berne, October (1999). See http://www.iam.unibe.ch/~famoos/handbook
3. Fugetta, A., Godart, C. and Jahnke, J.: Arquitectural Views and Alternatives. In: Derniame, J-C., Kaba, B.A., and Wastell, D. (eds.): Software Process: Principles, Methodology and Technology. Lecture Notes on Computer Science, Vol. 1500. Springer-Verlag (1999), 95-116
4. ISO/IEC: JTC1/SC7/WG4 15940 working draft 5, Information Technology - Software Engineering Environment Services, June (2000)
5. Kitchenham, B.A., Travassos, G.H., Mayrhauser, A. von, Niessink, F., Schneidewind, N.F., Singer, J., Takada, S., Vehvilainen, R. and Yang, H.: Towards an Ontology of Software Maintenance. Journal of Software Maintenance: Research and Practice. 11 (1999), 365-389
6. MDC: Meta Data Coalition, Open Information Model, v.1.0, August (1999)
7. Morgenthal J.P. and Walms, P.: Mining for Metadata. In Software Magazine, Feb/Mar (2000); Wiesner Publishing. Available in http://www.softwaremag.com/archive/-2000feb/MiningMetadata.html
8. OMG: Object Management Group, Meta Object Facility (MOF) Specification, v. 1.3 RTF, September (1999). In http://www.omg.org
9. OMG: Object Management Group, XML Metadata Interchange (XMI), v. 1.1, November (2000). In http://www.omg.org
10. Park, J. and Lee, K.: A XML-based Approach to Software Process Improvement Environment on The Internet. Proceedings of the IASTED International Conference on Software Engineering and Applications. Anaheim-California, USA (2001), 76-80

11. Pigoski, T.M.: Practical Software Maintenance. Best Practices for Managing your Investment. John Wiley & Sons, USA (1996)
12. Polo, M., Piattini, M., Ruiz, F. and Calero, C.: MANTEMA: A complete rigorous methodology for supporting maintenance based on the ISO/IEC 12207 Standard. Third Euromicro Conference on Software Maintenance and Reengineering (CSMR'99). Amsterdam (Netherland), IEEE Computer Society (1999), 178-181
13. Polo, M., Piattini, M., Ruiz, F. and Jiménez, M.: Assessment of Maintenance Maturity in IT Departments of Public Entities: Two Case Studies. Proceedings of Third International Conference on Product Focused Software Process Improvement (PROFES'2001). Kaiserslautern, Germany, 86-97
14. Rout, T.: SPICE: A Framework for Software Process Assessment. Software Process Improvement and Practice. vol 1, no 1 (1995), 57-66
15. Ruiz, F., Piattini, M., Polo, M. and Calero, C.: Audit of Software Maintenance. In: Auditing Information Systems, USA, Idea Group Publishing (2000), 67-108
16. Ruiz, F., Piattini, M. and Polo, M.: An Conceptual Architecture Proposal for Software Maintenance. International Symposium on Systems Integration (ISSI, Intersymp'2001). Baden-Baden, Germany (2001), VIII:1-8
17. Tichelaar, S., Ducasse, S. and Demeyer, S.: FAMIX and XMI. Proceedings of the Seventh Working Conference on Reverse Engineering (WCRE'2000). Brisbane, Australia (2000), IEEE Computer Society Press, 296-299
18. W3C: World-Wide-Web Consortium, Document Object Model (DOM) level 1 specification, v. 1.0. October (1998). In http://www.w3.org/DOM/
19. W3C: World-Wide-Web Consortium, XML Schema Part 0: Primer, May (2001). In http://www.w3.org/TR/xmlschema-0/
20. W3C: World-Wide-Web Consortium, XQuery 1.0: An XML Query Language, working draft, June (2001). In http://www.w3.org/TR/xquery/
21. WfMC: Workflow Management Coalition TC00-1003 1.1, The Workflow Reference Model, January (1995)
22. ISO/IEC: ISO/IEC TR 15504-5: Information Technology – Software Process Assessment - part 5: An assessment model and indicator guidance, (1999)
23. García, F., Ruiz, F., Piattini, M. and Polo, M.: Conceptual Architecture for the Assessment and Improvement of Software Maintenance. 4th International Conference on Enterprise Information Systems (ICEIS'02). Ciudad Real, Spain, 610-617

Software Solutions to Internet Connectivity in Mobile Ad Hoc Networks

Christer Åhlund[1] and Arkady Zaslavsky[2]

[1] Luleå University of Technology
Centre for Distance-spanning Technology, Department of Computer Science
SE-971 87 Luleå, Sweden
christer@cdt.luth.se
[2] School of Computer Science & Software Engineering, Monash University
900 Dandenong Road, Caulfield East, Vic 3145, Melbourne, Australia
a.zaslavsky@monash.edu.au

Abstract. In recent years wireless Internet access and wireless communications between peers have become the focus of intensive research efforts in various areas of information and communication technologies. Mobility aspects, software development and support for mobile users are currently of major interest within this research area. The Mobile IP protocol is deployed for mobility management of hosts moving between networks. Ad hoc routing is also of major importance for connectivity between communicating mobile hosts without backbone infrastructure. In this paper we propose and describe an integrated connectivity solution and its software implementation between an ad hoc network running the Ad Hoc On-Demand Distance-Vector Protocol (AODV) and a wired IP network where Mobile IP is used for mobility management. The article also describes a project called Mobile City in which our software solutions and support infrastructure are tested and validated.

1 Introduction

Current network and distributed systems are unthinkable without sophisticated software solutions that require non-stop evolution and improvement [24, 25]. The IP protocol is the major network protocol used in modern computer networks. This protocol was developed for a wired network topology with stationary routers and hosts. The IP address is used to reach a node in a network (like a router and a host) by determining a route to the destination and identifying the host within the destination network. IP addresses are hierarchically organized with a major network part identifying the network, an optional subnet part identifying a subnetwork within the major network and a host part identifying the host within the network or the subnet. The hierarchical IP address allows routers to only look at the network part when finding a route to a destination. The only router looking at the host part of an IP

M. Oivo and S. Komi-Sirviö (Eds.): PROFES 2002, LNCS 2559, pp. 559–571, 2002.

address is the router(s) connected to the network where the destination host resides. To overcome the static network topology problems and to support mobility within IP networks, Mobile IP (MIP)[7] is proposed and partly deployed. MIP can be used for hosts connecting to a foreign network and still function as if they were connected to the home network. Because of the mobility aspects, wireless connections are becoming very popular and are considered the preferred way for a mobile host's (MH) connectivity. Wireless technologies like 802.11a and 802.11b [9] among other technologies are used instead of wired connections and do create a one hop connection to a wired network like Ethernet. To be able to connect to networks equipped with 802.11 access points (AP), the mobile host must be within radio communication range to the AP.

Another type of network becoming popular because of the wireless capabilities in computer communications is an ad hoc network [10]. In ad hoc networks there is no such fixed infrastructure as a wired backbone with routers. Instead, all mobile hosts (MHs), which are ad hoc hosts, usually both work as end user hosts and routers within the ad hoc network. The address space in an ad hoc network enables to work within the ad hoc network regardless of the wired IP network topology. Some ad hoc network proposals make use of clustering to create a hierarchical network scheme, while others use a flat address space. Ad hoc routing protocols can be classified into two major types of routing protocols: proactive and reactive routing protocols [21]. The proactive routing protocols always try to maintain a route to every host in the ad hoc network regardless of whether user data is being sent or not. The proactive approach is the one used in IP networks by routing protocols like RIP and OSPF [13]. In ad hoc networks where mobility might be high, the proactive routing protocols may not be the most optimal protocols to use, since the path created to a destination may be obsolete when the destination is addressed. The reactive routing protocols create a path to a destination when packets need to be sent there. If no user data is sent in the ad hoc network no routes are created. In ad hoc networks reactive routing protocols have been proven to be efficient [11, 12].

Our goal with the work described in this article is to enable mobile users to communicate ad hoc when connecting without a backbone, and at the same time have connectivity to a wired IP network infrastructure (the home network or a foreign network) accessing the Internet. When outside communication range to an AP, an intermediate adjacent ad hoc host should be used if possible to reach the AP.

We propose and describe an approach connecting wired IP networks with ad hoc networks running the Ad Hoc On-Demand Distance-Vector Protocol (AODV) [14] for routing in the ad hoc network. Ad hoc hosts will have connectivity with hosts in the ad hoc network as well as in the Internet. For mobility of hosts between networks we use the MIP protocol. Our approach integrates ad hoc networks with IP networks and the Internet.

The contribution of the work proposed and described in this article is an integrated connectivity solution and its prototype software implementation. We propose a new functionality for gateways between IP networks and ad hoc networks for „global connectivity", so that MHs can move between wired IP networks and ad hoc networks while maintaining network connectivity. We also propose protocol changes so that the AODV protocol and the MIP protocol can function together.

In section 2 we describe the Mobile City project. Section 3 describes our design and implementation. Related work is described in section 4. Section 5 concludes the paper and describes future work.

2   Mobile City

Mobile City (www.mobilecity.nu) is an EU funded research and development project that develops both a wireless communication infrastructure and diverse mobile applications that can support various activities of individuals as well as communities. The project involves extensive wireless infrastructure and a number of research initiatives in mobile communications and applications development. The work described in this article is discussed in the context of bringing wireless communication to every person/potential user. The real city in the focus of this project is Skellefteå, located in the northern part of Sweden in the Internet-Bay area. Skellefteå is a typical representative of a regional community in a sparsely populated area of the country (see figure 1), with well-developed infrastructure, mostly small and medium-sized enterprises and a broad range of applications that users might need. Rather than focusing on one technology, the project involves a variety of communication and networking technologies, including 802.11, Bluetooth, GPRS/EDGE, UMTS, etc with each technology supporting a class of applications. In addition, Mobile City addresses the additional important aspect of utilization of mobile Internet-based services.

Fig. 1. Regional map

Current work within Mobile City to support people, companies and business with wireless network connectivity in the community of Skellefteå is described in [18-20].

3   Connecting IP Networks with Ad hoc Networks

3.1   Design Considerations

For ad hoc networks to be integrated with IP networks, ad hoc networks should adapt to the network functionality within IP networks. Often ad hoc networks are seen as self-contained and are of limited size. Ad hoc networks are considered a complementary to IP networks in this article, where Internet connectivity can be extended into the ad hoc network, making ad hoc networks a part of the Internet. We assume that an ad hoc network uses a flat address space.

The location of a host in IP networks is identified by the network bits within the IP address (the major network bits and the subnet bits). When a packet arrives at the router connecting the network hosting the destination, and if the destination is connected to a network being a Local Area Network (LAN), the hierarchical IP address is converted to a MAC address using the ARP protocol [15] in IPv4 or the Neighbour Discovery Protocol [3] in IPv6, before the packet is sent in a frame in the last hop using the MAC address as the identifier of the destination. The MAC address represents a flat address space without information about the host's locality within the LAN.

Considering the ad hoc network has a flat address space, it can be seen as a network (major network or subnetwork) within Internet. This will identify an ad hoc network connected to the Internet by its own network number. There is, however, a major difference between a LAN and an ad hoc network. Hosts connected to a LAN are within the same broadcast domain, and are managed as one hop connections by the IP protocol. A packet broadcasted in the LAN will reach all hosts connected to the network. In the ad hoc network a broadcast sent by one ad hoc host may not reach all other hosts. A broadcast need to be retransmitted by hosts in the network so that it will reach all hosts. A broadcast in the ad hoc network running the IP protocol uses the time to live (TTL) value to limit the spreading of a packet. A packet's TTL when arriving at a router connected to a LAN requires a value of 1 to reach a host connected to the network. In the ad hoc network a TTL of 1 when forwarded on the ad hoc network will be discarded after the first hop. This behaviour needs to be managed by gateways connecting ad hoc networks with IP networks.

Instead of using the ARP or the Neighbour Discovery Protocol, the ad hoc routing protocol needs to be used in what is defined as the last hop in IP networks. The functionality in reactive ad hoc routing protocols maps well to the functionality in the ARP protocol and the Neighbour Discovery Protocol, with a request for the host in the last hop and a soft state table. The route request (RREQ) in reactive ad hoc routing protocols can be compared to the ARP request, and the soft state ad hoc routing table to the ARP table.

We assume all MHs in the ad hoc network to have an IP address and to be able to connect to hosts within the Internet. MHs should be able to move between ad hoc networks and still function as if they were connected to the home network. Peers in the ad hoc network should be able to communicate one-hop or multi-hop regardless of their network part in the IP addresses. This means that two hosts homed in different networks will be able to communicate peer-to-peer. MHs homed in an ad hoc network will have the network number given the ad hoc network, and MHs visiting the network will either use their home address as an identifier, an address given by a DHCP server, or if IPv6 is used, stateless auto configuration [3] can be used.

MHs connected to the home ad hoc network will be reached through the IP network by IP routing to the gateway connecting to the ad hoc network. Then the ad hoc routing protocol is used to locate the destination in the ad hoc network. If however the gateway already has an active path to the destination, the packet will be forwarded without a prior RREQ creating a route.

When an MH in the ad hoc network addresses a correspondent host, we use the way proxy ARP [15] works to manage where to send a packet for a destination in the same network or in another. In the proxy ARP approach a router looks at the IP address requested, and if the router sees that the destination is in another LAN it responds with its own MAC address. All packets to the IP address will be sent to the router and the router will forward the packet to the destination. The source does not need by itself to investigate if the destination is within the same LAN or not, the router will support this. If the destination is within the same network it will itself respond.

In ad hoc networks we must be able to manage a multi-hop distance between hosts and the gateway, compared to the mechanisms in IP networks with one hop. Instead of the link layer address used in LANs to reach a gateway or a correspondent host in the same network, the IP addresses of the gateway and the MH have to be used, since the gateway may be multiple hops away. If the ad hoc routing protocol uses link layer addresses for routing within the ad hoc network, link layer addresses can be used. But in our work the IP address within the ad hoc network is used to identify MHs and to make route decisions.

To manage mobility of MHs connected to an IP network and trying to connect to different ad hoc networks, MIP is used. In MIP, messages for advertisement, solicitation and registration are sent using local links. For ad hoc networks the MIP messages must be able to travel multiple hops in the ad hoc network. To enhance the performance of our implementation, routes should be installed to the source of the MIP messages.

3.2 Design

In our design and implementation described below we make use of MIPv4, and the AODV routing protocol within the ad hoc network.

The design principles described in this section underlie our design considerations discussed in the previous section. We will describe:

- How MIPv4 messages are managed in the ad hoc network.
- How an MH decides what foreign agent (FA) to register with, if it knows several FAs.
- How a destination address from the ad hoc network is found being in the ad hoc network or in the Internet.

For an MH to be able to communicate ad hoc and to visit foreign ad hoc networks, the MH needs to run both the MIP and the AODV protocols. The same stands for a gateway connecting an ad hoc network to an IP network hosting the AP functionality. For the MIP messages specified to be sent link-local in a LAN, with a TTL value of 1, we have changed the value to indicate the size of the ad hoc network or the length in hops to an MH.

We have made the AODV protocol MIP-aware to recognize MIP messages so that ad hoc hosts (MH and gateway) can install routes based on the messages. Hosts forwarding agent advertisements will install a route to the FA. When an MH then registers with an FA by sending a registration request to the agent, a route will be available, without the need to do an explicit RREQ for the FA. The registration request creates a route for the registration reply, and the agent solicitation message creates a route for the unicasted agent advertisement.

An MH discovers a path to a destination by sending an RREQ for the destination. If the destination is known to be outside the ad hoc network, the gateway replies with a proxy RREP (ProxyRREP) to the source. For a destination within the ad hoc network the gateway will function as an ad hoc host forwarding the RREQ.

For a gateway to know which hosts are in the ad hoc network the AODV protocol requires the knowledge of the visitor list in the FA, and all hosts homed in the ad hoc network have to have the same network number as the gateway connecting to the ad hoc network. These requirements are the same as for a LAN in IP networks managing mobility. When a route is requested for a destination with a network number different from the ad hoc network, the visitor list is searched by the AODV process to see if the destination is available in the ad hoc network. If the destination in not within the network the gateway sends a ProxyRREP to the source. If the destination is a foreign MH visiting the ad hoc network, normal AODV operations are used to discover the destination within the network. Figure 2 illustrates this process. A ProxyRREP is also sent if a destination homed in the ad hoc network is connected to a foreign network. The home agent (HA) functionality used is as specified in MIPv4. Packets coming to the gateway will be processed as shown in figure 3.

To manage several FAs covering an ad hoc network there is a need to synchronize the visitor information between the FAs. Without synchronization, a gateway may conclude that a destination is within the wired IP network and send a ProxyRREP to the source, while the destination is, in fact, within the ad hoc network but registered with another FA. The FAs synchronize their visitor lists using the wired IP network to offload the ad hoc network, the information is synchronized when an entry is added or deleted from the visitor list in a gateway. In this way, all gateways will be able to see if a visiting host is within the ad hoc network even though it is not registered with the gateway receiving the RREQ. The HA binding cache does not have to be synchronized between the gateways since the gateway responding with a ProxyRREP will be the gateway acting as a HA for the MH connected to a foreign network. Other gateways will believe that the MH is in the ad hoc network.

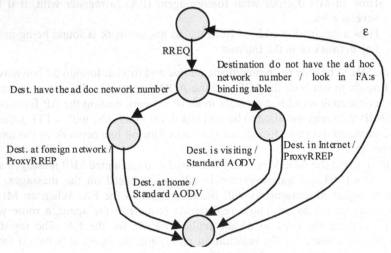

Fig. 2. The process in the gateway to manage AODV RREQ messages

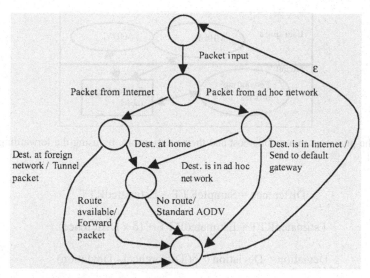

Fig. 3. The flow in the gateway to process an incoming packet

When several FAs serve an ad hoc network, an MH must be able to choose the best FA to register with. In our approach, the FA closest to the MH will be used based on the roundtrip time (RTT) between the MH and the FA. For each agent advertisement received at an MH, an icmp echo request message is sent to the FA to measure the RTT.

3.3   Implementation

The gateway as well as the MHs run the MIP software and the AODV software (see figure 4). The MIP software used is the HUT distribution [16] and the AODV software is a distribution from Uppsala University[17]. The operating system used is Linux 2.4 [22].

The MIP and the AODV software operate by modifying the forwarding table within the Linux kernel. In the kernel, the forwarding process forwards the packets using the information in the forwarding table.

The software in the gateway looks as in figure 4 with the extension of a shared memory between the MIP process and the AODV process, so that the AODV process will be informed of visiting MHs. If the gateway hosts an HA as well, the shared memory will also contain the hosts homed in the ad hoc network connected to a foreign network.

To measure the RTT we use the icmp echo request sent to the FA that the MH knows about. To calculate the metric used to select an FA we use the Jacobson/Karels algorithm [23] for the retransmission timer in the TCP protocol (see formula 1).

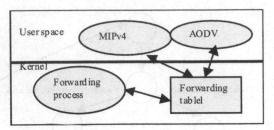

Fig. 4. The processes in a mobile host and their relationship, by using the forwarding table in the kernel

$$Difference = SampleRTT - EstimatedRTT. \tag{1}$$

$$EstimatedRTT = EstimatedRTT + (\delta \times Difference).$$

$$Deviation = Deviation + \delta(|Difference| - Deviation).$$

$$Metric = \mu \times EstimatedRTT + \phi \times Deviation.$$

By using the deviation in the metric calculation the variance will affect the FA selected. A big variance creates imprecise measurements and needs to be considered as a special case.

To switch between FAs the difference between the MeanRTTs must be bigger than a threshold.

In MIP, an MH receiving an agent advertisement assumes the previous link layer sender to be the FA, and uses this address as the default gateway. This must be modified to function in ad hoc networks, otherwise the MH will believe an intermediate host in the ad hoc network forwarding the agent advertisement to be the FA. We reserve the first care-of address field in the agent advertisement to the FA address within the ad hoc network (see figure 5). The MH can then discover the address of an FA being multiple hops away.

The agent solicitation message is also modified to function in the ad hoc network for the same reason as the agent advertisement. We have also added a sequence number to limit the broadcast of the solicitation and for the creation of a route to the sender. The solicitation message used in the standard MIP is the same as the router solicitation message. The extension in figure 6 shows the agent solicitation extension added to the router solicitation.

0 1 2 3 4 5 6 7 8 9 0 1 2 3 4 5 6 7 8 9 0 1 2 3 4 5 6 7 8 9 0 1

type	length	sequence number		
registration lifetime		R B H F M G V	reserved	
foreign agent address on the ad hoc network				
zero or more care-of addresses				

Fig. 5. The modified agent advertisement extension for the ad hoc network

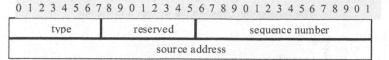

Fig. 6. The agent solicitation extension added to the router solicitation

Since we create a route based on the route request as well to enhance the performance, we use an extension field in the message to add the source address.

In today's 802.11 connectivity solutions, a host registers with an AP using a PC-card configured in infrastructure mode. In this mode the MH can only associate with one AP at a time. If two hosts want to communicate without a backbone infrastructure, they can do so ad hoc by configuring the PC-card in ad hoc mode. With this standard network interface configurations, it is not possible to communicate with one physical interface in both modes simultaneously. To manage connectivity with several APs as well as MHs in the ad hoc network, all interfaces are used in ad hoc mode.

3.4   Evaluation

We have thus far created some basic measurements to evaluate the performance of a TCP flow and the RTT from a source in the IP network to an MH connected to a foreign ad hoc network being between 1 and 4 hops from the gateway (see figure 7).

The links in the wired IP networks are 100Mbps, and for the wireless connectivity Orinocco 11Mbps Silver cards are used. The agent advertisement is sent every 5 seconds and the ad hoc route timeout is 10 second. The results are shown in figure 8. All MHs are within 10 meters radius. We filter frames by the MAC-address to control the connectivity between MHs, and to create the ad hoc connections shown in figure 7. The performance degradation in figure 8 is due to the link layer protocol and it shows how an overheard flow will affect the delay and the throughput.

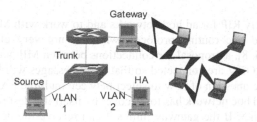

Fig. 7. The topology for our evaluation

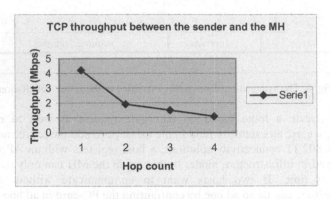

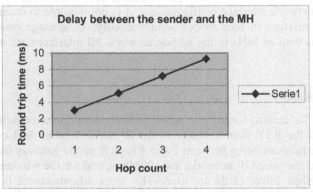

Fig. 8. A basic performance measurement

4   Related Work

In [6], authors modify RIP for ad hoc networks and to work with MIP. This approach uses a proactive ad hoc routing protocol, which is not very efficient in ad hoc networks. In [2, 4, 5, 8], a proposal for connections between MIP and AODV is made. In [5] MIPv4 and AODV are connected so that MIP messages will be managed in the ad hoc network. The question of how to select between multiple FAs is not addressed, and an MH in the ad hoc network has to discover by itself if a destination is within the ad hoc network or not. If the gateway thinks it can receive the destination it replies with an FA RREP (FA-RREP). But before an MH can use the gateway, it first needs to conclude that the destination is not within the ad hoc network and this will delay the connection setup time. MIPv6 management with AODV is proposed in [4] using the neighbour discovery protocol. The same approach for destinations in the IP network is taken as in [5] and it is proposed that router advertisements should not be sent without router solicitation. However, in [2] measurements show that it is more efficient to use the normal MIP behaviour where advertisements are sent without solicitations. In [2] and [8] an approach to selecting between multiple FAs is described, the selection in made on the hop count between the FA and the MH. Hop count may not be the best way to measure what FA to register with since network load is not considered. In [1] MIP and the ad hoc routing protocol DSR are addressed.

A number of software engineering aspects related to wireless and distributed systems are discussed in [24, 25].

5   Conclusion and Further Work

In this article we propose and describe an integrated connectivity solution and its implementation connecting IP networks and ad hoc networks running the reactive AODV routing protocol, where MIP is used to manage mobility. The software supports the creation of areas covered by gateways connecting wireless MHs to the Internet. MHs will be able to communicate peer-to-peer or with hosts in the IP network. Our approach proposes a new way to locate a destination inside the ad hoc network or in the IP network, and the selection of a FA based on the RTT between the MH and the FA.

The solution will support the creation of applications requiring global connectivity. An application using a software socket (TCP or UDP) and one or more network interfaces can rely on the networking software within the MHs and the gateway to find a route to a destination, in the ad hoc network as well as in the Internet. This avoids complexity within the applications.

Fig. 9. A hot-spot area – university campus in Skellefteå

We are currently running additional performance tests and collecting statistics. We will compare our proposal to select between multiple FA with the proposals in [2] and [8]. The performance and the time to discover a destination in the ad hoc network or in the IP network will be evaluated and compared to the proposal in [2,4,5,8]. The evaluation is currently carried out in our network laboratory. The Mobile City project is currently creating a hot spot area in the campus area (se figure 9) where the infrastructure can be used for further evaluation in a real environment. The campus hosts two universities among other educational institutions and companies.

References

1. Broch, J., Maltz, D.A., Johnson, D.B.: Supporting Hierarchy and Heterogeneous Interfaces in Multi-Hop Wireless Ad Hoc Networks. Proceedings of the Workshop on Mobile Computing held in conjunction with the International Symposium on Parallel Architectures, Algorithms, and Networks, IEEE, Perth, Western Australia, (June 1999)
2. Jonsson, U., Alriksson, F., Larsson, T., Johansson, P., Maquire, G.M., Jr.: MIPMANET-Mobile IP for Mobile Ad Hoc Networks. MOBIHOC (2000) 75-85
3. Thomas, N.: Neighbor Discovery and Stateless Autoconfiguration in IPv6. IEEE Internet Computing. (July 1999) 54-62
4. Wakikawa, R., University, K., Malinen, J.T., Perkins, C.E., Nilsson, A., Tuominen, A.J.: Global connectivity for IPv6 Mobile Ad Hoc Networks. IETF Internet Draft, draft-wakikawa-manet-globalv6-01.txt (July 2002)
5. Belding-Royer, E.M., Sun, Y., Perkins, C.E.: Global Connectivity for IPv4 Mobile Ad hoc Networks. IETF Internet Draft, draft-royer-manet-globalv4-00.txt (November 2001)
6. Lei, H., Perkins, C.E.: Ad Hoc Networking with Mobile IP. EPMCC'97 (Oct 1997)
7. Perkins, C.: Mobile IP. IEEE Communications Magazine (May 2002) 66-82
8. Sun, Y., Belding-Royer, E.M., Perkins, C.E.: Internet Connectivity for Ad hoc Mobile Networks. To Appear in International Journal of Wireless Information Networks special issue on „Mobile Ad Hoc Networks (MANETs): Standards, Research, Applications"
9. Gast., M.S.: 802.11 Wireless Networks, The Definitive Guide. O'Reilly (2002)
10. Perkins, C.E.: Ad Hoc Networking. Addison-Wesley (2001)
11. Johansson, P., Larsson, T., Hedman, N., Mielczarek, B. and Degermark. M.: Scenario-based performance analysis of routing protocols for mobile ad-hoc networks. Proceedings of the Fifth Annual International Conference on Mobile Computing and Networking (August 1999)
12. Holland, G., Vaidya, N.: Analysis of TCP Performance over Mobile Ad Hoc Networks. Proceedings of IEEE/ACM MOBICOM (1999) 219-230.
13. RIP, OSPF http://www.cisco.com/univercd/cc/td/doc/cisintwk/ito_doc/
14. Perkins, C.E., Belding-Royer, E.M: Ad-hoc On Demand Distance Vector Routing. 2nd IEEE Workshop on Mobile Computing Systems and Applications (1999)
15. Stevens, W.R.: TCP/IP Illustrated, Volume 1: The Protocols. Addison-Wesley (1994) 53-64
16. Dynamics-HUT Mobile IP, http://www.cs.hut.fi/Research/Dynamics/
17. AODV-UU, http://www.docs.uu.se/~henrikl/aodv/
18. Ahlund C., Zaslavsky A.: „Mobile City" Ad Hoc Wireless Network Support for Regional Communities. The Path to 4G Mobility (September 2001)
19. Ahlund C., Zaslavsky A.: Wireless Network Support for Connectivity in Regional Communities. International Conference on Emerging Telecommunications Technologies and Applications, Steps towards the Information Society of the Future, ICETA (2001) 17-19

20. Ahlund C., Zaslavsky A., Matskin M.: Supporting Mobile Business Applications in Hot Spot Areas with Pervasive Infrastructure. The First International Conference on Mobile Business, M-BUSINESS (2002)
21. Royer, E., Toh, C.-K.: A Review of Current Routing Protocols for Ad-Hoc Mobile Wireless Networks. IEEE Personal Communications Magazine (April 1999) 46-55
22. Linux, http://www.linux.org
23. Peterson, L.L., Davie, B.: Computer Networks a Systems Approach. Morgan Kaufman Publishert (2000) 391-392
24. Roman, G.-C., Murphy, A. L., Picco, G. P.: A Software Engineering Perspective on Mobility. In A. C. W. Finkelstein, editor, Future of Software Engineering. ACM Press, (2000).
25. Rover, D.T., Waheed, A., Mutka, M.W., Bakic, A.: Software Tools for Complex Distributed Systems: Toward Integrated Tool Environments, IEEE Concurrency, (April-June, 1998), 40-54.

Mobile Application Architectures

Pasi Alatalo[1], Jarkko Järvenoja1, Jari Karvonen[2], Ari Keronen[1], and Pasi Kuvaja[1]

[1] Department of Information Processing Science, University of Oulu
P.O.Box3000, FIN-90014 OULU, Finland
[2] Department of Economics, University of Oulu
P.O.Box4600, FIN-90014 OULU, Finland
{Pasi.Alatalo,Jarkko.Järvenoja,Jari.T.Karvonen,
Ari.Keronen,Pasi.Kuvaja}@oulu.fi

Abstract. Modern computer architectures are large containing thousands of lines of code with complex and often distributed forms. Mobile and multi-platform solutions even increase this complexity. Modeling and managing a software architecture is important way of handling these complex systems, describing it to different actors inside software business and for analyzing and improving system performance. In this paper we go through mobile architectural structures and analysis of these with empirical mobile application development. We used different architectural views for analyzing mobile architectures and architecture role in development. The architecture and architectures role on the development has been studied in mobile application- and multi-platform service development.

1   Introduction

Telephone, mobile and fixed-line, has connected people for a long time. At mid of 90's the GSM (Global System for Mobile) provided mobile phones with short message (SMS) based communication channel. Data started to be part of the communication. The development in wireless communications generated many services that were based on data transactions. Valuable information services as well as entertainment services became part of mobile communication.

The market of wireless communication is developing. Data transactions enabling technologies, GSM and SMS got new properties and requirements with the introduction of Wireless application protocol (WAP). Wap facilitated online-connection between two terminals possible and converged Internet into the mobile communication.[2] Next steps on the development rout were to integrate digital television (already partly functioning), third generation mobile phones and local networks working together.

This integration created a new problem called entity management. The main question is how to manage application development in certain platform so that it would work also in multi-channel environment? One possible answer is reasonable architecture that allows flexibility in development. Keeping attention on the

M. Oivo and S. Komi-Sirviö (Eds.): PROFES 2002, LNCS 2559, pp. 572-586, 2002.

architecture during the development helps in focusing on the right tasks at the right time. In this paper mobile application development is considered from the product idea to the final product from the architecture development point of view. The paper is based on experimental research performed in MONICA and MOOSE-projects.

2   Software Architectures in General

Software architecture describes and demonstrates the content of created software. The form of software descriptions varies. Diverse need of information and requirements of architecture have caused variety in software architecture definitions. One definition of the software architecture is to describe the relationship between static and dynamic parts of the software. In other words it alludes in two important characteristic of the computer program: the hierarchical structure of procedural components and the structure of data. [5]

In the 90's software architectures have increased to one of the most significant part of software engineering. Different technologies that are handled especially from software architecture point were spreading to industrial use. In addition there are continually developed more complicated applications that include thousands of lines of code and that are complicated to maintain and to reuse. Those are the real-world problems and demand that caused the emergence of different software architectures and will develop in the area of changing technologies and system requirements. In that way software architecture definition can nowadays be seen as a critical part of the software application development.

Borderline between architecture and structure of lowest part of software is thin, which may affect overlapping in software architecture design. One definition could be that software architectures include those features of software that do not change during the software process. [5]

2.1   Purpose of the Software Architecture

Modeling and documenting software architecture is important for many reasons. Stakeholders can look at structural features of software with the help of modeling and documentation. Using architectural model developers can analyze software at very early phase of the software process. Architecture is the first step in designing software itself and it defines stable ground for software development. Different architecture models can be standardized and named, and can be re-used in many subsequent applications. This leads to identification and documentation of general architecture models that are application independent. The architecture models are called architectural styles. Examples for architectural styles are layered architecture and repository architecture. [4][5]

2.2   Product Line Architecture

The set of software programs, which have similar structure and functionality, are called software product families. The software architecture, which is common to software product family, is often called product line architecture. Layers, components and frames have significant role in product line architecture. The use of product line architecture is continuously increasing in software industry. In specific the increasing use of the product line architecture is motivated by the fact that they make reuse of software modules easier, that leads further into more reliable software programs, better time controlled projects, increased productivity of the development, less development risks, easier prototyping etc. [10]

2.3   Layered Software Architecture

Layered software architecture means software structure that consists of layers that are logically similar on different abstraction levels. The function of layered software architecture is that higher layer can use services, which lower layer produces. Normally that leads into a situation where the lower layers produce the most common services. On the other hand this means that the higher level the layer is described to the more independent the layer is from the application itself.

Layered software architecture can be described in three-layered architectural model, which consists of application layer, middleware layer and platform layer. Middleware offers platform independent common services like support for user interface. Platform layer offers for example operating system, communication software and other hardware dependent software (drivers etc.). See Figure 1.

Most common structure of layered software architecture is hierarchical and bypassing forbidding. Hierarchy means that direction of service request is always from higher level to lower level or service request is send to same level. To forbid bypassing means that service request do not bypass next layer. Structures that allow bypassing are possible but are not so common. See Figure 2.

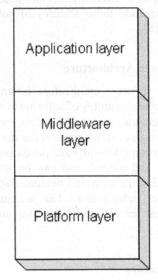

Fig. 1. Three-layer architectural model

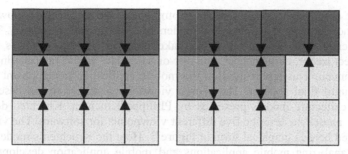

Fig. 2. Non passing and passing hierarchical layered software architectures

Independent layer needs interfaces to serve and request service for. Services are produced to serve higher layer requests that could be used via the interface. This interface is called service interface or utilization interface. On the other hand services, which layer is requested, could be used via implementation interface. Utilization interface of layer is the same as implementation layer of the higher layer. Implementation interface of the lowest layer and utilization layer of the highest layer connects system to physical environment.

Benefits of layered software architecture are clear, simple structure, which make possible to develop and understand software as sets of independent layers. Because of the independent nature of the architectures the designers who are specialized in different layers can focus onto their own layers without knowing anything about another layer. Additionally, layered software architecture makes understanding of system easier to them who are not so familiar with software designing and implementation for example customers and managers. [4][5][9]

2.4 Distributed Systems

Nowadays more and more applications work in distributed environments either in wired or wireless systems. Due to this, new distributed technologies are created and architectural solutions based on these new technologies are developed. The most significant of these technologies are CORBA (Common Object Request Broker Architecture) and Java RMI (Remote Method Invocation). CORBA is common distribution standard for objects and it is independent from implementation language and operating systems. Java RMI is Java implementation for distribution mechanism of objects. [11][12]

3   Different Views of Software Architectures

Different software architecture models and their representations have been used for different purposes. When analyzing more precisely the architectures and their representations, one dimension is the abstraction level. Higher abstract levels are used in general description of the software or parts of the software. The abstraction levels of the representations allow describing the basic functionality and structure of the software level by level and that makes it easier and faster. The more detailed architecture descriptions we go the more complicated the architecture show-ups are. This also increases the requirements to understand the given information. The view that is under study is dependent of the stakeholder in question, such as end-user, client, project leader, implementer, manager or salesman, whose interests in software vary quite much. This report used on the mobile application development from the early idea until final product. The chosen views for architecture are based on the software architecture models presented by Philippe Kruchten. Kruchten defined so called „4+1 model" to describe five different viewpoints for software. The viewpoints are illustrated here in graphical form in Figure 3. Here the Kruchten's models will be applied in analyzing mobile applications and mobile application development. On each level of development the analysis will be performed through Kruchten's viewpoints in order to find out conveniences of the mobile application development. [6]

The five viewpoints are as follow:

- **First view** is the use case view where the system is looked at from outside, as the user looks at it. This view emphasizes outer functionality of the system.
- **Second view** is called logical view and it describes static software models (classes, interfaces etc.) and dynamic relationship of different software models of the system. This view emphasizes inner functionality of the system.
- **Third view** is called process view and this view describes interaction and organization between parallel processes and threads. This view emphasizes performance, scalability and distribution of the system.
- **Fourth view** is called implementation view. This view divides system to physical parts (files etc.), which are gathering together to be represented in special way. This view emphasizes controlling of software product.
- **Fifth view** is called deployment view. This view describes hardware composition of the system; connections needed by hardware and software modules and processes locate in different hardware component. This view emphasizes distribution of the system, delivery of the system and assembly of the system.

Using software architecture gives quite good new concepts like classes, interfaces, components, modules, sub-systems, inheritance of classes, processes, messages, files, hardware components, communication models etc. Architecture model may concern either static structure of software like classes or dynamic structures like objects. It may also concern static relationships as well as dynamic behavioral models. Architecture can be described either as abstract model, which has not direct relation to software, or as concrete model. An example of applying the views in mobile music service will be presented in **Figure 3**.[4][6]

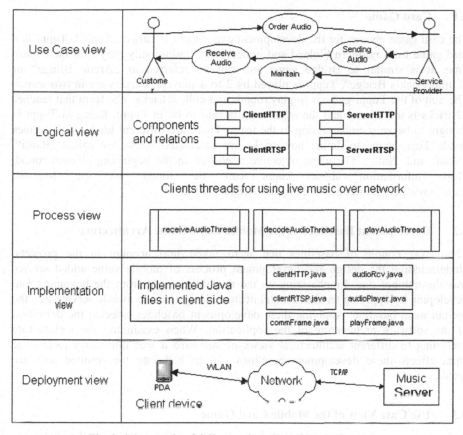

Use Case view	
Logical view	
Process view	
Implementation view	
Deployment view	

Fig. 3. An example of different views in mobile music service

4   Experiences of a Mobile Service Development

The experiences presented here are based on mobile card-game application development during MONICA[1] and MOOSE[2] projects. The projects have theoretical proportion where concepts in this area are studied and practical proportion in which the concepts were tested in real mobile application development. As a case example of mobile service a game service development was chosen. There were number of reasons for the decision; for example entertainment business is one of the most growing part of the mobile business and games have always being the best test bed of new technology.

---

[1] The target in MONICA project was to improve production facilities of value added services
    in mobile telecom area. More information: www.monica.oulu.fi
[2] MOOSE-project is studying software engineering methodologies for embedded systems

4.1   Card Game

The card game chosen for the development experiment is called „Tuppi". Tuppi is a card game from northern Finland and lumberjacks traditionally play it in their spare time. It is similar to Bridge game and can be referred as „Arctic Bridge" or „Lumberjack's Bridge". Tuppi is played by 2 to 4 players. Players are in two teams. The aim of the Tuppi-game is to play rounds and collect tricks. The team that reaches 52 tricks is the winner and the other team is said to be in Tuppi. Being in Tuppi is thought to be very embarrassing to the team. There are different kinds of objectives inside Tuppi-game to define how tricks are calculated: these are called „Rami", „Nolo" and „Solo". The game objective is chosen in the beginning of each round. More information about Tuppi can be found on the Internet: http://www.geocities.com/TimesSquare/Arena/5911/ .

4.2   Development Baselines of the Mobile Card Game Architecture

There was couple of baselines that were taken into account in the projects. Understanding the design and development process of mobile value added service was the number one. Emphasizing on the reusability right from the beginning and developing by applying an abstract architecture design for the mobile service was the second main baseline. Applying these development baselines affected the definition of the software architecture of the application. When examining the architecture according to different architectural views of software it was quite easy to analyze what effects these development baselines chosen had into the resulted software architecture.

4.3   Use Case View of the Mobile Card Game

In use case view the system is looked from the user viewpoint. During the card game development a sample of case studies were used to describe the system from the user perspective. The case studies helped quite much in finding out additional requirements and new feature ideas. In use case development an approach defined by Dzida and Freitag [1] was applied.

According to this approach use cases have three perspectives: use scenario, indented system use and context scenario. Use scenario describes the use situation. Who is using the system and what is the motivation of the user. Indented system use tells us what kind of system we are dealing with and for what purpose for we are using it. Context scenario describes the backgrounds of the use and the context in which the use scenario is valid.

In the projects a metaphor of game house to represent Mobile Tuppi was generated. In game house players may meet and play different games. The game house architecture is described in the subsequent Figure 4 from the use case view. New player has a key to the game house where he can chat with other players in the lounge. When they decide they can go to one of the game rooms and start to play a game. Game rooms have tables where players have card decks and cards. The room, where the player is, defines the game that can be played. New games are added by adding new game rooms. This was done in Mobile Tuppi by defining rules for the new game. Players can have cards on the hand and other cards on the table. This metaphor is well descriptive since the objects in the metaphor are the actual objects in the logical level of the architecture description.

4.4   Logical View of the Mobile Card Game

During the MONICA and MOOSE projects different distributed mobile client-server systems were studied and found that there is quite similar basic functionality in many of the systems. Therefore, there are similarities in the architectures. When considering the application from the logical viewpoint it can be found that the most of the components that are used are the same. Major differences in server and clients are in the components that manipulate and present data instead of entire architectural structure of the application system.

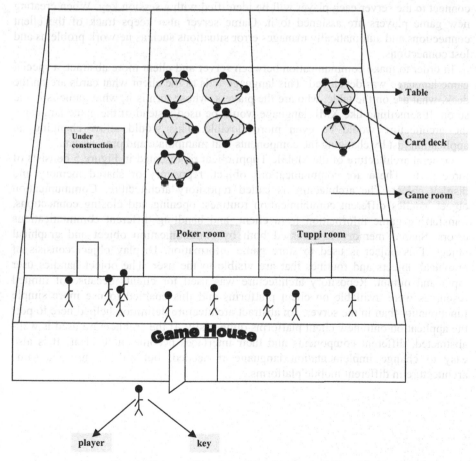

Fig. 4. Use case view for a Game house –architecture

When defining a reusable architecture solution it is essential to differentiate those components from other components. The use of layered architecture in server helped this differentiation. The higher level the layer is described, the closer onto that layer becomes the independent application. Layered software architecture gives a clear and simple structure with a possibility to develop and understand software as sets of independent layers. Previous solution makes a possibility to reuse most of the layers in other software development. For example communication classes are just focusing on transmitting data, they don't take a stand for the transmitted data itself. This approach emphasis data, data structure and data manipulation as the key points to consider when aiming towards abstract reusable architectures.

Mobile Tuppi-server architecture consists of five main objects: game server, serial gateway, router, encoding server and wireless access server. These objects can physically reside in same device. Task of the game server object is to administrate games, players and game sessions and to handle actual play of a game. When clients connect to the server each player will be identified with a session key. When creating new game players are assigned to it. Game server also keeps track of the client connections and automatically manages error situations such as network problems and lost connections.

In order to make communication between server and client more abstract, a special game language was developed. This language tells to the client what cards are on the deck, what are on the table, who are the players, whose turn is it, what game is it and so on. If something like XML language would be used instead of the game language, the architecture would be even more flexible. This would allow changing an application just by changing the components that manipulate and present data.

General architecture of the Mobile Tuppi client represented in Figure 5 consists of three parts. These are communications object, repository or shared memory and display object. The architecture is called repository architecture. Communication object handles different communication routines: opening and closing connections, transferring game information from client, and handling different communications errors. Shared memory is accessed both by communication object and graphical object. This object is used to store game information. Display object consists of graphical objects and routines that are visible to the user. The object handles user input and output. Repository architecture was used for clients because of limited resources were available on client platforms and this enabled to use more simple functionality than in the server. An abstract architecture definition helped here to port the application onto new client platforms quite easily. If the architecture used is well-abstracted, different components and their interfaces become quite clear. It is also easy to change implementation language if needed, but still to use the same architecture in different mobile platforms.

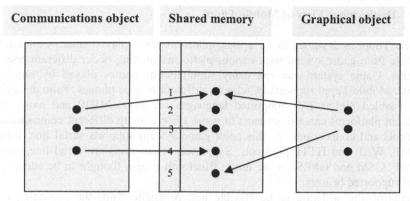

| Communications object | Shared memory | Graphical object |

Fig. 5. General Tuppi-client architecture

4.5   Process View of the Mobile Card Game

Tuppi clients have two different threads. Communication classes are run in one and user interface and data manipulation classes in other. These threads communicate through blackboard or data repository. It is easier to distinguish data and data manipulation from the rest of the application by using repository architecture in the client application. This makes client application more abstract and reusable. For defining new applications you just change the parts of the client that handles UI and data. Other benefits are better performance since communication routines do not have to wait for the UI routines to finish and easier synchronization between communication classes and UI. This is quite important when working with devices of very limited resources like mobile phones.

4.6   Implementation View of the Card Game

Implementation view to architecture consists of physical parts (files etc.) of the software. Building mobile multi-platform software makes this view challenging, because software has different files for different platforms, and different distribution channels for them. Mobile Tuppi that supports a variety of platforms has different files for MIDP implementation, Java implementation etc., and number of ways to deliver them to different platforms. The MIDP applications can be delivered to the mobile terminal with SMS message and installed automatically.

At the time of the case study of mobile technologies didn't support dynamic downloadable libraries or components. Client applications were delivered in single packed file. This is yet relatively simple. When component technologies can be used in mobile platforms you can have dynamically downloadable components and libraries. You need to have a good plan how to organize them.

This view for architecture has the advantage in large and complex applications where number of delivered files can be thousands and you need to plan the structure of the files. In addition to that there is a need to plan, how to maintain the files, and how to deliver them to customer.

4.7   Deployment View of Mobile Tuppi

Mobile Tuppi is designed to be a multi-platform multi-player game. Connection is possible from game system with various platforms running under different operating systems. Game system can run many simultaneous games played by number of people. Mobile Tuppi supports PC-clients, different mobile phones, Palm devices and Java enabled digital TV. Supported languages are Java, MIDP and native Epoc. Different platforms can also connect to game system using different communications protocols and connections. At this point game system supports serial line, infrared, TCP-IP, WAP and HTTP protocols. Supported connections are serial line, infrared, TCP-IP, GSM and GPRS. In the future Bluetooth is also thought to be added to the list of supported bearers.

Planning the software to be flexible and re-usable from the beginning of the development proved to be on the right track. It was possible to start from very simple implementations and add more complicated platforms as the technology developed. When using layered software architecture, it was possible to add new bearer in a quite simple way, just by adding new modules for one layer and leave the other layers untouched. Figure 6 shows the deployment view of Mobile Tuppi. [2][7][8]

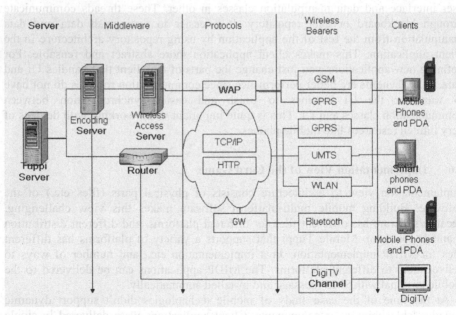

Fig. 6. Tuppi-game architecture

5   Tools Used during the Experiment

Tools that were used in mobile card game development consist of modeling tools (Rational Rose), programming tools (KAWA, Visual Studio), platform specific tools, finishing tools and from emulators (PALM, Symbian OS etc.) and devices (palm, mobile phones etc.). Platform specific tools and finishing tools are used for code pre-verifying, packaging and exporting to environment running software in portable clients. See Figure 7.

In the beginning a study of different development tools supporting development for mobile applications was performed. Different tools both for programming and modeling was explored. Mobile platforms set special requirements for application development on the behalf of memory handling, building graphical interfaces and communications. There are a variety of solutions for mobile application development. Many tools for development support only standard solutions and it is not possible to add new libraries for mobile development. Some tools however support this kind of possibility, but configuring them for mobile application development is a tricky task. Mobile solutions are developing fast and development tools must be kept up-to-date. There is a need for tools that support the use of standard description methods also for new mobile applications. In the ideal situation the whole software architecture can be modeled and programmed with the integrated CASE environment that supports automated code generation for different solutions, debugging and reverse engineering. This makes it possible to easily maintain architecture description for the entire mobile service.

Rational Rose was selected for modeling tool as it supports both C/C++ and Java programming languages. The process of development is a circular. First the base model for the game was done with Rational Rose and UML-modelling. This model was then engineered to code with Rose code generator. KAWA (KAWA IDE Integrated Development Environment) and Visual Studio was then used to further development of the code. Rose supports reverse engineering and that was used to keep the model up to date. If any changes were needed in the model, updated model was then engineered back to code. Code was ported to actual devices or emulators. Clients run a program in KVM (Kilobyte Virtual Machine), which is a Java Virtual Machine for Java for small and resource constraint devices. Different language libraries can be added to Rose so that it can do reverse engineering also for these new platforms. This made possible to make common architecture descriptions for both server and different mobile clients.

For Java development JDK version 1.3 was used together with J2ME (Java 2 Micro Edition), which is a modified Java platform for small devices. Early in the development KJAVA was used. It is a package of Java for PalmOS devices released at the 2000 in JavaOne show. It was renamed by Sun and is part of the J2ME packages. Figure 8 shows picture about Java architectures. Configurations define API's and features of the VM for the devices with certain amount of resources. For example amount of memory can limit which configuration can be used. Profiles define API's for certain domains such as MIDP profile for mobile phones and two-way pagers.[2]

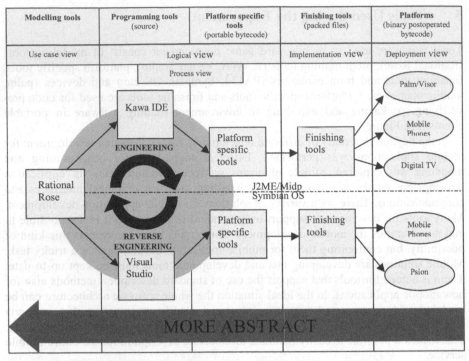

Fig. 7. Mobile application development tool chain in Monica project

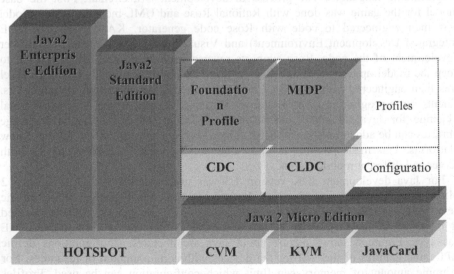

Fig. 8. Java architectures [2]

Symbian OS is customised C/C++ based development environment from Symbian that is used for example in Nokia phones. This produces native code applications that run faster than interpreted code in these devices.

6   Conclusion

It is evident that distributed technologies have a major role in future of mobile applications development. Mobile platforms have opened from restricted systems to allow use of third party software. Downloadable libraries and entities force developers to rethink existing architectures. Different architectural solutions are grouping into product line architectures that allow simultaneous programming of applications in several product lines for the platform in question. Trade of software and architecture solutions between different software companies will evolve since this kind of technology fits well in mobile software development business.

It is essential to success of the project to keep different stakeholders involved in software development process. Kruchten's model can be used to divide architectural information in different views for the same architecture. These views can be used as a tool for different stakeholders to communicate from the development. It also makes it easier to analyze the architecture from different viewpoints in order to create comprehensive solutions. This model can also be used to divide development tools with the same category see Figure 7. Traditional development methods works well in the development where goals of the software are clear from beginning of the project. This is not often the case in rapidly developing mobile business. This is why more flexible methods like prototyping are often used. Kruchten's model can be used to analyze traditional methods as well as prototyping but it does not suite well to agile methods that have totally different approach to development. Agile approaches are very interesting in mobile application development viewpoint. Their approach for development is emphasizing focusing on development and user involvement. They start with minimal documentation, try to produce only vital information and software features and reduce unnecessary documentation work (less is better). This kind of approach makes it easier to adapt to changing world and keep documentation and the system in synchronization.

Mobile application development belongs to the complicated, but quite regular software development area that includes many different solution possibilities in the development. The experiences from the mobile card-game development lead to the development process covering many distribution channels (different client platforms). Architecture and the readiness to react to changes that were caused by technology requirement changes became key points in successful development. Changes that came during the application development required clear architecture.

Identifying, standardizing and naming general architecture models helps to reuse same models and code in several applications. A normal life example about cars and roads instead of software business helps to understand how important is the re-use. New road is not build (infrastructure for content delivering) for every car (application) that is made. Same road is used that is made safe, well-defined and documented. This allows carmakers to focus onto their key business that is car making and users to safely use them. When new cars (platforms) were built the same road that before was used or there could be a new fast line (new bearers) to speed up the driving. New roads are also built to go new places (new type of applications) but these are added to existing infrastructure. In the sense of software production this means that well-tested solutions are re-used for content delivery of different applications. This increases productivity, QoS (Quality of System) and keeps users happy.

Mobile Tuppi architecture, in which data manipulation and UI are well isolated from the rest of the application functionality, give new ideas on how multi-platform applications may work. Different platforms have different capabilities. There can be platforms with limited memory and screens and multimedia platforms that have 3D UI with possibility to use speech and sound. During the card game development an idea came out to change the ways that the data is represented in different platforms by informing the application about the capabilities of the platform. This would mean content aware plug and play-architecture for mobile devices. With downloadable components new UI could be loaded to the phone when it is connecting to the system first time. There could even be different producers using same architecture that could do this UI component. Well-abstracted and documented game architecture could also mean that someone else could do new games or game creation could be automated (see also J. Orwant paper of automated programming for game generation [3]).

References

1. Dzida,W., Freitag, R.: Making Use of Scenarios for Validating Analysis and Design. IEEE Transactions on Software Engineering, Vol .24, No. 12, December (1998)
2. Nokia: MITA, Mobile Internet Technical Architecture, IT Press, Finland (2001)
3. Orwant, J.: Automated programming for game generation. http://www.research.ibm.com/journal/sj/393/part2/orwant.txt, IBM (2000)
4. Koskimies, K.: Oliokirja. 2nd edn. Satku – Kauppakaari, Gummerus Kirjapaino Oy, Jyväskylä (2000)
5. Pressman, R.S.: Software engineering – a practitioner's approach. 3rd edn, McGraw-Hill Book Company, Berkshire, England (1994)
6. Kruchten., P.: The 4+1 view model of architecture. IEEE Software, volume 12, No 6 (1995) 42-50
7. Sun Microsystems: J2ME[tm] Mobile Information Device Profile (MIDP) http://wireless.java.sun.com/midp/ (2002)
8. Lewins, J., Loftus, W.: Java software solutions – Foundation of program design, Addison-Wesley (1998)
9. Garnegie Mellon Software Engineering Institute: Software architecture documentation in practice – Documentating architectural layers. http://www.sei.cmu.edu/publications/documents/00.reports/00sr004.html (2002)
10. Garnegie Mellon Software Engineering Institute: A Framework for software product line practice – version 3.0. http://www.sei.cmu.edu/plp/framework.html (2002)
11. Seetharaman, K., The Corba Connection, Communications of the Acm, volume 41, No.10 (1998)
12. Sun Microsystems: Java Remote Method Invocation (RMI), http://java.sun.com/products/jdk/rmi/ (2002)

Wireless Games – Review and Experiment

Dan Bendas and Mauri Myllyaho

Department of Information Processing Science, University of Oulu
P.O.Box 3000, FIN-90014 OULU, Finland
{bendas.dan,mauri.myllyaho}@oulu.fi

Abstract: This paper is an introduction to the domain of wireless games. It presents a brief history of mobile gaming, a number of important technologies and introduces classification and evaluation concepts and criteria. A multi-player, multi-platform card game developed in the University of Oulu, is used to present authors' own experiences in this field.

1   Introduction

Computer gaming is often thought as children's free time hobby, but IDSA surveys show that more than half of computer and video game players are over 18 years old. The three top reasons to play games are related to entertainment: fun, challenge, and playing with company. [6] The major challenge of creating a computer game is to make a game for almost everyone, and in the mobile environment reality-based games have drawn "special interest".

This paper aims to rise the interest of the reader towards issues of mobile and wireless gaming. In doing so we'll present results from a study aimed at finding new methods, processes, tools and technologies for developing mobile content. One critical assumption of the study is that entertainment services will be one of the key revenue streams for the 3G wireless industry. Findings of our background research about the current status of the wireless entertainment industry support the assumption and they are presented in the first part of this paper. For the experiments, a card game called "Four Players' Tuppi" (which is a traditional card game from Northern Finland, similar to Bridge or Whist) was developed to be playable with mobile devices.

This paper suggests that multi-platform wireless games have higher chances of commercial success than games running on a single type of handset. The practical development of a server-based game helped us to identify a possible architectural approach for this type of applications.

This paper is organized so that it starts with a presentation of the electronic gaming history followed by a short market analysis and a classification of wireless games by type of connectivity. Next chapter analyses the leading technologies used for implementing wireless games. Issues affecting the development of wireless games are discussed. An original solution for multi-device gaming is introduced. Lastly, the finding of the paper are synthesized.

M. Oivo and S. Komi-Sirviö (Eds.): PROFES 2002, LNCS 2559, pp. 587–600, 2002.
© Springer-Verlag Berlin Heidelberg 2002

2   Background

Most gaming history related articles forget to present, that first computer games were created for educational and simulation purposes. The first games were done in 1950's for the army scenarios and business management purposes, an example is Top Management Decision Game in 1957 [21, 24]. Digital gaming includes besides computer games also different mobile phone games, electronic games, video games, arcade games, and TV-games from the end of 1970's [25]. 1970's and 1980's created many arcade and computer game classics. Here are some examples: in 1978 Space Invaders created a "public" concept of game addiction [17], 1980 brought the most copied game title Pac-Man, and 1988 was the year of Tetris that was brought to all possible gaming platforms.

Nintendo is the most important mobile game company up to date. In 1980 it started selling portable Game & Watch product line having LCD displays, including two game alternatives and a watch (utility feature). Game Boy was introduced in 1989 and has already over 700 game titles from various game genres. It has sold close to 120 million units by March 2002 [14]. History of digital gaming shows that superior technical level is not a guarantee of success, as Game Boy has shown. The most important factors by Saarikoski [18] are quality and amount of games, and the naughty troll called "Chance".

1989 brought the public Internet and in 1993 Doom generated many Internet downloads and was a big success for ID software. Introduction of Doom established the concept of networked game in the mind of the public [10], and it invited later on new players with the abilities to create their own game environments (level-builders) and avatars (character builder kits).

The big amount of digital games has created the need to classify games into genres (categories). Many game companies have simplified their genres to very few numbers like arcade, adventure, role-playing, simulations, strategy, sport & racing [4]. Probably this simplified categorization will change in near future: the most popular genre for the adult gamers (over 50 years) was "puzzle/board/card"-games [7], and mobile phone gaming has introduced in few years forgotten and really successful game genres.

3   Mobile and Wireless Games

Mobile games are electronic games that are played using portable devices such as handheld game console, personal digital assistant (PDA), or mobile phone. A special category is wireless games that are played using network-enabled devices.

3.1   Market Analysis

Mobile phone content (MPC) market is pretty young worldwide: in Japan it started in 1999. Estimation of Japanese MPC market size for 2002 is 140 billion yen, from which downloadable Java games are thought to be 20 billion yen [19].

Table 1. Mobile entertainment and gaming users, millions [28]

Entertainment application	by 2001	2006	Games sub-application	by 2001	2006
Information services	47.2	901.0	SIM/embedded	34.3	263.7
Gambling	25.7	572.4	Online (SMS/net)	12.0	508.8
Gaming	42.9	848.0	Downloadable	5.7	206.7
Music	71.5	689.0	Multi-platform	3.0	197.8
Pictures	34.3	636.0			
Moving Images	1.4	318.0			

Biggest U.S entertainment field in 2001 was music, and after that follow digital gaming (sales of hardware and software) and movie ticket sales [11]. Global markets' of 3G service revenues are estimated to be $320 billion, and mobile gaming worth $23.7 billion in 2010 [20; 27]. In Western Europe five big countries generate over 70% of the mobile entertainment revenue, and the estimates for the Finnish mobile gaming market size are: 3.55 million EUR in 2001, and 31.13 million EUR in 2005 [17]. In 2001 PC and video game market in Finland was 59.3 million euros [26].

The ARC Group's predictions from the growth of the global mobile entertainment usage are given in Table 1. This shows that gaming is expected to be popular compared to other entertainment applications, and that online (connected) gaming is expected to become the most popular sub-category.

The mobile gaming value chain can be expressed with three main players, presented in Figure 1. Their tasks are following: game developer provides the content, portal is the distribution channel, and operators charge for the service or for the data transfer.

IDSA study [5] shows that more than one-third of Americans owning game consoles or computers say "they play also games on mobile devices like handheld systems, PDAs, and cell phones". Nintendo has also noticed the growing interest to multi-player games and it has introduced link cable to connect 4 Game Boys (GB). In 2001 Mobile Adapter GB system was introduced in Japan to enable linking Game Boy to cell phones [2].

The current situation of the wireless gaming field is best synthesized by D. Kushner's [11] words: "Despite puny screens, primitive to nonexistent graphics and conflicting standards, cell phones and other wireless devices are the hottest electronic playspace around."

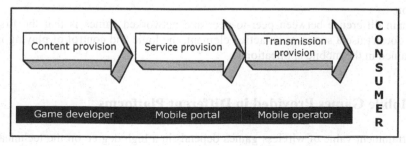

Fig. 1. Mobile gaming industry value chain [15]

3.2   Classification of Wireless Games

Kushner [11] defines wireless game as an "entertainment application, that is played on the Internet-enabled portable device such as PDA and, particularly, with a mobile phone". From the connectivity point of view there are three main categories of wireless games:

1. *Stand-alone game* involves only one non-connected handset and one player.
2. *Peer-to-peer game* involves two or more handsets and players and some data transfer channel.
3. *Networked game* resembles a distributed system that is played by many players over a cellular network while connecting to some mobile entertainment server.

Stand-alone games typically come embedded with handsets. These games can be specifically optimized for one platform, and take full advantage of the handset's features such as sound, vibration, or a color display. Since there is no need to deal with I/O (networking) induced uncertainty, stand-alone games can provide high quality presentation, good response time for the user interface and are robust. Typical embedded games are Snake on Nokia, and Kung-Fu on Siemens. The idea of playing games was introduced to consumers in year 1997, when Nokia launched the model 6110 with its Snake game [15, 29].

The channel of data transfer for peer-to-peer games can be infrared interface (IrDA), short range radio (Bluetooth), or Circuit Switched Data Call (CSDC). They bring additional challenge for the player when compared to stand-alone games: the player can now have an intelligent human partner, not an algorithm, to compete with. The interface with the communication channel (I/O subsystem) adds always some delays and uncertainty into the application – no matter how simple the implementation is. Need of available game partner(s) requires physical proximity or at least a previous agreement between players. An example of peer-to-peer game is Nokia's Snake when played via infrared.

Networked game includes many players using different computing devices to participate in a game, aiming common goals and sharing the same virtual realm. Networked games always involve a server. An example is Alien's Fish Exchange by nGame. The data capacity of the connection and its latency directly affects the quality of the interaction. The nature of games dictates their bandwidth needs: for example a deep thinking board game like chess may be enjoyed when it's played over WAP, and a fast-paced multi-player action game requires a fast and low-latency broadband connection.

The main difference between peer-to-peer and networked games is that the first category doesn't use a server as an active element, the logic and control of playing is self-contained in the mobile application.

4   Mobile Games Provided in Different Platforms

The entertainment value of wireless games depends in a high degree on the technical abilities of that game, on its presentation, on its complexity and speed of response.

Moreover, customers want to have a large variety of games to choose from, not to be limited to a few of them, that came embedded with the terminal.

The first embedded games were coded into the firmware, and powered by the extra processing abilities of devices that were not used for controlling the main functions of the phone. Since then, the hardware evolved bringing up the possibility and interest for applications developed by 3rd parties that can be installed by end-users.

Different software solutions (platforms) have emerged, trying to solve the complex problem of accommodating and running foreign application in a small and restrictive medium such as a mobile telephone's operating system. Between them J2ME and BREW are competing to become accepted as standard platform for high-end handsets, while WAP and SMS are still dominating the lower range of devices. Some manufacturers choose proprietary solutions such as ExEn or Mophun™ in order to obtain the desired quality. There are more competitors such as the Symbian consortium or Microsoft's Pocket PC 2002 Phone Edition, which have the potential to induce big changes in the near future.

4.1   J2ME

The Java™ application environment, designed and maintained by Sun Microsystems through an open process, is a de-facto industrial standard. Characteristics like the structure of the language, portability of binaries, and inherent protection mechanisms recommend Java as a possible candidate for an universal application environment for mobile devices. The "Micro Edition" of Java (referred as J2ME) was developed to fulfill the need for small version, suitable for portable devices [23]. The Mobile Information Device Profile (MIDP) is the J2ME variant aimed for small, connected appliances, especially mobile telephones and PDAs.

There are already many MIDP enabled devices on the market from most of the major mobile telephone manufacturers. This first generation portable Java technology (based on MIDP 1.0) suffers from a series of inconveniences. Each manufacturer has proprietary, incompatible extensions of the MIDP standard, the networking is restricted to HTTP (the only protocol required by the standard), and many device-specific features can't be accessed by Java applications (ex. infrared or Bluetooth interfaces). A series of improvements are expected in the future, including higher execution speed with optimized virtual machines and hardware acceleration, more networking possibilities (datagrams, sockets, secure HTTP), game-oriented graphical functions, etc. MIDP 2.0, the next version of the standard, which is going to be introduced in 2003, will contain many of those additions, eliminating though the need for proprietary extensions.

MIDP applications are called "MIDlets". They can be downloaded and installed into a device in multiple ways. One possibility is via the device's wireless network connection (ex. GPRS), following a link in a WAP page. A PC can also be used to download the MIDlet, and to upload it into the handheld using a short range connection (cable or infrared or Bluetooth).

Industry analysts forecast J2ME to have a significant market share as a platform for mobile entertainment in the coming years [15]

4.2   i-mode and i-appli

i-mode is a mobile data service and a brand name of the Japanese operator NNT DoCoMo. It is designed to provide Internet connection and access to special designed services to cell phone users

The network's transmission protocol for i-mode is a variant of low bandwidth Code Division Medium Access (CDMA) that allows efficient usage of the radio spectrum. CDMA doesn't reserve one channel for each link like in the GSM's CSDC system. i-mode's maximum speed is only 9600 bauds that is anyway appropriate for optimized applications [3].

i-appli is an extension to i-mode service that allows downloading and executing applications locally on handsets, see Figure 2. The environment is based on J2ME and on the i-mode extensions library similar to MIDP defining terminal-specific features like the user-interface, and HTTP protocol.

The first generation of games were simple server-based applications like fortune telling or virtual horse racing. i-appli made it possible to have downloadable stand-alone micro-games.

Well-established games companies like Sega and Sony have launched titles for the i-mode platform (many of them being adapted from other restricted platforms). The potential is even higher: in the beginning of 2001 the Japanese company Dwango Co. launched a massive multi-user role playing game (RPG) called Samurai Romanesque. It includes nice graphical capabilities and impressive features: up to 500.000 simultaneous users, real-time interaction, complex scenario and graphics [9].

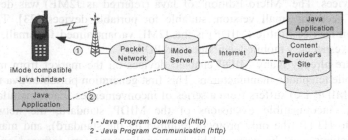

1 - Java Program Download (http)
2 - Java Program Communication (http)

Fig. 2. Downloading Java applications in i-mode handsets[1]

4.3   BREW

Binary Runtime Environment for Wireless™ (BREW) is an application environment developed by Qualcomm Inc. Initially it was intended for Qualcomm's CDMA chipsets, but now BREW is available for most of the existing mobile platforms.

The advantages of BREW are small footprint (it is a binary kernel and the applications are native, not interpreted), fast execution speed, optimized for one platform, and seamless integration with the device. These characteristics as well as

---

[1]   modified after NNT DoCoMo, Specifications of Java for i-mode,
http://www.nttdocomo.co.jp/english/p_s/i/java/index.html [checked September 3rd ,2002]

support from large telephone corporations (Qualcomm, Sharp, Sanyo, Samsung, LG, etc.) have assured success for BREW on Asian and American markets.

On top of a wide-band CDMA air interface, with the support of a powerful processor and a color screen, BREW provides some of the most advanced entertainment applications in our days. Korean operators are offering entertainment services such as video clips for movie previews, sports highlights, full-color music videos, casino gaming, video gaming, downloading of images, and Karaoke services [12]. In addition to increased throughput CDMA2000 technology makes it possible to have concurrent voice and data sessions. By July 2002 more than 1 million BREW-enabled handsets were sold worldwide (in Korea, Japan, and U.S) [13].

4.4   SMS, MMS and WAP

The built-in messaging ability of GSM looked like a promising delivery medium for mobile entertainment. Despite the large number of commercial and experimental applications that have been deployed since the beginning of '90s the results are rather disappointing. Very few major SMS based services did managed to capture the interest of the consumers. Some companies that tried to offer such services in Finland include: iobox, 2ndhead, speedytomato. The factors that contribute to this situation include price, text entry method, small carrying capacity, and latency.

With game interaction limited to text through triple-tap, there's not a lot room for interface innovations. One thing SMS has in favor, though, is a definite revenue stream. SMS-enabled handsets are available worldwide and every carrier knows how to bill for messages. [30]

The income model of SMS, as well as the technical implementation, is specifically designed for person-to-person communication and not for turn-based computer games, and especially not for machine to machine data links.

Successful SMS games are those where the amount of sent messages is low while the stakes are high. Examples are "Who wants to be a millionaire", and cross media games with TV interface. In Finland SMS-based real-time chat brought the IRC to television, and generated over $90.000 in revenue during the first month [16]. „Who Wants To Be A Millionaire?" is world's most widely played mobile game, for SMS and WAP, and it is available to over 150 million users across the globe (in May 2002 also for i-mode).

Three ways of employing SMS in games can be detected:

- As carrier – where actual game information is transported over SMS, as in "Who wants to be a millionaire?"
- As a controller for a cross-media applications. Some or all interactions are performed using a mobile phone, while game's graphical display is shown in another media, for example on a TV channel (WaterWar and Katapultti on Finnish SubTV cable channel) or in Internet (Pumpui).
- As a payment instrument. Premium-priced SMS adds credits for games performed on other media (ex. Habbo Hotel, or arcade rally machines).

Technically, SMS is used as carrier for other types of mobile entertainment such as downloadable ring tones and display logos.

MMS (Multimedia Messaging Service) is a multi-channel messaging system, able to transfer pictures, sound and text between mobile phones and also to desktop PCs. It is going to be an enabler application for the new generation of handsets with color screens, embedded cameras (like Nokia 7650), and fast data interfaces (GPRS, HSCSD). At this time there are already games for MMS, for example the dating game LUVM8, in China, developed by a local company in collaboration with Nokia. The penetration of high-end terminals supporting MMS is still low so the commercial success of such services can't be yet assessed.

WAP is an open standard for mobile Internet, largely adopted by European phone manufacturers. A typical WAP system includes a server, an access gateway and a browser, residing on the handset. Its main usage is for static and low-dynamic information retrieval.

The first public WAP services started in the beginning of 1999. Between the different proposed applications have been games and entertainment services, but the level of acceptance from the consumers was low. Affecting factors include the high price and the technical limitations of the implementations on top of GSM. The most suited games for WAP are turn-based board games, played between one human and a computer. In this case, the player decides the move, submits it to the server, the response is computed instantaneously and it's sent in response. The lack of a push mechanism prohibits real-time or multi-player games.

GPRS (General Packet Radio System) is an upgrade to GSM networks (so called the 2.5 generation), allowing always connected links, faster transfer speeds and flat-rate monthly fee for data transfers. WAP over GPRS is a much more attractive option that it was over CSD calls, but our opinion is that downloadable applications (i.e. J2ME) makes it irrelevant for the future mobile games.

4.5   Crossmedia

The interest for interactive TV programs has brought a number of interesting applications where one mobile technology (especially SMS) is used as a control channel in a television show.

One example is the successful Finnish game WaterWar [22]. SubTV, a small cable TV station run this shows daily for about two hours. The players are organized in two teams, competing for the control of the battlefield. Mobile phones are used to send SMS controlling the characters on the screen. Up to 30 persons can play simultaneously. There is also a chat on the screen allowing players and spectators to exchange messages. Automatic players are available during non-peak hours. WaterWar is developed using a special platform for TV games developed by Frantic Media.

This technology can be perceived as a pioneer for real digital TV applications.

4.6   Other Platforms

Outside from widespread standards, a number of proprietary solutions for embedding games into mobile devices exist on the market.

InFusio is a French company who started activity in the field of mobile games in 1998. In September 2000 they launched their own platform for games called ExEn.

Early in 2001, the first GSM handsets with ExEn technology has been launched on European markets, providing for the first time the ability to add 3rd party games into devices.

The platform has been licensed to several major manufacturers, and has been deployed in different networks in Europe and Asia. In August 2002, the list included D2 Vodafone, SFR, Orange , China Mobile, Telefonica [8].

ExEn technology contains three elements: an executive kernel that is embeddable in handsets (at manufacturing time), a server and a collection of games.

The executive kernel is available for licensees to be included in cell phones. It offers a core language based on J2ME and a library of game-enabling routines such as sprite animation, image resize, collision detection, accelerated scroll, etc. The server supports downloading of games (via CSDC) and some services like high score listing and access control. This allows mobile network operators to monitor the usage of the games and to implement different billing policies or extensions to the system. The games are provided by In-Fusio – at the moment of writing the platform is closed for third party developers. They are stand-alone games built around successful ideas from the 8 bit home computers generation: sports games, platform-jumping, etc.

According to Sony Ericsson "Mophun™ [2] is a software based gaming console for mobile terminals." It is a proprietary solution developed by Stockholm-based Synergenix. Sony Ericsson schedules to introduce it in their new model T300 in Q4 of 2002. It uses C/C++ applications called "gamelets", deployed in a sandbox environment. There is an SDK available, WEB support for individual developers and prototype games that can be played on the Internet.

Until a standard mobile gaming platform will become mature enough and will be commonly accepted by the telecom industry, the proprietary solutions will continue to exist and to provide optimum performance for specific devices

5   Wireless Game Development Characteristics

Creating and operating successful wireless games is a complex process requiring certain managerial and technical abilities. This might be a surprising assertion, given that the average wireless game appears to be by far simpler that most of the PC games. In fact, a number of factors affect the development process of wireless applications, making it more difficult the development of traditional, desktop applications. The distribution chain is longer in the wireless case, and the deployment environment is restricted and controlled by telecom operators. Platforms are less familiar for average developers, the know-how is less accessible. The wireless platforms are also less mature, more prone to undocumented behavior than desktop computers.

In order to be commercially profitable a wireless game should feature a set of characteristics that are often conflicting or hard to reach: 1) playability – to be fun,

---

[2] Mophun ™ White paper
http://www.ericsson.com/mobilityworld/sub/open/devices/T300/docs/Mophun_WP.html
(2002)

2) reasonable reliability, 3) low cost of playing, 4) interoperability across different devices, 5) usability of the UI, and 6) enough fast response time (multi-player games).

In the same time a multitude of devices coexist in one operator's network rising up the dilemma: which one of them to support?, see Figure 3.

The perceived entertainment value of a wireless game is constrained from the beginning by the natural device's limitations. Small screen, miniature keyboard, low consumption processor – all contribute to a rather unattractive environment. A game idea must stand by itself. Unlike in the PC or console world, there can't be any fancy graphics, sound or effects to back it up. High creativity and talent must be invested in the earliest design phases, this is a essential precondition of success. Companies owning intellectual property rights for older games (for 8 bit home computers or consoles) are in particularly good positions in the wireless entertainment market. Newcomers are faced with the difficult situation when many good ideas that seem to be new are already implemented and copyrighted.

As [1] notes, there is a first basic option for a customer: to use a complex, integrated device, offering both a mobile phone and information processing functions, or to chose a PDA with separated telephone which can also act as a wireless network interface.

Fig. 3. Choice of two devices [modified after Canalys, 2001]

The variety of mobile devices is much larger than that of desktop computers and the diversity of the software platforms is even larger. Even closely related platforms, like J2ME implementations on telephones from the same manufacturers have slightly different features, like the size of the screen or the color depth. Each technology may require investments in new tools (ex. WAP server, MMS access point) and in know-how.

A specific problem of wireless games is losing the connection in the middle of one session. Especially in the case of action or multi-player games, these situations need to be detected and recovered both for the player who is (temporarily) disconnected and for those who are continuing their session.

6   Monica Experiment

The Monica Project was established in 1999 at the University of Oulu aiming to research topics about value-added service development for 3G mobile phones. One experiment consisted of the practical implementation of a multi-client, multi-platform mobile card games. By analyzing similar systems developed by industrial companies, it was evident that a special approach was needed in order to be able to support a large variety of client devices.

Most of the existing solutions were built around one platform and one bearer media. There were solutions for WAP over GSM link or Java applets over IP, or dedicated systems for connected Palm PDAs, and so on. This type of approach seems to be the most robust and successful since it leverages the strengths of one single platform and eliminates the risks associated with combining different, incompatible technologies. A common characteristic of the analyzed solutions was the tight coupling between the business logic of the application and the presentation layer.

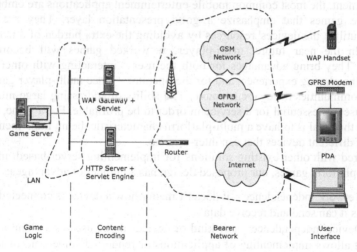

Fig. 4. "Monica" architecture for mobile entertainment services

The first step in our approach was to define a generic architecture for mobile entertainment services to separate as much as possible the logic and the presentation aspects, see Figure 4. The solution is to encode game's logic in a process called "game server", which is separate from the preparation of data in the client device's format. The second activity is carried in a process called "content encoder". In this way, the simultaneous multi-platform access to the service is realized by adding an encoder for each of the supported end-user platforms.

Another characteristic of the Monica's approach is that all the information processing is performed by the server, the end-user client devices act as simple "remote user interfaces", or as browsers. This brings the advantage that virtually any device that is capable of bi-directional communication can be used as a terminal for the game, and the adaptation process is relatively simple.

The content (in our case, a card game) can be presented in an as simple or complex way that is required. For instance, on the screen of a WAP phone the cards can be presented with numbers and letters, and they can be manipulated via menus, while in a PC's Java client, the same game can display animation, play sounds, etc. Another advantage is that a centralized logic allows simpler maintenance, defects can be fixed and features can be added by modifying only one repository of code (the server).

The most important drawback of this idea is that the game is very sensitive to network latency. Each of the user's actions have to be validated and applied by the server via a network link, so the roundtrip transfer time of one message between client and server is the minimum response time of the interface. In the case of SMS for example, the result of pressing one button in the user interface can be perceived only after one minute.

7   Conclusion

At the moment, the most common mobile entertainment applications are embedded or stand-alone games that emphasize a good presentation layer. They are able to optimally utilize the devices' resources by avoiding the extra burden of a networking channel. In the near future, multi-player, networked games will become more important. They bring advantages for both the user – interacting with other humans improves the playing experience, and for the operator – since multi-player games help building communities of loyal customers. The ability of addressing large numbers of potential users is essential for a service in order to be profitable. For a game, one way to achieve this goal is to have a multi-platform characteristic, being implemented for a number of different devices that can inter-operate.

Compared with other existing solutions for implementing server-based, multi-user and multi-platform games, our proposed design has a number of advantages:

- Network independence – it doesn't matter how a device is connected, as long as it can send and receive data
- Device independence – any kind of device can be used as a client as long as it allows implementing of applications or rendering some kind of language. The level of usability can vary greatly, but essentially, the usability of the game is similar with the usability of that environment
- Easiness to port to new platforms – since the model of application is well defined, the modifications are related especially to platform specific issues. Our implementation supports six different client platforms, each one of the having multiple configuration variants.

References

1. Canalys.: Choice of one or two devices. Mobile analysis. Volume 2001, Issue 13. http://www.canalys.com/download/mr200113.pdf (2001) [checked August 2nd, 2002]
2. CNN.: Nintendo wins new software maker. February 7, 2001. http://www.cnn.com/ (2001) [checked August 2nd, 2002]
3. Fujii, K.: iMode: The first smart phone service in the world. http://www.fujii.org/biz/csom/imode.html (2002) [checked October 3rd, 2002]
4. Games Top 10.: Genre. http://www.gamestop10.com/genres/index.htm (2002) [checked August 12th, 2002]
5. IDSA.: Computer And Video Games Are Here To Stay. http://www.idsa.com/5_22_2002.html (2002) [checked July 16th, 2002]
6. IDSA.: Essential Facts about the Computer and Video Game Industry. May 2002. http://www.idsa.com/pressroom.html (2002) [checked July 16th, 2002]
7. IDSA: Interactive Digital Software Association Reports Popularity Of Computer And Video Games With Adults. http://www.idsa.com/releases/9_13_2000.html (2000) [checked August 2nd, 2002]
8. InFusio.:Customers. http://www.in-fusio.com/fond_references/customers_ref.php (2002) [checked June 15th, 2002]
9. Hall, J.: Be an iMode Mifune?. Wireless Gaming Review, Somerville. http://www.wirelessgamingreview.com/reviews/samurai021402.php   (2002) [checked August 11th, 2002]
10. Holmquist, L.E., Björk, S., Falk, J., Jaksetic, P., Ljungstrand, P., Redström, J.: What About Fun and Games?. In Ljungberg, F. (ed.) Informatics in the Next Millennium, Lund: Studentlitteratur, 1999 (1999)
11. Kushner, D.: The Wireless Arcade. Technology Review. July/August 2002. Cambridge (2002) 46-52
12. Mobileinfo.: Market Outlook & Trends: CDMA2000 Providing Operators With Significant 3G Advantages. News: Issue #2002 – 28, July 2002 http://www.mobileinfo.com/news_2002/issue28/cdma2000_penetration.htm (2002) [checked July 25th, 2002]
13. Mobileinfo.: Technology: Qualcomm the Bearer of Good News. News: Issue #2002 – 25, July 2002. http://www.mobileinfo.com/news_2002/issue25/qualcom_brew.htm (2002) [checked July 25th, 2002]
14. Nintendo.: Consolidated Financial Statements: May 30, 2002. http://www.nintendo.com/corp/report/financialstatements_5-30-02.pdf (2002) [checked October 3rd, 2002]
15. Partanen, J-P.: Mobile Gaming: A Framework for Evaluating the Industry 2000-2005. Gaptime Century, Espoo http://www.gaptime.com/mobilegaming.pdf (2001) [checked October 3rd, 2002]
16. Puha, T.: Wireless Entertainment: The State of Play. Gamasutra, San Francisco http://www.gamasutra.com/resource_guide/20010917/puha_pfv.htm   (2001) [checked July 18th, 2002]
17. Ranta, P.: Tietokonepelien lyhyt historia (timeline). http://www.urova.fi/home/pranta/ptimeli.htm (2000) [checked July 22nd, 2002]

18. Saarikoski, P.: Kauniit ja rohkeat – videopelien värikäs historia. MikroBitti, 2000, Vol. 3. (2000)
19. Sambe, Y.: Mobile Phone Content and Java Game Market in Japan. Santa's Games. April 18th-19th 2002, Rovaniemi. (2002)
20. Scherlis, D.: Culture Clash. Mobile Entertainment Analyst. Volume 1, Number 1, July 2002, http://www.wirelessgamingreview.com/mea/ (2002) [checked October 3rd, 2002]
21. South-Western College Publishing.: The Global Business Game: A Brief History of Business Games. http://www.swcollege.com/management/gbg/history.html (2000) [checked August 6th, 2002]
22. SubTV.: WaterWar. http://www.sub.tv/subtv2002/index_html.shtml (2002) [checked August 12th, 2002]
23. Sun Microsystems.: Java™ 2 Micro Edition (J2ME™). http://java.sun.com/j2me (2002) [checked October 2nd, 2002]
24. Suominen, J.: Elektronisen pelaamisen historiaa lajityyppien kautta tarkasteltuna. http://www.tuug.org/~jaakko/tutkimus/jaakko_pelit99.html (1999) [checked July 24th, 2002]
25. Suominen, J.: Kiehtovat pelit – elektroniikkapelien suosion salaisuudet. http://www.utu.fi/hum/satakunta/digi/esitelmat/digiesitelma05_2001.html (2001) [checked July 24th, 2002]
26. Toptronics.: Lehdistötiedote 11.02.2002: Pelimarkkinat Suomessa 2001. http://www.toptronics.fi/ (2002) [checked July 20th, 2002]
27. UMTS Forum.: Forum revises market study. UMTS Forum Secretariat, London http://www.umts-forum.org/mobilennium_online/2002.02/story5.htm (2002) [checked August 13th, 2002]
28. Wireless Web News.: Gaming the only way out for struggling operators. Vol 2, Num 42. Visiongain House, London (2001)
29. Zeime, G. Great things in small packages. Contact No. 10 1998. Ericsson publication http://www.ericsson.com/about/publications/kon_con/contact/cont10_98/ (1998) [checked August 2nd, 2002]
30. Zsigo, K.: Making Money Writing Wireless Games. http://www.wireless-gamingreview.com/articles/konny071602.php (2002) [checked July 18th, 2002]

Analysis of Risks in a Software Improvement Programme

Emmanuel Chauveau, Claire Lassudrie, and David Berthelot

France Telecom R&D, DTL/TAL,
2 Avenue Pierre Marzin, 22307 Lannion Cedex, France

Abstract. In a fast changing world, with more and more demanding clients, quality needs increase. To satisfy it, a lot of organizations producing software chose the Software Process Improvement approach. At France Telecom R&D, we develop this approach using the ISO/IEC TR 15504(SPICE) process model. The improvement programme we implemented was combined with risk management. To optimise the risk management in the programme, we chose to analyse statistically the risks of the programme. In this communication, we present how we set up the programme, the risk management implementation and the risk data analysis methods and results.

1 Introduction

In a fast changing world, with more and more demanding client, quality needs increase. To keep the pace, industries need to improve continuously and most of them chose a process approach known in the software engineering world as Software Process Improvement (SPI). It's the approach chosen by France Telecom.

Starting from ISO/IEC TR 15504 (SPICE) [1] process model, we launched a SPI programme focusing on a subset of SPICE processes. In this programme, we implemented risk management to have a better control on the programme. In order to optimise the way risks are managed in the programme and consequently the programme itself we chose to implement a statistical analysis on the risks to understand the risks and their evolution in the programme better. This communication intends to explain how we implemented the different steps and the results we obtained.

Section 1 shows why and how we implemented a SPI programme at France Telecom then, in Sect. 2 we describe the risk management within this programme: its principles, implementation and results. Section 3 gives the data analysis methods, the description of the data used and then the results we obtained. Finally, we conclude and give tracks of possible future work.

M. Oivo and S. Komi-Sirviö (Eds.): PROFES 2002, LNCS 2559, pp. 601–614, 2002.
© Springer-Verlag Berlin Heidelberg 2002

2   The Software Process Improvement Programme at France Telecom R&D

In this section, we introduce first the business goals of France Telecom R&D then its improvement approach and finally how we organised the SPI programme.

2.1   France Telecom R&D Business Goals

France Telecom R&D is the vector of France Telecom group's innovation, in France and on an international level. However, in a fast changing world, where customers are more and more demanding in terms of quality services, France Telecom R&D has to keep on anticipating its products to the demand.

For this reason, it is necessary:

- To create durable value and competitive advantages,
- To be the first to propose innovation to our customers,
- To provide powerful, diversified and simple services,
- To develop the use of telecommunications services,
- To reduce the costs and to optimise architectures of the network.

In this context of strong competition, development of innovative software is a key activity for France Telecom R&D. A Software Process Improvement (SPI) programme [6] was launched in 1999 having for goals:

- To improve the products quality,
- To increase cost control,
- To reduce time and costs of development.

2.2   France Telecom R&D Improvement Approach

The process approach has become natural and integrated in the majority of companies. Telecommunications operators (ATT, Sprint, BT, Bell Atlantic...) or companies considered to be the best of their category (Xerox, Texas Instrument, IBM, SGS Thomson...), support their development by the process approach.

An in-depth work on the processes provides a response and a better knowledge of the organisation in order to identify and to exploit all the layers of progress.

Our software process model is based on the process model defined in ISO/IEC TR 15504 Part 2(SPICE) [1]. The improvement approach used in the SPI programme is a continuous improvement methodology based upon the application of Deming's wheel known as PDCA Cycle (Plan-Do-Check-Act).

- P - " Plan" which consists in defining and planning the selected improvements,
- D - " Do" which allows the implementation of the improvement,
- C - " Check " is the stage of assessment of the results,
- A - "Act": if the goals of improvement are met we propose new improvements; else we redefine the improvement plan.

According to our specific context and needs, we selected a subset of the software processes from SPICE reference process model. Reducing time to market can be achieved by reinforcing configuration management and project management. Improving requirements management, quality control and supplier monitoring could achieve improving product quality.

According to these objectives, 5 priority processes were chosen:

- Configuration management,
- Quality assurance,
- Acquisition,
- Requirements management,
- Software project management.

For each priority process, a target level was set to be reached three years after the programme launch. To monitor process improvement, software process assessments compliant to SPICE assessment model (ISO/IEC/TR 15504 part 2,3 [1]) were periodically performed in the operational units. Outputs of these assessments are process profiles, which assess the maturity of each process on a 5-levels-scale, together with a list of strengths and weaknesses, from which an improvement plan can be built for each process.

In a first step, the perimeter involved in the improvement programme contained the operational units developing software for creation of telecom services. It is intended to extend this perimeter at the end of the first three years of the programme.

2.3   Structure and Organisation
of the Software Process Improvement Programme

The structure at the heart of our SPI programme is the SEPG (Software Engineering Process Group). The members of the SEPG are the process owners and the SPI correspondents of the organisational units.

Roles and responsibilities of the SEPG are:

- To help organisational units to define their processes,
- To co-ordinate training sessions on the processes,
- To perform systematic measurements on the software processes by leading SPICE compliant assessments and collecting metrics relative to processes and projects in the operational units (such as delays, budget overflow ...),
- To help operational units to build and implement improvement plans.

For each priority process, a **process owner** is responsible for the whole improvement activity on this process within France Telecom R&D. In addition to this structure, an improvement **programme team** was set up in order to manage the SPI programme and to perform support activities such as quality assurance, assessments, training, documentation, configuration management, and **risk management**.

The programme has been divided into the following tasks:

-   Programme management,
-   Baseline management (definition and maintenance of the software process baseline),
-   SPI support (including process assessment and support for building improvement plans),
-   Training management,
-   Measurement management.

Each task is under responsibility of a task leader (which is member of the SEPG). The whole programme is under responsibility of the programme leader. The sponsor of the SPI programme is the director of France Telecom R&D strategy department.

3   Risk Management in the SPI Programme

Because of the strategic importance of the improvement programme, we decided to implement risk management from the very beginning of the programme to increase its probability of success.

3.1   Risk Management Principles and Implementation

Project Risk Management [2-4] is a process than can be split in five parts or phases interacting as described in the fig. 1. The five phases are: strategy definition, risk analysis, risk treatment, risk control and risk capitalisation. The different phases principles and the implementation we made are described in the following sections.

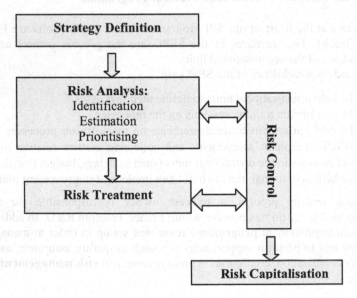

Fig. 1. Risk Management Phases

Strategy Definition. The goal of this phase is to define the risk management strategy for the programme. At this step of the process, guidelines of the process instantiation are to be defined as for example human and material resources, kind of estimation (symbolic or quantitative), treatment strategies, classes of risks to focus on or documents and methods to use.

In the SPI programme, the following strategy was defined:

1. A first risk analysis is performed by an external risk assessment team in order to benefit from an external view on the programme and to develop inner competences on risk management.
2. A risk manager belonging to the programme team performs risk follow-up all along the improvement programme.
3. The dispositions taken in this phase are written in the Programme Risk Management Plan. Four classes of risks are taken under consideration: contract, human, management, and technical.

Risk Analysis. Risk analysis is the key phase of the process. This phase consists in three activities: identification, estimation and prioritising of the risks, which are described below.

Identification.
The goal here is to identify the risks of the programme. Each risk should be described as precisely as possible, as well as its causes and consequences. To identify risks, some techniques and methods exists as for example:

- Documents analysis
- Brainstorming and others group techniques
- Interviews of projects members and/or experts
- Questionnaires and catalogues.

Estimation.
The goal of this activity is to give values (numeric or ordinal depending on whether the analysis is quantitative or symbolic) to characteristics of each risk like probability, impact and maybe detectability. Risk exposure is henceforth defined by a mathematical function (or more likely a matrix in symbolic analysis) of those characteristics.

Prioritising.
The criterion the more generally used to prioritise risks is the exposure but other criteria can be used as for example the possible time of occurrence. Risk exposure can be defined as a combination of risk impact and risk occurrence probability.

Implementation.
Risk identification and estimation were performed using a combination of interviews of the main actors of the programme, of analysis of the management documentation and of brainstorming sessions.

Risk estimation of impact and probability were performed on a symbolic four-levels scale: *very low, low, high, very high.*

	OCCURRENCE PROBABILITY			
IMPACT	Very low	Low	High	Very high
Very low	Minor	Minor	Acceptable	Acceptable
Low	Minor	Acceptable	Acceptable	Unacceptable
High	Acceptable	Acceptable	Unacceptable	Major
Very high	Acceptable	Unacceptable	Major	Major

Fig. 2. Exposure Matrix

Four levels were defined for risk exposure, which was determined according to Fig. 2

Risk Treatment. The first task of this phase is to choose the kind of response to each risk: transfer (insurance), passive acceptation (emergency procedure), active acceptation (preventive actions) or suppression (suppressing actions).

Once it is done, the actions and emergency procedures should be decided. We should keep in mind that actions can have consequences (positive or negative) on other risks and that they may bring up new risks. Metrics and indicators are also defined in order to control the risks and the linked actions.

In the SPI programme, the treatment strategy consisted in reducing risk probability whenever it was possible, by identifying specific actions that aim at eliminating or reducing potential risk causes. One action may reduce several causes and several risks. We focused on major and unacceptable risks.

Risk Control. In this phase, we follow the evolution of risks (probability, impact, exposure...), of actions (completion rate, efficiency...) and of metrics and indicators defined in the treatment phase. Regularly, risk analysis is relaunched (especially the estimation) and possibly risk treatment (in case of lack of efficiency, new risks to treat, etc.). If a passively accepted risk occurs we launch the emergency plan.

Risk evolution, status and completion of actions are continuously monitored all along the improvement programme. Communication on risk management is a key point in our improvement programme. Reports on evolution and status of risks and actions are produced regularly.

As risk management is an iterative process involving continuous identification of new risks, periodic risk reviews take place every three months and a complete risk analysis is launched every year.

Risk Capitalisation. At the end of the project, we capitalise both on the process and on the risks in order to share experience. Capitalising on the process means that we analyse how the process was applied, the problems we had with the process and eventually suggestions to improve it. This way, we can have a continuous improvement. Capitalising on risks consists in collecting information about the risks of the project (their classes, if they occurred...) in the organisation database. The risks should be as generic as possible to be re-usable.

3.2   Results

During the initial risk analysis, 33 risks were identified:

- 5 major risks
- 17 unacceptable risks
- 11 acceptable risks.

Most of the risks were from the technical and management classes. The five major risks belonged to these two classes.

New risks were continuously identified along the programme. At the time of this study, that is two years and a half after the programme launch of the programme, 66 risks were identified from which 33 were closed.

These new risks concern specifically:

- Assessment methodology and planning,
- Development and maintenance of the process baseline,
- Implementation of improvement plans.

These risks were mainly from technical and human classes. On the whole, 201 causes and 170 mitigation actions were identified.

We experienced that the risk management approach provided the following benefits in the improvement programme:

- Improved communication between the different actors,
- Valuable help in problems understanding and resolution,
- Better resource allocation,
- Increased capacity to cope with evolving context.

However, some risks that have been identified during the initial risk analysis are still active. Some other risks occurred in spite of the actions planned for their reduction. In order to understand risk evolution, we decided to use data analysis techniques.

4   Data Analysis

The goal of the data analysis we performed was to improve our knowledge of programme risks by the study of relations (correlations and oppositions) between risks and between characteristics [8,10]. These relations permit to form coherent risk groups.

4.1   Input Data

Input data consist of sixty-six individuals described by thirteen variables. The individuals correspond to the risks and the variables to the characteristics.

Each of the sixty-six risks of our analysis is described by the following characteristics. For each characteristic, we give the categories (values taken by the characteristics) used. For some characteristics we will give an explanation of what they represent.

- Class: management, technical, human and contract.
- Programme task: measures, baseline, programme management, SPI support and training.
- Programme phase: preparation of the programme, definition of the SPI strategy, improvement deployment and assessment.
- Risk owner: person who has competence or authority to collect information on a risk, to follow this risk and to give ideas of treatment for this risk. The risk owners identified correspond to different roles in the project (programme leader, tasks leaders, sponsor of the programme…).
- Initial exposure: major, unacceptable, acceptable and minor.
- Current exposure: major, unacceptable, acceptable and minor.
- Status: this characteristic inform on the aptitude of the risk to appear or not; categories are closed, active.
- Occurrence: occurred, not occurred.
- Detectability: weak, strong.
- Risk persistence: persistent, not persistent.
- Repeatability: repeats itself, does not repeat itself.
- Evolution trend: controlled (risk exposure has become acceptable), stable, reduced (risk impact/probability has decreased but the exposure is still not acceptable).
- Process related to the risk: This process is the most related to the origin of the risk: the occurrence of the risk may result from a poor performance of the implementation of this process in the programme. The processes considered belong to the process reference model ISO/IEC 15504 TR part 2[1].

Figure 3 shows an example of a risk with all its characteristics.

4.2   Analysis Methods

On account of data nature, the procedure of analysis will consist in subjecting the set of the risks to a Multiple Correspondence Analysis then to a Hierarchical Classification. These methods intend to summarise and to explain the information contained in data sets like the set of risks we study and simultaneously to provide a clear visual or geometric representation of the information [7,9].

"Lack of efficiency of a SEPG meeting"

Class: Management	**Owner:** Programme Leader
Task: Baseline	**Phase:** SPI Strategy Definition
Process: Project Management (MAN.2)	**Repeatability:** Yes
Persistence: Not Persistent	**Detectability:** Weak
Initial Exposure: Unacceptable	**Current Exposure:** Acceptable
Evolution Trend: Controlled	**Occurrence:** Not Occured
Status: Active	

Fig. 3. Risk example

Multiple Correspondence Analysis (MCA). The MCA [11] is the most fertile method of the data analysis and is a pillar of the factor analysis success among the experts. It is especially well fit to the treatment of questionnaires and to the exploitation of surveys, when all the variables are symbolic.

This method is the application of the Correspondence Analysis to the study of tables including more than two symbolic variables. Whereas the Correspondence Analysis studies the relationship between two characteristics I and J observed on a given population, the MCA studies the relationships between an unspecified number k of characteristics J1...Jk.

The MCA resides primarily on the interpretation of axes called principal axes. Indeed, the objective is to give sense to these axes in order to highlight oppositions between groups of categories and groups of individuals.

The first step of the method is to define the characteristic elements of each principal axis, namely:

1. The active categories, which are explanatory for it. The active categories are those that were used to determine the principal axes.
2. The illustrative categories, which are significant for it. The illustrative categories were not used for the determination of the principal axes but they are connected to them a posteriori.
3. The individuals that are explanatory for it i.e. the best represented on the axis.

Next, projections of the set of categories and the set of the individuals on the axes permit to define relationships between these various elements.

Finally, the results of a MCA are illustrated with graphs that represent the configurations of the individuals and the categories in projection planes formed by the first principal axes taken two at a time.

The software package used for the analysis is SPAD [1]

Hierarchical Classification (HC). The methods of classification [12] are widely used in the conception of questionnaires as well as in the definition and the classification of the surveyed units, as in the coding of the answers. They permit to determine a definition and a simplified view of the studied "reality".

The HC is used to group objects or individuals described by a number of variables or characteristics. This method gives relatively fast, economical, and easily interpretable results.

Moreover, a MCA rarely provides an exhaustive analysis of a set of data. It is sometimes useful to use a classification method in addition to a MCA because it will help to reduce the complexity of the analysis. Additionally, use of a classification method permits to summarise the configuration of points obtained from a MCA. In other words, a further reduction in the dimensionality of the data is valuable and leads to results that are easier to analyse.

The most systematic and earliest algorithm for HC is the Lance and Williams's one. It creates a hierarchical tree of individuals. By "cutting" this tree, we then obtain a partition of the set of individuals, thus making it possible to form homogeneous groups of individuals.

---

[1] SPAD is software edited by the CISIA (Centre International de Statistiques et d'Informatique Appliquées) in Montreuil, France.

4.3   Results Interpretation

We first present the results of the MCA, then the groups obtained by the HC before discussing these results.

Multiple Correspondence Analysis Results. The principle is to interpret the principal axes, to give them sense, in order to highlight oppositions between groups of risks. We noticed that the proportion of information accounted for by the first three principal axes is larger than the one that is accounted by the other axes, so we focused on interpreting these three principal axes.

The first axis opposes:

- Risks related to assessment: They depend on the SPI support task and they are linked with the Process assessment (ORG.2.2) process as well as the support task leader. Moreover, these risks are largely characterised by a minor current exposure and by the fact they are not persistent. An example of these risks is: *"Lack of availability of an assessor"*
- Risks connected with management: These risks depend on the baseline task and on the management one. They are described by a weak detectability and they have the specificity not to repeat themselves. Moreover, they are linked to the programme leader and to the Project Management (MAN.2) process. A representative risk is: *"Undertaking of the organisational units workload in the SPI programme"*

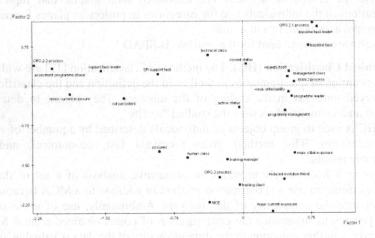

Fig. 4. Representation of the categories in the plan formed by the two first factorial axes

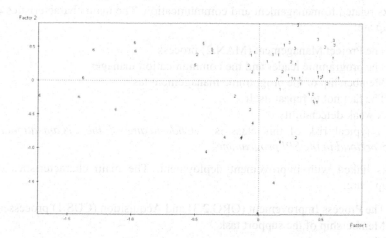

Fig. 5. Representation of the risks groups on the two first factorial axes

Next, the second axis opposes:

- Risks related to human resources: They depend on the training task and on the management one. They are related to the Human resource management (ORG.3) process and they are associated with the training manager and with the SPI resource manager. Furthermore, these risks are largely described by a major initial exposure, by a major current exposure and also by a reduced evolution trend. Last, they have the specificities to have occurred and to be still active. The risk *"Turn-over of key SEPG members"* is significant of these risks.

- Technical risks, connected with the baseline task: These risks are linked with the baseline task leader and the Process establishment (ORG.2.1) process is related to them. They are also generally characterised by a closed status. *"Difficulty to make the baseline converge"* is a good example of these risks.

Finally, the third axis doesn't show a clear opposition but characterises risks related to the measurement task. These risks are associated with the measurement task-leader and the Measurement (ORG.5) process is linked with them. Moreover, they are largely described by a stable evolution trend and by an active status. This group of risks is slightly opposite to closed risks along the axis. *"Reject of the SPI Programme indicators by the organisational units"* is a risk significant of this group.

We can then visualise these oppositions of groups of risks and groups of characteristics in projection planes formed by the first three principal axes taken two at a time. For example, Fig. 4 provides us with the representation of the set of the categories in the plane formed by the first two principal axes.

Hierarchical Classification Result. The hierarchical classification highlighted a partition of the risks in six groups. Each group is characterised by some categories. Combined with the result of the MCA we affined the results to obtain the six following groups:

1. Risks related to management and communication. The main characteristics of this group are:

   - The Project Management (MAN.2) process
   - The programme leader and the communication manager
   - Membership of the programme management task.
   - The fact not to repeat itself
   - A weak detectability
   - A typical risk of this class is: ``Undertaking of the organisational units workload in the SPI programme"

2. Risks linked with improvement deployment. The main characteristics of this group are:

   - The Process Improvement (ORG.2.3) and Acquisition (CUS.1) processes
   - Membership of the support task
   - The contract class
   - An unacceptable current exposure
   - Moreover, we can notice that these risks are particularly related to programme delays, to difficulties in meeting the deadline. A risk of this class is for example: ``Late transmission of the organisational units improvement plans"

3. Risks connected with baseline task. The main characteristics of this group are:

   - The baseline task leader
   - The Process establishment (ORG.2.1) process
   - The programme phase related to the definition of the SPI strategy
   - A closed status
   - ``Difficulty to make the baseline converge" is a good example of these risks.

4. Risks related to human resources. The main characteristics of this group are:

   - The Human Resource Management (ORG.3) process
   - The training manager and the SPI resource manager
   - Membership of the training task and of the programme management one
   - The fact it occurred
   - A major initial exposure
   - A major current exposure
   - A reduced evolution trend
   - An active status
   - The risk ``Turn-over of key SEPG members" is significant of these risks.

5. Risks linked with measures task. The main characteristics of this group are:

   - The measures task leader
   - The Measurement (ORG.5) process
   - A stable evolution trend
   - An active status
   - ``Reject of the SPI Programme's indicators by the organisational units" is a risk significant of this group.

6.   Risks related to assessment. The main characteristics of this group are:

- The Process assessment (ORG.2.2) process
- The SPI support task leader
- Membership of the SPI support task
- The fact not to be persistent
- A minor current exposure
- An example of these risks is: ``Lack of availability of an assessor''.

Figure 5 shows the representation of the risks in the two first factorial plans. The number of his group represents each risk. It confirms the pertinence of the formed groups.

5   Discussion

Results of MCA combined with those of HC have shown six distinctive groups of risks based both on contextual characteristics of risks and characteristics related to risk evolution and mitigation. From these results, we can see that risks from group 4 (human resources) and group 2 (improvement deployment) are still major and unacceptable, whereas risks of group 3 (baseline) and group 6 (assessment) have been closed or became acceptable. This can be explained by the efficiency of reduction actions for risks concerning assessments and baseline development. These actions relied on competencies of SEPG members in the field of process definition, process improvement and process assessment based on ISO 15504 standard.

Actions proposed for reduction and control of human risks were dependent on the human resource process that was outside the scope of the programme. It led to a lower control of these risks. Moreover, some risks related to improvement deployment suffered from the absence of specific resources dedicated to training management and to communication management (both roles were assumed by the programme leader).

These findings showed us that in the future, we should have to concentrate our efforts on reduction of human risks, by changing our strategy regarding these risks and to involve more the human resource management in the improvement programme. It also put in evidence the necessity of having specific resources dedicated to training and communication in the programme.

We can note the measures related risks are a little isolated. Reticence was shown on this task and as it isn't a major objective of the project, less effort was put on it.

The combined results of MCA and HC provide a classification of risks in six groups, each of these groups being associated to a process (these processes are those used to manage, define, evaluate, ... the SPI programme strategy, baseline and results). This demonstrates the importance of the related process concept to structure and guide the risk management approach. A similar use of this concept can be found in [5].

Results of risk analysis have been presented to the programme leader and the task leaders who have found that it provided a true representation of what had happened in the programme by highlighting difficulties and success encountered until now, and that it was so an important part of programme evaluation.

6   Conclusion and Future Trends

Statistically analysing risks is very rich. Opposing categories, regrouping others give very interesting information on characteristics of risks as well as on the SPI programme. The analysis highlighted classes combining static characteristics (fixed once for all) with dynamic ones (which change along the programme). This classification will allow us to improve the treatment actions or to define better-aimed actions.

The future step in this study will be to analyse in the same way the actions. For this we will try to see which characteristics can be used to describe in the most pertinent way the actions. Once done, we will launch a predictive analysis in order to see if according to some characteristics values, we can predict the evolution of the related risks and the efficiency of the actions.

Acknowledgement

The authors would like to thank Dominique Hediguer, and Bernard Haug from CR2A-DI/Transiciel, and Hervé Courtot from France Telecom for their support to risk analysis and risk management implementation. We would also thank Richard Castanet, Professor at the University of Bordeaux I, who is Emmanuel Chauveau's Ph.D. Thesis director and Jian-Feng Yao, University of Rennes, who is David Berthelot's training period supervisor.

References

1. ISO/IEC TR 15504-2, "Information Technology – Software process assessment – A reference model for processes and process capability", 1998
2. B.W. Boehm, "Software Risk Management: Principles and Practices", IEEE Software, Jan.1991, pp 32-41
3. R.M. Wideman, "Project and programme risk management", PMBOK Handbook Series, Vol. 6, Project Management Institute, 1992
4. H. Courtot, "La gestion des risques dans les projets", Economica, 1998
5. C. Völker, H. Stienen and R. Ouared, "Taking SPICE to the third dimension: Adding risk analysis to ISO/IES TR 15504", ICSSEA 2001, 2001
6. C. Lassudrie and G. Gulla-Menez, "Risk Management in Software Process Improvement, SPICE 2002, pp. 245-260, 2002
7. L. Lebart, A. Morineau and K.M. Warwick, "Multivariate Descriptive Statistical Analysis", Wileys & Sons, 1984
8. W.W. Cooleys and P.R. Lhones, "Multivariate Data Analysis", Wileys & Sons, 1971
9. G. Saporta, "Probabilités, Analyse des données et statistique", Ed. Technip, 1990
10. J.M. Bouroche and G. Saporta, "L'analyse de données", Presses universitaires de France, 1980
11. H.H. Harman, "Modern Factor Analysis (3rd edition)", Chicago University Press, 1976
12. J.A. Hartigan, "Clustering Algorithms", Wiley, 1975

Generation of Management Rules through System Dynamics and Evolutionary Computation

Jesús S. Aguilar-Ruiz[1], José C. Riquelme[1], Daniel Rodríguez[2], and Isabel Ramos[1]

[1]Department of Computer Science, University of Seville
41012 Sevilla, Spain
{aguilar,riquelme,Isabel.ramos}@lsi.us.es
[2]Department of Computer Science, The University of Reading
Reading, RG6 6AY, UK
d.rodriguez-garcia@rdg.ac.uk

Abstract. Decision making has been traditionally based on a managers experience. This paper, however, discusses how a software project simulator based on System Dynamics and Evolutionary Computation can be combined to obtain management rules. The purpose is to provide accurate decision rules to help project managers to make decisions at any time in the software development life cycle. To do so, a database from which management rules are generated is obtained using a software project simulator based on system dynamics. We then find approximate optimal management rules using an evolutionary algorithm which implements a novel method for encoding the individuals, i.e., management rules to be searched by the algorithm. The resulting management rules of our method are also compared with the ones obtained by another algorithm called C4.5. Results show that our evolutionary approach produces better management decision rules regarding quality and understandability.

1 Introduction

Decision making is an important part of software processes. Most organisations allocate resources based on predictions and improving their accuracy of such predictions reduce costs and make use of resources in a more effective way.

In this work we have combined System Dynamics and Evolutionary Computation to achieve high quality decision rules. On the one hand, dynamic models such as System Dynamics are becoming popular among the Software Engineering research community as they may provide a better solution to some of the problems found in Software Engineering when compared with traditional static models. In principle, dynamic models can help in making good decisions with data that are scarce and incomplete. On the other hand, Evolutionary algorithms allow us to find an approximate optimal solutions in a large search space, i.e., management rules in a database generated by the project simulation based on System Dynamics.

M. Oivo and S. Komi-Sirviö (Eds.): PROFES 2002, LNCS 2559, pp. 615-628, 2002.
© Springer-Verlag Berlin Heidelberg 2002

The organisation of the paper is as follows. Section 2 discusses the related work. Section 3 presents the approach taken for generating management rules. Section 4 discusses a series of scenarios to prove our approach. Section 5 discusses its validation with a generic framework. Finally, Section 6 concludes the paper and future work is outlined.

2   Related Work

2.1   System Dynamics and Software Project Simulators

System Dynamics is a method for studying how complex systems change over time where internal feedback loops within the structure of the system influence the entire system behaviour [9]. In System Dynamics, it is necessary first to understand the behaviour of the real word so that important cause-effect relationships, which are called base mechanisms, can be modelled. The formal model consist of a set of mathematical equations which can be represented graphically as flow graphs.

The application of system dynamics to software projects provides the perspective of considering them as complex socio-technological systems. Their evolution will be determined by their internal structure as well as the relations established inside the working team. This allows the development of dynamic models to describe the feedback structure of the system being modelled as well as the mental process followed by project managers in making decisions.

The building of a dynamic model for a software project is based on the evolution of the project and the attainment of the project goals such as meeting the deadlines, a project phase being within budget, etc. depends on (i) a set of initial parameters that define the initial estimations and (ii) the management policies to be applied. These policies are related with the project (number of tasks, time, cost, number of technicians, software complexity, etc.) and the organization (maturity level, average delay, turnover on the project's work force, etc). Using of software project simulation environments based on dynamic models such as Vensim, iThink, etc., project managers can experiment different management policies without additional cost including the following:

1. A priori, project analysis, to simulate the project before initiation.
2. Project monitoring, to simulate the project during its development phase for adapting the project estimation to its actual evolution.
3. Post-mortem analysis through the simulation of a finished project, to know how the results obtained could have been improved.

2.2   Abdel-Hamid's System Dynamic Model

Abdel-Hamid [1] developed an model in order to study the effects of project management policies and actions on software development. Developed to help

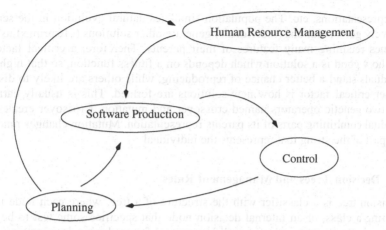

Fig. 1. High Level View of Abdel-Hamid Model of Software Project Management

understanding the software development process, it allows to evaluate the impact of management policies. Being the software development of complex systems difficult to understand in its entirety, Abdel-Hamid's model is partitioned into four subsystems that are manageable and understandable (see Figure 1):

1. Human Resource Management Subsystem deals with hiring, training, assimilation and transfer of the human resources.
2. Software Production Subsystem models the software development process excluding requirements, operation and maintenance. This subsystem has four sectors: Manpower Allocation, Software Development, Quality Assurance and Rework, and System Testing.
3. Control Subsystem deals with the information that decision makers have available. The model takes into account that it is difficult to know the true-state of a process during development as usually such information is inaccurate.
4. Planning Subsystem takes into account the initial project estimates. Such estimates need to be revised through the software project life cycle

2.3   Evolutionary Algorithms

Evolutionary Algorithms (EA) are a family of computational models inspired by the concept of evolution and natural selection. These algorithms employ a randomised search method to find approximate optimal solutions to a particular problem [12]. Generally, this approach is applied to search spaces that are too large to use exhaustive techniques.

Based on a generally constant size population of individuals, an EA follows an iterative procedure based on selection and recombination operators to generate new individuals in the search space. Such individuals are usually represented by a finite string of symbols called chromosome. They encode a possible solution in a given problem search space which comprises of all possible solutions to the problem. The length of the string and the population size are completely dependent of the problem in hand and the finite string of symbol alphabet can be binary, real-valued encodings, tree representations, etc. The population simulates natural evolution in the sense that iteratively good solutions (individuals) generate other solutions (offsprings) to replace bad ones retaining many features of their parents. Therefore, a critical factor is to know how good is a solution which depends on a fitness function, so that high-fitness individuals stand a better chance of reproducing, while others are likely to disappear. Another critical factor is how new solutions are formed. This is usually carried out using two genetic operators named crossover and mutation. Crossover creates a new individual combining parts of its parents representation. Mutation changes randomly a small part of the string that represents the individual.

2.4   Decision Trees and Management Rules

A decision tree is a classifier with the structure of a tree, where each node is a leaf indicating a class, or an internal decision node that specifies some test to be carried out on a single attribute value. A well-known tool for producing decision trees is C4.5 [14] which basically consists of a recursive algorithm with a divide and conquer technique that optimises a decision tree. The main advantage of decision trees is their immediate conversion to rules (in the form of *if ... then ...*) that can be easily interpreted by decision-makers. For example, assume a hypothetical database that associates weight (in kilograms) and height (in meters) of a person with having a paper accepted in a relevant conference. The database is a sequence of tuples such as (83, 1.71, no), (71, 1.62, yes), etc. A rule describing the relationship among attribute values and class might be: *if weight in [60, 70] and height in [1.60, 1.68] then he/she is a candidate for having a paper accepted*. It is to note that (i) the finding of these rules can be tackled with many different techniques, one such technique being evolutionary algorithms and (ii) such rules may produce relationships between variables that are not be evident.

In software engineering, it is possible to generate management rules automatically for any project and to know the managerial policies that ensure the achievement of its initial aims. The deviations from the initial estimates could be detected (monitoring) and the behaviour of the process is well understood through the management-rule set. In short, management rules make it possible to:

- obtain values considered as *good* for any variable of interest (time, effort, quality, number of technicians, etc.), independently or together with other variables;
- analyse managerial policies capable of achieving the aims of the project;
- know to which range of values the parameters must belong in order to obtain good results.

3   Our Approach

Our goal is to find management policies that produce good results for variables of interest in every scenario taking into account that quality must be prioritised, i.e., we must consider only high quality projects. Based on these constraints, we try to obtain policies that minimize the delivery time (independently of the effort), the effort (without taking into account the delivery time) or both delivery time and effort at once. Figure 2 shows the process to obtain decision rules:

1. Define the intervals of values for the attributes of the dynamical model (see Table 2 which will be discussed in the case studies).
2. Define the goals of the project (values for time and cost).
3. Generate the database: each simulation produces a record with the values of the parameters and the values of the variables as it is shown in Table 3 in the next Section.
4. Assign labels to the records according to a threshold for every variable.
5. Generate decision rules from the previously generated database using our evolutionary algorithm.
6. Compare generated decision rules with those produced by using the C4.5 algorithm.

It is to note that the first two steps previously are performed by the project manager and the next two items are executed automatically (see Figure 2).

3.1   System Dynamics

In our approach, decision rules are generated by the evolutionary algorithm based on the database generated by the Abdel-Hamid's dynamic model [1] simulating the temporal behaviour of the project. It contains the controls for setting three groups of required parameters: the parameters of the project (size, number technicians etc.), the parameters of the organisation (average delays related to hiring, dismissals etc.) and finally, the parameters controlling the simulation process. Our generated database consist of a sequence of tuples with continuous attributes and a class label.

Abdel-Hamid's work was chosen because in addition to emphasise project management, descriptions, validation and conclusions of his model are extensively reported.

3.2   Evolutionary Computation

Evolutionary computation provides an interesting approach for dealing with the problem of extracting knowledge from databases. In this case, the search space comprises of management rules for decision making and we will try to find a rule set

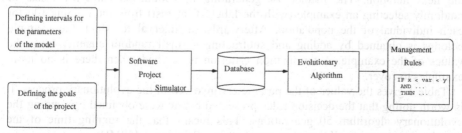

Fig. 2. Generation of Rules

that describes the knowledge within data in order to classify it. For an attribute a_i, the rules take the form of „if a_j in $[l_j, u_j]$ then *class*", where l_j and u_j are two real values belonging to the range of the attribute and $l_j < u_j$.

Two critical factors influence the decision rules obtained by using evolutionary algorithms: (i) the selection of an internal representation of the search space (coding) and (ii) the definition of an external function that assigns a value of goodness to the potential solutions (fitness).

3.2.1 Coding

Our approach, called „natural coding", uses one gene per continuous attribute leading to a reduction in the search space, i.e., the space of all feasible solutions. This reduction has a great influence on the convergence of the evolutionary algorithm, i.e., finding approximate optimal rules. Our coding method uses natural numbers so that a value per attribute is necessary, i.e., every interval is encoded by one natural number, leading to a reduction of the search space size. Natural Coding is formally described in [2]. The reader can have a better understanding of this coding method, for continuous as well as discrete attributes, by referring to that work.

3.2.2 Fitness Function

The fitness function must be able to discriminate between correct and incorrect classifications of samples. Finding an appropriate function is not a trivial task, due to the noisy nature of most databases. The evolutionary algorithm maximizes the fitness function f for each individual and it is given by the equation (1).

$$f(i)=2(N-CE(i))+G(i)+coverage(i) \tag{1}$$

where N is the number of examples being processed; $CE(i)$ is the number of class errors, which is produced when an example belongs to the region defined by the rule but it does not have the same class; $G(i)$ is the number of examples correctly classified by the rule; and the *coverage* of the *i-th* rule is the proportion of the search space covered by such rule.

3.2.3 Algorithm

The algorithm is a typical sequential covering EA [13], i.e., it chooses the best individual of the evolutionary process, transforming it into a rule which is used to eliminate data from the training file [17]. In this way, the training file is reduced in the next iteration. The method of generating the initial population consists of randomly selecting an example (with the label of interest) from the training file for each individual of the population. Afterwards, an interval to which the example belongs is obtained by adding and subtracting a small random quantity from the values of the example. A termination criterion is reached when there is no more examples to cover.

Table 1 gives the values of the parameters involved in the evolutionary process. It is worth noting that the decision rules presented below were obtained by running the evolutionary algorithm 50 generations. This means that the running time of the algorithm was very small (less than a minute in a Pentium II 450MHz).

Table 1. Parameters of the evolutionary algorithm

Parameter	Value
Population Size	100
Generations	50
Crossover probability	0.5
Individual Mutation probability	0.1
Gene mutation probability	0.1

4   Case Studies: Generation of Rules for Software Development Projects

By simulating the Abdel-Hamid's dynamic model [1] we obtained three different scenarios. These scenarios are defined by intervals of values that the attributes can take. It is worth noting that the initial values were almost the same as those described by Abdel-Hamid. Only four attributes were modified, taking random values from previously defined intervals. Each row comprises of the name of the attribute in the model, the range of values it can take, a brief description of its meaning and its estimated value at the beginning of the project.

The attributes ASIMDY, HIREDY, TRNSDY (related with the new personnel management enrolled to the ongoing project) and MXSCDX (related with the decision of imposing constraints to the delivery time) described in Table 2, will allow us to analyse their influence on the variables of the project (mainly, delivery time, cost or effort, and quality) described in Table 3. Table 2 shows attribute names and their description, range and initial estimated input value. Table 3 shows attribute names, description and initial estimated output value. These input and output parameters will be used to generate the following scenarios:

- Scenario 1: Attributes can take any value within the range (as defined in Table 2).
- Scenario 2: Attributes related with the personnel management take the low values in their range, i.e., ASIMDY in [5,15], HIREDY in [5,10] and TRNSDY in [5,10], so that the personnel management is fast. Moreover, the date extension can not be greater than 20% of the initially estimated value.
- Scenario 3: Personnel management is the same as in the previous scenario and MXSCDX can take any value within its range.

Table 2. Parameters of the environment of the project and organisation

Attribute	Interval	Description	Estimated Value
ASIMDY	[5,120]	Average assimilation delay (days)	20
HIREDY	[5,40]	Average hiring delay (days)	30
TRNSDY	[5-15]	Time delay to transfer people out (days)	10
MXSCDX	[1-50]	Max schl completion date (dimimensionless)	3

Table 3. Variables of the environment of the project and organisation

Variable	Description	Estimated Value
EFFORT	Effort for the project development (tech. per day)	1.111
TIME	Delivery time (days)	320
QUALITY	Quality of the final product (errors/task)	0

Table 4. Number of Software Development Projects satisfying the constraints. Rows indicate constraints over variables and columns over attributes: (1) None; (2) EFFORT < 1888; (3) TIME < 384

Constraint	(1)	(2)	(3)
NONE	300	42	37
QUALITY < 0.35	8	1	8
QUALITY < 0.45	227	26	27

4.1 Scenario 1

The results for this scenario are as follows: the variable EFFORT take values within the range [1589,3241], TIME in [349.5,437] and QUALITY in [0.297,0.556]. In order to assign a label to the records, the variables were discretised, taking one threshold for TIME and EFFORT and two for QUALITY. The constraints over the attributes and variables are shown in Table 4, where rows indicate constraints over variables and columns over attributes. Only 8 out of three hundred simulations had QUALITY less than 0.35, whereas when QUALITY is less than 0.45 there were 26 records with EFFORT under 1888 and 27 records with TIME under 384. Only one record satisfied both constrains EFFORT and TIME simultaneously.

We used the evolutionary algorithm to find rules that provide an adequate effort, a good delivery time or an excellent quality (three independent analysis).

Rule for effort: a rule covering 22 records (C4.5 produces two rules covering 23 records).

> if $101 \leq$ ASIMDY
> and $20.2 \leq$ HIREDY
> and $6.9 \leq$ MXSCDX
> then EFFORT$\leq$ 1888 and QUALITY$\leq$ 0.45

If the assimilation and the hiring are slow then the effort is optimised.

Rule for time: a rule covering 20 records (C4.5 produces two rules covering 21 records).

> if $7 \leq$ ASIMDY$\leq$ 17.9
> and $5.6 \leq$ HIREDY$\leq$ 39.5
> and $2.3 \leq$ MXSCDX
> and $5.4 \leq$ TRNSDY
> then TIME$\leq$ 384 and QUALITY$\leq$ 0.45

This rule shows that the intervals for the attributes HIREDY, MXSCDX and TRNSDY are very unrestricted, i.e. these attributes might take any value within the range. Therefore, the rule could only consider the attribute ASIMDY: a fast assimilation should enough to fulfil the time constrains.

Rule for quality: if QUALITY must be less than 0.35, only 8 records with TIME less than 384 were obtained. The evolutionary algorithm needs one rule (while C4.5 needs two rules).

> if ASIMDY≤ 23.2
> and 5.9≤ HIREDY≤ 32.8
> and 13.1≤ MXSCDX≤ 47.1
> and 5.5≤ TRNSDY≤ 10.8
>   then TIME≤ 384 and QUALITY≤ 0.35

This rule is similar to the previous one but there is a warning about minimising the average delay to transfer people.

4.2   Scenario 2

For this scenario the variable EFFORT takes values in [1709,3395], TIME in[349.5, 354.3] and QUALITY in [0.235, 0.661]. The thresholds for labelling the database were 1999 for EFFORT, 352 for TIME and 0.35 and 0.45 for QUALITY. The number of records satisfying these constraints are shown in Table 5.

Rules for time: two rules covering 31 records out of 45. (C4.5 produces 3 rules covering 22 records).

> if 11.6 ≤ ASIMDY
> and 6.3 ≤ HIREDY
> and 1.1≤ MXSCDX ≤ 1.15
>   then TIME≤ 352 and QUALITY≤ 0.45

> if 8.6 ≤ ASIMDY
> and 6.8 ≤ HIREDY ≤ 9.5
> and 1.16 ≤ MXSCDX
>   then TIME ≤ 352 and QUALITY ≤ 0.45

These rules are complementary in relation to the schedule completion date extension: the first one has a fixed schedule and the second one has not.

Table 5. Number of Software Development Projects satisfying the constraints. (1) None; (2) EFFORT < 1999; (3) TIME < 352

Constraint	(1)	(2)	(3)
NONE	300	105	297
QUALITY < 0.35	13	0	12
QUALITY < 0.45	47	1	45

Rules for quality: for 12 records with QUALITY less than or equal to 0.35 the evolutionary algorithm produced a rule covering six of them (C4.5 produced three rules covering 8 out of 12):

> if $11.8 \le$ ASIMDY
> and $7.8 \le$ HIREDY ≤ 9.8
> and $1.1 \le$ MXSCDX ≤ 1.19
> and TRNSDY ≤ 6.8
> then TIME ≤ 352 and QUALITY ≤ 0.35

To improve the quality, the rule must limit the time delay to transfer people out.

4.3   Scenario 3

The model is again simulated 300 times with the following values for the variables: EFFORT in [1693,2415], TIME in [349.5,361.5] and QUALITY in [0.236,0.567]. The threshold for labelling the database are the same that in the second scenario. The number of records satisfying the constraints is shown in Table 6.

Rules for effort and time: the scenario 3 is the only one that has a case which both constraints over time and effort were satisfied: when EFFORT < 1999 and QUALITY <0.45 there are 11 cases matching TIME <352 by chance. Two rules cover these records (C4.5 needs three rules).

> if $8.4 \le$ ASIMDY ≤ 11.5
> and $8.8 \le$ HIREDY
> and $9.3 \le$ MXSCDX
> then EFFORT ≤ 1999 and TIME ≤ 352
> and QUALITY ≤ 0.45 (7 records)

> if $9.8 \le$ ASIMDY ≤ 11.2
> and $6.8 \le$ HIREDY ≤ 8
> and MXSCDX ≤ 39.5
> then EFFORT ≤ 1999 and TIME ≤ 352
> and QUALITY ≤ 0.45 (4 records)

> if $9.8 \le$ ASIMDY ≤ 11.2
> and $6.8 \le$ HIREDY ≤ 8
> and MXSCDX ≤ 39.5
> then EFFORT ≤ 1999 and TIME ≤ 352
> and QUALITY ≤ 0.45 (4 records)

Table 6. Number of Software Development Projects satisfying the constraints (1) None; (2) EFFORT < 1999; (3) TIME < 352

Constraint	(1)	(2)	(3)
NONE	300	164	226
QUALITY < 0.35	43	0	9
QUALITY < 0.45	116	11	49

These rules point out that for obtaining good results simultaneously (TIME) and EFFORT) is essential a fast assimilation of technicians. The two rules are complementary in relation to HIREDY and MXSCDX.

Rules for time: if we only wish to minimise the variable TIME, we can produce similar rules as before by relaxing the assimilation (ASIMDY). In this way, we can accept values for this parameter less than 14.

5   Validation and Discussion

Kitchenham *et al.*[11] propose a framework for validating a bidding system, which can also be used for evaluating Dynamic Systems. The evaluation framework is composed of five quality aspects: (i) syntactic quality, (ii) semantic quality, (iii) pragmatic quality, (iv) test quality and (v) value quality. For each quality aspect, the authors define goals and means to achieve them. We will use this framework for discussing our approach.

The syntactic quality goal is syntactic correctness. Systems Dynamics have a well defined syntax based on graphs and formal models so that they are amenable to automation. Rules and decision trees have also a well defined syntax.

The semantic quality goal comprises of feasible validity and feasible completeness. In the context of System Dynamics, feasible completeness mean that the model include all the relevant causality relationships in the domain. Feasible validity refers to the correctness of such relationships to the domain. Kitchenham *et al.* define 'traceability to the domain' as the model property that supports the semantic quality goals.

As we have stated previously, Abdel-Hamid's is not only well documented, but it was also semantically validated in several ways: (i) replication of reference models based on extensive review of the literature, (ii) face validity based on interviews with software project managers at major organizations to fill in gaps in the literature, (iii) extreme conditions simulation, (iv) case study parameterising it for a NASA software development project and reproducing the patterns of the completed software project (cost, schedule, and work force loading).

In our opinion, semantic quality goals are the most difficult to achieve in the context of System Dynamics and since they are related to the problem of knowledge elicitation. Another important point highlighted by Kitchenham *et al.* is the difference between generic and specialized models. The same applies to System Dynamics, where causal relationships of software processes could be defined in a generic way but once these generic processes are modelled it can be difficult to adapt them to other more concrete environments.

The pragmatic quality deals with the issue of how to express a model and it comprises of two goals: feasible comprehension and feasible understandability. Methods to facilitate comprehension include visualization, explanation and filtering which can be assessed through empirical studies. Expressive economy and structuredness are model properties that enable the feasible understandability quality aspect. In our case, the documentation and guidelines provided by Abdel-Hamid help to customise and improve the model. In relation to the set of rules are intuitive and self-documented.

Test Quality The goal for the test quality aspect is feasible test coverage. Simulation studies can be used to assess this quality aspect.

Value Quality refers to practical utility. Kitchenham *et al.* include appropriate user manuals, training etc. as means to achieve it. In the context of System Dynamics, project managers and quality assurance engineers need to understand the underlying models to apply them correctly. In relation to the quality of the set of rules produced by the evolutionary algorithm, there are many advantages of our approach in comparison with C4.5 [14]. For example, our algorithm searches for rules which cover records with the label identified by the user whereas C4.5 generates a decision tree in which all the labels appear, i.e., including those not helping to manage the project properly; from these rules we cannot extract useful knowledge related to management policies. C4.5 always produced more rules covering less records. In many cases, the intervals found by C4.5 for some parameters had a very small range, which is inappropriate if project manager want to vary such parameters to achieve a goal.

Finally, we must comment that System Dynamics models may not be applied in all software organisations. There are constrains that need to be born in mind. First, expertise is required to model the entities, attributes and cause-effect relationships that compose such models. Second, models need to be customised, i.e., calibrated for each organization. To do so, organizations may need a well established process for applying System Dynamic properly. If we consider the Capability Maturity Model (CMM) [15], at level 3, Key Process Areas (KPA) related to managerial issues and organization-wide standards are introduced. At this level, data collection is integrated in the development process. Moreover, it is only at Level 4 that an organisational measurement program is established for measuring the quality of the products and processes. As a result, availability of data in order to calibrate the System Dynamic model is usually only available in mature organisations.

6   Conclusions and Future Work

In this paper, we have shown an approach that combines system dynamics and evolutionary computation to produce rules automatically for the decision-making task in project management. Our technique may contribute to coping with the complex problem of decision-making within the software project development framework, and it facilitates the use of dynamic models, since the project manager only has to provide the aims of the project and the range of the parameters, especially for those having a high degree of uncertainty. Such management rules can be applied before, during and after the execution of a project.

In our approach, we first generate a database using the Abdel-Hamid's model [1] simulating the temporal behaviour of the project. Then, decision rules are constructed by the evolutionary algorithm, which is based on a new method for coding. Such rules were compared with the ones obtained by another well-known algorithm (C4.5[14]). It produces better solutions in the search space, covering more *good* examples with less number of rules being the results more applicable and beneficial.

In addition to further improvement such evolutionary approaches, we are currently working on the application of other machine learning techniques (fuzzy logic, association rules, etc.) to the databases generated by the simulation. From the software engineering point of view, our future work is related to how to integrate such approach into the development process and visualisation. We have detected as a basic prerequisite the lack of a methodology for interpreting all the information that project managers collect from multiple sources. Usually, project management tools and control panels inform the project manager about the state of the project. Corrective actions are taken on the basis of the manager's experience and assessed on the basis of management rules, in order to fulfil the desired goals. Further efforts are also directed towards improving the visualization of such rules including all kind of data generated by processes and products.

Acknowledgements

The research was supported by the Spanish Research Agency (CICYT-TIC1143-C03-02 and CICYT- TIC1143-C03-01)

References

1. Abdel-Hamid, T.K.: Software Project Dynamics: an integrated approach. Prentice-Hall, 1991.
2. Aguilar-Ruiz J.S., Riquelme J.C., and Del Valle C.: Improving the Evolutionary Coding for Machine Learning Tasks. *15th European Conference on Artificial Intelligence*, ECAI'02, IOS Press, 173-177, 2002.
3. Aguilar-Ruiz J.S., Riquelme J.C., Ramos I. and Toro M.: An evolutionary approach to estimating software development projects. *Information and Software Technology*, 14(43):875-882, 2001
4. van Leeuwen, J. (ed.): Computer Science Today. Recent Trends and Developments. Lecture Notes in Computer Science, Vol. 1000. Springer-Verlag, Berlin Heidelberg New York (1995)
5. Michalewicz, Z.: Genetic Algorithms + Data Structures = Evolution Programs. 3rd edn. Springer-Verlag, Berlin Heidelberg New York (1996)
6. Dolado, J.J.: On the problem of the software cost function. *Information and Software Technology*, 43:61-72, 2001.
7. Fayyad, U.M. and Irani, K.B.: Multi-interval discretisation of continuous valued attributes for classification learning. In *Proceedings of the Thirteenth International Joint Conference on Artificial Intelligence*. Morgan Kaufmann, 1993.

8. Finnie, G.R., Wittig, G.E., and Desharnais, J.-M.: A comparison of software effort estimation techniques: using function points with neural networks, case-based reasoning and regression models. *Journal of Systems and Software*, 39(3):281-289, 2000.
9. Forrester, J.W.: *Industrial Dynamics*, Productivity Press, 1961.
10. Holte, R.C.: Very simple classification rules perform well on most commonly used datasets. *Machine learning*, 11:63-91, 1993.
11. Kitchenham B.A., Pickard L.M., Linkman S.G. and Jones, P.: A Framework for Evaluating a Software Bidding Model, *Empirical Assessment in Software Engineering (EASE)*, Keele University, 2002.
12. Koza, J.R.: *Genetic Programming*. The MIT Press, Cambridge, Massachusetts, 1992.
13. Mitchell, T.: *Machine Learning*. McGraw Hill, 1997.
14. Quinlan, J.R.: *C4.5: Programs for machine learning*. Morgan Kaufmann, San Mateo, California, 1993.
15. Paul, M.C., Curtis, B., Chrissis, M.B. and Weber, C.V.: Capability Maturity Model, Version 1.1, *IEEE Software*, 10:18-27, 1993.
16. Shepperd, M. and Schofield, C.: Estimating software project effort using analogies. *IEEE Transactions on Software Engineering*, 23(12):736-743, 2000.
17. Venturini, G.: Sia: A supervised inductive algorithm with genetic search for learning attributes based concepts. In *Proceedings of European Conference on Machine Learning*, pp. 281-296, 1993.
18. Walkerden, F. and Jeffery, R.: An empirical study of analogy-based software effort estimation. *Empirical Software Engineering*, 42:135-158, 1999.

Heterogeneous Information Systems Integration: Organizations and Methodologies

Ricardo J. Machado[1] and João M. Fernandes[2]

[1] Dep. Sistemas de Informação, Universidade do Minho, Guimarães, Portugal
[2] Dept. Informática, Universidade do Minho, Braga, Portugal

Abstract. In this paper, a methodology for integrating heterogeneous industrial information systems is presented. The methodology is strongly based on the extensive reuse of already-made components and is conceptually divided in three levels, one for each kind of designer that is typically involved in this type of projects. To accomplish a better integration of the activities and tools necessary to develop industrial information systems with the proposed methodology, three appropriate organizational configurations are adopted.

1   Introduction

The development of industrial information systems is mainly centered in design activities where the re-usage and integration of previously implemented technologies become the main tasks. This reality is imposed by the need to extend the life-cycle of legacy systems, and also as a means to reach final solutions in fewer time and with more robust characteristics. It is important to state that the main goal of an *industrial control-based information system* (ICIS) is the management of the information that flows in the factory plants between the lower and the upper CIM (computer integrated manufacturing) levels [1]. These integration-based design activities are normally executed within an ad-hoc approach, without a strong framework to methodologically support the global process model.

In the context of industrial information systems design, this approach is motivated by the technological diversity of the components, where embedded systems, web-services, and control applications must work together to accomplish the easy interconnection between the lower (0, 1 and 2) and the upper (3 and 4) CIM levels [2]. These solutions are complementary, within the industrial organizations, to the well-known management information systems (MISs) [3]. *Industrial information systems* (IIS), which result from the integration of a MIS with an ICIS, are the answer to accomplish the definition of an applicational platform, based on ERP (enterprise resource planning) approaches, in order to integrate and unify the management and control of all organizational information.

The design and open implementation of this new kind of heterogeneous information systems demand some methodological and architectural issues to be carefully treated

M. Oivo and S. Komi-Sirviö (Eds.): PROFES 2002, LNCS 2559, pp. 629-643, 2002.
© Springer-Verlag Berlin Heidelberg 2002

[4], which are discussed in this paper. The usage of a UML-based approach to model the organizational configurations that support the execution of IIS integration projects are also presented in this paper. The final goal is to derive an architecture of a tool-set that can aid in the design of the software components that are needed to integrate the IIS solutions. The proposed approach identifies the team structure of an IIS project and, in parallel, defines the software engineering activities that are to be executed by the multiple-organization team members.

This paper does not discuss how helpful is the methodology across organizations, neither does it explicitly report on the benefits of the method compared to others, by presenting a practical assessment of the advantages and weaknesses of the approach, compared with previous ways of working.

This paper intends to justify, in a non-formal way, the methodological steps followed during the execution of an industrial project [5] in which the authors have been involved to apply the approach. In relation to the UML notation, although it is used in some diagrams of this paper, it is not explained here (for details please refer to [6-8]). The UML diagrams that were considered vital for heterogeneous software-based systems design are: use cases, objects, classes, sequence, and statecharts [9].

2   Overview

The presented methodology, designated *virtual automation* (VA), is a complete design and run-time environment, based on software tools, on library modules and on shop-floor software components. In the VA terminology, these components are called *functional modules off-the-shelf* (FMOTSs). VA allows the rapid and easy integration of a distributed network of FMOTSs (that collectively correspond to the ICIS) with the corporate MIS. VA includes the following (in this paper, only the 2 first topics are covered):

- A CAE (Computer-Aided Engineering) software tool.
- A CASE (Computer-Aided Software Engineering) software tool.
- A library composed of several middleware implementation components.
- A FMOTS library composed of several software components.
- A RTOS (Real-Time Operating System).
- A family of embeddable target architectures.
- A run-time execution engine for real-time gateway computation.

Integrating a MIS and an ICIS is a hard task due to the semantical, cultural, temporal, and informational gaps that exist between the development process models that are typically followed for the two subsystems [10]. The main purpose of the VA methodology is to fill the gap between those two subsystems in order to easily and rapidly develop IIS solutions. Additionally, the VA approach guarantees the technological transparency in the virtual modeling of the FMOTSs and also copes with the system's design complexity, by offering a unified development environment that allows the system-level design of the IIS' integrating parts.

The VA methodology is based on co-design principles [11], by promoting the cross fertilization between the hardware and the software domains. Additionally, co-design allows the semantical unification of the relevant concepts for system-level modeling, the application of data abstraction (object-orientation) to design target architectures and the use of executable specifications to evaluate the system's requirements in its initial developments steps [12]. The research in cross fertilization between both domains has been given excellent results and the work in this field must continue to promote the systems' virtual prototyping (totally in software) and to incorporate the operational approach and the spiral process model into design methodologies.

The hardware/software partitioning and the global scheduling of heterogeneous systems are co-design problems not consensually solved up to now, since they impose the complex conciliation of the synchronization of pseudo-concurrent software with inherently parallel hardware, together with the minimization of communication costs between several partitions [13]. These tricky problems can be even more difficult to tackle if hard real-time systems are considered, with their additional non-functional requirements that enormously constrict the allowable design space exploration.

3   Organizational Configurations

Any engineering project possesses an environment defined by: (1) the *project technical background*, which consists on a scientific and technological framework that defines methodologies, techniques and tools used by the engineer within the execution of the project activities; (2) the *nature of the economical activities*, which defines the application scope of the project deliverables.

3.1   Canonical IT Activities

Taking into account the execution context of an IIS integration project, three canonical classes of organizational IT (*information technology*) activities can be defined:

1. *#A activities (R&D)*. These activities produce generic goods and services for a set of economical activities, but without a binding with a concrete instance of those economical activities. These #A activities are typically R&D activities and are developed by universities, research centers, hi-tech enterprises, and R&D departments of important corporations. An organization that executes these activities possesses ECAD (Electronic Computer-Aided Design) and CASE development tools and produces embeddable target architectures and software elements for compositionally implementing IISs.

2. *#B activities (integration)*. These activities use the generic goods and services (furnished by #A activities) within a concrete instance of economical activities, by adapting and customizing the reusable technological components. These #B activities typically integrate technological solutions, and are developed by engineering companies and engineering departments of important corporations. An organization that executes these activities detains embeddable target architectures and software elements (produced by type #A activities) and produces IIS final solutions for supporting the supervision and monitoring of production, maintenance and quality indexes of industrial processes.

3. *#C activities (production)*. These activities correspond to the economical activities that constitute the target problem domain.

For implementing ICISs with the VA approach, there are several professional profiles that do contribute for the accomplishment of the 3 types of activities, previously indicated:

-   the hardware engineer, which conceives embeddable target architectures at level 1 of the VA methodology (see sec. 4), directly contributing to execute type #A activities;
-   the software engineer, which conceives FMOTSs at level 2 of the VA methodology (see sec. 4), directly contributing to execute type #A activities;
-   the systems engineer, which constructs final solutions at level 3 of the VA methodology (see sec. 4), directly contributing to execute type #B activities;
-   the maintenance technician, which technically supports the systems engineer with respect to the processes and equipments used for type #C activities and assures that all the procedures for installing and maintaining the final solution are done;
-   the manager that is responsible for type #C activities.

3.2   Configurations

Based on the 3 types of activities and the 5 profiles involved with them, the authors obtained 5 organizational configurations that serve as a reference for the same number of environments where ICISs can be developed.

In configuration I (fig. 1a), there is a different organization for each type of activity: (i) an organization (of type #A) that just executes type #A activities, by recurring to hardware and software engineers; (ii) an organization (of type #B) that just executes type #B activities, by recurring to systems engineers; (iii) an organization (of type #C) that just executes type #C activities, by recurring to maintenance technicians and managers. This configuration requires the organizations to have a high degree of specialization, since each one only supports one type of activity.

Configuration II (fig. 1b) differs from configuration I by the fact that the maintenance technician is included in the organization of type #B instead of type #C. This configuration requires the maintenance technicians (and also the systems engineers) to be sufficiently able to adapt themselves to the specific details of all the type #C organizations where they develop ICIS projects.

In configuration III (fig. 1c), there are only 2 different organizations involved in the project: (i) an organization (of type #A) that just executes type #A activities, by recurring to hardware and software engineers; (ii) an organization (of type #B + #C) that executes types #B and #C activities, by recurring to systems engineers, maintenance technicians and managers. This configuration covers the situation where a big corporation (organization of type #B + #C) is capable of promoting the conception of final solutions.

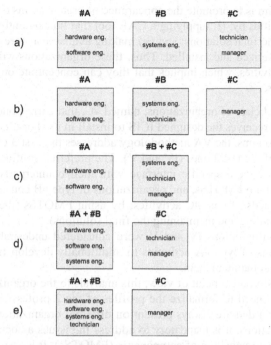

Fig. 1. Organizational configurations

In configuration IV (fig. 1d), there are only 2 different organizations involved in the project: (i) an organization (of type #A + #B) that executes types #A and #B activities, by recurring to hardware, software, and systems engineers; (ii) an organization (of type #C) that just executes types #C activities, by recurring to maintenance technicians and managers. This configuration concentrates, on a single corporation (organization of type #A + #B), all the R&D effort and the way technology is transferred to the industrial parties capable of promoting the final solutions conception.

Configuration V (fig. 1e) differs from configuration IV by the fact that the maintenance technician is included in the organization of type #A + #B instead of type #C.

It is possible to obtain more organizational configurations than those discussed above. However, there is no real interest, for example, to concentrate the 3 types of activities on a single organization or to separate in distinct organizations the hardware and the software engineers, since the VA methodology has two main goals:

- The first one is to free the organizations that execute type #A activities from: (i) having a deep knowledge of all the application areas where the technologies developed by them can be used; (ii) developing final solutions; and (iii) installing and maintaining final solutions. Thus, organizations that only execute type #A activities can have less dispersion on their work, which implies more time and attention to research and to develop industrial prototypes and integratable components. The desire of only assigning type #A activities to these organizations is related to the need of having final products with higher quality standards, i.e., more versatile, robust and effective FMOTSs.

-   The second aim is to promote the appearance of organizations only responsible for type #B activities by: (i) supplying a CAE tool that transparently supports the construction of the final solutions; and (ii) making available a store of FMOTSs ready to be parameterized and installed. Thus, these organizations will not have to pursue R&D activities, which implies that they can concentrate on the integration of final solutions.

There is a third class of organizations, named #C, that corresponds to the industrial organization that receives the designed ICIS to install in its shop-floor.

With these two aims, the VA methodology addresses the first 3 configurations (I, II and III) instead of the last 2 ones (IV and V). The preferred configurations assure that the organizations have a specific interface with their counterparts: organizations of type #A only develop FMOTSs, and organizations of type #B construct final solutions that satisfy the needs of type #C activities, by using FMOTSs (they may also be responsible for installing and maintaining the final solutions).

Contrarily, configurations IV and V were considered undesirable, since they require organizations of type #A activities to additionally develop final solutions and, even, to install and maintain them.

From a methodological point of view, this analysis to the organizational configurations justifies the need to formalize the profiles of the 2 professionals (software and systems engineers) that are always present on different organizations. By working on different organizations, it is mandatory to address the issues associated to the design, the reuse and the composition of components (FMOTSs). It is also obligatory to take into account that the components must be fully documented in what concerns their functionalities and the way they can be interconnected.

Within the VA approach, the systems engineer should: (1) know the FMOTSs behavioral interface; (2) know the final solution's requirements; and (3) be able to parametrize and interconnect the selected FMOTSs to fully accomplish the requirements of the final solution. The software engineer should: (1) know the target architecture designed by the hardware engineer; (2) know the algorithmic requirements to implement over the target architecture; and (3) be able to develop generic components (FMOTSs).

4   The VA Approach

This section discusses how to obtain a design environment for system-level integration of real-time embedded FMOTSs capable of implementing ICISs. Within that environment, models should be iteratively reified until the system is implemented, without the need for manual macro-refinements, with the transparent reuse of embeddable target architectures and software modules, and supporting, throughout the design process, the activities of the three professionals typically involved (hardware, software and systems engineers).

To accomplish this objective, it is necessary to decouple the traditional top-down one-all-going project approach into three feed-forward quasi-independent project levels, each one with a different design flow, but organized by a common middle-out macro-process design flow (fig. 2):

- *Hardware level* (level 1 of the VA methodology), where the embeddable target architectures are provided to computationally support the parameterisable FMOTSs [14]. It is possible to make use of reconfigurable technologies to implement, directly in the hardware, algorithmic primitives that should be transparently used in level 2. The introduction of these reconfigurable technologies promotes the execution of typical co-design tasks, like the pre-partitioning tasks.

- *Software level* (level 2 of the VA methodology), where the parameterisable programs to run on the FMOTSs are constructed with a CASE tool [15]. At this level, the software engineer must decide which functionalities will run directly on the processor and which ones will be synthesized for the reconfigurable devices.

- *Information system level* (level 3 of the VA methodology), where the final heterogeneous IIS solution is designed with a CAE tool, by integrating the previously designed FMOTSs and the existing MIS [7]. The systems engineer can decide whether to use the algorithms embedded in the FMOTSs or to conceive new ones (or complement the existing ones) to run on the real-time gateway (the component responsible for stubbing the interconnection of the ICIS with the MIS).

This decoupling must assure that it can be possible to establish, with the three kind of engineering professionals, a co-design community within the same project, each one with the responsibility of implementing the control primitives corresponding to his capabilities and duties. This approach can be better explained by reinterpreting the 5 T's analysis [16].

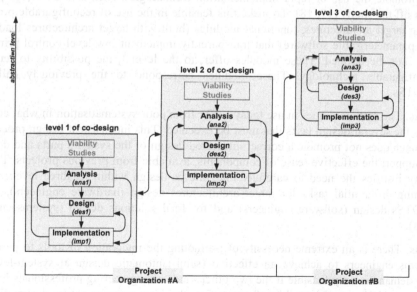

Fig. 2. Macro-process of the 3-level methodology

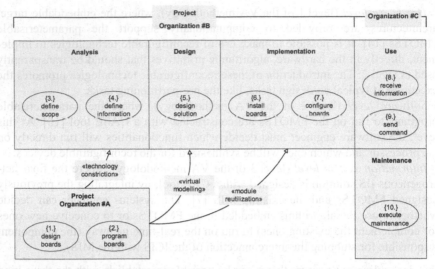

Fig. 3. Final solutions life-cycle diagram

Timelines. The time to market pressure, together with the usual requirements modifications, suggests that methodologies try to address the reduction of development times and promote the use of rapid implementation technologies, such as COTS (components off-the-shelf) [17, 18]. To make this feasible in the use of reconfigurable processing target architectures, functional modules (built with target architectures loaded with parameterisable software) that transparently implement low-level control primitives must be defined. These modules offer, to the level 3, the possibility to reuse reconfigurable technology. These modules correspond to the previously called FMOTSs.

Tasks. The methodologies in use today suffer from poor systematisation in what concerns the several design tasks that must be executed. This inconsistent design process approach does not promote a correct integrated design of the system's parts and does not support the effective reuse of components, available from previous projects. This reality justifies the need to carefully integrate co-design within its three levels, by defining differential tasks for target architectures design (hardware engineers), for FMOTSs design (software engineers) and for final solutions design (systems engineers).

Tools. There is an extreme necessity of promoting the integration of tools to permit systems engineers to achieve an effective (semi-)automatic design at system-level. This demand is only feasible if the two other kinds of engineering professionals have access to design tools capable of supporting the intra-communication design flow levels, in what concerns the semantical manipulation of unified representations and the automatic code generation.

Technology. Taking into account the Moore's Law, custom solutions are only interesting in a narrower time-window. In this context, it is advantageous to adopt methodologies capable of supporting technologies that allow the periodic update of components (model year upgrade) for performance increase, but assuring, at least, the same functionality. This model year upgrade of components benefits from the co-design level decoupling, since each engineering professional is only concerned with the update within its design level, but contributing for the global updating of the final solution.

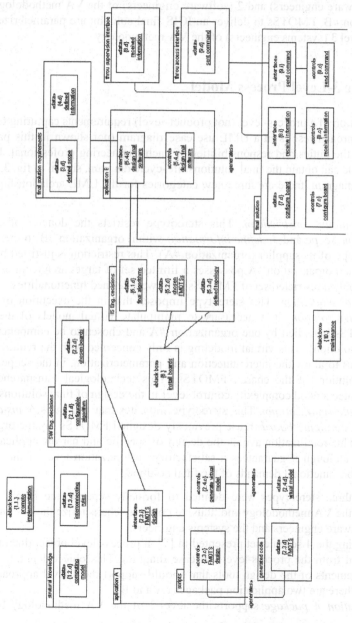

Fig. 4. Process-level object diagram of the 3-level approach

Talent. Besides all the R&D work that this co-design approach demands, the training of the three engineering professionals in this new way of executing and designing with heterogeneous implementations must not be ignored.

Fig. 2 illustrates two kinds of projects, each one executed within a different organization. At organization #A, ready-to-use FMOTSs are delivered, which support levels 1 (hardware engineers) and 2 (software engineers) of the VA methodology; and at organization #B, FMOTSs to deliver an ICIS final solution are parameterized, which support level 3 (systems engineers) of the VA methodology.

5   The 3-Level Process Model

The execution of a process-level (not product-level) requirements capturing task of the 3-level approach results in a UML use case diagram (not shown in this paper) that represents the duties and responsibilities of each engineering professional. From this diagram one can obtain the final solutions life-cycle diagram, shown in fig. 3.

In this diagram, there are three new categories for the UML «relationship» stereotype:

1. «*technology constriction*». This stereotype restricts the domain of use cases *3. define scope* and *4. define information* within organization #B to the economical scope of its supplier (organization #A). This restriction is justified by the fact that each organization #A possesses a limited set of target architectures and supplies only a restricted set of FMOTSs with well-defined functionalities.
2. «*virtual modeling*». This stereotype imposes that in the execution of use case *5. design solution*, it is necessary to manipulate virtual models of the selected FMOTSs (supplied by one organization #A and chosen to be components of the final solution). This virtual modeling is only concerned with the required characteristics to allow the interconnection and parameterization, in the scope of the final solution, of the chosen FMOTSs. This technological transparency should guarantee a good complexity control level in the design of final solutions.
3. «*module reutilization*». This stereotype indicates that use cases *6. install boards* and *7. configure boards* reuse previously designed FMOTSs (by the organization #A). This reutilization avoids the design of specific and narrow application solutions, although it guarantees a satisfactory customization level of the functional and non-functional demands of the final solution.

These three stereotypes were defined to formally separate the level 2 from the level 3 of the VA methodology and, thus, to correctly characterize the design activities of the software engineers and the systems engineers.

Following the 4-set rule set presented in [7], a process-level object diagram (fig. 4) is obtained from the process-level use case diagram. This object diagram represents the requirements of the design tools that should support the 3-level approach. In this diagram, there are two application packages (A and B).

Application A package supports the level 2 of the VA methodology by making available:

4. one environment with an user interface (*2.3.i FMOTS design*) capable of assisting the design tasks of software engineers, who possess the structural knowledge of the target architectures (*1.2.d computing model* and *1.3.d interconnecting rules*) and who take some previous decisions (*2.1.d configurable algorithm* and *2.2.d chosen boards*);

5. one engine capable of (semi-)automate both the design of FMOTSs (*2.3.c FMOTS design*) and the generation of final code (*2.3.d FMOTS*) for the system synthesis and implementation in the chosen target architecture;

6. one engine capable of (semi-)automate the generation of virtual models (*2.4.c generate virtual model*) to allow, in the application B package, the configuration, in a technological transparent way, of the previously designed FMOTSs (in application A package).

Application B package supports the level 3 of the VA methodology by making available:

1. one environment with an user interface (*5.4.i design final software*) capable of assisting the design tasks of information systems engineers, who possess the knowledge of the final solutions requirements (*3.d defined scope* and *4.d defined information*) and who take some previous decisions (*5.1.d final algorithms, 5.2.d chosen FMOTSs* and *5.3.d defined topology*);

2. one engine capable of (semi-)automate the generation of final solutions (*5.4.c design final software*).

For implementing the application A package, a Java-based tool is being used and for the application B package, the LabVIEW CAE tool is being adopted (fig. 5) [5]. In LabVIEW, the technological transparency in the remote invocation of the shop-floor embedded components is accomplished by the use of VIs (*virtual instruments*) that represent their behavioral interface for pre-run-time parameterization and for establishing the run-time interconnection with their distributed implementations.

Note that the *final solution* package corresponds to the ICIS final solution to be installed in the organization #C shop-floor. This final solution executes the FMOTSs configuration (*7.c configure board*) and then executes the supervision and monitoring algorithms included in the FMOTSs (*8.c receive information* and *9.c send command*). LabVIEW is also the central element of the final solution that gathers and distributes the information from all the processing elements; i.e., LabVIEW performs at run-time the role of a semantical gateway between the shop-floor elements and the corporate MIS.

Fig. 6 depicts the global 3-level environment with the cascaded ECAD, CASE and CAE tools supporting the three engineering designers in the implementation of heterogeneous IIS final solutions.

6   Conclusions

This paper has presented a 3-level methodology, especially tuned to apply the basic co-design principles to the open component-based design of parameterisable modules, capable of supporting the integration of heterogeneous industrial information systems. The methodology is intended to help various IT practitioners to design systems that can be reused and adapted by others. The paper starts by identifying three classes of activities for building an IIS:

- The R&D activities that produce generic and embeddable hardware/software elements.
- The integration activities that adapt the previous software to a specific application/system.
- The production activity that makes sure that the application/system runs in the target environment.

To achieve a comfortable integration of the activities and tools necessary to develop industrial information systems with the proposed methodology, the authors have selected three organizational configurations that are considered appropriate to support the global methodology. The activities can be split over three different organizations or be tackled within the same organization. The paper describes a methodology to support the design and development to be integrated softly among these three groups of practitioners. The systematic analysis and metric assessment of other comparable methodological approaches were not considered to be presented in this paper.

Within this context, from the process-level use case diagram (final solution life-cycle diagram), a process-level object diagram was obtained, which specifies the requirements of the design tools supporting the 3-level approach.

Based on these requirements, a set of design tools has been assembled to support the VA methodology. Both, the methodology and tools, have been already used in real projects for developing industrial information systems.

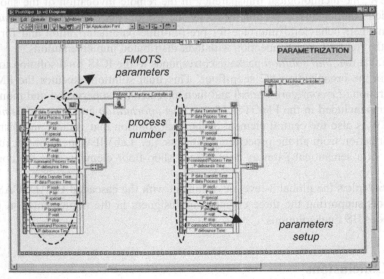

Fig. 5. The LabVIEW CAE tool

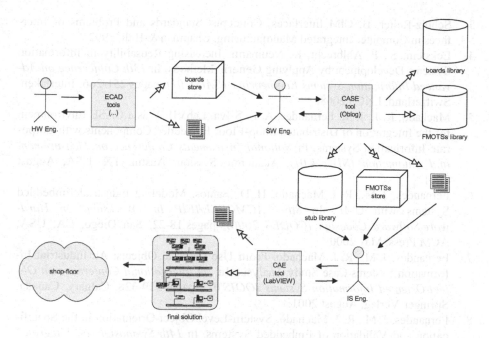

Fig. 6. Global 3-level environment

The LabVIEW environment proved to be a powerful and mature CASE tool, by providing the essential mechanisms to benefit from the component-based design approach in the reuse of components, the rapid prototyping in the user's requirements validation, and high-quality user interfaces easily programmed for the final solutions. Additionally, the environment supports the system life-cycle evolution, requirements modification and software maintenance, which greatly contributes to deal with the development of heterogeneous information systems.

Acknowledgments

We gratefully acknowledge financial support from Fundação para a Ciência e a Tecnologia (FCT) and Fundo Europeu de Desenvolvimento Regional (FEDER) under project „METHODES: Methodologies and Tools for Developing Complex Real-Time Embedded Systems" (POSI/37334/CHS/2001).

References

1.   Waldner, J.-B. CIM: Principles of Computer-Integrated Manufacturing. John Wiley & Sons, 1992.
2.   Ranky, P. G. Computer Networks for World Class CIM Systems. CIMware Limited, 1990.

3. Scholz-Reiter, B. CIM Interfaces: Concepts, Standards and Problems of Interfaces in Computer Integrated Manufacturing. Chapman & Hall, 1992.
4. Eckstein, S., P. Ahlbrecht, K. Neumann. Increasing Reusability in Information Systems Development by Applying Generic Methods. In *13th Conference on Advanced Information Systems Engineering (CAISE'01)*, pages 251-266, Interlaken, Switzerland, LNCS 2068.
5. Machado, R. J., J. M. Fernandes, A. F. Silva. LabVIEW as a CASE Environment for the Integration of Distributed Shop-Floor Embedded Components with Corporate Information Systems. In *National Instruments Conference on Measurement and Automation (NIWeek'01)*, Academic Session, Austin, TX, USA, August 2001.
6. Fernandes, J. M., R. J. Machado, H. D. Santos. Modeling Industrial Embedded Systems with UML. In *8th   ACM/IEEE/IFIP Int. Workshop on Hardware/Software Codesign (CODES 2000)*, pages 18-22, San Diego, CA, USA, ACM Press, May 2000.
7. Fernandes, J. M., R. J. Machado. From Use Cases to Objects: An Industrial Information Systems Case Study Analysis. In *7th International Conference on Object-Oriented Information Systems (OOIS'01)*, pages 319-328, Calgary, Canada, Springer-Verlag, August 2001.
8. Fernandes, J. M., R. J. Machado. System-Level Object-Orientation in the Specification and Validation of Embedded Systems. In *14th Symposium on Integrated Circuits and System Design (SBCCI'01)*, pages 8-13, Pirenópolis, Brazil, IEEE Computer Society Press, September 2001.
9. Köhler, H. J., U. Nickel, J. Niere, A. Zündorf. Integrating UML Diagrams for Production Control Systems. In *22nd International Conference on Software Engineering (ICSE 2000)*, pages 241-251, Limerick, Ireland, ACM Press, June 2000.
10. Derynck, R. R., T. Hutchinson. Integrating Real-Time Systems with Corporate Information Systems, *The Hewlett-Packard Journal*, 50(1):26--28, 1998.
11. Rozenblit, J., K. Buchenrieder. Codesign: Computer-Aided Software/Hardware Engineering, IEEE Press, 1995.
12. Machado, R. J., J. M. Fernandes, H. D. Santos. A Methodology for Complex Embedded Systems Design: Petri Nets within a UML Approach. In B. Kleinjohann, editor, *Architecture and Design of Distributed Embedded Systems*, pages 1-10, Kluwer Academic Publishers, 2001.
13. Yen, T.-Y., W. Wolf. Hardware-Software Co-Synthesis of Distributed Embedded Systems. Kluwer Academic Publishers, 1996.
14. Machado, R. J., J. M. Fernandes, A. J. Esteves, H. D. Santos. An Evolutionary Approach to the Use of Petri Net Based Models: From Parallel Controllers to HW/SW Co-Design. In A. Yakovlev, L. Gomes, and L. Lavagno, editors, *Hardware Design and Petri Nets*, pages 205-222, Kluwer Academic Publishers, 2000.
15. Machado, R. J., J. M. Fernandes. A Petri Net Meta-Model to Develop Software Components for Embedded Systems. In *2nd IEEE International Conference on Application of Concurrency to System Design (ACSD'01)*, pages 113-122, Newcastle Upon Tyne, U.K., IEEE Computer Society Press, June 2001.

16. Madisetti, V. K., M. A. Richards. Advances in Rapid Prototyping of Digital Systems. *IEEE Design & Test of Computers*, 13(3):9-11, 1996.
17. Voas, J. The Challenges of Using COTS Software in Component-Based Development. *IEEE Computer*, 31(6):44-45, 1998.
18. Wang, Y., S. Patel, D. Patel. On Built-in Test Classes for Object-Oriented and Component-Based Information Systems In *7th International Conference on Object-Oriented Information Systems (OOIS'01)*, pages 307-316, Calgary, Canada, Springer-Verlag, August 2001.

Author Index

Lecture Notes in Computer Science

For information about Vols. 1–2455

please contact your bookseller or Springer-Verlag